Performance
of Textiles

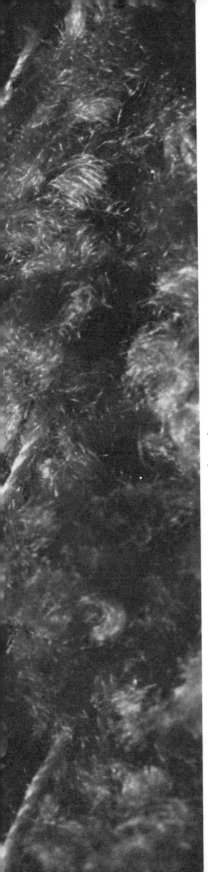

Performance
of Textiles
Dorothy Siegert Lyle

JOHN WILEY & SONS

New York   Santa Barbara   London   Sydney   Toronto

Library of Congress Cataloging in Publication Data

Lyle, Dorothy Siegert.
Performance of textiles.

Bibliography: p.
Includes index.
1. Textile fibers—Testing. 2. Textile fabrics—
Testing. 3. Dry cleaning. 4. Laundry. I. Title.

TS1449.L88   677'.0287   76-54110
ISBN 0-471-01418-4

Printed in the United States of America

10 9 8 7 6 5 4 3

TO my family and to the
professional and business friends
who helped and encouraged me
to develop my unique career

Foreword

The textile industry is increasingly becoming one of fashion *plus*–price *plus*. The "plus" implies performance and value in addition to the usual aesthetics and cost that have earlier dominated textile purchases. More and more consumers are expecting performance and quality in their textile purchases. State and federal government are demanding performance of textile products in such areas as safety and renovation, as evidenced by their continuing activity in textile flammability and care labeling. It is no longer sufficient for textile products to simply look good in the store; many now carry guarantees for one to five years of normal service; more textile products than ever are being marketed with labels that claim adherence to various performance specifications. Cleanability and care are becoming more technological and are as important as any other aspect of performance. Textile products, as with many other consumer products, are being sold subject to scrutiny and recourse under the powerful concepts of implied warranty or strict liability.

The measurement and evaluation of these several aspects of performance is based on a recognized and uniform system of test methods and standards. Such methods are used by industry in evaluating their products, either in process or when sold. The same test methods may be used by government when checking compliance with the several statutes that regulate textile products in commerce. Clear, concise, and accurate care labels must be provided for the consumer. Testing for compliance with industry certified performance programs and government regulations must also be conducted.

Thus, the entire field of textiles needs people with skills that require a level of professionalism and training never before demanded of the textile, apparel, home furnishings, retailing, care, and related industries. Even these brief words illustrate an obvious need for a second-level textile course to provide students with an awareness and working knowledge of the many ways in which textile product testing, labeling, use, and care information can and must be integrated into the total distribution process, from product development and manufacturing through to the ultimate consumer.

Dorothy Lyle's book meets the needs for teaching, training, information, and reference needed by a varied and broad spectrum of students and professionals who will deal with many of the above aspects. However, the book does not replace the extremely detailed *AATCC Technical Manual* or *ASTM Book of Standards,* although it can be very useful for the synopses of many of the methods contained there. Second, it does not provide a detailed theoretical framework for an advanced study of textiles involving fiber science, fabric geometry, finish analysis, or the like.

This book does provide an excellent and very comprehensive overview for a broad base of textile students directed toward any number of diverse careers. Although the careers may be different, all are related by their need for a working knowledge of consumer-oriented textile performance. Vital to this knowledge is a familiarity with the standard (and not so standard) methods by which textile performance is gauged; the technology of soiling, staining, use, and care; and an understanding of the key channels of communication between the various participants in the total system, that is, business and industry, the consumer they sell, and the government that affects them both.

Performance of Textiles fills the need as a text for such a second-level textile course. Similarly, it can be a "building block" for further study and courses in some of the areas highlighted in this book. Such areas include the testing of fiber, yarn, and fabric for product performance; renovation, use, and care of textiles; and consumer-government-business relations in textiles. The book is, similarly, a ready reference for many who presently are practitioners of its information but have lacked a compendium that outlines many of the test methods and discusses many important concepts not previously available.

Finally, the book takes advantage of the unique professional experiences that Dr. Lyle, through her unusual, multifaceted career, has brought to this field. This book is an information source for the present and future, insuring that end-use performance of consumer textiles will indeed continue to receive the attention and recognition it deserves.

Steven M. Spivak, Ph.D.

Associate Professor,
Textiles and Consumer Economics
University of Maryland

Preface

It is said that schools are teaching skills that may be obsolete before a student reaches 30 years of age. It is difficult, if not impossible, to predict the specific skills and techniques needed in the next 5 years, let alone the next 25. This is why every effort must be made continuously to update training and education as a reflection of constant change. Education and business must prepare for the talents needed in the year 2000.

As a result of a recent survey, an administrator stated that some administrators do not realize what potential there is for incorporating significant experiences into a curriculum of textile technology; they are not aware of opportunities for support in making testing equipment available for undergraduate-level experiences. With the emphasis on consumerism, consumer preferences, and consumer economics, industry is hiring people trained with experience in these areas as well as textile technology itself.

Students of textiles should be trained to develop an appreciation for the technology involved in producing satisfactory consumer products. The generalist should understand how standards are made, how test methods are developed, how specifications are written, and how laws are made.

Before writing *Performance of Textiles,* I contacted several administrators, teachers, and researchers to find out what they thought objectives for a first- and second-level textile course should consist of. I also asked whether or not textile testing was taught, if students used textile equipment, and what equipment was used. In addition, I asked several leading business and industry firms what they expected and required of people trained in textiles.

Because there was a lack of unanimity among educators as to what subject matter should be taught at the first- and second-level courses in textiles, it was a great challenge in developing this text. I hope it meets the needs of the students planning a career as a consumer specialist, a consumer educator, buyer or merchandiser, a laboratory technician, or researcher, for in these career areas one must understand and have an appreciation for textile technology, textile care technology, product testing, test method development, standardization, and labeling. These varied areas led me to set up the following objectives for this text, giving the student:

1. An understanding and appreciation for the development of test methods, specifications, and standards.

2. An acquaintance with the equipment developed and used in making textile measurements.

3. An appreciation of the honesty and integrity required in order to evaluate and report test findings.

4. A realization that research is never static; it is always in a process of evolution.

5. An understanding of the basic concepts of stain removal, soil removal from fabrics by laundering, and dry cleaning.

6. A sound basis for counseling consumers on care procedures and specialty cleaning.

7. An insight into voluntary and mandatory labeling.

8. A realization of the interrelationships in the tripartite dynamics of government, business and industry programs, and their relation to consumer textiles.

9. An overview of the performance of textiles in consumer use—the problem and the possible solution.

This text does not stand alone. It must be supplemented by the use of the *Technical Manual of the American Association of Textile Chemists and Colorists,* the *Book of Standards of the American Society for Testing and Materials,* and colleges and universities that are properly equipped to supplement the text with meaningful laboratory experience.

Dorothy Siegert Lyle

Acknowledgments

No text can be written without the help and guidance of many people—too many to list here. However, I do acknowledge the generous support of the people in managerial positions of the International Fabricare Institute, especially Charles R. Riggott, General Manager and Dr. Manfred Wentz, former research director and now professor at the University of Wisconsin.

I also appreciate the permission for the use of materials from the *Technical Manual of the American Association of Textile Chemists and Colorists* granted to me by W. R. Martin Jr., Executive Director, Dr. George S. Wham, President, and G. J. Mandikos, Technical Secretary, for the use of materials from the American Society for Testing and Materials granted to me by Delores G. Collyer, Administrator, Information Services. The scientific equipment manufacturers were extremely cooperative in supplying photographs and illustrations. Their use, however, is not an endorsement. I also appreciate the permission of the American Association for Textile Technology for the permission to use material from their monograph, The Technology of Home Laundering granted by Joseph J. Crowley, President of AATT and Vice President of the United States Testing Company. I also thank T. R. Bainbridge, Tennessee Eastman Company, for permission to use his paper on Normal Distribution presented at the 1975 spring meeting of the ASTM Committee D-13 on textiles.

I acknowledge my professional friends who provided information, particularly Dean Laura M. Odland, the University of Tennessee; Dean Ruth Hoeflin and Dr. Theresa Perenick, Kansas State University; Dean Laura J. Harper, Oris Glisson, and Dr. W. L. Mauldin of Virginia Polytechnic Institute and State University; Dean J. Anthony Samenfink and Dr. Marcia D. Metcalf of Stout University of Wisconsin; Dean Lela O'Toole and Dr. Lynn Sider of Oklahoma State University; Dr. Ruth Galbraith, Auburn University; Patricia A. Wilson,

Colorado State University; Dr. Mary Lapitsky, Ohio State University; Dr. Lois Lund and Dr. Robert R. Rice, Michigan State University; Dean Norma Compton and Dr. Constance M. Chiassan, Purdue University; Dr. Virginia Carpenter and Dr. Patricia Helms Darling, University of Rhode Island; Dean Naomi Albanese and Dr. Pauline Keeney, University of North Carolina; Dr. Joan Lare, California State University (Long Beach); Dr. Betty Smith and Dr. Steven Spivak, University of Maryland; Dr. Arthur Price, Fashion Institute of Technology; and to my many friends in business, but particularly Genevieve M. Smith, Sears Roebuck and Company; John Anderson, Mary Stapleton, and Maurene Grasso, J.C. Penney Co. Inc.; Helen Horn Wheeler, Manager, Seal Laboratory, International Fabricare Institute; Lee Johnston, Manager, Laundering Laboratory and A. C. Lloyd, Technical Director, IFI Research Center, International Fabricare Institute and Rose White, American National Standards Institute; and to the unknown reviewers for their helpful and constructive criticisms and suggestions.

I deeply appreciate the counsel, assistance, and direction given me by Dr. Theresa Perenick, Kansas State University; Dr. Steven M. Spivak, University of Maryland; Dr. Manfred Wentz, University of Wisconsin; and Mary Hawkins, former editor of the National Association of Science Teachers. Special thanks go to my brother, John Siegert, and his wife, Anne, for the hours of effort spent in typing, retyping, and proofreading the manuscript, and to my husband, Ernest Tyrrell, for his patience, helpfulness, and understanding during the long hours I spent in the evenings and weekends in preparing this manuscript. At last, but by no means least, I thank Deborah Wiley and these people at Wiley for their guidance and support: Penny Doskow, Production Supervisor; Malcolm Easterlin, Manager of College Editing; Susan Giniger, Senior Editor; Vic Corvino, Illustration Supervisor; and Maura Fitzgerald, Designer.

D. S. L.

Contents

Performance
of Textiles

Introduction
An Overview

1

It's all in the eyes of the beholder!" In 1976, there are those who insist that this is the age of quality and value. The consumer wants more performance for the clothing dollar spent. For example, equipment has been designed—at a cost of $1 million—to assure quality in tricot knits. The unit uses radioactive tracer materials to monitor the production and finishing of tricot to insure quality in fabric width, weight, construction, and finishing. On the other hand, some mill men are turning back the clock to give the fashion designer fabrics that have a homespun, wrinkled, trashy, natural appearance. Does this mean that "trash fabrics" do not offer quality and value? One fashion editor expressed it this way:

> The quality and value of the homespuns and trash cotton is that very look. They don't look plastic, uniform, or mass produced. They don't look like polyester, they look homemade, different, natural, interesting. That's where the value is. That's what the fashion world wants.

Some consumers want colorfast dyes and uniform, clean stitches; others want dirty yarns, bows and skews (fabrics off grain), faded dyestuffs, and imperfect fabric construction.

For the consumer who wants and expects good performance from textiles during use, storage, laundering, or dry cleaning, it is necessary to set up a system of standards of serviceability and attitude measurements. Consumers should ask themselves: Why do I want to buy this item? What do I expect of it in way of performance? How long do I expect it to last? What did the salesperson tell me about it? Did I misuse or mistreat the item in use or cleaning? Why has it failed to live up to my expectations?

It has only been in recent years that consumer performance of textile merchandise has taken on significance. Amazingly, few laboratories keep statistics on fabric performance.

Some years ago, Dr. Jules Labarthe, Senior Fellow of the Kaufman Fellowship, Mellon Institute, Pittsburgh, Pennsylvania, studied 10,001 or more complaints. He found that 66 percent of the complaints were not the fault of the merchandise. This means that in some 6000 cases the consumer, the laundryman, or the dry cleaner had either misused or mistreated the textile item, thus causing its early failure, and that the fabric itself was not at fault. Thirty-four percent of the complaints was in the merchandise itself. In studying these figures, Dr. Labarthe pointed out that it is well to remember that many consumers do not bother to return merchandise when it fails to give satisfaction. Hence, the significance of a single complaint is great.

The Mellon Institute studies show that women's wear accounts for the greatest number of returns (71.3 percent), followed by men's wear (13.4 percent), children's wear (8.3 percent), and all other types of textiles (7.0 percent).

A recent survey of the Phillips Fibers Corporation was reported on by Arthur Dunham* entitled "The Wear-Dated Goals: 'Point of No Return.'" Mr. Dunham states: "Let's face it! No matter what steps are taken to manufacture good quality apparel, things can go wrong . . . 14,000 somethings that went wrong culled from unsatisfactory garments covered under the Wear-Dated program which were returned by customers last year (1974). They illustrate what fiber producers, mills, manufacturers, retailers, and consumers do wrong. Better yet, they show what can be done to make 14,000 wrongs all right."

Over the years, the International Fabricare Institute's Textile Analysis Laboratory has compiled textile damage statistics. Although the percentages for responsibility vary from year to year, an average indicates that the service industry is responsible for one-fourth of the complaints, the consumer for one-fourth and the manufacturer for about one-half. There are cases where responsibility cannot be assigned. Typical types of damage and responsibility assignments are shown in Table I–1.

Many times there is no easy answer as to who is responsible when textile damage occurs. The circuitous route through which textile items travel from fiber production to consumer use is a complex one. Sometimes it is impossible to pinpoint the responsibility.

Responsibility for satisfactory performance of textile items in end use is fourfold:

1. *Control at the source.* The manufacturer should produce merchandise that will give consumer satisfaction.

2. *Control by the retailer.* The retailer should purchase goods for resale that will give satisfactory consumer performance.

3. *Remedy of soil and stain conditions.* The service industries should study and develop proper methods of handling and cleaning of textile items, recognizing the fact that some merchandise requires special processing techniques.

4. *Prevention and care in use.* The consumer should exercise discrimination in the selection of textile merchandise, and use the article as it is intended to be used, giving it the proper care in wear, cleaning and storage.

Progress is being made in developing test methods and specifications that predict more accurately fabric performance under condi-

* The Clemson University *Textile Marketing Letter,* Vol. X, No. 5 (May 1975), College of Industrial Management and Textile Science, Clemson, South Carolina.

Table I-1 Types of Damage and Responsibility Assignments[a]

Consumer	Manufacturer	Service Industry
Mechanical damage	Loss of finish	Color loss—prespotting
Mineral acid damage	Color fading—pigment prints	Redeposition
Insect damage	Stiffness—plastic coated fabrics	Wool felting
Color loss—bleach	Acid and alkaline color change	Mechanical damage
Oxidized oil stains	Solvent-soluble dyes or pigments	Carbon
Shrinkage and stretching	Fluorescent dye discoloration	Heat damage
Carmelized sugar stains	Water-soluble dyes	Color loss—spotting
Fused fibers	Shrinkage	Delustering
Miscellaneous stains	Solvent-soluble dyes—leather	Stains in dry cleaning
Medicine and cosmetic stains	Sun fading	Acid and alkaline color change
Food and beverage stains (other than specified)	Bonding and inter-facing separation	Color loss (other than specified)
Albumin stains	Solvent-soluble sizing or coating	Stains—prespotting
Contact dye stains	Design damage (other than specified)	Color fading (other than specified)
Chemical damage (other than specified)	Foam laminate yellowing and deterioration	Nonvolatile material
Sulfuric acid damage	Finish damage—fur-type pile fabrics	Change in appearance (other than specified)
Scorch	Mechanical damage (other than specified)	Stretching
Streaks in drapes	Stains (other than specified)	Stains (other than specified)
Color loss (other than specified)	Change in appearance or odor (other than specified)	Fabric damage—bleaching
Ink stains	Sun tendered curtains and drapes	Pilling
Paint	Loss of flock print	Loss of finish

Table I-1 (Continued)

Consumer	Manufacturer	Service Industry
Color loss—perfume	Stretching	Color change (other than specified)
Carbon	Low-strength fibers	Color fading—wet cleaning
Oxycellulose	Color loss—physical	Failure to follow label instructions
Adhesive stains	Mechanical damage—leathers	Shrinkage (other than specified)
Metallic stains	Damaged velvets	Stiffening

[a] Ranked from highest to lowest number of complaints as recorded in 1975 by the International Fabricare Institute's Textile Analysis Laboratory.

tions of use. The National Bureau of Standards, the American Society for Testing and Materials, the American Association of Textile Chemists and Colorists, and the American National Standards Institute are working toward test methods that more accurately predict fabric behavior in end use. Such efforts will result in greater satisfaction for the consumer.

Some of the test methods currently used in testing fabrics fail to predict actual wear performance, the error being more often that the test is too mild than because it is too rigorous. It is also very difficult to simulate actual use or wear conditions in laboratory tests. There is a committee of the American Association of Textile Chemists and Colorists, RA 75, studying the correlation of laboratory tests and end-use performance.

No book could possibly cover all the consumer performance problems of fabrics during use, storage, or care.

I decided to discuss representative consumer performance problems along with specific test methods available today, in order that you may study the purpose and scope of the test method, the principles of the test, and the evaluation and reporting of test results, and to determine their relation to consumer end-use performance.

1

The Role of
Textile Testing

7

The textile industry has created a consumer appetite for product performance that often exceeds the capability of the item purchased. Business, industry, and the government spend a large part of their budget for research and development to give the consumer the desired properties he wants or *thinks* he wants.

According to Booth*, the subject of textile testing can be answered by the "W" questions: Why do we test? What do we test? Who does the test?

Textile testing is undertaken at different stages in the development, production, and distribution of goods and after items fail to give good performance in wear, use, and storage.

Why do we test fabrics? The most important reasons are:

1. *Research and Development.* Through research, new products are developed and old ones improved. Research gives the direction to solve a problem and determines which theories are sound.

2. *Quality Control.* A manufacturer or converter must exercise quality control and evaluate its performance before he sells to the cutter. Only by pretesting can the cutter know if the fabric will be satisfactory for a specific end use. Companies can set certain levels of quality control to produce the kind of product they sell.

The National Bureau of Standards and the Apparel Research Foundation in July 1968 published *Testing Programs for the Apparel Industry—Evaluation of Material and Components* to provide standard testing procedures for evaluating those essential properties that determine the compatability, appearance, and performance of materials and components. The proposed testing programs provide minimum, intermediate, and advanced levels of testing programs.†

3. *Comparative Testing.* This function is necessary in developing and improving a product. It makes possible a comparison of two or more products from identical or different sources.

4. *Analyzing Product Failure.* This is the first step in product performance. It is necessary to detect, analyze, and correct certain errors. Is the fabric better, identical, or poorer than another lot? Has a new process resulted in an improvement? If not, what changes need to be made? Who is responsible for the failure?‡

* J. E. Booth, *Principles of Textile Testing,* Chemical Publishing Co., Inc., New York (1969), p. 1.

† J. M. Blandford and Phyllis L. Bensing, *Testing Programs for the Apparel Industry—Evaluation of Materials and Components,* Part I and Part II; American Apparel Manufacturers Association.

‡ A. G. Blackman, *Manual For Fabric Defects in the Textile Industry* (1975); Granitville Company, Granitville, South Carolina.
Terms Relating To Fabric Defects; *Annual Book of ASTM Standards.*

5. *End-Use Performance.* How an item is to be used must be considered in testing programs because the consumer needs must be satisfied. End-use specifications are taking on new importance.

There has been a growing demand for textiles to meet specifications commensurate with their end uses. The use of specifications has many advantages: (1) the prevention of deterioration in quality by using inferior raw materials, (2) the production of goods of known performance, and (3) the opportunity to produce exactly what is required by the consumer. The consumer may be the garment manufacturer, the retail buyer, or the public. For example, a designer for a particular garment maker may approach a fabric house with a small sample of fabric of a particular color or design with a request to "reproduce this for me." Or specifications may be drawn up by a purchaser and the item is subjected to tests to prove whether it falls within the limits allowed in the specification. As an example, the government purchases garments for the military that must meet its own specifications.

The American National Standards Institute published a book, referred to as the L-22, which contains standards of performance for textile fabrics based on end use. The end uses include garments for girls, women, boys, and men and household textiles. A typical format of the standard is shown on page 14. The book is intended as a guide to aid the manufacturer, the consumer, and the general public. It is not a binding industry standard. Some companies use higher standards, while there are others that use lower ones. Many textile organizations are represented on the Committee for Textiles, L-22, which develops the standards. The first book was published in 1952, with revised and expanded standards published in 1960 and 1968.* The work, begun by the American National Standards Institute, has been transferred to the American Society for Testing and Materials Committee D13-56 Textiles (see Chapter 12). At the moment the entire manual is under revision and will appear with an ASTM format at some future date.

6. *Quality-Tested Programs.* Some manufacturers use testing and quality control programs in their advertising and promotion programs. The end product is the result of all the care, or lack of care, in the choice of raw materials, processing, finishing, and the making of an item. The objective is to produce an item that will satisfy the consumer's requirements both in serviceability and in price.

A number of organizations have been formed that test the performance of textiles. Some of these organizations are independent

* Performance Requirements for Textile Fabrics, ANSI Standard, L-22 (1968); American Society for Testing and Materials, Philadelphia, Pa.

organizations who carry out tests on items submitted by manufacturers. They issue a certification mark that allows the manufacturer to indicate on their labels that the goods have been tested and found satisfactory.

Some programs are controlled by the manufacturer, an association of firms with a common purpose, or trade associations. Some of these programs have fallen by the wayside because of lack of economic or consumer support. You can see that some of the reasons for textile testing are textile-manufacturer oriented; others are consumer oriented.

Many people have devoted a lifetime to the study of developing test methods and specifications that measure fiber and fabric performance. Some of the fiber and fabric properties are readily understood; others are not so easily understood; still others defy accurate objective measurements. One of the most baffling problems is the failure of some laboratory measurements to correlate with performance in consumer use and care of textiles.

There are some simple tests that can be performed relatively quickly and at little cost. They require little training and the minimum of equipment. But, for research and development, or when one needs to have specific and accurate data, training and experience in the use of sophisticated and expensive equipment is absolutely necessary.

CORRELATION OF TESTS

The data from fabric tests must be studied in relationship to its intended end use. Is the fabric strong enough to make into work clothes? Is the fabric fire resistant to meet the needs of a fireman? Is the fabric dimensionally stable for use in children's clothing? Are the colors fast enough to resist the ravages of sunlight and weathering? Many more similar questions need to be raised.

We must make realistic judgments in selecting test methods and making evaluations. Why should a fabric designed to be used in evening clothes possess lower strength and colorfastness properties than one designed for a drapery fabric? Why should a fabric designed for men's shirts resist chlorine bleach and high water temperatures? Why should a fabric designed to be washable meet the requirements of a dry-cleanable fabric? These and many other judgments need to be considered to determine the acceptance or rejection of fabrics designed for consumer use.

The correlation of textile text methods or procedures with consumer use is not an easy task. The problems involved are the following: (1) When is it necessary to duplicate actual use conditions? (2)

When is it acceptable to only correlate test methods and procedures with actual use conditions? (3) Where does the break-even point occur in the volume of tests required and subsequent assurance of quality and the cost to the manufacturer, which is passed on to the consumer in the final price of the merchandise?

The reason that the correlation of test methods with actual use conditions is so difficult is because we are dealing with human beings, and no two people are alike. There are more variables in the area of wearing apparel than in household items. But even in the use of household fabrics there are many variables due to individual differences in use and locations. For example: a journalist wearing a corduroy suit and sitting at a typewriter desk where the suit is subjected to abrasion of the underside of the desk on the knee area shows a different wear factor than a salesman wearing the identical suit. In some cases the laboratory test method and results give a higher measurement than that which might occur in use. The opposite may also be true. Frequently, laboratory test methods do not measure a combination of wear factors, cleaning methods, and storage of an item from one year to the next. For example, a window fabric may be affected not only by its placement in a room but in what part of the country it is used.

Consumers are at a loss to properly evaluate a garment or household item unless the performance information is given on a label or hang tag. Even then he can do so only if he is educated to understand the meaning of test methods, test results, and test evaluations. This is a very difficult task. The majority of consumers must depend on the reputation of the manufacturer and the retail store where the merchandise is purchased. This is why pretesting is important to the consumer, members of the service industries, the retail stores and the manufacturer.

AGENCIES ENGAGED IN TEXTILE TESTING

There are two technical and scientific organizations that are the leaders in publishing methods for testing textile materials. One—the American Society for Testing and Materials—specializes in physical properties and the other—the American Association of Textile Chemists and Colorists—concentrates on dyeing and chemical treatments. Both organizations are comprised of many technical committees whose members include a wide cross section of the textile industry. The recommended test methods of both organizations have generally been accepted and are used by the textile industry. The test methods are also used as an aid to governmental agencies and the general public. For more detail on these organizations, see Chapter 12.

The U.S. government also publishes a book containing methods for testing textile materials entitled *Federal Test Method Standard No. 191*. It is used for testing fabrics for government purchase. Many of the test procedures contained in the *ASTM Annual Book* and the *AATCC Technical Manual* are also in the Standard No. 191. The Defense Personnel Support Center publishes a Qualified Laboratory List.*

Many mills, manufacturers, retail stores, magazines, and trade associations have their own textile testing laboratories. There are also companies that do independent testing. These firms perform tests on textile samples submitted and send the results to the company requesting the information. For more detail on these organizations, see Chapter 12. For a listing of independent textile testing laboratories, see Appendix A.

CLASSIFICATION OF TEXTILE TEST METHODS

Textile test methods or procedures may be classified in different ways. Some authorities group test procedures according to (1) physical testing, (2) chemical testing, and (3) microscopic testing. Still others classify test methods as (1) fiber identification including burning tests, microscopic tests, and solubility tests, (2) fiber and yarn analysis, (3) fabric analysis, (4) physical performance tests, and (5) performance to care—laundering and dry cleaning. For the purpose of our discussion, we shall review fiber characteristics, yarn analysis, and physical fabric properties. For the discussion of the physical performance tests we shall consider those tests designed to measure (1) aesthetic appearance, (2) durability, (3) comfort (4) safety, (5) care, (6) biological resistance, and (7) environmental resistance.

PARAMETERS NECESSARY FOR TEXTILE TESTING

Anyone who wishes to pursue a career in research or textile testing, or to interpret test methods, procedures, and results even to the lay public, must understand the parameters that are a part of laboratory analysis: (1) the use of statistics, (2) methods of sampling, (3) moisture relationships, (4) the necessity for calibrating equipment, and (5) the validity or reproducibility of test results.

There are some subjective tests in which a numerical result is difficult to produce. One fabric may be judged softer in handling than another. Usually a series of tests is made on a group of individual items and the results from each test recorded and subsequently analyzed

* Qualified Laboratory List No. 21, Defense Personnel Support Center, 2000 South 20th Street, Philadelphia, Pa. 19101.

by suitable methods. The use of statistical methods enables you to extract the maximum amount of information about the tested material from the available data and to use this information for various purposes such as quality control and research. Without an understanding of the elements of statistical methods, the study of testing methods and instruments becomes rather pointless. The instruments used are means to an end and are not ends in themselves.

STATISTICS

The study of statistics in depth is very important to the person who plans to go into research. Many individuals have to write research papers and reports as well as read them.

In order to interpret test results, the minimum you need is a general understanding of frequency distributions, of calculating the usual statistics such as the average and standard deviations, and of designing and analyzing simple comparative experiments. An excellent reference for the study of statistics is *Introduction to Statistical Analysis* by W. J. Dixon and F. J. Massey, Jr.* You should also study STP-15-C, the *ASTM Manual on Quality Control of Materials*† and the *Handbook of Textile Testing and Quality Control*.‡

T. C. Bainbridge, of the Tennessee Eastman Company, presented a paper at the 1975 spring meeting of the ASTM Committee D-13 on Textiles§ in which he described the nature of frequency distributions in general, the specific properties of a normal distribution, the calculations of confidence limits and critical differences, and the testing for normality. His presentation is an excellent example of how data can be handled accurately so that it is understandable. Permission to use parts of his paper here has been granted, to show how statistics can be used to make data understandable.

Normal Frequency Distribution

Any mass of data can be simplified by condensing it into a frequency distribution. For example, 270 individual values can be reduced to a table like that shown in Figure 1–1. The data in such a table can then be plotted in any of several ways, the most common of which are frequency polygons and histograms (see Figure 1–2).

* McGraw Hill Book Company, Inc., New York, New York (1957).

† American Society for Testing and Materials, Philadelphia, Pa.

‡ E. B. Grover and D. S. Hamby, *Handbook of Textile Testing and Quality Control*, Textile Book Publishers, New York (1960).

§ T. R. Bainbridge, Paper, "The Normal Distribution," Tennessee Eastman Company, Kingsport, Tennessee.

USA Standard Performance Requirements for Women's and Girls' Woven Blouse or Dress Fabrics

PROPERTY	MINIMUM REQUIREMENTS					TEST METHOD See Part VII*
IDENTIFICATION:	L22.10.3-B Washable 160 F	L22.10.3-W Washable 160 F No Bleach	L22.10.3-C Washable 120 F No Bleach	L22.10.3-H Washable 105 F No Bleach	L22.10.3-D Drycleanable	
BREAKING STRENGTH						USAS L14.184
Dry (See Note 1)	20 lb	20 lb	20 lb	20 lb	20 lb	Grab Test
Wet	12 lb	12 lb	12 lb	12 lb	12 lb	(ASTM D 1682)
RESISTANCE TO						USAS L14.102
YARN SLIPPAGE	15 lb	15 lb	15 lb	15 lb	15 lb	(ASTM D 434)
TONGUE TEAR STRENGTH						USAS L14.207
(See Note 2)	1 lb	1 lb	1 lb	1 lb	1 lb	(ASTM D 2261)
YARN SHIFTING						USAS L14.103
Maximum Opening						(ASTM D 1336)
Satins	0.10 in.	0.10 in.	0.10 in.	0.10 in.	0.10 in.	1 lb load
Others	0.05 in.	0.05 in.	0.05 in.	0.05 in.	0.05 in.	1 lb load
MAXIMUM DIMENSIONAL CHANGE —						USAS L14.138 (AATCC 96) (ASTM D 1905) Table II
EACH DIRECTION	2.5%	2.5%				Test No. III
(See Note 3)			2.5%			Test No. II
				2.5%		Test No. I
					2%	AATCC 108
ODOR	Class 3	Class 3	Class 3	Class 3	Class 3	TDI No. 3
COLORFASTNESS TO						USAS L14.54
Atmospheric Fading after						(1 cycle)
Washing (See Note 4)	Class 4	Class 4	Class 4	Class 4		(AATCC 23)
Drycleaning (See Note 4)					Class 4	
Laundering	Test IVA	Test IIIA	Test IIA	Test IA		USAS L14.81
Alteration in Shade	Class 4	Class 4	Class 4	Class 4		(AATCC 61)
Staining	Class 3	Class 3	Class 3	Class 4		Intl Gray Scale
Drycleaning (See Note 5)	Class 4	Class 4	Class 4	Class 4	Class 4	AATCC 85
Crocking						
Dry	Class 4	Class 4	Class 4	Class 4	Class 4	USAS L14.72
Wet	Class 3	Class 3	Class 3	Class 3	Class 3	(AATCC 8)
Wet-Washed Crock Cloth (See Note 6)	Class 4	Class 4	Class 4	Class 4	Class 4	Color Transference Chart
Perspiration						USAS L14.56
Alteration in Shade	Class 4	Class 4	Class 4	Class 4	Class 4	(AATCC 15)
Staining	Class 4	Class 4	Class 3	Class 3	Class 3	Intl Gray Scale
Light	L4-20 hr	L4-20 hr	L4-20 hr	L4-20 hr	L4-20 hr	USAS L14.53 (AATCC 16A)

NOTE 1: Fabrics known to exhibit a wet strength which is in excess of the dry strength requirement need not be subjected to a wet test.

NOTE 2: Use of USAS L14.203 (ASTM D 1424—Elmendorf) Test Method is permitted if preferred with existing requirements as given in this standard. However, in case of controversy, USAS L14.207 (ASTM D 2261) shall prevail.

NOTE 3: Use AATCC Test Method 99 when applicable. Use FLA Tests No. 1 and No. 2 for laminated (bonded) fabrics.

NOTE 4: Use corresponding test methods as provided in the columns under laundering and drycleaning.

NOTE 5: Under this standard, a washable fabric shall also be colorfast to drycleaning, unless specifically labeled: DO NOT DRYCLEAN. Drycleanable goods are drycleanable only.

NOTE 6: For wet-washed crock cloth use CS 59-44, Part VIII, Colorfastness to Crocking, Para 31a.

*The references to the test numbers in this column give only the permanent part of the designation of the USA Standard, AATCC, ASTM, and other test methods. The particular edition for year of issue of each method used in testing the material for conformance to the requirements here specified shall be as stated in the current edition of Part VII of these L22 Standards.

Figure 1-1

Cell midpoint	Frequency
300	1
450	1
600	6
750	38
900	80
1050	83
1200	39
1350	17
1500	2
1650	2
1800	0
1950	1
Total	270

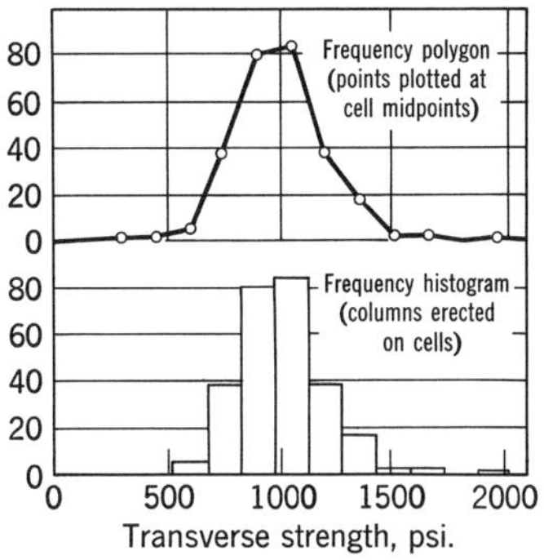

Figure 1-2 Presentation of distributions.

In reducing data to a frequency table, it is often necessary to group a range of values into a single "cell" in order to obtain the 10 to 20 cell groupings that tend to represent the original data with a minimum loss of information.

Either grouped or ungrouped data can be summarized by obtaining the arithmetic average (or mean) and the standard deviation using Equations 1.1, Eq 1.2, or their algebraic equivalents:

$$\bar{X} = \Sigma X/n \qquad (1.1)*$$

$$s = [\Sigma(X - \bar{X})(n - 1)]^{1/2} \qquad (1.2)\dagger$$

where

$\bar{X}$ = the arithmetic average or mean
s = the standard deviation
x = the value of an individual observation
n = the number of individual observations
Σ = the summation sign

X	(X − X̄)
8	+2
6	0
7	+1
4	−2
5	−1
Totals 30	0

Figure 1-3

For example, given the five observations shown in Figure 1–3, the value of $\bar{X} = (8 + 6 + 7 + 4 + 5)/5 = 30/5 = 6$.

The standard deviation is just what its name implies: a standard measure of variability. The lower-case Greek letter sigma, σ, is used as the symbol for the standard deviation for a whole population, while lower-case s is used for an estimate of the standard deviation obtained from a sample.

In working with ASTM methods, we are usually interested in calculating s, an estimate of the standard deviation, instead of σ, the

* STP 15-C, *ASTM Manual on Quality Control of Materials,* American Society for Testing and Materials, 1916 Race Street, Philadelphia, Pa. 19103 (February 1951), pp. 5–11.

† STP 15-C, pp. 14–20.

15   *The Role of Textile Testing*

value of the standard deviation for all possible values in a population. The term "variance" is nothing more than the square of the standard deviation or the value obtained by Equation 1.1 prior to extracting the square root.

Using the differences between each observation and the average shown in the second column of Figure 1–3, $s^2 = (+2)^2 + (0)^2 + (+1)^2 + (-2)^2 + (-1)^2/(5-1) = 10/4 = 2.5$. In turn, $S = (2.5)^{1/2} = 1.58$.

Equation 1.2 defines the standard deviation and works well when the average can be expressed as an exact value. There are other equations that are easier to use with a calculator and not subject to rounding errors in the value of the average.*

Equation 1.2 uses degrees of freedom as a divisor, or one less than the number of observations in estimating the standard deviation. The concept of degrees of freedom has been mistakenly thought to be very complex.

Figure 1–4 shows that for any set of five observations having a specific average, four of the observations can have any value and may be considered free because adjusting the fifth value can still give the desired average. For example, if it is required that a group of five people average having 53¢, four of them can have any amount of coins they wish. By adjusting the amount of change in the possession of the fifth person, including the possibility of an I O U to represent a negative amount, the total change in the possession of these persons can be made to equal $2.65 or an average of 53¢ a person.

Thus, obtaining a statistic such as an average can be considered as fixing the value of one of the observations, resulting in $n - 1$ degrees of freedom for the set of data.

Every distribution has three primary characteristics: location on the x axis, spread along the x axis and shape. The average and the standard deviation are our best measures of the location and spread of the distribution. Shape can be observed and categorized in a general sense, or more elaborate tests can be made to determine whether the shape of the observed distribution can reasonably be said to agree with an expected shape.

Frequency distributions, like people, come in many shapes and sizes. Figure 1–5 shows four typical shapes of distribution. Figure 1–5a shows a J-shaped distribution. Counting data and data on percent defective often form J-shaped distributions. Figure 1–5b is a "skewed" distribution; it is not symmetrical but has a longer tail on one side as compared to the other. When the longer tail is toward the higher values of the distribution (as in this figure) the skewness is pos-

	Free
Degrees	Free
of	Free
Freedom	Free
	Fixed
	Average

Figure 1-4

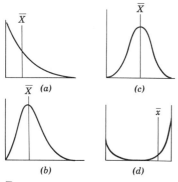

$\overline{X}$ (a) $\overline{X}$ (c)

(b)   (d)

Figure 1-5

---

* STP 15-C, pp. 14–20.

itive. When the longer tail is toward the lower observations, the skewness is negative. Again, counting data and data on percent defective can form skewed distributions. In addition, many data based on measurements of observed values show some skewness.

Figure 1–5c is a symmetrical distribution or a distribution with the average exactly at the center of a symmetrical bell-shaped distribution. At times, counting data and data on percent defective form symmetrical distributions. In fact, there are many symmetrical distributions of which the normal distribution is one.

Figure 1–5d is a U-shaped distribution. This type of distribution is not very important but is included to show that rather surprising shapes do occur for distribution of actual data.

PROPERTIES OF THE NORMAL DISTRIBUTION

The normal frequency distribution is a specific symmetrical bell-shaped distribution in the family of curves illustrated in Figure 1–5c. There is a specific equation for describing the normal curve, and symmetrical bell-shaped distributions that do not conform to that equation are not normal. For example, a curve may have more observations near the mean than a normal curve. Such a curve has more peakedness than a normal curve and is said to have a positive excess of kurtosis. In the same way, a somewhat flat-topped curve with relatively few observations near the mean has a negative excess of kurtosis. These differences may occur even when the average and standard deviations for the distributions are equal but usually have relatively small influence on most statistical conclusions.

As shown in Figure 1–6, the standard deviation for the normal curve equals the horizontal distance from the mean to the inflection point. The inflection point is the point at which the curve stops turning downward and begins to turn upward as it moves out from the average. Figure 1–6 also illustrates the fraction of observations

Figure 1-6

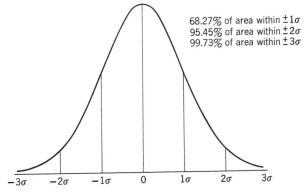

68.27% of area within $\pm 1\sigma$
95.45% of area within $\pm 2\sigma$
99.73% of area within $\pm 3\sigma$

-3σ $\quad -2\sigma$ $\quad -1\sigma$ $\quad 0$ $\quad 1\sigma$ $\quad 2\sigma$ $\quad 3\sigma$

17   *The Role of Textile Testing*

that are expected to fall within multiples of one, two or three standard deviations from the average. For example, 95.45 percent of the observations should fall within plus or minus two standard deviations from the average. There are numerous extensive tables showing this and other properties of data from normal distributions.

The normal distribution and its use to explain the probabilities of games of chance was first established by de Moivre in 1733. Laplace later gave a proof for the curve and, as a result, the curve is sometimes called the Laplacean curve. Carl Friedrich Gauss (1777–1855) approved the law, used it, and gave an original proof of it. Because of his reputation as a mathematician, the term "Gaussian curve" is the most frequently used alternate name for the normal curve.

The normal curve is a continuous function that lends itself well to mathematical treatment. It has been explored thoroughly and many useful relationships have been developed, one of the most useful of which is shown in Equation 1.3*:

$$s_{\bar{x}} = (s^2/n)^{1/2} = s/\sqrt{n} \tag{1.3}$$

where $s_{\bar{x}}$ = the standard error (or standard deviation) of an average and where the other terms are as previously defined. This relationship permits us to calculate the variability for averages of any size when knowing the variability for individual observations.

The normal curve is the basis of virtually all tests of significance and of many statistical tables. Unless a test of significance is specifically labeled as nonparametric, or independent of the underlying distribution of the data, it is almost surely based on the normal distribution.

The tables for the normal distribution allow us to construct a frequency distribution based on a specified average, standard deviation, and number of observations that is an excellent approximation of the original distribution yielding those statistics when the original distribution was a mound-shaped one approximating the normal curve.

The sampling distributions of averages, standard deviations, and many other parameters are either exactly or approximately normal. Averages can be used to form a frequency distribution just as individual observations can be formed into a distribution. A distribution of averages of as few as four observations per average will be normal for all practical purposes regardless of the shape of the distribution for the individual observations. For example, averages of four drawn from a distribution like that in Figure 1–5d will have an essentially normal distribution instead of a U-shaped one.

* STP 15-C, pp. 23–25.

The normal curve can be used as a starting point for generating other curves of statistical importance.

If two averages, $\bar{X}_1$ and $\bar{X}_2$, each containing n observations, are drawn independently from the same normal distribution, their difference $(\bar{X}_1 - \bar{X}_2)$ is an important statistic. If many such differences were obtained by drawing many such pairs of averages, a frequency distribution of the differences can be obtained. The average of such a distribution of differences would be zero and the standard error for such differences could be calculated by Equation 1.4*:

$$s_{(\bar{X}_1 - \bar{X}_2)} = (2s^2/n)^{1/2} = 1.414s/\sqrt{n} = 1.414s_{\bar{X}} \qquad (1.4)$$

where $s_{(\bar{X}_1 - \bar{X}_2)}$ = the standard error (or standard deviation) for a difference between two averages of n and where the other terms are as defined earlier.

The theory permits the user to calculate the expected variability for differences between two averages of any size based on the variability for individual observations.

Equation 1.3 shows how to calculate the standard error for averages of any specified size. Using the grand average for all individuals and such a standard error, we can calculate a frequency distribution for averages of that size. Such a distribution is shown as the inner curve in Figure 1–7. Equation 1.4 may be used to calculate the standard error for differences between two such averages. Using zero as the mean and the calculated standard error, we can construct a frequency distribution for the difference between two averages as shown by the outer curve in Figure 1–7.

Note that the distribution for differences between two averages is 1.414 times as wide as the distribution for single averages of the same size. This means that confidence limits based on the distribu-

Figure 1-7

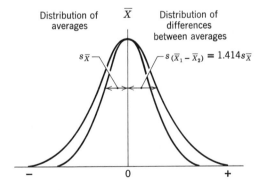

Distribution of averages $\bar{X}$ Distribution of differences between averages

$s_{\bar{X}}$

$s_{(\bar{X}_1 - \bar{X}_2)} = 1.414s_{\bar{X}}$

$-$ 0 $+$

* ASTM Recommended Practice D-2906-74, Statements on Precision and Accuracy, *1974 Annual Book of ASTM Standards,* Part 32, Section 8.

19   *The Role of Textile Testing*

tion for single averages cannot be used realistically to determine if an observed difference between two averages is significantly large.

In order to calculate confidence limits for single averages, it is only necessary to multiply the standard error for single averages by a constant (3,4). To obtain the critical difference for comparing two averages, the standard error for the difference in two averages is multiplied by the same constant. The value of the critical difference is larger than the confidence limit as a result of the larger standard error when evaluating the difference between two averages.

Testing for Normality

Unfortunately, there is no foolproof way to test for normality. The care with which a test should be made is, of course, dependent on the importance of being correct and of detecting relatively small departures from normality.

In most tests of significance based on the normal curve, no serious errors will be caused by moderate departures from normality. At worst, the odds will be changed slightly: the actual probability level will be slightly higher or lower than the assumed probability level. If the departure from normality is due only to skewness, two-sided confidence limits will include essentially the predicted percentage of results with fewer than half of the anticipated values being outside one limit but with more than half of the anticipated values being outside the other limit. Skewness will, therefore, have some effect on one-sided confidence limits as, for example, a limit that states 95 percent of test results would be expected to equal or exceed a specified value.

In the simplest situations, a judgment can be made about significant departures from normality based only on a subjective evaluation of a frequency polygon. Two more formal tests frequently used are plots on normal probability paper and the chi-square test.*

To use normal probability paper,† list the data as a cumulative frequency distribution. Such a distribution shows the percentage of the observations that equal or exceed a series of specified values. Figure 1–8 shows two plots of such cumulative frequency distributions on a simplified version of normal probability paper. The data points indicated by circles represent a distribution of averages of 10.

The straight line formed by the points is a strong indication of normality. The data points indicated by X's represent a distribution of variances for samples of 10. The curved line formed by the points indicates a departure from normality.

* W. J. Dixon and F. J. Massey, Jr., *Introduction to Statistical Analysis,* McGraw-Hill Book Co., New York, (1957), pp. 55–57 and pp. 226–227.

† The equivalent of Keuffel and Esser Co., Style 46-8000, or of Codex Book Co. Inc., Norwood, Mass., 02060. Style 3127 is acceptable.

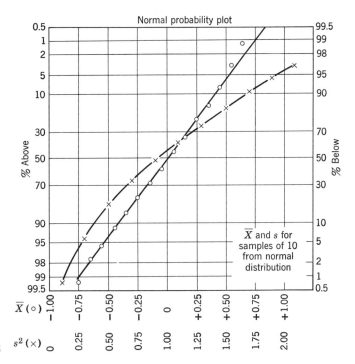

Figure 1-8

The chi-square test is performed by comparing observed frequencies to frequencies calculated from tables of the normal curve and the observed average and standard deviation. The contribution of each observed frequency's departure from the anticipated frequency is added to obtain a total that is evaluated by comparison to a critical value from a table of the chi-square function.

All of these methods of testing normality require a frequency distribution. This means that we cannot realistically evaluate normality or conformance to any other type of frequency distribution from a group of observations consisting of a number of small groups obtained under different circumstances, such as in different laboratories, on different materials, or the like. The entire group, preferably of at least 50 to 100 observations, must all be taken under the same set of conditions. This means that questions about normality cannot be answered by the type of data obtained from a typical interlaboratory test.

SAMPLING

The manufacture of textiles is largely a system of mass production; a spinning mill produces thousands of bobbins of yarn every day; a weaving mill weaves hundreds of yards of fabric. To test every item would be impossible. Furthermore, many tests are destructive in character and this in itself limits the amount of testing. In testing products in a testing laboratory, this can become very costly. Therefore, testing may be made on a "test sample."

The sampling method is governed by the following: (1) the form of the material, (2) the amount of material available, (3) the nature of the test, (4) the type of testing instrument, (5) the information required, and (6) the degree of accuracy required.

The material available for testing is called the population, and the sample is a relatively small number of individual members that are selected to represent that population. If all the members of the population were identical, we would be justified in testing just one item. The characteristics thus measured would be that of the population. Unfortunately, one of the major problems in textiles is that of variation. Fibers in the same bale of cotton vary in length and fineness, bobbins from the same yarn frame vary in count and strength, fabrics woven on the same loom vary in appearance and freedom from defects, and garments made from two lots of fabric may give different performance in end use.

It follows that in order to get an answer that represents the population, a sample must consist of a number of individuals. An individual is one member of the population. The method of selecting the individuals to make up a sample ensures that a random sample is obtained. In such a sample every individual in the population has an equal chance of being selected. This means that it is possible to eliminate bias in the sample. Test methods and procedures specify how and where samples should be taken for the specific test.

Acceptance Sampling

Acceptance sampling, which could be called rejection or decision sampling, is the process of choosing a portion of a lot or unit of production to test for acceptability. It is the first step in a system to determine whether or not a manufacturer is meeting the specifications that apply to his product. Acceptance sampling has been used widely by the military, and it has come to be a part of contracts between private companies.

Recently, the Consumer Product Safety Commission issued a proposed sampling plan (see Chapter 5, Part 4). If a product is a risk to the consumer, 100 percent testing provides maximum insurance. When testing is destructive or costly, some sort of accepted sampling procedure is essential. For a complete discussion of acceptance sampling, refer to the articles published in *ASTM Standardization News*, Volume 3, No. 9 (September 1975).

MOISTURE RELATIONSHIPS

Some of the most important properties of textile fibers and fabrics are closely related to their behavior in various atmospheric conditions. Most fibers and fabrics are hygroscopic, that is, they are able to absorb water vapor from a moist atmosphere and, conversely, lose water in a dry atmosphere. Many physical properties are affected by the amount of water absorbed such as dimensions, tensile strength, elastic recovery, electrical resistance, and rigidity. In fabrics, moisture relationships of a fiber play a major part in deciding whether the fabric is suitable or unsuitable for a particular purpose. The importance of this point is appreciated when fabrics for clothing, both outerwear and underwear, are considered. Additional factors arise in these cases since the structural details of the fabric can modify the behavior of the fiber. For example, fabrics made from a hydrophobic material such as polyester can pick up water by a "wicking" action along the fiber and yarn surfaces. The amount of moisture in a sample of material may be expressed in terms of Regain or Moisture Content.*

Regain is defined as the weight of water in a material expressed as a percentage of the oven dry weight. Moisture content is the weight of water in a material expressed as a percentage of the total weight (or conditioned weight as measured under standard conditions).

Let oven dry weight $= D$
weight of water $= W$
regain $= R$
moisture content $= M$

Then,

$$R = \frac{100W}{D} \qquad \text{and} \qquad M = \frac{100W}{D + W}$$

Also,

$$R = \frac{M}{1 - (M/100)} \qquad \text{and} \qquad M = \frac{R}{1 + (R/100)}$$

$$W = \text{conditioned weight} - \text{dry weight}$$

$$R = \frac{\text{conditioned weight} - \text{dry weight}}{\text{dry weight}} \times 100$$

$$M = \frac{\text{conditioned weight} - \text{dry weight}}{\text{conditioned weight}} \times 100$$

The regain of a fabric depends on the amount of moisture present in the surrounding air. The dampness of the atmosphere can be described in terms of "humidity," either absolute humidity or relative

---

* J. E. Booth, Principles of Textile Testing, Moisture Regain and Testing, p. 100.

humidity. Absolute humidity is the weight of water present in a unit volume of moist air, that is, grains per cubic foot or grams per cubic meter.

Relative humidity is the ratio of the actual vapor pressure to the saturated vapor pressure at the same temperature, expressed as a percentage.

$$\text{r.h. (percent)} = \frac{\text{actual vapor pressure}}{\text{saturated vapor pressure}} \times 100$$

An alternative definition for relative humidity is the ratio of the absolute humidity of the air to that of air saturated with water vapor at the same temperature and pressure. This ratio may then be expressed as a percentage. At ordinary temperatures such as those at which processing and testing are carried out, the two ratios are almost identical. It is convenient to describe a given atmosphere in terms of relative humidity rather than absolute humidity because the regain of fabrics appears to depend on the relative humidity rather than the actual amount of water vapor present.

Since the relative humidity affects the regain of a fabric, and since the properties of the material are influenced by the regain, it is necessary to specify the atmospheric conditions in which testing should be carried out.

CONDITIONING OF TEXTILES FOR TESTING

Standard conditions are designed so that reproducible results may be obtained on the fabrics tested.*

The physical properties of textiles and, consequently, the results of tests, are usually affected by temperature and relative humidity. The specified temperature of $70 \pm 2°F$ ($21 \pm 1°C$) and a relative humidity of 65 ± 2 percent are used as the standard atmosphere in the United States for testing textiles. Conditioning and testing under these conditions provide assurance that reliable comparisons may be made between laboratories, mills, and manufacturers.

The results of tests obtained on textile materials and products under varying or nonstandard conditions may not be comparable with one another. Differences in temperature of 20°F should not cause too much variation in physical characteristics. With regard to humidity, most man-made fiber fabrics, being hydrophobic, do not absorb much moisture and so will not be greatly affected by changes in relative humidity. More significant differences may be evident, because of their hydrophilic nature, in the results of the tests of rayon, cotton, and wool at different relative humidities. In the absence of laboratory conditioning facilities, a room may be equipped with an

* Conditioning Textiles and Textile Products for Testing; ASTM Designation D-1776-74, (1975).

air conditioner and, when necessary, a humidifier or dehumidifier to achieve a temperature within a range of 65 to 85°F (18 to 29°C) and a relative humidity of less than 65 percent, preferably between 45 and 65 percent. The standard conditions used in various countries come within this range of temperature and relative humidity.

The instruments used for the determination of the humidity are known as hygrometers or psychrometers. There are methods such as the gravimetric, chemical, and the dew point methods that may be used, but they are not commonly used in testing laboratories.

The three main types of instruments used to determine humidity are (1) wet-and-dry bulb hygrometer, (2) hair hygrometer, and (3) electrolytic hygrometer.

CALIBRATING INSTRUMENTS

Standard test methods that include requirements for calibration of apparatus are included under the names of the equipment or the test method (see *Annual Book of ASTM Standards*). For example, in the test method Standard Specifications for Tensile Testing Machines for Textile Materials'* instructions are given for the verification of indicated load and verification of recorded elongation of constant-rate-of-extension type machines, verification of recorded elongation of constant-rate-of-traverse type and constant-rate-of-load type testing machines, and verification of nominal gage length. The verification should be done or supervised by a qualified person competent to exercise scientific judgment.

Another example is the calibration of the carbon-arc lamp in a Fade-Ometer. Light-sensitive paper and a booklet of standard faded strips of the paper are obtained from the National Bureau of Standards for calibration of commercial fading lamps. The standard faded strips are produced in the Bureau's Master Fading Lamp, which is adjusted to produce in 20-hours exposure appreciable fading of the American Association of Textile Chemists and Colorists (AATCC) Standard L_4. The booklet contains faded strips exposed for stated intervals of standard fading hours, and is suitable for use in calibrating fading lamps in a length of run about equivalent to the life of a trim of carbons, or 20 fading hours.

The importance of accuracy in testing cannot be overemphasized. A piece of equipment is as good as the operator using it. Routine care of equipment is essential, but calibration of the instruments is equally important. It is important to know the degree of tolerance that is acceptable. Any test equipment that needs calibration should be verified at intervals of 12 months and, if used only occasionally, every two to three years. If delicate equipment is moved or when there is

* Tensile Testing Machines for Textile Materials; ASTM E-4-72 (1975).

reason to doubt the accuracy of results, the equipment should be calibrated and verified.

REPRODUCIBILITY OF RESULTS

Again, we repeat: ACCURACY IS REQUIRED IN TEXTILE TESTING. Conditions of tests must be reproducible for data to be reliable. Many research studies are planned to involve many laboratories and many technicians. Before cooperative research is begun, the scope and purpose of the interlaboratory test must be established and should include (1) the class of material or type of test method being studied, (2) the quality characteristics being measured, (3) the conditions whose effects are being studied, (4) the conditions under which the tests are being made, and (5) the objectives being reached by the interlaboratory test.

The objectives to be achieved should include (1) a definition of the precision or reproducibility or repeatability on essentially the same material, (2) a definition of the overall reproducibility, that is, how close the averages come to the grand average of all tests or to the value adopted as the reference standard, (3) a statement of desirable commercial sample sizes, accompanied by the associated confidence level and sampling error percentages when necessary, (4) a statement of the limitations found during the test, and (5) a statement of the agreement among laboratories, among operators, and such other breakdowns as are necessary to extract from the data all the information possible.

EVALUATING COLORFASTNESS OF TEXTILES

There are general practices and procedures for evaluating colorfastness, color staining, and color transfer.

The American Association of Textile Chemists and Colorists has established standard terminology for rating colorfastness properties of fabrics to various test methods as well as evaluating color staining and color transfer. Each class of fastness is defined with respect to the test method. A standard is usually indicated. In other words, each test method has a yardstick for rating the property to be measured.

Eight classes are provided for fastness to light, ranging from Class 9, very high lightfastness, to Class 1, very low lightfastness.*

Five classes are provided for most other properties, ranging from Class 5, high, to Class 1, low.

Fastness lower than Class 1 is seldom of interest, but it may be designated Class 0. Any material that does not qualify for Class 1 in a test falls in Class 0.

* AATCC Nomenclature for Colorfastness Ratings; *AATCC Technical Manual,* p. 96.

Words may be used to express the relative fastness of the classes as determined by the tests. One should become familiar with the nomenclature used for colorfastness ratings as given in the following table:

Terms for Fastness to Light		Degree of Alteration in Shade and Strength	
Class		Class	
9	Superlative	5	Negligible or no change
8	Outstanding	4	Slightly changed
7	Excellent	3	Noticeable change
6	Very good	2	Considerably changed
5	Good	1	Much change
4	Fairly good		
3	Fair		
2	Poor		
1	Very poor		

Terms for Most Other Properties		Terms for Describing Differences in Color (shade and strength)	
Class		Class	
5	Excellent	Br	Brighter
4	Good	B1	Bluer
3	Fair	D	Duller
2	Poor	G	Greener
1	Very poor	R	Redder
		S	Stronger
		W	Weaker
		Y	Yellower

Dischargeability of Dyeings		Degree of Crocking or Staining of Effect Fibers	
Class		Class	
5	Discharge is white	5	Negligible or no staining
4	Discharge is slightly tinted	4	Slightly stained
3	Discharge is noticeably colored	3	Noticeably stained
2	Discharge is considerably colored	2	Considerably stained
1	Does not discharge	1	Heavily stained

Gray Scale For Color Change

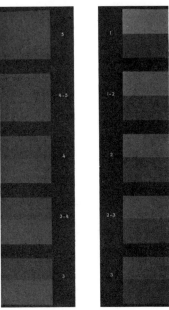

Figure 1-9 Gray Scale for Color Change. (Courtesy: American Association of Textile Chemists and Colorists)

This scale* consists of nine pairs of standard gray chips, each pair representing a difference in color or contrast (shade and strength) corresponding to a numerical fastness rating (see Figure 1–9). The results of colorfastness tests are rated by comparing the difference in color of tested specimen and original fabric with the differences represented by the scale.

The fastness ratings and corresponding color differences, determined by the Adams chromatic value formula, are given in the first two columns of Table 1–1.

Fastness rating 5 is represented on the scale by two identical chips that are mounted side by side, are neutral gray in color, and have a reflectance of 12 ± 1 percent. The color difference is 0.

Fastness ratings 4.5 to 1, inclusive, are represented by a "reference" chip identical with those used for Step 5, paired with similar but lighter neutral gray chips, the visual differences in the pairs being in geometric steps of color difference, or contrast, shown in Table 1–1.

The original fabric and the test specimen are placed side by side. The lengthwise and crosswise yarns of each sample should be in the same direction. The Gray Scale is placed along side of the fabrics under standard conditions of lighting. The visual comparison is made between the original sample, the tested fabric, and the Gray Scale, and the difference noted and rated. The overall difference or contrast is the basis for evaluation. If it is desired to observe and record the character of the color change (hue, depth, brightness) the terms listed in Table 1–2 may be used.

Gray Scale For Staining†

This scale is used to evaluate undyed fabrics. The scale consists of one pair of white and nine pair of gray and white color chips each representing a visual difference in color or contrast (shade and strength) corresponding to a numerical rating for staining (see Figure 1–10). The staining of undyed cloth in colorfastness tests is rated by comparing the difference in color of the stained and unstained cloth with the differences represented by the scale.

The fastness ratings and corresponding color differences, determined by the Adams chromatic value formula, are given in the first two columns of Table 1–3.

Fastness rating 5 is represented on the scale by two identical white chips mounted side by side, having a reflectance of not less than 85 percent. The color difference is 0.

* AATCC Evaluation Procedure 1, Gray Scale of Color Change.
† AATCC Evaluation Procedure 2, Gray Scale For Staining.

Figure 1-10 Gray Scale for Staining. (Courtesy: American Association of Textile Chemists and Colorists)

Table 1-1

Fastness Rating	Color Difference (AN units)	Tolerances for Working Standards (AN units)
5	0	0.0
4–5	0.8	±0.2
4	1.5	±0.2
3–4	2.1	±0.2
3	3.0	±0.2
2–3	4.2	±0.3
2	6.0	±0.5
1–2	8.5	±0.7
1	12.0	±1.0

Table 1-2

Rating		Meaning
3	Contrast equal to Step 3 of the Gray Scale	Change is a loss in depth of color only
3 Redder	Contrast equal to Step 3 of the Gray Scale	No significant loss in depth but color has become redder
3 Weaker, yellower	Contrast equal to Step 3 of the Gray Scale	Loss in depth and change in hue have occurred
3 Weaker, bluer, duller	Contrast to Step 3 of the Gray Scale	Loss in depth and change in both hue and brightness have occurred
4–5 Redder	Contrast intermediate between 4 and 5 of the Gray Scale	No significant loss in depth but color has become slightly redder

NOTE. When the space available for recording qualitative terms is restricted as on pattern cards, the following abbreviations may be used:

Bl	bluer	W	weaker
G	greener	S	stronger
R	redder	D	duller
Y	yellower	Br	brighter

Table 1–3

Fastness Rating	Color Difference (C.D. units)	Tolerances for Working Standards (C.D. units)
5	0.0	0.0
4–5	2.0	±0.3
4	4	±0.3
3–4	5.6	±0.4
3	8	:0.5
2–3	11.3	±0.7
2	16	±1.0
1–2	22.6	±1.5
1	32	±2.0

Fastness ratings 4.5 to 1, inclusive, are represented by a reference white chip identical with those used for rating 5, paired with similar but neutral gray chips, the visual differences in the pairs being in geometric steps of color difference, or contrast, shown in Table 1–3.

A piece of an unstained fabric and the test specimen is placed in the same plane (oriented in the same direction) and the Gray Scale for Staining is placed beside them under standard conditions of lighting. The visual difference between the original sample and test specimen is compared and the difference noted as represented by the gray scale. The rating of the test specimen is the number on the gray scale that corresponds to the contrast between the original and test specimens.

Color Transference Chart*

The chart uses 24 color chips from the *Munsell Book of Color* comprising six colors: neutral gray, red, yellow, green, blue, and purple. The neutral gray and the various hues are each shown in four depths, ranging from a very light tint to a moderately deep shade. In terms of the Munsell nomenclature defining hue, value, and chroma, the neutral grays are shown at values 9, 8, 7, and 6 and the hues 5R, 5Y, 5G, 5B, and 5P are correspondingly shown at 9/1, 8/2, 7/2, and 6/2 value and chroma (see Figure 1–11).

The chips on the chart are mounted on white cardboard in four horizontal rows, each starting with a neutral gray and ending with the purple hue. The rows are placed and aligned so that every color shows a similar gradation in depth in a vertical line, the lightest tints being on the top and the heaviest on the bottom, and for rating pur-

* AATCC Evaluation Procedure 3, AATCC Color Transference Chart.

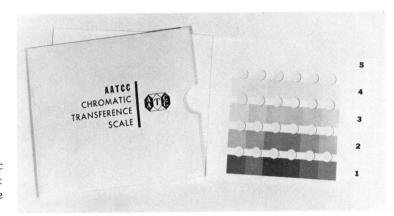

poses the rows are designated numerically, No. 4 being assigned to the top row or lightest colors, down to No. 1 for the bottom row or heaviest colors. The rows are mounted with sufficient separation between them to show circular holes cut in the card over each chip in the four rows. A white cardboard mask is provided containing three holes in a straight line, so that when held vertically over the chart, the rectangular opening in the middle of the mask discloses one of the circular openings in the color chart, and the two circular holes on either side of the rectangular opening in the mask will expose circular areas of the vertically adjacent color chips, equal in area to the sample visible through the hole in the card itself. The middle hole in the mask is rectangular rather than circular, in order to make the placing of the mask easier and less critical to show the full circular area of the sample being rated.

The fabric showing the transferred color is placed behind the card on which the chips are mounted so that a representative part of the colored portion is visible through one of the circular holes in the vertical column closest to it in character of shade. It is then moved up or down in this column so that it is intermediate between a chip showing greater intensity of color and a chip showing less intensity.

Numerical ratings are used for comparison with the numbered rows on the chart.

The ratings are as follows:

Stain	Rating
Practically unstained	5
Stain equal to Row 4	4
Stain equal to Row 3	3
Stain equal to Row 2	2
Stain equal to Row 1	1

31   The Role of Textile Testing

2
Methods for
Fiber Identification

33

For review, the generic names of the man-made fibers and natural fibers are given in Table 2–1. Fiber trademark names, along with the manufacturer, are listed by generic fiber name in Appendix B, along with fiber producers and associations.

It is not possible for the average consumer to identify fabrics by look or feel. Yet the fiber content is of great importance to the consumer. If you buy silk, you want silk—not acetate. Fiber identification is not a simple matter. Knowledge and skill are important. Even the simple burning tests are not always reliable. In some cases laboratory facilities and expensive equipment are required.

There are five relatively simple methods that may be used to identify fibers:

1. A burning test.
2. Microscopic examination (longitudinal and cross section).
3. Solubility tests in various reagents.
4. Staining tests (fibers are dyed or stained with specific dyes).
5. Fiber density.

Burning tests may give a clue to fiber type, that is, whether it is natural or man made. Microscopic examination and staining tests may help confirm identification by burning. Solubility and fiber density tests are particularly necessary when we want to separate the individual fibers used in a blend. However, in some instances, the use of the burning test, microscopic, staining, solubility, and fiber density tests are of little value for fiber identification purposes. The use of more sophisticated equipment, methods, and techniques are necessary for fiber identification. Examples are (1) infrared spectroscopy (IR), (2) gas chromatography (GCO), and (3) thermal analysis.

BURNING TESTS   Textile fibers are complex chemical substances. As such, when they burn they exhibit different fume odors, smoke colors, and residue types. The burning test is a simple method to identify fibers because all we need is a flame and the knowledge of the burning properties.

The burning test is useful to those who have no other means of identification. It is also useful as a confirmatory test. For example, under the microscope, regular nylon and polyester have the same appearance. While it is usually not possible to tell them apart solely by using the microscope, it is usually possible to distinguish between these two fibers by burning them.

This test does have certain limitations. The burning behavior of the fiber may be affected by the finish applied to the fabric. For ex-

Table 2-1 Modern Textile Fibers

Man-Made Fibers			
Petroleum Based		Cellulosic	Mineral and Metal
Acrylic	Nytril[a]	Acetate	Glass
Anidex[a]	Olefin	Rayon	Metallic
Aramid	Polyester	Triacetate	
Azlon[a]	Rubber		
Lastrile[a]	Saran		
Modacrylic	Spandex		
Nylon	Vinal[a]		
Novoloid	Vinyon		

Natural Fibers			
Cellulosic	Protein	Mineral	Rubber
Cotton	Wool	Asbestos	Rubber
Linen	Silk		
Jute	Specialty hair		
Ramie			
Hemp			

[a] Not currently produced in United States.

ample, a flame-retardant finish on a cotton fabric greatly reduces the degree of flammability, while napping or brushing of the same fabric increases the rate of burning. Also, the presence of some finishes will mask the odor from the fumes.

The use of fiber blends may also complicate the identification of fibers by burning. Two or three different kinds of fibers burning together in one yarn or fabric may be difficult to distinguish.

Some fibers burn almost identically because they are the same chemical substance. Cotton, linen, and rayon are examples. Other methods must be used to differentiate these fibers.

When making a burning test of fiber or a sample of fabric, look for three things:

1. How it burns: Does it burn rapidly? Does it go out quickly? Does it smolder?
2. How it smells: when the flame goes out, smell the smoke.
3. The ash: note its color and its shape. Can you crush it, or is it hard?

Study the reaction of textile fibers to heat and flame as given in Table 2–2.

Table 2-2 Reaction of Textile Fibers to Heat and Flame

Fibers	Typical Behavior of Fiber Specimen				
	When Approaching Flame	When in Flame	After Removal of Flame	Odor	Typical Ash Characteristics
Cellulose Fibers					
Cotton	Does not fuse or shrink away from flame	Burns quickly without melting	Continues to burn without melting afterglow	Burning paper	Small, fluffy gray ash
Linen	Does not fuse or shrink away from flame	Burns quickly without melting	Continues to burn without melting afterglow	Burning paper	Small, fluffy gray ash
Protein Fibers					
Natural silk	Fuses and curls away from flame	Burns slowly with some melting	Burns very slowly; sometimes self-extinguishing	Burning feathers	Round black bead, brittle, pulverizes easily
Weighted silk	Fuses and curls away from flame	Burns slowly with some melting	Burns very slowly; sometimes self-extinguishing	Burning feathers	Leaves ash the form or shape of fiber or fabric. Glows like a red-hot wire
Wool	Fuses and curls away from flame	Burns slowly with some melting	Burns very slowly; sometimes self-extinguishing	Burning hair	Lumpy, blistered ash, brittle, breaks easily
Man-Made					
Azlon	Fuses and curls away from flame	Burns slowly	Sometimes self-extinguishing	Burning hair	Brittle black bead
Mineral Fibers					
Natural asbestos	Does not ignite	Does not melt Glows in high heat	No change	No odor	Remains unchanged May blacken
Man-Made Mineral					
Glass	Does not burn	Softens and glows	Hardens	None	Changes shape. Hard bead
Metallic					
Pure metal	Does not burn	Glows red	Hardens	None	Original shape
Coated metal	Fuses and shrinks	Melts	Depends on coating used	None	Hard bead
Man-Made Fibers (Cellulose)					
Rayon	Does not shrink away from flame	Burns very rapidly	Leaves a creeping ember	Burning wood	Small or no ash
Man-Made Modified (Cellulose)					
Acetate	Fuses away from flame	Burns with melting	Continues to burn with melting	Acetic acid or vinegar	Leaves brittle, black, irregular-shaped bead

Table 2-2 Reaction of Textile Fibers to Heat and Flame (Cont'd)

		Typical Behavior of Fiber Specimen			
Fibers	When Approaching Flame	When in Flame	After Removal of Flame	Odor	Typical Ash Characteristics
Triacetate	Fuses away from flame	Burns with melting	Continues to burn with melting	Burning paper	Brittle, black irregular shaped bead
Man-Made Fibers Acrylic	Fuses away from flame	Burns rapidly with melting	Continues to burn with melting Shreds material	Acrid	Leaves hard, brittle, black, irregular-shaped bead
Anidex	Fuses away from flame	Burns with melting	Continues to burn with melting	Chemical	Leaves black charred ash
Aramid	Fuses and shrinks away from flame	Burns slowly with melting	Self-extinguishing	Sweet	Leaves a hard brown ash
Mod-acrylic	Fuses away from flame	Burns very slowly with melting	Self-extinguishing	Acrid	Leaves hard, black irregular shaped bead
Novoloid	Fuses and shrinks from flame	Burns slowly with a glow	Self-extinguishing	Phenolic	Retains shape but turns black
Nylon	Fuses and shrinks away from flame	Burns slowly with melting	Usually self-extinguishing	Boiling string beans	Leaves hard, tough gray, round bead
Nytril	Fuses away from flame	Burns slowly with melting	Continues to burn with melting	None	Leaves hard, black irregular shaped bead
Olefin	Fuses, shrinks and curls away from flame	Burns with melting	Continues to burn with melting	Chemical	Leaves hard, tough tan, round bead
Polyester	Fuses and shrinks away from flame	Burns slowly with melting	Usually self-extinguishing	Chemical	Leaves hard, tough black, round bead
Rubber	Fuses away from flame	Burns rapidly with melting	Continues to burn with melting	Sulphur	Soft, tacky, irregular mass
Saran	Fuses and shrinks away from flame	Burns very slowly with melting	Self-extinguishing	Sharp, acrid	Leaves hard, black, irregular bead
Spandex	Fuses but does not shrink away from flame	Burns with melting	Continues to burn with melting	Chemical	Leaves soft, fluffy, black ash
Vinal	Fuses and shrinks away from flame	Burns with melting	Continues to burn with melting	Chemical	Leaves hard, tough, tan bead
Vinyon	Fuses and shrinks away from flame	Burns slowly with melting	Self-extinguishing	Acrid	Leaves hard, black, irregular bead

Footnote on following page

MICROSCOPIC FIBER IDENTIFICATION

The microscope is an indispensable tool in textile analysis, used for fiber identification and to study surface characteristics of yarn and fabric. It aids the fabric designer and fabric analyst in determining the fabric structure. It may be used to analyze damage to a fabric. The longitudinal and cross sections of fibers and fabrics may be viewed through a microscope. Many quantitative determinations may be made and recorded in the form of drawings or photomicrographs.

There is a large number of different types of microscopes on the market ranging from very simple forms or designs to complex electron microscopes used to study the internal structure of fibers. Each one is designed for a specific purpose.

Two instruments are required in the study of textiles: (1) a microscope with a revolving stage for fiber analysis; and (2) a stereoscopic binoocular microscope for fabric analysis (see Figures 2–1 and 2–2).

The microscopic test procedure and a descriptive microscopic appearance of textile fibers are given in Table 2–3. Photomicrographs of the fibers are shown in Appendix C. For the student who has never used the microscope, instructions are given in Appendix C, as is a new rapid method of preparing fiber cross sections.

SOLUBILITY

A solution is a molecular dispersion of the polymer in a solvent. The solution process is governed by time (kinetic) and equilibrium conditions (thermodynamic).

Solubility depends on the structure of the fiber, that is, its chemical structure, molecular weight, crystallinity, and cross linking.

Chemical structure determines polymer solubility. Solubility decreases as the molecular weight increases. The higher the degree of crystallinity, the more difficult it is for the fiber to dissolve. Crystalline polymers dissolve near their melting points. Cross-linked polymers do not dissolve—they swell. The exception may occur if they are degraded.

Test Procedure: A specimen of the fiber is moved slowly toward a small flame, and the reaction of the fiber to heat is observed. One end of the specimen is then pushed directly into the flame to determine the burning characteristics of the fiber. After removal from the flame, the fiber's burning characteristics are again observed and the burning odor is noted. (The bruning odor can be compared with that of known fibers.) The specimen is then allowed to cool, and the characteristics of the ash are checked.

Groups of fibers, short lengths of yarn or small pieces of fabric can be used as test specimens unless the product to be tested contains a combination of yarns or a blend of fibers. In such cases, individual fibers selected from the textile material with the aid of a magnifying glass may be used.

Caution: This test should be made with care to prevent burning of the fingers and to avoid inhaling excessive amounts of smoke from the burning sample. Hold the yarns or fabric with a pair of tweezers. Do not allow molten material to drop on your skin. It can cause a severe burn.

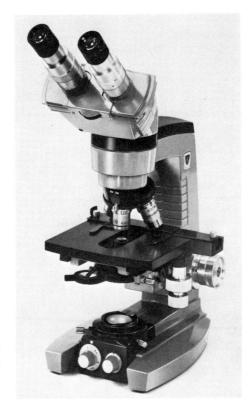

Figure 2-1 The microscope and its parts are used to study textile fibers effectively. (Courtesy: American Optical Corporation)

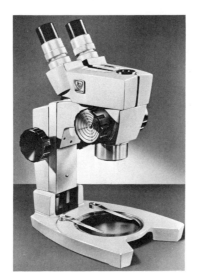

Figure 2-2 A stereoscopic binocular microscope is used for fabric analysis. (Courtesy: American Optical Corporation)

Table 2-3 Microscopic Test

Fiber	Microscopic Appearance*	
	Longitudinal	Cross Section
Cellulosic Fibers		
Cotton (mercerized and not mercerized)	Ribbonlike. Convolutions sometimes change direction. No significant lengthwise striations.	Tubular shape with tubes usually collapsed and irregular in size.
Linen	Bamboolike. Pronounced cross markings nodes and fissures. No significant lengthwise striations.	Tubular shape with tubes often collapsed and very irregular in size as well as shape.
Ramie	Similar to linen but much larger. Very heavy cell walls and well defined lumen or broad and flat wall with indistinct lumen.	Thick, irregular convolutions.
Jute	Long cell elements with frequent joints. Uneven in diameter. Broken tissue usually evident. Broad lumen.	Irregular shaped with central lumen.
Protein Fibers		
Natural		
Silk (weighted silk)	Smooth surface like a glass rod. No significant lengthwise striations.	Triangular. Points of triangle are rounded. Irregular in size and shape.
Wool	Serrated surface and cross markings due to surface scales.	Round or nearly round.
Man-made		
Azlon (Chinon)	Smooth surface like a glass rod.	Similar to silk. Irregular shape with six rounded lobes that are irregular in size and shape.
Mineral Fibers		
Natural		
Asbestos	Straight surface like a finely polished metal rod.	Irregular striated shapes.
Man made		
Glass	Rodlike with smooth surface.	Round cross sections.
Metallic		
Pure metal	Long, smooth, rodlike.	Round, smooth.
Coated metal	Irregular widths, pigmented. Varies with method of construction.	Rounded lobes that vary according to construction.
Man-Made Fibers (cellulose)		
Rayon		
Viscose	Very distinct lengthwise striations. No cross markings.	Irregular shape. Serrated outline.
High tenacity	Smooth, rodlike. No irregular striations.	Irregular in shape with few serrations.
High wet modules	Smooth, rodlike.	Oval or round shape.
Cuprammonium	Smooth glasslike rod.	Round.
Man Made (modified cellulose)		
Acetate Tiracetate	Glasslike rod with distinct lengthwise striations. No cross markings.	Irregular shape. Serrated outline.

Table 2-3   Microscopic Test (Cont'd)

| Fiber | Microscopic Appearance* | |
	Longitudinal	Cross Section
Man Made Fibers		
Acrylic		
Acrilan, Creslan, Zefran	Rodlike. Smooth surface and outline.	Round or nearly round. May include bean shape.
Orlon	Broad. Indistinct lengthwise striations. No cross markings.	Dog bone.
Bicomponent Orlon	Lengthwise striations. No cross markings.	Irregular—mushroom or acorn.
Anidex		
Anim/8	Wide translucent with lighter central canal.	Round.
Aramid	Smooth surface like a glass rod.	Dog bone
Modacrylic		
Dynel	Lengthwise striations. No cross markings.	Ribbonlike; irregular.
Verel	Broad and often indistinct lengthwise striations.	Dog bone.
Nylon	Glass-rod. Smooth surface.	Round or nearly round.
Antron	Broad rod-shape, indefinite lengthwise striations.	Trilobal (three lobes).
Novoloid	Amorphous (shapeless). No micro structure.	Amorphous (shapeless).
Nytril	Distinct lengthwise striations.	Irregular shape. Serrated outline.
Olefin	Rod-like with a smooth surface and outline.	Round or nearly round.
Polyester	Rod-like with a smooth surface and outline.	Round or nearly round.
Trevira	Broad rod shape, indefinite lengthwise striations.	Pentalobal (five lobes).
Dacron (T62)	Broad, sometimes indistinct lenghtwise striations. No cross markings.	Trilobal (three lobes).
Dacron 8	Broad rod shape, indefinite lengthwise striations.	Octolobal (eight lobes).
Rubber		
Extruded	Opaque, pigmented ribbon-like.	Round, oval with crystal particles on wall.
Cut	Opaque, pigmented ribbon-like.	Square, rectangular.
Saran	Rod-like with a smooth surface and outline	Round or nearly round.
Spandex	Broad. Indistinct lenghtwise striations. No cross-markings.	Dog bone.
Globe DC100	Vary in size. Flat ribbon-like with striations.	Irregular, round.
Vinyon	Resembles mercerized cotton; lumen-like channel running through the middle of filament with an occasional twist.	Dog bone.

Test Procedure (Longitudinal)
1. Pull a yarn from the warp or lengthwise direction of the sample.
2. Tease the yarn apart into fibers.
3. Mount the fibers on a slide with a drop of distilled water. Place a cover glass over the mount.
4. Examine at low magnification (50 to 60×).
5. Examine under high magnification (250 to 500×).
6. Compare with a known sample or photomicrograph.
7. Repeat with a yarn pulled from the filling or crosswise direction of the fabric.

Test Procedure (Cross section)
Considerable technique is required to make cross sections of textile fibers. See the *Technical Manual of the American Association of Textile Chemists and Colorists,* Method 20-1973, or the method of the American Society of Testing Materials, Test Method D-276-60T.

Trade names are used only when longitudinal or cross sections differ from generic names.

* Photomicrographs in Appendix C courtesy of E. I. DuPont de Nemours and Company, Inc.

Table 2-4 Chemical Solubility of Fibers

	Acetic Acid	Acetone	Sodium Hypochlorite	Hydrochloric Acid	Formic Acid	1.4-Dioxane	m-Xylene	Cyclohexanone	Dimethyl Formamide	Sulfuric Acid	Sulfuric Acid	m-Cresol	Hydrofluoric Acid
Concentration (%)	100	100	5	20	85	100	100	100	100	59.5	70	100	50
Temperature (C)	20	20	20	20	20	101	139	156	90	20	38	139	20
Time (minutes)	5	5	20	10	5	5	5	5	10	20	20	5	20
Acetate	S	S	I	I	S	S	I	S	S	S	S	S	
Acrylic	I	I	I	I	I	I	I	I	S	I	I	P	I
Anidex	I	I	I	I	I	I	I	I	I	I	I	I	
Azlon	I	I	S										
Cotton and flax	I	I	I	I	I	I	I	I	I	I	S	I	I
Glass	I	I	I	I	I	I	I	I	I	I	I	I	S
Modacrylic	I	SE	I	I	I	SP	I	S	SP^a	I	I	P	
Nylon	I	I	I	S	S	I	I	I	N	S	S	S	
Nytril	I	I	I	I	I	I	I	S	S	I	I	SP	
Olefin	I	I	I	I	I	I	S	S	I	I	I	I	
Polyester	I	I	I	I	I	I	I	I	I	I	I	S	I
Rayon	I	I	I	I	I	I	I	I	I	S	S	I	I
Saran	I	I	I	!	I	S	S	S	S	I	I	I	
Silk	I	I	S	I	I	I	I	I	I	S	S	I	
Spandex	I	I	I	I	I	I	I	I	S	SP	SP	SP	
Teflon	I	I	I	I		I	I	I	I	I	I	I	I
Vinal				S	S	I	I	I	I	S	S	I	
Vinyon	I	S	I	I	I	S	S	S	S	I	I	S	
Wool	I	I	S	I	I	I	I	I	I	I	I	I	

S = soluble.

I = insoluble.

P = forms plastic mass.

SP = soluble or forms plastic mass.

SE = soluble except for one modacrylic fiber characterized by low flammability and liquid inclusions visible in cross section.

N = nylon 6 is soluble, nylon 6/6 is insoluble.

^{a} = Soluble at 20°C without plastic mass.

Courtesy American Association of Textile Chemists and Colorists.

Solubility tests are valuable to determine the fiber content of an unknown fabric, and verify other tests used to identify fibers.

There are many solvents that may be used to distinguish one fiber from another. The principle of solubility of the natural fibers is based on their reactions to common acid and alkaline solutions. Solubility becomes more complex when dealing with the man-made fibers, requiring the use of organic solvents in addition to acid and alkali solutions.

Many of the tests must be carried on under carefully controlled conditions. Some of the liquids are hazardous and must be handled with care. Exhaust hoods, gloves, aprons, and goggles should be used for fiber solubility work.

For tests at room temperature (20°C) place a small sample of the fibers in a watch crystal, test tube, or 50-ml beaker, and cover it with the test solvent. Use about 1 ml of solvent per 10 mg of fiber.

If the test is conducted at the boiling point of the solvent, first bring the solvent to a boil (use boiling chips) in a beaker on an electric hot plate in a ventilated hood. Adjust the hot-plate temperature to maintain slow boiling and keep watch so that the solvent does not boil dry. Drop the fiber sample into the boiling solvent.

If the test is conducted at some intermediate temperature, heat a beaker of water on a hot plate and adjust the temperature with a thermometer. Place the fiber sample in the test solvent in a test tube and immerse in the heated water bath.

Note if the fiber dissolves completely, softens to a plastic mass or remains insoluble. Compare the data on fiber solubility with the chemical solubility of fibers* in Table 2–4.

Test Procedure For Unknown Fibers

If the composition of the textile material is not known or indicated, a representative sample of the textile material or fibers selected from the sample should be immersed in the liquids prescribed in Table 2–5 in the numerical sequence shown. The concentration and temperature of each liquid should be as specified.

When small clumps of fibers or individual fibers are used in the test, they should be selected carefully to insure that each of the different classes of fibers in the textile material are tested in every liquid. Good illumination is required for observing the effect of the liquids or single-fiber specimens. The liquids must be used in the numerical sequence specified if each class of fibers is to be systematically removed. The order of removal of the fiber classes by the series of liq-

---

* *Solubility of Fibers.* Reprinted with the permission of the American Association of Textile Chemists and Colorists.

Table 2–5 Scheme for Identification of Fibers by Chemical Solubility

Solvent	Removes
1. Acetic acid (glacial) 75°F	Acetate, triacetate
2. Hydrochloric acid (20% conc.) 75°F	Nylon 6, nylon 6.6
3. Sodium hypochlorite (5% available chlorine) 75°F	Silk, wool
4. Dioxane (212°F)	Saran
5. Xylene (meta) at boil	Olefins
6. Ammonium thiocyanate (70% by weight) at boil	Acrylics
7. Butyrolactone (70°F)	Modacrylics, Acrylics
8. Dimethyl formamide (200°F)	Spandex—veriify
9. Sulfuric acid (75% by weight) 75°F	Cotton, flax, rayon, nylon, acetate
10. Cresol (meta) (200°F)	Polyester, nylon acetate

1. Take a sample of the fabric to be analyzed. The sample should remain in the solvent for five minutes before proceeding to next step. Observe the sample to determine removal of fiber(s) after each test.

2. Proceed in numerical order given in the table. Always rinse the residue thoroughly after each step.

3. For verification, examine the residue for microscopic identification.

uids is also shown in the table above. If certain fibers are known to be absent from the textile material, the solvents for these fibers can be omitted from the tests.

Safety Precautions

The handling of chemicals require certain safety measures. Laboratories should have normal precautionary procedures posted for quick reference. One of the most critical of these is to protect the eyes and skin. If chemicals come in contact with the eyes, rinse the eyes immediately with water.

Some chemicals can be used without a fume hood, provided there is adequate ventilation. However, the fumes from cresol, phenol, and formic acid are unpleasant, and a hood makes their use less annoying. Dioxane and metaxylene should not be used near a direct flame, for they are highly flammable. Consult a chemical handbook for safety precautions in the use of chemicals.

DYE AND STAIN TESTS

Dyes and stains may be used to confirm the identity of fibers and to study the various fiber structure. A number of different stain tests are used to identify man-made textile fibers. Various dye manufacturers prepare dyes and stains for this purpose. These tests are applicable only to white or light-colored fibers. In order to identify a colored fabric or fiber, it is first necessary to strip the dye. Most dye manufacturers provide instructions on staining procedures as well as cards showing the typical color of each fiber after staining. It is sometimes difficult to distinguish one fiber from another in blended yarns or fabrics because they are stained approximately the same color. In such a case, examine the stained material under a microscope and compare it with a standard colored specimen. It is advisable not to rely on one staining solution—if several different identification stains give the answer then you will be certain it is right.

Methods of staining may vary slightly, but in all cases the fiber should be wet out thoroughly in hot water before dyeing. Place the fiber in the dye solution recommended by the manufacturer. Remove the material, rinse lightly and dry before evaluation is made. See Appendix D for a representative method of fiber identification using a stain.

SPECIFIC GRAVITY TEST

The specific gravity test provides another method of differentiating between fibers, or of confirming identifications made by other methods. In this test, a specimen of the unknown fiber is placed in a liquid of known specific gravity and observed to determine whether the fiber sinks or floats.

The test procedure for determining specific gravity of textile fibers is as follows:

To test for specific gravity, place a single filament or single fiber specimen in a series of specially prepared liquids of known specific gravity. If the specific gravity of the fiber is greater than that of the liquid, the specimen will sink in the liquid; conversely, if the specific gravity of the fiber is lower, the specimen will float. (The fiber's surface must be free of air bubbles since they can affect the results of the test.)

A suitable series of liquids for this test may be prepared by mixing, in various proportions, carbon tetrachloride (specific gravity of 1.60 at room temperature) with xylene (specific gravity of 0.87 at room temperature). Before using any of the liquids for fiber identification, their specific gravity should be checked with a calibrated hydrometer. Fibers and their specific gravity are given in Table 2–6.

Table 2-6 Fibers and Specific Gravity

	Fibers	Specific Gravity[a]
	Man-Made	
Acetate	Secondary (Acele[b]) and triacetate ("Arnel")	1.32
Acrylic	All (including orlon[b] and orlon Sayelle[c])	1.14 to 1.19
Modacrylic	"Dynel"	1.30
	"Verel"	1.36
Nylon	Nylon 6 and nylon 6.6 (including Antron[d] and DuPont type 501)	1.14
Nytril	"Darvan"	1.18
Olefin	Polyethylene and polypropylene	0.92
Polyester	Dacron[b], "Fortrel," "Terylene," "Toray-Tetoron"	1.38
	"Kodel"	1.22
	"Vycron"	1.37
Rayon	All	1.52
Saran	All	1.70
Spandex	Lycra[b]	1.21
	"Vyrene	1.35
	Natural	
Cotton	All (including mercerized and not mercerized)	1.52
Flax	Bleached	1.52
Silk	Boiled off	1.25
Wool	Cashmere, mohair, and regular (merino)	1.32

[a] These are average values; hence, individual determinations on the same fiber specimen may produce values that vary by as much as 0.02.
[b] DuPont-registered trademark.
[c] DuPont's registered trademark for its bicomponent acrylic fiber.
[d] DuPont's registered trademark for its trilobal multifilament nylon yarn.

ALTERNATE METHODS

There are alternative methods that may be used in confirming the relative simple tests just described, for example, (1) infrared spectroscopy, (2) gas chromotography and (3) thermal analysis.

Infrared Spectroscopy (IR)

An infrared spectroscopy instrument is shown in Figure 2–3. When infrared radiation is passed through a substance, certain frequencies are absorbed and others are transmitted. This is similar to the absorp-

Figure 2-3 Infrared spectrophotometry is being used an increasing extent for the recognition and quantitative analysis of structural units in unknown compounds. Each textile fiber has its own identifying infrared absorption band. (Courtesy: International Fabricare Institute)

tion of visible light that causes materials to show color. Infrared spectroscopy, therefore, consists of determining the frequencies at which absorption occurs. The absorption in the infrared region is associated with molecular vibration. The vibrational modes involve localized motions of small groups of atoms and emit absorption bands at frequencies characteristic of these groups and the type of motion they undergo.

Most infrared spectrophotometers use a glowing light source to provide electromagnetic radiation from 2.5 to about 15 microns (μ). In practice, the usual absorption spectrum in the infrared region is shown as a plot of absorption versus the wavelength (μ), or absorption versus wave number (cm^{-1}). The wave number is defined as the reciprocal of the wavelength. Since the wavelength is given in microns (μ) and the wave number or frequency in reciprocal centimeters (cm^{-1}), we must convert the dimensional units from microns to centimeters (1 μ = 10,000 cm). Thus: wave number (cm^{-1}) = 1/wavelength, $\mu \left(\dfrac{1\ \text{cm}}{10,000\ \mu} \right)$ = 10,000/wavelength, cm.

Some typical IR-absorption bands of interest to textile chemists are shown in Table 2–7 and Figure 2–4.

There are several methods used in the preparation of man-made fibers for IR analysis:

1. Pressed-disc technique. This method consists of mixing the finely divided fiber with powdered potassium bromide. The disc is formed under pressure.

2. Mulling. Fibers are cut to short length and mixed with a nonvolatile and nonabsorbing mulling liquid. The mull is transferred to rock salt plates for IR analysis.

47 *Methods for Fiber Identification*

Table 2-7 Typical IR Absorption Bands of Interest To Textile Chemists

Group	Frequency Range, cm^{-1}
OH—stretching vibrations	
free OH	3610–3645 (sharp)
intramolecular H bonds	3450–3600 (sharp)
intermolecular H bonds	3200–3550 (broad)
NH—stretching vibrations	
free NH	3300–3500
H bonded NH	3070–3350
CH—stretching vibrations	
$\equiv$C—H	3280–3340
$=$C—H	3000–3100
CH$_2$	2853 ± 10, 2926 ± 10
CH	2880–2900
C$=$O-stretching vibrations	
nonconjugated	1700–1900
conjugated	1590–1750
amides	~1650
C$\equiv$N-stretching vibration	
nonconjugated	2240–2260
conjugated	2215–2240
C—O—C vibration in esters	
formates	~1175
acetates	~1240, 1010–1040

3. Solvent-cast films. A solution of a fiber in an appropriate solvent is poured on a glass plate where the solvent is evaporated off. When the film is formed, it can be peeled from the glass plate. This film is then put into a suitable holding device for IR analysis.

Textile laboratories usually establish a library of known fiber spectra charts. The spectrum of an unknown fiber is matched with the spectrum of the known fiber which allows the identification of the unknown. Reference spectra can also be found in the *Technical Manual of AATCC*.

ATR Attachment

ATR is the attenuated total reflectance. The attachment to the spectrophotometer permits spectral determination of solids, powders,

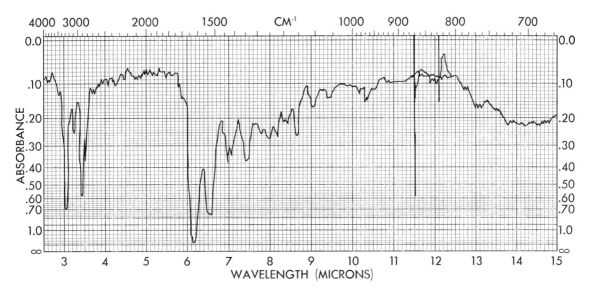

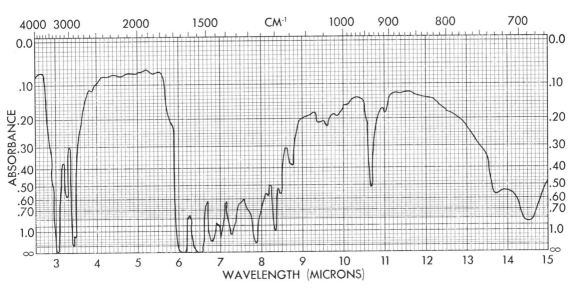

Figure 2-4 An infrared spectra of nylon 6, nylon 6.6.

and fabrics without destroying the sample. This is extremely important when working with samples that cannot otherwise be presented to the beam because of poor solubility or because it is difficult or impractical to present them as a thin film. The heart of the ATR attachment is a prism of high refractive index. The light beam traversing this prism is reflected from the sample face up to 25 times, resulting in good, easily read spectra.

Gas Chromatography (GC)

A gas chromatograph instrument is shown in Figure 2–5. Gas chromatography is a method of separating volatile compounds in a mixture. Separation is achieved in a long separation column packed with a solid material of high surface area, which may be coated with a nonvolatile liquid (stationary phase). The compounds to be separated are carried through the column in a stream of carrier gas, normally helium (mobile phase). The components move through the columns at different speeds, and so become separated. After the gaseous phase leaves the column, it enters a detector. The individual components initiate a series of signals that appear as a succession of peaks on the recorded curve (chromatogram).

A principal limitation of gas chromatography is its restriction to volatile substances. Since textile polymers are nonvolatile, they must be pyrolyzed in an inert atmosphere. Pyrolysis under controlled con-

Figure 2-5 Gas chromatography is an instrumental method of analysis for the separation, identification, and quantities of volatile mixtures. The series of peaks and valleys on the strip chart may identify not only the generic classification of a fiber but the trade-name fiber and manufacturer within a generic classification. (Courtesy: International Fabricare Institute)

ditions breaks down the polymer into a series of volatile products that can be analyzed by gas chromatography. Pyrolysis is the chemical decomposition by the action of heat. The volatile pyrolysis products are characteristic of the polymer. This pyrolysis chromatogram or "pyrogram" may be used as a "fingerprint" to help in the identification of polymers and fibers in a manner similar to that of the IR spectrum.

Thermal Analysis (TA)

Thermal analysis is the measurement of changes in physical or chemical properties of materials as a function of temperature. The sample is placed in a regulated and controlled temperature environment. Changes in the sample are monitored by an appropriate transducer that produces an electrical output. This output is amplified and applied to a readout device. Four different techniques are used in fiber and polymer analysis.

DIFFERENTIAL THERMAL ANALYSIS (DTA)

This is a technique in which the difference in temperature (ΔT) between a sample and an inert reference material is recorded as a function of temperature. When the sample is not changed physically or chemically, both materials are at the same temperature, and ΔT is zero. But when a change occurs, a temperature difference results. This ΔT is recorded by the instrument as a function of time or temperature. A curve or thermogram is obtained, which reflects characteristic properties of a fiber. Changes detected may include the glass transition, desorption of moisture, polymer crystallization or fusion, and irreversible decomposition processes (see Figure 2–6).

Figure 2-6 A thermogram for an undrawn commercial polyester fiber.

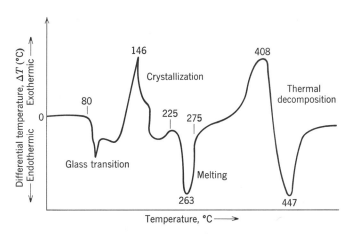

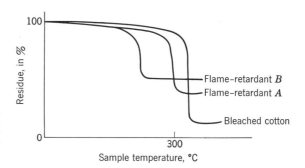

Figure 2-7 A schematic thermogram for cotton, bleached and treated with two different flame-retardant finishes.

DIFFERENTIAL SCANNING CALORIMETRY (DSC)

Differential scanning calorimetry differs from differential thermal analysis in that the differential energy connected with a transition is recorded, instead of the temperature difference. Early literature refers to this technique as differential enthalpic analysis. The differences in energy required to maintain the same temperature in both the sample and the reference during heating and cooling are measured in mcal/sec as a function of time and temperature.

This technique lends itself to quantitative measurements of heat of transition as well as the specific heat of textile polymers.

THERMOGRAVIMETRIC ANALYSIS (TGA)

Thermogravimetric analysis is a technique for measuring the loss or gain of weight of a sample as a function of temperature. A temperature range from ambient to 1200°C can be covered. The basic instrumentation consists of a recording balance, a temperature-programmed furnace, and a chart recorder.

Information on rate of evaporation, thermal stability (flame retardancy), fiber blends, rate of pyrolysis, plasticizers, and finishes can be obtained from thermogravimetric analysis. A schematic thermogram for cotton, bleached and treated with two different flame-retardant finishes, is illustrated in Figure 2–7.

THERMOMECHANICAL ANALYSIS (TMA)

This is the newest of the four techniques. It measures the change in linear dimension (expansion, shrinkage) of a sample as a function of temperature. The glass-transition temperature (T_G) is observed as a change in expansion coefficient (second-order transition), whereas the melting temperature (T_M) is seen as change in dimension (first order transition).

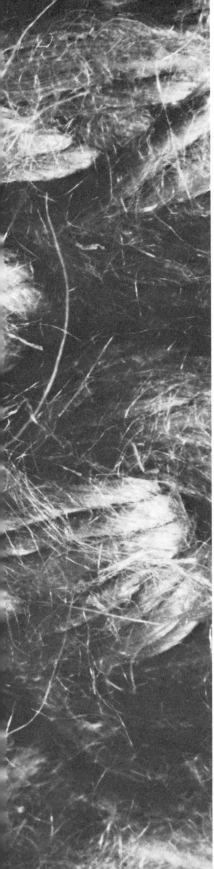

3

Fiber and
Yarn Analysis

The discussion in this chapter on fiber and yarn analysis is presented to develop an understanding and appreciation of why and how fibers and yarns are tested.

Fiber and yarn testing is usually done at the mill level and is also important in research. A researcher may need to dissect yarns and fabrics for testing in order to separate individual variables that affect fabric performance.

Most students do not realize that a fiber, from the time it is grown or manufactured until it is made into a yarn, is under close scrutiny and tested every inch of the way until it becomes a part of a fabric.

Scientists have written in detail about the inherent properties of textiles and their importance to yarn and fabric production, such as J. E. Booth, *Principles of Textile Testing;* Ernest R. Kaswell, *Textile Fibers, Yarns and Fabrics;* and John H. Skinkle, *Textile Testing.*

STAPLE LENGTH

Staple is the finite length of a textile fiber. As commonly used, it means the average length of a sample of fiber. Staple is usually associated with the grade of cotton and wool fibers. However, there is a distinction between staple and grade that is important in testing because one is measurable and the other is the expression of opinion of an expert. "Grade" as used to describe a textile fiber is a summation in the mind of the person examining the material of the color, handle, evenness, staining, and fineness of the fiber; this summation can be learned only by long experience and comparison with standards. The grading of fibers should not be attempted by the ordinary technician but should be left to an expert.

Cotton has nine grades, ranging from Middling-Fair, which is the best grade, to Good-Ordinary, which is the poorest grade. Wool has seven grades ranging from Fine (the best) to Braid (the poorest) in the American system. The fineness of the fiber is the most important factor in grading wool; a microscopic projection method of measuring this fineness has been devised and is in more or less general use. The grading of silk varies with the locality from which the silk comes.

Recommended for reading is *The Classification of Cotton,* Miscellaneous Publication No. 310, U.S. Department of Agriculture and Official Standards of the United States for *Grades of Wool* SRA-C&M 135, also from USDA.

LABORATORY METHODS FOR DETERMINING COTTON QUALITY

The use and standardization of laboratory test measurements have been developed to provide information to supplement the classer's art or skill. Laboratory instruments are available to determine color, foreign matter content, fiber length and length uniformity, fiber fineness and maturity, and fiber strength. Most of the test methods are standardized and published by the American Society for Testing and Materials to promote uniformity in testing. A small group in the International Organization for Standardization is also working toward international agreement on the standardization of the various cotton-fiber test methods. The International Calibration Cotton Standards Committee (ICCSC) sets the policies for the operation of a program by the Cotton Division of the Consumer and Marketing Service (C&MS) to provide uniform cottons with standard values for use in calibrating instruments used in commercial trading. The cotton division of C&MS also furnishes other calibration cottons with standard values for use in calibrating test measurements not included in the International Calibration Cotton Standards.

COLOR TESTS

A visual type of disk colorimeter was used for many years in measuring the color of cotton in preparing the cotton grade standards. In 1950 the Nickerson-Hunter Cotton Colorimeter was developed to replace the visual method (see Figure 3–1). It is a fully automatic, self-standardizing, photoelectric instrument provided with a color diagram of the upland cotton grade standards. The color scales on the instrument are in terms of percent reflectance (Rd) and a degree of yellowness (Hunter's + b factor). The hue in cotton color is fairly constant, thus these two scales provide a satisfactory picture of the visual lightness and chroma differences in the various upland cottons. To operate the instrument a representative sample of cotton is placed over a window ($3\frac{3}{4} \times 4$ inches) and a button is pressed to open a shutter so that the sample is visible to the photocell-filter combination of the colorimeter head. Automatic indicators move to a position of balance showing the degree of lightness on a vertical scale and the degree of yellowness on a horizontal scale. Because these color factors are indicated against a diagram of the color of the grade standards, the color of a cotton sample may be read directly in terms of the average color of the grade standard it most nearly matches.

Figure 3-1 Technician performing raw stock color test on colorimeter. (Courtesy: U.S. Department of Agriculture)

FOREIGN MATTER

Cotton usually becomes contaminated by leaf and other trash in various amounts from exposure in the fields and harvesting methods. Much of the foreign matter is removed by the cleaning and drying

Figure 3-2 Technician performing fiber-length tests on cotton using the Suter-Webb fiber sorter. (Courtesy: U.S. Department of Agriculture)

process during ginning. What remains must be removed as waste in the manufacturing process. Cottons that contain the least amount of foreign matter, other conditions being equal, are those with the highest spinning value. Official grades of cotton are established and are available from the U.S. Department of Agriculture.*

The foreign matter content in samples of cotton are obtained with a Shirley analyzer. The machine makes an almost perfect separation of lint and trash in a cotton sample.

LENGTH AND LENGTH VARIATIONS

Array Method

The measurements obtained by the array method are used mostly in research studies of cotton (see Figure 3–2). In performing these tests, the fibers in a small representative sample of cotton are parallelized by pulling them through a series of combs. The fibers are arrayed according to length and placed on velvet-covered boards. They are measured for length and separated into different length groups at $\frac{1}{8}$-inch intervals. Each group is accurately weighed to obtain the length-weight distribution. Upper quartile length, mean length, coefficient of variation, and percentage of fiber in each $\frac{1}{8}$-inch-length group are usually calculated for each sample.

Fibrograph Method

This test method is fast and is used widely in fiber laboratories for measuring fiber length and length distribution. These tests are

* *The Classification of Cotton,* U.S. Department of Agriculture Miscellaneous Publication No. 310.

Figure 3-3 Technician performing fiber length test on cotton using the Digital Fibrograph method. (Courtesy: U.S. Department of Agriculture)

performed with a Fibrograph instrument, a photoelectric device (Figure 3–3). In performing the tests, the fibers in a representative sample of cotton are placed at random in the teeth of a pair of combs to provide the test specimen. The portion of the fibers protruding from the outside edge of the combs is combed to form a parallelized test board. The Fibrograph instrument scans the test board from the short fiber portion to the long fiber portion at the board's extremity. The amount of light passing through the board to the photocell increases as its bulk decreases. Information on the length-frequency of the fibers in the sample is registered as a special curve for the manual and Serno models, or as a direct reading at selected points on the curve for Digital models. Measurements are then calculated according to the formula for the particular equipment used.

AIRFLOW TESTS AND MICRONAIRE READINGS

Micronaire, Fibronaire, Port-ar, and other commercial airflow instruments are used in this test (Figure 3–4). They provide a rapid measure of fineness and maturity of the sample. The tests provide measures that cannot be determined accurately visually. Mass production methods, including conveyor belts, automated instruments, and separate stations for weighing and testing of the samples, have been developed for these tests. In performing these tests, a representative standard weight sample is placed in the instrument's sample holder where it is compressed to a standard volume. The specimen is then subjected to standard air pressure and the flow of air through the sample is read on a direct scale in terms of Micronaire reading. A fine, immature cotton causes more resistance to airflow that results in a low

Figure 3-4 Technician performing tests for Micronaire reading by use of airflow instrument. (Courtesy: U.S. Department of Agriculture)

Micronaire reading. A coarse, mature cotton causes less resistance to airflow, resulting in a high Micronaire reading.

When separate readings of fineness and maturity are desired, they can be obtained by a special technique known as the Causticaire method for measuring fineness and maturity. In making these tests, the airflow instrument is used with a special Causticaire scale that is proportional to airflow. Tests are performed on samples of cotton both before and after being treated with sodium hydroxide. The caustic treatment swells the fibers causing them to fill out, become more cylindrical in shape, and offer less resistance to airflow. The ratio between the untreated and the treated airflow readings provide an index of maturity or degree of cell-wall development. Fiber fineness can also be calculated from the treated reading and the maturity index. This method is particularly useful when dealing with different botanical types of cotton that have different inherent fiber fineness chararacteristics.

FIBER STRENGTH TESTS

Pressley, Stelometer, and Clemson flat bundle testers are commercial instruments that can be used to measure fiber strength (Figure 3–5). These instruments provide measures that cannot be determined accurately by a classer. They are not as rapid as the airflow tests but they are used widely in the cotton industry. In making the tests, cotton is hand combed and the fibers are parallelized in the form of a flat ribbon about one-quarter inch wide and then placed in a set of breaking clamps. The fibers are cut to a definite length, broken in the tester, and then weighed. The strength of the bundle divided by the weight of the broken bundle provides an index of fiber strength that can be converted to 1000 pounds per square inch or grams per tex (see page 67).

OTHER FIBER AND PROCESSING TESTS

Laboratory procedures have also been developed to provide comparative measures of various items of fiber properties, processing efficiency, and product quality for different cotton samples from closely controlled fiber and spinning or processing tests.

WOOL GRADING

Fineness is one of the most important characteristics of wool. It mainly determines whether wool will be used in a suit, sweater, blanket, or in a pair of socks.

Fibers vary widely in fineness or diameter, whether they are taken from a single animal or from different sheep. The value and use of the wool is primarily determined by the average fiber diameter and the distribution of the various fiber diameters in a fleece or group of fleeces. Grade standards for wool are based on these value-determining characteristics.

The U.S. Department of Agriculture grade standards for wool as it comes from the sheep and for wool top, a partially processed wool product, have served as reliable guides in national and international trading for many years. Separate, but closely related, federal grade standards exist for wool and wool top, and these standards classify the entire range in fiber fineness.

The first operation is putting the wool through a string breaker machine. There are two belts moving in opposite directions with teeth on them, clawing a string of wool fibers into small lengths. The

Figure 3-6 A fiber-fineness laboratory is housed in a carry case. The operator places 12.5 grams of wool on a balance pan. The sample is transferred to the sample chamber. The fibers are compressed in the chamber. The atomizer bulb is pumped a few times to fill the pressure tank and the fineness reading is recorded. Theoretically, the flow of air or resistance of air is related to specific surface, fiber diameter, and fiber length. (Courtesy: Spinlab Special Instruments Laboratory, Inc.)

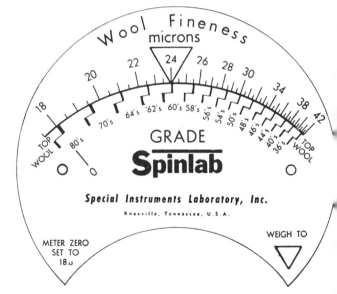

graders then separate the fleeces for variation in length, diameter, and condition. Figure 3–6 shows a unit that may be used in the field to test wool for fiber fineness and fiber length.

The current wool top standards became effective January 11, 1969. On that date two new grades, "Finer than Grade 80s," and "Coarser than Grade 36s," were added. A dual grade designation provides for wool top in which the average fiber diameter and fiber diameter distribution do not meet the requirements of the same grade.

The official grades of wool top and their measurement specifications are shown in Table 3–1. Wool top, which qualifies for any of the grades on the basis of its average fiber diameter, but fails to meet the fiber diameter dispersion requirements for that grade, is assigned a dual grade designation. In such case, the first designation indicates the grade based on the average fiber diameter. The second designation indicates that of the next coarser grade. This indicates that the

Table 3–1 Wool Top Grades and Specifications

Grade	Average Fiber Diameter Range, Microns	25 Microns and Under, Min.	30 Microns and Under, Min.	40 Microns and Under, Min.	25.1 Microns and Over, Max.	30.1 Microns and Over, Max.	40.1 Microns and Over, Max.	50.1 Microns and Over, Max.	60.1 Microns and Over, Max.	Number of Fibers Required Per Test[b]
					Fiber Diameter Distribution Percent[a]					
Finer than 80s	Under 18.10	95	—	—	5	1	—	—	—	400
80s	18.10–19.59	91	—	—	9	1	—	—	—	400
70s	19.60–21.09	83	—	—	17	3	—	—	—	400
64s	21.10–22.59	—	92	—	—	8	1	—	—	600
62s	22.60–24.09	—	86	—	—	14	1.5	—	—	800
60s	24.10–25.59	—	80	—	—	20	2	—	—	800
58s	25.60–27.09	—	72	—	—	28	—	1	—	1000
56s	27.10–28.59	—	62	—	—	38	—	1	—	1200
54s	28.60–30.09	—	54	—	—	46	—	2	—	1400
50s	30.10–31.79	—	44	—	—	56	—	2	—	1600
48s	31.80–33.49	—	—	75	—	—	25	—	1	1800
46s	33.50–35.19	—	—	68	—	—	32	—	1	2000
44s	35.20–37.09	—	—	62	—	—	38	—	2	2200
40s	37.10–38.99	—	—	54	—	—	46	—	3	2400
36s	39.00–41.29	—	—	44	—	—	56	—	4	2600
Coarser than 36s	over 41.29	—	—	—	—	—	—	—	—	2600

Courtesy U.S. Department of Agriculture.

[a] The second maximum percent shown for any grade is a part of, and not in addition to, the first maximum percent. In each grade, the minimum percent and the first maximum percent total 100 percent.

[b] Research has shown that when wools of average uniformity in fiber diameter are measured, the prescribed number of fiber to measure per test will result in confidence limits of the mean ranging from approximately ±0.4 to ±0.5 micron at a probability of 95 percent.

63 *Fiber and Yarn Analysis*

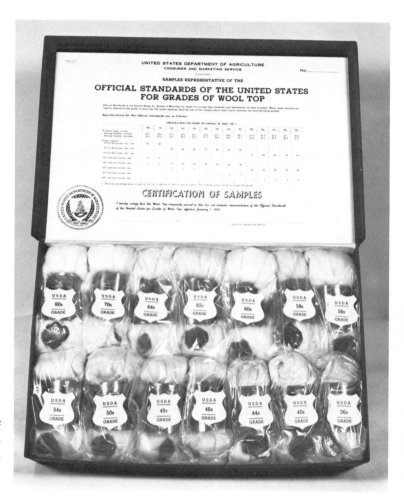

Figure 3-7 Complete set of samples representative of the official standards of the United States for grades of wool top. (Courtesy: U.S. Department of Agriculture)

fiber diameter dispersion does not meet the requirements specified for the grade, corresponding to the average fiber diameter. Official standards for grades of top wool are shown in Figure 3–7.

LABORATORY MEASUREMENT OF WOOL FIBERS

The average fiber diameter and fiber diameter dispersion are determined by sectioning the fibers in a sample to a designated short length, mounting the sections of fibers on a slide, projecting the magnified image onto a scale, and measuring the diameter of a minimum number of fibers. This requires knowledge and skill in preparing cross-sectional slides and microprojection, sampling, calibration, and calculating measurements (see Figures 3–8 to 3–12).

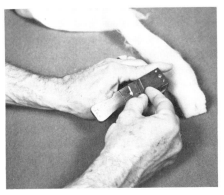

Figure 3-8 Cutting fibers from test specimen for short-fiber measurement. Note fiber pieces adhering to the razor blade. (Courtesy: U.S. Department of Agriculture)

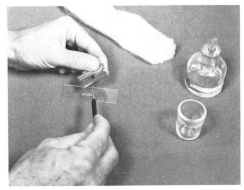

Figure 3-9 Transferring out fibers from blade to oil on the slide. (Courtesy: U.S. Department of Agriculture)

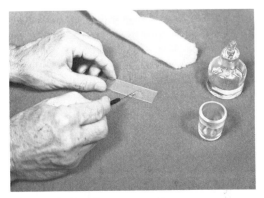

Figure 3-10 Dispersing fibers thoroughly in oil with dissecting needle. (Courtesy: U.S. Department of Agriculture)

Figure 3-11 Microprojector. (Courtesy: U.S. Department of Agriculture)

Figure 3-12 Marking wedge scale at point where wedge and fiber image correspond. (Courtesy: U.S. Department of Agriculture)

COUNT AND DENIER

Two systems of expressing weight-length ratios are in use:

1. Counts or number—the number of units of length in a unit of weight (used on all spun yarns).
2. Denier—the number of units of weight in a unit of length (used on all continuous filament yarns).

In the counts system, the unit of length is a "hank" or standard skein, and the unit of weight is (in the United States) the pound. The hank varies with the branch of the textile industry and also somewhat with geographical location. In cotton mills, for example, the standard hank is 840 yards; in worsted mills, the standard hank is 560 yards. Because of the variation from country to country, ASTM has proposed that the "Typp" system be used for all fibers. The Typp system is based on a standard hank of 1000 yards as indicated by the name which consists of the initial letters of the phrase "thousands of yards per pound."

The denier system was once in considerable confusion because different localities adopted different units of weight and length but, in this country, the adoption of the so-called "legal denier" has eliminated the confusion. The denier of a yarn is now expressed as the number of 0.05-gram weights (deniers) of a standard skein of 450 meters; another way of expressing it is the number of grams in a skein of 9000 meters.

The length of the yarn is obtained by use of a yarn reel (Figure 3–13). This consists essentially of six arms of such a length that the perimeter of the hexagon formed by wrapping the yarn around the arms is one yard, 1½ yards, or 112.5 centimeters. The reel is operated at constant speed by a motor. A revolution counter calibrated in yards is attached to measure the total length of the yarn reeled off.

Weighings of the yarn may be made by (1) grain scales at room conditions, (2) analytical balance at room conditions, (3) special

Figure 3-13 A motorized yarn reel makes it possible to make filament and spun yarns automatically into the selected skein length. (Courtesy: Alfred Sutor Co., Inc.)

quadrant scales at room conditions—usually direct reading, (4) torsion balance and drying oven, and (5) analytical balance and drying oven.

Weighing oven dry in the oven by means of a balance mounted on the oven is the most accurate method of getting the true weight.

TEX SYSTEM FOR LINEAR DENSITY OF FIBERS AND YARNS

A plan for the orderly introduction of the single system of numbering yarns made from all types of fibers is being introduced to the textile industry in most of the countries of the world.

Yarn number represents the "size," "fineness," or—more accurately—the relationship between weight and length of a yarn. The tex system has been chosen to replace the many conflicting systems now used.

It is proposed to make the changeover in easy stages over a period of years. The first stage started in 1960 and will run until the trade is thoroughly familiar with the new system. Dates for the second and third stages will be set when the trade becomes ready for them. It appears that the acceptance of this system is very slow.*

The first stage is designed to familiarize everyone working in the textile industry with tex numbers. The existing yarn count systems will continue in use, but a corresponding rounded tex number will be given in parentheses after the traditional yarn count or yarn number, for example, 18 cotton count (32 tex), 48 worsted count (18 tex), 100 denier (11 tex).

In the second stage, commercial transaction and manufacturing operations will be shifted to tex numbering. The equivalent traditional yarn number or count will be given in parentheses after the tex number, for example, 32 tex cotton yarn will be written 32 tex (18.5 cotton count); 18 tex worsted yarn will be written 18 tex (48 worsted count).

In the third stage, the traditional yarn number in parentheses will be deleted; only tex numbers will be given.

The rounded tex numbers can be obtained readily from short tables relating them to the numbers or counts in the system now used. Condensed tables are available for cottons, worsted, woolen, and denier numbers or counts, with directions for their use. The tex number of a yarn, fiber or other strand is defined as the weight in grams of one kilometer of yarn. Constants have been calculated for converting yarn numbers or counts of all systems currently in use to tex numbers. For the present, however, only rounded equivalent numbers are used.

* "Will Tex Ever Take Over World Wide?" *Textile World,* 125:101 (April 1975).

Agreement on the tex system for yarn numbering is a notable achievement in international standardization in a field where standardization in long overdue. The advantages* of the system are:

1. The various yarn systems now in use with different fibers—English cotton counts, French cotton counts, metric counts, Yorkshire woolen skeins, American woolen runs, English worsted counts—will all be replaced with the tex system, eliminating time spent in converting units from one system to the other and avoiding mistakes that occur when technicians are forced to think in unfamiliar units.

2. Efficiency in mills spinning yarns from any fiber will be increased. Picker laps, slivers, rovings, and yarns will all be numbered in the same units, thus facilitating the calculation of drafts at all stages of spinning and eliminating confusion due to changing systems between laps and slivers, slivers and rovings, tops and gills, rovings and yarns.

3. Operating procedures will be simplified in mills simultaneously spinning yarns from fibers numbered in different systems, for example, wool and man-made fibers on both the worsted and woolen systems. Sales of these products to different customers will also be simplified.

4. The buying and selling of yarns that must meet specifications given in different traditional numbering systems will be simplified by eliminating the time spent in converting and checking results.

5. Efficiency in cost accounting and inventory control will be increased, since all yarns, regardless of the fiber used, will be based on the same yarn-numbering system.

6. Fabric design work will be simplified, since the same amount of yarn—the same length of yarn of a given number or count—will be needed to make the same weight of fabric, regardless of the fibers involved.

7. Calculation of the resultant count of all plied yarns that are numbered in indirect numbering systems will be much easier, since with tex numbers the equivalent single number can be calculated by simple addition.

8. Efficiency of quality control and cost comparisons will be improved since all derived or calculated yarn properties, such as breaking tenacity or lea product, will be in the same units regardless of fiber used.

* *1970 Annual Book of ASTM Standards,* Appendix VI.

9. It will be easier to interpret and use the findings of textile research workers published anywhere in the world.

10. Any spinning or blend study involving the number of fibers in a yarn will be easier to make, since the yarn and the fibers used will both be numbered in the same or closely related systems.

11. The time spent in technical textile schools teaching and practicing the use of various yarn-numbering systems will be eventually eliminated.

12. The U.S. textile industry will avoid being placed at a further disadvantage in production costs with respect to competition from foreign countries who are expected to adopt the tex yarn-numbering system.

PLIES AND FILAMENTS

In review, a ply yarn is composed of two or more single yarns twisted together. The number of singles in a yarn is designated by a number (2, 4, 6) that precedes the word "ply."

Silk is the only natural filament fiber. The size of a silk yarn depends on the number of cocoons reeled off at one time. Filament yarns are man made either by a continuous or discontinuous process. The number of filaments in a yarn made by the continuous process is predetermined at the time it is spun. In the discontinuous method, the filaments are extruded, placed on a cone and shipped to the yarn manufacturer. The yarn manufacturer determines the number of filaments he wants in a particular yarn. Plies and filaments are units that make up a yarn.

If you have two yarns of the same denier but one contains more filaments than the second, you will find that the first yarn will be more pliable and flexible and softer than the second. It is customary to give the number of filaments as well as the denier; thus, a 150-denier yarn composed of 40 filaments would be given as 150d 40f or as 150/40. The usual number of filaments in a yarn are 16, 18, 24, 36, 40, 42, 60, 66, 88, and 100, but the two most common numbers are 40 and 60 filaments.

When filaments are fairly coarse, the easiest way to count them is to cut a piece about an inch long and untwist the yarn, if any appreciable twist is present. Withdraw the filaments from the bundle one at a time by means of a pair of tweezers, counting the filaments as they are withdrawn. If the filaments are fine but not too numerous, a mount may be made and the filaments counted through a binocular microscope. If the filaments are fine and numerous, it is safest to stain the fiber and make a cross section. Using a microscope, count the number of cross sections in the mount.

In the case of the spun yarns, the basis is the single yarn that is made up of a large number of individual fibers held together by a certain amount of twist. If two or more single yarns are twisted together we have a ply yarn and the number of plies is indicated when giving the counts, thus 40/2 or 2/40 means that two 40's single yarns have been twisted together to give a ply yarn.

TWIST

Twist is the number of turns per inch given to a yarn in order to hold the constituent fibers or yarns together. Up to a certain point, an increase in the twist tends to make a stronger staple yarn; but above this point, the additional twist adds a strain to the fibers that results in a weaker yarn. In general then, there is a certain limited range of twist that is desirable; for certain effects, however, less twist (soft twist) or more twist (hard twist) may be necessary. According to the kind and amount of twist, yarns may be classified as single yarn; ply yarn, cord, and core yarn.

The most common method of measuring twist is the "twist counter" (Figure 3–14), which untwists a given length of yarn and measures the number of turns necessary.

The twist counter consists of two jaws, one nonrotating but movable on a rod. The distance between the jaws may be varied. The jaw is fixed in position and rotates by means of a handle. A revolution counter is attached to read the number of turns.

The ASTM method of describing direction of twist is preferred. This system describes the twist as "S" or "Z." According to the definition: "a yarn or cord has S twist if, when held in a vertical position, the spirals conform in slope to the central portion of the letter 'S,' and Z twist if the spirals conform in slope to the central portion of the letter 'Z.'" Figure 3–15 illustrates both types of twist.

A yarn is said to be in balance if the amount of twist is just enough to keep the component yarns or fibers in position. If more twist than

Figure 3-14 A twist tester and counter is used for determination of twist and take-up of yarns. An enclosed drive unit provides two counters that are mechanically interlocked to provide automatic counting of "S" and "Z" twists. Both the direct counting method and the untwist method can be used. (Courtesy: U.S. Testing Co.)

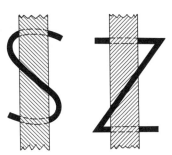
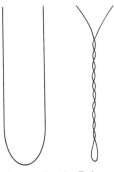

Figure 3-15 "S" and "Z" twist.

Figure 3-16 Balanced and unbalanced yarn.

this is put in, the yarn will kink and snarl; if less twist is put in, the yarn will tend to untwist and will kink again. For knitting machines and sewing machines especially, the question of balance in the yarn used is very important. A yarn is tested for balance by taking a one-yard length in the hands, each end held by thumb and forefinger of one hand and bringing the ends together. If the yarn hangs in a loop without twisting about itself, it is in perfect balance; if it twists about itself, it is not balanced. A rough indication of unbalance is obtained by noting the number of times the yarn twists about itself, but usually a yarn is reported simply as "balanced" or "not balanced." Figure 3–16 illustrates balanced and unbalanced yarns.

YARN UNIFORMITY

The most common way of comparing yarns for uniformity is by means of the inspection board or "seriplane." The seriplane (Figure 3–17) was originally devised for use in the silk industry but its use has been extended to other textiles. It consists essentially of a device for

Figure 3-17 The seriplane is used for detecting imperfections and gauging evenness, neatness, and cleanliness in all types of yarns. Yarns are wrapped on boards under controlled tension and at a predetermined number of warps per inch. The panels are compared with photographic standards of grading prescribed by the U.S. Department of Agriculture, ASTM, and the International Silk Association. (Courtesy: U.S. Testing Co.)

winding yarn at even intervals around a board of a color contrasting with the yarn. The seriplane, in its simplest form, winds yarn from one or two packages on a black board; machines are made that wind a large number of boards at a time. After winding, the board is viewed at a little distance for general evenness or density of yarn, looking especially for streaks. The boards are then examined more closely for (1) thick and thin places, (2) slubs—bunches of loose fiber caught in the yarn, (3) uneven twist, (4) corkscrew twist (yarns made of different diameter, size, fiber content or direction of twist), (5) oil or rust spots, (6) hairiness (excessive number of protruding fibers), and (7) broken filaments.

The test is qualitative but it may be made roughly quantitative by counting the number of imperfections per board. Permanent records may be made by photographing the boards, to be compared later with other photographs.

YARN STRENGTH

There are two standard methods of test for breaking strength of yarns: the single-strand method* and the skein method.†

Single-strand Method of Test

This method determines the breaking load and elongation of monofilament, multifilament, and spun yarns, either single, plied, or cabled, with the exception of yarns that stretch more than 5.0 percent when the tension is increased from 0.5 to 1.0 grams per tex.

METHOD OF TEST

A specimen is placed in the clamps of a tensile testing machine, stretched or loaded until broken, and the breaking load and elongation observed. Elongation at a specified load or the load or tenacity at a specified elongation may also be obtained.

This method offers three options with respect to moisture content of the specimens at the time of testing:

Option 1: Conditioned (in moisture equilibrium for testing with the standard atmosphere for testing).
Option 2: Wet.
Option 3: Oven dry.

* Breaking Load (Strength) and Elongation of Yarns by the Single-Strand Method; ASTM-D-2256-75.

† Breaking Load (Strength) of Yarn by the Skein Method; ASTM-D-1578-67 (1972).

The method also offers three options for the physical conformation of the specimen:

Option A: Straight.
Option B: Knotted.
Option C: Looped.

The strength of a yarn influences the strength of fabrics made from the yarn, although the strength of a fabric also depends on its construction and may be affected by finishing operations.

Since, for any fiber type, breaking load is approximately proportional to linear density, strands of different sizes can be compared by converting the observed breaking load to breaking tenacity (grams/tex or grams/denier), (see Figure 3–18).

The single-strand method gives a more accurate measure of strength and elongation and more information on the amount of variation present in the material than does the skein method. On the other hand, the single-strand method, while using less material, requires more of an operator's time and accordingly is more costly.

Elongation, combined with strength, indicates the ability of a yarn or fabric to absorb energy (energy absorption = work = strength and elongation). If the elongation at break of warp yarns is too low, weaving becomes difficult or even impossible. On the other hand, low-elongation yarns (and fabrics made from them) have greater dimensional stability. Garments made from such yarns are less likely to become "baggy" at the knees, elbows, or other points of stress.

The reduction in strength due to the presence of a knot or loop is considered a measure of the brittleness of the yarn. Elongation in knot or loop tests is not known to have any significance and is not usually recorded.

Tests in the wet condition are usually made only on yarns that show a loss of strength when wet or when exposed to high humidity—for example, yarns made from animal fibers and man-made fibers based on regenerated and modified cellulose. Wet tests are made on flax yarns to detect adulteration by failure to gain strength.

Tests in the oven-dry condition are usually made only on yarns that will be used at elevated temperatures or will be used under very dry conditions that will affect the observed strength—for example, on rayon yarns intended for use in tire cords and yarns for other industrial purposes.

Skein Method

A skein is a continuous strand of yarn in the form of a flexible coil having a large circumference in proportion to its thickness.

The standard method of test for breaking load (strength) of yarn (skein method) determines the breaking load of yarn in skein form.

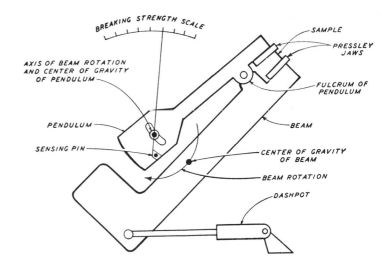

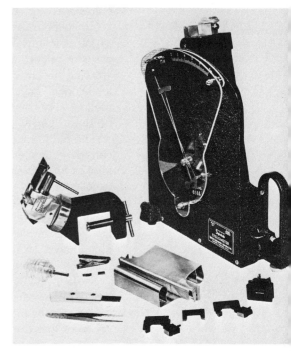

Figure 3-18 This is a fiber strength and elongation instrument. A fiber sample is taken from the hand comb. Loose fibers are combed from the sample by raking the fibers across the comb. The sample is then placed in the vise and clamped under measured torque. The ends of the sample are cut off and the testing jaws put into place. The beam is released and the results read directly on the scale. The sample is removed and weighed. (Courtesy: Special Instruments Laboratory)

The observed breaking load is expressed in units of force, and equations are provided to convert breaking load to skein breaking tenacity and to break factor.

Skein strength is the force required to rupture a skein of yarn, expressed in units of weight, as breaking load. The skein-breaking tenacity is the breaking load of a skein divided by the product of the yarn number in a direct numbering system and the number of strands placed under tension (twice the number of wraps in the skein).

The skein-break factor is the comparative breaking load of a skein of yarn adjusted for the linear density of the yarn expressed in an indirect system. It is the product of the breaking load of the skein and the yarn number expressed in an indirect system, for example, pounds force times cotton count (also called count-strength product).

The method is applicable to spun yarns, either single or plied, composed of any fiber or blend of fibers, but is not suitable for yarns that stretch more than 5 percent when the tension is increased from 0.25 to 0.75 gf (grams-force)/tex.

This method provides three options based on the perimeter of the reel, the number of wraps in the skein, and the machine speed or time to break.

Option 1 is 80, 40 or 20 turns on a 1.5-yard reel, broken at 12 inches per minute.

Option 2 is 50 turns on a 1-yard reel, broken at 12 inches per minute.

Option 3 is 50 turns on a 1-meter reel, broken in 20 seconds.

Option 1 is in general use in the United States; Option 2 is used for woolen yarns; and Option 3 has been proposed in the International Standards Organization (ISO) for international use.

This method is frequently combined with the determination of linear density carried out on the same skeins.

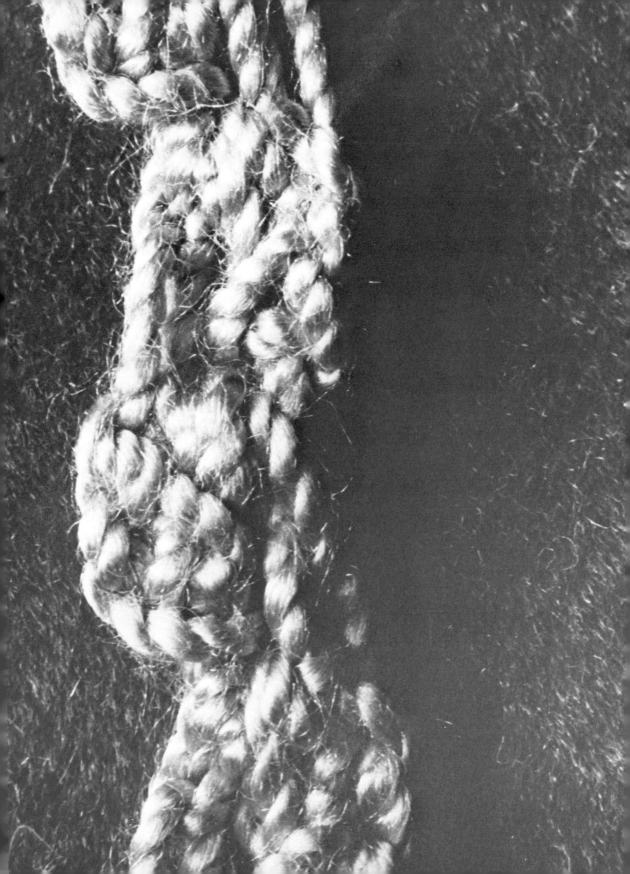

4

Analysis of Physical Fabric Properties

It is important to know the dimension and construction properties of fabrics. These properties play an important role in the buying and selling of fabrics, as well as in consumer use.*

LENGTH

Fabric length is simply the distance from one end of the fabric to the other. Measurement is made at the edge of the fabric or along the fold while it is lying flat under no tension and no wrinkles. The length may be expressed in yards or meters and fractions thereof. Most suppliers and retail stores use automatic measuring devices to measure length.

WIDTH

Fabric width is the distance across the filling or course direction of a fabric or from one edge or selvage to the other. An average of several measurements are made in several areas with the fabric lying flat under no tension or wrinkles. The width is expressed in inches or centimeters and expressed as a whole number or as a range. For example: 40 inches or 58/60 inches. Fabric width is an important consideration of the apparel manufacturer, the tailor, coutourier, and the home sewer. It determines the cutting advantages of the particular garment pattern or pattern for a household item.

Fabrics are made in a range of widths. The width variations of finished fabrics occur because of the variations in size of looms and knitting machines. Another variable is the degree of shrinkage that occurs when the fabric is finished by the manufacturer.

Most fabrics sold to garment manufacturers or for retail sales are wound around a cardboard tube. A full roll or piece of woven fabric usually contains from 60 to 100 yards. Knit fabrics are usually shipped in 35- to 50-pound rolls, in either open width or tubular form.

Some fabrics are doubled and rolled. They are folded in half lengthwise and then wound around a flat piece of cardboard. Fabric is sold on full-length rolls usually in 60- to 100-yard lengths; knit fabrics are in 35- to 50-pound rolls. (Retail is 30 yards.)

Velvet and other pile fabrics, such as simulated fur pile fabrics, are usually not rolled because the pressure would flatten the surface. The

* J. J. Pizzutto, *Fabric Science,* Fairchild Publications, Inc., New York (1974). Pp. 345–353.

fabric is placed on a frame so the surface does not contact any other part of the fabric.

Pieces of woven or knit fabric less than 40 yards are called shorts. They are sold either on 20- to 40-yard pieces (called 20s to 40s), 10- to 20-yard pieces (called 10s to 20s) or 5- to 10-yard pieces (called 5s to 10s). Jobbers are the usual buyers of these short pieces of fabric. Fabric mill end shops and discount mill outlet stores are also buyers of short lengths. Remnants are usually 1- to 10-yard pieces of fabric.

Pound goods are usually very short pieces of fabric (often containing pieces less than one yard). They are sold by the pound and not by the yard. Fabric that cannot be sold in any other manner is sold this way. These goods are bought at the buyer's risk and usually at a low price. End uses include stuffing for furniture and clothes for dolls.

Length-Width Relationships

In the analyzing and testing of fabrics, a textile technician must be able to identify the length (warp or wale direction) and width (filling or course direction). The warp or length is always parallel to the selvage. It is equally important to recognize the face (right side) and back (underside) of a fabric.

Besides having a face and a back, some fabrics have a top and a bottom on the face side. Most fabrics, when resting on a flat surface with the face side up and the warp yarns vertical, have the same appearance as the bottom. Thus, it will not make any difference in appearance in this case if a garment is made with its parts placed from top to bottom or if its parts are turned 180 degrees around and placed from bottom to top. Often, some of the parts are made top down while others are bottom down to facilitate the cutting process. No difference is noticed in the garment made. However, in some fabrics there is a difference. It may be the weave or the finish. For example, fleece, a fabric with a long nap, has an obvious top and a bottom to the face. It is made into garments with the nap brushed downward. In pile fabrics like velveteen and corduroy, the pile is not perfectly erect but lies at an angle. The color may vary from dark to light as the fabric is turned 180 degrees on a flat surface. This is due to the difference in the angle of light reflection. Sometimes these fabrics are used in garments with the pile upward to obtain a richer or darker color. In most cases the garment should be made with all its parts in the same top down or bottom down direction. A fabric with a woven or printed figure having an upright position can be cut only in one direction because the figure must be in the upright position in every piece forming the garment.

WEIGHT*

Weight is an important fabric property when comparing two similar fabric constructions. In some cases, but not in all, it is an indication of quality. For example, a heavier muslin is usually a better quality than a lighter one. Weight is often a consumer consideration in the selection of a fabric. A lightweight wool fabric, for example, may be desired over a heavyweight wool fabric.

Fabric weight is expressed as mass per unit area, that is, ounces per square yard, (grams per square meter), ounces per linear yard (grams per linear meter), or linear yards per pound (meter per kilogram). Ounces per square yard is the weight of a piece of fabric 36 inches × 36 inches. Ounces per linear yard is the weight of a piece of fabric 36 inches long and as wide as the entire fabric. In both these methods, the lighter the fabric, the lower the number of ounces, and vice versa. Linear yards per pound is the number of yards of the cloth equal to one pound. In this method, the lighter the fabric, the higher the yards per pound, while the heavier the fabric, the lower the yards per pound. A gauze fabric may be as light as 25 yards per pound while a wool coating fabric may be as heavy as 1 or 2 yards per pound.

When we want to determine the weight of a fabric, identical-size samples must be compared. For example: a six ounce per square yard of fabric 52 inches wide is heavier than a four ounce per square yard piece of fabric 52 inches wide. An eight ounce per linear yard fabric 54 inches wide is heavier than a seven ounce per linear yard fabric of the same width. A two linear yard per pound fabric 40 inches wide is heavier than three linear yards per pound fabric 40 inches wide.

Even though fabric widths vary, you can make an immediate comparison by using the ounces per square yard basis because you are examining the exact same area. The other two methods of determining fabric weight require additional calculations.

Calculating Fabric Weights

The following formula is used for calculating the ounces per square yard of fabric.

$$\frac{\text{Area in square inches of fabric weighed}}{\text{Weight in ounces of fabric weighed}}$$

$$X = \frac{\text{square inches in one square yard} \times \text{weight of fabric}}{\text{ounces per square yard of fabric}}$$

For example: assume that we cut a 20- × 22-inch sample from a 40-inch width fabric. The sample weighs 1.75 ounces. Calculate the ounces per square yard. Recall that 36 inches = one yard.

* Construction Characteristics of Woven Fabrics; ASTM-1910–64 (1975).

$$36 \times 36 = 1296 \text{ square inches}$$

$$\frac{(20)\ (22)}{1.75} = \frac{1296}{X} \qquad X = \frac{(1296)\ (1.75)}{(20)\ (22)}$$

$$X = 5.15 + \text{ounces per square yard}$$

If it is necessary to work with small samples of fabric the weight can be calculated in grams; remember that 28.35 grams equals 1 ounce.

The following formula is used for calculating the ounces per linear yard.

$$\frac{\text{Width from selvage to selvage}}{\text{Number of inches in a yard (36)}} = \frac{X \text{ (ounces per linear yard)}}{\text{ounces per square yard}}$$

$$X = \frac{\text{width of fabric}}{36} \text{ (ounces per square yard)}$$

In this calculation, the ounces per square yard of the fabric must first be calculated.

$$\frac{40}{36} = \frac{X}{\text{ounces per square yard}} \qquad X = \frac{40}{36} \ (5.15)$$

$$X = 5.72 \text{ or } 5.7 \text{ ounces per linear yard}$$

The following formula is used for calculating linear yards per pound (16 ounces equals one pound).

$$(\text{Linear yards per pound}) \ X = \frac{16(\text{ounces per pound})}{\text{ounces per linear yard}}$$

$$X = \frac{16}{6.3} \qquad \text{or} \qquad X = 2.81 \text{ linear yards per pound}$$

COMPARING WEIGHTS OF FABRICS OF DIFFERENT WIDTHS

No calculations are necessary in determining the ounces per square yard because one square yard or an equal length and width of fabric is being examined. For example:

Fabric No. 1 is 40 inches wide. One square yard weighs 4 ounces.
Fabric No. 2 is 50 inches wide. One square yard weighs 6 ounces.
Fabric No. 2 is heavier than Fabric No. 1.

To calculate the ounces per linear yard we need to either proportionally increase or decrease the weight when comparing two fabrics. For example:

Fabric No. 3 is 50 inches wide and one linear yard weighs 10 ounces.

Fabric No. 4 is 56 inches wide and one linear yard weighs 12 ounces.

Either Fabric No. 3 must be proportionally increased in weight to equal the 60-inch wide fabric (No. 4) or Fabric No. 4 must be proportionally decreased in weight to equal the 50-inch wide fabric (No. 3).

The formula for calculation is:

$$\text{Original weight of fabric} \times \frac{\text{new width}}{\text{original fabric width}}$$

$$= \text{new fabric weight}$$

1. *Proportionally increasing the weight of Fabric No. 3.*

$$\frac{10 \text{ ounces} \times 56 \text{ inches in width}}{50 \text{ inches in width}} = 11.2 \text{ ounces per linear yard}$$

2. *Proportionally decreasing the weight of Fabric No. 4.*

$$\frac{12 \text{ ounces} \times 50 \text{ inches in width}}{56 \text{ inches in width}} = 10.7 \text{ ounces per linear year}$$

Thus, Fabric No. 4 is heavier.

Linear Yards Per Pound

The calculation of linear yards per pound must be based on equal fabric widths. Let us assume, for example:

Fabric No. 5 is 40 inches wide and weighs 2.00 linear yards per pound.

Fabric No. 6 is 44 inches wide and weighs 1.75 linear yards per pound.

Either the width of Fabric No. 5 must be increased to equal 44 inches and its linear yards per pound reduced proportionally, or the width of Fabric No. 6 must be decreased to equal 40 inches and its linear yards per pound increased proportionally.

The formula for calculation is:

$$\text{Original fabric weight} \times \frac{\text{original fabric width}}{\text{new fabric width}} = \text{new fabric weight}$$

1. *Proportionally reduce the linear yards per pound of Fabric No. 5.*

$$2.00 \times \frac{40}{44} = 1.82 \text{ linear yards per pound}$$

2. *Proportionally increase the linear yards per pound of Fabric No. 6.*

$$1.75 \times \frac{44}{40} = 1.925 \text{ or } 1.93 \text{ linear yards per pound}$$

Thus, Fabric No. 5 is heavier.

The range of fabric weights is given in Table 4–1.

FABRIC COUNT*

Consumers should be aware of fabric count and its relationship to performance. The over-the-counter buyer of yard goods should be aware of variations in fabric construction from one shipment to another of the same fabric. Usually the higher the fabric count, the

Table 4–1   Range of Fabric Weights

Type	Weight Ounces Per Square Yard	Examples of End Uses
Very light weight	Less than 1	Curtains Sheer blouses Gauze Mosquito netting
Light weight[a]	2–3	Linings Summer dress fabrics Shirtings Summer pajama fabrics
Medium weight[b]	5–7	Summer suitings Slack fabrics Tablecloths Lightweight jacket fabrics

Heavy weight	9–11	Lightweight
		  coats
		Winter suitings
		Fabrics for work
		  clothes
		Toweling

Very heavy weight	Over 14	Winter coats Heavy sweaters Canvas (duck)

Courtesy: Fairchild Publications Inc.

  [a] Fabrics in this approximate weight range used for shirts, blouses, and so forth, are frequently called top-weight fabrics.

  [b] Fabrics in this approximate weight range used for slacks, shorts, and so forth, are frequently called bottom-weight fabrics.

  * Construction Characteristics of Woven Fabrics; ASTM-1910–64 (1970).

83   *Analysis of Physical Fabric Properties*

better the feel, durability, weight, hand, and stability of the fabric. Higher-count fabrics usually cost more than lower-count fabrics, all other factors being equal. A higher-count fabric usually has higher fabric strength; lower count, a lower strength for a given weight. Sometimes fabric manufacturers will add a finish to low-count fabrics to give them added hand and weight. This sometimes reduces both fabric or tensile strength and tear strength.

The yarns per inch in a fabric is given by two numbers with an × between. For example, 100 × 80 means 100 yarns per inch in the warp and 80 yarns per inch in the filling. The first number is for warp yarns per inch and the second is for filling yarns per inch. A fabric with the same number of yarns per inch in both directions is said to be square. An 80 square print cloth has 80 warp and 80 filling yarns per inch. The yarns per inch in the warp and in the filling is called the fabric count. In some cases you will only find one number given. This is known as a type number. For example: sheeting is classed on the number of yarns per square inch. The sum of the yarns per inch in the warp and the yarns per inch in the filling is given as type number. For example, if a sheeting has 80 warp and 80 filling yarns per inch, the type number is 160 (80 plus 80).

Fabric Count Measurements

Fabric count is the number of ends (warp) or picks (filling) per inch for woven fabrics, or the number of wales or courses per inch for knit fabrics. Measurement is made with the fabric in a flat and relaxed condition.

The yarns per inch in different parts of the same fabric often vary. Because of this, if a full-width piece of fabric is available, the warp count should be taken at several points along the width and the filling count taken at several points along the length of the fabric. Counts of full-width pieces of fabric should not be made within about four inches of the selvage because the yarns may be packed closer together near the edges. If only a small swatch is available, the counting should be done in the middle and not at the edge.

Determine if it is easier to make the count on the face or the back of the fabric. There are different ways that measurements can be made: (1) counting individual yarns; (2) groups of yarns; or (3) by line gratings (Figures 4–1 and 4–2).

INDIVIDUAL YARNS

Look through the pick glass and determine whether the counting can be done more easily on the face or on the back. It is often easier to see one set of yarns on the back and the other set on the face. If the fabric is dark, place it against something light, and vice versa.

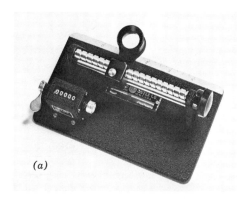

(a)

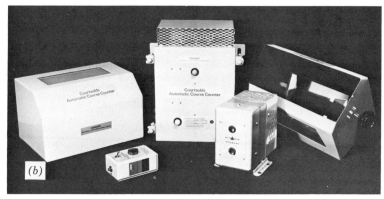

Figure 4-1 (a) An automatic thread-counting micrometer. (b) An automatic course micrometer. [(a) Courtesy: Alfred Suter Co., Inc. (b) Courtesy: Courtalds]

(b)

Figure 4-2 Line gratings may be used to measure yarns per inch in a fabric. (Courtesy: Shirley Development Ltd.)

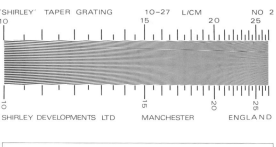

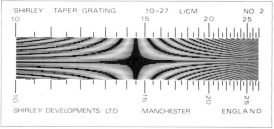

Line up the left edge of the opening in the base of a pick glass with the first yarn to be counted. Use a pick needle to point to the yarns as they are counted from one edge to the opposite edge of the opening in the base. If 60 yarns are counted with a one-inch glass, the yarns per inch is 60. If a half-inch glass is used, or if the yarns are counted for only one-half inch, the yarns per inch would be 60 times 2, or 120. It is best to count a full one inch, however, because if a mistake is made in counting, or if the counting is done in a nonrepresentative area, the error will increase when calculating the number of yarns in one inch.

Fabric count is an average of measurements made in the length and width directions and is reported to the nearest whole number. If the fabric is not of uniform construction (a dobby design or a stripe), the following formulas can be used

$$\frac{\text{Ends per repeat}}{\text{Inches per repeat}} = \text{average ends per inch}$$

$$\frac{\text{Picks per repeat}}{\text{Inches per repeat}} = \text{average picks per inch}$$

The above formulas can also be used for determining wales and courses per inch for nonuniformly constructed knit fabrics.

COUNTING GROUPS OF YARNS

In counting yarns per inch in a fabric having a check pattern like a gingham, groups of yarns instead of individual yarns can be counted. If every colored stripe has 10 yarns and every white stripe has 10 yarns, the number of complete stripes in the inch is counted and then multiplied by 10. The yarns in the incomplete stripe at the end are then added. If, in a striped fabric, there are 10 yarns per inch in a white stripe and 10 yarns per inch in the colored stripe and there are 8 yarns of an incomplete stripe at both edges of the fabric, the total is 10 × 10 + 16 (8 + 8) or 116 yarns.

Finding the yarns per inch can also be done by counting weave repeats instead of individual yarns. The yarns are counted in groups, with the group depending on the weave used.

LINE GRATINGS

The gratings are specially prepared plastic plates measuring about $3\frac{1}{4}$ inches × $4\frac{1}{4}$ inches, which are placed on the fabric. The number of fabric yarns per inch is then read off the scale. The gratings are composed of ruled, accurately spaced sets of lines. When placed on a piece of fabric, a moiré pattern of light and dark bands appears on the grating. This is because of the partial coincidence of the lines on the grating and the yarns of the fabric.

The range of each grating is limited to about 40 yarns per inch. To count any number between 10 and 200 yarns per inch, a set of different gratings is required.

The gratings can only be used if the yarns in a fabric are clearly visible.

The grating is placed on the fabric with the longest edge parallel to the yarns to be counted. The grating is then adjusted until a cross appears. The number of yarns per inch is indicated where the arms of the cross cut the scale (Figure 4–2).

YARN DISTORTION

Yarn distortion in woven fabrics occurs when the symmetrical surface appearance of the fabric is altered by the shifting or sliding of warp or filling yarns.

Causes Of Yarn Distortion

There are several reasons why yarns distort or shift: (1) Thread count—if the number of yarns per inch is low, the yarn can move from side to side. A good example is the ease with which yarns can shift in gauze because the yarns are woven far apart. (2) Type of yarn—filament yarns are smoother and more even than spun yarns, so filament yarns slip more easily than spun yarns. Rayon yarns shift more than cotton yarns because the rayon fiber has a smooth rodlike shape while cotton has an irregular surface. (3) Weave—the plain weave, which has many interlacings, holds the yarns in place better than a satin weave, which has a minimum of interlacings. (4) Finish—a finish may affect yarn movement. For example, a resin finish on a fabric binds the yarns so that they tend not to slip.

A SIMPLE THUMB-AND-FINGER TEST

A preliminary test for yarn distortion may be made with the thumb and forefinger touching opposite surfaces of the fabric and exerting a shearing motion to produce a frictional force.

The device used to determine yarn distortion is a fabric shift tester (Figure 4–3). Patterns of shift openings are shown in Figure 4–4. In the test method,* a piece of fabric is subjected to a specified shearing force acting in the plane of the fabric. The degree to which

* *Distortion of Yarns in Woven Fabric;* ASTM Test Method D-1336-72 (1973).

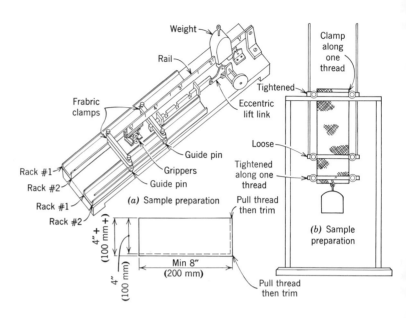

Weight

Rail

Frabric clamps

Rack #1
Rack #2

Rack #1
Rack #2

Eccentric lift link

Guide pin
Grippers
Guide pin

(a) Sample preparation

Clamp along one thread

Tightened

Loose

Tightened along one thread

Pull thread then trim

(b) Sample preparation

4" + (100 mm +)
4" (100 mm)

Min 8"
(200 mm)

Pull thread then trim

Figure 4-3 The fabric shift tester is an instrument that measures yarn distortion in woven fabrics after surface friction has been applied. This condition, known as "blistering," impairs the surface appearance of the fabric by displacement of the warp or filling yarns through sliding or shifting. Low-count filament yarn structures are particularly susceptible to "blistering." The widest opening of each shift mark is measured. This instrument may also be used to evaluate finishes. (Courtesy: U.S. Testing Co.)

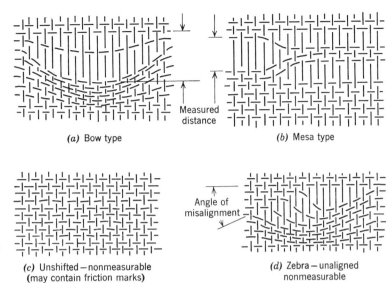

(a) Bow type

(b) Mesa type

(c) Unshifted—nonmeasurable
(may contain friction marks)

(d) Zebra—unaligned
nonmeasurable

Figure 4-4 Patterns of shift openings. (Courtesy: American Society for Testing and Materials)

the force causes yarns to shift distorting the original symmetry of the weave is taken as a measure of yarn distortion in the fabric. The amount of the widest opening between the yarns in the test areas is measured to the nearest $\frac{1}{100}$ inch. An average of the four measurements is taken and reported in the direction (warp or filling) of the yarns distorted.

5

Testing for
Product Performance

1 AESTHETIC APPEARANCE

Consumers rate aesthetic appearance as an important value when they purchase, wear, use, and care for their clothing and household items. Therefore, this quality cannot be ignored or underestimated.

Test methods designed for testing fabrics have been designed to help the various segments of the textile industry (1) evaluate their own product and (2) settle a dispute over a product when it arises. It has only been relatively recently that thought has been given to designing tests that may measure or predict consumer performance of fabrics.

In studying consumer performance of textiles, a single test method may be classified in more than one consumer performance category. For example, if a color of a garment changes in the underarm area from perspiration, then this is a change in aesthetic value; if the fabric is deteriorated by perspiration this is classed a durability value. However, the fact that the cause of perspiration is due to secretion of the glands and bacterial action it may be considered as a biological function. Thus it can be seen that consumer performance is a complex phenomenon. This is why judgments need to be made in the selection of a test method and evaluation of the results.

As stated earlier, we have chosen to group test methods as to function in end use: (1) aesthetic appearance, (2) durability, (3) comfort, (4) safety, (5) care, (6) biological resistance, and (7) environmental resistance. In those cases where the end-use function of a test method may or could be classified in one or more areas, this is mentioned and referenced.

APPEARANCE TEST METHODS

There are four test methods in the technical manual of the American Association of Textile Chemists and Colorists to measure appearance. They are:

1. *Test Method 124.* Appearance of Durable Press Fabrics After Repeated Home Launderings.

2. *Test Method 88B.* Appearance of Seams in Wash-and-Wear Items After Home Laundering.

3. *Test Method 88C.* Appearance of Creases in Wash-and-Wear Items After Home Laundering (a new method, appearing for the first time in the 1975 *AATCC Technical Manual*).

4. *Test Method 143.* Appearance of Apparel and Other Textile End Products After Repeated Home Launderings.

The four tests measure fabric smoothness, seams, creases, and apparel. The apparel method is a combination of the first three methods adapted slightly for evaluating end-use items rather than fabric samples.

In principle, the test methods are simple. Fabric samples or garments are washed, then evaluated. All four of the test methods use a standard lighting arrangement where the sample is hung against a viewing board with overhead fluorescent lighting. The crease test method uses an additional light source placed at an angle to the sample in order to highlight the creased area. In all methods, test samples are compared against a series of five rating steps where No. 5 is the best and No. 1 is the worst rating. Fabric smoothness is evaluated using three dimensional replicas while seams and creases are judged by photographic standards. The replica or photo standard that has the appearance most nearly like the test specimen determines the rating the specimen receives.

Since the test methods were originally developed for resin-treated wovens, the fabrics used in the development of the replica and photo standards were woven fabrics. This presents a problem when we try to evaluate knits using these same methods and replicas. In the purpose and scope of each of the basic methods, knits are not mentioned. The apparel method is intended for all types of applications.

Recently, Di Modica* made a survey of AATCC members for their experience in using the appearance test methods. She found that:

1. Method 124 (fabric samples) presented no major problems.

2. Method 88B (seams) also provided no serious problem although there was significant interest in developing component rating standards. The most often mentioned component areas were shirt plackets, pockets, and zippers.

3. On method 88C (creases), there was almost unanimous opposition directed toward the crease test method. There is zero correlation, zero reality, and zero validity according to Di Modica.

4. No questions were asked about the apparel method because it is so new.

Each of these test methods are discussed later.

---

* Genevieve M. Di Modica, *The Appearance Test Methods and their Application to Knits. Sense and Nonsense in Knit Testing No. 17,* American Association of Textile Chemists and Colorists, pp. 58–61.

DURABLE PRESS

"Durable Press," "Wash and Wear," and "Easy Care," are terms used interchangeably by manufacturers on hang tags and in advertising. Today, "Wash and Wear" is used infrequently. "Easy Care" is used quite frequently but, as one large merchandiser states, "We have found that 'Easy Care' items require ironing." The term "Durable Press" is used quite frequently. You might question then, why the AATCC Technical Manual lists test method 88C to evaluate wash-and-wear items. The test method uses the term "Wash and Wear" in a broad sense to describe a large range of fabrics and garments that are designed for easy care or durable-press (sometimes referred to as "permanent press") garments and fabrics.

Manufacturers advertise the following consumer benefits of durable-press suits: they retain shape and pressed-in creases; they resist wrinkling during wear; they need only minimum care when cleaning instructions are followed; they retain no oil and grease spots; and they pick up no soil in cleaning.*

Manufacturers who feature "Dry Clean Only" on their labels say the suiting fabric itself is washable, but that the linings and other trim required by fine tailoring are not. Therefore, they recommend dry cleaning, either professional or coin operated.

Complaints made by consumers on durable-press garments are (1) abrasion in wear and (2) odor problems. Abrasion in wear usually shows up in the knees, seat, and pockets where keys, a wallet, or lighter may cause abrasion.

Consumers who have odor problems usually inquire, "Will dry cleaning or laundering remove the odor from my durable-press garment?"

The odor that develops in a fabric is due to a lack of proper rinsing in the final step of producing durable-press fabrics and garments. It is claimed that any odor in a new durable-press garment may be removed by washing. If this is done at the point of garment construction, the garment will no longer be regarded by buyers as "new." This explains why many consumers complain about odor in new garments. Odor in a garment constructed to be dry cleaned presents a special problem because dry cleaning does not remove the odorous durable-press finish.

There have also been consumer complaints of skin irritation from durable-press garments. The remedy is to launder or wet clean the garment to remove residual chemicals in the fabric. If garment construction is such that there is a risk in wet cleaning the durable-press item, the responsibility for the decision must rest with the consumer. Many consumers ask: "How can I remove the creases in my

---

* "Drycleaning Durable-Press Garments," *Fabrics-Fashions Bulletin FF-168,* National Institute of Drycleaning (1968).

durable-press garments?" At the present time, there is no home method or professional method of removing durable-press crease lines. This creates a problem if a garment needs to be altered.

APPEARANCE OF DURABLE PRESS FABRICS AND GARMENTS

The durable-press concept seeks to provide the consumer with fabrics that require no ironing. Durable-press garments are not the same as wash-and-wear articles. Durable-press garments should retain their original appearance throughout their wear life. These include:

1. Smooth fabric appearance. The fabric should be highly wrinkle resistant so that the garment may be worn after being washed and dried without need of ironing. Also, objectionable wrinkles should not occur while the garment is being worn.

2. Flat seams. The garment seams should not pucker, from either cleaning or wearing. They should remain smooth in appearance.

3. Crease retention. Creases or pleats should remain sharp and not become less defined after being washed or worn.

Solid shades show wrinkles and creases more readily than printed or patterned fabrics. It is recognized that prints and patterns mask the mussiness present in durable-press fabrics.

The test method* used to evaluate the retention of the original smooth appearance of durable-press items is designed to reflect the capabilities of laundry equipment that is currently used in the homes of the vast majority of consumers.

Fabric samples are subjected to procedures simulating home laundering practices. A choice is provided of three alternative washing temperatures, and two alternative drying procedures.

The samples are mounted on a viewing board (Figure 5–1), with the warp in a vertical direction. Three-dimensional plastic replicas are placed on each side of the test sample to facilitate comparative rating. The overhead fluorescent light is the only light source for the viewing board. All other lights are turned off.

It has been the experience of many observers that light reflected from the side walls near the viewing board can interfere with the rating results. It is recommended that the side walls of the room or viewing cabinet be painted black or that blackout curtains be mounted on either side of the viewing board to eliminate the reflective interference.

---

* Appearance of Durable Press Fabrics After Repeated Home Launderings; AATCC Test Method 124 (1975).

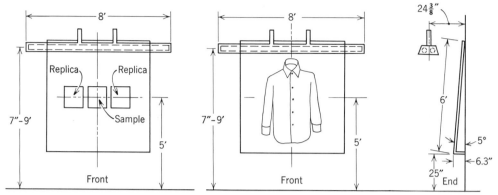

Figure 5-1 Lighting equipment for viewing test specimens. Materials list:

2—8′ type F96 CW (cool white) preheat rapid start fluorescent lamp (without baffle or glass).

1—white enamel reflector (without baffle or glass).

1—general-type swatch mount, spring loaded. Fabricate using light sheet metal (22 ga).

1—one-quarter in. plywood mounting board, overall dimensions 6′ × 4′. Paint gray to match No. 2 rating on International Gray Scale for Staining.

(Courtesy: American Association of Textile Chemists and Colorists)

Three trained observers rate each test specimen independently. Each sample is assigned the number of the replica that most nearly matches the appearance of the test sample (Figure 5–2). Each sample is rated on a 5-4-3-2-1 scale, class 5 being the best rating and class 1 the worst. Intermediate classes are also used.

In 1975, the AATCC Committee RA61 developed a test method* to evaluate the appearance of apparel and other textile end products after repeated home laundering. The test method is not a standard of performance for any textile item but only a standard method to evaluate performance of the item. Components, such as seams, pockets, and the like, vary with the item tested. Each component is assigned an absolute minimum performance value (see Rating Chart, Figure 5–3).

It is necessary to designate those components that are considered to be important to the item's appearance. Three trained observers rated each item's components independently after the item is mounted on a viewing board.

* Appearance of Apparel and Other Textile End Products After Repeated Home Launderings; AATCC Test Method 143 (1975).

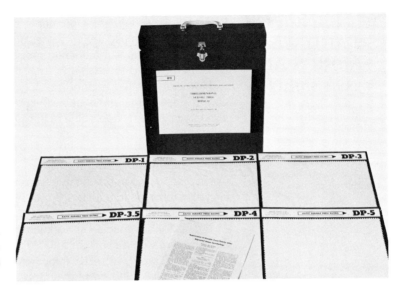

Figure 5-2 AATCC 3-0 durable-press replicas. (Courtesy: American Association of Textile Chemists and Colorists)

Figure 5-3 Rating chart of appearance of apparel and other end products. The weighting factors assigned to each component are 3—very important to overall item appearance; 2—moderately important to overall item appearance; and 1—slightly important to overall item appearance. The formulas for calculating the two options for reporting results are given in the AATCC Test Method 143(1975). (Courtesy: American Association of Textile Chemists and Colorists)

Identification:

Component (Characteristic, Attribute)	Weighting Factor (8.1.1)	Average Rating (8.1.2 or 8.2)	Point Value
	×	=	
	×	=	
	×	=	
	×	=	
	×	=	
	×	=	
	×	=	
	×	=	

Total weighting factor → × 5 = point value → Maximum point value

Total point value → × 100 = Percentile value

APPEARANCE OF WASH-AND-WEAR FABRICS AND GARMENTS

Wash-and-wear fabrics or garments only claim wrinkle resistance. They do not normally retain creases or pleats, nor do they necessarily possess flat seams. Frequently special washing and drying instructions are attached to wash-and-wear garments.

However, the test method* is designed for evaluating the retention of pressed-in creases in wash-and-wear fabrics. The method is also expected to be applicable to the evaluation of creases in finished garments.

Creased fabric samples are subjected to procedures simulating home laundry practices. A choice is provided of two alternative washing temperatures and three alternative drying procedures (drip, line, and tumble). In addition, a hand-washing procedure using drip drying is included.

Evaluation is made by supplementing the overhead lighting arrangement with a spotlight suitably placed to highlight the creased area (see Figure 5–4). The appearance of the specimen crease is compared with standard photographs. Five appearance classes are used for ratings. Standard 5 represents the best level of appearance of crease retention while Standard 1 represents the poorest appearance.

Figure 5-4 Lighting and viewing arrangements. (Courtesy: American Association of Textile Chemists and Colorists)

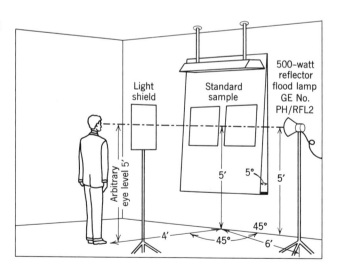

* Appearance of Creases in Wash-and-Wear Items After Home Laundering; AATCC Test Method 88C (1975).

APPEARANCE OF SEAMS IN WASH-AND-WEAR ITEMS

The appearance of a garment can be aesthically changed if the seams pucker or wrinkle. The test method* is designed for evaluating the appearance of seams in wash-and-wear fabrics. The method is also applicable to the evaluation of seams in finished garments or items.

Seamed fabric samples are subjected to procedures simulating home laundry practices. Two washing temperatures and three drying procedures (drip, tumble, and line) are provided. In addition, a hand-washing procedure using drip drying is included.

The evaluation is performed by using an overhead lighting procedure and comparing the appearance of seams with the standard photographs (see Figure 5–5a and b). Five appearance classes are recognized. Standard 5 represents the best level of appearance while Standard 1 represents the poorest level of appearance.

Figure 5-5 (a) Photographic comparative ratings for single-needle seams. (Courtesy: American Association of Textile Chemists and Colorists) (b) Photographic comparative ratings for double-needle seams. (Courtesy: American Association of Textile Chemists and Colorists)

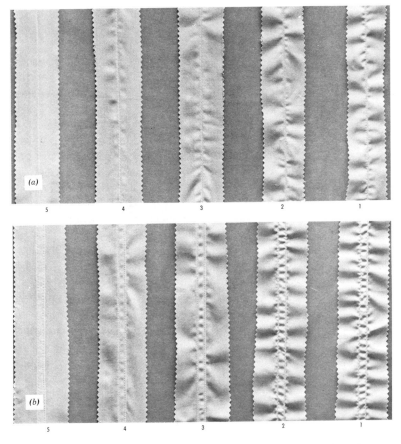

* Appearance of Seams in Wash-and-Wear Items After Home Laundering; AATCC Test Method 88B (1975).

COLORFASTNESS

There are many conditions that influence the performance of color in solid hues or prints. Some fabrics change colors greatly while they are in use; others change very little and some not at all. When considering a printed fabric, each color in the print requires testing and evaluation.

When a color changes in hue, value, or intensity it usually results in an aesthetic consideration. Color change may be attributed to abrasion, atmospheric conditions such as ultraviolet light, oxides of nitrogen, or ozone; acid and alkaline substances; bleaches in laundering or from products one may come in contact with; crocking or rubbing off of color during wear; drycleaning in perchlorethylene, petroleum, or fluorocarbon solvents; perspiration; washing in either cold or hot water alone, or in combination with detergents; and rainwater, chlorinated pool water, or seawater. The ability to evaluate a change in colorfastness of a fabric requires a thorough knowledge of dyes and pigments and why they change color; a knowledge of test procedures and their limitations; and how color changes are rated, evaluated and reported.

Colorfastness, color staining, and color transfer are standardized ways to evaluate colorfastness and are discussed in Chapter 1.

In evaluating colorfastness, changes due to the conditions of use or test are compared with the colors or shades of the original fabric. The terms most generally used are excellent, good, fair, poor, and very poor colorfastness. There are variations to these ratings for some tests. Each term is assigned a number ranging from a high number such as Class 9 very high lightfastness to Class 1 (very low lightfastness). Any fabric that does not qualify for Class 1 in a test, falls in Class 0 (see Chapter 1).

It is also important to observe and study color bleeding or color migration and color staining. This phenomenon can occur with a printed fabric or when two colors are combined in garments or household items. The transfer of color and the staining of a lighter fabric may make a garment unwearable or a household item no longer usable. The bleeding and staining of a fabric may be studied by attaching a multifiber test fabric* to the fabric being tested. The test cloth is evaluated for the transfer or pickup of color. This is rated by degrees of staining: Class 5—negligible or no staining, Class 1—heavy staining. Some colored fabrics may changed in color, hue, or intensity and not show any staining. The reverse is also true. Some fabrics may not change color but may show staining of the test fabric.

---

* Available from Testfabrics, Inc., 200 Blackford Avenue, Middlesex, New Jersey 08846.

Colorfastness To Abrasion

Color loss due to abrasion is called "frosting," "differential wear," or "fibrillation." * It is a change of color caused by localized abrasive wear.

Fibers, yarns, and the dye may be disturbed by rubbing or flexing of the fabric surface against a like or an unlike surface. In some cases the dye rubs off (crocks); in others, microscopic examination shows that disturbance of the yarns or fibers causes a difference in light reflection that makes the fabric appear lighter or darker.

This type of color change may occur as a result of rubbing a spot or stain in an attempt to remove it; natural abrasion in use and wear, such as the rubbing action of the elbows on a desk or the shoulder and seat area against a chair; and excessive mechanical agitation during cleaning of the garment.

The surface of a fabric should never be rubbed in an attempt to remove a spot or stain. Proper techniques of stain and spot removal, as well as cleaning, usually prevent this kind of color change. However, after long periods of wear, some change in color can be expected.

Color change may also occur because of differential wear in a fiber blend in which the fibers differ in shade, or the abrasion of a fiber in a 100 percent composition fabric in which there may be variation of the penetration of dye.

Discoloration in fiber blends, for example, has been noted in fabrics made of yarn containing black polyester fibers and light rayon fibers. The rubbing of the fabric against something carried in the pocket, like a wallet or a key case, weakens the rayon fibers leaving the polyester, which has greater abrasion resistance, intact. The worn areas appear black because the weakened rayon fibers are rubbed away and only the black polyester remains.

It is known that certain chemical finishes used in manufacture to impart crease resistance also reduce abrasion resistance. Rayon and cotton fibers that withstand wear reasonably well when they do not contain this finish deteriorate rapidly when they do. Even without a special finish, rayon and cotton do not perform nearly as well as polyester.

Abrasion and test methods for evaluation of this property is discussed in Part 2, of this chapter, Durability.

Loss Of Color From The Crocking Of Dye

Crocking is defined as the color transfer from one colored textile material to another by rubbing. The scope of the crocking test does not include how well a textile material withstands rubbing action before physical signs of wear or a color change begin to appear. These

* Frosting, Color Change Due to Flat Abrasion; AATCC Test Methods 120 (1974) and 119 (1974).

are examined in an abrasion test or a colorfastness to frosting test (see p. 133).

Some dyes have very low resistance to crocking or rubbing. The loss of color may occur as localized streaks, as streaks throughout a garment or in spots and blotches. It is common to find light areas where a fabric is folded and subjected to abrasion during wear, such as along the hemline and cuffline. The mechanical action in dry cleaning, wet cleaning, and laundering may also remove color and cause this type of damage.

Dark shades are more likely to crock than light shades. There is more dye in and on the fabric, so there is more dye that can be rubbed off. Printed fabrics may crock more readily than dyed fabrics because most of their dye is on the surface and not inside the fabric as with dyed fabric. A wet fabric will crock more than a dry fabric because the moisture assists in removing dye.

Colorfastness to crocking is important for wearing apparel fabrics, and equally important for household fabrics. Some manufacturers give colorfastness information on their color cards.

The occurrence of the loss of color by crocking or rubbing in wear, dry cleaning, wet cleaning, and laundering may be attributed to the type of dye, the method of application, or to improper cleaning techniques. This problem may be controlled in manufacture by the selection of dyes that possess good colorfastness to crocking or rubbing, and in dry cleaning by good plant practices on the part of the dry cleaner.

TEST FOR COLORFASTNESS TO CROCKING

Colorfastness to crocking tests* may be made by two methods, depending on the objective of the test:

1. The Crockmeter test determines the degree of color that may be transferred from the surface of colored textile materials to other surfaces by rubbing. It is applicable to textiles made from all fibers in the form of yarn or fabric, whether dyed, printed, or otherwise colored (see Figure 5–6).

2. The Rotary Vertical Crockmeter test determines whether or not color may be transferred from the surface of colored textile materials to other surfaces by rubbing. It is applicable to textiles made from all fibers in the form of yarn or fabric, whether dyed, printed, or otherwise colored, and especially to prints where the singling out of areas smaller than possible to test with the standard AATCC Crockmeter is required (see Figure 5–7).

* Colorfastness to Crocking; AATCC Test Methods 8 (1974) and 116 (1974).

Figure 5-6 (a) Test samples are mounted on the flat base of the instrument that is covered with abrasive paper to prevent sliding. The sample is held in place with a stainless steel sample holder or rubber bands. A 2 in. × 2 in. (5 cm × 5 cm) square of standard white Crockmeter test cloth is mounted on the rubbing finger with a spring clip. The finger rests on the sample with a pressure of 32 oz (900 g) and inscribes a straight path $4\frac{1}{8}$ in. (10.5 cm) long with each turn of the handle. The stroke length may be adjusted to 2 in. (7.6 cm) or 2 in. (5 cm) when the test material is limited in size.

(b) A motorized crockmeter is equipped with an electric motor operating at the specified 60 revolutions per minute and an automatic shut-down counter. The counter may be set for any desired number of strokes between 1 and 999. (Courtesy: Atlas Electric Devices Co.)

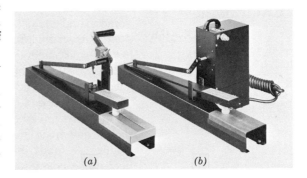

(a)   (b)

In both tests, the procedure uses test squares either dry or wet with water or other liquids. The test may be made before or after laundering, dry cleaning, pressing, or finishing since these procedures may affect the degree of color transfer from a fabric.

The test squares are backed with three layers of white test cloth while being evaluated. Evaluation of the amount of color transferred from the specimen to the white test square is done by means of the AATCC Color Transference Chart or the Gray Scale for Staining with intermediate steps.

Figure 5-7 The Rotary Vertical Crockmeter provides a reciprocating rotary motion to the test finger and a selected pressure on the test figure. (Courtesy: Atlas Electric Devices Co.)

Both dry and wet crocking fastness is rated from Class 5—negligible or no color transfer—to Class 1—color transfer equivalent to Row 1 on the AATCC Color Transference Chart or Step 1 on the Gray Scale for Staining.

Colorfastness To Light

Sunlight can be devastating to colors (aesthetic) and can cause deterioration and loss of strength. The cause of the damage may be considered as an environmental function in end uses since sunlight is a natural environmental factor that affects fabric performance.

Dyes are very complex in their chemical makeup. Some have limitations when applied to certain types of fabrics. For example, to obtain the brilliance of color desired on silk fabrics, a certain degree of colorfastness must be sacrificed. Also, the intended use of a fabric should determine the degree of colorfastness to light required. For example, a fabric that is being dyed or printed for evening wear needs little colorfastness to light, whereas a fabric being dyed or printed for draperies would require a high degree of colorfastness to light.

Color change because of exposure to light is caused by either the direct or the indirect rays of sunlight. Ultraviolet rays cause the greatest degree of change in most dyes. It is always possible to detect the degree of colorfastness to light by comparing an unexposed area (underside of hem, collar, cuffs) with an area that has been exposed to light.

When the end use of the fabric is known, dyes should be selected in manufacture that will meet the specific lightfastness requirements.

TESTING FOR COLORFASTNESS TO LIGHT

There are different methods* and procedures used to give a measure of the fastness of color to light: (1) daylight, (2) sunlight, (3) the carbon-arc lamp, and (4) the xenon-arc lamp. The test methods that use the carbon-arc and the xenon-arc lamps may be varied by (1) alternating the light and darkness or using continuous light exposure. Each method may also be varied by laundering the specimens between exposures.

It is important to recognize that there is a distinct difference in spectral distribution of the carbon arc and the xenon arc. There is no overall correlation between them; hence, they cannot be used interchangeably.

DAYLIGHT EXPOSURE

In the daylight-exposure method, the test specimens are allowed to remain in a test cabinet 24 hours a day. This method is typical of

---

* Colorfastness to Light (General Method); AATCC Test Method 16 (1974).

actual end-use exposure conditions. In this test the specimens are exposed to low-intensity radiation occurring before 9 A.M. and after 3 P.M., and on cloudy days, when the specimen temperature may be low and the moisture content high.

SUNLIGHT EXPOSURE   The standard method for a number of years was the sunlight method. In this method, specimens are exposed against standards or for specified amounts of radiation expressed in a unit of solar radiation called langleys. Tests are conducted only on sunny days between the hours of 9 A.M. and 3 P.M. The specimens are exposed only at high radiation intensity, high temperature, and low moisture content of the fabric. This test method is recognized as a dry test and as the most reproducible natural-light test.

It is a common practice to expose materials by both sunlight and daylight methods. Exposure is made at more than one location in order to obtain better information as to their acceptability for general overall use under widely varying conditions. In interpreting the results of natural light tests, it must be recognized that the amount and character of the color change produced depends on such factors as (1) the spectral distribution (the makeup or proportion of ultraviolet, infrared, and visible light) and the density of the incident radiant flux (light intensity), (2) the temperature and moisture content of the specimen, and (3) the action of atmospheric contaminants (Figure 5–8).

Figure 5-8 An outdoor exposure cabinet meets the requirements of a well-ventilated cabinet in which samples may be left on a 24-hour-a-day basis protected from the weather. Test samples are mounted on a removable tray consisting of a wooden frame covered with aluminum screening. The cover is easily removed. The cabinet is supplied with a metal cover for limiting exposures between certain hours without removing the samples. (Courtesy: Atlas Electric Devices Co.)

THE CARBON-ARC LAMP METHOD

A sample from a fabric to be tested and a set of standards (usually AATCC Blue Wool Lightfastness Standard L-2 to L-9) are exposed simultaneously under specified conditions for sufficient time to produce a specified amount of color change. The carbon-arc method produces results that correlate with those obtained by the natural light methods (Figure 5–9a and b).

THE XENON-ARC LAMP METHOD

The spectral radiation distribution of the xenon arc is altered by infra-red absorbing inner and outer filter glasses and is very close to that of average or typical sunlight. It is to be expected that the results of the xenon-arc methods on all materials, except those sensitive to atmospheric contaminants, will agree with the results of comparable natural-light methods. However, this requires verification by comparative testing of accelerated exposure and natural exposure.

GENERAL PRINCIPLES

The rates of the fading of fabrics and the standards do not necessarily change to the same degree. Changes in color depend on the spectral distribution, the intensity of the radiation, and the temperature and moisture content of the fabric. The relative fastness of textiles under the various test methods may vary considerably.

It is necessary to indicate the method use in the evaluation and rating of colorfastness. Significantly different fastness can occur in terms of standards between the various methods. It is also important that color changes be evaluated under standard lighting conditions.

REPORTING COLORFASTNESS TO LIGHT

There are different ways to report colorfastness to light. "Just appreciable fading" means a change in color of any kind, whether a change in hue or becoming lighter or darker. Color change or color difference is immediately noticeable in comparing the exposed area of the specimen with an unexposed area. Samples should be viewed in north-sky light or an equivalent source with illumination of 50 foot-candles or more on the surface. If closer inspection or a change of angle is required to make certain that there is a change in color, the fading is not considered to be "appreciable."

"Just appreciable fading" is also the degree of contrast between the exposed and unexposed specimen. This color change is visually equal to the contrast between the pair of pieces of paper of the International Geometric Gray Scale for Evaluating Change in Color.

There is also an AATCC Blue Wool Lightness Standard that is used to evaluate color changes. By this method, "just appreciable fading" is 1.5 units of color difference when the exposed area of the

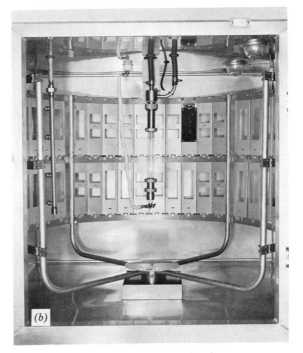

Figure 5-9 (a) The first Fade-Ometer was developed in 1918 and immediately found application in the testing of textiles. The first unit consisted of an enclosed carbon arc lamp, housed in a cylindrical chamber. Little thought was given to controlling radiation, temperature, or humidity of the test environment—the samples merely sat around the lamp. After several years of experience it was concluded that the radiation intensity and temperature in the test chamber did indeed play an important role. Therefore, thermostatically controlled fans, arc voltage regulation, and the rotating specimen rack were all introduced. It was also discovered that sample moisture had an effect and test chamber humidity must be considered. First absorbent wicks and later, in the early 1950s, the automatic electric humidifier was added to control this variable. (Courtesy: Atlas Electrical Devices Co.) (b) The samples to be tested are placed in specimen holders and arranged on a revolving rack for a specified time of exposure. (Courtesy: Atlas Electrical Devices Co.)

specimen is compared with the unexposed area. Computation is by the Adams-Nickerson color difference formula (AN(40)), or with formulas other than Adams-Nickerson.*

Exposures of various standards and specimens of different hues, values, and chromas may, by visual comparison, show "just appreciable fading" equal to Step 4 of the Gray Scale,† but when measured instrumentally the number of Units of Color Difference, computed by the Adams-Nickerson color difference formula, may vary considerably from the 1.5 + 0.2 value of the pair of pieces of paper on the Gray Scale illustrating Step 4.

The L-22 standards for performance requirements for textile fabrics gives specifications for colorfastness to light. Most apparel fabrics are tested for periods of up to 40 standard fading hours. An evening fabric is usually tested for only 10 SF hours because fabric for this end use requires little resistance to sunlight. Material to be used for a man's suit usually is tested for 40 hours, because this fabric will have to resist the fading effect of the sun to a much greater degree. Drapery fabric is usually tested for 80 hours.

WHITENESS OF FABRICS

Different compounds are used to produce a brightening or whitening effect on fabrics. Depending on the compound selected, a fluorescent brightener may produce a reddish, bluish, greenish, or neutral white. Fluorescent brightening agents are also used on pastel-dyed fabrics and furs.

Exposure to light causes some brighteners to change from white to yellow. On wool, silk, and fur the change is always permanent. Washable cottons may be re-treated. Fluorescent brighteners vary in their fastness to light. The fastness properties of a single brightener varies considerably on different fibers. Some fluorescent brighteners have poor colorfastness to hypochlorite bleach. Detergents containing an optical bleach can make a fluorescent-dyed fabric become more sensitive to light. Some fluorescent dyes change from the heat of steam pressing.

Whether an article that has lost original whiteness can be satisfactorily whitened depends on how badly it is discolored, as well as other factors. Some wet-cleanable items can be treated with a fluorescent brightener or detergent that contains an effective bright-

---

* See Color Measurement of the Blue Wool Lightfastness Standards: Instrumental, AATCC Test Method 145 (1975).

† See Chapter 1, p. 28.

ener. At present, there are no successful fluorescent brighteners that can be applied in dry-cleaning solvents. Chemical manufacturers are striving to develop fluorescent dyes and brighteners with better color-fastness properties. The dyer of fabrics should be selective in choosing the best brightener for the particular fiber to be dyed.

There is no test method used to test fabrics that have fluorescent dyes and tints applied to them. The test method* for reflectance, blueness, and whiteness of bleached fabrics has two objectives: (1) measuring the effectiveness of bleaching and (2) evaluating the whiteness of bleached, untinted fabrics.

Most of the impurities in unbleached fabrics absorb a portion of the blue light that falls on them. Bleaching removes these impurities. Measurement of blue reflectance gives a measure of the degree of purification during bleaching. This measurement can be made by a reflectometer.

Whiteness is attributable partly to luminosity (green reflectance) and partly to freedom from yellowness. Therefore, to evaluate this properly, blue and green reflectances are measured and an empirical relationship is used to calculate relative whiteness.

Whiteness measurements are discussed in Chapter 8. As reflectance is affected by the nature of the surface of the fabric, comparisons can be made only between samples of the same type of fabric.

PHOTOCHROMISM

Some dyes become darker rather than lighter when exposed to light. This is particularly true when some finishes such as crease and crush resistance are applied to dyed fabrics. The test method† does not consider color changes in consumer use. The test method is intended for detecting and assessing colored textiles that change in color after brief exposure to light but that return to their original shade when stored in the dark.

A sample of the fabric is exposed to light of high intensity for a time much shorter than that necessary to cause a permanent change. The change in color of the specimen is assessed immediately after exposure with the standard Gray Scale. The specimen is then stored in the dark and assessed again.

---

* Reflectance, Blue and Whiteness of Bleached Fabric; AATCC Test Method 110 (1975).

† Colorfastness to Light: Detection of Photochromism; AATCC Test Method 139 (1972).

LOSS OR CHANGE IN FINISHES AND DESIGNS

A fabric may be of a construction that in itself would give good performance in use and care. However, a design or finish applied to the fabric may impart limited serviceability.

Applied surface designs and finishes may cause poor fabric performance due to the method of application or the lack of quality control at the time of application.

There is no test method that is used for evaluating loss or change in finishes or designs to laundering. There is a test method* that indicates the effect of repeated dry cleanings on the applied design or finish on textiles and other materials. It is also applicable for evaluating the durability of applied design materials and finishing agents manufactured for use on fabrics and other products intended for apparel and household use that are renovated in consumer service by commercial dry-cleaning procedures. This test is not applicable for evaluating the resistance of colors to spot and stain removal procedures used by the dry cleaner.

The test consists of agitating a sample in a solution of solvent and a dry-cleaning detergent. Steel balls are used to simulate the kind of mechanical action that occurs in a dry-cleaning machine. A large specimen is used to produce a correlation with commercial conditions. Unfortunately, this test does not correlate very well with fabrics that are worn and cleaned in plant-size equipment.

The durability of applied designs by this test method are judged for appearance as follows:

Class 5—Negligible or no change in appearance.
Class 4—Slightly changed in appearance.
Class 3—Noticeably changed in appearance.
Class 2—Considerably changed in appearance.
Class 1—Much changed in appearance.

The durability of fabric hand is judged for change as follows:

Class 5—Negligible or no change in hand.
Class 4—Slightly changed in hand.
Class 3—Noticeably changed in hand.
Class 2—Considerably changed in hand.
Class 1—Much changed in hand.

Finish performance characteristics are evaluated in accordance with AATCC test methods (e.g., AATCC Test Method 22: Water Repellency: Spray Test) (see p. 244).

---

* Drycleaning: Durability of Applied Designs and Finishes; AATCC Test Method 86 (1973).

OBJECTIONABLE ODOR FROM TEXTILES

Textile producers use many types of resin finishes to impart crease resistance and shrinkage control to fabrics. Urea formaldehyde or melamine formaldehyde resins, when improperly cured in textile finishing, may break down and the objectionable odor may not become noticeable until after wear, storage or cleaning. Some of these give off a fishlike odor. This problem may occur if a textile finisher fails to wash out the excess chemicals after the curing or heat-setting operation, if he cures the fabric for too long a time or at too high a temperature, or if he uses an old resin solution that has been stored for too long.

These improperly cured resins break down and produce odor-forming compounds (aliphatic amines) at any time after manufacture. Proper curing of the resin finish by the textile finisher is the only sure method of control. There have been cases where such an odor has been removed by laundering or wet cleaning in an alkaline solution of water and detergent, but there is no guarantee that this treatment will always be effective. Frequently, fabric combinations and garment design do not lend themselves to a wet processing treatment.

Some firms are in the business of removing odors from fabrics, including smoke odors. This may be achieved by two methods: exposure to ozone, and the use of masking compounds (see Chapter 9).

Odor In Resin-Treated Fabrics

This test is designed to determine the presence of odor caused by the breakdown of a finish under certain conditions of temperature and humidity. The odor may not be noticeable in a garment or household item at the time of purchase. The odor may develop in wear or when such a garment or fabric is stored. This odor could be described as similar to fish, wet dog, burnt chemical, pyridine, bad chemical odor, excessive formaldehyde, or excessive aromatic odor.

There are two test methods used to determine formaldehyde odor in fabrics: (1) the steam method* and (2) the jar method.† Both tests are applicable to textile fabrics that may have been given a formaldehyde resin finish. They provide an accelerated means for determining the amount of formaldehyde likely to be released in storage conditions or wear.

In the first method, a sample is exposed to low-pressure steam for a short period of time. The steam is condensed and the amount of

---

* Determination of Formaldehyde Odor in Resin Treated Fabric, Steam Method; AATCC Test Method 113 (1975).

† Determination of Formaldehyde Odor in Resin Treated Fabric, Sealed Jar Method; AATCC Test Method 112 (1975).

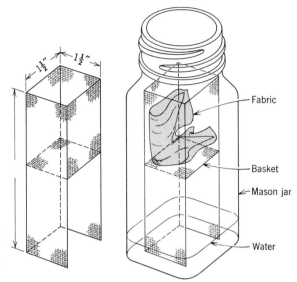

Figure 5-10 The wire mesh basket detailed on the left is suspended in a sealed jar with one fabric specimen as shown on the right. (Courtesy: American Association of Textile Chemists and Colorists)

formaldehyde evolved from the specimen is determined from the characteristic color developed by formaldehyde in the presence of phenylhydrazine and ferric ion.

In the second method, a weighed fabric sample is suspended over water in a sealed jar. The jar is placed in an oven at a controlled temperature for a specified length of time. The amount of formaldehyde absorbed by the water is then determined colorimetrically (Figure 5–10).

The odor potential rating indicates the degree of formaldehyde likely to be evolved. The ratings are given in Table 5–1.

Table 5–1 Qualitative Rating of Formaldehyde Odor Potential

Color Comparator Rating (from 7.4)	Formaldehyde Odor Potential
4.1 to 5.0	None
3.1 to 4.0	Trace
2.1 to 3.0	Slight
1.1 to 2.0	Moderate
0.6 to 1.0	Strong
Less than 0.5	Extremely strong

PLEATING

"Permanent" means continuing or enduring in the same state, place, or the like without marked changes. "Permanently pleated" means that the pleats are not subject to change or alteration. Pleats in a garment may be functional or used for aesthetic appearance of design. Pleating may result in two performance problems: (1) separation and removal and (2) color change in pleating.

Pleat separation and removal may be traced to one or more conditions of fabric production, wear, or cleaning, for example, fiber content of the fabric, construction of the fabric, the method of pleating used, the condition of pleating (time, temperature, cooling and method of forming), garment design and fit, conditions of wear, and method of cleaning.

Loss of pleats may occur in wear, for example, sitting on pleats may cause them to separate. Perspiration or spilling a beverage on some pleated fabrics causes the pleats to separate and to be lost. Some pleats are lost in washing, others in dry cleaning, drying, spotting, or finishing.

There is a need to clarify the term "permanently pleated." Pleated garments are expected to have some degree of pleat sharpness and smooth appearance after cleaning. If pleats loosen up in wear and cleaning, then resetting of the pleats is necessary. Pleats that cannot be conveniently reset include fluted, corrugated, pinch, crystal, mushroom, accordion, and pettipleats. These can be reset by the manufacturer although this requires taking the garment apart, resetting the pleats, and then resewing the garment. This is quite costly and, in most cases, impractical.

Colorfastness To Pleating

Some colors in fabrics may change in shade or intensity when subjected to the steam required to pleat a fabric. This test method* is intended for evaluating the resistance of the color of fabrics of all kinds and in all forms to the action of steam-pleating processes. The test samples are not pleated for the test. A sample of the fabric is placed in contact with specified undyed fabrics and is steamed under specified conditions of pressure and time and then dried. The change in color of the sample and the staining of the undyed fabrics are evaluated with standard gray scales.

PILLING

Pills are bunches or balls of tangled fibers on the surface of a fabric that are held to the surface by one or more fibers. The ease and extent to which a fabric will form pills is called "pilling propensity." The

* Colorfastness to Pleating: Steam Pleating; AATCC Test Method 131 (1973).

resistance to the formation of pills on a fabric is known as "pilling resistance." Pills should be distinguished from fuzz, which is untangled fiber ends projecting from a fabric surface.

PILLING

Pilling may occur on both woven and knit fabrics, and may be related to fiber, yarn, and fabric construction. Natural fibers will break away shedding the pills. Synthetic fibers are so strong that they do not break away readily from the fabric. Pills usually occur in areas that are especially abraded or rubbed during wear, as in the underarm area. The condition can be accentuated by the action of laundering or dry cleaning. It is very difficult, if not impossible, to card the pills from the synthetic fabrics satisfactorily. They can be shaved off with an electric razor, but great care must be taken not to damage the fabric.

Although several test methods for the evaluation of pilling resistance have been published over the years, their limitations still exist.* The recognition of these limitations is essential if test procedures are not to be used indiscriminately. Results that are obtained without knowledge of, or regard for, their validity can be misleading. Continued refinement and development of methods for the evaluation of pilling will result in procedures that offer good reproducibility and a sound basis in correlation with use.

The American Society for Testing and Materials defines pills as "bunches or balls of tangled fibers which are held to the surface of a fabric by one or more fibers." In order to better understand the laboratory simulation of the pilling process, it is helpful to examine the mechanism of pill formation during wear. Qualitatively, it proceeds in three distinct stages. During the first stage, fiber ends must either be present on the surface of the fabric or they must be brought to the surface during wear. Once present, these fibers then begin to entangle with other fibers present, and, as a result of abrasive action, form into pills. The final stage of this process is the wearing away of the pills as the fibers holding them to the surface break under the stress of abrasion.

Of these three stages, the one having the greatest effect on the overall pilling is the initial stage of fuzz formation. It is, therefore, es-

* Peggy A. Quinn, *Evaluating Pilling Sensibly: Sense and Nonsense in Knit Testing, No. 17;* American Association of Textile Chemists and Colorists, pp. 54–57 (1976).

sential that the laboratory test procedure involve sufficient mechanical action to introduce fiber ends to the surface of the fabric if they are not already present. The test should not be too severe in abrasive action or the degree of pill wear off will be accelerated, thereby giving erroneous results.

Pilling Resistance Tests In Use

Recognizing the complexity of the pilling mechanism, and the inherent difficulties in developing procedures to simulate end-use performance, it is not surprising that several evaluation methods have been proposed over the years.

When ASTM Method D1375, Pilling Resistance and Other Related Surface Changes of Textile Fabrics, was originally published in 1955, five procedures were detailed, including the Inflated Diaphragm Test, the Reciprocating Table Test, and the Appearance Retention Test. However, these procedures have been deleted over the years because of lack of use, and currently only the Brush Test and the Random Tumble Test appear in the *ASTM Book of Standards*. A new method, the Elastomeric Pad Test is within the ASTM balloting process, and will likely be approved as a standard method shortly. Each of these methods utilizes a somewhat different principle in attempting to simulate pilling in use.

The Brush Test utilizes nylon brushes mounted on a rotating platform to brush the surface of the test specimen, and in so doing, bring fiber ends to the surface. Fiber pills are then formed by rubbing these specimens together in a circular manner. The brushing operation is often critical in this procedure, since the degree of pilling is dependent upon the presence of fiber ends at the surface. This test has received wide usage in the evaluation of woven shirtings and blouse fabrics.

The Random Tumble Test employs a less severe type of abrasion as it tumbles specimens multidirectionally against each other and the sides of a cork-lined cylindrical chamber. Short cotton fibers added to the chamber become entangled with surface fuzz created during the tumbling, and form into lint pills. This method has enjoyed wider usage than the Brush Test, and can be applicable to a range of fabrics and uses.

The Elastomeric Pad Test, which has been described in the *Textile Chemist and Colorist,* utilizes a surface abrasion tester equipped with two elastomeric friction pads. Fiber pills are formed on the specimen, which is mounted over one pad, and it is abraded multidirectionally by the other pad. The severity of the test can be adapted by varying both the amount of rubbing and the load applied to the friction pad.

Evaluation of Results

Evaluation of results obtained during testing is often one of the most variable features of any procedure involving subjective interpretation. The availability of a standard rating scale serves to facilitate the evaluation. It was not until 1975 that a scale was made available for use in evaluating pilling. Photographic standards for the Random Tumble Test were published. To date, the Brush Test does not have a rating scale.

The use of standardized viewing conditions is helpful in evaluating results. Such conditions are prescribed in D-1375. Correct usage remains a point of contention. The ASTM Apparatus for Fabric Evaluation, known as the ASTM Viewing Box, is used, but ratings are based solely on what is observed under these viewing conditions. Tactile observations, as well as scrutiny outside the box, results in ratings that are often more critical than they would be otherwise.

Lack of reproducibility of results can plague users of these methods. It should be guarded against by calibrating each instrument with fabrics of known pilling propensity. Calibration techniques are recommended in D-1375, and should be used to assure that test conditions are controlled.

Interpreting Results

These test methods are used daily by textile evaluation laboratories. The results that are derived, and their interpretation, can be of questionable value, perhaps even worthless. Users of the methods sometimes fail to recognize their limitations. A single procedure is not suited for the evaluation of all fabrics in every end use.

Contained within D-1375 is a statement on significance that urges each user of these methods to develop criteria for his own use based on correlation with actual performance. This may sound like a hedge until we recognize that no single test method can be expected to duplicate the pilling incurred under the diverse wear conditions of the multitude of fabrics used today. Not only do wear conditions and pilling performance vary from fabric to fabric and garment to garment, but they also vary within different areas of the same garment.

In attempting to reproduce the different types of pilling observed in use, different test methods, and variations in severity of methods, are necessary. The fact that 30 to 60 minutes of testing by the Random Tumble Test has become almost sacred after so many years of use does not preclude that 15 or 75 minutes can also produce meaningful results. And when using the Brush Test, it may not be necessary to brush the fabric surface at all; fabric-to-fabric rubbing may be sufficient to produce desired results on napped or other soft finish fabrics.

There are many factors that affect the pilling resistance of any fabric in a given end use. It is impossible to specify which method and variation is best suited for the evaluation of a particular fabric. Quinn concludes that the factors that govern the pilling performance of fabrics under service conditions are too complex to be simulated by a single laboratory test. Nevertheless, those procedures that are adopted for use in the evaluation of this property should be as refined as technically possible. The reduction in test variability can improve within-laboratory reproducibility and help establish good between-laboratory correlation. However, given the test procedures available, it is essential to recognize their limitations and to continue to correlate test results with actual performance data to evaluate pilling sensibly.

Pilling Resistance Tests

There are two procedures,* which utilize different equipment and test methods, used to measure pilling resistance: the Brush Pilling Tester and the Random Tumble Pilling Tester.

Both procedures are used by the textile industry for the evaluation of a wide variety of fabrics. The selection of a particular procedure for a particular fabric depends on various factors, including the availability of equipment and prior experience with the procedure.

The resistance of a fabric to pilling and other surface effects, such as fuzzing, is determined in simulated wear tests on these laboratory machines. The fabric is evaluated by comparison with visual standards, actual fabrics, or photographs showing a range of pilling resistance.

Pills observed in worn garments vary appreciably in size and appearance. The appearance of pills depends particularly on the presence of lint and degree of color contrast, factors that are not evaluated when pilling is rated solely on the number of pills. The development of pills may be accompanied by other surface phenomena such as loss of cover, color change, or the development of fuzz. Since the overall acceptability of a fabric depends on both the characteristics of the pills and the other factors affecting surface appearance, it is considered desirable that fabrics tested in the laboratory be evaluated subjectively with regard to their acceptability and not rated solely on the number of pills developed. A series of standards based on graduated degrees of wear of the fabric type being tested may be set up to establish and aid subjective ratings. The latter offer the greatest advantage when the laboratory test specimens correlate closely in appearance with worn garments, that is, show similar color contrast, presence of lint in the pills, and a similar ratio of pills to fuzz.

* Pilling Resistance and Other Surface Effects of Textile Fabrics; ASTM D-1375 (1973).

The pilling resistance of a fabric in actual wear varies with individual wearers and general conditions of use. As a consequence, it can be expected that worn garments will show a fairly wide pilling resistance after wear and much greater variation in wear than in replicates from laboratory tests. This experience must be borne in mind when adopting levels of acceptability for any series of standards.

Finishes and fabric surface changes may exert considerable effects on pilling tests. Therefore, with some fabrics, it may be desirable to test before and after laundering or dry cleaning or both.

THE BRUSH PILLING PROCEDURE

The brush pilling procedure determines the resistance of fabrics to pilling and fuzzing (see Figure 5–11). Samples are subjected to simulated wear conditions by first brushing the fabric to form free fiber ends, and then subjecting the fabric to a circular rubbing action with a sponge that rolls the fiber ends into pills. This is accomplished by the Brush Pilling Tester. The instrument utilizes a circular rubbing motion to produce pills. It consists of a table that is driven by a ratio motor and a jack shaft at approximately 56 RPM and a $\frac{3}{4}$-inch radius. Two rubbing surfaces are provided, one is with cellulose sponges and the other is with a nylon brush. Both the radius of rotation and the rubbing surfaces may be varied.

The appearance of the fabric is then evaluated by comparison with visual standards in a low-angle illumination apparatus. The samples are rated subjectively on a scale ranging from: 1—very poor resistance (very severe pilling) to 5—excellent resistance (no pilling).

No general test procedure has been developed that is applicable to all types of fabrics. For *loosely constructed knit fabrics,* the brushing step is usually omitted and the tests made by rubbing the sponges for a given length of time, usually five minutes. For clear fin-

Figure 5-11 This Brush Pilling Tester accommodates six samples of fabric. The fabrics are supported in one of two type holders. The standard sample holder is the circular holder on the right for fabric-to-fabric tests. This holder consists of a circular sponge covered base with an "O" ring for clamping the specimen. This test requires brushing the face of the six samples. The holders are then run face to face (three sets on tester) to produce the pills. (Courtesy: Custom Scientific Instruments, Inc.)

ished woven fabrics, a satisfactory test procedure is to brush the fabrics for a given time, usually five minutes, and to allow this with a period of rubbing with the sponges, also usually five minutes. Blended fabrics containing wool frequently pill more by the brush pilling procedure than in wear. Fabrics of this type can be tested by using only the sponges and rubbing for a series of time intervals and noting the pilling after each interval. Fugitive (nondurable) finishes and other added materials affect the pilling of new fabrics so that pilling before and after washing or dry cleaning frequently gives valuable information.

THE RANDOM TUMBLE PROCEDURE

The random tumbler test is the most widely used test to measure pilling. This method determines the tendency of fabrics to form pills or to fuzz under conditions intended to simulate normal wear. It is generally applicable to all apparel-type fabrics including both knit goods and woven goods. Some finishes commonly applied to fabrics greatly change the pilling tendency of the fabric. It is suggested that any fabric being tested for pilling or fuzzing should be tested in both the original finished condition and after laundering or dry cleaning, whichever is appropriate, in this way simulating the conditions under which the fabric will be used.

The machine used to run this test is called the Random Tumble Pilling Tester (see Figure 5–12). It has a series of covered cylinders in which the fabrics rotate for a specified length of time.

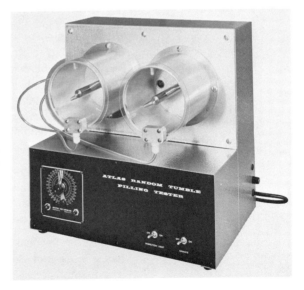

Figure 5-12 The Random Tumble Pilling Tester produces results under controllable test conditions that correlate well with a fabric's end-use performance. The instrument conforms to the requirements of ASTM designation D-1375. This method causes fabric test samples to form typical pills by a random rubbing motion produced by tumbling specimens in a cylindrical chamber lined with a mildly abrasive material. Small amounts of gray cotton fiber (short length) are introduced into each chamber at the beginning of a test. When a test is run, susceptible fabrics will develop lint pills typical to normal wear. The method is applicable to either knit or woven apparel-type fabrics. (Courtesy: Atlas Electrical Device, Inc.)

For the pilling test, the cylinders are lined with a thin layer of cork. Three $4\frac{3}{16}$-inch square samples are cut from the fabric for use as test swatches. The samples are placed in separate cylinders which then rotate for 30 minutes for sheer fabrics, 60 minutes for slack fabrics, and 75 minutes for shirting fabrics. The amount of time chosen for test rotation is predetermined by wear trials carried out with actual garments and correlates directly to a specific number of hours of actual garment use.

Samples are related by comparing them to numbered, standard test photographs. Pilling ratings are reported on a scale of 1 (severe pilling) through 5 (no pilling).

TESTS FOR SNAGGING

One of the problems in knitted fabrics made of filament yarns is their tendency to snag.

Knit fabrics have consumer appeal because of their properties of ease of care, hand, stretch and recovery, and general comfort of wearing. Due to their loop configuration and makeup, they are subject to quality problems as *barré* or defects in loop formation, snagging, and dimensional stability. Snagging has developed as probably the most serious of the problems.

Snagging of a knitted structure is a complex action extremely difficult to measure and evaluate. The results can be confusing and misleading, depending on the technique used. As a result, several methods and apparatus have been developed dealing with this problem. Some methods are more successful and realistic than others. Probably the one most widely known and accepted in the industry at present is the Mace Tester. This method is described shortly. Other methods range from single points and sandpaper surfaces to a fabric being dragged across rows of pins.

In the early investigations of a study at North Carolina State University, a "turntable and stylus" device was developed using an old U.S. Testing Company hosiery snag tester. In addition to such factors as yarn size, bending rigidity, torsion, and so forth, having effect on the degree of snagging it was noted that:

1. Snagging was directional and depended on the movement and pressure of the pin or stylus point.

2. Snagging severity varied with the tension of the fabric and the surface over which it was mounted.

In order to measure the effects of yarn and construction properties, a "loop pull" test was developed using the Instron tensile tester. The method consisted of clamping the fabric around a two-inch cylinder, inserting the hook of a knitting needle into a loop, and measuring the force resulting from pulling the loop. In addition to other variables it was noted that the tension in the mounted fabric specimen had a varied effect on the length of snag and force involved.

Snag testers that are commercially available at the present time are:

1. The J.C. Penney snag tester—a variation of the AATCC hosiery snag tester.

2. The DuPont snag tester.

3. The Mace tester.

These testers were developed to make overall subjective comparisons of snagging resistance between various fabrics, rather than the specific measures obtained using the loop pull test.

The investigation undertaken at the North Carolina State University was designed to try to find the "why" of snagging relative to fabric construction, type of yarn, yarn size, number of yarn filaments, bending rigidity, yarn torque, and various treatments and chemical finishes. The attempt was to understand how a fabric was caught and snagged, and how it responded or reacted to this condition. The instrument developed is called the Bean Bag Snag Tester.* It was developed to eliminate some of the problems associated with all of the methods and especially the Mace tester. It consists of a technique where the fabric to be tested is fitted as a cover around a bean bag and is tumbled inside an eight-inch diameter rotating cylinder. The inner surface of the cylinder has eight rows of pins fixed at an approximate angle of 30 degrees. They hook and snag the bean bag covering as it tumbles randomly within the cylinder.

The test fabric specimen is sewn as a pouch within which the bean bag is placed. It is not prestressed or under tension as it fits around the bean bag. Thus the fabric is subjected more nearly to conditions of actual wear snagging as opposed to being tightly stretched over a testing surface. Tension is applied to the surface of the test specimen only when hooked by the wire points as the bean bag shifts and tumbles during the testing cycle. The random tumble action of the specimen eliminates the necessity for separate directional testing in the course and wales directions of a knit fabric. The total number of tests required for proper evaluation of a fabric is thus reduced from what would normally be required by the Mace and other testers.

As the cylinder rotates the bean bag specimen is snagged by one or more pins and carried to the top of the cylinder where it is released

* W. C. Stuckey and A. E. Shiekh, Snags In Snag Testing of Knits: Sense and Nonsense in Knit Testing No. 17, American Association of Textile Chemists and Colorists. (1976)

from the pins. It falls to the bottom of the cylinder to be snagged again. The weight of the bean bag hanging on the pins at the apex of the cylinder rotation creates the snag in the fabric. The weight of the bean bag as well as the number of revolutions are the two major variables in determining how much a particular fabric will snag.

The investigation showed that the Bean Bag Snag Tester has certain advantages over the Mace Tester. It is claimed:

1. Snagging is multidirection on the Bean Bag as it tumbles randomly, compared to the directionally snagged specimens of the Mace. It has been questioned if there is a proper way to combine the directional effects, course, and wale of the Mace.

2. Bean Bag test data is less variable than that taken with the Mace, giving more precision and confidence in assessment.

3. One-half the number of test specimens required for the Bean Bag because of the resulting low variation and the multidirectional random tumble.

4. The test fabric is sewn around the Bean Bag in its relaxed state (under no tension). Tension is applied to the fabric only when the mass of the bean bag shifts and moves during testing. It is felt that the bean bag more simulates the firmness of the human form, and the manner in which a textile conforms to it in actual wearing, than in the case of the Mace where the specimen is stretched over a drum. Thus, the snag of the Bean Bag is more realistic.

5. More than one test specimen may be tested at the same time in the test chamber of the Bean Bag tester, whereas the Mace tests only one specimen per test position.

6. Test conditions may be varied in degree of severity by changing the speed of the drum, the number of cycles, or the weight of the Bean Bag.

The Mace Test

In this test, which was developed by Imperial Chemical Industries, Ltd., an instrument very much like the mace used by medieval knights is bounced against rotating samples of fabric (see Figure 5–13). Two 6-inch by 13-inch samples from the length and width directions of the fabric are tested and rated by comparing them to numbered, standard photographs. The average of the two ratings in the most critical direction is reported as the snagging results.

The ratings for the laboratory tests have been correlated with actual performance in garment wear trials. The test ratings range from 1 (severe snagging) to 5 (no snagging). A 3 rating is considered passing for polyester double knits for women's casual wear. A 4 rating is considered passing for men's double-knit slacks and suits.

Figure 5-13 The mace test determines a fabric's ability to resist snagging. (Courtesy: International Fabricare Institute)

WRINKLE RECOVERY

Wrinkle recovery is defined as that property of a fabric that enables it to recover from folding deformations. Wrinkle resistance is that property of a fabric that enables it to resist the formation of wrinkles when subjected to folding deformations. Wrinkle recovery depends on several factors:

1. Fiber content (wool and polyester have an inherent resilience).

2. Yarns (highly twisted yarns reduce the tendency of fabrics to wrinkle).

3. Fabric construction (a closely woven fabric shows wrinkles more than one that is loosely woven). Thick fabrics do not wrinkle as much as thinner ones. A plain weave fabric will wrinkle more than a 4 × 4 basket weave.

4. Color (a print does not show wrinkles as readily as a solid color).

5. Finishes (finishes can be applied in textile finishing to improve the resiliency of a fabric, especially fabrics containing the cellulose fibers such as cotton, flax, and rayon).

Wrinkle Recovery Of Fabrics

The test methods* cover the determination of the wrinkle recovery of woven fabrics. They are applicable to fabrics made from any fiber, or combination of fibers. The two methods are (1) the Recovery Angle and Vertical Strip Method that uses the Wrinkle Recovery Tester and accessories (Figure 5–14) and (2) the Appearance Method that uses

* Wrinkle Recovery of Woven Textile Fabrics Using the Vertical Strip Apparatus; ASTMD-1295; Wrinkle Recovery of Fabrics: Recovery Angle Method; AATCC Test Method 66 (1968).
Wrinkle Recovery of Fabrics: Appearance Method; AATCC Test Method 128 (1974).

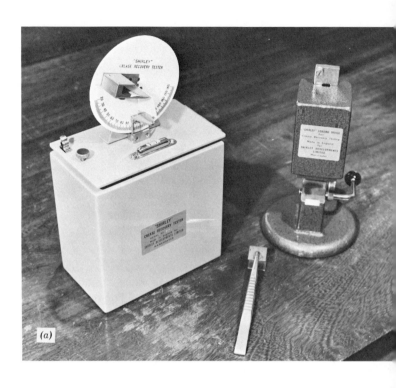

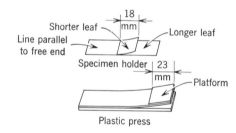

Figure 5-14 (a) Shirley Crease Recovery Tester. (b) Disk and protractor are mounted coaxially on a vertical support so that they are free to rotate about a horizontal axis. The center of the disk-protractor assembly is marked, and a vertical guide line is drawn in the support from the center mark to the base. The disk is provided with a vernier having a central zero point that indicates on the protractor the angle formed by the creased specimen when it is mounted on the clamp. (Courtesy: Shirley Development Ltd.)

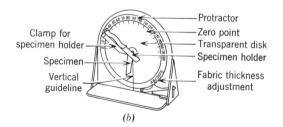

Figure 5-15 This wrinkling device measures the wrinkle recovery of fabrics. The specimen fabric is twisted and wrinkled in the tester under a predetermined load for a prescribed period of time at standard atmospheric conditions. The specimen is then reconditioned in the standard atmosphere and evaluated for appearance by comparing it with the standard AATCC wrinkle-recovery replicas. (Courtesy: American Association of Textile Chemists and Colorists)

a Wrinkle Tester and the 3-Dimensional Durable Press Replicas (Figure 5–15).

In the Recovery Angle and Vertical Strip Method, a test specimen is creased and compressed under controlled conditions of time and load, then suspended in the test instrument for a controlled recovery period, after which the recovery angle is measured. This method is used both as a research tool and for production quality control. Although the between-laboratory precision is poor, the within-laboratory precision can be good.

Because the arbitrary values that determine wrinkle recovery in actual use vary widely, no single set of test conditions can be selected to give good correlation with actual wear. The arbitrary values that must be controlled in the test are relative humidity, temperature, applied pressure, time under pressure, and recovery time. This method specifies arbitrarily selected values for the latter three factors, based on a compromise between conditions likely to be encountered in service and the expeditious conduct of the test. Two conditions of temperature and relative humidity are specified as being representative of normal experience.

Warp tests and filling tests are usually both performed, with the average angle that the specimens remain bent for the warp direction and the filling direction given as the result.

In the Appearance Method, the method of test is for determining the appearance of textile fabrics after induced wrinkling. It is applicable to fabrics made from any fiber or combination of fibers. A test specimen is wrinkled under standard atmospheric conditions in a standard wrinkling device (Wrinkle Tester) under a predetermined load for a prescribed period of time. The specimen is then reconditioned in the standard atmosphere for textile testing and evaluated for appearance by comparison with three-dimensional reference standards.

Three trained observers rate each test specimen independently. The test specimens are mounted on a viewing board and rated against the three-dimensional wrinkle-recovery replicas under special lighting conditions. Each sample is assigned the number of the replica that most nearly matches the appearance of the test specimens by the observer.

The other two observers proceed in the same manner assigning ratings independently. An average of the nine observations on each test fabric (three judgments on each of three specimens) is reported.

A WRINKLE TESTER DEVELOPED BY INDUSTRY

The Celanese Wrinkle Tester was developed at the Summit Research Laboratories of the Celanese Corporation of America (Figure 5–16). The Celanese Wrinkle Tester is a helpful tool in evaluating

Figure 5-16 The Celanese Wrinkle Tester consists of an air system that alternately pumps the air out of specimen tubes and into specimen containers. The transparent specimen tubes open to the air. Rubber diaphragms are sealed in the tubes. Both set into a head piece and are connected with the air system. The fabric samples are attached to the center post in a hoselike manner. A recycling timer controls solenoid valves so one set of sample containers is open two minutes to pressure; the other set under vacuum. Under vacuum, the rubber diaphragms collapse and wrinkle the fabric. The samples under pressure hang freely and relax. A timer controls the length of the test. The pressure under which the fabrics are crushed is recorded on a vacuum gauge. (Courtesy: Custom Scientific Instruments, Inc.)

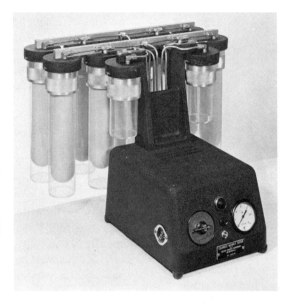

the resilience and wrinkle behavior of fabrics under conditions very similar to those occurring in actual use. Instruments on the market today tend to produce the same deformation regardless of the inherent resistance to wrinkling of fabrics and measure solely the recovery rather than the resistance. The Celanese Wrinkle Tester takes into account that fabrics, in actual wear, display wide differences in the pattern and degree of wrinkling due to their inherently different wrinkle resistance. The instrument simulates the widely accepted clenched fist test by performing a repetitive cyclic wrinkling action under precisely controlled conditions.

After the test the fabric samples are removed from the instrument for evaluation. A special viewing box has been designed to provide proper light conditions. Care must be taken that all fabric samples be hung in the viewing box in a uniform manner. The subjective evaluation of the wrinkled fabric samples as they appear in the viewing box are conducted as follows. (1) Five observers are selected to individually indicate their choice of the best or least wrinkled fabrics from among the fabrics. (2) The scorer may utilize a semiquantitative scoring system whereby the least wrinkled fabrics attain the lowest individual point scores. (3) The fabrics may be examined in several stages: (a) immediately after insertion into the viewing box, (b) after a 1-hour relaxation period, (c) after 24 hours, and (d) at the end of 48 hours.

These point scores may further be subdivided into a relative ranking order, whereupon statistical analysis may be utilized. Colored stereo photography may be used to advantage in recording the appearance of the wrinkled fabrics at the various examination stages in order to provide permanent records.

2 DURABILITY

Durability tests are used to compare the wear resistance qualities of products with competitive products, research and develop better quality materials, improve existing materials, analyze and isolate defective materials, and extend the serviceable life of products.

Durability of fabrics must be considered in relationship to end use of a product. For example, one expects the durability of boys' trousers to be greater than a girl's party dress. Durability or lack of it may also influence appearance, comfort, and care. Improper care methods may hasten the loss of durability in some fabrics.

Durability is a complex function because of the interrelationships of fiber content, yarn construction, fabric construction, color application, and finish and applied fabric design. In wearing apparel and household items the satisfaction in end use frequently depends on the durability of the weakest component. For example, a lining in a coat may wear out sooner than the face fabric used.

ABRASION

Abrasion is defined as the wearing away of any part of the fabric by rubbing against another surface. It has been very difficult to correlate conditions of abrasion of a textile in wear or use with test methods.

The resistance to abrasion is affected by many factors, such as the inherent mechanical properties of the fibers, the dimensions of the fibers, the structure of the yarns, the construction of the fabrics, and the type, kind, and amount of finishing material added to the fibers, yarns, or fabric.

The resistance to abrasion is also greatly affected by the conditions of the tests, such as the nature of abradant, variable action of the abradant over the area of specimen abraded, the tension of the specimen, the pressure between the specimen and abradant, and the dimensional changes in the specimen.

The test methods and equipment used have been designed to measure "flat" abrasion. It is only recently that attention has been focused on "edge" abrasion.

Edge Abrasion

Edge abrasion may occur on some resin-bonded pigment prints, fabrics that are given a stiff finish, some coated urethanes, vinyls, and flocked fabrics (see Figure 5–17).

Figure 5-17 This flocked fabric shows a loss of flock along the seam line due to edge abrasion. (Courtesy: The International Fabricare Institute)

Attention was focused on edge abrasion at the AATCC Symposium on Flocked Fabrics in 1974. Genevieve Smith, Manager of Sears Laboratories, stated:*

"One of the laboratories with whom I talked regarding flat abrasion mentioned that in their experience the flocked fabrics with satisfactory flat abrasion results usually have poor edge abrasion and vice versa. The adhesive employed appears to be responsible for this occurrence. They have concluded that where 'the adhesive is quite pliable or soft, edge abrasion is good, but flat abrasion allows the fibers to cut themselves at the adhesive line because of too much maneuverability of the fibers. When the adhesive is not so pliable the flocking seems to be more rigidly adhered and has good flat abrasion. However, the edge abrasion results in chunks of the adhesive and flocking coming loose.'"

Ronald J. Pacheco, J.C. Penney Company, Incorporated, said:†

"In the past the Penney lab has used the Accelerator test for evaluating edge abrasion. Three sets of two specimens each are abraded

* Genevieve M. Smith, "Flocked Fabrics: Performance and Evaluation,"; American Association of Textile Chemists and Colorists Symposium, Flocked Technology Paper, New York (1974).
† Ronald J. Pacheco, "Flocked Fabrics and the Consumers, the Manufacturers Responsibilities (ibid.)."

129 Testing for Product Performance

at 2000 RPM against a number 250 abradant cylinder liner and evaluated after one, two and three minutes. In conjunction with this, we would wash and/or dryclean a finished item to compare the accelerated test with the abrasion occurring in renovation.

"Recently we have experimented with a new AATCC test method from RA81-Appearance of Flocked Fabrics After Repeated Home Laundering and/or Coin-Op Drycleaning. This method uses simulated pant legs which are washed and/or drycleaned and then evaluated for edge wear abrasion at the hems, cuffs and seams. As of this date it appears to be an excellent method."

In 1973, the Textile Analysis Department of the International Fabricare Institute received 15 damaged flocked velvet garments. The first eight months of 1974 showed an increase to 40 per month. During the next four months of 1974, the average monthly number jumped to 83. Whether the great increase in the number of damaged garments was caused by the use of flocked fabrics in more garments, or if it was due to the use of adhesives that are less resistant to drycleaning solvents, was not known.

Since many of these garments are labeled as dry cleanable, customers expect them to be returned undamaged. When the problem with flocked velvets first came to IFI's attention, they ran tests to try to find a satisfactory dry-cleaning procedure. They found that even a five-minute wash cycle, which removed a satisfactory amount of soil, resulted in considerable loss and removal of flock from the fabric.*

The fabrics were not uniformly damaged by dry cleaning, some parts of the fabric withstanding dry cleaning while others did not. This indicates that dry-cleanable flocked fabrics can be produced if the proper technology and properly formulated adhesives are used in manufacturing. Westfall and Mayfield†, as well as Kantner‡, have illustrated that properly formulated adhesives do withstand repeated cleanings. The need for a realistic test method tailored to predict the end-use performance of flocked fabrics is necessary. Meaningful laboratory test methods are needed as screening or quality control methods. However, they are only valid if they adequately predict end-use performance under actual cleaning conditions. Therefore, laboratory methods must be correlated with actual field conditions.

In a limited laboratory test, three flocked fabrics, each with a dif-

---

* Manfred Wentz and Norman Oehlke, "Performance of Flocked Fabrics in Drycleaning"; AATCC Symposium, Flocked Technology Paper (1974).

† P. M. Westfall and H. Mayfield, "Breathable Acrylic Latex Flock Adhesives"; *Book of Papers,* 1974 National Technical Conference, American Association of Textile Chemists and Colorists (1974).

‡ G. C. Kantner, "The Effect of Formulation Variables on the Performance of Acrylic Flocking Adhesives (ibid.)."

ferent adhesive base of acrylic copolymer, were used. An AATCC Crockmeter [AATCC Test Method 8 (1972)] was used as a reproducible source of mechanical action with 320 grit Emery abrasive paper on the peg. Fifty strokes were applied to each sample.

The original flocked fabric samples, not wet with solvent, did not show any noticeable abrasion when subjected to the mechanical action of the Crockmeter.

Samples of each fabric were immersed, with no mechanical action, for 10, 30, and 120 minutes in each of the dry-cleaning solvents (perchlorethylene, petroleum solvent, and solvent 113).

The objective of selecting time as a variable was to find out whether the absorption of dry-cleaning solvent by the flocked adhesive is slow enough to prevent excessive swelling and loss of adhesive strength.

The samples were then squeezed between paper towels to remove excess solvent. The wet pickup was approximately 65 percent. The mechanical action of the Crockmeter removed a significant amount of flock from the fabric immersed only 10 minutes in perchlorethylene while the fabrics immersed in petroleum solvent or in solvent 113 showed no noticeable flock removal even after 120 minutes immersion.

The mechanical force applied during crocking was sufficient to overcome the adhesive force so that sections of the flock were removed along the direction of the rubbing motion. It was noted that the dry fabric withstood crocking under the same conditions. This leads to the conclusion that the flocked fabric is most susceptible to mechanical abrasion in the solvent-swollen state.

The same flocked fabrics, after immersing 10 minutes in the three solvents, showed varying resistance to scratching with the fingernail. The fabric immersed in perchlorethylene for 10 minutes had very little resistance to abrasion when scratched with the fingernail. The flock from the fabric wet with solvent 113 could be removed slightly but only with difficulty and not at all from the sample wet with petroleum solvent.

The solubility theory of polymers (the adhesives) probably explains the greater damage caused by perchlorethylene. Simplified, this theory states that a solvent with the characteristics of perchlorethylene will be more likely to dissolve or produce maximum swelling of the polymer (adhesive) than will a solvent with the characteristics of petroleum solvent or solvent 113.

Samples of the same flocked fabrics were subjected to a 15-minute perchlorethylene cleaning cycle in a regular dry-cleaning unit. Before cleaning, each sample was folded and sewn on one side to simulate a seamed edge. After one cleaning, the edge abrasion was hardly detectable but after two or more cleanings it was quite apparent and increased as the number of cleanings increased. However, on no samples, even after 10 cleanings, was any pile loss observed on the flat surface of the fabrics.

The test results with these samples indicate that they could be safely cleaned if the fabric remained perfectly flat and had no seamed edges. These conditions are not possible during a normal dry-cleaning and drying cycle and with normal garment construction. The tumbling action during dry cleaning and drying cycles necessarily results in folding and creasing. The edges of these areas are subjected to greater mechanical action and damage occurs.

Norman Oehlke, IFI analyst, points out that all flocked fabrics are not as resistant to solvents as those used in the experimental tests. Many garments received by the Textile Analysis Laboratory show complete removal of the flock except for a few small pieces held by sewing threads at the seams.

In 1975, AATCC Committee RA81 developed and published a new test method* for evaluating the appearance of flocked fabrics after repeated home laundering or coin-op dry cleaning. The method covers a procedure for evaluating the durability of flocked fabric to home laundering or coin-op dry cleaning. The method uses a simulated pant leg to evaluate loss of flock and appearance of edge abra-

Figure 5-18 Simulated pant leg for edge-wear evaluation. Directions for construction are given in the test method AATCC 142 (1975). (Courtesy: American Association of Textile Chemists and Colorists)

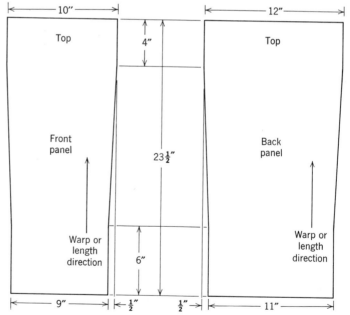

* Appearance of Flocked Fabrics After Repeated Home Laundering and/or Coin-Op Dry Cleaning; AATCC Test Method 142 (1975).

sion (Figure 5–18). The number of launderings or dry cleanings are agreed to by the laboratory personnel. After the specified cleaning cycles, the simulated pant legs are opened and laid flat with the side seam in the center of the examination area. The edge wear is compared with AATCC photographs and ranked as follows: 5—None, 4—Slight, 3—Noticeable, 2—Considerable, and 1—Severe.

Testing For Abrasion Resistance

It has been very difficult to correlate laboratory tests with wear. This may explain why there are many different types of abrasion testing machines, abradants, testing conditions, testing procedures, methods of evaluation of abrasion resistance, and interpretation of results.

The methods used may be described by the equipment or the machines used in testing.*

1. *Inflated Diaphragm* (Figure 5–19). Fabrics are tested first by

Figure 5-19 This surface abrader is designed to evaluate the surface abrasion of a fabric to determine the serviceability of most materials. Accessory attachments may also be used to measure frosting of fabrics. See text for discussion of this instrument's operation). (Courtesy: Custom Scientific Instruments, Inc.)

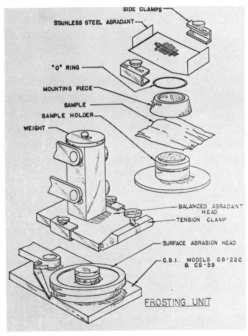

* Abrasion Resistance of Textile Fabrics; ASTM D-1175-71; AATCC 93 (1974).

placing the rubber diaphragms into a rotating head. The specimen is then laid on top of the diaphragm. The specimen centering ring is then placed on the specimen with the groove slide fitting the head of the diaphragm. Next, the clamping ring is placed into position and turned onto the rotating head until it clamps firmly.

An abrasive paper suitable for the fabric is clamped on the abradant plate. The specimen is inflated to a pressure suitable for the fabric. The pressure is adjusted by the diaphragm pressure regulator and indicated on the pressure gauge. The balanced head is then loaded with the desired weights and lowered into the inflated specimen. The table reciprocates through one inch of movement at a rate of 112 cycles per minute. The surface abrasion head makes one revolution in approximately 100 cycles of the reciprocating table. If unidirectional abrasion is required the rotary motion pawl may be disengaged. After the material has been worn through the contact in the diaphragm and the balanced head will come together completing an electrical circuit, thus automatically stopping the instrument and recording the number of cycles on the counter.

2. *Flexing and Abrasion* (Figure 5–20). The general method of flex abrasion tests is to determine the resistance of fabrics to flexing and abrasion when the specimen under controlled compression and tension is subjected to unidirectional reciprocal folding and rubbing over a flex bar.

Tests may be run wet or dry. One end of the flex specimen is clamped in a quick-acting clamp of the balanced head and then carried around the carbide-tipped flexing bar. The other end of the specimen is then clamped in the flexing block and as the table reciprocates, the specimen flexes and bends around the flexing bar. The mechanical linkage activates the electrical flex control switch when the specimen ruptures, thus automatically stopping the instrument and recording the number of cycles at the end of the test. An automatic timer may be used to flex a specimen to the desired number of cycles as an alternative to having the specimen rupture. The tension load placed on the specimen and the load of the balanced head are adjustable in accordance with the requirements of the test.

3. *Oscillatory Cylinder.* This method determines the abrasion resistance of woven textile fabrics using the oscillatory cylinder tester.* Abrasion resistance is measured by subjecting the specimen to unidirectional rubbing action under known conditions of pressure, tension, and abrasive action (Figure 5–21).

4. *Rotary Platform* (Figure 5–22a and b). The specimens are subjected to rotary rubbing action under controlled conditions of

Figure 5-20 The Stoll Flex Tester is used in quality controlled testing as well as in research departments. This instrument provides for flex abrasion, bending, roll and fold testing, and gives reproducible results using the automatic electrical end point. See text for discussion of this instrument's operation. (Courtesy: Custom Scientific Instrument, Inc.)

* Available from J. K. Industries, Villa Park, Ill.

Figure 5-21 An oscillatory cylinder abrasion machine. (Courtesy: J. K. Industries)

Figure 5-22 A double-head rotary platform abraser. See text for discussion of this instrument's operation. (Courtesy: Teledyne Taber)

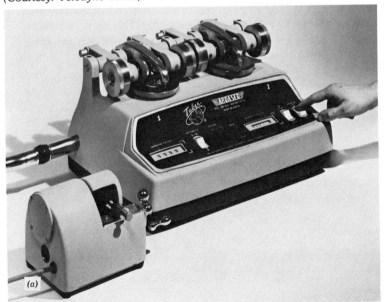

(a)

Abradent wheels, weighted on test specimen, are driven in opposite directions

(b)

Figure 5-23 The Schiefer Abrasion Testing Machine produces uniform abrasion, as predicted by Dr. Schiefer's mathematical theory that forms the basis for this machine. (Courtesy: Frazier Precision Instrument Co.)

pressure and abrasive action. Different models of the Taber Abraser are available for testing single specimens or two different or identical specimens, separately or simultaneously. The fabrics to be tested are subjected to the wear action of two abrasive wheels at a known pressure in grams. The results are evaluated by four different methods: (1) end point or general breakdown of material, (2) comparison of weight loss between materials of the same specific gravity, (3) volume loss in materials of different specific gravity, and (4) measuring the depth of wear.

5. *Uniform Abrasion.* This method covers the determination of the resistance to abrasion of a wide range of textile materials using uniform abrasion testing.*

Abrasive action is applied uniformly in all directions on the surface of the specimen. The machine can be varied in settings depending on the nature of the fabric to be tested and the use to be made of the test results (see Figure 5–23).

6. *Impeller Tumble.* In this test, the specimens are subjected to flexing, rubbing, shock, compression, stretching, and other forces during a test (Figure 5–24). The accelerotor is an instrument for rapidly determining the abrasion resistance and wear characteristics of textiles. The instrument was developed and patented by the American Association of Textile Chemists and Colorists. It simulates the various types of dry, moist, and wet abrasion that are encountered in end use. The factors of speed, time, size, and type of rotor, size of specimen, and type of liner employed are all interrelated and together they determine the severity of the test.

The tests are rapid, 3 to 12 minutes, and both reproducibility and repeatability of test results are of a high order. The random motion principle of an unfettered specimen employed in the accelerotor

Figure 5-24 The impeller tumble method uses the accelerotor. (Courtesy: Atlas Electric Device Co.)

* Available from Frazier Precision Instrument Company, Silver Spring, Md.

frees it from the limitations of rigidly mounted specimens. This principle produces samples with a close and completely realistic relationship to end-wear use.

COLORFASTNESS TO ACIDS AND ALKALIES

One may question why the subject of colorfastness to acids and alkalies is discussed under the subject of durability of fabrics. The purpose is to emphasize that in consumer use fabric deterioration or loss of durability due to loss of fabric strength is more common than change of colors due to acids and alkalies. Yet there is no test method or procedure that takes this fact into account.

Acid Damage: Hydrochloric and Sulfuric

Hydrochloric and sulfuric acid are strong mineral acids that attack and weaken most textile fibers. Even diluted concentrations will harm most fabrics. Sometimes a diluted acid may be spilled on a fabric. As it dries, the water evaporates and leaves a less volatile and more concentrated acid in the fabric.

The damage usually results when a person brushes against an object on which acid has been spilled. Hydrochloric and sulfuric acid are used extensively in industrial plants and in dental, medical, photographic, and in all chemical laboratories. Hydrochloric acid, commonly called muriatic acid, is used in some medicines. Some scouring compounds and deodorants will form hydrochloric acid under certain conditions of use and storage. Storage batteries contain sulfuric acid. Accidental contact with them is a common cause of this type of fabric damage. Some deodorants contain salts of sulfuric acid that can, under certain conditions, form sulfuric acid.

Some shoulder pads and some jacket linings are made from wool fibers held together with a thin film of synthetic rubber containing chlorine. Under certain conditions, the synthetic rubber breaks down and gives off hydrochloric acid strong enough to cause the lining fabric to weaken. Although this type of damage often shows up during cleaning, its cause must be attributed to the presence of chlorine-containing synthetic rubber. This type of damage may be controlled by selection of a binder that does not contain chlorine in the manufacture of bonded materials.

Sometimes chemical damage to a fabric looks like a stain. The yarn in the fabric may be a mixture of dark-colored polyester fibers and light-colored cotton or rayon fibers. What appears to be a stain is actually the loss of cotton or rayon fibers in the yarns. As they are removed, the lightening effect on the dark polyester yarn is lost. When the fabric is held up to light, the affected area is noticeably thinner because of the missing fibers. Polyester fiber is resistant to acid but the acid can damage rayon and cotton.

Alkali Damage

This type of damage is frequently found on wool fabrics, wool blends, and wool combinations. Wool is very sensitive to alkaline substances. Even diluted solutions of strong alkalies damage wool very readily. This type of damage can also occur on silk, hair fibers, and synthetic protein fibers.

The damage may occur when a wool fabric comes in contact with caustic soda, caustic potash, or strongly alkaline washing compounds. Caustic alkalies are used in many household cleaning aids such as lye, Drano, and floor-scouring products. Many times the consumer is not aware that such substances have come in contact with wearing apparel or household items. Frequently the damage is not evident until the item has been subjected to the normal flexing action necessary to clean it.

Precaution in wear and use is the only way this type of damage may be avoided. If an acid or alkaline substance comes in contact with the fabric, flush the area immediately with water. Often damage from acids or alkalies is not evident until after a garment is cleaned. The flexing of the fabric in dry cleaning, wet cleaning, and laundering, and the heat of drying and pressing causes the damaged areas to disintegrate.

Acid Color Change

A limited number of dyes used to color wool fabrics change color when exposed to acidic conditions. The color change occurs most frequently in blue, tan, and gray dyes. It is a common practice to use acidic spotting reagents on fabrics to remove certain spots and stains. This practice does not affect many colors used to dye fabrics. However, dyes used to color wool are very sensitive to certain acidic reagents. They change color, either temporarily or permanently. Certain kinds of stains, such as ink, rust, tannin, and caramelized sugar, cannot be removed satisfactorily from many of the colored wool fabrics.

In some cases color changes may be restored by spotting the area with water, followed by neutralization of the area spotted. Most cases require soaking the fabric in a detergent and water solution. However, these methods are not effective on some dyes, and the color change may be permanent.

Color Change Caused By Alkali

Alkaline color changes are often noted on dark blue and black acetate fabrics. The color usually changes to a red. The color change is mistaken frequently for atmospheric gas fading (fume fading). A very common type of alkaline color change occurs on bright green wool fabrics and bright green silk fabrics. The color changes to a yellow. These color changes are caused by contact with alkaline liquids, foodstuffs, perspiration, and cosmetic preparations that have been allowed to remain in the fabric.

Alkaline color change will occur if alkaline staining substances and perspiration are allowed to remain in the fabric. Stains of this type should be removed as soon as possible. The use of alkaline spotting and dry cleaning reagents can also cause this type of color change.

Most alkaline color changes can be restored to the original color by the dry cleaner. Success depends on the type of dyestuff. If a fabric is allowed to remain in an alkaline condition for a long time, the color change may become permanent.

In the test for colorfastness to acid and alkalies,* test specimens are evaluated for resistance to simulated action of acid fumes, sizes, alkaline sizes, alkaline cleansing agents, and alkaline street dirt. The samples are steeped in or spotted with the required solution and examined for color changes. The effect on the color of the test specimen can be expressed and defined by reference to the Gray Scale for Color Change. Class 5 is negligible or no change as shown in Gray Scale Step 5 and Class 1 is a change equivalent to Gray Scale Step 1 (see Chapter 1, p. 28, Gray Scale for Color Change).

LAMINATED AND BONDED FABRICS

For review, let us describe the fabrics that fall into this classification. Some authorities refer to this class of fabrics as *multiple-component fabrics*.

1. *Laminated urethane foam.* The outer fabric or the outer and backing fabric are joined by bonding fabric to foam by either fusion, chemical adhesives or vulcanizing.

2. *Chemical quilted fabrics.* A face fabric and a backing fabric is held to the urethane foam or a fiber batt by adhesive and heat in a variety of patterns or designs.

3. *Fabric-to-fabric bonding.* The outer fabric is bonded to an acetate or nylon backing fabric either by urethane foam or chemical adhesives.

4. *Press-on interlinings, interfacings, and linings.* Woven and nonwoven fabrics are made with a thermoplastic resin on one side that melts under heat and pressure to form a bond with the fabric it is joined.

* Colorfastness to Acids and Alkalies; AATCC 6 (1975).

5. *Double-faced fabrics.* A reversible fabric may be made by bonding two fabrics together with an adhesive.

6. *Film-bonded fabrics.* A clear or opaque polyurethane or vinyl film is bonded by an adhesive to the face side of a fabric.

Performance In Consumer Use

In 1959, consumers were introduced to a new and different fabric formulation called "laminated fabrics." With this new development, consumer problems were encountered. They were:

1. Delamination or separation of the face fabric from the backing due to a loss of adhesion between the foam and fabric.

2. Discoloration of the foam

3. Deterioration of the foam. The degraded foam is usually badly discolored and deteriorated to the point where it crumbles away from the fabric.

Foam Laminates

There appears to be no real understanding among foam manufacturers and laminators as to why discoloration and deterioration of foam occurs. Following are some of the theories that have been advanced:

1. Aging. It has been found that foam products, stored over a long time, react differently—some remain in their original condition, others become dark brown in color and badly deteriorated. An acid condition has been noted, but degradation may be a matter of one to several years.

2. Light. Polyester-type foam is affected by light. The color of the foam will change from white to yellow to brown without any real loss of strength. Excessive exposure may cause a complete breakdown of the foam.

3. Bleaching. In wet processing, polyester foam is discolored by hypochlorite bleaching agents turning it yellow to brown. Highly concentrated oxidizing bleaches, such as hypochlorite, may also cause deterioration.

4. Treatment of foam in manufacture. Some manufacturers use a caustic soda treatment in the manufacture of the foam and it is believed that a residual alkaline condition may accelerate deterioration.

5. Short cuts in manufacture. It is believed that if short cuts are taken in the manufacture of foam by omitting certain compounds or elements to produce a less expensive product, then this may result in discoloration or deterioration of the foam.

Chemically Quilted Fabrics

The problems with chemically quilted laminates may be described as follows:

1. Complete loss of design. When this occurs, either the adhesive is completely dissolved or a finish applied to the face fabric interferes with adhesion. In the case of fabric laminated to foam, the face fabric or lining in a sandwich construction separates from the foam. This is also true in the fabric-to-fiber batt quilted fabrics. The batting in some cases falls down to the hemline between the outer face fabric and the lining fabric.

2. Partial loss of design. In some cases, the adhesive is dissolved in only one panel or section of a garment. This results when fabric from two different production lots are combined in a garment design. This occurs because of the practices used in mass production of wearing apparel.

Fabric-To-Fabric Bonding

In 1963, consumers saw the introduction of fabric-to-fabric bonding. They also experienced poor performance due to partial or complete separation of the face fabric from the acetate or nylon tricot. Separation was directly related to construction of the face fabric, type and amount of adhesive used, the method of adhesive application, the curing temperatures, or the agitation of cleaning that causes separation because of poor adhesion.

Customer complaints fall into four categories: partial or complete separation of the face fabric from the lining fabric, shrinkage in cleaning or in finishing with steam, stiffening or change of hand after drycleaning and finishing, or adhesive staining or transfer to the face fabric. The staining assumes the pattern in which the adhesive is applied.

These problems will even occur in controlled cleaning processes where agitation is reduced, temperatures lowered and where finishing is done with only light steaming. In many cases, the outer fabric bubbles, blisters, or separates. The dry cleaner or consumer cannot press the outer fabric flat nor can the two fabrics be resealed.

Press-On Interfacings

In 1964, the dry-cleaning industry was baffled by garments that developed what looked like the "measles." In some cases, the damage looked like mildew stains. This was the introduction of the fusible press-on nonwoven or woven interfacings.

The garments affected included raincoats, dresses, blouses, jackets, trousers, and children's garments. The fabrics ranged from lightweight cotton to medium-weight butcher's linen and heavyweight fabrics for jackets, trousers, and rainwear, such as poplin and gabardine. The colors ranged from white and pastels to the darker colors, such as tans and browns.

The discoloration that occurs from press-on interfacing, nonwoven and woven, is a complex problem. The factors involved are the kind of thermoplastic resin used to make the facing, the weight of the nonwoven or woven interfacing fabric, the color and weight of the woven fabric to which the nonwoven or woven facing is attached, the type of solvent and the temperature to which the material may be exposed, and time, heat, and pressure in the finishing or pressing operation.

Press-On Linings

Early in 1966 coats and suits made of knitted or woven fabrics with press-on lining fabrics made their appearance. This new development caused the consumer to complain about the separation of the press-on lining from the face fabric and shrinkage to the face fabric.

Manufacturers of both fabrics and garments with press-on woven linings pointed up two definite advantages: the press-on lining may serve as a built-in interlining and also helps to stabilize the fabric against shrinkage or stretching.

Two basic principles of fabric performance were ignored:

1. If a face fabric separates from the lining and the face fabric has not been stabilized for shrinkage control, shrinkage in the garment may occur. Shrinkage may occur without separation of the two fabrics.

2. If there is a differential shrinkage of the face and lining fabrics, puckering along the construction details of a garment are such that a smooth acceptable appearance cannot be obtained when the garment is finished or pressed.

Double-Faced Fabrics

In 1967, double cloth, adaptations of double cloth, and double-faced fabrics became popular. It is important to identify each type and understand why they react as they do in cleaning.

A true double cloth is a fabric made of a double-cloth weave. Two fabrics consisting of a set of warp and filling yarns are bound together with an extra set of yarns.

An adaptation of a double cloth is made with three sets of yarns. Usually the fabric appears to be made of only a warp and filling yarn of contrasting colors, one color thrown to the face of the fabric and the other thrown to the back. Yet the fabric is reversible.

Double-faced fabrics are made by taking two-face fabrics and binding them together with an adhesive.

Some of the double-faced fabrics dry clean satisfactorily, while some cause consumer complaints because of partial separation.

There is a very simple way to differentiate between a double cloth and a double-faced fabric. Examine a seam in an unexposed part of a garment. Pull the seam apart. If there is an extra set of yarns that holds the two sets of fabrics together, the fabric can be drycleaned satisfactorily. The adhesive that holds the two fabrics together in a double-faced construction can be seen.

Polyurethane Film Bonded To Fabric

One of the newer ideas in "wet look" apparel is a "see through" effect made by bonding a sheet of clear plastic film to finished fabric so that the color and pattern are visible. It is popular in ladies wear and provides a plastic protection that does not hide the fabric, but in a unique way enhances it. Still another effect is achieved by bonding an opaque polyurethane to fabric.

Although the film itself is not affected by dry-cleaning solvent, satisfactory performance in dry cleaning depends on the adhesive's resistance to solvent, the bond's effectiveness, and the nature of the backing cloth. The fabric bond must be strong enough to prevent separation of the film from the fabric. Sometimes the film also becomes tacky or sticky and causes the film to stick together. Some films discolor or yellow when exposed to light.

TESTING BONDED AND LAMINATED FABRICS

Separation of the face fabric from the back fabric, partial or complete, is a function of durability to wear, washing, or dry cleaning.

The ASTM test method* covers procedures for characterizing the delamination, strength of bond, appearance, and shrinkage of the bonded and laminated fabrics after dry cleaning and laundering.

Samples are prepared and marked for shrinkage measurements. They are dry cleaned, laundered and dried, or both, through a prescribed cycle that is repeated a specified number of times. The dry cleaned or wash specimens are examined for appearance and delamination and measured to determine if any shrinkage occurred.

The samples may also be tested to determine the strength of the bond. These methods are used to estimate the durability and strength of the bond, the change in appearance, and the amount of shrinkage that may be expected when the garments made from bonded or laminated fabrics are washed or dry cleaned.

* Bonded and Laminated Apparel Fabrics; ASTM Test Method D-2724-72 (1973).

The alteration of appearance is really an aesthetic property. Aesthetic changes of appearance may be described as puckering, crack marks, bubbling or blisters, face fabric pilling, loss or gain of stiffness, color change, and wrinkles.

The AATCC test method* measures bond strength only. Bond strength tests may be made on fabric as bonded or laminated or after a specified number of dry cleaning or laundering and drying cycles.

This method estimates the durability and strength of the bond that may be expected when the garments made from bonded and laminated fabrics are washed or dry cleaned.

BREAKING OF YARNS AND FABRIC

Low tensile strength and low tear strength of the fabric may contribute to its susceptibility to mechanical damage. This can occur when tension is put on the fabric during wear or during cleaning. Sharp objects in contact with a fabric may also cause rips, tears, or holes.

In some cases, mechanical damage may be attributed to the basic construction of the fabric itself; carelessness in wear or mishandling in cleaning may also be responsible. It is frequently impossible to pinpoint the exact cause when this type of damage occurs.

The interrelationships of tensile strength, tear strength, and abrasion resistance are complex. Add to this the factors of wear and cleaning and one can see that it is frequently impossible to specifically analyze why a fabric fails to give good consumer performance.

Dr. Steven Spivak,† explains the interrelationship of tensile strength, tear strength, and abrasion resistance to fabric structure. He points out that many factors are interrelated and shows it in Table 5–2.

Table 5–2 Interrelationships ÷ Fabric Structure To Tensile and Tear Strength and Abrasion Resistance

Key	Fabric Structure	Tensile Strength	Tear Strength	Abrasion Resistance
1. Low	Loose	1	3	1
2. Medium	Moderate	2	2	3
3. High	Tight	3	1	2

* Bond Strength of Bonded and Laminated Fabrics; AATCC Test Method 136 (1972).

† Lectures on Interrelationships of Yarn/Weave Structure, Tensile Strength, Tear Strength and Abrasion Resistance; University of Maryland.

Table 5–2 shows that differences in fabric structure (i.e., loose–moderate–tight) can influence performance properties in very different ways. For example, if other factors such as fiber type, fabric finish, and the like, are held constant, it can be seen that a tighter fabric construction generally contributes to high tensile strength but also lower tear strength and vice versa. A moderate structure, not too tight or too loose, could be expected to yield best abrasion resistance.

Let us briefly try and understand why fabric structure can have such differing influences on performance properties. For tensile strength, tighter fabric structures have more yarn interlacings and yarn crimp, contributing greater resistance and strength. However, the mechanism of fabric tearing is very different from tensile strength, and relates to the ability of individual yarns to slide and pack together or "jam" into a bundle, thereby increasing the tearing force. Thus, in the case of tearing, a looser fabric structure contributes to more yarn sliding and jamming, and higher tear strength. Try and tear a woven gauze or knitted fabric to understand this concept.

In abrasion resistance, the problem is more complex. Basically, very loose yarn or fabric structures are prone to snagging, which can readily rupture yarns and ruin the fabric. Alternately, very tight structures inhibit fiber movement during abrasion, causing fibers to be stressed and fatigued beyond their yield point, resulting in fiber breakage. A moderate structure, somewhere between tight and loose, is a reasonable compromise between the two.

This simple table and discussion shows very clearly that one fabric may have very different performance properties due to the interactions of durability factors. Hence, one test method may or may not predict how a fabric may perform in consumer use.

We mentioned in Chapter 5, Part 1 that sunlight could be considered as an aesthetic value in color measurement but a durability value in damage caused by sunlight. Measuring the breaking strength of fabrics is an important scientific measurement in research studies. This is particularly true in measuring fabric resistance to sunlight.

Sunlight Damage

Fiber deterioration in curtain, drapery and sportswear fabrics results from exposure to either direct or indirect rays of the sun. All fibers are subject to this type of damage, but the rate of deterioration varies according to fiber content, yarn and fabric construction, the textile finish applied, and the type of dyeing and printing applied to the fabric.

Conditions of use also contribute to this type of damage. Grime and dirt added to atmospheric acid fumes, heat from heating equipment, and moisture in the air, all work together to reduce the tensile strength and tear strength of these fabrics. Frequently the weakened fabric does not go into shreds or holes until it is subjected to the flexing action of cleaning.

Some factors may be controlled at the point of manufacture, for example, by controlling the amount of delusterizing pigment used, or selecting dyes that are not supersensitive to light. Eye appeal rather than durability and serviceability often influences the purchase of this class of merchandize.

BREAKING LOAD AND ELONGATION OF TEXTILE FABRICS

Three machines can be used to measure the forces required to break a fabric when it is under tension:*

1. Constant-Rate-of-Extension Tensile Testing Machine (CRE). A machine in which the rate of increase of specimen length is uniform with time (see Figure 5–25).

2. Constant-Rate-of-Traverse Tensile Testing Machine (CRT). A machine in which the pulling clamp moves at a uniform rate and the

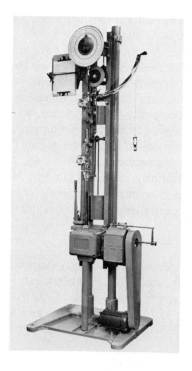

Figure 5-25 Constant-rate-of-traverse type testers are used for determining strength, elongation, and adhesion characteristics of textiles, skein yarns, and fabrics. It is used for seam slippage tests, zipper testing, and grab and strip tests. (Courtesy: GCA/Precision Scientific)

* Breaking Load and Elongation of Textile Fabrics; ASTM D-1682 (1970).

Figure 5-26 Tensile testing equipment has become very sophisticated and versatile. This constant rate of extension electronic tester can accommodate material measurements from one gram to 2000 lb. It consists of a pulling unit, strip chart recorder, set of grips, and sentronic load cell. Many optional features are available. (Courtesy: Instron Co.)

load is applied through the other clamp which moves appreciably to actuate a weighing mechanism, so that the rate of increase of load or elongation is dependent upon the extension characteristics of the specimen (see Figure 5–26).

3. Constant-Rate-of-Load Tensile Testing Machine (CRL). A machine in which the rate of increase of the load being applied to the specimen is uniform with time after the first three seconds.

Three methods may be used to measure strength:

1. Grab Test. Only a part of the width of the specimen is gripped in the clamps. For example, if the specimen width is four inches (100 mm) and the width of the jaw faces one inch (25 mm), the specimen is gripped centrally in the clamps.

2. Modified Grab Test. Only a part of the width of the specimen is gripped in the clamps and in which lateral slits are made in the specimen to sever all yarns bordering the portion whose strength is to be tested, reducing to a practical minimum the "fabric assistance" inherent in the grab method.

3. Strip Test. The full width of the specimen is gripped in the clamps. (a) Raveled Strip Test. A strip test in which the specified specimen width is secured by raveling away yarns. (b) Cut Strip Test. A strip test in which the specimen width is secured by cutting the fabric.

The basic principle of the test is that a continually increasing load is applied longitudinally to the specimen. The test is carried to rupture in a specific time. Values for the breaking load and elongation of the test specimen are obtained from machine scales or dials or autographic recording charts. Breaking elongation is the increase in length that has occurred when the fabric breaks.

It has been found that the wear life of a fabric correlates with both strength and elongation and not with strength alone.* With all other factors equal, a fabric with lower breaking strength and higher elongation may remain wearable for as long a period as a stronger fabric but with lower elongation. The extra elongation enables fabrics to better withstand the normal wear forces.

Most woven, nonwoven, or felted textile fabrics may be tested by at least one of the methods. The methods are not recommended for knitted fabrics (see Bursting Strength, p. 149). All of the procedures are applicable for testing fabrics either dry or wet.

The results obtained may depend on the type of machine used for the test. Constant time-to-break has been specified because it is the best known way of providing good agreement between the results from different types of machines. However, data obtained on constant-rate-of-load testers may differ from that obtained on constant-rate-of-traverse or constant-rate-of-extension testers when testing fabrics made from fibers whose behavior is strongly dependent on the rate of extension used, for example, high density polyethylene.

The grab method is used whenever it is desired to determine the "effective strength" of the fabric in use, that is, the strength of the yarns in a specific width together with the additional strength contributed by adjacent yarns. The breaking load determined by the grab method is not a reflection of the strength of the yarns actually gripped between clamps and cannot be used for direct comparison with yarn strength determinations. Grab tests are as precise as raveled strip tests and the specimens require much less time to prepare though they require more fabric per specimen. There is no simple relationship between grab tests and strip tests since the amount of fabric assistance depends on the type of weave, fabric count, mobility of yarns, and the like.

The raveled strip method is applicable whenever it is desired to

* J. Pizzuto, A. Price, and A. Cohen, *Fabric Science,* Fairchild Publications, Inc., New York (1974), p. 313.

determine the breaking load required to rupture a specific width of fabric. The information is particularly useful for comparing the effective strength of the yarns in the fabric with their strength before weaving. If a fabric cannot be raveled readily, a grab or cut strip test can be used.

The cut strip method is used instead of the raveled strip method for heavily fulled fabrics, felted fabrics, or any fabric that cannot be readily raveled.

The modified grab method is applicable when it is desired to determine the breaking load required to rupture a specific width of fabric for those constructions in which the application of testing stress on raveled strip specimens produces further unraveling. This method is desirable for high strength fabrics.

In addition to making and evaluating a fabric's strength and elongation with others, the breaking strength test can be used to evaluate the effects of destructive forces on woven fabrics, including sunlight, abrasion, laundering, bleaching, and some finishing processes such as napping, embossing, and resin-treated fabrics.

BURSTING STRENGTH

Bursting strength is the amount of pressure required to rupture a fabric. This test* is designed for fabrics that do not have yarns or where the yarns are not in any given direction, such as knits, felt, nonwoven material, lace, and net. Elongation cannot be determined.

The machines used for this test are the Mullen Tester (for the diaphragm bursting test, see Figure 5–27), and a breaking strength tester with a ball bursting attachment (see Figure 5–28).

The force is applied at right angles to the plane of the fabric. Either a rubber diaphragm is expanded by light pressure until it pushes its way through the fabric clamped over it or a steel ball is pushed through the fabric. All yarns or areas are tested simultaneously for the weakest point because the testing force is applied radially and not in one direction as in breaking or tearing strength tests. Bursting strength is expressed in pounds and is an average of 10 tests.

At the Knit Symposium sponsored by AATCC Committee RA84, Knit Fabric Technology, Braham Norwick, Joseph Bancroft and Sons, presented a paper, "Bursting Strength and Consumer Performances."† He stated that the Bursting Strength Knit Goods Test is

* Bursting Strength Knit Goods; ASTM Test Method D-231 (1970).

† Braham Norwick, "Bursting Strength and Consumer Performance," *Sense and Nonsense in Knit Testing No. 17;* American Association of Textile Chemists and Colorists, pp. 36—38. (1976)

Figure 5-27 Mullen Diaphragm Bursting Tester. (Courtesy: B. F. Perkins Division Standard International Corp.)

Figure 5-28 Ball bursting attachment to tensile strength machine. (Courtesy: GCA/Precision Scientific)

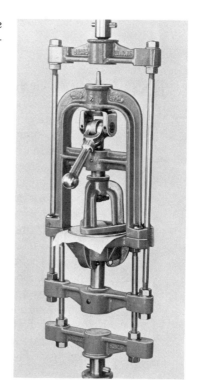

useful as in laboratory quality control but has no relation to performance of fabrics in end use.

TEAR RESISTANCE OF WOVEN FABRICS

At one time the tearing resistance of a fabric was judged when a technician grasped one end of a specimen in each hand and tore it. There was a slight difference between the two specimens, but an analytical value could not be placed on the results. The findings could not be related to someone else, nor could a comparison be made on that day's production with that of a day, week, month or year earlier. Today, modern equipment provides a meaningful value that can be used to compare different production runs.

There are a tremendous number of basic and combined materials that must resist the forces of tension, torsion, folding, and puncture associated with normal handling and use. Textiles for clothing and packaging must have high tear resistance in addition to other desirable qualities. Nonwovens must have tearing resistance equal to the materials which they are to replace.

Tearing strength is the force required either (1) to start or (2) to continue or propagate a tear in a fabric under specified conditions. Tearing strength is expressed either in pounds or grams. The average of the warp tests and of the filling tests is given as the result. The devices for this test are (1) the Elmendorf Tearing Tester, (2) the Constant-Rate-of-Extension Tester and Constant-Rate-of-Traverse type tester.

Falling Pendulum (Elmendorf) Method

This method* is used for the determination of the average force required to continue a single-rip-tongue-type tear starting from a cut in a woven fabric by means of a falling-pendulum (Elmendorf) apparatus (see Figure 5–29). This method is not suitable for knit fabrics, felts, or nonwoven fabrics. It is applicable to treated and untreated woven fabrics, including those heavily sized, coated, or resin treated (e.g., wash and wear), provided the fabric does not tear during the test in the direction crosswise to the direction of the force applied.

The Elmendorf Tearing Tester utilizes the energy conversion principle (potential to kinetic) to determine the work done. The potential energy is stored in the sector-shaped distance above its neutral point. In the raised position, the two sample holding clamps—one stationary and attached to the base, the other movable and attached to

* Tearing Strength of Woven Fabrics, ASTM D-1424-63; ASTM-D-2261-71; ASTM 2262-71. (1971)

Figure 5-29 The Elmendorf Tearing Tester. See text for a description of how this equipment determines the tear strength of a fabric. (Courtesy: Thwing Albert Instrument Co.)

the pendulum—are aligned and ready for the sample. The sample is centered in the clamps. Both clamps are secured. An initial slit is made using a cutting knife, which is centered between the clamps and adjusted in height to produce a slit $20 \pm .15$ millimeters in length. This provides a tearing length of $43 \pm .15$ millimeters. The principal reason for this slit is to eliminate edge tear forces and to restrict the measurement to the internal tearing force only. After the slit has been made, the pendulum stop is depressed, allowing the pendulum to swing under the force of gravity. The specimen is torn as the pendulum clamp moves away from the stationary clamp. The work done on the specimen is the difference between the initial potential energy and the sum of the remaining kinetic and potential energies at the completion of the tear.

Results obtained with this method are similar to those obtained by other methods for tongue-type tears but differences in level of test occur. The level of test will depend in part on the rate of tearing. This method is advantageous insofar as simplicity and speed in testing since (1) specimens are cut with a die and (2) results are read directly from the scale of the pendulum. The specimens are relatively small in area and, thus, require less fabric. The reading obtained is directly proportional to the length of the material torn.

Tongue (Single Rip) Method On Constant-Rate-Of-Extension Machine (CRE)

A rectangular specimen, cut in the center of the shorter edge to form two "tongues" (or "tails"), is gripped in the clamps of a recording tensile testing machine and pulled to simulate a rip. The force to continue the tear is calculated from precalculated readings as the average force to tear, or from a moveable automatic pen on the chart as the median-peak load or the average of the five highest peaks.

The force registered in a tear test is irregular. Consequently, empirical methods have had to be developed to obtain usable values related to tear strength. In spite of the empirical nature of the reported values, it is believed they reflect comparative performance of similar fabrics tested and measured in the same way. No procedure is available that can be used with all fabrics to determine the minimum tearing strength.

Depending on the nature of the specimen, the type of testing machine used, and its rate of operation, the recorder will show the force required to break each successive yarn, or to shift one or more yarns and break two or more yarns simultaneously, forming peaks on the chart. The height of the peak will depend on the number and strength of yarns broken at one time. The highest peaks appear to reflect the strength of a yarn needed to stop a tear in a fabric of the same construction. The valleys recorded on the chart between the peaks have no specific significance. It is indicated, however, that the minimum force to tear single yarns is above the lowest valleys.

The highest peaks, which may reflect the force required to break several yarns, bear no simple relationship to the average force required to break successive individual yarns. As a consequence the average of the five highest peaks reflects both the strength of the yarn and the ease with which it shifts in the fabric.

The intermediate peaks reflect the force needed to shift or break an individual yarn or a fewer number of yarns than cause the highest peaks. Under some conditions the force required to break successive individual yarns can be detected and measured. This value represents the minimum force required to tear the fabric, but it will not do so under other conditions that permit yarn slippage.

The median peak value by definition must be above the average load required to break successive, individual yarns. The median peak value, however, does give a figure that reflects the minimum force required to tear the fabric much more closely than the average of the five highest peaks.

Tongue (Single Rip) Method On Constant-Rate-Of-Traverse Machine (CRT)

Tearing strength, as measured in this method, is the force required to continue a tear started previously in the specimen. The reported value includes the force required to shift yarns and to break one or more yarns at the same time. The reported value is not directly related to the force required to initiate or start a tear.

A rectangular specimen, cut in the center of the shorter edge to form two "tongues" (or "tails"), is gripped in the clamps of a recording tensile testing machine and pulled to simulate a rip. The force to continue the tear is estimated by averaging the five highest peak loads registered by a recorder.

Figure 5-30 Thickness gauge—there are a variety of thickness gauges, thickness testers, compressometers, and indention machines available from commercial equipment sources. (Courtesy: Custom Scientific Instruments, Inc.)

FABRIC THICKNESS

In textiles, fabric thickness* is the distance between the upper and lower surfaces of the material, measured under a specific pressure (see Figure 5–30 and Table 5–3). Fabric thickness is usually measured in thousandths of an inch and is usually an average of tests taken at random over the fabric.

This property is important when warmth and bulk properties depend on the fabric thickness-to-weight rates such as in pile fabrics, blankets, and carpeting. It indicates shrinkage and abrasion resistance. The garment manufacturer relies on this measurement in calculating the number of fabric lays in cutting garments and determining settings to use for stitching on sewing machines.

The determination of the thickness of a textile material is a delicate operation because of the ease of compression of most fabrics. The usual type of thickness gauge has a broad anvil on which a presser foot is pressed by a spring. The sample is placed on the anvil and the presser foot is lowered onto the sample by releasing the raising lever very slowly, the dial then indicates the number of thousandths of an inch between the anvil and the presser foot. The variables that affect

* Thickness of Textile Materials Measuring; ASTM D-1777-64 (1975).

Table 5–3 Guide for Selection of Pressures in Measuring Thickness of Material[a]

Type of Materials	Examples	Pressure Range (psi)
Soft	Blankets, fleeces, knit fabric, lofty nonwovens, woolens	0.005 to 0.50 (0.35 to 35 g per sq cm)
Moderate	Worsteds, sheetings, carpets	0.02 to 2.0 (1.4 to 144 g per sq cm)
Firm	Ducks, asbestos fabrics, felt	0.1 to 10 (7 to 700 g per sq cm)

[a] This table is intended as a general guide for the selection of pressures for various materials. In general, the use of the minimum pressure in the range listed for that material is appropriate. Specific pressures for certain products are given in ASTM Methods D-418. Testing Woven and Tufted Pile Floor Covering, stipulates that the thickness of woven pile floor coverings shall be determined under a pressure of 0.100 psi.

the result are (1) size of presser foot (the greater the size, the less it will sink into the fabric), one inch suggested; (2) form of presser foot; (3) weight on presser foot (the greater the weight, the more it will sink into the cloth); (4) velocity of presser foot (the faster the foot is allowed to drop the more it will penetrate the fabric); (5) time elapsing during measurement (the presser foot does not come to equilibrium immediately), five seconds is suggested; (6) stability of the machine (jarring will cause foot to penetrate deeper), a solid support is necessary; and (7) condition of the specimen during measurement (the fabric should be free of wrinkles but not under tension).

SEAM SLIPPAGE, SEAM STRENGTH

Seam slippage is described as the amount or degree a fabric pulls away at the seam. Sometimes the thread used to stitch a seam breaks. Seam strength relates to the force required to break the stitching thread at the line of stitching.

In Chapter 4, yarn distortion, patterns of yarn shifting and a method of test to measure yarn shifting was discussed. Fabrics in which yarn distortion is a problem may also experience a problem with yarns slipping in the seam area. As a result, a distortion area may result adjacent to the seam. Sometimes the seam actually may open without any yarns breaking and with the sewing thread still intact.

There are several reasons why a fabric performs unsatisfactory yarn and seam slippage. Seam slippage may occur in a garment or household item because of (1) a low number of warp or filling yarns to an inch (known as thread count) in relation to particular yarn and fabric construction characteristics, (2) too shallow seam allowances (any strain on the fabric at the seams causes the yarns to shift), (3) too tight a fit (undue strain during wear may cause yarns to shift at the seam line), and (4) improper seam construction (this could be too shallow a seam or not enough stitches per inch of machine stitching).

Strain on the fabric or just a rubbing action in some cases may result in the yarns shifting. Moisture from perspiration may remove the sizing that holds the yarns in place. Slippage of yarns may occur in areas thus affected. The solvent action and the flexing action of dry cleaning, wet cleaning, and laundering may also break up the sizing and allow shifting of yarns.

This type of problem may be controlled by adding more twist to the yarns, increasing the thread count of the particular fabric, establishing the correct relationship of balance of warp and filling yarns, and the selection of a sizing that will not be disturbed by wear, water, or solvent.

Measuring Resistance To Yarn Slippage

During wear and care, some filament-type fabrics with low count may exhibit yarn slippage at points of strain. The test method* applies to the measurement of the resistance to slippage of filling yarns on warp yarns or warp yarns on filling yarns in silk, rayon, acetate, and man-made woven fabrics and combination weaves of these fibers.

Resistance to slippage is the pounds pull (across a seam) per inch of width necessary to produce an elongation of $\frac{1}{4}$ inch in excess of the normal stretch of the fabric under the same load on a pendulum-type testing equipment. An average of five tests is the resistance of the yarns to slippage.

Seam Strength

Many times the serviceability of an item is limited because of poor seam strength or breaking of the stitching thread at the seam. The test method† covers the determination of the breaking load of sewn seams when the load is applied perpendicularly to the seam, using

---

* Yarn Slippage in Silk, Rayon and Acetate Woven Fabrics; ASTM D-434-42 (1970).

† Seam Breaking Strength of Woven Textile Fabrics; ASTM Designation: D-1683 (1973).

the Grab Test of ASTM Methods D-1682, Test for Breaking Load and Elongation of Textile Fabrics. The sewn seams may be taken from sewn articles such as garments or may be prepared from fabric samples.

This method requires a straight seam line, and is not applicable if the seam line is curved. The seam line of the seamed samples must be parallel to either the warp yarns or the filling yarns, or as nearly parallel as the practical limitations permit (as in taking seams from previously sewn articles).

Preparation of sewn seam test specimens from fabric samples requires separate prior specification of sewing details that represent acceptable trade practice for the parties interested in the test results. These details vary with the end-use article and include the seam allowance or the width of fabric used in making a seam bounded by the edge of the fabric and the farthest stitch or the repeating unit of sewing thread formation in the production of sewn seams and stitching.

If the breaking load of the fabric is required in addition to the breaking load of the seam, the fabric adjacent to the sewn seam is tested in the fabric direction(s) that is perpendicular (or approximately perpendicular) to the seam direction, using the Grab Test of Methods D-1682, with sampling and selection of fabric specimens meeting the requirements of both test methods.

This test method may be used for several purposes: (1) to determine optimum sewing conditions such as seam type, stitch type, number of stitches per unit length of seam, sizes of sewing threads, sizes of sewing machine needles, and so on, (2) to measure a fabric property, (3) to evaluate seam quality competence of personnel making seams, (4) to obtain an integrated composite of all of the preceding factors by measuring one aspect of quality in sewn seams taken from previously sewn articles, and (5) to determine seam efficiency. The breaking strength of the seam is divided by the breaking strength of the fabric and multiplied by 100.

3 COMFORT

One of the most complex and intricate measurements to make and evaluate is *comfort*. Most clothing is designed primarily for fashion with little or no thought to comfort. Consumers seldom think of comfort in selecting clothing unless the design of a garment is restrictive, or if the desire is for something that will keep one "warm" or perhaps something that will keep one "cool." Occasionally you may hear a complaint that a certain fiber cannot be worn because it makes the wearer feel "itchy," hence "uncomfortable."

Fiber choices and structural features of knits affect comfort.* One question is constantly asked: What fabric criteria should be examined to predict comfort acceptance in knits?

One feature that distinguishes knits from woven goods of equal weight is that there is much more openness in knits and a definite lower limit to the tightness that can be achieved. Thus, knits tend to be more transparent to the passage of light, air, and water vapor than woven fabrics.

The natural openness of knits makes them sensitive to the passage of air with air permeability values generally in excess of 200 ft³/ft²/min. For garments requiring wind protection, knits are of limited use. Very open knits are desirable for warm weather clothing, where air motion through the clothing can serve to give much needed ventilation. But the open spaces have to be particularly large to contribute any substantial "breathing" effect in the absence of wind.

The thermal insulation that clothing provides for wear in most climates has been established to be proportional to fabric thickness. Two important factors are (1) type of yarn and (2) fabric surface. Fabric thickness is determined by yarn bulk in a polyester shirting fabric. In a cotton shirting, additional thickness is provided by the fibers of the staple yarn that not only stick out from the yarn but project above the fabric surface as well.

There is another way in which the type of yarn used in knitting affects the comfort of a fabric. Filament yarns in knits when bulked still give smooth fabrics that, in clothing, give good skin contact and a cool feel. Conversely, staple yarns in knits give a fuzzy surface that, on contact with the skin, feels warm. There is evidence that these surface fibers play a very important role in determining the comfort

* N. R. S. Hollies and P. L. Hall, "Comfort Acceptance In Knit Structures," *Sense and Nonsense in Knit Testing No. 17;* American Association of Textile Chemists and Colorists. (1976)

acceptance level of next-to-skin clothing, particularly when the skin is wet.

The historical reason for associating water absorption or regain along with the wetting properties of fabrics with their comfort is based on the fact that hygroscopic natural fibers give more comfortable clothing fabrics. For example: a 100 percent knit cotton garment is more comfortable under mild conditions of perspiration than a 100 percent knit polyester of the identical construction. Attempts to relate regain or wicking properties to comfort level have been unsuccessful.

USEFUL METHODS FOR ASSESSING COMFORT OF KNITS

Table 5–4 lists methods with references that can be used at least to establish the relative comfort acceptance level of different knits depending on the clothing use proposed for each fabric. There is no substitute for actual wearing studies on subjects under both the work and climatic conditions of wear for determining what contribution each fabric property makes to overall comfort. This is particularly true of the new method for measuring surface wetness of knits under dynamic conditions actually encountered in clothing use. More work is definitely needed to establish over what range of conditions, for which fabric and fiber choices, a simple measure of fabric surface wetness can truly reflect comfort sensations of the wearer.

The U.S. Army Research Institute of Environmental Medicine, Natick, Massachusetts, has done more research in the United States

Table 5–4 Suggested Fabric Test Methods for Assessing Clothing Comfort

Property Examined	Test Method Used	Reference
Thickness	Compressometer methods	ASTM Method D-1777
Surface smoothness	Compression, thermal, and photographic	Clothing: Comfort and Function
Air permeability	Permeometer and permeability	ASTM Method D-737
Vapor resistance	Vapor-cup weighing methods	Clothing: Comfort and Function
Wettability	Drop absorption test	
Surface wetness	Dynamic surface moisture device	AATCC Method 39-1974

in measuring the comfort factor of clothing systems than any other laboratory. Many people have overlooked the scientific design of military clothing.

Dr. Ralph F. Goldman* points out that there has been a great deal of work on assessment of comfort usually by a "comfort vote." Other studies have shown that subjective interpretations of comfort differ from those of pleasant versus unpleasant and differ also from those of temperature sensation. All are related to pleasantness, comfort, and temperature sensations reported by subjects and depend on change from an existing baseline. There are differences in comfort sensations associated with the seasons of the year, age, sex, and physical conditions. Such studies merely attempt to define the zone of comfort and at what point there is a deviation from the comfort zone due to temperature, humidity, air motion and radiant heat exchange. Dr. Goldman takes a nonsubjective approach to comfort. Instead of trying to define comfort and its associated ranges, he considers tolerances to heat, cold, and work. Instead of working from comfort to discomfort, he works from discomfort or limits of physiological tolerance on approaches to less severe conditions. Thus, he interprets comfort as those conditions where significant physiological changes do not occur. This approach involves expressing physical factors in the environment, physiological factors in the individual. This is done by either direct physical measurement or biophysical simulation such as a heated copper manikin by development of predictive models of what the physiological responses would be to any given combination of work, temperature, humidity, air motion, and clothing and, finally, by controlled physiological studies to refine and ultimately validate the biophysical models developed (see Figures 5–31 and 5–32).

The measurement of comfort involves the interaction of multidisciplinary factors drawing from (1) the theoretical physics of heat transfer, (2) the biophysics of clothing, (3) the physiology of metabolic heat production, distribution, and elimination, and (4) related atmospheric conditions. Figure 5–33 illustrates how these factors relate in the case of a soldier.

In this part of the text we shall discuss those test methods that relate to the comfort of an individual: absorbency, air permeability, resistance of fabrics to static charge, comfort provided by elasticity, stiffness, hand and drape, heat transfer, and resistance of fabrics to cling.

* Ralph F. Goldman, "Comfort, A Non-Subjective Approach," paper, U.S. Army Research Institute of Environmental Medicine, Natick, Ma.

Figure 5-31 Heat injury and the athlete has much in common with the military research on heat injury and the soldier. The copper manikin is dressed in a military uniform. The control unit measures voltage level, amperage level, total "on" time, and total elapsed time. (Courtesy: Ralph F. Goldman, Ph.D., Director, Military Ergonomics Laboratory, U.S. Army Research Institute of Environmental Medicine)

ABSORBANCY OF WOVEN FABRIC

Absorbancy of water is one factor that determines the suitability of a fabric for a particular use. It is important in fabrics that are to be dyed, since the completeness and uniformity of the dyeing are dependent on the absorbancy. Where fabrics are to be given resin or other specialized finishes, absorbancy is a factor to be considered. Absorbancy is also a factor that may result in either comfort or discomfort in wear. Wettability or absorbancy of textile fabrics or yarns can be determined by a test method* that allows a drop of water to fall from a fixed height onto the taut surface of a test specimen. The time required for the specular reflection of the water drop to disappear is measured and recorded as wetting time.

* Absorbancy of Bleached Woven Cloth; AATCC Test Method 79 (1972).

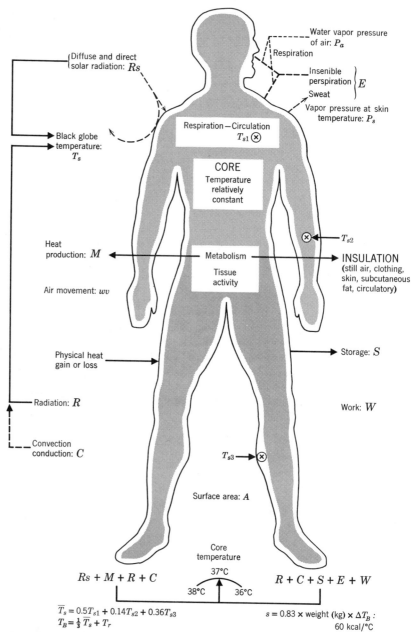

Figure 5-32 The complexity of comfort measurements is shown in the diagram that summarizes the factors in human energy balance. Activity is an important source of internal heat that must be eliminated from the body or stored in the body where it produces a direct increase in body temperature thus reducing physiologic tolerances below levels tolerable at rest, while clothing directly alters the body's heat exchange with its environment by radiation, conduction-convection, and evaporation. (Courtesy: Ralph M. Goldman, Ph.D., Director, Military Ergonomics, U.S. Army Research Institute of Environmental Medicine; and Gordon and Breach, Science Publishers Ltd.)

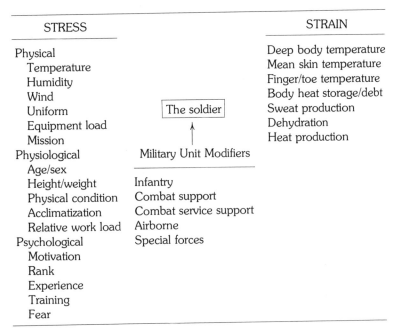

STRESS		STRAIN

STRESS

Physical
  Temperature
  Humidity
  Wind
  Uniform
  Equipment load
  Mission
Physiological
  Age/sex
  Height/weight
  Physical condition
  Acclimatization
  Relative work load
Psychological
  Motivation
  Rank
  Experience
  Training
  Fear

The soldier

Military Unit Modifiers

Infantry
Combat support
Combat service support
Airborne
Special forces

STRAIN

Deep body temperature
Mean skin temperature
Finger/toe temperature
Body heat storage/debt
Sweat production
Dehydration
Heat production

Figure 5-33 Diagram of a systems analysis of the stress inputs and physiological strain output responses of "the soldier." (Courtesy: Ralph M. Goldman, *Environment, Clothing and Personal Equipment, and Military Operations.*)

AIR PERMEABILITY OF FABRICS

Air permeability* is an important factor in the performance of such textile materials as filters, fabrics for clothing, tentage, mosquito netting, sails, and parachutes. In filtration, for example, air permeability is directly related to efficiency (pressure differential between the surfaces of a filter in use). Air permeability can also be used to provide an indication of the "breathability" of weather and rainproof fabrics or of coated fabrics in general.

Performance specifications, both industrial and military, have been set up on the basis of air permeability and are used in the purchase of materials where permeability is of interest.

Air permeability may be affected by several factors. (1) Construction or finishing techniques can have an effect upon air permeability by causing a change in the length of airflow paths through a fabric. (2) Yarn twist is important in that as twist increases, the circularity and density of the yarn increases, thus reducing the yarn diameter and the cover factor and increasing the air permeability. (3) Yarn crimp and weave influence the shape and area of the interstices between yarns, and may permit yarns to extend easily. Such yarn ex-

---

* Air Permeability of Textile Fabrics; ASTM D 737-69 (1975).

Figure 5-34 The Air Flow Tester is used for measuring air flow (permeability) characteristics of fabrics. The apparatus consists of a suction fan for drawing air through a known area of fabric defined by the circular orifice of 2.75 in. and a means of measuring the rate of air flowing through the test area of the fabric. Vertical manometer reading are converted to air flow in cubic feet/ minute/square feet of fabric. Pressure drop across the sample is read on the inclined manometer. (Courtesy: U.S. Testing Co.)

tension opens up the fabric, increases the free area, and increases the air permeability. (4) Hot calendering may be used to flatten yarns, thus reducing air permeability.

By definition, air permeability is the rate of air flow through a material under a differential pressure between the two fabric surfaces.

Air permeability is expressed in U.S. customary units as cubic feet of air per minute per square foot of fabric at a stated pressure differential between the two surfaces of the fabric. In this test method, the rate of air flow through a known area of fabric is adjusted to secure a prescribed pressure differential between the two fabric surfaces in the test area. From this rate of flow the air permeability of the fabric is determined (Figure 5–34).

STATIC CHARGE

Static electricity can be defined in both passive and active terms: it is both the accumulation of an electric charge on an isolated body and the electrical discharge resulting from that accumulation.

About 1600, it was discovered that there were two kinds of electricity—positive and negative—and that each was repelled by itself and attracted to its opposite.

One of the classic studies in the field is still practiced by schoolboys today: a glass rod is rubbed by silk and small bits of paper attracted to it. After a time, however, the bits of paper absorb the rod's charge. The paper bits are thus repelled because they contain the same "kind" of electricity.

The attraction of opposite charges explains the well-known clinging slip. Three qualities determine the amount of attraction between the two charged bodies involved in this event: the size of the charges, the distance between them and the properties of any medium between them. Since a clinging slip and human body are often highly charged, very close and rarely with much medium of any kind between them, they have been known to cling tenaciously for a long time. Static dissipation is slow static buildup fast. The problem is a continual one, especially in dry, cold weather.

Static cling challenged the textile fiber producer, so we now have some antistatic fibers made by (1) a recomposition of the chemistry of the fiber prior to the yarn stage, (2) a chemical conductor spun into the yarn, evenly distributed throughout each filament, and (3) an additive put into the fiber at the manufacturing stage.

Everyone at some time has probably experienced a static charge when putting a wool sweater over the head or walking across a wool or nylon rug and then touching a metal light switch.

Sometimes consumers seek help from professional dry cleaners to remove static charges from their garments. In some cases a cleaner is able to dry clean the garment and eliminate the clinging condition. In the garment pictured in Figure 5–35, the fabric was dry cleaned and dried, and steamed on a press. But all attempts to remove the static charge were unsuccessful. After each treatment the skirt became charged with electricity. It is suspected that some fabrics, when treated with finishes to make them wrinkle resistant, causes the condition.

Electric charges can also cause soil and dirt to deposit on fabrics treated with a water repellent finish; on curtain and drapery fabrics that decorate walls and windows.

There are two methods that may be used to measure static charges: (1) measuring the electrical resistance or (2) measuring the cling tendency.

The test method* used to measure the clinging tendency of fabrics under use conditions integrates the effect of fabric weight, stiffness, construction, surface character, finish application, and other fabric properties that affect the static clinging tendency of fabrics during use. The test method makes use of a basic law of physics that states that oppositely charged materials attract each other. Since a

Figure 5-35 This wool skirt is charged with static electricity; hence it clings to the wearer. When the skirt was held about a quarter of an inch above an ash tray, the cigarette ashes were drawn to it as was a pice of cotton thread held within six to eight inches of the fabric. (Courtesy: International Fabricare Institute)

---

* Electrostatic Clinging of Fabrics: Fabric-to-Metal Test; AATCC Test Method 115 (1973).

165   *Testing for Product Performance*

metal plate exhibits the same phenomenon of instantaneous charge induction when placed in the field of a charged material, a metal plate is used to simulate the problems of clinging observed between charged garments and the human body; (t_d) is the minutes required for the charge on the sample to detach itself from the metal plate. It is the level where the electrical attractive forces between the fabric and the metal plate (human body) are overbalanced by the gravitational forces of the fabric acting to pull the fabric away from the plate.

The test method*,† used to measure electrical resistances of fabrics and yarns is designed to determine the surface electrical properties of all textile fabrics containing natural or man-made fibers. Electrical resistivity influences the accumulation of electrostatic charge and, therefore, provides one measure of the electrostatic properties of a textile fabric.

Fabric samples to be tested are brought to equilibrium at a specified humidity and temperature. They are measured for resistance to the passage of current by means of an electrical resistance meter.

ELASTIC YARNS

Plain and shirred elasticized banding and trim are very much a part of fashion in women's, men's, and children's garments. Both exposed and covered elastic are being used by garment manufacturers to make a garment fit well and add comfort value in wear, and add fashion appeal to the garment.

Elastic yarns or elastic webbing may be used alone or together to achieve a fashion look. You find them in the backs and sides of jackets, around cuffs or across pockets, and around the waistline of jeans, slacks, trousers, and skirts.

Elastic yarns differ chemically and physically. They are made of natural rubber, synthetic rubber, and spandex.

The Federal Trade Commission defines rubber as a manufactured fiber in which the fiber-forming substance is comprised of natural rubber or a chemically defined synthetic rubber bearing a name like Lastocarb, Lastrile, and Lastochlor. However, these terms are never used on labels or hangtags.

Natural rubber fibers are made from concentrated sap of certain trees, while synthetic rubber fibers are produced from a synthetic polymer made from petroleum products by the chemical industry. The softened rubber is extruded as a monofilament yarn.

An uncovered or monofilament yarn, sometimes called thread, can be inserted within the main body fabric of a slack or jacket to

* Electrical Resistivity of Fabrics; AATCC Test Method 76 (1972).
† Electrical Resistivity of Yarns; AATCC Test Method 84 (1973).

achieve a gathered or smooth-fitting waistband. Multicolored yarns can be used for fashion effects.

Monofilament yarn or thread can be woven into a webbing. The webbing may be used in waistbands on men's, women's, or children's slacks, jeans, or shirts.

An uncovered monofilament yarn may be the core around which yarns or other fibers are wrapped or wound, thus protecting it from abrasion. Rubber core yarns are used where stretch and elasticity are required. They may also appear as stitching yarns to create decorative designs or stretch fabrics.

Some elastic yarns swell in dry-cleaning solvent. This causes the yarn to become shorter and shrink. This shrinkage may be progressive through, say, five dry cleanings.

In some cases, when a rubber core yarn is used, stretching can occur. Textile yarns do not swell in dry-cleaning solvent. If the rubber core yarn swells and the textile yarn does not, in time the textile yarn cuts into the swollen rubber yarn and segments or cuts it. This causes the rubber yarn to lose its elasticity and to stretch.

In still other cases, aging and flexing in wear and cleaning along with mechanical agitation and heat can cause a rubber yarn to lose elasticity. Stretching is the results.

Permanent care labels must disclose fully, clearly, and thoroughly "regular" care and maintenance required by the mere use of the product. This includes the component parts of a garment, including trim.

There are manufacturers who produce dry-cleanable elastic yarns (see Figure 5–36). If elastic yarns are not dry cleanable, the garment should be labeled "Do Not Dry Clean."

If the garment maker fails to provide the correct sewn-in care instructions, he is responsible for poor performance of elasticized yarns

Figure 5-36 Pictured here is a graphic example of how a new dry-clenable elastic webbing is an improvement over the old version. The bottom swatch is the old-type webbing that stretched out of shape after just one dry cleaning; the top swatch shows how even though it has been dry cleaned it goes back to its original size. Both swatches were originally the same size. (Courtesy: International Fabricare Institute)

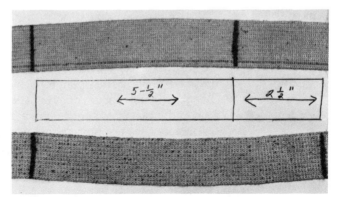

in wear and care. If shrinkage or stretching occurs in removable or replaceable parts of garment design, such as the waistband, the problem can be corrected by replacement; however, this is an added cost.

ELASTIC FABRICS

Stretch fabrics are designed for specific end uses. There are two types of stretch: comfort stretch (25 to 30 percent) and power stretch (30 to 50 percent). Stretch is important in swimwear, active sports clothing such as ski wear, snowmobile suits, and athletic clothing, and foundation garments. In some uses power stretch fabrics are required that have extensibility and quick recovery. Comfort stretch fabrics are designed for low loads (two pounds per inch); power stretch at considerably higher loads.

J. P. Stevens Company* has established the following recommendation for stretch or elastic fabrics:

Tailored Clothing: 15 to 25 percent unrecovered growth.

Spectator sportswear: 20 to 35 percent; no more than 5 percent growth.

Active skiwear: 30 to 50 percent; no more than 6 percent growth. Growth is the difference between the original size and that measured after elongation.

An elastic fabric is one made from an elastomeric fiber either alone or in combination with other textile fibers. An elastic fabric, when conditioned in the standard atmosphere for textile testing, will stretch under tension and return immediately and forcibly to substantially its original dimensions and shape when tension is removed. The elastic fabric may be manufactured by weaving, braiding, or knitting.

When testing elastic fabrics there are three properties that should be examined: (1) the amount of stretch a given length of fabric possesses under various loads (percent stretch), (2), the force or pounds it takes to stretch the fabric a certain elongation (power), and (3) the degree of return after being stretched (recovery). In all three cases the degree of each property will vary as the fabric is repeatedly stretched. It is also important to know to what extent the properties change. The test method does not take into account the load of elasticity in dry-cleanable stretch fabrics (see Figure 5–37a and b).

There are five test procedures† designed to test elastic fabrics: (1) Tension by Constant-Rate-of-Load Type Tensile Testing Machine,

* American Fabrics No. 64 (Summer 1964), p. X1.

† Tension and Elongation of Wide Elastic Fabrics; ASTM D 1775-74 (1975).

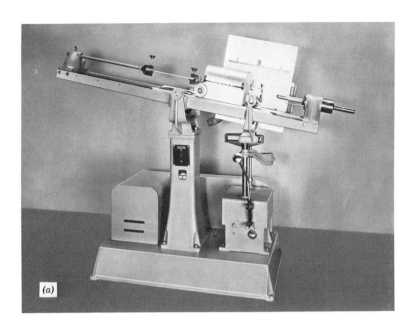

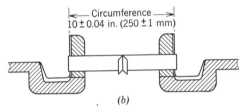

Figure 5-37 (a) Constant rate-of-load-type tester. Used to cycle (stretch and relax) elastic fabrics. (Courtesy: GCA/Precision Scientific) (b) Loop Specimen in place on pins.

Circumference
10 ± 0.04 in. (250 ± 1 mm)

(b)

(2) Stretch by Constant-Rate-of-Load Type Tensile Testing Machine, (3) Change in Tension Due to Oxygen Pressure Aging, (4) Change in Tension Due to Dry Heat, and (5) Change in Tension, Dimension, and Appearance Due to Laundering.

The tension testing machine used may be either a Scott Tester IP-4 model or IP-2 model, equipped with A-7 clamps. However, results from the model IP-2 machine are not interchangeable with results from the model IP-4 machine.

Tension and Stretch By Constant-Rate-of-Load Tensile Testing Machine

Conditioned specimens are subjected to a prescribed load, using a selected or agreed-on effective carriage weight. The specimens are then unloaded, and the cycle repeated to determine the tension (or load) at the specified stretch. Load-elongation curves are plotted by an autographic recording instrument.

This method of test specifies the use of constant rate of load machines of the Inclined Plane type.

169   *Testing for Product Performance*

Conditioned specimens are subjected to a prescribed load recovery cycle run on the prescribed machine to determine the stretch at a specified load produced by a specified effective carriage weight.

This test is used to determine the stretch of an elastic fabric when subjected to a specified load less than the load required to rupture the fabric.

Change in Tension Due To Oxygen Pressure Aging

The tension of an elastic fabric is determined before and after exposure to accelerated aging by oxygen under pressure and reported as the percent change in tension due to oxygen aging. Aging may be carried out for one or more agreed upon times at a temperature of 158°F (70°C) or at a temperature agreed on by the parties concerned.

When used as a comparative test, the data obtained gives information on the relative resistance of aging (oxidation, etc.) of elastic fabrics.

Change in Tension Due To Dry Heat

The tension of a fabric is determined before and after exposure to dry heat for a specified period at a specified temperature. The change in tension is reported as percent loss of the original tension.

For change in tension due to dry heat, the times and temperatures generally accepted are (1) Test No. 1—two hours at 300°F (150°C), (2) Test No. 2—one hour at 275°F (135°C), and (3) Test No. 3—other times and temperatures may be agreed on by the parties interested in the test results.

If an elastic fabric shows less than 20 percent tension loss in Test No. 1, the fabric is considered as capable of withstanding commercial laundering. If the tension loss is 20 percent or greater in Test No. 1 but less than 20 percent in Test No. 2, the elastic fabric is considered satisfactory for home or domestic laundering.

Change in Tension, Dimensions, and Appearance Due To Laundering

The effect of laundering on the gain or loss in tension, on length and width changes, and on changes in appearance of an elastic fabric is determined by this test method.

This test is used to determine the changes in tension, dimension, and appearance of an elastic fabric when subjected to specified commercial or home laundry procedures. Tests for all three changes are made even though testing for only one or two changes may be of primary importance. The test and laundering conditions must be agreed upon by the parties interested in the test results.

Figure 5-38 A newly designed elastic tester. See text for description of the instrument. (Courtesy: Custom Scientific Instruments, Inc.)

Figure 5-39 A newly designed static extension tester. See text for description and use of this instrument. (Courtesy: Custom Scientific Instruments, Inc.)

New Equipment

Two new pieces of equipment have been developed to test: elastic fabrics (see Figure 5–38) and woven and knit stretch fabrics (see Figure 5–39).

ELASTIC TESTER

The Elastic Tester was designed to give the technician a versatile unit. Elastic fabrics may be tested for initial set, permanent set, and failure. The number of samples tested at one time may vary from one to four. The unit flexes four 1½-inch, two 3½-inch, or one 8-inch-wide samples. The stroke of the unit can be set up to eight inches on a nine-inch-long sample.

STATIC EXTENSION TESTER

The Static Extension Tester was developed to determine the stretch and recovery properties of woven stretch fabrics. Although particularly designed for woven fabrics, this test may also be applicable for knit fabrics, provided that the elongation at two pounds per inch is less than 85 percent. In the determination of fabric stretch good correlation between percent fabric stretch at two pounds per inch and "hand stretch" has been observed for a broad range of stretch fabrics.

The single-station tester consists of a vertical frame with a fixed clamp at the top, a 50-cm vertical scale, and a sliding clamp that operates within the scale range. With this unit is furnished a four-pound weight. The multistation unit consists of five fixed clamps and one single-station unit. The multistation units allow three tests each for two specimens at one time. The single-station unit is used to determine the fabric stretch and the five fixed station as well as the single station unit are used to determine the growth after elongation to a predetermined extension.

FABRIC HAND, RESILIENCE, STIFFNESS, DRAPE

Hand may be defined as an individual's reaction of the sense of touch when fabrics are held in the hand. There are many factors that give character or individuality to a material observed through handling. A fabric may feel* light, velvet soft, mellow, satin smooth, dry, papery, crisp, scroopy, sandy, bristly, heavy, harsh, rough, scratchy, furry, waxy, fuzzy, or downy soft.

The effect of finishing fabrics with starch, gums, lacquer, wax, water repellent compounds, or plastic or softening them with glycerine or oils require study to obtain the desired results. Hand or "handle" of a fabric is an illusive property and depends on the sense of touch. The term "smooth" has different meanings to different people. A satin is smooth; so is a cotton chintz but it is also stiff. Buckrum is stiff; chiffon limp; cashmere is soft, tweed is rough. Hand of a fabric is evaluated by the sensations of smoothness or roughness, hardness or softness, stiffness or limpness. These feelings may determine if a fabric is comfortable or uncomfortable to a wearer.

Resilience is a property that causes a fabric to spring back when it is crushed in the hand. The resilience of a fabric may be a very important psychological as well as physical value to the comfort of a fabric in wear or use.

Stiffness is defined as the resistance to bending. This property can influence the aesthetic appearance as well as the comfort of a fabric. For example: a stiff horsehair braid used to give a bouffant look to a skirt may make the wearer uncomfortable because of its stiffness. Some men object to wearing a 100 percent mohair suit because it is uncomfortable due to the stiffness of the fabric. Resistance to bending or flexual rigidity is called flex stiffness. There are several factors that affect fabric stiffness. For example, (1) a dress of 100 percent acetate has better drapability than one made of 100 percent polyester. (2) Highly twisted spun yarns usually reduce the draping qualities of fabrics. (3) Fine filament yarns are more pliable than the thicker filament yarns which are stiffer. (4) The thickness of a fabric also affects its stiffness and draping qualities. A coating or women's

* R. M. Hoffman, "Measuring the Aesthetic Appeal of Textiles," *Textile Research Journal*, Vol. 35, No. 5 (May 1965).

winter suiting will be quite stiff compared with a blouse. (5) Fabric finishes often reduce the drapability, especially the resin finishes used on cotton cloth.

Bending length is a measure of the interaction between fabric weight and fabric stiffness as shown by the way in which a fabric bends under its own weight. It reflects the stiffness of a fabric when bent in one plane under the force of gravity, and is one component of drape. Bending length is called drape stiffness.

Stiffness and resiliency tests are used to (1) aid in quality control and evaluation of products and materials, (2) provide standard for comparison of competitive products, (3) provide means of evaluating resilience (elastic or springlike) qualities of a variety of materials and products, and (4) provide standard for building in stiffness or elasticity.

There are two methods* used to test the stiffness of fabrics: (1) the Cantilever Test (preferred) and (2) the Heart Loop Test.

Both methods are applicable to fabrics of any fiber content. In general, these methods are more suitable for testing woven fabrics than for testing knitted ones.

Cantilever Test

This is the preferred method because it is simpler to carry out. It is, however, not suitable for testing fabrics that are very limp or that have a marked tendency to curl or twist at a cut edge. In many of these latter cases, the Heart Loop Test may be used.

The device used for this test is a Stiffness Tester (see Figures 5–40 and 5–41).

Shirley Stiffness Tester

A test specimen is cut to size with the aid of the template and then both template and specimen are transferred to the platform. Both are slowly pushed forward. The strip of fabric will commence to droop over the edge of the platform and the movement of the template (i.e., the scale) and the fabric is continued until the tip of the specimen viewed in the mirror cuts both index lines. The bending length can be read immediately. Each sample is tested four times, at each end and again with the strip turned over. Mean values for the bending length in warp and filling directions can be calculated and, if required, values for flexual rigidity and bending modulus.

Gurley Stiffness Tester

The Gurley Stiffness Tester consists of a balanced pendulum or pointer that is center pivoted and that can be variously weighted below its center. The pointer moves parallel to a ''sine'' scale, grad-

* Stiffness of Fabrics; ASTM Test Method D-1388 (1970).

Figure 5-40a Fabric stiffness, cantilever principle. A rectangular strip of fabric, 6 inches × 1 inch, is mounted on a horizontal platform so that it overhangs, like a cantilever, and bends downward. From the length *l* and the angle θ a number of values are determined.

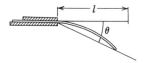

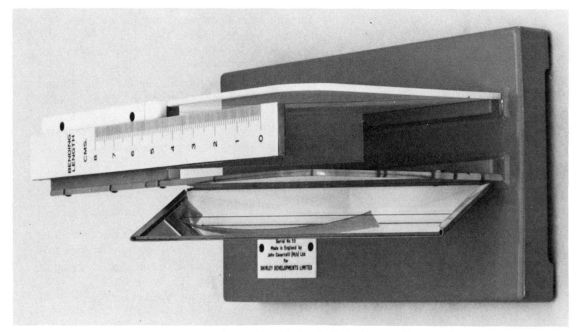

Figure 5-40b Shirley Stiffness Tester. See text for discussion of the use of this equipment. Fabric Stiffness Cantilever Principle. (Courtesy: Shirley Development Ltd.)

uated in both directions. In the test, the pointer is deflected by a sample of material pressed against its top end. The sample, cut to a standard length from one to four inches, and standard width, from one-half to two inches, overlaps the top of the pointer by one-fourth of an inch. The sample, being bent by the weight of the pointer, releases it. The point of release is taken as the test reading.

Heart Loop Test

Some fabrics are too flexible or limp to be tested using the cantilever principle.

A strip of fabric is formed into a heart-shaped loop. The length of this loop is measured when it is hanging vertically under its own

Figure 5-41 Gurley Stiffness Tester. See text for the use of this equipment. (Courtesy: Teledyne Gurley)

weight. From this length the bending length and flexual rigidity may be calculated (see Figure 5–42).

The two methods will not necessarily give the same numerical values or rank different types of fabrics in the same order. Both methods, however, can give an excellent correlation with a subjective evaluation of a given fabric type.

Figure 5-42 (a) The Heart Loop Test (stiff fabric) (b) The Heart Loop Test (limp fabric)

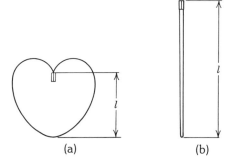

(a)   (b)

175 *Testing for Product Performance*

Drape

Draping qualities are related to fabric stiffness. How a fabric bends under its own weight is one indication of its drapability.

A highly drapable fabric is one that when hung can be arranged in folds. Many times the quality of "drape" is important to the designer who wants to achieve a graceful look. It has taken many years for scientists to develop test methods to measure these qualities objectively.

Booth* describes a simple method for measuring drape in which the warp and filling interacts and produces a graceful fold.

Figure 5-43 The circular specimen is "draped" over the circular support.

A circular specimen about 10 inches in diameter is supported on a circular disk about 5 inches in diameter and the unsupported area drapes over the edge (see Figure 5–43). If the specimen were a 10-inch piece of cardboard, no draping would occur and the area of projection from the periphery would equal the area of the cardboard. With fabrics the material will assume some folded configuration and the shape of the projected area will not be circular but something like the shape shown in Figure 5–44.

The FRL^R Drapemeter is one of the first instruments to be developed that can measure differences in draping properties among materials with equivalent or different bending rigidities (see Figure 5–45).

The FRL^R Drapemeter is useful for characterizing the draping properties of knitted and woven fabrics, apparel and decorative fabrics, nonwoven and disposable materials, and films. It is especially valuable in assessing changes in draping characteristics resulting from changes in fabric or nonwoven construction and from the use of special finishes or softeners. It finds application in quality control, product development, and consumer and textile research laboratories.

Figure 5-44 The projected outline of the "draped" specimen.

The instrument uses a circular sample of material that is draped over a table of substantially smaller diameter than that of the sample. A light source and lens located below the specimen projects an image of the draped sample shape upward where the image outline can be traced on paper. Materials are characterized in terms of a drape coefficient, which is obtained from the original area of the unsupported fabric annulus and the projected image of this same annulus of a fabric hanging in a draped configuration. The drape coefficient can, theoretically, range from zero to 100 percent.

HEAT TRANSFER OF FABRICS

Comfort in clothing is a complex interrelationship of temperature, humidity, air motion, and thermal radiation. It involves the physical principles of conduction, convection, radiation, and evaporative heat

* J. E. Booth, *Principles of Textile Testing,* Chemical Publishing Company, New York (1969), p. 287.

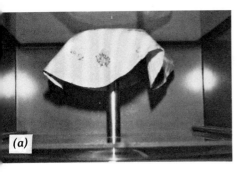

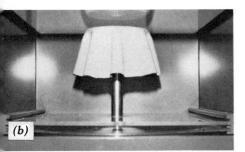

Figure 5-45 The FRL^R Drapemeter, an instrument used to measure fabric drape. A circular specimen is draped over the circular support. See text for discussion of the use of this equipment [(a) and (b) Courtesy: Rowena Dowlen, Textile and Clothing Laboratory, Mid-Atlantic Area, Agriculture Research Service, USDA, Knoxville, Tennessee. (c) Courtesy: IMASS]

losses from the human body. The test method* used to measure thermal transmission of fabrics is intended for use in determining overall thermal transmission coefficients due to the combined action of conduction, convection, and radiation. It measures the time rate of heat transfer from a warm, dry, constant-temperature, horizontal flat-plate up through a layer of the test fabric to a relatively calm, cool atmosphere.

By definition, "thermal transmittance" is a term that takes into account the overall heat transfer through the test fabric at a steady state and calculated in terms of BTU per hour per square foot of the fabric per degrees Fahrenheit difference between a hot plate and the cool atmosphere.

* Thermal Transmittance of Textile Fabric and Batting Between Guarded Hot Plate and Cool Atmosphere; ASTM D-1518-72.

4 SAFETY (TEXTILE FLAMMABILITY)

There is an increased awareness of the problems relating to textile flammability. This has resulted in investigating the fundamental burning characteristics of (1) fabrics, garments (sleepwear), carpets and rugs, and mattresses, (2) the development of testing methods, equipment and evaluation and (3) the development of products that offer increased protection from fire. Flammability standards presently exist for all fabrics used in wearing apparel, deriving from the Flammable Fabrics Act of 1954 and 1967. A recent series of additional flammability standards begun about 1970 include carpets and rugs (DOC FF1, 2-70), children's sleepwear sizes 0–14 (DOC FF3-72, FF5-74), and mattresses and mattress pads (DOC FF4-72). At this time, further deliberation is being given to proposed flammability standards for upholstered furniture (PFF6-74) and either specified apparel items (PFF7-74) or general wearing apparel [Mushroom Apparel Flammability Tester (MAFT)]. Table 5–5 summarizes the past federal flammability legislation. Under PFF7-74, it has been proposed that flammability standards for women's sleepwear, night robes, pajamas, dresses, and men's shirts and pants may proceed on à staggered basis, with 1976 set for women's sleepwear. Compounding PFF7-74 is the recent development of the MAFT tester by the National Bureau of Standards and recommended to the Consumer Product Safety Commission as a possible alternative to PFF7-74. It should be apparent that changes in fabric flammability legislation requires continual study in order to be aware of the items covered, the requirements for meeting the standards, and the conditions of compliance.

Although property and financial losses from fire are statistically large, most of the attention and concern has been directed toward the saving of lives. As it turns out, many of the improvements made for lifesaving reasons also result in a reduction of property loss and manufacturers' liability.

The Consumer Product Safety Commission is responsible for the safety of consumers. The functions of this Commission are discussed in Chapter 11. The National Fire Prevention and Control Administration (Chapter 11), has four responsibilities: (1) information gathering and analysis through the National Fire Data Center, (2) research and development utilizing as a part of this program the Fire Research Center at the National Bureau of Standards, (3) public education,

Table 5–5 Current Status of Fabric Flammability Legislation

Items Covered	Requirements for Meeting Standard	Effective Date	Extent of Compliance
Wearing apparel General standard (CS-191-53).	45° test. Samples exposed to a small flame and time measured to burn a fixed lenght of fabric is determined for comparison with test criteria.	July 1, 1954	All fabric must meet standards, unless replaced by a later standard below.
DOC-FF-2-70 Large carpets and rugs.	"Pill" test. In test sample, fire from a burning tablet of menthenamine does not spread more than 3 inches before going out. Test must be repeated on sample after 10 launderings.	April, 1971	All items must meet standard. Those not complying will be banned from the market.
DOC-FF-2-70 Small carpets and rugs, including bath mats less than 6 feet long and area no greater than 24 square feet.	Same as for large carpet and rugs.	December 1971	Items not meeting standard must be labeled: "fails U.S. DOC Standard FF-2-70. Should not be used near source of ignition."
DOC-FF-3-71 Children's sleepwear (sizes 0-6X), including fabrics intended for use in children's sleepwear.	"Vertical forced ignition" test. Samples exposed to flame before and after 50 launderings. Average char length of all samples must not exceed 7 inches in length and no single sample to have char length in excess of 10 inches. Afterflame period of melting and dripping can be no longer than 10 seconds.	July 1972 to July 1973	Garments not meeting the standard must be labeled "Flammable (does not meet U.S. DOC Standard FF-3-71). Should not be worn near sources of ignition."
	(As originally promulgated in 1970, no failure of any sample was allowed. Standard since amended to a more realistic sampling plan.)	July 28, 1973	All garments must meet standard. Those not complying will be banned from the market.
DOC-FF-4-72 Mattresses and mattress pads.	"Cigarette" test. Mattresses must resist ignition from 18 burning cigarettes placed at specified locations both on the bare mattress and between two sheets on the mattress.	May 31, 1972	Final standard issued, but "year of grace" to be allowed before compliance required.
	(Note: Cigarettes are used as ignition source because they have been found to be the principal cause of bedding fires.)	May 31, 1973	All items must meet standard. Those not complying will be banned from the market.
FF-5-74 Children's sleepwear, sizes 7-14.	Same as DOC FF-3, but no residual flame-time criteria.	May 1, 1975	All sleep garments must comply after effective date.
PFF-6-74 Upholstered furniture	"Cigarette" test on upholstery mockup.	Effective date undetermined	
PFF-7-74 Specified apparel.	Similar to FF-5 method. Requires 35 launderings. It is a fabric rather than a garment standard.	Proposed September 1, 1976	Includes six end-use garment categories.
MAFT (NBS) Mushroom Apparel Flammability Test.	Based on two tests: (1) surface ignition and (2) heat transfer.	Effective date undetermined	

and (4) establishment of an academy for fire fighters and fire prevention personnel.

One cannot appreciate the complexity of the flammability problem until he becomes actively involved. "The young child knows what fire is, yet the best technical brains cannot agree on a definition of a 'standard fire,'" said Lomartire.* A short trip into this ill-defined world suddenly brings one face to face with questions of economics, production capability, degree of protection required, original performance and performance in use.

One might raise the question, "What are we trying to protect against?" Pressures are at work to achieve the following objectives:

- Suitable flame-retardant apparel for children to protect them from garment involvement on exposure to a small ignition source.
- Carpeting that will not propagate a flame from a fully developed fire to another area that is not involved within a building of "fire-resistant" construction.
- Elimination of those fibers in building furnishings that add significantly to the smoke produced by the total fuel load.
- Suitable flame retardant apparel for the elderly to protect them from garment involvement on exposure to a small ignition source.
- For all wearing apparel, a general tightening of the current regulation CS-191-53 by another notch.

These objectives cannot be reached without giving consideration to the economic environment. Costs go up and the customer pays more. In addition to increased costs as a major tradeoff with improvements to be achieved, other tradeoffs or compromises generally include reduced fabric aesthetics, reduced choices, and related performance problems.

You will find that sometimes industry representatives approach the Consumer Product Safety Commission to present an alternate method of testing. For example, in 1975 J.C. Penney representatives† presented an alternative apparel flammability test method. They pointed out that the existing children's sleepwear test method is only for a vertical flame test with ignition at the bottom edge of the fabric while the Penney test is capable of edge ignition and plane surface ignition (see Figure 5–46). Testing specialists believe plane surface ignition provides a more realistic flammability test.

---

* John Lomartire, "Fibers and the Environment," paper given at the National Symposium on Fiber Frontiers, June 10, 1974.

† John Anderson, Maureen Grasso, and Martin Gavlak, "The Development of the Semi-Restrained Fabric Flammability Test," *Textile Chemists and Colorists,* Vol. 7, No. 6 (June 1975), p. 23.

Figure 5-46 A test sample showing the twin post, pilot light control, and ignition flame—the J. C. Penney tester. (Courtesy: J. C. Penney Co.)

There are three basic differences in the test methods used by the Consumer Product Safety Commission and Penney. They are (1) sample size, (2) the method of mounting the sample, and (3) the source of ignition.

The existing Consumer Product Safety Commission standards (DOC-FF3-71, FF5-74) consist of an inverted U-shaped frame which exposes a swatch of material, 2 inches by 10 inches, in place. The bottom edge of the fabric is ignited with a sliding flame which is pulled away after three seconds. Penney's semirestrained test method uses a larger piece of fabric, 6 inches by 15 inches, there is no frame, and a different ignition source is used. A clamp on top holds the chains on either side, which holds the material in place on the bottom. The chains are anchored one-fourth of an inch above the raw edge to simulate the hem of the apparel.

In the Penney test, with just a metal frame on top leaving the sides free, it is claimed that the researchers could get a more accurate picture of burn direction and time lapse before flame extinguishing.

The ignition source is the third difference in the two test methods. While the Consumer Product Safety Commission uses a sliding frame pointed in a 25-degree angle at the fabric, Penney uses twin posts that are placed on either side of the fabric. Flames are released from both posts simultaneously and join together to form a single flame to ignite the fabric.

This feature permits both edge and plane surface testing because the fabric can be lowered so the twin posts ignite the fabric separately and on either side of the fabric. Measurement of ease of ignition also is facilitated with this method.

At the same time, the National Bureau of Standards also developed a new type of test method different from those previously used. It measures two new fabric characteristics: ease of ignition and heat transfer.

NBS ACTIVITIES IN APPAREL FLAMMABILITY

The National Bureau of Standards (NBS) is under contract to the Consumer Product Safety Commission to investigate concepts for a new general apparel flammability standard. This led to the "Mushroom Apparel Flammability Test" (MAFT). The MAFT concept is that flammability standards should fulfill several requirements:

1. The test used should resemble real-life accidents as closely as possible in a laboratory environment.

2. The standard should provide a measure of the real-life hazard.

3. The test should be simple, repeatable, and reproducible.

4. The pass-fail criteria should be chosen to remove as many hazardous materials from the market without creating a shortage and yet be consistent with minimal decrease in consumer choice, serviceability, comfort, appearance and ease of care, as well as minimal increase in cost.

The draft proposed test simulates garment burns by using a vertical cylindrical specimen that is closed on top. The cylindrical specimen behaves during ignition and burning much like garments do and eliminates the need for frames and other unrealistic specimen suspension methods. This appears to be particularly important for 100 percent nylon and polyester fabrics that burn somewhat differently when held in frames than in garment form.

The hazard in apparel fires, according to Braun, Krasny, Peacock, and Stratton,* is a function of (a) garment configuration, (b) fabric ignitability, (c) rate of flame spread and heat transfer from the fabric to the victim's body, and (d) the duration of the burn, which should be related to extinguishability. The draft proposed standard, based on

* E. Braun, J. F. Krasny, R. D. Peacock, and A. Stratton, NBS Activities in Apparel Flammability; National Bureau of Standards, Washington, D.C. 20234 (December 1975).

the MAFT test, considers the first three items. Extinguishability is being explored under research grants to the University of Maryland and the Massachusetts Institute of Technology.

Garment fit affects hazard in two ways: loose-fitting garments are more likely to be exposed to ignition sources than tight-fitting garments. The draft proposed standard requires that the more hazardous loose, long garments be made from low flammability Class 1, fabrics—fabrics that, even when they burn, would transfer heat to the skin at a low rate. Tighter, shorter garments could be made of Class 2 and 3 fabrics that would transfer heat at a higher rate.

In addition to the garment classification, the proposed standard stipulates pass-fail criteria for two fabric flammability characteristics: ease of ignition and heat transfer to inside the cylindrical specimen. The first test consists of exposure of the specimen to surface ignition for a given time (one second). If the specimen fails to ignite, it would be in Class 2; if it ignites, in Class 3. If the specimen ignites in one-half second it is in Class 4 and the fabric could not be used in garments.

The second test measures the total heat transfer to the inside of the specimen. Skin suffers second-degree burns when exposed to approximately 8.4 joules per square centimeters [2.0 calories per square centimeters (cal/cm^2)] if the heat is delivered at the rate that usually occurs with burning cellulosic fabrics. If the heat is delivered at a lower rate more total heat is required for a second-degree burn. A test should measure the area of a simulated body exposed to this heat load. Such tests would be expensive, complex and very dependent on specimen and simulated body geometry. The MAFT compromises by measuring total heat flux rate received on specified surfaces inside the burning, cylindrical specimen. The assumption is that the heat delivered to the outside of the specimen is of secondary importance and that the more heat delivered to the inside, the greater the potential for large or deep burns, or both.

MAFT TEST PROCEDURE

A schematic drawing of the Mushroom Apparel Flammability Tester is shown in Figure 5–47. The specimen, 61 centimeters × 30 centimeters (24 inches × 12 inches), is suspended from a collar and pinned together. The collar is fitted over the top place, so that the specimen forms a cylinder.

Ignition is by a methane flame emerging from a No. 18 hypodermic needle. The flow rate of the methane is 110 cubic centimeters per minute. This results in an approximately 1.9-centimeter (three-fourths of an inch) flame length. A hook protrudes 0.9 centimeters (three-eighths of an inch) from the orifice of the needle. During ignition, it is brought in contact with the specimen, regulating the relative

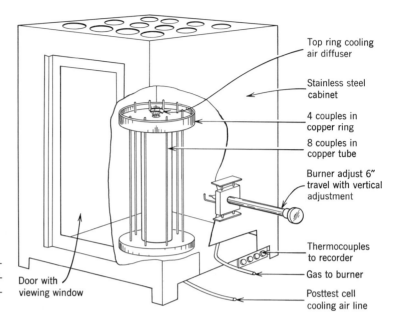

Figure 5-47 The Mushroom Apparel Flammability Tester. (Courtesy: Custom Scientific Instrument, Inc.)

Top ring cooling air diffuser

Stainless steel cabinet

4 couples in copper ring

8 couples in copper tube

Burner adjust 6" travel with vertical adjustment

Thermocouples to recorder

Gas to burner

Posttest cell cooling air line

Door with viewing window

position of flame and fabric. Ignition is on the specimen surface, 10 centimeters (4 inches) from the bottom of the specimen; flames can thus spread sideward and downward as well as upward. The heat transferred to the inside of the specimen is measured by 16 thermocouples attached to the inside of the blackened copper cylinder and 4 thermocouples attached to a sensor ring in the top plate. The joint output of all thermocouples is summed, weighted by the appropriate constants for the cylinder and top sensor. The total rate of heat transfer can thus be measured.

Ease of ignition is tested by letting the flame impinge on the surface of the fabric specimen, because this would be the normal way of ignition in real-life accidents. On the other hand, the heat transfer test is intended to be a simulation of the worst case conditions when the flames burn on both sides of the fabrics. This is achieved by cutting a small hole in the ignition area. Burning on both sides even without this hole begins soon after ignition in most fabrics; but some heavy or fire-resistant treated fabrics burn only on the outside in the MAFT. However, when the resulting char is broken, the flames spread to the inside, and the heat transfer rate increases significantly. Chars are generally very brittle and could be broken in real-life accidents by stresses on the garment due to the movement of the victim. The cutting of the hole thus appears a realistic way to simulate accidents.

In the heat transfer test, the maximum rate of heat transfer rather than the total heat is measured. The total heat depends greatly on test geometry, the fabric weight, and the duration of the burn. The maximum rate can be considered to be a material constant and more typical of the injury potential of the fabric.

The following is the tentative test procedure:

Ease of ignition: the specimen is mounted and the flame permitted to impinge for a specified time, for example, one-half or one second. If the fabric does not ignite, it is turned 90 degrees and the test repeated. If ignition occurs in a certain percentage of tries (yet to be determined) in one-half-second exposure to the flame, the fabric is Class 4. If ignition does not occur in one-half second, but in one second, the fabric is Class 3; it is does not occur in one second, the fabric is Class 2.

Heat transfer: the specimen is mounted and a hole made in the ignition area. Ignition time is 3 and 12 seconds. If the maximum heat transfer rate per unit area is less than 0.40 J/cm^2 s (0.096 cal/cm^2 s), the fabric is Class 1.

The standard error obtained in three replicate heat-transfer tests of commercial cotton, polyester/cotton, acrylic, acetate, and acetate blend fabrics ranged from 7 to 33 percent and averaged 14 percent. It was somewhat higher for 100 percent polyester and nylon fabrics that had very low heat transfer rates. The reproducibility of the ignition test is under investigation.

According to present thinking, no testing would be needed for fabrics that would be labeled "4." Only the ignition test would be needed for Classes 2 or 3 fabrics, which could be used in relatively tight-fitting garments covering about half of the body, for example, slacks, shirts, tight blouses, and so on. Only a heat transfer test would be needed for Class 1 fabrics that could be used in all garments, including robes, nightshirts, and dresses. Guidelines for definition of the tightness of fit required for Classes 1, 2, and 3 garments have been proposed. They are based on "ease" or "oversize" of garments, that is the garment-body distance as determined from the body dimensions listed in the U.S. Voluntary Sizing Standards for Apparel and the girth of the garment laid flat. A similar method for determining tightness or looseness of fit is used in the Australian children's sleepwear standard.

Drafts of the garment classification and drawings of the MAFT apparatus are available from NBS (Program for Fire Prevention—Products, Room B06, Building 225, National Bureau of Standards, Washington, D.C. 20234).

THE THERMO-MAN

Another example of independent flammability research is the Du Pont project on a new highly instrumented mannequin that can measure potential skin damage from flames and heat to a degree never before realized* (see Figure 5–48).

The mannequin has 114 heat-sensing devices. Computers connected with the mannequin produce data that enable researchers to plot the depth and extent of skin damage that would occur on a continuous time scale when various types of fabrics are ignited and burned.

Bercaw points out that the studies are planned to develop a more thorough understanding of the fundamental facts of fabric ignition and combustion and the transfer of heat from burning fabric to a human body. He says that while burning a yarn in an ash tray or aiming a flamming blow torch at a garment on a hanger may create a dramatic impression, such demonstrations bear little resemblance to real-life exposure. These demonstrations serve only to obscure facts rather than to reveal them.

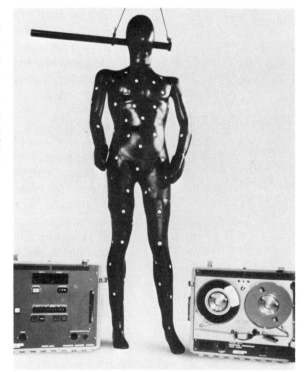

Figure 5-48 The Thermo-o-Man was constructed originally for a U.S. military study of protective clothing by the Aerotherm Division of the Acurex Corporation. The DuPont version of the mannequin is modified to provide data more pertinent to conventional wearing apparel and actual fire accident conditions. The 114 heat sensors record heat flow and intensity that can be translated by computer into a record of skin surface and tissue temperature and damage at varying depths and over precise areas of the body. (Courtesy: E. I. duPont de Nemours and Company, Inc.)

* J. R. Bercaw and K. G. Jordan, "Use of 'Thermo-Man' For Estimating Injury From Burning Garments." Paper presented at the Eighth Annual Meeting of the Information Council For Fabric Flammability 12/5/74.

The Thermo-Man studies are designed to provide highly detailed estimates of heat transfer from burning fabrics and a more quantitative understanding of apparel flammability from ignition to extinction.

Future studies are designed to develop basic data about the effects of garment design, fit, and condition, fabric composition, construction, finishes and maintenance, the conditions of ignition, the victim's reactions, and other factors involved in fabric flammability.

Information from the studies could assist in the development of improved fibers, as a guide in the development of new flammability tests for apparel fabrics to assure adequate protection without penalizing fabrics with demonstrated low injury potential.

From these examples it can be seen the interrelationship of business-industry-government in their concern that the consumer be offered fabrics or clothing for sale that may not contribute to a wearer's personal injury in a fire.

MINOR CONSUMER TEXTILE USE PROBLEMS OVERLOOKED

There are some consumer performance problems related to safety that have been overlooked. They are not covered by any test method.

There were a number of white quilted pads* that developed brown spots on them four to six inches in diameter accompanied by stiffness in the colored area. Microscopic and chemical tests showed that the batting in the pads was made up chiefly of polypropylene with some nylon and cotton.

The cause of the spots was the polypropylene. Polypropylene fiber is oxidizable. In a tumbler dryer, heat causes greater oxidation of the fiber and this produces more heat. If the fiber is covered or insulated so that the heat cannot escape, the kindling temperature of the polypropylene may be reached and a fire may result.

It is possible for a fiber manufacturer to put a wash-resistant antioxidant into the fiber to prevent this oxidation, but not all manufacturers of this fiber do so.

It is not unusual for a consumer, as well as a launderer or dry cleaner, to have a tumbler dryer fire. IFI's Textile Analysis Laboratory has received packages of charred material, metal hooks, and eyes on oxidized rubber. The normal heat of a tumbling operation rarely gets above 250°F. This temperature should not cause a fire with cotton and nylon fabrics unless some other factors are present that would raise the tumbler dryer temperature to the danger point.

* International Fabricare Institute Textile Notes 73 and 49.

Foam rubber used as stuffing of toys and some nonwoven fabrics used in garment design have also been responsible for fires. Foam rubber used in shoulder pads, and stuffed animals may reach the point of smoldering or burning under conditions of dry cleaning and laundering. Foam rubber pads should not be used in dry-cleanable garments unless they are recognizable and removable. Buttons made of cellulose nitrate can be a potential fire hazard in tumble drying.

Fingernail polish is seldom thought of as an incendiary. Certain lacquers, such as fingernail polish and collodion, will ignite or burn when heated to a temperature of between 400 and 500°F. Thus, the presence of a nitrocellulose lacquer on a fabric may cause a hole to burn in the fabric during ironing.*

FLAMMABILITY TEST METHODS

There are many tests methods and standards used in the United States for the evaluation of flammability of textile products. One of the best sources of information on this subject is *Textile Flammability, A Handbook of Regulations, Standards and Test Methods,* published by the American Association of Textile Chemists and Colorists. The book contains the standards of the Consumer Products Safety Commission, the Department of Transportation and the Federal Aviation Agency, sampling plans, requirements for various federal programs, state and city regulations, building codes, and existing and proposed test methods from various sources.

Flammability Of Clothing Fabrics (45° Angle Method) (CS-191-53)

This test† is designed to indicate textiles that ignite easily and, once ignited, burn with sufficient intensity and rapidity to be hazardous when worn. The method can be applied to the testing of textiles generally; however, the scale of evaluation is applicable only to textiles used for apparel, for which three classes of flammability are defined:

Class 1. Normal flammability. These textiles are generally accepted as having no unusual burning characteristics.

Class 2. Intermediate flammability. These textiles are recognized as having flammability characteristics between normal and intense burning.

Class 3. Rapid and Intense Burning. These textiles are considered dangerously flammable and unsuitable for clothing because of their rapid and intense burning.

* IFI's Textile Notes 10 and 33.

† Flammability of Clothing Textiles; AATCC Test Method 33 (1962). Flammability of Clothing Textiles; ASTM D-1230-72.

Preparation of samples for this method is very important. Preliminary tests are made to determine which face to test. For textiles with a pattern formed by varying depths or density of pile, tufting, and the like, the test samples are taken from the area that preliminary tests show to have the fastest rate of flame spread. Samples from garments are normally taken from the outer face of the garment; however, if the lining fabric has the fastest rate of flame spread in preliminary tests, then the lining surface is tested.

In the preliminary tests, samples are tested on both faces and in the lengthwise and crosswise direction and with and against any discernible lay, on a raised-fiber surface. For fabrics with a raised-fiber surface it has been found that the long dimension of the specimen should be parallel to the lay of the pile, and also that flame propagation is most rapid when progressing against the lay of the pile.

While all fabrics are to be tested in their original state, it is also necessary to dry clean, wash, and retest those fabrics known to contain a fire-retardant finish or to have any other condition that could cause their flammability classification to be changed by dry cleaning and washing. The samples are dried before testing. This puts the fabric in its most flammable condition.

The Flammability Tester measures the flammability of fabrics under carefully controlled conditions (see Figure 5–49). A mounted

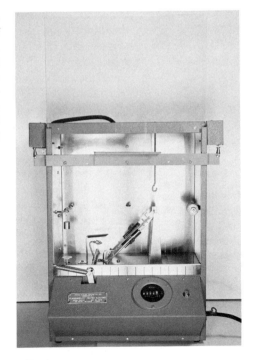

Figure 5-49 This flammability tester is an electromechanical device used to measure the flammability of clothing and textiles used for clothing (CS 191-53). The ignition medium consists of an electric-driven motor driven butane gas jet formed around a hypodermic needle. Timing starts automatically at the moment of flame contact and is stopped automatically. The panel-mounted electric timer registers the flame-rate spread in 0.1 sec. (Courtesy: U.S. Testing Co.)

specimen is placed in position on the rack in the chamber of the apparatus. The stop cord is strung through the guides in the specimen holder and through the guides at the rear of the chamber. The weight is hooked in place close to and just below the guide ring. The stop watch is set at zero and the door closed. The starting lever is brought over to the extreme right and released. This starts the timing mechanism and applies the flame for one second to the specimen. Timing is automatic, starting on application of the flame and ending when the weight is released by the burning of the stop cord. The time of flame spread of each specimen is recorded. The time of flame spread, the number of specimens tested, and the reporting of test results are made in accordance with procedures outlined in AATCC Test Method 33 (1962) and Commercial Standard CS 191-53.

Flammability Of Children's Sleepwear

Figure 5-50 The vertical flammability tester is used to make determination of the resistance of children's sleepwear. See text for discussion of the use of the equipment. (Courtesy: U.S. Testing Co.)

There are two standards for the flammability of children's sleepwear: (1) children's sleepwear sizes 0 up to 6X (DOC FF 3-71 as amended) and (2) children's sleepwear sizes 7 through 14 (FF 5-74).

The principal difference between DOC FF 3-71 and FF 5-74 is that the standard for the smaller sizes contains an additional test criterion that limits the length of time-flaming molten materials otherwise other fragments from any individual test specimen may continue to burn on the base of the test cabinet after exposure to a gas burner flame. Information available to the Commission, including accident data and reports of investigations, indicate that the risk of injury is less to older children because they are better able to protect themselves from fire. Therefore, the two standards should be different because they are directed toward reduction of different levels of hazard.

Under DOC FF 3-71, "Children's Sleepwear" means any product of wearing apparel up to and including size 6X, such as nightgowns, pajamas, or similar or related items, such as robes, intended to be worn primarily for sleeping or activities related to sleeping. The standard* provides a test method to determine the flammability of items of children's sleepwear. All items of children's sleepwear must meet the acceptance criterion.

Test specimens are cut so that they are tested in the direction that gives the greater flammability. Samples may be taken from yardage of a fabric lot or garments.

Five conditioned specimens, 8.9 × 25.4 centimeters (3.5 × 10 inches), are suspended one at a time vertically in holders in a steel test chamber (see Figure 5–50).

---

* Standard for the Flammability of Children's Sleepwear (DOC FF 3-71, as amended).

The chamber consists of a stainless steel draft-free cabinet with a hinged glass paneled door for observation of specimen during burning. The side mounted burner is manually positioned under the test specimen. The barrel of the burner is inclined at an angle of 25 degrees from the vertical. A needle valve is used for adjusting flame height. Accessories include five specimen holders, a stopwatch, a set of four weights, and a metal ruler to make length determinations. An asbestos pad is placed on the bottom of the cabinet and asbestos sheets are used for specimens that drip molten material.

The samples are subjected to a standard flame along their bottom edge for a specified time of three seconds under controlled conditions. The char length and residual flame time are measured. "Char length" means the distance from the lower edge of the specimen exposed to the flame to the end of the tear in the charred, burned, or damaged area.

"Residual Flame Time" is defined as the time from removal of the burner from the specimen to the final extinction of molten material or other fragments flaming on the base of the cabinet.

"Afterglow" means the continuation of glowing of parts of a specimen after flaming has ceased.

The procedure described above is carried out on finished items (as produced or after one washing and drying) and after they have been washed and dried 50 times according to Test Method AATCC 124 (1969). Items that do not withstand 50 launderings are tested at the end of their useful service life.

Alternatively, a different number of times under another washing and drying procedure may be specified and used, if that procedure has previously been found to be equivalent.

Laundering is not required of items that are not intended to be laundered. Items that are not laundered and labeled "dry clean only" are dry cleaned by a procedure which has previously been found to be acceptable.

All items of children's sleepwear must be labeled with precautionary instructions to protect the items from agents or treatments that are known to cause deterioration of their flame resistance. If the item has been initially tested after one washing and drying, it must be labeled with instructions to wash before wearing. The labels should be permanent and otherwise in accordance with rules and regulations (see Chapter 10).

Test Criteria And Sampling Plans

The test criteria of the DOC FF 3-71 standard are as follows: (1) the average char length of five specimens does not exceed 17.8 centimeters (7.0 inches); (2) no individual specimen has a char length of 25.4

centimeters (10 inches); and (3) no individual specimen has a residual flame time greater than 10 seconds.

However, in order to determine whether a specific fabric or garment passes or fails the standard, the test criteria noted above must be considered along with the detailed sampling plans incorporated in the final version of the standard as amended from the original version.

The amendment provides that (1) a manufacturer who can demonstrate similar operating characteristic curves (OC's) in his *own* sampling plan may submit it for approval as a substitute for DOC's sampling plan; (2) different colors or prints of the same fabric may be considered as a single production unit provided the test results demonstrate no significant difference in flammability performance; (3) *piece goods* that rely on fibers rather than finishes or additives for fire-resistant performance do not need to be washed 50 times by the fabric producer; (4) garments made from fabrics that are *warranted by the fabric supplier* to meet DOC FF 3-71, including the 50 wash provision, do not need to be laundered 50 times when testing the garment.

The method of sampling of *fabrics* is illustrated in Figure 5–51. In a 5000-yard sample, five specimens are taken at the beginning of the

Figure 5-51 Fabric production acceptance testing. [From *Textile Industry Products Safety News Letter,* Vol. 2, No. 4 (April 1974).]

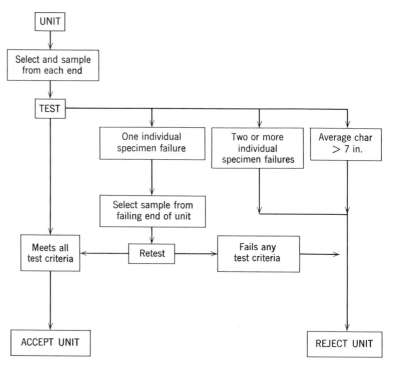

5000 yards. The sampling plan permits certain individual failures of items (2) and (3) of the test criteria (specimen char length and residual flame time) provided item 1 of the criteria is met, that is, the sample char length must be 17.8 centimeters (7.0 inches) or less. Therefore, if 1 specimen fails the standard provides for a retest of 5 specimens from the end that produced a failing specimen. On retest, all 5 must pass. If any 1 fails, the lot fails. If 2 or more of the original 10 specimens fail, the lot fails.

Reduced and tightened sampling involves testing procedures on piece goods that are to be followed in the event: (1) the fabric tests consistently are passing (reduced sampling) (2) the fabric tests give failing results (tightened sampling).

In the disposition of rejected units, the amendment provides for reworking a failed piece goods unit and retesting after the fabric is reworked. The amendment provides that the Federal Trade Commission will establish records of piece goods test results that must be maintained by the textile producer.

In prototype garment testing (see Figure 5–52), the amendment provides that all seams on designer or prototype garments must be

Figure 5-52 Garment prototype qualification. [From Textile Industry Products News Letter, Vol. 2, No. 4 (April 1974).]

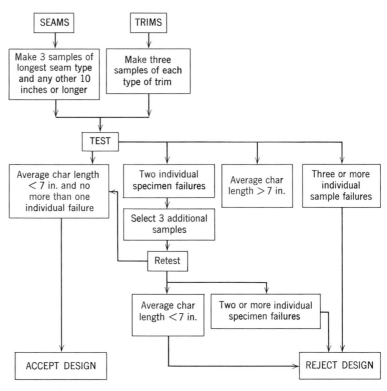

tested before the style is accepted for the line. For each seam that is different (merrow side seams would be the same even though there are two in the garment) 15 specimens must be prepared. For seams that are different (single needle, double needle, merrow, merrow shirr, flat lock, etc.) and that are less than 10 inches long in the garment, it is necessary to seam pieces of fabric to the 10-inch length and test 15 specimens. Again, the average char length criteria must always be met. Then, if none or one seam specimen from a group of 15 on the same seam fails, the design is accepted. If 2 out of 15 specimens fail, it is necessary to retest the same designs. If 3 or more specimens fail, the design is rejected.

In retesting the seam design after 2 specimen failures, if none or 1 specimen fails, the design is accepted. If 2 or more fail the design is rejected.

In testing the *prototype trim* it is necessary to sew the trim to a fabric to simulate the garment construction so that it is in the center of the specimen. For trim at hems, it is suggested that the trim be sewn between two pieces of fabric if the construction is merrow. If it is single needle or double needle, the trim is sewn in the center of a single 3½-inch × 10-inch specimen. The trim and design are accepted or rejected on the same basis as the seam prototypes.

In *production* testing, the amendment provides for testing only the longest seam. Production testing requires selecting 15 specimens, no more than 5 of which can come from one garment, on the longest seam from a unit of any size up to 500 dozen maximum. If the average char length criteria is met, and 3 or fewer specimens fail either residual flame time or char, the unit is accepted. If more than 3 fail, the unit is rejected. If the garments can be reworked, it is possible to do so and retest. If they cannot be reworked, they are rejected.

The prototype samples and results, both pass and fail, are kept with identifying records by the manufacturer. The failures are also retained to illustrate the design changes made to achieve garment styles that meet the standards.

The records and prototypes samples must be kept for three years. However, some save them for a longer period. In addition, another 15 prototype specimens, untested from each sample, are kept by the company so the tests could, if necessary, be duplicated later by the government.

It can be seen that considerable time, effort, and money are invested to assure the consumer that the products offered in the market place will give the safety quality desired to protect children.

TOXICITY

Toxicity may be defined as the state or degree of being poisoned. Toxicologists measure toxicity in biological systems. These quantitative measurements of toxicity, plus a knowledge of the conditions under which a material is used, enables an estimation of the hazards, or risks, associated with such use of a product. This traditional approach has been quite successful in anticipating harmful effects to man that could arise from the normal use of fibers and in preventing hazardous exposures.

Levinskas* defines toxicity as a quantitative measure of the capacity of a material to produce injury or death if enough of it reaches a susceptible tissue or organ. For example, cyanide is a toxic material, and a relatively small amount can sicken or kill a person if it gets absorbed into the body. This can be regarded as an inherent property of the cyanide ion. He defines hazard as the probability that harm will result from a given use of a material. The key word in the definition of hazard is "use." Despite the inherent toxicity of cyanide, cyanide baths are used in the electroplating of metals with relatively little hazard since the baths are kept alkaline to prevent evolution of gaseous hydrocyanic acid and workers are instructed to prevent direct skin contact with the cyanide solutions.

He further states that another feature of the term "hazard" is that it is a judgment, a qualitative decision, which is made on the basis of available information with respect to the degree of risk associated with a given use of a material.

Until recently, health concerns with fibers focused primarily on predicting reactions that could occur from wearing apparel. The probability of allergenic or dermatitic responses from synthetic fibers or from dyes and finishing agents for natural and synthetic fibers can be estimated and kept negligible by animal and/or human patch test. It is interesting to note that a report of even a few allergic responses to a synthetic fiber or a finish creates a rash of denunciations of that material even though the incidence of allergic responses may be low. Instead of recognizing that someone may be allergic to almost anything (the counterpart of toxicity) and that the synthetic fiber may even be beneficial to a person allergic to wool (the counterpart of hazard evaluation), we lose our objectivity in emotionalism.

News coverage of fires is dramatic and it fans the flame of concern over the flammability of synthetic polymers, including fibers, and the health hazards associated with their pyrolysis products. Certain unpleasant facts tend to be overlooked. People died in fires even be-

---

* George J. Levinskas, "Fibers and the Environment," paper given at the National Symposium on Fiber Frontiers, June 10, 1974.

fore synthetic fibers and other synthetic polymers were as widely used as they are today. In fact since the annual death toll from fires has been relatively constant in this country for about 20 years, and since our population has increased, the actual death rate from fires has been declining. To credit the use of synthetic polymers for this decreased death rate from fires is unfounded.*

The best fire retardants are halogenated materials. They can give off acid halides when they burn, thus adding other substances to a long list potentially hazardous pyrolysis products. A fire is an exceedingly complicated system that changes from moment to moment. At present, because of the impossibility of recreating and sustaining an average fire in a laboratory, it is virtually impossible to evaluate the relative contribution to the health hazards of any single component generated during the burning of even natural materials. Assessment of the added health hazards, if any, superimposed by the pyrolysis products of fire retardants is equally impossible.

In 1976 the Environmental Defense Fund (EDF) filed a petition with the Consumer Product Safety Commission against the chemical Tris (2.3-dibromopropyl phosphate).

An estimated 50 to 60 percent of the children's sleepwear and most other fire-resistant apparel contain the chemical that, according to the Environmental Defense Fund ". . . may represent a substantial cancer hazard to children and others. . . " The product is being investigated by the Consumer Product Safety Commission as a possible health hazard.

The manufacturer states that Tris is no hazard when properly applied to textiles.

The Consumer Product Safety Commission has been petitioned, by the Environmental Defense Fund to require warning labels for apparel of polyester fabrics treated with Tris, and urged washing new sleepwear three times to remove excess chemicals.

Tris is not easily water soluble, and trade sources say mills may not look favorably at afterwashing the treated fabric several times to remove the excess chemical, before shipping to customers, because of the increased time and cost factors.

Eight textile firms producing fire-retardant polyester fabrics for the children's sleepwear market are said to be evaluating a chemical that might compete with or replace the one now used. The new chemical is described as "a total phosphorous material . . . that is water-soluble." The treated fabric goes through an afterwash to remove the excess chemical that does not contain any bromine or halogens.

* Anon., "Fires and Fire Losses Classified," 1872. *Fire Journal*, 23–26 (September 1973).

5 CARE

Care of modern-day fabrics is dependent on the fiber content, yarn construction, and fabric construction, the variables of dyeing and printing that give a fabric its color and design, the variables of finishing that give a fabric aesthetic or performance properties and the variables of surface design application. But just as important are the design, construction, and fashion details and all the components combined to make wearing apparel and household items. Also, many times it is the degree and type of soil or staining that governs the selection of the best method of care.

In this chapter we consider the test methods and equipment devised to test products to bleaching, laundering, and dry cleaning and the resultant changes in fabrics, such as dimensional change, loss or change in color, finishes, and design applications.

BLEACHING Colorfastness of dyes and loss of strength from bleaching is an important consideration in both home and commercial laundering. Proper care methods for use of bleach are discussed in Chapters 7 and 8.

Oxidizing agents convert the cellulose in cellulose fabrics, such as cotton, linen, or rayon, into oxycellulose. Oxycellulose is much weaker than cellulose. The oxidizing agents are usually bleaching compounds such as hydrogen peroxide or sodium hypochlorite. Such agents are used in the home and in commercial laundering.

When a fabric comes in contact with a bleaching agent for too long a time or in too high a concentration, oxycellulose is formed and the fabric is weakened. Flexing of the fabric in laundering is sufficient to cause the weakened area to develop into a hole.

Some consumer problems result from the misuse of bleach. For example: household bleaches used full strength for cleaning purposes can seriously weaken the fibers in the cleaning cloth unless the bleach is thoroughly rinsed out. Furthermore, other fabrics that come in contact with the cleaning cloth can be damaged.*

Household bleaches containing sodium or calcium hypochlorite have been used for several years as disinfectants and deodorizers. Currently, many different brands are being recommended in na-

* IFI's Textile Note 34.

tional advertising for use in cleaning sinks and other porcelain surfaces as well as tile and linoleum.

When these bleaches are used full strength for cleaning such surfaces, the cleaning cloth will be weakened. This weakness is even more serious if the bleach is not thoroughly rinsed out. Further damage to other fabrics may result from contact with the unrinsed cleaning cloth. If a cloth saturated with a hypochlorite bleach is dropped into a laundry hamper or laundry bag, any cellulosic fabric that comes in contact with the cleaning cloth will be weakened by the household bleach.

In some cases, retention of chlorine can cause a problem. Manufacturers may use formaldehyde resins to improve the crease resistance of a fabric, to stabilize a fabric for shrinkage control, or to give permanency to embossed designs. This type of resin combines with chlorine from a chlorine-type bleach bath.

It is sometimes necessary to bleach fabrics treated with a formaldehyde resin. The presence of this resin in the fabric is usually not recognizable. When placed in a chlorine bleach bath, the fabric usually turns yellow and may be weakened. When the resin combines with chlorine, it is very difficult, if not impossible, to rinse the newly formed compound from the fabric. When the fabric is dried and pressed, the resin-chlorine compound breaks down, causing the yellow discoloration and releasing hydrochloric acid. The acid causes the fabric to become weakened and may cause it to disintegrate.

Fabrics treated with a formaldehyde resin should not be bleached in a chlorine-type bleach bath. If a fabric so treated is bleached in chlorine, it should be treated immediately with a neutralizing agent like sodium bisulfite before pressing. Other bleaches such as hydrogen peroxide and sodium perborate may be used safely on this type of fabric.

The test methods devised to evaluate the effect of bleach on fabrics include colorfastness to bleaching with chlorine, colorfastness to bleaching with peroxide, and loss of strength due to chlorine bleach.

Colorfastness To Bleaching With Chlorine

This test method* is applicable to cotton and linen textiles and mixtures whether dyed, printed, or otherwise colored, which may be subjected to solutions containing up to 0.3 percent available chlorine.

Bleached muslin or lightweight cotton cloth colored with standard dye solutions serve as a control. A test sample and samples of the appropriate control dyeings are washed in hypochlorite solution under controlled conditions.

* Colorfastness to Bleaching with Chlorine; AATCC Method 3 (1972).

The samples are evaluated for color changes and staining of multifiber test fabric. The effect on the color of test fabric by each of four tests with different concentrations of available chlorine, is evaluated and the colorfastness classified by comparison with the Gray Scale for Color Change: Class 5, negligible or no change and Class 1, staining equivalent to Row 1 on the AATCC Chart or Step 1 on the Gray Scale for Staining.

Colorfastness To Bleaching With Peroxide

This test method* is intended for evaluating the resistance of the color of fabrics of all kinds except polyamide to the action of bleach baths containing peroxide at concentrations commonly employed in textile processing. But the same principles may be adopted to testing fabrics for colorfastness to bleaching with peroxide in home washing.

A sample of the fabric is placed in contact with specified white cloths and is immersed in the bleaching solution, rinsed, and dried. The change in color of the specimen and the staining of the test cloths are evaluated. Color change is evaluated by alteration of shade and strength by classifying the effect on the color of the test specimens by reference to the Gray Scale for Color Change: Class 5, negligible or no change as shown in Gray Scale Step 5, and Class 1, a change in color equivalent to Gray Scale Step 1. Staining is classified by the AATCC Color Transference Chart or the Gray Scale for Staining: Class 5, negligible or no staining and Class 1, staining equivalent to Row 1 on the AATCC Chart or Step 1 on the Gray Scale for Staining.

Loss Of Strength Due To Chlorine Bleach

There are two test methods†,‡ used to measure loss of tensile strength: (1) a multiple sample method and (2) a single sample accelerated test. Many factors, such as pH, concentration, and time, significantly influence the amount of damage caused by retained chlorine.

In the multiple fabric test, the samples are chlorine bleached in a domestic-type laundry machine, rinsed, dried and pressed between hot metal plates (see Figure 5–53). The damaging action of the retained chlorine is calculated from the difference in tensile strength before and after pressing. The percent lost is calculated by the formula:

$$\frac{Tc - Tcs}{Tc} \times 100 =$$

* Colorfastness to Bleaching with Peroxide; AATCC Test Method 101 (1972).

† Chlorine Retained, Tensile Loss: Multiple Sample Method; AATCC Test Method 114 (1971).

‡ Chlorine Retained, Tensile Loss: Single Sample Method; AATCC Test Method 92 (1971).

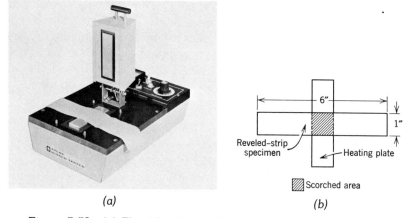

(a)   *(b)*

Figure 5-53 (*a*) The Atlas Scorch Tester provides controlled conditions of temperature and pressure that meet AATCC and ISO instrument requirements for retained chlorine, colorfastness to hot pressing, and colorfastness to dry heat (sublimation) tests. It consists of one or more sets of heated plates. The lower plate is set in a fixed position in the base of the instrument. The upper plate is mounted in a hinged head that may be raised to permit the loading or removal of samples. In its closed position the Scorch Tester head rests on four spring-loaded pins. These pins counterbalance a percent of the head weight and the plate pressure on specimen than conforms to chlorine retention test-method practice. One model is a multiple plate unit featuring five pairs of individually controllable plates. Each pair may be set at a different temperature allowing rapid identification of sample failure point. A typical test might use 15°C, with steps going to 140°, 155°, 170°, 185°, and 200°C. Failure at 170°C, would allow the sample to meet the ISO range II but not range III standard. This model is ideal for laboratories where large numbers of samples must be tested or screened. (*b*) Specimen on heating plate. (Courtesy: Atlas Electric Devices Co.)

percent loss in tensile strength due to damage caused by retained chlorine

where Tc = average tensile strength of chlorinated specimens, unscorched, and

Tcs = average tensile strength of chlorinated specimens, scorched

The single sample test has been designed for use on cotton and rayon fabrics, but may be used on any fabric or finish that is not damaged by heat alone.

The fabrics are treated in sodium hypochlorite solution, rinsed, dried, and pressed between hot metal plates. The damaging action of the retained chlorine is calculated from the difference in tensile strength before and after pressing. The calculation of damage caused by the retained chlorine is calculated by the formula given above.

DIMENSIONAL CHANGE

Fabric stability in wear and care is a very important consideration if wearing apparel or household items are to give consumer satisfaction. The Standards L22—Performance Requirements for Textile Fabric—establishes shrinkage tolerances for various classes of merchandise. Stretching of a fabric can be as great a problem as shrinking in cleaning; however, both can cause consumer dissatisfaction. This has resulted in using the term "dimensional change" to describe change in direction.

Dimensional change in fabrics is a very complex phenomenon. It can be explained by fiber, yarn, and fabric construction characteristics.

Relaxation Shrinkage

Most fabrics are produced under tension that leave strains in the fabric. Unless these strains are fully released by the manufacturer before the fabric is made into a garment, relaxation shrinkage will ultimately occur. Relaxation shrinkage is the tendency of the yarns to revert to their normal, unstretched dimensions. In many cases, sizings or finishes help keep the fabric in its stretched condition.

If a fabric has not been fully relaxed by the manufacturer, cleaning and steaming, using normal finishing practices, will cause the fabric to continue its relaxation and shrinkage. Usually several cleanings will be required to relax it completely. Laundering or dry cleaning may partially or wholly remove any sizings or finishes that tend to stabilize the fabric dimensions.

Many good methods are available to preshrink and to stabilize fabrics in textile manufacture. A fabric may be stretched, then relaxed and treated either mechanically or chemically to hold the shrinkage to a certain tolerance. The shrinkage that remains in the fabric is known as "residual shrinkage." Many consumers have learned that the added cost for a preshrunk or stabilized fabric is a worthwhile investment.

It has been observed that synthetic fibers of vinyl and vinyl copolymers (Movil, Kurchalon, Rhovyl, Saran, and Rovana) shrink in perchlorethylene. This is believed to occur because of molecular orientation and, consequently, fiber relaxation caused by a slight takeup of the solvent by the fiber, hence, shorter fabric dimensions.

Relaxation shrinkage occurs when these fabrics are dry cleaned in perchlorethylene. Therefore, fabrics made of these fibers should be dry cleaned in petroleum solvent. However, if construction of the item permits, they may be wet cleaned or laundered.

Swelling Shrinkage— Hydrophilic Fibers

Fibers that pick up moisture will swell. This can cause shrinkage in rib-weave fabrics and in rib variations. These include some failles, Gros de Londres, epingles, grosgrains, bengalines, and ottomans. Shrinkage is usually greatest in the rib-weave fabrics made of wool, rayon, cotton, acetate, or a combination of any of these. Shrinkage of rib-weave fabrics is due to two causes: (1) the fabrics are not relaxed, and (2) the fiber content and weave construction makes them susceptible to swelling shrinkage. Usually rayon or acetate yarn is used in the warp or lengthwise direction of the fabric. The heavy crosswise rib is usually made of rayon and cotton. These rib fibers swell more than acetate when wet. When they swell, they pull the ribs close together and shrinkage occurs.

Shrinkage may occur when these garments are dry cleaned, wet cleaned or laundered. Some may shrink even when steam is used in finishing them.

Fabrics may be preshrunk by methods available in modern textile finishing plants, although the relaxation of rib-weave fabrics is more difficult than that of others. This group of fabrics should be cleaned in solvent with low solvent relative humidity. Wet cleaning or laundering results in the risk of excessive shrinkage.

Felting Shrinkage

Felting shrinkage may occur in fabrics made of wool and hair fibers. The wool and hair fibers possess a natural tendency to shorten and mat together. This is called "felting" shrinkage. Any fiber that has a scaly surface structure has a natural tendency to felt. The tendency to mat is more pronounced in angora than in wool or other hair fabrics. Woolen fabrics, containing small percentages of angora, shrink much more readily than do all-wool fabrics. Soft, loosely woven wool fabrics, especially those of high-grade wool fibers, have a tendency to felt more than hard-finishing wool fabrics.

Felting shrinkage can result from: (1) excessive mechanical action during cleaning and drying, (2) high temperature along with tumbling action in drying, and (3) high relative humidity of the solvent during dry cleaning.

Recommended drycleaning plant practices and recommended home washing practices for handling these specialty items will usually control this problem. Once a fabric has become felted, it is impossible to stretch it back to its original size.

Heat Or Thermal Shrinkage

The physical properties of hydrophobic fibers change with the temperature.* It is well established that far below the glass transition temperature, every polymer chain is essentially trapped in one of its many possible geometrical arrangements. The polymeric material behaves as a glassy elastic solid. In the vicinity of the glass transition temperature or above, extensive deformation can take place.

Since most textile polymers are semicrystalline, that is, they possess amorphous and crystalline regions, their response to temperature changes is complex.

Thermal shrinkage of textile polymers occurs if the fibers are exposed to temperatures in excess of the glass transition temperature but kept below the crystalline melting point. The magnitude of the shrinkage depends on the fiber morphology and on external variables such as temperature, tension and time. It is believed that the thermal energy breaks the intermolecular cohesive forces between the polymer chains which leads to an increased mobility of chain segments. Residual orientation stresses in the fiber are released under these conditions. At even higher temperatures, the whole polymer chain can rearrange into a new configuration of lower free energy. As discussed earlier, the localized disruption of intermolecular order can also be generated by solvents that can act as plasticizers. A combination of both mechanisms may be involved during extreme drying conditions in dry cleaning. However, no experimental data have been published to verify this hypothesis.

Heat setting plays an important role with respect to end-use properties of hydrophobic textile fabrics. Hearle and Miles† have summarized the theoretical and practical aspects of this important operation. The setting of fibers or fabrics should be permanent so that no dimensional changes can occur during dry cleaning or laundering.

Progressive Shrinkage

Relaxation shrinkage and swelling shrinkage seldom reach their maximum in the first cleaning. These forms of shrinkage continue through successive cleanings. This is called progressive shrinkage.

* Manfred Wentz, "Knit Shrinkage in Drycleaning—Statistics and Causes," *International Fabricare Bulletin NOTCT-11* (1973).

† J. W. S. Hearle and L. W. C. Miles, *The Setting of Fibers and Fabrics.* Merrow Publishing Co. Ltd., Waterford, Herts, England (1971).

Progressive shrinkage may not become noticeable until the third or fourth cleaning in an overstretched, sized fabric. Some fabrics may continue to shrink a little each time they are cleaned. Maximums have been reached in tests anywhere from the second to tenth dry cleaning.

Progressive shrinkage may be controlled by relaxing or preshrinking fabrics before they are made into garments.

Unequal Shrinkage

No test procedure takes into account unequal shrinkage. This may be traced to yarn and fabric construction and is a common occurrence in towels and table linens.

Although towels develop a substantial shrinkage when first washed, the decrease in towel size caused by this shrinkage usually causes no consumer complaint. Manufacturers of towels do not use a preshrinking treatment on the theory that maintenance of original size of a towel, within limits, of course, is not essential to its utility. The important characteristic of a towel is that absorbency of the fabric, and the total absorbency is not affected by shrinkage.

Towels, however, are decorative as well as useful and, therefore, are produced in a multitude of colors and designs. A uniform shrinkage does not affect the appearance of a towel, but localized shrinkage causes the towel to become puckered and distorted, which naturally results in consumer dissatisfaction.

Distortion or damage in linen damask tablecloths may result from unequal shrinkage. This type of shrinkage is found chiefly in "double" damask linen tablecloths. It is not a problem in "single" linen damask or in cotton damask cloths.*

Unequal shrinkage is due to localized contraction of some of the warp yarns, which occurs during washing because of the residual shrinkage in these particular yarns.

In many cases this shrinkage occurs in lengthwise colored stripes or figured patterns. Excessive localized contraction of warp yarns just inside the selvages causes borders to pucker and often results in actual ruptures of the fabric near selvages. Unequal shrinkage may also cause linen damask to increase in thickness in local areas, sometimes as much as 20 percent.

Excessive cases of unequal shrinkage make good ironing and folding an impossibility. Similarly, breakage of the fabric may occur when yarns that have shrunk disproportionately are subjected to normal strain during ironing.

The fact that only a few of the yarns shrink excessively precludes the possibility of the unequal shrinkage being due to the washing

* IFI's Textile Note 1.

treatment. During washing, all sections of the material receive uniform detergent action. Regardless of the washing process used, a linen tablecloth that has a tendency to develop unequal shrinkage will eventually do so. Although the shrinkage may not be particularly noticeable during the first few washings, the cumulative effect of this unequal shrinkage becomes apparent after a number of washings.

Since unequal shrinkage of linen damask is a result of inherent residual shrinkage of certain yarns, and thus originates in the manufacturing process, variations in the washing formula will not eliminate this problem.

Shrinkage: Apparent—Not Actual

Increased weight of an individual will naturally make garments fit more snugly. When this occurs, the individual's first thought is that the garment has shrunk.

This apparent shrinkage occurs most often when a garment is cleaned and then stored for a period of time before wearing. Snugness is noted when the garment is brought out for the next season of wear. A simple check can be made to determine if the garment has shrunk. If a dress or suit fabric has actually shrunk, it will, in most cases, shrink to a greater degree than the lining, sewing thread, slide fastener, hem, and seam tape. If the garment has shrunk, the tape along the slide fastener, the seam line, or the lining will pucker. If the garment shows none of these tell-tale indicators, shrinkage has probably not occurred and an increase in the measurements of the wearer is most likely the answer.

Stretching— Loss Of Shape

There are several trends in the textile and fashion fields that have resulted in an increased number of problems or complaints of stretching during dry cleaning, finishing, and wet cleaning. They are increased use of acrylic fibers (Orlon, Acrilan, Creslan, Zefran) in knitting yarns and fabrics, both domestic and imported, texturizing of yarns, a greater variety in knitted fabric constructions, scarcity of finishes that inhibit sag and stretch in knit fabrics and permanently stabilize them, and an increase in the production and sale of knitting yarns.

Many knitting yarns on the market today are made of heat-sensitive fibers that shrink excessively when exposed to heat in drying and finishing. Many knitting yarns are made of acrylic or acrylic-blended yarns that may shrink or stretch in cleaning and finishing.

In some fabric construction, when a fabric shrinks in the lengthwise direction, it will stretch in the crosswise direction. Wear alone may stretch some fabrics out of shape, for example, bagging at the knees and the seats of trousers, or stretching of a knit garment in wear.

If some garments are hung to dry while they are dripping with water or solvent, they may be stretched out of shape. This is particularly true of knits, although not confined to them. Some garments may stretch with manipulation in steam finishing, while the fabric is warm and moist from steam.

The tendency to stretch in most cases may be controlled by yarn and fabric construction. Proper care of fabrics in use and cleaning will eliminate many such problems.

TEST METHODS FOR DIMENSIONAL STABILITY

We first consider the laundering of woven and knitted fabrics except wool. The test method* determines the dimensional changes of woven or knitted fabrics, made of fibers other than wool, to be expected when the fabric is subjected to laundering procedures commonly used in the commercial laundry and the home. Four washing test procedures are given, varying in severity from very severe to very mild. They cover the range of practical washing from commercial procedure to hand washing.

Five drying test procedures are given to cover the range of drying techniques used in the home and commercial laundry. Three methods for determining the dimensional restorability characteristics are given for those fabrics that require restoration by ironing or wearing after laundering. These tests are not accelerated and must be repeated to evaluate dimensional changes after repeated launderings (see Figures 5–54 to 5–57).

Table 5–6 contains the various washing, drying, and restoration procedures. The person using these tests must determine which combination of procedures is practical for any specific item in order to evaluate the dimensional changes of textile fabrics or garments after laundering procedures commonly used in the home or commercial laundry.

A specimen or garment is washed in a cylindrical reversing wash wheel, dried and subjected to restorative forces where necessary. Temperature and time of agitation in the wash wheel are varied to obtain different degrees of severity. Drying procedures and application of restorative force procedures are varied to conform with end-use handling during home or commercial laundering. Distances

* Dimensional Change; AATCC Test Methods 96 (1972); 99 (1972); 135 (1970); and ASTM D-1905.

Figure 5-54 A Flat Bed Press is used for distortion-free pressing. The perforated base plate is covered with a piece of felt or some similar moisture-absorbing material. The pad so formed is then covered with a piece of bleached sheeting or broadcloth. The press is turned on and allowed to heat to the desired temperature. The fabrics to be pressed are then dampened and placed on the pad of the press. The fabric is carefully and gently smoothed by hand to remove wrinkles but not distorted or stretched in any way. The head of the press is then lowered and left on the specimen until the sample is completely dry. (Courtesy: United States Testing Co.)

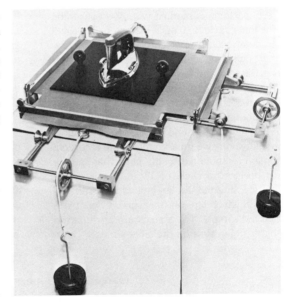

Figure 5-55 This method is intended for determining the dimensional restorability of woven fabrics. A marked specimen that has been laundered, pressed, and measured to determine dimensional change is rewet and pressed under tension until dry. The dampened specimen is placed on the bed of the Tension Presser. Using the chart below, select and apply the proper weights for both the warp and filling directions.

Dimension Change as Obtained after Flat-Bed Pressing		Calibrated Weight to be Applied on Tension Presser
Any gain	−1.0% loss	½ lb
1.1	−3.0% loss	1 lb
3.1	−5.0% loss	3 lb
5.1% or more loss		4 lb

The specimen is allowed to remain under tension during the drying operation. The perforated drying plate is heated and applied to the specimen. The specimen is measured at each of the appropriate reference points in both directions and the average change reported in the dimensions of the warp and filling. (Courtesy: U.S. Testing Co.)

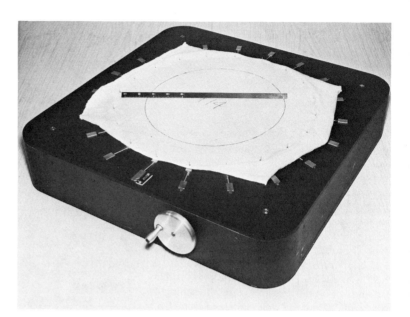

Figure 5-56 The Knit Shrinkage Gauge is designed for measuring knitted fabric shrinkage.

The test specimen is marked with two concentric circles. The inner circle is 10 in. in diameter. This circle is used to determine the percent shrinkage by comparing the original diameter with the diameter after laundering, drying, and being subjected to the tensions of restoring. The outer circle, which consists of 20 equidistant dots, is 14 in. in diameter and is used as a guide in mounting the sample on the tension pins.

After marking, the fabric is laundered, tumble dried, and the shrinkage measurements are recorded. Then the fabric is mounted on the pins when in their innermost position (a circle of 11 in. in diameter). Each pin is connected to an individual calibrated spring through which tension (measured in grams) is exerted on the sample. The springs are anchored to guides that travel in slots on the table surface. These guides are moved in and out by a slotted disc. A hand wheel operates the drive.

After the fabric is mounted on the pins the guides are driven to their outermost position. In this condition an equilibrium is reached between the restraining force of the fabric and the tension of the extended springs. The restored shrinkage measurements are then taken in both the length and width directions of the sample.

The measurement of percent shrinkage is simplified through use of a 10-in. scale calibrated in terms of percent shrinkage.

The determination of restraining force can be made from the extension of the springs or from the diameter of the sample under tension, expressed as percent shrinkage. A graph relates percent shrinkage to restraining force. (Courtesy: U.S. Testing Co.)

marked on the specimen in warp and filling directions (or wales and courses for knitted fabrics) are measured before and after laundering.

The preparation of test specimens will vary depending upon the type of dimensional restorability procedure (if any) to be used. In measuring garments, critical measurements in length and width directions should be taken before and after washing, drying, and restorative procedures.

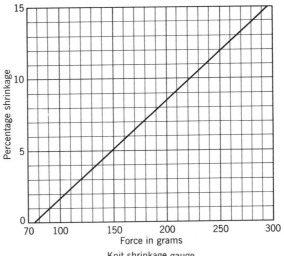

Figure 5-57

Knit shrinkage gauge
Shrinkage in percent vs. force in grams

In fabric samples, it is necessary to mark distances on a sample in both lengthwise and widthwise directions and to measure before and after laundering. The distances may be marked with indelible ink and a fine-point pen, by sewing fine threads into the fabric, or by a specially designed stamping machine. The marked distances are parallel to the respective yarns. Usually, the greater the original distances

Table 5–6   Washing, Drying, Restoration Procedures

Washing Procedure	Drying Procedure	Restoration Procedure
I. 100–109°F for 30 min	A. Drip dry	1. Tension presser
II. 120–129°F for 45 min	B. Flat-bed press dry	2. Knit shrinkage gauge
IIx. 140–149°F for 45 min	C. Screen dry	3. Hand iron
III. 160–169°F for 60 min	D. Line dry	
IV. 203–212°F for 60 min	E. Tumble dry	

The test used may be identified by a code, consisting of a Roman numeral, a letter, and an Arabic numeral. For example Test IIIE1 refers to a specimen that has been washed by procedure "III" at 160°F for a total of 60 minutes in the machine, has been dried in a tumble dryer by procedure "E" and has been subjected to restorative forces on the tension presser by procedure "1."

209   Testing for Product Performance

marked, the greater will be the accuracy of the test. Distances of less than 10 inches are not recommended. To facilitate ease of marking and measuring, the author prefers a 20-inch × 20-inch square measured with tempered metal rule graduated in 50 (0.2) inches. An average of three measurements are made in each direction. The following formulas are used for calculations:

$$\text{Percent shrinkage} = \frac{\text{original length} - \text{final length}}{\text{original length}} \times 100$$

$$\text{Percent stretch} = \frac{\text{final length} - \text{original length}}{\text{original length}} \times 100$$

Fractional measurements should be changed to decimals. A minus sign (−) in front of the percent indicates shrinkage; a plus sign (+) indicates stretch.

There is a specially designed test (AATCC 99-1972) for measuring felting and relaxation shrinkage in woven or knitted wool textiles. The method is an accelerated test for determining the relaxation and felting shrinkage of woven and knitted textiles containing at least 50 percent wool.

Relaxation shrinkage is determined by soaking measured specimens in a sesquicarbonate solution, hydroextracting, drying, and remeasuring.

Felting shrinkage is determined by washing measured specimens in a soap, polyphosphate, borax solution, or a soap, polyphosphate, sesquicarbonate solution in a rotary washer of the reversing type, rinsing, hydroextracting, drying, and measuring.

COLOR FASTNESS TO DRY CLEANING

Many people believe that although the color of a fabric may change in laundering, there is no need to worry about color change in dry cleaning. This is a misconception as the solvents used in the dry cleaning process can cause loss or transfer of dye in dry cleaning.

Several conditions during the dyeing and printing of a fabric may contribute to the transfer or loss of color in dry cleaning: (1) an excess amount of dye may be left in the fabric; (2) the proper amount of dye may be used, but it may not be fixed properly to the fabric; (3) a dye may be used that is solvent soluble—the dye bleeds in dry cleaning solvents; and (4) there may be improper selection of dyestuff for the particular fabric.

In some cases, the original hue remains; in others, it becomes lighter in color. The dye may be carried off in the dry-cleaning solvent, or it may transfer to a lighter background of the fabric or to lighter trim of a garment.

The dye may bleed and transfer in dry cleaning while the solvent is being removed from the fabric or while the fabric is being dried. In some cases the dry cleaner may be able to correct or improve this condition. Success depends on fiber content and construction of the fabric, garment construction, and the degree of intensity of the dye staining. This problem may be controlled by the textile dyer and printer. The danger of its occurrence can be minimized by careful color classification before dry cleaning.

Pigment Color Failures

Pigment printing differs from other methods of printing in that the colors are produced by finely ground, insoluble pigments instead of dyes. It is called "emulsion printing" because the pigment is dispersed in an emulsion of water and oil with a suitable resin binder. The emulsion is then applied to the fabric in a solid shade by "padding" or in design by screen or roller printing. The color and the design do not stand in relief to the fabric surface like paint. Pigment-colored fabrics look no different from fabrics printed by the roller method.

The agent that binds the color to the fabric is a thermosetting resin in pigment emulsion system. It must be "cured" by a timed exposure to heat after its application. This secures proper fixation of the color to the fabric. Failure to carry out the process correctly results in poor colorfastness.

The increasing incidence of complaints can be traced mainly to application shortcomings of the textile printer. These are variables that must be controlled to achieve good colorfastness: (1) colors must be carefully selected for resistance to solvent solubility; (2) the resin binder system must be suitable for the types of fibers and fabric involved, as well as the type of printing system; (3) the binder must be fully "cured"; and (4) when special finishes are applied, such as durable press treatments, they must not destroy the qualities of an otherwise properly applied color system.

Pigment colors are more readily affected in perchlorethylene than in petroleum or fluorocarbon solvent dry cleaning. However, some perform poorly in all three cleaning systems.

Resin-bonded pigment printing is popular because:

1. A full range of pigment colors are available to meet all practical requirements for good colorfastness including light, wet cleaning, laundering, and dry cleaning. Color effects can be achieved that are not always feasible with the use of dye pastes alone.

2. Pigment colors have been especially suitable for use on washable cotton fabrics, but today are applicable to all types of knitted and woven goods of natural and synthetic blends. They can also be used with dye in the same printing run.

3. Printing with resin-bonded pigment colors can often be done more economically than with dyes. There are also processing advantages to the printer.

4. Pigment color loss results from either or both of two causes: (a) the pigment itself or the binder is soluble in solvent, and (b) the binder does not have a sufficient grip on the pigment and fiber to resist rubbing off with the action of washing. Pigment colors are all fast to the same physical wear-off action of washing in laundering as in dry cleaning. All pigment color technologists agree that when the cloth to be printed or padded is properly prepared for application of color and the right color and binders are used, excellent colorfastness to dry cleaning and laundering is attainable.

Testing And Evaluating Colorfastness To Dry Cleaning

This test method* determines the resistance of the color of textiles of all kinds to dry cleaning.

The test is not suitable for the evaluation of the durability of textile finishes, nor is it intended for use in evaluating the resistance of colors to spot and stain removal procedures used by the dry cleaner. This test indicates results to be obtained with repeated commercial dry cleanings.

Four types of dry cleaning equipment can be used in testing: (1) the Launder-Ometer, (2) the dry-cleaning tumbler (see Figure 5–58), (3) the Atlas Electric Dry-Cleaner (see Figure 5–59), and (4) a coin-operated dry cleaner. Perchlorethylene solvent is used in the

Figure 5-58 The Dry Cleaning Machine is essential laboratory apparatus for investigating colorfastness and dimensional changes in fabrics during dry cleaning. It can also be used for testing colorfastness and dimensional changes during laundering. The dry cleaning machine consists of a motor-driven stainless steel tumbler that rotates on an axis 50 degrees off center. For shrinkage, a sample is marked with a known dimension, tumbled for 25 min in the dry-cleaning machine to which has been added 1000 parts Stoddard's Solvent and 67 parts dry-cleaning soap at room temperature. The sample is then given three 5-minute rinses in Stoddard's Solvent followed by a hydroextraction after which it is allowed to dry at room temperature on a horizontal ventilated screen. The sample is then pressed on a flat-bed press. Dimensional changes resulting from the dry cleaning are then measured. (Courtesy: U.S. Testing Co.)

* Colorfastness to Dry Cleaning; AATCC Test Method 132 (1969).

Launder-Ometer for the colorfastness test; petroleum solvent for the applied designs, finishes and shrinkage tests. Perchlorethylene is used in the colorfastness test because (1) it is as extensively used as Stoddard solvent (petroleum solvent) in commercial dry cleaning in the United States; and (2) it is slightly more severe in solvent action than Stoddard solvent. A color that is not affected by perchlorethylene will not be affected by petroleum solvents, whereas the converse is not always true. Any change in color of the specimen is then assessed with the standard Gray Scale for Color Change.

The evaluation of the effect of dry cleaning on color of a test specimen is done by a comparison with an equivalent piece of the original textile and with reference to the Gray Scale for Color. Colors are classified from Class 5, negligible or no change as shown in Gray Scale Step 5, to Class 1, a change in color equivalent to Gray Scale Step 1.

This test indicates what may happen to the color of fabrics after repeated commercial dry cleanings.

LOSS OF DURABLE WATER-REPELLENT

Textile mills apply water-repellent finishes not only to rainwear fabrics but also to many others. For example, many men's suiting fabrics are made water repellent so the suits will be resistant to spots and stains.

Some water-repellent finishes are removed by dry cleaning, wet cleaning, and laundering. Other finishes—called durable types—are

213 *Testing for Product Performance*

not removed readily. Some fabrics treated with the so-called durable finishes lose their water repellency when dry cleaned. The reason is probably not because dry cleaning actually removes the finish, but because the fabric, when dry cleaned under plant conditions, retains a minute film of soap or detergent that counteracts the water-repellent effect.

This is important to dry cleaners. Many garments are sold with the claim that their water-repellent or stain-resistant characteristics will not be affected by dry cleaning. After they are dry cleaned and lose their water repellency, the consumer feels the dry cleaner must have mishandled the garment.

A study on the effect of dry cleaning on durable water-repellent finishes showed:*

1. Most of the so-called durable water-repellent finishes lose their water repellency when dry cleaned. This is something the dry cleaner cannot avoid in practical plant operations.

2. There are some durable water-repellent finishes that withstand dry cleaning operations very well.

3. One of the main virtues of the durable type finishes is that after dry cleaning they regain their water repellency when retreated, while other fabrics usually do not.

Testing For Loss Of Durable Water-Repellent Finish

This test method† covers the determination of the effects of dry cleaning on the water repellency of fabrics treated with a durable water repellent. The method covers the laboratory evaluation of fabric swatches and not for the acceptance sampling of commercial deliveries without prior agreement between the parties. Fabric swatches cut from fabric that has been treated with a durable water-repellent finish are tumbled in a solution of dry cleaning detergent, perchloroethylene, and a small amount of water in a cylinder placed in a Launder-Ometer. Two rinses follow. Then the water repellency is evaluated using the Spray Test in Method D–583. Test results can be used to predict with good reliability the permanence of treatment of durable water-repellent fabric.

---

* "Effect of Dry Cleaning on Durable Water Repellent Finishes," *National Institute of Drycleaning Bulletin No. T-313* (1953).

† Effects of Dry Cleaning on Permanence of Durable Water-Repellent Finish; ASTM D-2721-72.

COLOR CHANGE TO HEAT

Heat-sensitive dyes on fabrics may change color slightly at temperatures lower than the setting for the particular fiber or fibers in the fabric. When this occurs, the color change is permanent or may be only temporary. Upon cooling, the dye reverts to its original hue. But when the fabric is pressed with the iron set on a higher setting than required by the fiber or fibers in the fabric and allowed to remain in contact with the fabric for a few seconds, the color change is permanent.

Some dyes used to give fabrics color take on a cast with successive pressings between cleanings. Any attempt to overcome this condition causes the dye to become darker.

Transfer or Bleeding of Dye in Pressing

The use of moisture and steam causes some dyes to bleed or become dulled on some crepes, satins, and taffetas containing acetate. This type of damage may occur during steam pressing in combination with the use of moisture to dampen the fabric. This may cause bleeding and loss of color in some fabrics.

This damage usually occurs when a garment has been altered by letting out seams or letting down the hemline. In an attempt to remove original creases or lines of stitching, the fabric is sprayed with water and then steamed while wet. This practice may result in dulling of the area pressed, bleeding of the dye, or both.

If delustering or dulling of the fabric has occurred, the area may be sprayed with water and pressed with a dry iron (without the use of steam) until dry. When loss of color has occurred, there is no satisfactory method of restoration. Even redyeing is often unsatisfactory.

Sublimation of Dye

Some dark-colored acetate and nylon fabrics (blue, black, brown, red, green, yellow), when in close proximity to white or light-colored acetate and nylon fabrics, cause dye streaks on the light fabric. The dye on the colored fabric sublimes. The dye changes from a solid to a gas and then forms again as a solid on the light fabric.

This may occur when a light or pastel fabric is combined with a dark-colored fabric in a garment design, for example, a dark-colored lining or trim to a lighter outer fabric. It may also occur when a light-colored garment is hung next to or near a dark-colored garment. Sublimation or transfer of dye may also occur during the drying of a fabric and while a fabric is being pressed.

This type of problem may be controlled by the selection and application of dyes by the textile dyer and printer.

Recent Evaluation Of Color Change To Heat

Since the discovery of dispersed dyes and their application to cellulose acetate, the transfer of colors from dyed fibers to other fibers by heat has been a problem.* Some dispersed dyes exhibit a significant vapor pressure and, when exposed to sufficient heat, will go from a solid to a gas without passing through a liquid phase. This is called sublimation.

Through the years, the term "sublimation" has been applied to all such cases of color transfer and staining due to heat. There are other mechanisms of color and transfer due to heat. It has been shown† that so-called "sublimation" staining of some dyes is primarily caused by vapor transfer, while for other dyes nonvapor or contact transfer causes the stain.

As new man-made fibers, such as nylon, polyester, and acrylics, grew in popularity, problems due to heat were intensified. Beside problems in the textile mill, there were also end-use problems of hot pressing, wet pressing, and storage sublimation. For example, there might be a color transfer from a face fabric to lining and trim during the pressing of a garment.

There were a number of tests used to predict and measure the colorfastness to heat of dyes and dyed fabrics. AATCC Research Committee RA 54, Colorfastness to Heat, was given an assignment of developing a test for colorfastness to sublimation that could be used throughout the textile industry. This committee developed an "In-Plant Method for Colorfastness To Heat." After much experimentation, the final method requires a dyed test specimen in contact with an undyed fabric exposed to dry heat by close contact with a medium that is heated to the required temperature. The change in color of the specimen and the staining of the undyed fabric is assessed with standard gray scales.

Since the heat in an end-use test is normally applied from only one surface, it was necessary to design a test method to accomplish this with laboratory instruments. This was accomplished by placing on the lower heating plate a piece of asbestos sheet at least 3 to 6 mm $\frac{1}{8}$ to $\frac{1}{4}$ inch) thick and then placing on this a piece of wool flannel. This allows the correct pressure to be obtained and it also allows the steam to escape in the damp- and wet-pressing procedure. A piece of undyed cotton fabric is placed above the wool flannel and then the test specimen. This entire surface simulates the surface of a press or ironing board.

* Charles L. Zimmerman, "Evaluating Colorfastness To Heat," *Textile Chemists and Colorists,* Vol. 6, No. 11 (November 1974), p. 254.

† "A Study of Sublimation of Dispersed Dyes on Polyester and Polyester/Cotton Blends," Rhode Island Section, AATCC, *American Dyestuff Reporter,* Vol. 54 (1965), p. 26.

The four temperatures in the AATCC test were reduced to three (110 ± 2, 150 ± 2 and 200 ± 2C) but the same range of temperature is covered.

Tests For Colorfastness To Heat

There are two distinct tests for evaluating colorfastness to heat:*,† (1) colorfastness to hot pressing and (2) colorfastness to dry heat excluding pressing.

The test method for colorfastness to hot pressing determines the resistance of the color of textiles of all kinds and in all forms to color change and color transfer when subjected to hot pressing. Tests are given for hot pressing when the fabric is dry, damp, and wet. The textile and use usually determines which tests should be made. Washable fabrics may be subjected to actual dry iron contact and also to wet pressing. Dry-cleanable fabrics may be subjected to actual dry iron contact and then either ironing over a wet press cloth or by steam pressing.

Samples are tested for hot, moist hot, or wet hot pressing under controlled conditions and evaluated for color change and color transfer. The change in color of the test sample is compared with the Gray Scale for Color Change at once and again after conditioning at room temperature and humidity (65 percent relative humidity and 70°F (21°C)) for two hours. Staining or color transfer to the upper press cloth is classified with the Gray Scale for Staining.

The test method for colorfastness to dry heat (excluding pressing) assesses the resistance of color of textiles of all kinds and in all forms.

Several tests differing in temperature are provided: one or more of them may be used, depending on the requirements. When this method is used for evaluating color changes and staining in dyeing, printing, and finishing processes it must be recognized that other chemical and physical factors may influence the results.

A sample of the fabric in contact with undyed fabrics is exposed to dry heat by close contact with a medium that is heated to the required temperature. The change in color of the specimen and the staining of the undyed fabrics are assessed with standard gray scales.

FABRIC RESISTANCE TO OILY TYPE STAINS

Oil repellency is defined as the ability of a textile fiber, yarn, or fabric to resist wetting by oily liquids.

This test method‡ is designed for detecting the presence of a fluorochemical finish, or other compounds capable of imparting a

* Colorfastness to Heat: Hot Pressing; AATCC Test Method 133 (1973).

† Colorfastness to Heat: Dry (Excluding Pressing); AATCC Test Method 117 (1973).

‡ Oil Repellency: Hydrocarbon Resistance Test; AATCC Test Method 118 (1972).

low energy surface, on all types of fabrics by evaluating the fabric's resistance to wetting by a selected series of liquid hydrocarbons of different surface tensions.

This test method does not give an absolute measure of the resistance of the fabric to staining by all oily materials; other factors such as composition and viscosity of the oily substances, fabric construction, fiber type, dyes, other finishing agents, and the like, also influence stain resistance, in that generally the higher the oil repellancy rating, the better resistance to staining by oily materials, especially liquid oily substances. This is particularly applicable when comparing various finishes on a given fabric.

Drops of standard test liquids, consisting of a selected series of hydrocarbons with varying surface tensions, are placed on the fabric surface and observed for wetting. The oil repellency rating is the highest numbered test liquid which does not wet the fabric surface.

The oil repellency rating is measured on two separate areas of the test specimen. If the two ratings are not in agreement, additional determinations are made and the modal value reported.

Stain Release

Many claims are being made about the effectiveness of soil-release finishes for stain removal as well as soil removal and these are being critically studied by retail and manufacturing organizations to determine their validity.

Consumers have been plagued with the problem of how to remove oily type soil from polyester-cotton blends. Typical is the letter from the Director of Service Standards of the Hot Shoppes, Washington, D.C. It reads: "Our new waitress uniforms, which are an olive green color, 65% Dacron and 35% cotton fiber blend, are giving us laundering problems. The grease spots that the girls pick up in a normal working day are not coming out with strong soap solutions. The green color is also bleeding onto the white color which prevents hot water from being used in the laundering process.

"Some of our waitresses have used the dry cleaning coin machines very successfully. However, I thought perhaps you might suggest a dry cleaning compound that we could use which would be more economical, or someone who could supply me with laundering or dry cleaning instructions."

Allied trade firms in the dry cleaning industry who handle accounts for garment manufacturers have also been asked for information on how to remove oily type soil and stains from polyester-cotton blends. A typical letter reads as follows: "We have several garment manufacturers who are having problems when removing oil-type stains from polyester-cotton blended fabrics as well as permanent crease-type materials treated with formaldehyde.

"When using a spot-removal product on oily stains, a circle is left on the material which is difficult to remove."

A standard working method of testing the stain and soil resistance of various fabrics is certainly needed. There is a proliferation of test methods designed to evaluate fabrics which have been treated with many different types of finishes so as to impart the desired resistance to soiling or staining. The American Association of Textile Chemists and Colorists have designed two test methods: (1) Oil Repellency: Hydrocarbon Resistance Test; and (2) Soil Release: Oily Stain Release Method.

Soil Release

All fibers become soiled, but most can be washed with good results because water, detergents, and optical brighteners can penetrate the fiber. The development of soil-release finishes became necessary following the growth of permanent press because the high percentage of resin and the presence of polyester fiber results in a fabric with very low absorbency. Soil-release finishes permit relatively easy removal of soils (especially oily soils) in laundering. The polyester fiber and the resin are hydrophobic—resist water and are oleophilic—like oil. Soil-release finishes help make the fiber more absorbent (hydrophilic) thus permitting better "wettability" for improved soil removal. Several added benefits result from the use of soil release finishes in permanent press fabrics. These include improved antistatic properties, improved fabric drapability, and somewhat greater comfort in hot weather.

A test method* has been designed to measure the ability of a fabric to release oily stains during home laundering.

A stain on a test sample is produced by using a weight to force a given amount of the staining substance into the fabric. The stained fabric is then laundered in a prescribed manner and the residual stain rated on a scale from five to one by comparison with standard stain-release replica showing a graduated series of stains (see release ratings in Table 5–7). An average of nine ratings for each fabric is made.

COLORFASTNESS TO WASHING

When a manufacturer sews a label in a sports coat or shirt that reads, "guaranteed to fade," it is taking a "bold" approach to the problem of fast colors. It is a good example of smart merchandising! A consumer cannot very well complain if the dye in his Madras jacket stains his shirt after the garment has been guaranteed to do just that.

* Soil Release: Oily Stain Release Method; AATCC Test Method 130 (1970).

Table 5–7 Stain Release Ratings

Class 5—Stain equivalent to Standard Stain 5.
Class 4—Stain equivalent to Standard Stain 4.
Class 3—Stain equivalent to Standard Stain 3.
Class 2—Stain equivalent to Standard Stain 2.
Class 1—Stain equivalent to Standard Stain 1.
Class 5 represents the best stain removal and Class 1 the poorest stain removal.

Color Bleeding

Madras is a hand-loomed cotton fabric made in Madras, India. Imported hand-woven Madras is yarn dyed with natural vegetable dyes. It has special characteristics—the colors run and bleed, it shrinks in laundering, it has a characteristic smell, and it has irregular imperfections in the weave.

In laundering or wet cleaning, the intense vegetable dyes in Madras wash out and bleed together, giving the fabric a soft, muted appearance.

Launder or wet clean Madras garments individually. The dye bleeds profusely and colors the water. White trim on a garment could be stained from this excess dye. The garment should be squeezed or wrung very lightly to avoid mottling the fabric.

The dyes in Madras perform differently in dry cleaning. Some colors change, others do not. Some dyes become much brighter, particularly when the fabric is dry cleaned in percholoroethylene. Some dyes also show very poor colorfastness to light on 24-hour exposure to the light of the Fade-Ometer.

Madras colors run when the fabric is exposed to moisture or perspiration. This should be taken into account when the garment is purchased.

Color Transfer

Several conditions during the dyeing and printing of a fabric may contribute to the transfer of color during laundry or wet cleaning: (1) an excess of dye may be left in the fabric; (2) the proper amount of dye may be used, but it may not be fixed properly to the fabric; and (3) the dye may not be colorfast to water.

In some cases the original hue remains the same; in others, it becomes lighter in color. The dye may be carried off in the water, or it may be transferred to a lighter background of the fabric or to lighter trim on the garment. The dye may bleed and transfer while the water is being removed from the fabric or while the fabric is being dried.

In some cases a professional dry cleaner may be able to correct or improve the condition by using dye-setting reagents or by bleaching.

Success depends on fiber content and construction of the fabric, the fabric finish, garment construction, and the degree and intensity of the dye staining. The problem may be controlled by the use of dyes which are fast to water.

Tests for Colorfastness

There are a number of variations used in the tests for fastness of color to washing.* These occur because there are differences in the washing procedures for different fibers and there are also variations in the washing procedures for the same fiber. For example, wool fabrics cannot be washed like silks or cottons. Wool fabrics should not be washed in hot water and for a long time. Shrinkage and felting can occur. Silks should be washed gently in warm water. Neither silk nor wool can be bleached with chlorine-type bleach. Some cottons can withstand high water temperature while others require low temperature. Some cottons can be bleached with chlorine-type bleaches while others cannot.

The important variables that must be considered in a washing test are:

1. *The proportion of water to the amount of fabric washed is important.* If the volume of water is too high, the fabrics just float around without the squeezing and twisting action that comes from tumbling in a smaller volume of water.

2. *The washing temperature has a very great effect on colors and shrinkage.* Often the dye is loosened from the fabric by the action of hot water and detergent solutions.

3. *The additions to the water besides detergent or soap also affect the test results.* Some wash tests are made with the addition of sodium carbonate or bleach. The alkaline sodium carbonate intensifies the washing action, making it more severe on the color. Bleach should not be used in washing 100 percent colored articles. It is used on fabrics that have both white and colored areas, as a white tablecloth with a colored border, or a white sheet with colored stripes.

Dyes used on such fabrics should be fast to bleaching. This is the reason bleach is added to the washing solution for some washing tests. Any test should include whatever action or chemical the article encounters in actual use.

4. *Time is also important.* For example, articles from which the dye runs should be washed without long periods of soaking because the dye will continue to bleed. Washing should be done quickly be-

---

* Colorfastness to Washing; AATCC Test Method 61 (1972).

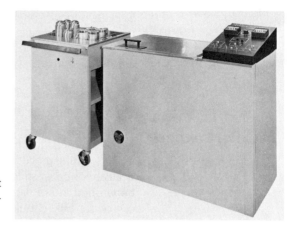

Figure 5-60 A Launder-Ometer and movable unit that holds the individual jars. (Courtesy: Atlas Electrical Devices Co.)

cause the longer the washing time, the greater the amount of color that comes out of the fabric.

5. *Mechanical action to which fabrics are subjected during laundering must also be included in the washing test.*

Study Table 5–8 and note the variables of temperature, water, additives, bleach, mechanical action and time.

The accelerated domestic washing and commercial laundering test for colorfastness is carried out in a Launder-Ometer or similar rotating small containers. (See Figure 5–60, 5–61) The water temperature can be controlled. Steel balls provide the mechanical action and can be varied and controlled. A multifiber cloth is attached to the samples being tested so that bleeding and staining can be evaluated.

These accelerated laundering tests are designed for evaluating the washfastness of fabrics that are expected to withstand frequent laundering. The color loss and abrasive action resulting from solution or

Table 5–8 Test Conditions

Test No.	Temp. °F	Temp. °C	Total Liquor Volume in ml.	% Detergent of Total Volume	% Available Chlorine of Total Volume	Steel Balls (number)	Time in Minutes
IA	105	40	200	0.5	None	10	45
IIA	120	49	150	0.2	None	50	45
IIIA	160	71	50	0.2	None	100	45
IVA	160	71	50	0.2	0.015	100	45

Figure 5-61 Inside view of the Launder-Ometer showing the arrangement of the individual jars. (Courtesy: Atlas Electrical Devices Co.)

abrasive action of five average hand, commercial, or home launderings, with or without chlorine, are closely approximated by one 45-minute test.

The effect on the color of the test samples are expressed and defined by reference to the Gray Scale for Color Change. Class 5 is negligible or no change as shown in Gray Scale Step 5, and Class 1 is a change in color equivalent to Gray Scale Step 1.

Staining is evaluated by means of the AATCC Color Transference Chart or the Gray Scale for Staining. Class 5 is negligible or no staining, and Class 1 has a staining equivalent to Row 1 on the AATCC Chart or Step 1 on the Staining Scale.

6 BIOLOGICAL RESISTANCE

Now we discuss those biological factors that have caused distress to consumers and the test methods that have been developed to measure the effectiveness of these destructive forces, such as insects and pests, mildew and rot, and perspiration.

INSECT DAMAGE

Many insects feed on certain fibers and certain finishes used in making fabrics. Many of these insects will feed on food or beverage stains that are allowed to dry on a fabric. These common insects include moths, beetles, crickets, roaches, silverfish, and termites.

Most common insect damage is caused by moth larvae to wool and hair fibers. Synthetic fabrics, if soiled, may also be damaged. Larvae can and will eat the fabric and cause considerable damage. Insects will cut most textile fibers when they are feeding on the food stains left on a fabric. Sometimes this damage is not noted prior to cleaning. The fibers may be weakened but not cut. Flexing of the fabric during cleaning causes these cut and weakened yarns to break and fall out, resulting in a hole.

Textile manufacturers have developed various types of moth-proofing finishes that may be applied at the time the fabric is manufactured. Some of these are permanent to cleaning; others are not. Dry cleaners are also in a position to treat garment and household items with a moth-repellent finish when they are cleaned. There is less risk of insect damage if items are cleaned and free from stains before storage.

Recent research has also shown that insects will damage clothing made from the man-made fibers. It was found to be considerable—if the clothing was marked with food stains.

Other insects with appetites for clothing are silverfish and crickets that have a taste for cellulose. They will eat cotton, especially if starch or glue or similar materials are present.

TERMITE DAMAGE

Termites* may be the cause of certain puzzling fabric damage problems for which there is no other logical explanation.

* Termite Damage—IFI's Textile Notes 23.

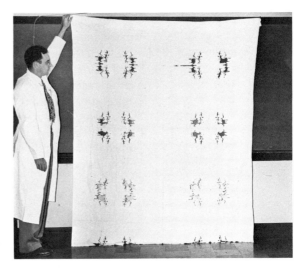

Figure 5-62 Termites in the linen closet were the cause of this damage to a sheet. (Courtesy: International Fabricare Institute)

The folded sheet pictured in Figure 5–62 was damaged in a peculiar pattern.

The damage passed entirely through every fold of fabric, and, in a letter from the laundry owner, it was reported that a stack of 16 sheets was similarly damaged. Edges of the damaged fabric in all layers were stuck together and held tightly by a hard substance with small specks of solid matter adhering to the edge.

There was no evidence of chemical deterioration, nor were there any damaging chemicals in the fibers. Apparently the damage was mechanical.

Damage by insects was suggested by the appearance of the sheet, and in examining the sheet carefully, a termite was found.

MILDEW Mildew is a fungus growth that attacks fabrics made of the cellulosic fibers under certain conditions of use and storage. It may appear as a stain, discoloration, or loss of color in the fabric.

Mildew will develop generally in warm, humid air. Lack of circulation of air, which is frequently found in clothes closets, garment bags, trunks, drawers, and basements, contributes to the formation of mildew after a musty odor can be detected. Under certain favorable conditions, some types of mildew fungus will remove color from the fabric as a result of chemical action. The fabric may or may not be weakened.

Mildew is a condition that may be quite easily identified. It usually produces grayish spots that are irregular in shape and size. Mildew in most cases results in a stain that is dark in appearance. However, some fungus growths are yellow, orange or red and result in yellow or orange stains. Since mildew is a fungus vegetablelike growth and is insoluble, it cannot always be removed entirely from fabrics, but its color may be reduced.

Many mildew preventives are now available to treat fabrics to make them resistant to mildew, or for use in clothes closets and drawers. Occasionally, mildew stains can be removed or lightened with bleaching. In some cases, bleaching is unsafe because of the color of the fabric.

PERSPIRATION

Garment manufacturers should consider colorfastness to perspiration in selecting fabrics where this property is desired. The consumer may do several things to prevent this type of damage. The underarm area may be protected with dress shields, antiperspirants and deodorants should be used as directed by the manufacturer, and clothes should be cleaned regularly to reduce the alkaline concentration in garments.

Perspiration may be very harmful to fabrics due to bacterial action that may cause (1) loss of fabric strength, (2) loss or change of color, (3) loss or change of finish, (4) odor problems, and (5) salt rings and deposits.

There are slight differences in the composition of human perspiration. Perspiration is 98 percent water and 2 percent dissolved solids. It is made up of organic matter (ammonium compounds, urea, amino acids, lactic acids, etc.) and inorganic matter (almost entirely chlorides). In addition, perspiration contains skin cells, dirt, and traces of 11 other chemical compounds. The variation that occurs from person to person results from differences in diet, drug intake, and general health.

Fresh (acid) and decomposed perspiration (alkaline) may cause considerable damage to dyes, especially those that are alkaline sensitive. Research studies show that many of the basic, direct, acetate and metallic dyes are affected by perspiration. Perspiration may cause bleeding of the dye and the staining of lighter areas of the fabric. In some cases it may change the hue, for example, a red dye may change to blue.

ANTIBACTERIAL FINISHES ON FABRICS

A great deal of time and effort has been spent in developing a test method for the evaluation of antibacterial finishes on fabrics.* The problem of evaluation of antibacterial finishes on fabrics involves the degree of antibacterial activity intended in the use of such fabrics. If only bacteriostatic activity (inhibition of multiplication) is intended, a qualitative procedure that clearly demonstrates antibacterial activity as contrasted with lack of such activity by an untreated sample may be acceptable. Several qualitative procedures must be available, due to the diversity of chemicals used as antibacterial agents on today's fabrics.

However, if bactericidal activity is intended or implied, quantitative evaluation is necessary. Quantitative evaluation also provides a clearer picture for possible uses of such treated fabrics. Through interlaboratory tests, a quantitative procedure, which simulates in-use conditions as much as possible, was developed. It is an outgrowth of the major test for bacteriostatic activity. As a result, a two-part procedure is recommended as follows:

1. Qualitative or presumptive tests.
2. Quantitative or reference test.

The test method recognizes four qualitative procedures for the demonstration of bacteriostatic activity. They are used to select fabrics that show promise of antibacterial activity. This method provides a quantitative procedure for the evaluation of the degree of activity. It is imperative that both the qualitative and quantitative tests be carried out by persons with training and experience in the use of bacteriological techniques.

Agar Plate Method

The Agar Plate Method† is recommended for evaluating antibacterial activity of fabrics. The objective of the test is the detection of bacteriostatic activity of fabrics. The method is suitable for a large variety of materials, but is not suitable for:

1. Certain materials that have an impervious or impermeable film or materials treated with finishes and coatings that produce impervious or impermeable films.
2. Antibacterial agents that, when applied to fabrics, are not readily diffusible through agar.
3. Fabrics with long nap that prevents contact with the agar.

* Antibacterial Finishes on Fabrics, Evaluation of: AATCC Test Method 100 (1970).

† Detection of Antibacterial Activity of Fabrics: Agar Plate Method, AATCC Test Method 90 (1970).

4. Materials treated with antibacterial agents that react with the culture medium.

Sterilized specimens of the test fabric are placed on AATCC agar that has been seeded with a test bacterium. After incubation, a clear area of no growth adjacent to the specimen indicates antibacterial activity of the fabric. A standard strain of Staphylococcus aureus and of Escherichia coli are used.

The test method is designed for use only by persons with training and experience in bacteriological techniques.

Finishes Used To Deter Insect Pests

This test method* covers the procedures for the evaluation of compounds or treatments designed to protect fabrics from damage by insect pests, such as moths or carpet beetles. It takes into consideration not only the initial protection furnished by the treatment, but also the permanency of the protection during conditions of ordinary use.

Treated and untreated samples are subjected to the action of insect pests under controlled conditions for one exposure period and then examined for evidence of damage. Additional exposure periods are given as necessary until visual damage is evident.

Test samples are prepared by applying the treatment of compound to be tested in the desired proportion to a piece of standard pure undyed scoured wool. After application, the specimen is thoroughly aired for a period of not less than seven days for the removal of all volatile constituents. The size of the piece is sufficient to furnish samples for all of the service tests to which it is to be subjected, such as washing, dry cleaning, hot pressing, sea water solution, perspiration, light and abrasion. Samples are rated from Class 1 to Class 5 based on the particular service test.

Resistance of Fabrics To Insect Damage

In this test procedure† biological methods are given for evaluating the resistance of fabrics that contain wool or other susceptible fibers to webbing clothes moths and to carpet beetles. The methods are *not* concerned with the evaluation of chemical finishes to deter insects or with subsequent handling, aging, washing, cleaning, and so on.

Two methods are provided for determining the extent of damage to test specimens: (1) the Excrement Weight Method is used only for tests with carpet beetles and (2) the Fabric Weight Loss Method is used for tests with webbing clothes moths and also may be used for

* Insect Pest Deterrents on Textiles, AATCC 28 (1971).
† Resistance of Textiles to Insects; AATCC Test Method 24 (1971).

Figure 5-63 A technician is inspecting the well-eaten swatch of wool fabric. In the background petri dishes contain two-inch squares of standard wool test fabric with 10 larvae being incubated in the dark cabinet for 14 days. (Courtesy: International Fabricare Institute)

tests with carpet beetles when preferred and when comparative tests with both insects are made.

These methods quantitatively measure the amount of feeding on the test specimen by the specified number and type of insects for a prescribed time under controlled conditions of temperature and humidity (see Figure 5–63).

At least four test samples and four control samples are required for the Excrement Weight Method and at least eight of each for the Fabric Weight Loss Method. The fabric must be free of any solvents or carriers used in application of chemical treatments and of any solvents or auxiliary agents used in subsequent durability test.

Test samples, each with an area of two square inches, are cut from widely spaced portions of the fabric.

Control samples of the standard control fabric each having an area of two square inches, are exposed under the same conditions as the test sample. If the fabric tested has been treated with some form of insecticide for the purpose of increasing its resistance to insect pests, samples of the same fabric in the untreated condition is exposed for comparison.

The procedure for the Excrement Weight Method is as follows: at least four samples to be tested and four control samples are prepared and placed face down in a separate covered dish. Ten larvae are placed on top of each specimen and put in a dark cabinet for 14 days at 80 $\pm$ 2°F and 55 $\pm$ percent relative humidity. At the end of the test a count is made of the living and dead insects. Damage to the fabric is determined by the quantity of the excrement deposited during the test period.

The test fabric is considered satisfactorily resistant to carpet beetles if an average quantity of excrement of not over 5 milligrams per specimen is deposited, provided that no single specimen shows more than 6 milligrams of excrement and that under the same conditions the controls show an average quantity of excrement of not less than 15 milligrams per specimen.

In the Fabric Weight Loss Method, the samples are weighed before and after the 14-day exposure and the loss of weight in milligrams, due to feeding of the test larvae is calculated as follows:

$$L = \frac{AC}{B} - D$$

where:

L = adjusted loss of weight in milligrams due to insect feeding
A = average weight of the four test specimens before testing
B = average weight of the four humidity check specimens before testing
C = average weight of the four humidity check specimens after testing
D = average weight of the four test specimens after testing

The number of live larvae and the number of pupated larvae are also reported. Tests may also be made on yarns and carpets.

Evaluation Of Fabrics For Resistance To Mildew And Rot

There are three test methods for the evaluation of fabrics for resistance to mildew and rot:* (1) Soil Burial, (2) Agar Plate Sterile Specimen, and (3) Agar Plate, Nonsterile Specimen. These methods determine susceptibility of textiles to mildew and evaluate treated textiles and textile-containing products attacked by mildew.

The test procedure selected for use will depend on the investigator's interest. For the determination of susceptibility of the fabric to mildew, one type of test may be desired. The type of exposure to which the fabric might be subjected may determine a more practical type test. For example, if the textile product will come in contact with soil, a test procedure simulating this exposure should be utilized; if the textile product is to be used inside buildings and would never come in contact with soil or tropical conditions, a much less severe test might be desired. The two important considerations when evaluating textile and textile-containing products in relation to mildew are (1) the actual deterioration of the textile product by action of mildew and (2) growth of mildew on the product not necessarily deteriorating the product but making it unsightly.

Certain preexposures of textile products may be important when specific end uses are critical such as leaching, weathering, or volatili-

* Fungicides, Evaluation on Textiles: Mildew and Rot Resistance of Textiles; AATCC Test method 30 (1971).

zation. When the end use is near high temperature and the fungicide may be volatile, a preliminary oven exposure may be desired. When the end use would be in tropical exposures or outside when rainfall is present, a leaching exposure should be performed before mildew evaluation is made. Another method is to actually expose the textile under the conditions expected of the textile and then expose it to mildew evaluation.

The Soil Burial Test Method is considered to be the most severe exposure for textile products. Only those fabrics that will come in direct contact with soil—such as sandbags, tarpaulins, and tents—are expected to perform well in this procedure. The procedure can also be used for testing the performance of experimental fungicides. Since it is severe, if a fungicide performs well it usually follows that it will perform well in less severe procedures.

The Agar Plate, Pure Culture, Sterile Specimen Test Method is used for evaluating fabric samples for mildew resistance that will not come in contact with soil. It is also used for evaluating the efficiency of fungicides and determining uniformity of fungicide distribution. The test organism is an organism that can attack cellulose: so this test is used in those areas where degradation of cellulose is important.

The Agar Plate, Pure Culture, Nonsterile Specimen Test Method is used for evaluation of fabric samples where surface growing organisms are important. Certain fungi can grow on a fabric but may not degrade it sufficiently to cause loss of tensile strength. Their growth on the fabric is undesirable and unsightly.

COLORFASTNESS TO PERSPIRATION

In designing a test to measure the colorfastness of a dye to perspiration,* researchers had to take in account the fact that three things may happen: (1) color change of the dyed fabric, (2) loosening and uneven redepositing of color, and (3) staining of material next to the colored fabric.

The device used for this test is the Perspiration Tester (see Figure 5–64). AATCC Test Method 15 has been criticized by many people for (1) indicating a degree of color transfer more severe than that encountered in actual performance and (2) unreliability of the alkaline phase of the tests on woolens, wool blends, acetate, and nylon. In response to the criticism, a task group of AATCC Committee RA 52, Colorfastness to Perspiration Test Methods, was formed to investigate Test Method 15 with actual wear performance† and to ascer-

* Colorfastness to Perspiration; AATCC Test Method 15 (1973).

† N. B. Gobell and B. J. Muller, "Evaluating Colorfastness to Perspiration: Lab Tests vs. Wear Tests," *Textile Chemists and Colorists,* Vol. 6, No. 11 (November 1974), p. 254.

Figure 5-64 The Perspiration Tester is used to determine colorfastness to perspiration and water (chlorinated pool, sea, distilled). For testing colorfastness to perspiration, samples of the test fabric and multifiber cloth are wet out in the appropriate solution. The Perspiration Tester is then loaded in the upright position with the $2\frac{1}{2}$ in. × $2\frac{1}{2}$ in. specimens centered between the $2\frac{1}{2}$ in. × $4\frac{1}{2}$ in. acrylic separator plates. One to 20 specimens may be tested simultaneously. The top plate along with the standard weight is then placed on the rack providing a 10-lb dead-weight loading. Thumb screws lock the top plate in place. The weight is removed, and the unit is turned over on its back and placed in the oven. (Courtesy: Atlas Electric Services Co.)

tain the need for modification of the existing test procedure, which tested color performance to both acid and alkaline solutions. With wool the alkaline phase showed more staining than is experienced in consumer wear. With acetate the staining was generally less than that of actual wear. The staining of nylon in the alkaline phase was comparable to that of the acid phase. So it was recommended that the alkaline phase be deleted from Test Method 15.

A slightly acid solution is used on a piece of colored fabric and tested and rated.

Unsatisfactory perspiration fastness may be due to bleeding or migration of color or it may be due to change in color of the fabric. It is possible that objectionable change in color may occur with no apparent bleeding. On the other hand, there may be bleeding with no apparent change in color, or there may be both bleeding and change in color.

The effect on the color of the test specimens is expressed and defined by reference to the Gray Scale for Color Change. Class 5—negligible or no change as shown in Gray Scale Step 5; Class 1—a change in color equivalent to Gray Scale Step 1.

Staining is evaluated by means of the AATCC Color Transference Chart or the Gray Scale for Staining. Ratings range from Class 5—negligible or no staining—to Class 1—staining equivalent to Row 1 on the AATCC Chart or Step 1 on the Staining Scale.

7 ENVIRONMENTAL RESISTANCE

John Lomartire* states that the so-called "environment" is made up of many subenvironments—political, social, economic, and geographic—where individual requirements are often in conflict with each other. Usually, the word "environment" suggests three other words: water, air, and land. The concern for pollution of these natural features of the world has increased recently. The textile industry, like every other business or industry, has reacted to this trend. For example, all dye houses color the water with discharge from the dye bath. To convert the colored water to clear water is very costly. This fact could lead to greater acceptance of the heat-transfer method of printing. Regardless of the route that industry takes, increased costs initially affect the manufacturer but ultimately the consumer. Odors arise from the bleaching and coating processes. This is an aesthetic problem. Undesirable smoke or odor is not known to be hazardous. Hence, industry has been slow to invest large sums to get rid of these. But there is no doubt that in future operations there will be additional air pollution control equipment. What to do with liquid and solid wastes will become a more serious problem. There are alternatives: improved operations that generate less waste, recycling waste, and use of waste as fuel.

Another consideration is the consumer environment: security protection, performance guarantees, customer notification procedures, care, and performance labeling.

It is estimated that air pollution is costing consumers some $2 billion a year in damage to textile materials exclusive of the cost of laundering or dry cleaning to clean the fabrics. In addition, it is estimated that color fading by atmospheric pollutants amounts to $350 million each year.

There are four basic categories of damage to textiles caused by air pollution: disintegration of natural and man-made fibers before the end of a normal wear cycle, damage that results from soiling in laundering and dry cleaning, fading of colors in nylon carpeting, acetate fabrics, cotton, and durable press fabrics, and discoloration of white

* John Lomartire, "Fibers And The Environment." Paper given at the National Symposium on Fiber Frontiers, June 10, 1974.

fabrics due to the effect of hydrogen sulfide and various chemicals on the fiber and finishes.

Smog formation can cause havoc to humans as well as textiles. There are many complex meterological conditions such as inversion layers, intensity of sunlight, and air turbulence that complicate the picture, but poor air dilution is one essential factor to smog accumulation.

The next fact of importance is that two distinct types of smog are recognized. One causes a problem in the winter and the other in summer and fall. The winter type of smog is caused by sulfur compounds in coal and fuel oil. Upon combustion of these fuels, sulfur dioxide gas is formed. In the atmosphere, sulfur dioxide undergoes a photochemical oxidation to sulfur trioxide. Sulfur trioxide reacts with water vapor in the air to form a mist. These aerosol particles are very acidic and can even cause death if the level gets too high.

The summer-fall type of smog is caused by interaction between the vapor of certain organic molecules and nitric oxide under the influence of sunlight. In this case, efforts to control smog have consisted of limiting the presence of both reactants in the atmosphere. Limiting the amount of nitric oxide in the air is a vast problem because the main cause of it is the combustion of gasoline. Oxides of nitrogen are not products of the burning of gasoline, but by-products. Whenever iron or steel is heated to redness in the presence of air, some of the oxygen and nitrogen in the air combine to form oxides of nitrogen (a mixture of nitric oxide and nitrogen dioxide).

When the oxides of nitrogen interact with organic molecules a complex series of reactions takes place stepwise leading to several products. The important products are ozone, aldehydes, and aerosols. In the course of the reactions, the organic molecules are extensively oxidized and decomposed into simpler molecules. However, some of the simple molecules can combine to form more complex substances that take the form of aerosols. Aerosols are stable suspensions in the air of tiny droplets of liquid or tiny particles of solids. Smoke and fog are typical aerosols, and it is from these two words that someone coined the word "smog."

Any one of the three products of the reaction between oxides of nitrogen and organic molecules could cause eye irritation. The aldehydes, for instance, have long been known as eye irritants, particularly two that have been detected in smog: formaldehyde and acrolein. Ozone also is irritating. The aerosols are a nuisance whether or not they cause eye irritation because of the dense haze they create.*
These *smog-forming* reactions are summarized in Figure 5–65.

---

* "Solvents and the Smog Problem," *NID Technical Bulletin T-422.*

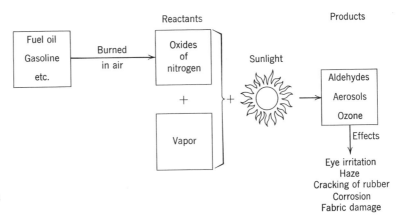

Figure 5-65 Schematic diagram of smog formation.

ATMOSPHERIC GAS FADING

The atmosphere is made up of a mixture of gases and pollutants. Fume fading, generally termed gas fading by textile manufacturers, is a color change of the dye. It is defined technically as "fading of a dyed fabric by acid gases in the atmosphere which are formed in combustion processes." The gases can be formed by gas burners, gas stoves, electric stoves, fireplaces, or furnaces burning coal, gas, or oil.

In the early 1930s when the first cases of fume fading were observed on acetate, the color changes were thought to be caused by unsatisfactory dyestuffs or unsuitable fabric. As the number of fume fading incidents increased, the source of the difficulty was found to be related to the chemistry of the fiber and the dyestuffs used in the fabric. By 1935, the cause was recognized as being the action of the oxides of nitrogen on dyed acetate.

Fume fading is most generally noticed in garments that have been hanging for a considerable length of time. Fumes from a stove or furnace in some other part of the building drift into the closet and accumulate there. They cause color changes on exposed portions of garments such as sleeve edges or the sides of skirts. The blue, violet, and red aminoanthraquinone dyes are most susceptible to gas fading. Certain of the azoacetate dyes are also subject to changes in shade.

Typical color changes are blue to violet, blue to red, and green to dull green, brown, or tan. Fume fading is not limited to one dye type. It may occur when dyes are combined to achieve a certain shade. For example, the dyer may wish to dye a fabric green. To do this he may blend a blue and yellow dyestuff. If the fabric so dyed is exposed to air containing oxides of nitrogen, the yellow dye may remain unaffected. But the blue dye might be affected by the oxides of nitrogen

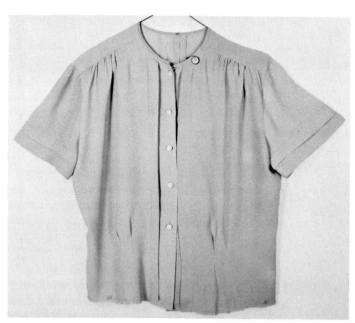

Figure 5-66 This blouse was made of two identical acetate fabrics, but one was treated with a fume-resistant finish. After a period of wear and cleaning, the treated fabric retained its original color; the untreated fabric changed color. (From a cooperative wear study made for the International Fabricare Institute by the Textile Department, School of Home Economics, University of North Carolina)

and change to a pink or red. After exposure, the fabric will appear as a blend of the original colorfast yellow dyestuff and a violet dyestuff or a color resulting from the combination of the original yellow dyestuff and a reddish violet dyestuff. The green will thus change to a dull green, then to a brown or tan.

This problem may be controlled by the textile industry by several methods: (1) solution dyeing of yarns, (2) selection of dyes that are known to have good colorfastness to atmospheric gas fading, and (3) aftertreatment of the fabric with a durable antifume finish (see Figure 5–66).

The dry cleaner may control this color change by (1) control of drying and finishing temperatures and (2) avoiding the use of a sour bath in wet cleaning.

The customer may control this color change by (1) protecting the fabric from direct contact with deodorants and antiperspirants and

(2) hanging garments in a garment bag and in a clothes closet that has good air circulation and is located a distance away from a chimney.

OZONE FADING

Recently, researchers have been studying color changes that result from what they call "atmospheric contaminants" and "ozone fading." Often this color change is confused with fume fading.

The oxide of nitrogen that is primarily responsible for gas fading is nitrogen dioxide. It has also been shown that if ozone is present in the atmosphere in sufficient quantities, ozone fading will occur. This is sometimes called O-fading. It may occur on dyes that are colorfast to fume fading. However, blue and red dyes seem to be affected to a greater degree than other colors. The change is most frequent in disperse and direct dyes.

In addition to ozone, oxides of nitrogen and the atmosphere may contain a number of other chemicals that react with dyes and fibers to produce color changes, such as sulfur dioxide, carbon monoxide, hydrocarbons from gasoline combustion, various peroxides of hydrocarbons, and industrial acid fumes. For example, in the Chicago area it has been found that a red dye on wool changes to yellow because of sulfur dioxide. In an atmosphere where there is high humidity, the action of these chemicals on the dyes and fibers is accelerated.

Although there has been a great amount of publicity on gas fading on acetate, this is not the only fiber subject to attack by ozone and atmospheric contaminants. Disperse dyes used on triacetate and polyester, as well as acetate, have changed color due to atmospheric conditions. Color changes have also been observed on nylon and wool.

Ozone may also cause bleaching in acetate, cotton, and nylon. The fading of ozone on nylon carpets is a problem that has faced many carpet manufacturers.

As a result, it has been necessary to choose improved dyes and modify nylon fibers to reduce the absorbency of ozone. These expensive color changes can be prevented. Such procedures have been adopted by responsible carpet manufacturers.

As a result of air pollution damage, manufacturers are improving dyes and modifying fibers to reduce the absorbency of ozone. This is being achieved by spending many dollars on research and development. Ultimately this cost is passed on to the consumer, but the added cost is small to obtain the added performance qualities needed to make merchandise serviceable.

The test methods discussed in this chapter include colorfastness to oxides of nitrogen, ozone, and water. Sunlight, which may also be considered an environment factor on fabrics, has been discussed in Parts 1 and 2 of this chapter.

COLORFASTNESS TO BURNT GAS FUMES

This method* is intended for evaluating the resistance of the color of fabrics of all kinds and in all forms when exposed to atmospheric oxides of nitrogen as derived from the combustion of illuminating or heating gas.

A sample of the fabric and a test control fabric are exposed in a gas-fading chamber (see Figures 5–67 and 5–68) simultaneously to oxides of nitrogen from burnt gas fumes until the control shows a change in color corresponding to that of the standard of fading. The change in color of the specimen is assessed with the standard Gray Scale for assessing change in color. If no color change is observed in the specimen after one exposure period or cycle, exposure may be

Figure 5-67 This instrument is used to study the effect of ozone, nitrogen dioxide, sulphur dioxide, or other gases on fabrics. The cabinet is designed to meet specifications calling for concentrations of gas under controlled conditions of temperature and humidity. Fresh room air is drawn into the machine through a charcoal and soda lime purifying filter to an air-mixing valve. This valve is manually adjustable to vary—from 0 to 100 percent—the amount of pure air drawn into the machine and eventually exhausted out the top, where it is vented outside. The air passing over the test samples is automatically maintained at any desired temperature from room up to 150°F (65°C) by thermostatically controlled electric heaters in the air stream. Relative humidity is controlled from the room up to 95 percent using heaters in the conditioning-chamber water bath. The regulated amounts of gas contaminants from either a generator or gas cylinder are also piped into this chamber where they are thoroughly mixed with the conditioned air. (Courtesy: Atlas Devices Co.)

* Colorfastness to Burnt Gas Fumes, AATCC Test Method 23 (1972).

Figure 5-68 The Gas Exposure Cabinet is equipped with a rotating rack having 10 horizontal support rods. Test specimens are hung directly on these rods in which case samples up to 18 in. long may be used exposing a total area of 1584 sq. in. Conventional sample holders can also be used with an average capacity of about 30. (Courtesy: Atlas Devices Co.)

continued for either a specified number of periods or for the number of periods required to produce a specified amount of color change in the specimen. The effect on the color may range from Class 5, negligible or no change to Class 1, a change in color equivalent to Gray Scale Step 1.

COLORFASTNESS TO OZONE

An ozoniter is used to test fabrics to ozone in the atmosphere (see Figure 5–69). The test* is designed to determine the resistance to color change of fabrics when exposed to ozone in the atmosphere. A test specimen and a swatch of *control sample* are simultaneously exposed to the atmosphere containing ozone until the control sample shows a color change corresponding to that of a standard of fading. This exposure is one cycle. The cycles are repeated until the specimen shows a definite color change or for a prescribed number of

* Colorfastness to Ozone in the Atmosphere Under Low Humidities; AATCC Test Method 109 (1972).
Colorfastness to Ozone in the Atmosphere Under High Humidities; AATCC Test Method 129 (1972).

Figure 5-69 The ozone exposure chamber is designed to provide a quick and reliable method of measuring colorfastness of fabrics or deterioration studies related to oxidation of materials. The contained ozone generator and exposure chamber is made of highly resistant materials. The generator provides a constant output of ozone. Uniform exposure of test specimens within the test chamber is assured by a fan and baffle arrangement between the generator and exposure chamber. (Courtesy: Atlas Devices Co.)

cycles. The effect on color of the test specimens after any specified number of cycles is made by reference to the Gray Scale for Color Change and report the number of cycles run. Class 5 shows negligible or no change as shown on Gray Scale Step 5; Class 1 shows a change in color equivalent to Gray Scale Step 1.

COLORFASTNESS TO WATER

It amazes some people that even water from the sky or any other source may cause a color change on their clothing. A red-blue dye that is used to dye rayon and rayon-blend fabrics of different weight and construction is very sensitive to clear water. Water tends to wick out the blue component of the dye. A similar color change may also occur when a spotter or consumer attempts to remove a spot or stain from the fabric. The color change may also occur as a result of slow drying when the garment is washed or wet cleaned. When this occurs, the color of the dye cannot be leveled out with steam spraying or even by completely wetting out the garment. Double areas or thicknesses of fabric do not dry as rapidly as single thicknesses. Staining usually occurs in areas of double thickness of fabric. A dye should withstand the amount of moisture a fabric is exposed to during normal wear to be serviceable.

Color Change From Water—Red Dye On Wool

Several theories have been advanced as to why a color change occurs in some red dyes used on wool. (1) The variables involved in manufacture and application of the dyestuff can cause a color change that may be the result of some inherent characteristic of the types of dye used or their application to wool fabrics, depending on the shade of red involved. (2) This type of water spotting problem is not unusual in colors that are clear and bright. It may occur in colors other than red. (3) The phenomenon is not caused by fading or any color change in the dyed fabric, but is a complicated change in light reflection due to the absorption of water by the fabric and individual fibers. For example, some broadcloths, flannels and gabardines other than red are known to water spot readily.

A person may get caught in the rain wearing a red wool fabric that water spots. The fabric may change color when treated with distilled water or steam from a spotting gun. The red color changes from a lighter to darker hue.

Dry cleaning will not remove the spots. The entire surface of the fabric may be sprayed lightly and evenly with a steam spotting gun, brushed lightly, and cabinet dried. This results in an even shade of color, although the hue may be slightly darker than the original color.

Method of Testing for Colorfastness To Water

The Colorfastness to Water Test Method* is designed to measure the resistance to water of dyed, printed, or otherwise colored yarns and fabrics.

Distilled water or deionized water is used in this test because natural (tap) water is variable in composition.

The sample, backed by multifiber test fabric, is immersed in water under specified conditions of temperature and time, and then placed between glass or plastic plates under specified conditions of pressure, temperature, and time. The change in color of the specimen and the staining of the attached multifiber test fabric are observed.

Evaluation for color change is classified by the effect on the color of the test sample by the Gray Scale for Color Change from Class 5 (rated as negligible or no change, as shown in Gray Scale Step 5) to Class 1 (has a change in color equivalent to Gray Scale Step 1).

Evaluation for staining is made by classifying the staining of the multifiber test fabric by the AATCC Color Transference Chart or the Gray Scale for Staining: Class 5 has negligible or no staining; Class 1 has staining equivalent to Row 1 on the AATCC Chart or Step 1 on the Staining Scale.

* Colorfastness to Water; AATCC Test Method 107 (1972).

COLORFASTNESS TO WATER AND LIGHT

This test method*,† is designed to provide a consumer end-use test for evaluating color change. This method simulates the effect of alternate water and light exposure on controlled fabrics.

A colored sample is immersed in water test solution or in seawater test solution for a specified period of time and immediately exposed to light in a carbon-arc lamp fading apparatus for a specified period of time. The test is repeated for a previously designated number of times or until the shade of the colored specimens has been altered to a "just appreciable fade," a change in color equivalent to Step 4 on the Gray Scale for Color Change.

A test is also designed to simulate the effect of high humidity and light on colored fabrics. The samples are tested in a carbon-arc lamp fading apparatus exposed first to darkness with high relative humidity for a specified period of time, then to light with low relative humidity for a specified period of time.

COLORFASTNESS TO SEAWATER

Color change in salt-sensitive dyes is a rather unusual type of color change that occurs on some dyes used to dye wool fabrics. Few people realize that their clothes can change color from seawater while they walk along the ocean. Colorfastness of fabrics to seawater is also an important consideration to owners of sea-going vessels and to the military. Materials containing salt, such as perspiration, and many food stains or sea spray may cause this color change.

This color change happens when salt (sodium chloride) comes in contact with the dye. The color change is usually toward red. It is most common on wool gabardine of brown, gray, and blue.

Discolored areas of this type may be removed by the dry cleaner by flushing the discolored area very quickly with a steam spotting gun.

The test method‡ is designed to measure the resistance to seawater of dyed or printed yarns and fabrics.

Artificial seawater is used because natural seawater is variable in composition and is often difficult to obtain.

The sample, backed by multifiber test fabric, is immersed in artificial seawater under specified conditions of temperature and time, and then placed between glass or plastic plates under specified conditions of pressure, temperature, and time. The change in color of

* Colorfastness to Water and Light: Alternate Exposure; AATCC Test Method 125 (1971).

† Colorfastness to Water (High Humidity) and Light: Alternate Exposure; AATCC Test Method 126 (1972).

‡ Colorfastness to Water: Sea; AATCC Test Method 106 (1972).

the specimen and the staining of the attached multifiber test fabric are observed.

Evaluation for color change is made by classifying the effect on the color of the test specimens by the Gray Scale for Color Change. Class 5 is negligible or no change as shown in Gray Scale Step 5; Class 1 has a change in color equivalent to Gray Scale Step 1.

Evaluation for staining is made by classifying the staining of the multifiber test fabric by the AATCC Color Transference Chart or the Gray Scale for Staining. Class 5 is negligible or no staining; Class 1 has a staining equivalent to Row 1 on the AATCC Chart or Step 1 on the Staining Scale.

COLORFASTNESS TO CHLORINATED WATER

This test method* is intended for evaluating the resistance to chlorinated pool water of dyed, printed, or colored yarns and fabrics.

The sample is backed by multifiber test fabric, immersed in diluted chlorine solution under specified conditions of temperature, time, and pH, and then placed between glass or plastic plates under specified conditions of pressure, temperature, and time. The change in color of the sample and the staining of the attached multifiber test fabric are evaluated.

Evaluation for color change is made by classifying the effect on the color of the test specimens by the Gray Scale for Color Change. Class 5 is negligible or no change as shown in Gray Scale Step 5. Class 1 has a change in color equivalent to Gray Scale Step 1.

Evaluation for staining of the attached multifiber test fabric is made by means of the AATCC Color Transference Chart or the Gray Scale for Staining. Class 1 has a staining equivalent to Row 1 on the AATCC Chart or Step 1 on the Staining Scale.

COLORFASTNESS TO WATER SPOTTING

Some dyes will change color to rainwater or water used to remove spots and stains. The test† method evaluates the resistance to water spotting of dyed or printed fabrics. The method does not determine whether the discoloration is removable.

Evaluation for change is made by classifying the effect on the color of the test samples by the Gray Scale for Color Change. Class 5 is negligible or no change as shown in Gray Scale Step 5. Class 1 has a change in color equivalent to Gray Scale Step 1.

* Colorfastness to Water: Chlorinated Pool; AATCC Test Method 105 (1972).
† Colorfastness to Water Spotting; AATCC Test Method 104 (1972).

WATER REPELLENCY

There are three test methods used to test the water repellency of a fabric (1) the Spray Test; (2) the Static Absorption Test; (3) the Tumble Jar Dynamic Absorption Test. These tests are applicable to any fabric that may or may not have been given a water-resistant or water-repellent finish. They measure the resistance of fabrics to wetting by water. The results obtained with the tests depends primarily on the resistance to wetting or water repellency of the fibers and yarns in the fabric, and not on the construction of the fabric.

Spray Test

Water repellency is defined as the ability of a textile fiber, yarn or fabric to resist wetting. This test* is made with a Spray Tester and results are rated with Standard Spray Test Ratings (see Figures 5–70 and 5–71). The test is especially suitable for measuring the effectiveness of water-repellent finishes applied to fabrics, particularly plain-woven fabrics. The portability and simplicity of the instrument and the shortness and simplicity of the test procedure make this method especially suitable for textile manufacturing control work. It is not intended for use in predicting the probable rain penetration resistance

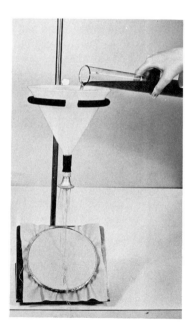

Figure 5-70 Water is sprayed against the taut surface of a test specimen under controlled conditions. The water produces a wetted pattern whose size depends on the relative repellency of the fabric. Evaluation is accomplished by comparing the wetted pattern with pictures on a standard chart (Figure 5.71) (Courtesy: American Association of Textile Chemists and Colorists)

* Water Repellency: Spray Test; AATCC Test Method 22 (1971).

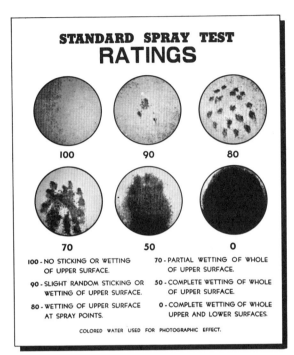

Figure 5-71 Spray Test Rating Chart (Courtesy: American Association of Textile Chemists and Colorists)

of fabrics, since it does not measure penetration of water through the fabric.

Static Absorption Test

This test* measures the resistance of fabrics to wetting by water. It is especially suitable for measuring the effectiveness of water-repellent finishes applied to fabrics, especially wool fabrics and napped fabrics of all fibers that are sometimes difficult to rate precisely by means of the Standard Spray Test. It is not intended for use in predicting the probable rain penetration resistance of fabrics, since it measures penetration of water into, but not through, the fabric.

A weighed sample is immersed in water at an average hydrostatic head of 3.5 inches for 20 minutes, removed from the water, reweighed, and evaluated by determining the percentage of water absorbed.

The increase in weight is divided by the original conditioned weight and multiplied by 100 to obtain the percent of water absorbed. The results for three test samples are averaged and reported (see Figure 5–72).

* Water Repellency: Static Absorption Test; AATCC Test Method 21 (1972).

245 *Testing for Product Performance*

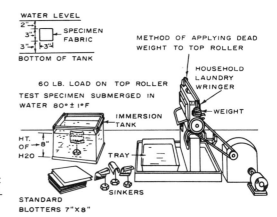

Figure 5-72 Static absorption tester. (Courtesy: American Association of Textile Chemists and Colorists.)

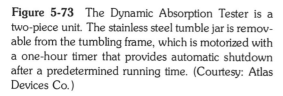

Tumble Jar Dynamic Absorption Test

This test* measures the resistance of fabrics to wetting by water. It is particularly suitable for measuring efficiency of finishes applied to fabrics, since it subjects the treated fabrics to dynamic conditions similar to those often encountered during actual use. It is not intended for use in predicting the probable rain penetration resistance of fabrics, since it measures penetration of water into, but not through, the fabric.

Preweighed samples are tumbled in water for a fixed period of time (see Figure 5–73) and are reweighed after the excess water has been removed from them. The percentage increase in weight is taken as a measure of the absorption or resistance to internal wetting.

The increase in weight of samples are divided by the original conditioned weight of the sample and multiplied by 100 to obtain the percent of water absorbed. The dynamic absorption of the fabric is

Figure 5-73 The Dynamic Absorption Tester is a two-piece unit. The stainless steel tumble jar is removable from the tumbling frame, which is motorized with a one-hour timer that provides automatic shutdown after a predetermined running time. (Courtesy: Atlas Devices Co.)

* Water Repellency: Tumble Jar Dynamic Absorption Test; AATCC 70 (1972).

obtained by averaging together the percent of water absorbed by each of the samples and reported to the nearest 1.0 percent.

WATER RESISTANCE

Water resistance is a general term denoting the ability of a fabric to resist wetting and penetration of water. There are three test methods designed to measure water resistance: (1) the Hydrostatic Pressure Test, (2) the Impact Penetration Test, and (3) the Rain Test. The methods are applicable to any fabric that may or may not have been given a water-resistant or water-repellent finish. The results obtained with this test depends on the water repellency of the fibers and yarns as well as the construction of the fabric.

Hydrostatic Pressure Test

This test* measures the resistance of fabrics to the penetration of water under static pressure, but not necessarily resistance to rain or water spray. It is suitable for testing heavy, closely woven fabrics that are expected to be used in contact with water, such as heavy ducks and tarpaulins. It is only of limited suitability for predicting the probable rain penetration resistance of garments.

A test sample is mounted under the orifice of a conical well of a hydrostatic pressure tester (see Figure 5–74). It is then subjected to

Figure 5-74 Standard 8-in. square test specimens are hydraulically clamped over a circular 4¼ in. diameter test area. Water is introduced through a constant level reservoir to the upper orifice chamber and onto the specimen from above. The hydrostatic head is raised at a fixed rate of 1 cm per second. The water is measured with a fixed indicator with traveling ruler to measure hydrostatic head and water cutoff. (Courtesy: Alfred Sutor Co., Inc.)

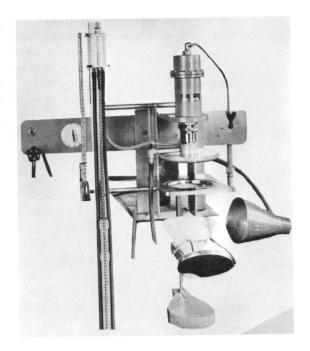

* Water Resistance: Hydrostatic Pressure Test: AATCC Test Method 127 (1971).

water pressure increasing at a constant rate until three points of leakage appear on its under surface. An average of the results obtained from three specimens is reported to the nearest 0.5 inch (1.0 centimeter) as the hydrostatic pressure resistance of the fabric.

Impact Penetration Test

This test* is applicable to any textile fabric, which may or may not have been given a water-resistant or water-repellent finish. It measures the resistance of fabrics to the penetration of water by impact, and thus can be used to predict the probable rain penetration resistance of garment fabrics.

Five hundred milliliters of water is allowed to spray from a height of two feet against the taut surface of a test sample backed by a weighed blotter. The blotter is then reweighed to determine water penetration and the sample is classified accordingly.

The increase in weight of the blotter in grams is calculated and the average result of the three test samples is reported. Individual determinations or average values of over 5.0 grams are reported as 5 + grams or > 5 grams (see Figure 5–75).

Rain Test

This test† measures the resistance of fabrics to the penetration of water by impact, and thus can be used to predict the probable rain penetration resistance of fabrics. It is especially suitable for measuring the penetration resistance of fabrics. With the instrument, tests may be made at different intensities of water impact to give a complete overall picture of the penetration resistance of a single fabric or a combination of fabrics.

A test backed by a weighed blotter is sprayed with water for five minutes under controlled conditions. The blotter is then reweighed to determine the amount of water which has leaked through the sample during the test (see Figure 5–76).

Water penetration, as indicated by the increase in weight of the blotter during the five-minute test period, is calculated and the average for at least three samples is reported. Individual determinations or average values of over 5.0 grams may be simply reported 50 5 + grams or > 5 grams.

In order to obtain a complete overall picture of the penetration resistance of a fabric or fabric combination the average penetrations with different pressure heads on the nozzle is obtained. The pressure head is varied by one-foot increments in order to determine (1) the

---

* Water Resistance: Impact Penetration Test; AATCC Test Method 42 (1971).
† Water Resistance: Rain Test; AATCC Test Method 35 (1971).

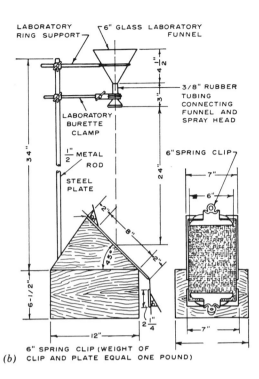

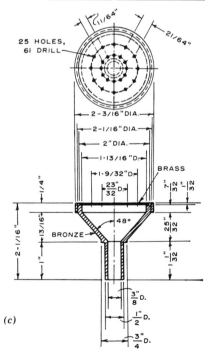

Figure 5-75 (a) Impact penetration tester. (b) Structural details of impact penetration tester. (c) Details of spray head. (Courtesy: American Association of Textile Chemists and Colorists)

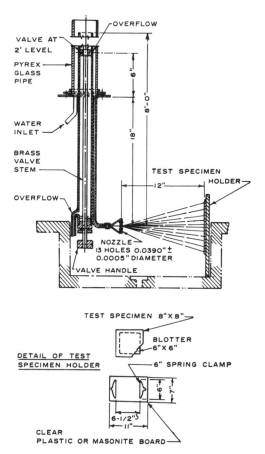

Figure 5-76 The Standard Rain Tester consists of an adjustable water column acting through a nozzle against the specimens to be tested. The center of the 13-hole nozzle lies in a horizontal plane with the center of the specimen holder. The face of the nozzle and the face of the specimen holder are in parallel vertical planes, 12 in. apart. The intensities of water impact are controlled by means of a glass pressure column. Each adjustment for the height of water in the column is made by a single setting of a valve, at the lower end of the drain or overflow pipe that extends up through the center of the glass pressure column. The 6-in. by 6-in. Standard Blotter, which is placed between the specimen holder and the specimen, is of standard weight, thickness, and absorbency. (Courtesy: American Association of Textile Chemists and Colorists)

250

maximum head at which no penetration occurs, (2) the change in penetration with increasing head, and (3) the minimum head required to cause "breakdown" or the penetration of more than 5 grams of water. At each pressure head a minimum of three specimens is tested in order to obtain the average penetration for that head.

WEATHER RESISTANCE

There are four methods used for testing weather resistance of fabrics:

1. Carbon-arc lamp exposure with wetting.
2. Exposure to natural light and weather.
3. Carbon-arc lamp exposure without wetting.
4. Exposure to natural light and weather without wetting.

Equipment used to carry out these tests is shown in Figure 5–77.

The first and second methods are intended for use in national and international trade in evaluating the resistance to degradation of textile and related materials, including coated fabrics, when subjected to natural or simulated weathering and radiant energy factors, and are further intended to check the level of durability represented in the material specification.

Figure 5-77 This instrument studies the effects of weathering of fabrics under controlled conditions. The cabinet is designed to meet specifications calling for simulations of sunlight and weather conditions. (Courtesy: Atlas Devices Co.)

The third and fourth methods are intended for use in evaluating the resistance to degradation due to weathering and sunlight exposure under milder conditions of a protected atmosphere, such as that found in the home. In these two methods, wetting during exposure is not a factor.

The four methods are applicable to fibers, yarns and fabrics, and products including coated fabrics, whether natural or dyed and whether finished or unfinished.

There are many considerations in interpreting the test results. Resistance to degradation under simulated or actual combined weather and sunlight exposure depends on:

1. The inherent properties of the material (physical state, mass, and compactness).
2. Special energy distribution and density of the radiant flux (from artificial source or sun).
3. The temperature and relative humidity of the air about the textile specimen during exposure.
4. The effect of leaching or degradation or additive products, including fiber stabilizers, by rain or water sprays.
5. Atmospheric contaminants.
6. The action of additive finishes and colorants including spectral absorption characteristics.
7. The action of residual laundry or dry-cleaning detergents.

The relative rates of degradation of different textile materials do not necessarily change to the same degree as those factors themselves change. Consequently, the relative durability of textile and related materials under the varying conditions of use cannot be predicted with certainty by any one test. It is, therefore, common practice to investigate the durability of materials by exposure to the variety of conditions under which they may be used in order to arrive at a full understanding of the performance that may be expected from them.

Having once established the acceptability of a given fabric, subsequent lots of it may be rated by direct comparison between them and the initially accepted material in any of the methods. Although the methods lead to results that are in general agreement for the majority of fabrics, they do not lead to the same results for all textiles. When significantly different levels of resistance to degradation are found between the natural sunlight and weather methods and their accelerated laboratory samples, the results obtained from exposure to direct sunlight and the elements of the weather is regarded as the level of durability of the particular material for the purposes of intended end use.

In research studies it is desirable to have an index when recording the relative durability of a series of fabrics to a common standard.

For the purposes of defining the relative durability of a test fabric to an agreed upon comparison standard an index, S_n5X, should be used. This index may be defined as the ratio of percent residual strength in the test specimen and the comparison standard at that number of Standard Weathering Hours* or langleys† required to produce an X percent loss of tensile strength in the comparison standard. With the index a specimen is considered to be as resistant to degradation as the standard when the S_nX value is 1, more durable when the S_nX index exceeds 1, less durable when the S_nX is less than 1.

Carbon-Arc Lamp Exposure With Wetting

This is a relatively rapid laboratory method‡ for assessing the resistance of textiles to degradation under radiant energy exposure conditions with periodic wetting to simulate unprotected natural sunlight and weather exposure.

Samples of the fabric to be tested in sufficient numbers to assure accuracy, are exposed to a specific calibrated carbon-arc source and to periodic wetting under defined conditions. Resistance to degradation is rated in terms of the number of standard weathering hours (SWH) of exposure and the percent loss in strength or percent residual strength (breaking or bursting) of the fabric when evaluated under standard textile testing conditions of $70 \pm 2°F$ and 65 ± 2 percent relative humidity.

When a standard of comparison is not available, the number of hours of exposure for a given fabric and the percent loss in, or residual, strength may be specified in the standard. When a comparison standard is available, the exposure period is that required to produce a specified or determined change in breaking (tensile) or bursting strength in the comparison standard, and the results for comparison standard and test material is reported either on an absolute basis of

---

* A "Standard Weathering Hour" (SWH) is defined as one-twentieth of the time of exposure to the NBS master standard lamp required to produce a 0.126 change in transmittance measured at 420 nm of an NBS-calibrated plate or chip, 0.060-inch thick, of yellow polymethylmethacrylate having an initial transmittance of 0.391.

† A langley is defined as a unit of solar radiation equivalent to one gram calorie per one square centimeter of irradiated surface.

‡ Weather Resistance: Carbon-Arc Lamp Exposure with Wetting; AATCC Test Method 111A (1972).

percent retained strength or percent loss in strength or on a relative ratio basis at the specified or determined level of the standard.

Terms of an agreed-on comparison sample or standard are (1) satisfactory—as durable or more durable than the comparison sample at the number of hours of exposure prescribed in the material standard and (2) unsatisfactory—less durable than the comparison sample when exposed for the number of hours prescribed in the material standard.

Carbon-Arc Lamp Exposure Without Wetting

This test method* is similar to the test method to the carbon-arc lamp with wetting. The difference is that this method for assessing the resistance of fabrics to degradation under radiant energy exposure conditions are mounted in the equipment without wetting to simulate the protected natural sunlight exposure, such as may occur with many fabrics used in the home or in protected environments.

Exposure to Natural Light and Weather

This method† serves as a reference method in the assessment of durability or resistance to degradation when results obtained by exposure to the carbon-arc lamp without wetting appears to be in conflict with those derived from direct sunlight and weather exposure.

The test is used to assess the resistance of textiles of all kinds, including coated fabrics, to degradation under solar energy and full weather exposure conditions.

Samples of the fabric to be tested, in sufficient number of replicates to assure accuracy, are placed on standard exposure racks exposed to sunlight and to the full elements of weather continuously, 24 hours a day, without cover under specified conditions. Resistance to degradation is rated in terms of the total number of langley units of radiation reaching the specimens and the percent loss in strength or the percent residual strength (breaking or bursting) of the material when evaluated under standard textile testing conditions.

When a standard of comparison is not available, the number of langleys of exposure for a given material and the percent loss in, or residual, strength is specified. When a comparison standard is available, the exposure period is that required to produce a specified or determined change in the breaking (tensile) or bursting strength in the comparison standard, and the results for comparison standard

* Weather Resistance: Carbon-Arc Lamp Exposure without Wetting; AATCC Test Method 111C (1972).

† Weather Resistance: Exposure to Natural Light and Weather; AATCC Test Method 111B (1972).

and test material is reported either on an absolute basis of percent retained strength or percent loss in strength or on a relative ratio basis at the specified or determined level of the standard.

Exposure to Natural Light and Weather Without Wetting

This method* serves as the reference method in the assessment of durability or resistance to degradation when results obtained by the carbon-arc lamp exposure without wetting appear to be in conflict with those derived from direct sunlight and protected weather exposure.

This method assesses the resistance of textiles to degradation under exposure to solar energy and the general elements of weather, excluding rain and precipitation. Standard samples are available and the evaluation is in reference to the degree of durability of the test samples relative to that displayed by the standard.

* Weather Resistance: Exposure to Natural Light and Weather without Wetting; AATCC Test Method 111D (1972).

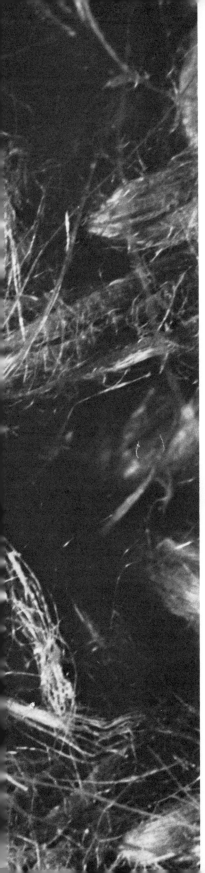

6
Fabric Care—
Soil, Spot, and
Stain Removal

257

The removal of soil and stains from textile products has never been easy, even with the natural fibers and relatively simple dye substances. Today, with constant introduction of new products into daily use, professional cleaning establishments as well as consumers must be constantly alert to new disasters to textiles. Some of these require new removal techniques. Others require only the recognition of the chemical makeup of the new substance and its proper classification into stain removal categories.

FABRIC SOILING

The type of soil in a fabric determines the methods to be used for its removal. The soiling of fabrics occurs as overall soiling, localized soiling (stains), or a combination of the two. The general accumulation of dust particles throughout a garment is an example of overall soiling. Ink, food, or other stains that usually appear as small spots are examples of localized soiling.

The obvious effect of soil on a fabric is a staining or dulling of it. Some less obvious effects are stiffening of fabrics from salts in foods and perspiration, color changes from acid or alkaline soils, fabric damage from salts, acids, or alkalies, and attraction of insects to soiled areas. Sharp embedded soil particles can cause fiber abrasion.

Types of Soil

Many soils have similar characteristics and can be grouped together. They are as follows:

SOLVENT-SOLUBLE SOIL

Solvent-soluble soils are those that are soluble in dry-cleaning solvents. Examples are oil, grease, and some waxes. These soils are insoluble in water.

WATER-SOLUBLE SOIL

There are two distinct types of water-soluble soil. One type is completely soluble in water; the other is partially soluble in water. Examples of the first type are common salt and sugar. Representative of the partially water-soluble soils are "built-up" food stains. Both types of water-soluble soils are commonly found on stained fabrics in the form of perspiration, food, or beverage stains.

INSOLUBLE SOIL

A soil not dissolved by dry-cleaning solvent, water, or special agents is an insoluble soil. Common examples are carbon, dust, lint, and sand. It is the most common type of soil in stained fabrics and comprises the bulk of the soil to be removed in dry cleaning.

SOIL INSOLUBLE IN SOLVENT AND WATER   Some soils are insoluble in dry cleaning solvent or water. These soils are either partially or completely soluble in special solvents or are removed by special agents other than solvents. Examples are nail polish, paint, ink, adhesive, albumin, and rust. This is called spotting.

Factors Affecting Soil Removal

Factors that affect ease of soil removal are type of soil, extent of soiling, age of the soil and the nature of the stained fabric.

How Soil Is Removed

Dry-cleaning solvent alone is capable of removing some soils. With the addition of dry-cleaning detergents and small amounts of water a greater variety of soils may be removed in the dry-cleaning washer (see Chapter 8).

Some soils do not lend themselves to adequate removal by dry cleaning methods. Many of these soils can be removed by laundering and wet cleaning techniques (see Chapters 7 and 8).

Some soil-removal methods do not depend on the solvent and lubricating actions of dry-cleaning solvent, water and detergents. These other methods involve soil removal by chemical or physical means.

SPOTS AND STAINS

Spot and stain removal can be quite complicated. Few people realize that as new products are developed, new spot and stain removal techniques must also be developed if the product comes in contact with fabrics during use.

A good example of a new source of stain is the child's delight, "Silly Putty"—a substance composed largely of silicone. Children get the dough in their hair, on clothes, and over furniture and rugs. Once the putty spreads and sets, the stain is difficult to remove. Energine or a similar spot remover should be used in attempting to remove the stain in the home. The professional cleaner has found that amyl acetate is effective in removing Silly Putty stains from most fabrics.

Some stains cannot be removed without damaging the fabric. An example is some of the new glues and paints that contain an epoxy resin as a base. When the resin dries, it becomes insoluble to both water and dry-cleaning solvent. There is as yet no method of removal for these resin stains.

Even the polyethylene bags widely used to protect garments when they come from the dry cleaners may cause stains that are difficult to remove. If these bags are subjected to excessive heat—for example, carrying garments in a car trunk across the desert or storing clothes in a closet that has a steam pipe—the polyethylene may melt and stain the garment the bag was meant to protect. The only method for removing this type of stain is immersion of the fabric in hot perchlorethylene. This procedure must be carried out in a laboratory. It cannot be done in the home or even in a dry-cleaning plant because of the risks in the vaporization of perchlorethylene. Moreover, the dye of the fabric must be colorfast to this treatment, otherwise the stain cannot be removed.

Some stains may be invisible in a garment. But with the heat of drying and pressing these stains become visible. They become brown stains. The reducing sugar in such common substances as fruit juices, artifically sweetened soft drinks, ginger ale, Tom Collins mix, and cocktails makes stains that are sometimes invisible when fresh. On wool, the heat required for drying and pressing fabrics caramelizes the sugar, causing a brown stain. Rarely can these stains be removed. This type of stain may develop even after the garment has been dry cleaned or after it has been stored for several months. This possibility should be kept in mind when one discovers stubborn brown stains. These stains should be flushed from the fabric with water while they are still fresh.

Ball-point pens have brought a new type of ink stain. Until a few years ago, most writing inks were of the iron gallo-tannate type. The ball-point inks are 40 to 70 percent glycols and glycol/ethers, solvent-soluble dyes, and basic dyes and resins. These inks are difficult to recognize. They are usually of standard colors and thus resemble other inks. If ball-point ink stains are worked on first with water, they become set and cannot be removed by dry solvents. They should be removed by prespotting with a dry solvent.

Ink stains have always required skill and special techniques for complete removal. With the advent of the new inks, however, removal requires not only skill and new techniques, but also time and patience.

STAIN IDENTIFICATION

Of prime importance in stain removal is identification of the stain. The first steps, and in many instances the only ones necessary, are observations of:

1. *Appeareance of the spot or stains.* (a) *Color* is often a clue. For example, a red color often identifies a lipstick stain; the brown color an iodine stain. (b) *Appearance.* A stain on the surface of the fabric also helps to identify a stain. For example, ink penetrates a fabric's surface; paint builds up on a fabric. (c) *Shape* is often a clue. For example, stains follow the yarns with the least degree of twist in a fabric.

If the yarns are of equal twist in both the warp and filling, a perfect cross will appear. (d) *Ultraviolet light* may be used to identify stains. For example, under ultraviolet or black light rust stains look black; oil stains on polyester glow; sugar stains fluoresces. The breakdown of a fluorescent dye or tint appears gray.

2. *Odor.* Smell may identify stains such as perfume, cold-wave solution (faint odor of bromine), or medicinal stains.

3. *Location.* For example, perspiration stains occur in the under-arm area of a suit or blouse, food stains on ties and on dress or suit fronts.

4. *Feel.* The sense of feeling may be used to identify some stains. For example, egg, a type of albuminous stain, may be recognized by its stiffness; glue and adhesives are sticky; paint may be rough or smooth; fingernail polish may feel built up on the fabric surface.

DYES AFFECT STAIN REMOVAL

Ninety-five percent of all fabrics handled in a dry cleaning plant have been dyed or printed with dyestuffs. These dyes are chemicals that may react with either the stain substance or the dry cleaning solvent. Therefore, the person who works with spot and stain removal must understand the types and characteristics of dyes. The main classifications of dyes are acids (anionic), cationic (basic), direct, developed direct, azoic, vat, mordant (metalized), sulfur, reactive, and dispersed dyes.

GENERAL PROCEDURES

Stain removal from modern fabrics is complex. It requires special tools and skill. The same stain on two different fabrics may behave quite differently, depending on fiber content, dye and finish characteristics, as well as construction of the fabric. No single prodecure, or basic method of treatment exists for removal of the hundreds of different types of stains that occur on the variety of fabrics used in wearing apparel and household items. Stain-removal procedures fall into four general categories.

Solvent Action

Solvent action occurs when one substance is dissolved in another. For example, sugar dissolves in water. The mechanical action of stirring hastens the solvent action. Sugar is not soluble in dry solvents, and no amount of stirring will dissolve it in these substances. On the other hand, a suitable dry solvent may be used to remove oils or greases, which do not dissolve in water.

A suitable solvent must be selected and used for each type of soluble substance in the stain. If the incorrect solvent is used, no amount of mechanical action will remove the stain.

Lubrication and Mechanical Action

Lubrication is particularly useful in removing insoluble and chemically inactive substances. It means the application of force in the presence of a "lubricant"—a surfactant. The washing of one's hands is an example of the physical action of lubrication. The soil is dislodged but not dissolved by mechanical work.

Chemical Action

Some stains must be removed by chemical action. In such procedures, a chemical spot remover reacts with the staining substance to produce a new compound. This compound does not have any characteristics of either the original stain or of the spotting reagent and may be rendered invisible or soluble and easily flushed from the fabric. An iodine stain is removed by treating it with ammonia. This results in ammonium iodide, a colorless water-soluble substance that can be rinsed from the fabric (see Group X, p. 275).

Digestion

Many stains require digestion for removal. Trade products used in commercial dry-cleaning plants contain enzymic materials. They convert insoluble substances into simpler substances that are more soluble and readily removed from fabric. In home use, the trade product Axion is used for presoaking to perform the same function. Enzyme detergents such as Gain and Biz are less concentrated but are formulated to convert some stains into soluble substances.

PROFESSIONAL REMOVAL OF STAINS

It is advisable to use a professional dry cleaner for cleaning and spotting when the stains are numerous or cover a large area, when they require a chemical procedure for which an individual is not equipped, when the fabric is fragile or highly sized, if the stain cannot be identified, or if there are doubts about the fabric itself.

Skill, specialized solvents, chemicals, and formulas are necessary to remove spots and stains. Commercial establishments have specialists, "spotters," who are responsible for stain removal.

The Work of the Spotter

The spotter must know or recognize and classify various types of stains and also have a knowledge of fabrics and dyestuffs and of the effectiveness of the various reagents on the stains, fabrics, and dye-

Figure 6-1 To remove stains, the professional spotter uses a specially designed spotting board with a sleeve attachment, a spotting gun, and a water spray gun—all controlled with steam, air, and vacuum attachments. (Courtesy: International Fabricare Institute)

stuffs. Even more important is the ability to use certain techniques and skills in the removal of stains. The spotter's job is to remove the maximum number of spots and stains with minimum damage to the fabric.

Before a spotter attempts to remove any spot or stain, he must first identify the stain and determine which spotting method would be most effective and whether wet or dry solvents should be used.

In the commercial dry-cleaning plant the spotter works at a so-called spotting board, a combination of a solid top and a perforated area at one end. A similarly fashioned sleeve board may be used with the spotting board for work on small areas (Figure 6–1). A tray under the board keeps garments off the floor.

The working surface of the board is hard and smooth. It may be made of glass, marble, Masonite, monel, or Formica. These materials are usually resistant to acids, alkalies and other spotting agents.

Spotting boards are equipped with steam and water guns and treadles to control air, steam, and vacuum. The operator holds the steam gun at right angles (90 degrees) to the fabric and at a minimm distance of four inches (when using both steam and air). The force of the steam holds the fabric to the board; the steam flushes the stain and spotting agents through the fabric, but at a distance of four inches the steam gun does not cause permanent yarn distortion.

With the usual 65 to 70 pounds of steam pressure, the temperature of the steam at the nozzle of the gun is above 300°F. At a distance of approximately four inches, the temperature of the steam is only about 110°F. The action of acids, alkalies, and bleaches can be accelerated by an increase in temperature.

When the vacuum treadle is depressed, a vacuum is created in the perforated area on the board to decrease the drying time after spotting. The vacuum also aids in flushing stains and agents used in stain removal and may decrease the building up of heavy rings. Warm air and vacuum decrease the drying time.

The water spray gun is effective in removing chemicals that are difficult to rinse. It may be more desirable than the steam spray in removing some spots, such as those containing blood, albumin, and starch.

Two brushes are usually kept on the board: one with white bristles, the other with black. The dark brush is used when spotting with dry-side chemicals. This avoids the danger of wet-side agents and dry-side agents contacting each other in the fabric, with resultant rings that may be difficult to remove.

Tamping is done on the solid area of the board. The tamping action is similar to driving a tack with a small hammer. The brush is held two to three inches above the fabric and hits it squarely without bending the bristles of the brush. The bristles strike the solid surface without spreading the distorting yarns.

The spotter also uses a spatula—a flat, smooth piece of bone pointed at one end. Bone is not affected by acids, alkalies, and bleaches. Metal might be affected by commercial rust removers or might accelerate the action of some of the spotting chemicals. The spatula is used to work spotting solutions back and forth over the stain and into the fabric.

The spotter freely uses medium weight turkish towels to absorb water and solutions from the surface of a garment, or to place underneath to absorb stains. Cheesecloth is used to feather when working a stain with dry-side agents. When a spot is "feathered out," the moisture is gradually reduced in quantity from the center of the stained area to the outside area, thus reducing the line of demarcation.

White blotters are used in the spotting department for testing dyestuffs on fabrics to determine their fastness to various chemicals and spotting agents. Blotters may also be used to absorb stains.

Since the spotter's work is on textile fibers of one type or another, he must be familiar with their properties as well as their behavior under various conditions of temperature, mechanical action, treatment with acids, alkalies, solvents, bleaches, and other chemicals.

HOME REMOVAL OF STAINS

The nonprofessional individual can successfully remove many small stains by carefully observing the basic steps for first aid for spot and stain removal (see Table 6–1). Before attempting to remove spots and stains at home, you should understand the basic concepts of stain removal (see Table 6–2).

After a stain is identified, it must be classified as to whether it is removable on the "wet" side (with water solutions) or on the "dry" side (with dry organic solvents or powders).

Table 6–1 First Aid For Spots and Stains

Absorb excess liquid with a clean, white cloth.
Avoid forcing staining material into the fabric.
Remove built-up surface stains with a spoon.
Sponge food stains with cool water.
Place towel under stained area.
Sponge with damp cloth to flush out staining material.
Sponge oily stains with drycleaning solvent. Do not allow drycleaning solvent to come in contact with skin.
Work only in a ventilated area. Avoid breathing solvent fumes.

Table 6–2 Basic Concepts—Spot and Stain Removal

Stain removal solutions should be used in the strengths recommended and for the length of time given. Directions and precautions given on the labels should be carefully observed.

Many stains react very slowly to the stain removal agent. Consequently, work carefully and have patience.

Aging and heat can set stains permanently. Remove stains immediately.

If the wrong method is used for a particular stain, the stain may be permanently set. For example, certain types of ball-point ink should be removed by prespotting with a dry spotter.

Oily stains should be sponged with a dry solvent.

Salad dressing and cooking oils contain polyunsaturated fats, which oxidize if not removed immediately. Oxidized oil stains cannot be removed by home methods. It is difficult, and sometimes impossible, for a dry cleaner to remove them.

Water is the most useful solvent for nongreasy stains.

A greasy or oily stain usually wicks along the fabric yarn.

Detergents for automatic dishwashers, heavy-duty household detergents, or laundry detergents may contain alkalies that could set some stains.

Some stains require professional treatment because of the solvents and techniques required to remove them.

Some stain removers sold in grocery and drug stores are a mixture of two or more solvents. Read the labels. Follow directions and precautions.

Chemical stain removers react with stains to form new compounds that are colorless or soluble, or both.

Chemical removers must be used cautiously to avoid fabric damage. Test reagent on an unexposed seam before proceeding.

Generally speaking, peroxygen bleaches are safer on more fibers and dyes than are chlorine bleaches.

Metal containers or metal objects should not be used with bleach for stain removal.

Color removers are generally used for stains on which bleaches are not effective.

Table 6-3   Items Needed To Remove Spots and Stains

Tools	Absorbent towels, cheesecloth, paper towels, facial tissue, sponge. Medium bristle brush with a handle. Medicine dropper; small syringe. Dull knife, spoon. Basin or bowl.
Solvents	Water Petroleum-based drycleaning solvent (Renuzit, Carbona). Perchlorethylene. Alcohol—denatured or rubbing for nongreasy stains. *Caution:* Flammable! Poison! Fades some dyes. Amyl acetate (chemically pure). *Caution:* Flammable! Poison!
Absorbents	Fullers earth. Cornstarch. Commercial products such as K_2R.
Enzymes, detergents	Commercial products such as Axion, Gain, Biz, or others.
Prespotters	Dry spotter (one ounce cocoanut oil to eight ounces drycleaning solvent.) If cocoanut oil is not available, use mineral oil. Wet Spotter (one part hand dishwashing detergent, one part glycerine, eight parts water). Commercial products such as Spray 'N Wash or Wisk.

The dry procedure is so named because it employs spot removal agents that contain no water. These agents are cleaning fluids or powders. Neither is effective on stains that must be dissolved in water. They are effective only on oily, greasy, or waxy stains. The powders contain a dry-cleaning solvent, which loosens the stain so the powder can absorb it out of the fabric. The procedure described below refers only to the liquid agents. Some stains require both "dry" and "wet" treatments in that order. Never use water and cleaning fluid together.

Any unidentified stains should be treated with the dry procedure first and then the wet procedure, if necessary.

Assemble the necessary tools and reagents before attempting to remove spots and stains. These are listed in Table 6–3.

There are certain precautions that must be taken to avoid accidents to a person, home, as well as the fabrics being worked on.

Table 6-3 Items Needed To Remove Spots and Stains (Continued)

Detergents and oily substances	Liquid detergent for hand dishwashing (Ivory, Lux, Joy, Vel). Glycerine (one part to one part water). Coconut oil.
Bleaches	Chlorine—Chlorox, White Sail, Purex or others. *Caution:* Poison. Peroxygen—Sodium perborate, (Snowy Bleach) hydrogen peroxide (3 percent). Color remover—commercial products such as Rit or Tintex. *Caution:* Poison.
Chemicals	Acetic acid or white vinegar—(5 to 10 percent concentration). Used to neutralize alkalies, for removal of some food and dye stains, and for restoring color changes due to alkalies. Ammonia or household ammonia—(10 percent concentration). Used to neutralize acids, for removal of some dye and food stains, and to restore colors changed by the action of acids. *Caution:* Poison. Tincture of iodine. Used only for stains containing silver compounds such as silver nitrate and some medical stains. Hypo crystals or sodium thiosulfate. Sold in drug stores or photo supply stores. Use one teaspoon of crystals dissolved in one cup of water. Used for removing iodine and chlorine stains. DO NOT USE ON SILK OR WOOL.

Study the precautions you should take in removing spots and stains

Test the fabric on an unexposed seam or hem with the solvent or chemical agent to be used. Observe for colorfastness of dye and finish. If unaffected, proceed.

Remove a built-up stain on the fabric surface with a spoon or dull knife.

Continue with the appropriate dry or wet procedure.

Spotting Procedures

Most stains can be classified into one of nine "families" or "groups." All the stains in each of these families or groups are removed by the same procedure and with the same removal agents. However, a few stains are too complex to fit into one of these groups, and will require more varied removal procedures. Some of these are listed at the end of group discussion under "Miscellaneous" or Group X. The dry procedure is as follows:

1. Place a towel under the stained area—preferably a white towel—to make it easier to detect transfer of staining material from stained fabric to towel.

2. Apply the solvent to the stain. Saturate the area.

3. Rub the stain lightly with your fingertips. Do not try to press it into the fabric. Let the solvent loosen the staining substance and rinse it through the fabric into the towel. Continue rubbing with the fingers until the staining material is gone.

4. Remove the towel.

5. Moisten a piece of cheesecloth with the cleaning solvent and wipe lightly around the outside edges of the spotted area. Wipe toward the center. This is to prevent a ring.

6. Allow to dry.

The wet procedure is as follows:

1. Place a towel under the stained area. A white towel is preferable because it will show the staining substance absorbed from the fabric.

2. Apply plain, cool water to the stain. Do not mix it with anything. Saturate the stained area.

3. Rub lightly with your fingertips to loosen the stain so it will wash through the fabric into the towel.

4. If water alone does not loosen the stain, add liquid detergent and work the same way with the fingertips.

5. Then wet a cheesecloth heavily with water and squeeze over the stained area to flush out the detergent. Detergent left in the fabric can cause a ring.

6. When the stain and detergent have both been washed out, remove the towel.

7. Then wipe a wet cheesecloth around the edges of the stained area to prevent a ring. Wipe toward the center.

8. Allow to dry.

In both the dry and wet procedures, work the stains slowly. Patience is necessary. Check frequently to see whether the staining substance has transferred to the towel. Change the position of the towel so that a clean portion of it is next to the stained area.

Also given are the steps to be followed in removing an unknown stain. Before proceeding, it is suggested that the directions given in Table 6–4, Table 6–5, and Figure 6–2 be studied.

Table 6–4   Stains That Require Chemical Stain Removers

Try mild treatment first.
1. Place absorbent towel under stain.
2. Dampen stain with cool water.
3. Apply liquid remover with medicine dropper or sprinkle powdered or crystalline removers on the dampened spot.
4. Do not allow remover to dry on fabric. Keep area wet with a pad of cotton or cheesecloth wet out with the stain remover solution. Use a pad dampened with water if a powder or crystalline remover is being used.
5. Rinse stain removal solvent or powder from washable fabric locally with water or rinse the entire garment in water.
6. If fabric is dry cleanable follow above procedure locally. Do not rinse entire garment in water.

For a stronger treatment:
1. Lengthen the time of the treatment.
2. Use a more concentrated stain-remover solution.

Table 6–5   Stains That Require Bleaches and Color Remover

Chlorine Bleaches
Do not use chlorine bleaches on fabrics that contain silk, wool, spandex, or special finishes unless the label or hang tag states it is safe to use chlorine bleach.
Test all dyed fabrics before using chlorine bleach. Follow directions on package for powder or granulated bleach. Do not put bleach solution in a metal container (see Figure 6–2).

Washable Fabrics
Mild Treatment
1. Mix two tablespoons of liquid bleach with one quart cool water.
2. Use medicine dropper to apply to small stains; soak large stains in solution.
3. Treat 5 to 15 minutes. Rinse with water. Repeat if necessary.
Strong Treatment
1. Mix equal parts of liquid bleach and water.
2. Use medicine dropper to apply to small stains; soak large stains in solution.
3. Rinse with water. Repeat if necessary.

Dry-Cleanable Fabrics
1. Mix one teaspoon of liquid bleach with one cup of cool water.
2. Apply to stain with medicine dropper.
3. Leave on stain for 5 to 15 minutes. Rinse well with water.

Table 6-5 Stains That Require Bleaches and Color Remover (Continued)

Powdered Peroxygen Bleaches
Do not use or mix in metal container.

Washable Fabrics

Mild Treatment
1. Mix one or two tablespoons powdered bleach with one pint lukewarm water for use on silk, wool, modacrylic fabrics. Use hot water for other fabrics.
2. Cover stained area with solution or soak entire article. Rinse well or wash.

Strong Treatment
1. Do not use this treatment on fabrics made of wool, silk, modacrylic, or heat-sensitive fibers.

Dry-Cleanable Fabrics
1. Sprinkle powdered peroxygen bleach on stain.
2. Cover with a cotton pad dampened with lukewarm water.
3. Keep damp until stain is removed. Rinse well.

Washable or Dry-Cleanable Fabrics

Hydrogen Peroxide
1. Moisten stain with a few drops of 3 percent solution of hydrogen peroxide.
2. Add hydrogen peroxide as needed to keep stained area moist until stain is removed. Rinse well.

Color Remover
1. Make test for colorfastness of fabric.
2. Do not use in metal container.

Mild Treatment
1. Dissolve ¼ teaspoon of color remover in ½ cup cool water.
2. Wet stain with a few drops of solution.
3. Dampen a cotton pad with solution and place on stain 1 to 5 minutes. Repeat if necessary. Rinse well.

Strong Treatment
1. Dissolve ¼ teaspoon of color remover in ¼ cup boiling water.
2. With medicine dropper, drop hot solution on stain. Repeat if necessary. Rinse well.

Group I
Fats, Oils, Waxes, Grease, Some Pigments and Dyes

Adhesive tape	Lotion: calamine, hand
Crayon	Makeup: powder, rouge
Dye: shoe polish	Nosedrops
Eye: liner, pencil,	Ointment
shadow, mascara	

Grease, oil	Paint
Hair spray	Smoke, soot
Ink: India, felt tip, marker, typewriter ribbon	Tar
Insecticides	Wax: car, floor, furniture

Method of Removal

Washable Fabrics

Sponge with dry solvent, apply dry spotter, and rub gently. Flush with dry solvent. If stain remains, repeat above procedure. Dry. Sponge with water, apply wet spotter and ammonia. Rub or tamp gently with brush. Rinse with water. Launder.

Dry-Cleanable Fabrics

Same as for washable fabrics, but do not launder.

Figure 6-2 (Courtesy: International Fabricare Institute)

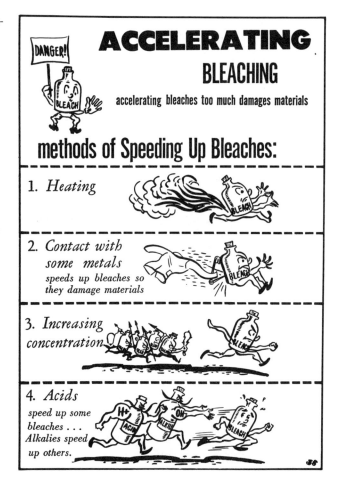

271

Group II
Food Stains Containing Oils and Fats

Catsup	Mayonnaise
Chili sauce	Milk
Chocolate	Pudding
Cocoa	Salad dressing
Cream	Sauce
Gravy	Soup
Ice cream	

Method of Removal

Washable Fabrics

Sponge with dry solvent, apply dry spotter, and rub gently. Flush with dry solvent. Dry. Soak in water solution of detergent and household ammonia. Rinse with water. Soak in water solution of enzyme product for 30 minutes. Launder. Repeat if stain remains.

Dry-Cleanable Fabrics

Sponge with dry solvent, apply dry spotter, and rub gently. Flush with dry solvent. Dry. Sponge with water. Apply wet spotter and ammonia. Rub.

Group III
Albuminous and Starchy Materials and Foods

Bath oil	Lotion, aftershave
Blood	Mouthwash
Body discharge	Mucus
Egg	Sherbert
Egg drops	Starch
Fish slime	Vomit

Method of Removal

Washable Fabrics

Soak in water solution of detergent and ammonia. Rinse with water. Soak in water solution of an enzyme product for 30 minutes. Launder. Repeat if stain remains.

Dry-Cleanable Fabrics

Sponge with water. Apply wet spotter and ammonia. Rub into stain. Rinse with water. Add an enzyme product and keep area moist for 30 minutes. Flush with water. Repeat if stain remains.

Group IV
Plastics, Some Pigments, and Dyes

Airplane glue	Lacquer
Carbon paper	Mimeograph ink
Cement, household	Mucilage, paste
Corn removers	Plastic
Correction fluid, mimeograph	Plastic glue
Cuticle oil	Solder, liquid
Cuticle remover	Typewriter ribbon
Fingernail polish	

Method of Removal

Washable Fabrics

Sponge with dry solvent, apply dry spotter, and rub gently. Tamp gently with brush after adding more dry spotter. Flush with dry solvent. Dry. If stain remains, repeat above procedure. Dry. Apply amyl acetate and rub or blot. Keep moist with amyl acetate for 15 minutes with occasional blotting. Flush with dry solvent. Dry.

Dry-Cleanable Fabrics

Same as for washable fabrics.

Group V
Tanin and Reducing Sugars, Some Vegetable Coloring Materials

Bath oil	Home permanents	Tea
Beer	Molasses	Tobacco
Berry juice	Mouthwash	Toothpaste
Caramelized sugar	Mud	Vegetables
Coffee	Shoe polish (white)	Vinegar (colored)
Casein glue	Shaving cream	Whiskey
Cordials	Soft drinks	Wine
Cough syrup	Suntan lotion	
Fruit	Syrup	

Method of Removal

Washable Fabrics

Soak in a water solution of detergent and vinegar. Rinse. Sponge with alcohol. Launder. If stain remains, soak in water solution of an enzyme product 30 minutes. Rinse and launder.

Dry-Cleanable Fabrics

Sponge with water. Apply wet spotter and vinegar. Rub into stain. Rinse with water. Apply alcohol and rub into stain. Dry. If stain remains, apply an enzyme product and keep area wet for 30 minutes. Rinse with water. Dry.

Group VI
Red Dyes, Deodorants, Perspiration, Urine

Antiperspirants	Merthiolate
Candy	Metaphen
Deodorants	Paint, water color
Dye: clothing, food, hair	Perspiration
Inks, red	Picric acid
Mercurochrome	Urine

Method of Removal

Washable Fabrics

Soak one hour in a water solution of detergent and ammonia. Rinse with water. Soak one hour in a water solution of vinegar. Rinse and dry. Apply alcohol and rub gently. Rinse with water. Launder.

273

Dry-Cleanable Fabrics

Sponge with water. Apply wet spotter and ammonia. Blot stain with blotting paper. Keep area wet for 30 minutes with occasional rubbing. Rinse with water. Apply wet spotter and vinegar. Rub gently. Rinse and dry. Apply alcohol and rub gently. Rinse with water. Dry.

Group VII
Blue, Black, Green, Violet Dyes
Bluing
Dye: clothing, food,
hair, shoe
Gentian violet
Ink: green, violet,
blue, black
Paint: water colors

Method of Removal

Washable Fabrics

Soak 30 minutes in a water solution of detergent and vinegar. Rinse with water and dry. Apply alcohol and rub gently. Dry. Soak 30 minutes in a water solution of detergent and ammonia. Launder.

Dry-Cleanable Fabrics

Sponge with water. Apply wet spotter and vinegar. Blot with blotting paper. Keep area wet for 30 minutes and blot occasionally. Flush with water and dry. Apply alcohol and rub gently. Dry. Sponge with water. Apply wet spotter and ammonia. Keep area wet 30 minutes and blot occasionally. Flush area with water. Dry.

Group VIII
Oxidizing Oils, Rubber Cement, Gum
Asphalt
Butter
Cement, rubber
Chewing gum
Corn oil
Linseed oil
Vegetable oil

Method of Removal

Washable Fabrics

Apply dry solvent and dry spotter. Rub or tamp gently with brush. Keep area wet with dry solvent and dry spotter for 30 minutes with occasional rubbing. Rinse with dry solvent. Dry.

Dry-Cleanable Fabrics

Same as for washable fabrics.

Group IX
Iodine, Penicillin, Silver Salts

Argyrol™*
Iodine†
Penicillin
Photo develop-
    ment fluid
Silver nitrate

Method of Removal

Washable Fabrics

Sponge area with water, add a few drops of iodine. Add a few drops of hypo solution and a few drops of ammonia. Flush well with water. Launder.

Dry-Cleanable Fabrics

Same as for washable fabrics, but do not launder.

* Use enzyme product first.
† Do not use iodine in method of removal.

Group X
Miscellaneous Stains

Acids*	Ink, ball-point pen
Alkalis*	Lipstick
Black walnut	Mildew
Brass	Mustard
Candle wax	Pencil
Chlorine	Rust
Cologne	Scorch
Grass	Shellac

Method of Removal
Acids

Washable Fabrics

Sponge with water, add ammonia, and let stand. Sponge and rinse well with water. Launder Immediately.

Dry-Cleanable Fabrics

Sponge with water, add ammonia and let stand. Sponge and rinse well with water.

Alkalies

Washable Fabrics

Sponge with water, add vinegar, and let stand. Sponge and rinse well with water. Launder immediately.

Dry-Cleanable Fabrics

Sponge with water, add vinegar, and let stand. Sponge and rinse well with water.

* See Figure 6-3.

275

Figure 6-3 (Courtesy: International Fabricare Institute)

Black Walnut

Washable Fabrics

Sponge with water, apply wet spotter and vinegar. Brush gently. Repeat if necessary. Flush area with water. Launder.

Dry-Cleanable Fabrics

Same as for washable fabrics, but do not launder.

Brass

Washable Fabrics

Take to dry cleaner.

Dry-cleanable Fabrics
    Take to dry cleaner.

Candle Wax

Washable Fabrics
    Remove excess with dull knife. Place stained area between blotting papers and iron. Replace blotters with fresh ones and iron until melting stops. Sponge with dry solvent. Dry.

Dry-Cleanable Fabrics
    Same as for washable fabrics.

Chlorine

Washable Fabrics
    Sponge area with solution of color remover and water.

Dry-Cleanable Fabrics
    Same as for washable fabrics.

Cologne

Washable Fabrics
    Sponge with water, apply wet spotter, and rub gently. Rinse with water. Apply alcohol and rub. Rinse with water. Launder.

Dry-Cleanable Fabrics
    Same as for washable fabrics, but do not launder.

Grass

Washable Fabrics
    Sponge with dry solvent, rub gently. Dry. Apply amyl acetate and rub gently. Flush with dry solvent and dry. Sponge with water, apply wet spotter and vinegar. Rub gently. Rinse with water and dry. Sponge with alcohol. Rub gently. Dry. Launder.

Dry-Cleanable Fabrics
    Same as for washable fabrics, but do not launder.

Ink, Ball-Point Pen

Washable Fabrics
    Apply lukewarm glycerine to stain, blot, and rub gently. Keep area wet with glycerine for 30 minutes with occasional blotting. Flush with water, apply wet spotter and ammonia, and tamp gently. Rinse with water. Dry.

Dry-Cleanable Fabrics
    Same as for washable fabrics.

Lipstick

Washable Fabrics
    Apply dry solvent, add dry spotter. Press area with clean blotter. Repeat until bleeding stops. If stain spreads, flush with dry solvent. Repeat until bleeding stops. Dry. Sponge with water, apply wet spotter and ammonia. Rub gently. Flush with water, apply wet spotter and vinegar. Rub gently. Rinse with water and dry. Sponge with alcohol, rub gently and dry.

Dry-Cleanable Fabrics
    Same as for washable fabrics.

Mildew

Washable Fabrics
    Gently brush off excess dried stain. Flush with dry solvent. Apply dry

277

spotter, amyl acetate, and brush gently. Flush well with dry solvent. Dry. Sponge with water. Apply wet spotter and vinegar. Rub gently. Flush with water. If stain remains, apply wet spotter and rub gently. Rinse and dry. If stain remains, apply alcohol and rub. Dry.

Dry-Cleanable Fabrics
    Same as for washable fabrics.

Mustard

Washable Fabrics
    Carefully scrape off excess dried mustard. Flush with dry-cleaning solvent. Tamp lightly with a brush. Flush with dry-cleaning solvent. *Allow to dry.* Sponge with water and vinegar. Tamp lightly with brush. Flush with water. Repeat the last step if staining substance remains. If any stain is left, wet the stain with hydrogen peroxide and add a drop of ammonia. Do not bleach longer than 15 minutes. Flush with water.

Dry-Cleanable Fabrics
    Same as for washable fabrics.

Pencil

Washable Fabrics
    Erase excess with soft eraser. Flush with dry solvent. Apply dry spotter and rub gently. Let stand 30 minutes. Flush with dry solvent and dry. Sponge with water, apply wet spotter and ammonia. Rub gently. Rinse with water. Repeat if necessary.

Dry-Cleanable Fabrics
    Same as for washable fabrics.

Rust

Washable Fabrics
    Send to dry cleaner.

Dry-Cleanable Fabrics
    Send to dry cleaner.

Scorch

Washable Fabrics
    If safe for fabric and dye, bleach with chlorine or peroxide.

Dry-Cleanable Fabrics
    Send to dry cleaner.

Shellac

Washable Fabrics
    Sponge with dry solvent, apply dry spotter, and tamp gently. Repeat. Dry. Apply alcohol and tamp. Dry.

Dry-Cleanable Fabrics
    Same as for washable fabrics.

Shoe Polish, White

Washable Fabrics
    Sponge with dry solvent, add dry spotter, and brush. Rinse with dry solvent. Sponge with amyl acetate and brush. Rinse with dry solvent and dry. Sponge with water, add wet spotter and vinegar. Brush gently. Rinse with water. Dry. Launder.

Dry-Cleanable Fabrics
    Same as for washable fabrics, but do not launder.

Steps To Be Followed in
Removing an Unknown Stain

Washable Fabrics

Sponge with dry solvent. Apply dry spotter and rub gently. Flush with dry solvent. Apply amyl acetate and rub gently. Flush with dry solvent. Dry. Sponge with water, apply wet spotter and vinegar. Rub. Flush with water, apply wet spotter and ammonia. Rinse with water and dry. Sponge with alcohol. Dry. Launder and bleach if safe for fabric and dye.

Dry-Cleanable Fabrics

Same as for washable fabrics but do not launder.

STAIN REMOVAL FROM SUEDE AND LEATHER GARMENTS

It is safest not to attempt any major stain removal from suede and leather garments. These articles are heavily impregnated with oils and finishes that are readily affected by dry-cleaning solvents. Consequently, any attempt to remove a grease or oil stain by using dry-cleaning solvent usually results in disturbance of the finish and this causes the development of a light-colored area. If any stain removal is attempted, only the surface of the skin should be very lightly sponged with a cloth containing barely enough solvent to dampen the sponging cloth.

Most dyes on suedes, especially the darker colors, are easily bled by stain removal agents containing water. Before trying any removal method, even for very small stains of foods or beverages, test the color of the article by very lightly sponging an unexposed seam allowance with a damp cloth. If the color is not transferred to the damp cloth, lightly sponge the small stained areas with a cloth that is barely damp with water only. Do not use detergent or other stain removal agents. When a suede or leather article becomes damp from water, whether from rain or stain-removal treatment, it must be dried in room temperature air without any heat applied in any manner.

Vinyls

Some of the many vinyl articles on the market are resistant to dry-cleaning solvents but many are likely to be damaged by solvents. Plasticizers used to soften vinyls are likely to be removed by dry-cleaning solvent and this will cause stiffening of the article and greatly reduce garment life. If any oil or grease stain removal is attempted, the procedure should consist of very lightly sponging the surface of the vinyl with a cloth barely dampened with dry-cleaning solvent. Do not make more than a few strokes of the sponging cloth over the surface of the vinyl as repeated rubbing will remove plasticizer and may change the appearance of the vinyl surface.

Vinyls are usually quite safe when stain removal is performed using water solutions. Stain-removal procedures using water and liquid hand dishwashing detergent with vinegar or ammonia are usually safe on vinyls. Follow the recommended stain-removal steps using these stain removers for stains listed after testing a hidden seam allowance for possible damage to fabric or color. A blotting action is the safest method to use in treating stains. Do not use a rubbing or tamping action as this may change the surface appearance of the fabric.

METHODS OF STAIN REMOVAL—RUGS AND CARPETS

Spot and Stain Removal

It is estimated that 90 percent of spots and stains from liquid spills can be prevented if immediate steps are taken to absorb the staining materials.

Spills, spots, or staining materials should be removed immediately or as soon as possible. If a guest causes the staining, a host should take immediate action to prevent a permanent stain and future embarrassment.

On liquid stains, us clean, white absorbent materials, such as face tissues, towels, or napkins, and blot. Solid materials can be removed mechanically by use of a rounded tablespoon. It is important to remove as much excess spillage as possible before using the removal techniques described below.

To prevent permanent stains, follow these basic rules:

1. Immediately blot up spills, using clean, white absorbent material (face tissues, napkins, towels).

2. Pretest spot-removal agent in an inconspicuous area. Put a few drops of reagent on each color in the rug and, using your white-absorbent material, hold it against each color. Wait about 10 seconds, then examine the results. If the dye has bled into the absorbent material, or if there has been a change in the colored area, call a professional cleaner for advice.

3. Do not overwet. Work with small amounts of the reagent and blot frequently. Problems result from using large amounts. Blot—do not rub or brush. Excessive mechanical action may cause distortion of the pile.

4. Work from the outer edge toward the center of the stain.

5. Have patience—some stains respond slowly.

6. After thorough blotting, the final step is to place a one-half-inch layer of the absorbent material over the damp area, weighting it down with a heavy object such as books. Allow at least six hours to dry. If necessary, brush the area after drying to restore original appearance.

7. Careless attempts to remove spots may result in permanent stains or permanent damage. If there are doubts about procedures, seek the advice of a professional cleaner. A few minutes on the telephone may help to prevent permanent stains or damage. Procedures for spot and stain removal on carpets and rugs are given in Tables 6–6 and 6–7. Careful drying methods are also important to prevent wicking actions that can cause complications. Always use small quantities of stain-removal solutions.

Table 6–6 Spot and Stain Removal—Carpets and Rugs

Group I	Group II	Group III
(Use Removal Method 1^a, followed by 2^b, 3, 4, and 5 for the following spills, spots, or stains)	(Use Removal Method 2^b, followed by 3, 4, and 5 for the following spills, spots, or stains)	(Use Removal Method 3 followed by 4 and 5 for the following spills, spots, or stains)
Butter	Acids	Alcohol
Chewing gum	Blood	Amonia or alkali
Cologne and	Candy	Beer
perfume	Chocolate	Bleach
Cooking oils	Cocktails	Coffee
Cosmetics	Crepe paper	Mustard
Dye	Egg	Soot
Food stains	Fruit	Syrup
Furniture polish	Fruit juices	Tea
Furniture stain	Gelatin	Urine
Grease	Glue	Wine
Household cement	Ice cream	
Inks	Milk	
Lipstick	Permanent wave	
Medicine	solution	
Metal polish	Soft drinks	
Nail polish	Vomit	
Oil		
Ointment		
Shoe polish		
Tar		
Unknown stains		
Water colors		
Water stains		
Wax		

^{a} If stain is removed, go to Method 5.
^{b} If stain is removed, go to Methods 4 and 5.

281 *Fabric Care—Soil, Spot, and Stain Removal*

Table 6–7 Stain-Removal Methods—Carpets and Rugs

1. Apply a small amount of a dry-cleaning solvent and blot; continue until no more staining material is evident. Use small amounts to prevent any possible damage to sizings, backings, or stuffing materials. Do not use gasoline, lighter fluid, or carbon tetrachloride.
2. Mix one teaspoonful of a neutral or light-duty detergent, a mild detergent containing no bleaches, with a cup of lukewarm water. Apply small amounts, blotting frequently until no more of the staining material is removable.
3. Mix a tablespoonful of ammonia with a half cup of water. Use small amounts on the spill or spot, blotting frequently until no more staining material is transferred to the absorbent material.
4. Mix one-third cup of white vinegar with two-thirds cup of water. Use small amounts and blot frequently continuing until no staining material remains.
5. Absorb as much moisture as possible. Place a half-inch layer of the absorbent white material on the entire remedied area, weight it down, and allow at least six hours to dry.

The professional rug cleaner is very interested in helping the consumer to take care of his own staining problems. He knows many stains will be permanent if the wrong remedies are used. It can happen that not even the professional expert can undo the damage. Untreated spills and spots will, with time, become hidden by soil, but after the carpet is cleaned and the soil is removed, the forgotten stain will reappear again.

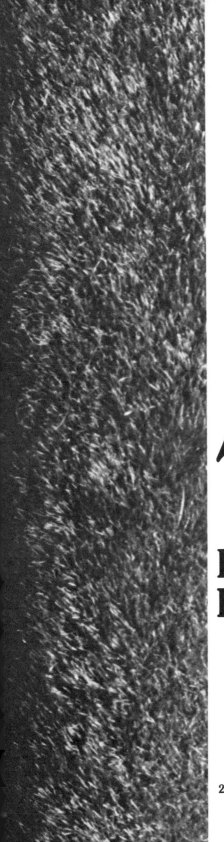

7
Fabric Care—
Laundering

285

Laundering detergency is complex technology. This complexity is illustrated in the remarks made by Richard L. Abbott,* Vice-President, Montgomery Ward and Co., who states:

> We do not believe it is possible to develop absolute standards with respect to washability and be practical in the market place. There are many reasons for our feeling this way:
>
> * No two persons will wash in identically the same way;
> * No two localities have identically the same water;
> * Customers will wash with many different detergents;
> * Water temperature will vary greatly by washing machine as well as by delivery from the heater itself;
> * No two washing machines are identical;
> * No two laundry loads are identical. We all know the effect that different garments have on each other when assembled together in a wash load.
>
> In other words, there is not a precise position that one can take with respect to how merchandise can and will be washed or cleaned.

For the purpose of discussion, laundering will be considered from the following points of view: (1) home laundering, (2) coin-op or self-service laundering, and (3) commercial laundering. It should be understood that some basic concepts apply to each of the three areas.

THE SCIENCE OF LAUNDERING

It is important to understand the basic concepts of laundering. Equipment alone does not guarantee satisfaction in laundering performance.

Laundering depends on certain factors: the kind, amount and temperature of water; the kind, amount, and basic functions of detergents; soaps and laundry aids, such as bleach; fabric softeners; enzymes; and brighteners. All these factors must be related to the mechanical and chemical effect on the variety of soils and stains deposited on or in fabrics.

Water—A Solvent

Laundry detergency is based on the aqueous medium—water. Water is a solvent for some soils. Water supplies vary from community to community or geographically. This accounts for the amounts and types of impurities. Four factors are most important: hardness, the presence of metals such as iron and magnesium, clarity or turbidity, and color.

* Richard L. Abbott, "Taking the Mystery Out of Fabrics," *Coin Launderer and Cleaner* (November/December 1971), p. 28.

WATER HARDNESS

Water hardness is generally reported in parts per million (ppm). Hardness depends on the amount of calcium or magnesium salt that has been dissolved in the water from various mineral sources in the earth. These salts may be carbonates, sulfates, chloride, or a mixture. Hardness is reported as equivalent calcium carbonate regardless of the form in which it exists. It is the metal part of the salt—calcium or magnesium—that causes the trouble.

Water usually falls between 3 to 30 grains per gallon (gpg) or 50 to 500 ppm. It is advisable to install a water conditioning unit to soften the water when water exceeds 2 grains or 25 to 35 ppm.

Some authorities list water hardness in terms of grains per gallon. These figures can be converted to parts per million by multiplying the number of grains per gallon by 17.1 ppm, for example, 17.1 ppm $\times$ 2 gpg = 34.2 ppm. Descriptive classifications are given as follows:

Range of Hardness mg/1 (ppm)	Descriptive Classification
1 to 60	Soft
61 to 120	Moderately hard
121 to 180	Hard
Above 180	Very hard

The water department of the municipal government in your community can tell you how hard the water is in your particular area.

Various methods can be used to soften water: boiling distillation, alkaline salts and limes, and ion exchange resins or a complex sodium aluminum silicate called zeolite. These methods of softening water are shown in Figures 7–1 to 7–4.

When it is not possible to have a water-softening system, packaged water softeners may be used. They may be classified as either the precipitating or nonprecipitating type. The latter is most convenient to use since it requires no skimming or settling of the curd or precipitate. When water softener is added to the wash water, it is equally important that it be added to the rinse water in order to prevent formation of "lime curd."

DISSOLVED METALS, TURBIDITY, AND COLOR

In addition to water hardness, you must also consider dissolved metals, turbidity, and color. Color in water is caused by industrial waste or decaying vegetation that may be present in the water system.

Water containing metal-ions iron and magnesium can cause staining of fabrics. Even a minute concentration of these metal ions can cause problems.

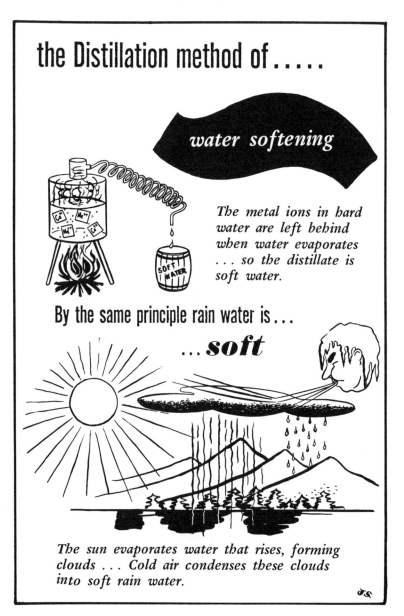

the Distillation method of.....

water softening

The metal ions in hard water are left behind when water evaporates ... so the distillate is soft water.

By the same principle rain water is...

...soft

The sun evaporates water that rises, forming clouds ... Cold air condenses these clouds into soft rain water.

Figure 7-1 (Courtesy: International Fabricare Institute)

Turbidity is caused by finely dispersed soil or clay in the water system. This condition may be caused from soil erosion or turbulence in the water supply such as a lake or reservoir.

Common water problems and their causes and cures are given in Table 7–1.

THE ALKALINE SALT method of . . . *water softening*

Eliminating water—hardening metallic ions like calcium (Ca^{++}) by precipitating them with alkaline salts such as soda ash (Na_2Co_3).

Figure 7-2 (Courtesy: International Fabricare Institute)

Soils   Soils that deposit in or on a fabric may be classified in different ways. They may be classified, according to their composition or appearance, as: (1) organic soils, (2) particle soils, and (3) spots and stains. They may also be classified on the basis of their solubility characteristics: (1) water soluble, (2) solvent soluble, and (3) water and solvent soluble.

the **COMPLEX SALT** method of ..

water softening

Metallic ions such as calcium ions (Ca^{++}) attack soap and make it insoluble.

Complex salts such as "Calgon" make the metallic ions harmless.

Figure 7-3 (Courtesy: International Fabricare Institute)

Organic soils—such as body oils, perspiration, waxes, fats, and fatty acids—are greasy or fatty in nature. Organic soils from the body are also concentrated in the neck, underarm, wrist, waist, and shoulder areas of the garment. Some of these soils may be removed by normal laundry procedures; others may require prespotting, brushing, or presoaking. Still others may require digestion with the aid of an enzyme product.

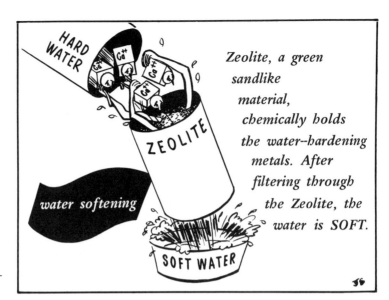

Figure 7-4 (Courtesy: International Fabricare Institute)

Zeolite, a green sandlike material, chemically holds the water--hardening metals. After filtering through the Zeolite, the water is SOFT.

Table 7–1 Common Water Problems

Problem	Cause	Cure
Grayed laundry "Ring" in bathtub.	Hardness from calcium and magnesium.	Increased detergent, packaged water conditioner, or water conditioning equipment.[a]
Brown to black stains on fabrics and porcelain.	Iron and manganese.	Water conditioner equipment with special filter.[a]
Cloudy water.	Sand, silt, or clay in suspension.	Filter.[a]
"Rotten egg" odor.	Hydrogen sulfide.	Chlorination and filtration.[a] For laundry, a very small amount of chlorine bleach.
Yellow or brown stains on fabrics and porcelain.	Organic matter.	Consult water equipment dealer for remedy.
Red stains from iron or galvanized pipes.	Corrosion of pipes.	Neutralizing filter.[a] New pipes if needed.
Blue stains from copper piping.	Corrosion of pipes.	Neutralizing filter[a] New pipes if needed.

[a] Consult water equipment dealer for proper units.

Particle soil may be salts, sugar, dust, clay, or carbon. While salts or sugar are water soluble, some of these materials deposit on a fabric and they do require a particular or special washing formula to remove them. For example, a higher detergent concentration necessitates a higher water temperature or more mechanical agitation is needed to obtain satisfactory cleaning results.

In either case, soil removal depends on (1) the application of energy (brushing, tamping, agitation of the washer cylinder) that exceeds the forces that binds the soils to the fabric and (2) physiochemical action (digestion, emulsification by the detergent) to weaken the forces that bind the soil to the fabric so that it may be removed by the mechanical action of the cleaning process.

In cleansing, whether it is laundering or dry cleaning, we need to maintain whiteness or brightness of the fabric and avoid redeposition of soil in the fabric that causes graying and yellowing.

Whiteness Retention

Whiteness is defined as the sum total of all colors. Most white materials contain various hues that cause us to describe them frequently as being "off-white" or "near-white." These near-whites may have a grayish hue when soiled but more often there is a mixture of hues that causes the white to look yellow, amber, or brown. If a blue hue predominates, the white may look quite pleasing to the eye. Most people like blue-whites but dislike yellow-whites; this is the reason for the age-old practice of using bluing agents for laundering whites.

In recent years the textile and detergent chemists have introduced a better method than bluing. They have developed a class of colorless dyes that fluoresce blue. This means that the dyed or tinted fabric absorbs ultraviolet light and reemits this energy as blue. The products used to achieve this effect are fluorescent whitening agents (FWA), also known as optical brighteners.

A truly white fabric would reflect 100 percent of all the light that illuminated it, regardless of wave length. Actually, no fabric does this, but some of them, notably bleached cotton, can reflect about 93 percent of the incident light. To be a neutral white, the fabric must reflect all wave lengths of light equally. Few fabrics (or papers) do this.

Redeposition of Soil

Redeposition is a term that is used widely, but the term has been very loosely used to describe graying, yellowing, or general dinginess of fabrics as it is judged by the eye.

It can also be measured by an instrument known as a photometer. The working principle of the photometer is very simple, illustrated in Figure 7–5.

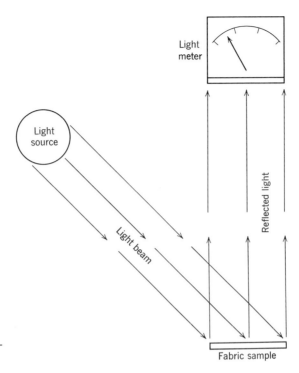

Light meter

Light source

Light beam

Reflected light

Fabric sample

Figure 7-5 Principle of the photometer.

To measure redeposition, a specified light beam (most often green light) is reflected off the sample of fabric, and the amount of reflected light is recorded by a light meter in the instrument. After the fabric sample has been dry cleaned, wet cleaned, laundered, or given some other treatment, another reflectance reading is taken. If the readings are the same as before the treatment, the samples are said to have the same brightness. If the brightness of the fabric has decreased, then the reading will be lower. Bleaching a white fabric, for example, results in an increased brightness, and a higher reading. Practically anything else that is done to a fabric results in a decrease in brightness. The following example illustrates redeposition:

The brightness of a white rayon swatch is usually around 80. In other words, it will reflect back 80 percent of the specified light beam. After cleaning, the reading may be 77. In practice then, this is often referred to as 3 percent redeposition, or three points redeposition. The relationship of various degrees of redeposition to the appearance of fabrics is shown in Table 7–2.

Causes of Redeposition

Usually when the term "redeposition" is used, it refers only to the fact that the fabric has darkened. Anything that absorbs light from the fabric reduces its reflectance and gives a low reading, which indicates

293 *Fabric Care—Laundering*

Table 7–2 Visual Comparison of Reflectance Readings on White Rayon

Percent Reflect-ance Drop	Appearance
over 6	Dingy work. Customer will notice it on casual inspection.
4 to 6	Garments not bright. Spotter may make light areas. Customers will probably not complain.
2 to 4	Good to fair. Skilled eyes can see it if there is a sample for comparison.
0 to 2	Invisible to the eye.

a high percentage of redeposition. True redeposition occurs when soil that is removed from the fabric returns to it and "redeposits." In a water system, detergents and soaps have a suspending action on the soil. The suspension must be sufficient to keep the soil from returning to the fabric. There are several conditions that may decrease the suspension power during cleaning and cause redeposition of soil on a fabric, such as overloading the washer, insufficient hot water, improper soaking, overlong wash period, improper use of suds-return system, and using insufficient or a poor detergent.

Soaps and Detergents

Soaps or detergents must be present in water to remove soil from fabrics in laundering. They must also hold the soil in suspension so they do not deposit on the fabric.

Until 1948, soap was a popular home laundry detergent. Synthetic detergents are used more widely at the present time. However, the use of a specially built soap has been recommended recently for washing flame-retardant fabric in order to retain the flame-retardant finishes. The U.S. Department of Agriculture* has developed a tallow soap that does not interfere with the protective finish to wash flame-retardant fabrics. A lime dispersing agent is used to prevent the buildup of insoluble calcium and magnesium soap deposits on the fabric and on parts of the washing machine. The detergent contains 64 percent tallow soap, 15 percent silicate builder, and 19 percent of the lime dispersing agent.

A soap is a metallic salt of a fatty acid. Not all soaps are soluble in water or beneficial for cleaning. Aluminum soaps, for example, are used as lubricants or greases. Sodium, potassium, or ammonium soaps are salts of fatty acids that are soluble in water and have cleansing power (see Figure 7–6).

* W. M. Linfield, Eastern Regional Research Center. Philadelphia, Pa.

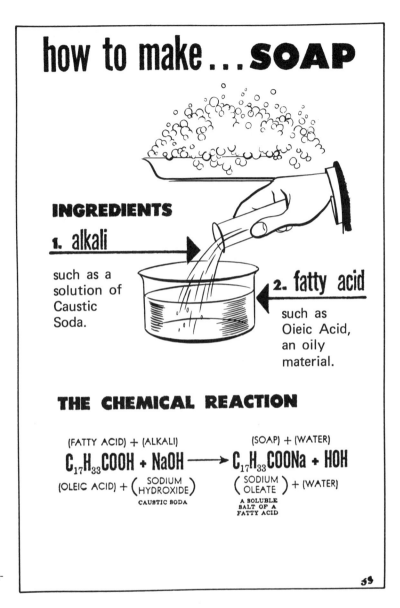

how to make... SOAP

INGREDIENTS

1. alkali

such as a solution of Caustic Soda.

2. fatty acid

such as Oieic Acid, an oily material.

THE CHEMICAL REACTION

(FATTY ACID) + (ALKALI)   (SOAP) + (WATER)

$$C_{17}H_{33}COOH + NaOH \longrightarrow C_{17}H_{33}COONa + HOH$$

(OLEIC ACID) + $\left(\begin{matrix}\text{SODIUM}\\\text{HYDROXIDE}\end{matrix}\right)$ $\left(\begin{matrix}\text{SODIUM}\\\text{OLEATE}\end{matrix}\right)$ + (WATER)

CAUSTIC SODA   A SOLUBLE SALT OF A FATTY ACID

59

Figure 7-6 (Courtesy: International Fabricare Institute)

A fatty acid is an organic acid that is insoluble in water. When a fat or oil containing fatty acid is boiled with an alkali-metal hydroxide such as sodium, potassium, or ammonium hydroxide, a water-soluble soap is formed. Most soaps for washing are sodium salts of fatty acids because of economics and because there is no difference in the cleaning ability of soaps of different alkali-metals. Sodium soaps make a hard or firm physical form. Potassium or ammonium soaps are soft and because they are more soluble, will make a more concentrated solution (see Figure 7–7).

Titer is the temperature at which the fatty acid of a soap solidifies (see Figure 7–8). It is best to use a high-titer soap in hot water because of its superior cleansing action. Low-titer soap has poorer

Figure 7-7 (Courtesy: International Fabricare Institute)

THE **Effect** OF HARD WATER ON **Soaps**

Calcium ions (a water hardening metal) combine with soaps and prevent sudsing and cleansing action.

However. . .if enough soap is used. . .sudsing and cleansing finally occur.

It often takes 4 or 5 times as much soap to make a suds in hard water as it does in soft water.

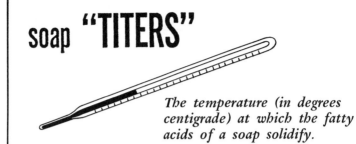

soap "TITERS"

The temperature (in degrees centigrade) at which the fatty acids of a soap solidify.

High titer soaps are __HARD__ soaps

These soaps are less soluble and harder to rinse in cold water but are excellent cleansers in hot water.

Low titer soaps are __SOFT__ soaps

These soaps are more soluble and are easier to rinse in cold water ... have poorer cleansing action in hot water.

Figure 7-8 (Courtesy: International Fabricare Institute)

cleansing action in hot water that does high-titer soap. A low-titer soap should be used in lukewarm or cold water where it retains its cleansing action.

A neutral soap is one that contains neither free alkali nor free fat.

Built soaps are products that have added alkalinity to increase detergent action. An alkali added to soap is called a builder. This mixture of alkali and soap is a built soap.

DETERGENT IN WATER

Anything that helps to remove soil is a detergent and the process of removing soil is called detergent action or detergency.

Soaps work as cleaning agents because each soap molecule has two distinct parts. One part, a carboxylate group, is attracted to water. The other part, a hydrocarbon chain, is repelled by water. These two distinct parts enable soap to work as a cleaning agent. Water alone will not remove the oily, greasy dirt on fabrics because the oil in the dirt repels the water molecules (Figure 7–9). When soap is added to the water, the hydrocarbon end of the soap molecule is repelled by water, but it is attracted to the oil in the dirt.

Meanwhile, the water-seeking end of the soap molecule is attracted to the water molecules. The soap molecule is active at these surfaces, as a surface active agent or "surfactant."

Surfactant molecules, like soap, are made of two distinct parts. One part is hydrophillic and attracts water, the other is hydrophobic and repels water. These are two distinct different parts within one molecule that enable soaps and surfactants to work as a cleaning agent.

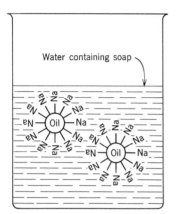

Figure 7-9 Soap keeps oil droplets apart.

WETTING ACTION

Water wets out fabrics but it is not effective in wetting out a greasy surface. Soil is oily and greasy, since most of it is covered with a minute film of oil or grease. The reason pure water does not wet out greasy substances is due to its high surface tension. When this tension acts between a liquid and air, it is called surface tension; when it acts between two liquids or between a liquid and a solid it is called interfacial tension. Surface tension may be described as a force that acts as though an elastic film covers the surface of the liquid. Detergents and soaps lower the surface tension.

The lowering of surface tension makes water penetrate rapidly into materials and wet out fabrics and greasy soil more readily.

FOAMING OR SUDSING

The reduction in surface tension by a soap or a detergent is often accompanied by foaming or sudsing. However, the degree of sudsing is not always a good measure of detergent action. Some detergents lower surface tension but make little suds (Figures 7–10 and 7–11).

Figure 7-10 Soap lowers surface tension of water.

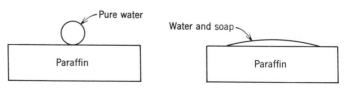

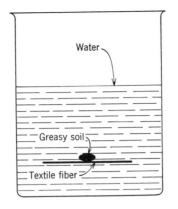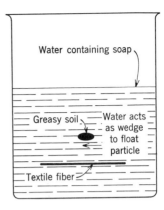

Figure 7-11 Soap helps water to dislodge greasy soil from textiles.

EMULSIFYING ACTION   Once oily or greasy material is removed from a fabric, it must be held in suspension so that it does not immediately settle back on a fabric but can be removed by rinsing. The emulsifying action of a detergent holds oil and greasy material so it does not settle back on the fabric.

SUSPENDING ACTION   Just as soap or detergent keeps oil in water and thus delays or prevents settling out, it also keeps particles of soil in water separated and keeps them suspended. This is a very important property of a soap or detergent for if it does not adequately suspend soil, the soil settles back onto the fabric and causes graying (Figures 7–12 and 7–13).

ALKALINE ACTION   The addition of the proper quantity of alkaline builders increases both wetting action that helps remove soil and also increases emulsification that keeps soil suspended. Alkali saponifies fats, making the fat water soluble.

Figure 7-12 Suspending action of soap.

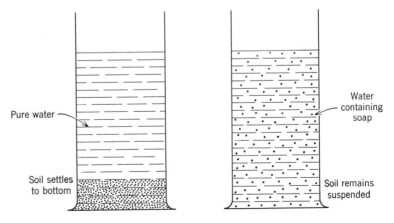

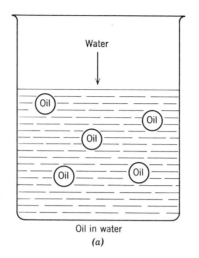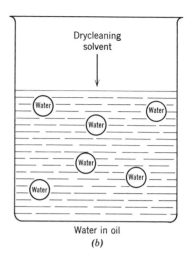

Figure 7-13 Two types of emulsion. (a) In water. (b) In drycleaning solvent.

Oil in water
(a)

Water in oil
(b)

What Is a Synthetic Detergent?

Synthetic detergents appeared in the 1930s. They are often called surfactants, which is an abbreviation for surface active agents. Many have been developed since. Some have cleansing powers similar to soap; some excel as wetting and emulsifying agents. They have many unique properties that are lacking in soaps and can be used under a wide variety of conditions.

Synthetic detergents are neutral (pH near 7). Sometimes a mild alkali is added to give better detergency. Synthetic detergents do not break down in diluted acid solutions or precipitate in hard water. They have sudsing action and detergency action in acid solutions and in hard water. They do not turn rancid. Small amounts of synthetic detergent may remain in the fabric and cause no trouble (Figure 7–14).

Types of Synthetic Detergents

Chemists describe electrically charged chemicals as positive or negative ions. For example, sodium and calcium are positive ions and are called cations; chlorine or sulfate as negative ions and are called anions. Detergents are classed according to their ionic characteristic (Figure 7–15).

ANIONIC DETERGENTS

Soaps are anionic detergents because the detergent portion of the molecule is an anion or negative ion. The synthetic detergents most commonly used in laundering are of the anionic type. Linear alkylbenzene sulfonates (LAS) are the most popular anionic compound in household detergents.

300   *Performance of Textiles*

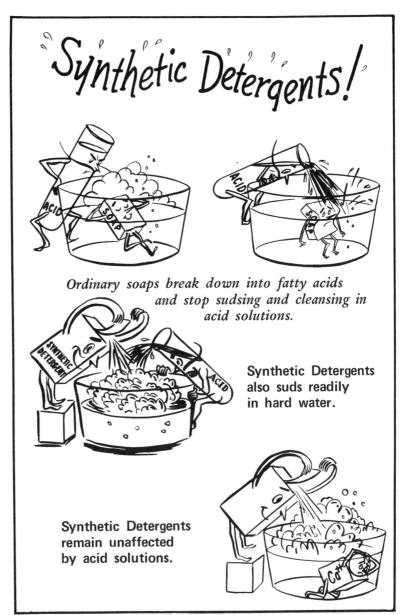

Ordinary soaps break down into fatty acids and stop sudsing and cleansing in acid solutions.

Synthetic Detergents also suds readily in hard water.

Synthetic Detergents remain unaffected by acid solutions.

Figure 7-14 (Courtesy: International Fabricare Institute)

CATIONIC DETERGENTS Some synthetic agents have reversed charges, that is, the organic or detergent portion of the molecule is positive or cationic while the water-soluble portion is negative or anionic.

Cationic detergents do not have as much cleansing action as soap and most anionic type synthetic detergents. They are used as house-

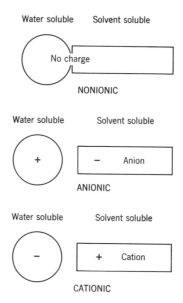

Figure 7-15 The three types of detergent molecules.

hold germicides and fabric softeners. They are not precipitated by hard water and are stable in acid and alkaline solutions.

NONIONIC DETERGENTS

Nonionic detergents are similar to other detergents in that one part of the molecule is soluble in water and another part in dry solvents. However, as the name implies, they are electrically neutral. Some nonionics are very good detergents. Some that clean well have very little lathering action in water. They have a neutral ph and are not affected by acids, alkalies, or hard water.

Composition of Detergents*

The components and functions of a typical detergent are given in Table 7–3.

SURFACE ACTIVE AGENTS (SURFACTANT)

Surface active agents is a general term that includes soluble detergents in liquid medium, dispersing agents, emulsifying agents, foaming agents, penetrating agents, and wetting agents (defined on page 303).

A detergent is produced by chemical synthesis and comprises an organic composition other than soap. It is a composition that removes soil.

* This discussion on detergents is adapted with permission from "Home Washing Products—The Technology of Home Laundry," American Association for Textile Technology, Inc., Monograph No. 108.

Table 7-3 Components and Function(s) of Detergents[a]

A. Surfactant (LAS, AS, nonionic, or soaps)	Loosen and disperse soil, provide or control suds; basic "cleaning" ingredients.
B. Builder	Soften water, aid surfactant in dispersion of soil, buffer detergent solution in alkaline region.
C. (1) Fluorescent whitening agents (combination of up to 3 or 4) (2) Bluing agents	Overcome yellowness on fabric and provide whiteness of blue-white hue.
D. Enzymes	Catalyze breakdown of protein or carbohydrate based stains to allow for removal by surfactant and builder.
E. Antiredeposition agents	Prevent removed soil from going back on fabric.
F. Sodium silicate, sodium sulfate, water	Carries free-flowing powder.

[a]"Home Washing Products—The Technology of Home Laundry," American Association For Textile Technology, Inc. Monograph No. 108.

A dispersing agent increases the stability of a suspension of particles in a liquid medium.

An emulsifying agent increases the stability of a dispersion of one liquid in another.

A foaming agent increases the stability of a suspension of gas bubbles in a liquid medium.

A penetrating agent increases the penetration of a liquid medium into a porous material.

A wetting agent increases the spreading of a liquid medium on a surface.

All these properties are necessary to carry out good laundering detergency. Described in another way, the surfactant molecule is a long organic body that is oillike in nature. It is hydrophobic or water hating. At the end of this body is a head that is hydrophillic or water loving.

Manufacturers achieve a balance of hydrophobic and hydrophillic portions of the molecule to achieve the wetting ability, an important property to penetrate and loosen soil from the fabric and hold it in suspension in the water. Antiredeposition agents are also used to prevent soil from going back onto the fabric until all agents are removed by rinsing the fabric.

Commonly Used Surfactants

In 1965, the detergent industry converted from an alkyl benzene in which the alkyl portion was derived from propylene tetramer to a more biodegradable one in which the alkyl was derived from paraffin or linear olefin sources. This was done to attain a surface active agent that would produce nonfoaming products when degraded by bacteria in water systems (Figure 7–16a and b). All alkyl benzene sulfonate used today in detergent products made in the United States is of the linear anionic type.

Figure 7-16a Alkyl benzene sulfonates. (Courtesy: American Association for Textile Technology)

ABS

LAS

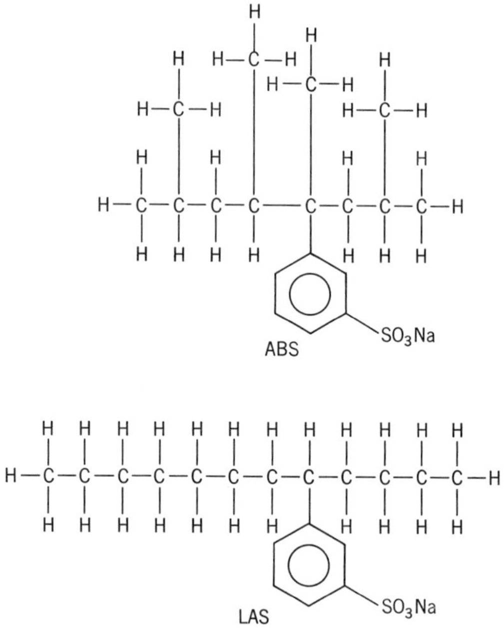

Figure 7-16b Alcohol-derived surfactants. (Courtesy: American Association for Textile Technology)

(a) Alcohol sulfate anionic

(b) Nonionic

304 *Performance of Textiles*

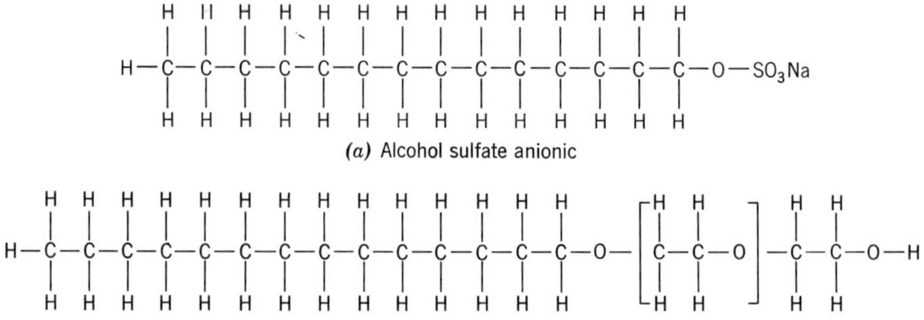

Another common type of anionic surfactant is derived from the sulfation of fatty alcohols. Alcohol sulfates are biodegradable and are excellent detergents.

Builders

Until recently the major builders used have generally been phosphates. Phosphates reduce water hardness by attaching themselves to the calcium and magnesium salts in solution and keeping them suspended in solution. Thus, detergent formulations differ from soaps in that they keep the calcium in a soluble form rather than allowing it to precipitate as a scum on the clothes. Phosphates also disperse and suspend dirt. They maintain the alkalinity that is necessary to neutralize the acidic materials found in the body soil, which can be retained on fabrics.

In recent years phosphates have come under attack from sources outside the detergent industry, mainly the government, because of their potential for producing nutrition for algeal growth in lakes, rivers, and streams. This phenomenon is called eutrophication, which is an abundance of minerals and organic nutrients in a lake or stream. This causes a reduction in the dissolved oxygen and favors the growth of plant over animal life. Excessive eutrophication destroys the essential ecological balance in bodies of water.

This problem has caused an intensified search for a suitable replacement, even though the amount of phosphate contributed by detergents to the waterways is small compared to the amount from other sources such as human waste and fertilizers.

The real solution to the eutrophication problem may lay in proper waste treatment. The detergent industry remains committed to replace phosphate generally when a satisfactory, safe replacement is available.

New products that use neither phosphates nor nitrilotriacetic acid (NTA) have been coming onto the market, claiming to do the laundering job as well as phosphate detergents. Some manufacturers are using sodium silicate and sodium carbonate but these materials have less sequestering ability. Experience has indicated that they do not perform quite as well. They are also corrosive to the skin. Other manufacturers are making products built with sodium citrate, products based on sodium silicate as the principal builder, and an unbuilt product that is essentially a highly concentrated detergent active solution with fluorescers.

Research on the reaction and performance of these new products is ongoing. Some people feel that none of these various types of "no-phosphate" detergent formulations performs as satisfactorily as do phosphate detergents. The no-phosphates are not considered as safe in case of accidental contact with eyes or if they are ingested by children; thus they require a warning statement on the package. In the case of carbonate-built detergents in particular there are several inherent disadvantages. Sodium carbonate is a precipitant-type builder. It combines with water hardness in the washing solution and precipitates as insoluble calcium carbonate that can (1) cause fabrics to become harsh, (2) cause apparent fading of colored clothes, (3) encrust on washing machine parts and plumbing systems, (4) cancel the effectiveness of the flame-retardant treatment on cotton fabrics, and (5) cause an adverse effect on the durability and aesthetic properties of chemical finishes such as permanent press, soil release and water repellency.

FLUORESCENT WHITENING AGENTS (OPTICAL BRIGHTENERS: FLUORESCENT DYES)

As stated previously, a bluing agent added in the form of a solution to the final rinse water causes the yellow of the fabric to look white. Bluing agents are being replaced with optical whiteners or brighteners that are incorporated into detergents. Optical brighteners are colorless dyes that makes white or colors appear brighter when exposed to light. They perform a similar function as bluing in that they create an optical illusion that the clothes are whiter. They are deposited on the fabric during the wash cycle.

The whitening agents function by converting some of the invisible light into a visible form. When natural sunlight strikes a fabric that has fluorescent whitening agent on its surface, the ultraviolet wave lengths are absorbed by the whitener, passed along their complex chemical structures, and reemitted in the visible region. Fluorescent whitening agents are activated by the ultraviolet light from daylight, fluorescent lighting, or, to a lesser extent, incandescent lighting. If the resulting light is of a suitable wave length, it can overcome yellowness on the fabric.

Fluorescent whitening agents (FWA) are very complex. A fluorescent brightener that is effective on cotton may not be effective on wool. Since fluorescent whitening agents are selective and do not all attach themselves to a given fiber to the same degree, manufacturers blend different fluorescent whitening agents for optimum results in a mixed fabric load. They are most effective when the soil has been removed properly from the fabric.

ENZYMES

Commercial launderers and dry cleaners have been using enzymes for many years to improve stain removal prior to the laundering or dry-cleaning process. Now some laundry products contain enzymes. Enzymes initiate a digestive action that breaks complex substances down into partially soluble forms so they can be removed from fabrics. They serve as catalysts, speeding the breakdown of certain stains made up of proteins and carbohydrates that are not normally removed by detergents alone. The breakdown products resulting from enzyme action are more easily loosened and removed by the detergent and washing process.

There are three major types of enzymes used in washing products: proteolytic for protein stains (milk, eggs, blood, etc.), amylolytic for starchy substances, and lipolytic for fats.

Enzymes have come recently under attack by sources outside the detergent industry. Questions are raised concerning consumer safety. Since positive research evidence is lacking, enzymes have been deleted from several laundry products except those made especially for presoaking.

There are two forms of enzyme washing products being marketed: (1) as an addition to a dry heavy-duty detergent (Lever Brothers' "Drive," Proctor and Gamble's "Tide X,K" and "Gain"), and (2) as a separate presoak item (Colgate's "Axion" and Proctor and Gamble's "Biz").

OTHER INGREDIENTS Antiredeposition agents are added to products to prevent "tattletale gray," which occurs during the washing cycle after the detergent has removed the soil from the fabric. Some of this removed soil has a tendency to redeposit on the fabric, and certain materials (antiredeposition agents) are added to prevent this. The most common antiredeposition agent is sodium carboxymethyl cellulose.

Lack of proper control of the washing cycle can lead to redeposition even though antiredeposition agents are present.

Perfumes and colors may also be included as part of a detergent. Colors are primarily for aesthetic purposes although some bluing of fabrics can be accomplished by certain dyes and pigments.

Silicates are added to detergents to help prepare free-flowing detergent powders as well as build in a resistance to corrosion of certain washing machine parts. Silicates used at higher levels may also become more important if phosphate levels are reduced significantly.

Laundry Aids

There is an ever-increasing number of laundry aids on the shelves of the supermarket and drugstores. It is sometimes difficult to decide what products will serve the consumer best.

BLEACHES Bleaches, which are designed to assist detergents to make the fabric look cleaner and brighter, can damage fibers, dyes, and finishes if not used correctly and must be used with caution.

There are three types of laundry bleach: liquid chlorine (strong), powdered chlorine (mild), and all-fabrics or oxygen (weak). All bleaches should be used according to the directions on the package.

The chemically active ingredient of the liquid chlorine bleach is the hypochlorite ion. This is an effective oxidizing agent. This effectiveness is both an advantage and a disadvantage of liquid hypochlorite bleach.

Liquid chlorine bleach offers the best stain removal but the greatest possibility of harming your clothes if used improperly. It should not be used on silk, spandex, acetate, wool, or fabrics that contain small percentages of these fibers. Chlorine bleach causes the above fibers to change to a yellow color that is permanent.

Chlorine bleach should not directly be poured onto clothes—it may cause holes in the fabrics. This damage may not be apparent until later. Liquid chlorine must be diluted, according to label directions, before being added to the wash water. Some laundry equipment is equipped with bleach dispensers. It adds bleach at the right time and in the right way. Check the directions for the amount to use; do not use more.

All dyed fabrics should be tested for colorfastness to bleach if no guarantee of colorfastness is given.

Certain resin finishes used on rayon, cotton, polyester-rayon blend, or polyester-cotton blend fabrics for wrinkle resistance or crease retention will retain some of the chlorine from chlorine bleaches. When heat is applied, for example, during ironing or tumble drying, hydrochloric acid is formed that weakens the fabric. Certain fluorescent whitening agents are destroyed if exposed to the chlorine bleach for a short period of time. This can be greatly reduced if the fluorescent whitening agent has had time to become attached to the fabric during laundering. This factor has influenced the design of washing machines in that delayed bleach dispensers have been developed so that the bleach is added during the washing cycle rather than prior to it. It has also led to development of "chlorine powders," which provide a delayed entry of the bleach into the water solution.

Powdered chlorine bleach offers the same general type of bleaching as the liquid, but is more gentle in action. It releases bleaching ingredients more slowly as it dissolves. Powdered chlorine bleach utilizes a group of chemicals known as "N-chloro compounds." Never sprinkle powdered bleach directly on clothes but add it after the washer has filled with water and started agitation. Although it is milder than liquid chlorine, powdered bleach can damage clothing if used improperly.

Oxygen bleaches are generally safer for all washable fabrics, producing little if any fabric damage. They are less damaging to most colors than chlorine bleaches and do not yellow chlorine-retentive finishes and fibers. They help maintain the brightness of white and colored items if used regularly.

Perborate-based oxygen bleaches do not become effective until quite high temperatures are reached. This means that they must be used in very hot water. This restricts the use of oxygen bleaches to fabrics that can be safely washed in very hot water.

One of the newer bleaching agents—the oxygen bleach potassium monopersulfate—is efficient at lower water temperatures and generally more effective than the perborates. Most dyes that are colorfast to washing are not affected by oxygen bleaches.

As low-phosphate detergents become more popular, bleach has taken on a larger role in trying to compensate for the decrease in cleaning strength of these types of detergents. However, many care labels on textile products warn against using bleach. (See the discussion on labeling of flame-retardant fabrics in Chapter 10.)

FABRIC SOFTENERS

Fabric softeners are laundry additives designed to reduce or eliminate static cling in man-made fibers, to make fabrics softer, fluffier, and easier to iron, to minimize wrinkling, and to help prevent lint from sticking to garments.

Fabric softeners provide a lubricating film on the fibers allowing them to move more readily against each other, minimizing wrinkling. Softeners also make many fabrics feel soft to the touch and imparts fluffiness to fabrics.

Static cling is caused by static electricity resulting from friction between fibers. Static charges are dissipated by the natural moisture content of such natural fibers as cotton, linen, and wool. However, synthetics like polyester, nylon, and acrylic have very little moisture content of their own, and static charges may build up on garments causing clinging and crackling. When fabric softener is used on synthetic fibers, the lubricating film absorbs moisture from the air, providing a path for discharge of the static electricity.

There are three types of fabric softeners available: (1) those added to the wash cycle; (2) those added to the rinse cycle, and (3) those added to the drying cycle. These products should be used according to manufacturer's directions. The proper concentration should be used and the product should be added at the proper time of the washing or drying cycle.

Laundry detergents are anionic as are such other additives as packaged water softeners. These react with the softener and nullify its effectiveness in some cases. Some softeners are made to be compatible with detergents and other laundry additives. Since the softeners that are added to the wash cycle are concentrated, they should never be poured directly on fabrics because staining may occur. The proper concentration should be used and the product should be added at the proper time in the wash cycle. Otherwise, there is a danger of buildup of excess softener on the fibers that can feel greasy and, in some cases, render a fabric surface water repellent. This is undesirable on fabrics that are used because of their absorbent property.

Undiluted fabric softener coming in contact with fabric will cause an oily, greasy looking spot although it will not damage the fabric. This type of spot can be removed by rubbing the dampened spot with hand soap and rewashing the item in the usual manner, using chlorine bleach if suitable for the fabric. A fabric softener stain will attract rust or soil from the wash water in subsequent washes causing the stain to look like gray or black grease.

Fabric softeners added to the rinse cycle may be purchased in a concentrated or diluted form. The addition of most softeners to the final rinse is important because there should be no other materials present in the water to interfere or react. If a cationic softener is added to the wash it will react with whatever anionic materials are present and both the softener and detergent become ineffective.

This reaction will cause a white, sticky residue (which is sometimes mistaken for lint) to appear on the clothes. For this reason rinse-added fabric softeners should be used only in the final rinse and never with soap, detergent, bleach, bluing, or packaged water conditioners.

If the washer is equipped with an automatic fabric softener dispenser, follow the directions in the washer instructions for the softener to be added properly to the final rinse. If the washer does not have a dispenser, add the softener according to label directions as soon as agitation begins in the final rinse.

Fabric softeners added to the drying cycle may be purchased in the following forms: (1) aerosol spray, (2) tear-off sheets of a non-woven fabric, and (3) a slow dispensing packet that attaches to a baffle in the dryer or on the dryer drum itself. Check the manufacturers' directions before using any dryer-added fabric softeners.

DISINFECTANTS

Disinfectants need not be used in every batch of laundry, but should be added if there is sickness in the family or neighborhood or if a self-service washer is used.

Research by the U.S. Department of Agriculture* has shown that

* See Bibliography, Chapter 7, for references.

certain types of disinfectants greatly reduce the number of bacteria that survive the hot water and detergents as used in home laundering. If ordinary home laundry methods do not kill bacteria, there is danger of spreading disease-causing bacteria in the family wash.

Quaternary ammonium, phenolic and pine oil disinfectants, and liquid chlorine bleaches (for fibers on which chlorine can be used) are effective in reducing the number of bacteria on textiles. Quaternary ammonium disinfectants should be added to the rinse water. Phenolic disinfectants may go into either the rinse or wash cycles. Chlorine bleaches and pine oil disinfectants should be added to the wash water.

In a recent laundering study, in which cold-water detergent was used, quaternary ammonium disinfectants and chlorine bleach were effective in reducing the number of bacteria when applied as indicated above. Addition of phenolic or pine oil disinfectant to the wash cycle in which cold-water detergent was used had little effect.

Hypochlorite is an effective germicide; as little as 20 ppm (1 cup = 200 ppm chlorine in top-loading washers) in the washing solution can destroy the bacteria in the normal family wash load.

STARCH
Starch is probably one of the oldest laundry aids.

Starch is still used in the home laundry for several reasons: (1) to replace the original finish which the manufacturer put into the fabric, (2) to impart crispness to the fabric, (3) to obtain a stiff, smooth, and shiny appearance for certain types of collars or cotton uniforms, (4) to help keep a garment clean for a longer time by covering and holding down tiny surface fibers that catch dust, and (5) to facilitate soil removal (soil is removed from starched fabrics more easily because soil attaches to the starch rather than to the fabric and is removed with starch during washing).

Starches may be classed as precooked vegetable starches, starch substitutes (such as PVA), and aerosol starches.

Precooked vegetable starches are available in dry and liquid forms. They are diluted with either hot or cold water and the garment is dipped into the solution. There are some aerosol vegetable starches, which are sprayed onto the fabric.

The synthetic polymer starches may be classified as soluble plastic type or durable plastic type. Some are sold in spray cans.

The aerosol starches are convenient to use. Follow the manufacturer's directions for application.

Washing Equipment*

Home equipment is available for washing and drying clothes. While most drying equipment is automatic, at least to some degree, washers are available both as conventional and automatic models. Combination washer-dryers are also available. Because there is such a wide variation in the capabilities and costs of the various models, each one should be considered in terms of personal laundry needs. Consider each of the following factors in relation to the equipment available when purchasing it for the home:

1. Size and frequency of wash loads.
2. Types of garments to be laundered.
3. Flexibility and degree of automatic control needed.
4. Special features desired or needed.
5. Installation and servicing requirements necessary.
6. Space available.
7. Warranty responsibility of the manufacturer.

A typical home washer is designed to wash, rinse, and extract water from the clothes automatically according to the sequence set on the time dial. Washers and dryers may be operated by electricity or gas and at a water pressure available at the point of installation.

Fashion and convenience has been built into washing equipment. There is a wide choice of color, designs, and sizes to meet specific needs.

MECHANICAL FUNCTIONS

A washing machine must perform three major functions: (1) it must wash soil from the clothing, (2) it must rinse out soap or detergent and soil from the wash process, and (3) it must extract the greater part of wash and rinse water prior to a drying process.

TOP-LOADING MACHINES

These machines are equipped with an agitator. The agitator transfers mechanical energy from the drive motor to the wash water and then to the clothes. The mechanical energy combines with the chemical energy (detergent) to remove soil and keep it in suspension. This energy transfer is controlled by the rate of oscillation or movement of the agitator expressed in strokes per minute and the degrees of arc through which the agitator turns.

The central cylinder (usually steel coated with porcelain enamel) that holds the items to be washed may be solid or perforated. Take care not to damage the cylinder either mechanically, such as chip-

---

* The material on washing equipment is adapted with permission from "Home Washing Products—The Technology of Home Laundry," American Association for Textile Technology, Inc., Monograph No. 108.

ping by metal closures on clothing, or chemically, by using corrosive laundry aids. Upon completion of the detergent cycle, the water is extracted from the fabric by force up and over the sides of the cylinder or drained through the perforations of the cylinder. Draining may take from two minutes up to six minutes; extraction cycle is usually six minutes.

FRONT-LOADING MACHINES

Front-loading machines also have a cylinder, but do not have an agitator. The clothes are cleaned by rotating the cylinder containing the clothes through the detergent solution. Baffles built into the interior of the cylinder lift the clothes from the water and then drop them back into it. Washing, rinsing, etc., proceed in the same sequence as described above in the top-loading machine.

DISPENSERS

The most common dispensers are for fabric softeners and bleach. At present, bleach is added about four minutes before the end of the detergent cycle (as discussed earlier) and fabric softeners during the rinse cycle.

WATER LEVEL

The water level can be preset according to load size on modern equipment and may vary with the design of the equipment. An average top-loading machine holds 16 to 18 gallons of water for both the detergent cycle and the rinse cycle. Some machines have additional sprays, so that 35 to 40 gallons of water per load of clothes can be used. Machines are also designed for higher capacity, especially those used in self-service launderies.

Some equipment manufacturers have adapted their machines for the smaller wash load by inserting a minibasket of water-volume control that can be preset on the control panel or sensor systems in self-service machines.

Front-loading machines generally use smaller amounts of water for each cycle, but they use more cycles than do top-loading machines.

WATER TEMPERATURE

A water-temperature control unit is usually found on the control panel of a washer. This control determines the mix or percentage of hot and cold water. On some machines this is accomplished by thermostatic controls. Hot water temperature ranges from 140°F, warm 100 to 120°F, cold water is the temperature as it emerges from the cold water tap.

WASH CYCLES Wash cycles vary in the length and degree of mechanical agitation given to a load of wash, the length of draining water, and the extraction of water from the load. For example, a "Regular" or "Normal" cycle might provide 60 to 100 agitations per minute with an average detergent cycle of 10 minutes in hot water followed by draining and a 2-minute extraction period of approximately 500 revolutions per minute. This may be followed by four spray rinses. The machine then refills for a 2-minute rinse, drain, and 2- to 6-minute extraction and another three to four spray rinses. This involves a total running time of 30 to 38 minutes.

From this average wash cycle manufacturers have programmed "Super Wash Cycle" for heavily soiled items, "Presoak" cycles for heavily soiled items or items with soil that require digestion with enzymes, "Permanent Press Cycle" where the cycle is longer and requires more water and a cold water temperature, and a "Gentle" or "Delicate Fabrics" cycle for delicate items and blankets that require a higher water level, low mechanical agitation, and lower water temperature.

AUXILIARY ITEM A suds saver is an auxiliary item found on some machines. This is an important consideration in areas where water is in short supply. Lightly soiled clothes are washed first, followed by medium- to heavily soiled items. The rinse water is stored during the progressive rinse cycles and then used in the successive detergent cycle.

Cold-Water Washing

This is a relatively new concept that is used advantageously in certain situations. For example, washing in cold water saves hot water for other uses and thus conserves energy. It results in less wrinkling—especially washable polyester or nylon knits and permanent press items that wrinkle if washed in hot water and then spun dry or put through a wringer while still hot. It lessens the the danger of shrinkage, particularly with knitted fabrics, chino pants, and some nonsanforized items and prevents the "setting" of certain types of stains—such as milk, eggs, blood, and other protein soils that can become permanent if washed in hot water. However, it is better when grease and oil stains are removed in hot water.

Cold water can vary in temperature from the freezing point to water of body temperature. However, for best results in laundering, the water temperature for cold water washing should not be lower than about 80°F.

Detergents for use in cold water have been developed. They dissolve readily and clean adequately in cold water. Cold-water detergents may also be used in hot water; in fact, for heavily soiled items, even when a cold-water detergent is used, warm or hot water will remove more soil.

Cold washing has raised certain questions, particularly concerning pathogenic bacteria. Some researchers* have stated that to obtain a relatively fungus-free fabric, factors important to prevent growth are water temperature between 120°F and 140°F, detergent, and longer washing cycles. The researchers state that survival on the fabric after drying at a delicate setting (126°F) cannot be relied on for sanitation and that viable test organisms remaining in the dryer can be transferred to items dried in subsequent wash loads. Some researchers have stated that cold-water washing followed by tumbling drying at a standard 160°F will produce clean clothing with little or no bacterial contamination. Laundering followed by steaming or ironing on a hot-head press has been shown to provide adequate disinfection.† If there is a family illness, it may be desirable to sanitize certain items. One cup of chlorine bleach is sufficient to sanitize a wash load.

Automatic Drying Equipment

The first automatic dryers actually began to appear on the market during the last 1930s. Growth since that time has been at a steady rate.* In 1974, the number of households using dryers was 36.3 million—26.1 million electric units, 10.2 millions gas units.‡

The modern home laundry dryer serves two distinct needs: (1) it dries laundered items safely and rapidly and (2) it returns items for which "no ironing" properties are claimed to a finished condition, essentially ready to wear with little or no touch-up pressing.

A dryer consists of a rotating drum driven by a motor-belt arrangement. A fan driven by the same motor draws room air into the machine. Heat is added and the moisture-laden air is exhausted to the outside. Entering air is heated by passing around either electric heating elements or gas flames before entering the dryer drum where it encounters the wet clothing. A lint screen is inserted into the air stream and traps lint, preventing its deposition in the room.

Most drums are constructed of painted or porcelainized steel. The drum rotates in one direction at a rate of approximately 40 to 50 revolutions per minute. The speed is controlled to give the clothing an acceleration just below one gravity (gravity is the force of attrac-

* C. S. Witt and J. Warden, "Can Home Laundering Stop the Spread of Bacteria in Clothing," *Textile Chemists and Colorists,* Vol. 3, No. 81 (July 1971). J. Warden and T. Highly, "Survival and Redeposition of Fungi During Laundering," *Home Economics Research Journal,* Vol. 3, No. 2 (September 1974).

† A. R. Martin, W. K. Rhodes, R. M. Wagg, and F. McNeil, "Should Drycleaners Use Bactericides?" *Technical Bulletin T. 463,* National Institute of Drycleaning (September 1970).

‡ 1970 Census of Housing Series (HC(SI)-6.

tion between two masses). If one gravity is exceeded the clothes become set and stick against the wall of the drum and will not drop, hence they will not drop through the air and dry properly.

As the drum rotates, three or four baffles, mounted to the inside of the drum, lifts the wet clothing, elevates them through about 120 degrees of revolution and then drops them back to the bottom of the drum. As they are dropped, the clothes open and are exposed to the evaporative action of the heated air entering the dryer drum.

There are two basic types of dryers: gas and electric. For several years, gas-heated dryers outsold electric dryers, but in recent years the electric dryers have been outselling the gas dryers.

Almost all electric dryers must be wired for 230 volts. Heating elements vary from about 4300 watts to 5600 watts of power, necessitating the higher voltages. Several manufacturers offer a 120-volt, small-volume dryer. In any case, the heating elements are of nichrome wire or of Calrod-type construction. Air is drawn from the outside at a rate of 80 to 120 cubic feet per minute over these heating elements where it is heated.

Input to gas dryers varies from about 24,000 to 36,000 BTU per hour. This amounts to 23 to 35 cubic feet of natural gas per hour. Gas dryers can be easily converted to operation with bottled gas by qualified service personnel. All manufacturers offer conversion kits for this purpose.

The growth of man-made fibers, beginning with the wash and wear garments of the early 1950s made dryer controls necessary. These man-made fibers are thermoplastic, that is, they remember the position they were in when heat-set and they try to recover to the remembered position. If heated to 180°F in the dryer, and allowed to cool to room temperature in a wrinkled condition, they maintain the permanently set wrinkles.

Manufacturers added a "Cool Down" setting to take care of this problem. The heat is cut off during the last 10 minutes of the drying cycle. Cool air is blown through the fabrics to cool them down before the end of the drying cycle. Thus the thermoplastic fibers are not permitted to remember their wrinkled condition; however, even this does not always solve the problem. The accumulation of lint on the fabrics may cause them to overdry. There are systems of detecting the degree of dryness of the load to control the overdrying condition: (1) a dryer control system based on the water retained in a load and (2) a system based on the temperature of the outgoing air from the dryer drum. More recently a sensory system has been developed to eliminate permanent wrinkling. The clothes are tumbled three or four turns of the drum every 5 to 10 minutes up to several hours after drying is completed. No heat is added.

Combination Washer-Dryers

Combination machines are engineered to carry on all the functions of the automatic washer and then dry the clothes in the same machine. All are loaded from the front. When the load is dry, the machine shuts itself off. For special loads, the combination machine can be used as just a washer or just a dryer. It has two big advantages over separate machines: clothes need not be transferred from one machine to the other and the unit takes only half the space of two machines. Its disadvantages lie in the fact that its general makeup does not allow for effective extraction of water. Consequently, the machine is in use for a long, expensive amount of time while extremely wet clothing is dried. Too, when one mechanism breaks, both the washer and dryer are usually out of operation until repairs can be made.

Hand Washing

Garments that do not have fast colors or with seams that may fray and pull apart or any special finishes or ornamentation may require special handling. Hang tags or labels should give recommendations for washing.

For hand washing, the water temperature should be 100 to 110°F. Soft water is desirable, but if water is hard, a water softener can be added before the soap, or a detergent can be used.

The soap or detergent should be dissolved completely before putting garments into the water. Suds should be squeezed carefully through the fabric. Excess suds may reduce the cleansing action. Water should be removed by squeezing rather than wringing. Drip-dry fabrics should not be squeezed.

Rinsing should be done in two or more waters. If the water is hard, and a soap and water softener have been used, the water softener should also be added to the first rinse. Water may be squeezed out, and additional water can be pressed out by rolling the item in a bath towel and patting.

If colors have a tendency to run, items should be rinsed often until the rinse water looks clear, then hung in front of a fan or in a breeze so that the garment will dry quickly.

Fabrics that are to be drip-dried should be hung without squeezing or wringing.

Ironing and Pressing Equipment

Modern irons are electric and depend on heat rather than weight to smooth fabrics. Controls maintain proper heat for the type of fabric. Most irons have dials that can be set for silk, rayon, cotton, linen, and so on. Steam irons and steam-and-spray irons have eliminated the need to sprinkle any garments. All irons come with operating instructions that should be followed for best results.

Using a professional laundry service makes it easy to total dollars-and-cents expenses. Home laundry makes it difficult to ascertain this cost. The following factors should be determined.

- How much of the initial investment and installation charges on home laundry equipment is charged off with each load of washing?
- Is the cost of repairs, replacement of parts, and service added?
- How much water is used? What is the cost? How much does it cost to heat it?
- How much gas and electricity is used to run the washing machine, dryer, ironer and iron?
- How much do laundry supplies (water softener, detergent and soap, bleach, bluing, and fabric conditioner) cost per load?
- When laundering procedure is misjudged and a garment or load of clothes is ruined, how much of this loss is charged off against the home laundry bill?

Before deciding how much of the laundry to do at home, determine the value placed on the time that would be saved by using a professional laundry service. This is especially important to the working person.

Self-Service Laundering

Using a self-service or coin-operated laundry may save time, work, and money for the consumer. You can use as many washers and dryers as needed and do the entire weekly task in a short hour or two.

There is no hard work required in using coin-store equipment. There is no cleaning of equipment or laundry area either before or after use. There is no "cluttering" up of the home equipment, supplies, and soiled clothing.

When using a self-service laundry the same general principles that apply to home laundering should be followed.

SORTING AND PREPARING ITEMS FOR WASHING

Some simple rules to follow are:

1. Sort clothes:

(a) According to soil. Heavily soiled or greasy clothes should be washed separately.

(b) According to color. Whites and very light fast colors may be washed together.

(c) For best results, nylons and delicate washables should not be mixed with sturdy, heavy fabrics and garments.

2. Empty pockets, zip-up fastenings, hook the hooks, and remove any trimmings or buttons that might be damaged or fade.

3. Mend rips and tears, sew on loose buttons. Pretreat any deeply imbedded soil or spots by brushing with a solution of detergent and water intended to be used in washing.

4. Follow washing instructions provided by the garment manufacturer or provided on machines or instruction signs in the coin-op store.

5. Wash white nylon with white items only. Nylon picks up color easily from other clothes.

6. Separate silk, wool, spandex, and chlorine-sensitive fabrics from loads that are to be bleached with a chlorine product.

7. When in doubt as to what bleach can be used, play it safe by using an all-fabric bleach.

8. Corduroy, some synthetic fibers, and certain finishes pick up lint. Napped and quilted items, such as chenille robes and fleecy coats, produce lint and should be washed together for best results.

9. Dark colors that tend to fade may "bleed" onto lighter colored fabrics. It is safer not to mix them.

10. Sheer, lace-trimmed, and delicately made blouses, dresses, and lingerie should be washed in delicate loads. Use "Delicate or Gentle" cycle if the machine has one.

11. Heavily soiled clothes (except wool) frequently require prewashing or soaking. Soaking or a prewashing also aids in stain removal and should be done in warm or cold water with a detergent added to give best results.

Soaking helps loosen soil and is similar to prewashing except that the clothes are not agitated or tumbled. There are two types of soaking: (1) soaking delicate garments such as washable woolens or fabrics that have becomed weakened with wear (add detergent to water and soak no longer than 15 minutes) and (2) soaking stained garments with an enzyme presoak laundry aid or an enzyme detergent, which removes certain soils and stains. Follow manufacturer's directions on the product used.

Water may be softened with a mechanical water softener or by the introduction of a nonprecipitating water conditioner available in small packages in coin dispensers.

WASHLOAD SIZE AND COMPOSITION

The bulkiness or volume of the load to be washed is more important than the dry weight. For best washing action, combine both large and small items in each load.

319   *Fabric Care—Laundering*

LOADING THE WASHER   Many people have a tendency to overload the washer. This can result in poor cleaning. Place large, unfolded articles loosely in the bottom of the washer basket and distribute the smaller items at random.

WATER TEMPERATURE   Correct water temperature is necessary for good washing results. Hot water (140–160°F) is essential for washing heavily soiled white and colorfast cottons and linens to keep them white and bright. Warm water (100–120°F) is recommended for washing lightly soiled delicate fabrics, noncolorfast colors, and bright colors. Cold water is suggested for washing lightly soiled fragile or delicate items, plastic shower curtains, and very bright colored fabrics. Common laundry problems are shown in Table 7–4.

COIN-OP DRYING   Dryers in the self-service store are efficient, economical, and easy to use. They accommodate several washer loads at one time. Because they are much larger than home dryers, they provide the room and tumbling action most desirable to help keep clothing and other fabrics wrinkle free.

Never overload a dryer. Properly loaded, there will be less wrinkling and more even drying. Remember, the finer the fabric, the lower the temperature setting. It is best to remove clothes as soon as they are dry—especially permanent press. "Cool-down" finishing is offered by many coin stores. Overdrying tends to impart a harsh feel to fabrics. Knitwear should be removed while there is still moisture in them and gently pulled into shape. Nylons and wash and wear garments do not retain as much water.

Never put foam rubber or plastic items in the dryer. Do not use laundry dryers for removing solvent odor from items that have been dry cleaned. Before putting items into the dryer be sure that all oil or grease is removed from the clothes before drying.

COMMERCIAL LAUNDERING

The first steps in handling items are identifying and classifying. During classification, the fabrics are separated into groups such as white, light color, dark color, white shirts, wool, man-made and heavily soiled white. Up to 12 classifications may be used depending on such things as color, fiber content, and degree of soil.

After identification and classification, the fabrics are washed. The method used to wash a particular article is determined by its classification. Laundries differ in their procedures, each utilizes its own experiences.

Table 7–4   Common Laundering Problems

Problem	Probable Cause	Remedy	To Prevent
Dingy white permanent press, nylons, or blends.	Washing with pastel colors (permanent press, blends, ets., pick up even trace of loose dye).	Nylon whitener may help. Bleach according to garment manufacturer's instructions.	Wash whites by themselves. Use adequate detergent.
	Washing with heavily soiled or greasy items.	Try using a spot lifter. Brush off white powder with clean dry cellulose sponge. Or sponge grease spot with dry-cleaning fluid, then, before it dries, saturate areas with liquid detergent. Wash. For old or heavy grease spots, clean article in coin-operated dry cleaner.	Remove grease spots while fresh. Wash clothes in hot water, using plenty of detergent. Do not wash permanent press with other greasy items, since it readily absorbs greasy soils.
Harsh or gray clothes.	Soap or detergent combined with soil left in clothes. Can be caused by overloading washer.		Place unfolded laundry loosely in basket. Do not overload. Use more water for bulky items. Always measure detergent. Always use a low sudsing detergent in tumbler washers. When washing in soft water, try a low sudsing detergent to avoid excess suds in top loading washers. Soap must not be used in hard water unless a nonprecipitating water conditioner is added to the water.
Holes in clothes, torn clothes.	Improper use of chlorine bleach.	Misuse of chlorine bleach can weaken cotton fibers and in time cause holes. Also, the weakened fabric tears easily.	Always measure bleach. Always dilute measured bleach in at least one quart of water before adding to washer. Do not pour bleach directly onto clothes. If washer does not have bleach dispenser, add diluted bleach solution after washer has filled with water, being careful not to pour directly onto clothes.

Table 7-4 Common Laundering Problems (Contd)

Problem	Probable Cause	Remedy	To Prevent
	Failure to mend rips and tears.		Check clothes before washing.
	Failure to close zippers.		Fasten hooks, zip zippers. Wash sheer garments in mesh bags.
	Hooks, buttons with rough or sharp edges.		Remove buttons.
Reddish-brown or yellow-brown stains or deposits on clothes (rust).	Iron in water supply, storage tank, or plumbing.	Remove from clothing, using commercial rust remover, following label directions. Rinse clothes thoroughly before placing in washer. After rinsing, clothes should be washed.	Iron may be present in water supply. To correct, check with a water treatment company. Be sure not to use chlorine bleach in water containing iron unless you add a nonprecipitating water conditioner to the wash water before adding the diluted bleach solution. May be necessary to flush out hot water tank. If pipes carrying water to washer are iron, they could cause the trouble.
Lint on clothes.	Failure to sort clothes.	Brush lint from clothes or use lint remover roller.	Separate lint givers (terry towels, chenille) from lint receivers (corduroy, permanent press, knits). Man-made fabrics, blends, and permanent press readily attract lint from cottons due to static electricity. This can be lessened by using a fabric softener in the final rinse.

Only soft water is used since hard water wastes supplies and forms deposits on washers and in water lines. In most cases, a laundry man will use soap and builders rather than a detergent because he generally has a water softener.

Periodically, samples of water from each operation are taken to determine whether the concentrations of alkali, soap, bleach, and sour are within prescribed limits.

If white clothes are being washed at the usual 140 to 160°F, a high-titer soap will be used because it gives the best suds and cleansing action at these temperatures. For washing wools at 90°F, a low-titer soap or a specially formulated detergent is used because this gives the best suds and cleansing action at low temperature.

For woolen articles, a special machine is used. It gently rolls the articles through heavy suds at a very low speed. A neutral soap or detergent is used. No alkali is added to this formula to prevent a deteriorating effect on the wool. Three to five rinses are generally used. If this is not done, an off-color discoloration in the fabric may result. The souring operation (fluoride compounds) that follows acts as a final rinse. On wool, the souring operation may act as a mothproofing treatment if sufficient amounts of sour are used.

Because silk is chemically similar to wool, it is washed in the same manner. A neutral soap or detergent is used. Chlorine-type bleaches are never used because they would yellow and damage the silk. Also, highly alkaline material would damage the silk. Curtains and draperies are washed gently like woolens, because they may have been weakened by light.

Light-colored fabrics of all fibers are washed at temperatures between 100 to 120°F. Because dark colors have a greater tendency to bleed than have light colors, the dark colors are washed at lower temperatures, 90 to 100°F.

In commercial laundering only white articles are bleached. If stain removal is necessary on colored items, they receive a special treatment.

After articles are washed, they are taken out of the washers and placed in extractors, which spin the clothes to remove excess water. Overextraction is avoided, especially for articles containing man-made fibers in order to avoid setting permanent wrinkles in the fabrics.

After extraction, the articles are sorted and sent to different areas of the laundry for proper finishing or drying. Generally, consumers may choose among a variety of services offered by the laundry. They may have everything tumble dried, only the flat pieces (sheets, tablecloths, and pillow cases) pressed, and the rest of the bundle tumble dried, or everything pressed, in which case all wearing apparel would be finished and returned to the consumer ready to wear or use.

Flat pieces are finished or pressed on what is called a flatwork ironer. Fabrics pass between a smooth, heated metal surface and large cloth-covered rolls. This dries the fabric, removes wrinkles, and applies a sheen to the surface.

Heated puff irons, small presses, handkerchief presses, sock forms, large flat presses for curtains, special curtain stretchers, and blanket carders and shapers are all used to finish various types of articles. Special equipment has been designed to press a shirt in a minute.

After finishing, the articles are brought to one location for sorting and packaging and delivery to the home.

8

Fabric Care—
Dry Cleaning

The purpose of dry cleaning is identical to that of laundering—to remove soils from fabrics. Instead of using water, as in laundering, dry cleaning uses organic solvents. Because of the absence of water, the term dry cleaning was introduced since the solvents used are dry solvents.

DRY-CLEANING SOLVENTS

A dry-cleaning solvent must possess certain qualities. It must have the following properties: minimum toxicity, nonflammability, safety for use on all common textile fibers and dyes, good solvency for fats and oils to insure a good cleaning job, an unobjectionable odor incapable of becoming a residual odor in fabrics after its use, chemical stability under all use conditions, noncorrosiveness toward ordinary metals used in machines, pipe, and pump construction, sufficient volatility to permit economical reclamation by distillation and rapid, economical, and safe drying conditions, and compatibility with detergents designed for use in solvent.

Dry-cleaning solvents serve various uses, some of which are to dissolve greases and oils, act as dilutents for dry-cleaning detergents, carry or flush soil from a fabric, and rinse nonvolatile material from fabrics. Today, the dry cleaning industry uses three types of solvents.

Petroleum Solvents

Petroleum dry-cleaning solvents have been used for many years. Petroleum is not a suitable product in its crude form and it must be refined to produce the useful products. Dry-cleaning solvent is a small fraction or part of crude petroleum.

The term "Stoddard Solvent" * is not a trade or copyright name. It is used to describe any solvent that meets the Stoddard solvent specifications. Some petroleum solvents are known as "fast-drying" solvents. These conform to Stoddard solvent specifications but are more volatile than Stoddard solvent. Other types of petroleum solvents are high-flash solvents. They are sometimes required to conform to local fire codes.

Synthetic Solvents

The synthetic solvents (see Figure 8–1) used by dry cleaners are man-made products and are known as chlorinated hydrocarbon solvents. Perchlorethylene is almost exclusively used because it is nonflammable and has powerful solvent action on oils and greases and relatively low boiling points and high volatility.

* U.S. Department of Commerce, National Bureau of Standards (S3–41).

Chlorinated and fluorinated hydrocarbons used as drycleaning solvents

Perchlorethylene (C_2Cl_4)

$$\begin{array}{ccc}
Cl & & Cl \\
| & & | \\
C & = & C \\
| & & | \\
Cl & & Cl
\end{array}$$

"Valclene" solvent ($C_2Cl_3F_3$)

$$\begin{array}{ccc}
F & F \\
| & | \\
Cl-C & -C-Cl \\
| & | \\
Cl & F
\end{array}$$

Key: C — Carbon
Cl — Chlorine
F — Fluorine

Figure 8-1

Fluorocarbon Solvents

A new dry-cleaning solvent was introduced by DuPont in 1960, called Valclene®. It is a fluorocarbon solvent that contains a detergent.

Fluorocarbon solvents possess all the qualities necessary for a good dry-cleaning solvent. However, they also have several limitations: the cost per pound is high and they are very volatile, so that they can be used only in special machines.

SOAPS AND DETERGENTS

Soaps and detergents are discussed in Chapter 7. Just as you get improved cleaning with the use of detergents with water, the same principle holds true in dry cleaning.

RELATIVE HUMIDITY

The natural moisture content of fabrics is affected primarily by the relative humidity of the air they are exposed to rather than by its temperature.

The amount of moisture carried into a dry-cleaning system by the fabrics to be cleaned is very critical and must be controlled. Excess moisture may cause shrinkage, wrinkling, and redeposition of soil.

CHARGED SYSTEMS— SOLVENT RELATIVE HUMIDITY

The charged system is a method of dry cleaning in which the dry-cleaning solvent contains or is "charged" with a solvent-soluble dry-cleaning detergent. Most charged systems have the ability to dissolve water, which will aid in removal of water-soluble soils. The detergent remains in the solvent at all times and is used repeatedly with constant filtration on successive loads. Additional water and detergent are added as required. The ability of a charged system to remove some water-soluble soils is its main advantage over previous methods of dry cleaning. It requires an exact control of the relative humidity of the added water.

The concept of moisture control is based on a discovery of the National Institute of Drycleaning that water in a charged system reaches equilibrium with the textile load. From this was coined the term "solvent relative humidity" (SRH), which refers to the relative vapor pressure of water in solvent. Three factors control SRH: (1) the nature and concentration of the particular detergent in the solvent, (2) the amount of water present in the system, and (3) temperature. Lower levels of solvent relative humidity are preferable for soft, luxury woolens that are susceptible to felting shrinkage. Higher solvent relative humidity is required to clean rainwear. The solvent relative humidity should not exceed 75 percent. Hence, very sophisticated moisture controls are required and vital in the proper operation of the charged system.

MARKING AND PRESPOTTING

Items received from consumers for cleaning are handled at least 15 times. The first is a "marking in" process. The items are classified into light and dark colors as suits and coat loads, dresses and similar items, draperies and slipcovers, special items, leather, and fur items (see Figure 8–2).

The attendant also separates those items that require prespotting. The term "prespotting" refers to spotting done before a garment is dry cleaned.

The principles of prespotting are the same as those discussed in Chapter 6.

THE DRY-CLEANING WASHER

All dry-cleaning washers consist basically of a shell and an inner cylinder. The shell provides a container for the solvent and the cylinder is a container for the load.

Washer cylinders revolve to supply the mechanical action necessary for efficient cleaning. A reversing mechanism changes the direction of rotation of the cylinder to help prevent tangling of the load (see Figure 8–3).

CLARIFICATION OF DRY-CLEANING SOLVENT

Dry-cleaning equipment is quite complex because of the various processes used to clarify dry-cleaning solvent. Dry-cleaning solvents are too costly to throw away after a single use, thus impurities must be continually removed to keep the solvent in usable condition.

There are three major methods for controlling the impurity level in the solvent. Most efficient solvent clarification requires the use of all

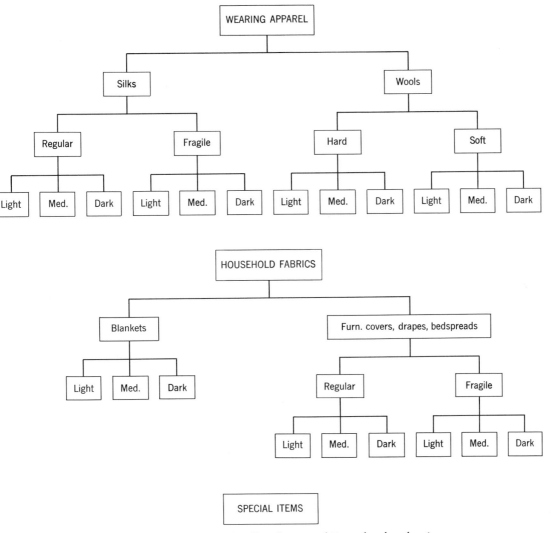

Figure 8-2 Classification of items for dry cleaning.
The term "silk" also refers to fabrics made of synthetic
fibers.

three: filtration, absorption, and distillation (see Figure 8–4 and
Table 8–1).

METHODS OF DRYING

Drying of garments may be done by three methods: a reclaiming
tumbler, drying cabinet, and room or air drying. In petroleum dry
cleaning the tumblers used consist basically of a perforated cylinder

Figure 8-3 A dry-cleaning room showing modern dry-cleaning equipment, automatic dry-cleaning machines, and a reclaimer tumbler. (Courtesy: American Drycleaner)

mounted in a shell through which is forced a stream of warm air. The air entering the tumbler passes over steam coils that heat the air. The heated air flows through the garments in the tumbler cylinder and is exhausted outside the building.

In perchlorethylene dry cleaning, drying is done in an enclosed tumbler with no air or solvent vapors leaving the unit. These vapors are recovered during drying by condensing them into a liquid form, which is drained back to the dry-cleaning machine.

At the end of the drying period, fresh air is brought into the tumbler from the room and passed through the garments, then exhausted. This is done for deodorizing purposes in order to remove the last traces of solvent vapors from the garments.

In a plant using perchlorethylene, washing, extraction, and drying may be done in one machine (called a "hot" unit—such as a typical coin-op machine) or washing/extraction may be done in one ma-

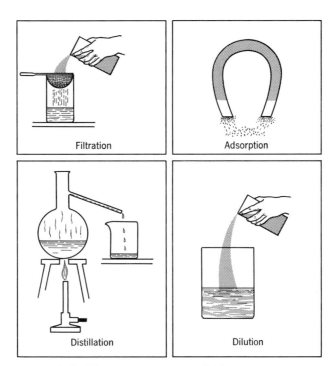

Figure 8-4 Filtration removes insoluble impurities from the contaminated solvent. The process of absorption is the adhering of a liquid or a gas to the surface of a solid body. Some soluble impurities can be removed from solvent by absorption. Distillation will remove practically all impurities from contaminated solvent. It is especially effective in removing dissolved greases and oils that are not removed by filtration or absorption. Replacement or addition of new or distilled solvent the percentage of impurities are reduced by dilution.

chine with drying done in a separate machine (a "recovery tumbler")

Some items handled in the dry-cleaning plant are either air dried or are dried in drying cabinets. Drying cabinets are enclosed shells through which warm air flows to evaporate the solvent. Garments are hung in drying cabinets. These recover solvent in much the same manner as do recovery tumblers.

Fabric conditioning units are used by both the professional dry cleaner and the coin or self-service cleaner (see Figure 8–5).

331   *Fabric Care—Dry Cleaning*

Table 8-1 Impurities Removed by Filtration, Absorption, and Distillation

Will Remove	Will Not Appreciably Remove
Diatomaceous Earth and Volcanic Ash Powders	
Insoluble soil	Coloring
	Cosolvents
	Mineral oils
	Greases and waxes
	Dissolved soaps and detergents
	Water
	Fatty acids
Sweetener Powder and Activated Carbon	
Insoluble soil	Mineral oils
Some soaps and detergents	Greases and waxes
Coloring	Water
Fatty acids	
Distillation	
Insoluble soil	Some cosolvents
Color	
Soaps and detergents	
Mineral oils	
Greases and waxes	
Some cosolvents	
Most fatty acids	
Water (in aftertreatments)	

The most recent innovation for finishing garments is called a "fabric conditional cabinet." There are two types: a continuous-type finishing and batch-process finishing.

The continuous-type finishing unit is an open-end cabinet that has a mechanical conveyor that moves the garments in one open end and out the other. Most batch processing cabinets work on the same principle as the continuous type except there is no automatic conveying of clothing.

Regardless of which equipment is used, the control of temperature and steam are important. Basically, all of the equipment operates on the same principles:

1. A steam cycle that relaxes the fabric.

Figure 8-5 A fabric-conditioning cabinet showing the batch-processing method. (Courtesy: Huebsch Originators, McGraw Edison Co.)

2. An air cycle (sometimes heated) that dries the fabric in a relaxed condition.

During both the steam and air cycles the garments are shaken to remove wrinkles.

SPOTTING

After dry cleaning, all garments are inspected by a person known as a "spotter." The spotter may find, in a few cases, that the article should be spotted and dry cleaned again. Otherwise, the spots and stains that fail to come out in the process must be treated separately.

FINISHING AND MINOR REPAIRS

When the cleaning operations have been completed and the inspector has passed the article as ready for final processing, it is routed through the sewing and finishing departments.

A number of sewing services may be included in the price charged for the plant's work, others being charged at established rates. Retacking of trouser cuffs, closing a seam, and securing a button are typical of simple services that would be performed at no extra charge. Lowering or raising cuffs and hems and replacing all buttons removed for safety and other major repairs are extra services and subject to extra charge.

What is the Difference Between Pressing and Finishing?

The term "pressing" means the removal of wrinkles only. "Finishing," on the other hand, implies more: it suggests that the finisher has the necessary skill and knowledge to restore the original appearance and "feel" of the fabric, finish details correctly, and do nothing to distort or alter the fit of the garment.

The finisher must be able to recognize, by appearance, all fabrics and the possible effects that steam, pressure, and vacuum will have on them. It is important to know that soft, nappy fabrics should not be flattened and made glossy, that cottons must look smooth and crisp, and that synthetics may easily be glazed, especially when pressing over seams and hems. In short, the finisher must be an expert in two things: how a fabric should look when finished correctly and how to achieve this look by the correct application of steam, pressure, and vacuum in the finishing procedure.

Steam is used to relax wrinkles, to make the fabric more pliable. Enough steam should be used to accomplish this and no more. Oversteaming a fabric has many disadvantages: (1) excess steam reaching portions of a garment already pressed may wrinkle it again, thus slowing production, (2) more time is needed for thorough drying by the vacuum—if the finisher fails to take this extra time, the work will suffer in quality, (3) chances of shrinking the fabric are greater, especially if the fabric has not been preshrunk in manufacture, and (4) some fabrics are softened and relaxed so much that stretching takes place almost automatically. This was a common occurrence when acrylic knits first appeared in the consumer market.

Pressure is needed, not so much to remove wrinkles, as to form a firm crease or impart the crispness desirable with some fabrics. The amount of pressure used must vary according to the fabric, with the softest fabrics at one extreme needing little or no pressure and the hard-finished fabrics at the other extreme, needing maximum pressure.

Pressure may be applied with the press head or a foam hand pad or a brush. In using the press head, pressure may vary from a light or contact pressure to medium or heavy pressure.

Vacuum is used chiefly to draw the steam away from the fabric, to dry and give it a firmer finish.

Equipment Use in Finishing

The equipment used in finishing garments and household items represents a considerable investment. The equipment is engineered to perform certain functions. Typical finishing equipment is shown in Figure 8–6.

Figure 8-6 A wool-finishing department showing a mushroom press, a grid-head press, and a steam-air former. (Courtesy: American Drycleaner)

WET CLEANING

Wet cleaning is a process of cleaning garments in water and water-soluble detergents, using precautions to prevent shrinkage, loss of color, and fabric distortion. There are several general steps in wet cleaning: (1) the garment or other article is first placed in water or in water containing soap or detergent, (2) the item is laid on a table and brushed by hand or processed in a washing machine, (3) the item is given several rinses in clear water, (4) the item is placed in the extractor to remove excess moisture, (5) some items are treated with sizings or dressing oils, and (6) the item is dried at room temperature or in the tumbler, whichever is most suitable.

How Does Wet Cleaning Differ From Washing?

Wet cleaning differs from washing in the following ways:

1. Garments are usually dry cleaned before they are wet cleaned.

2. If necessary, garments are measured carefully before wet cleaning and after wet cleaning are restored to original size.

335   *Fabric Care—Dry Cleaning*

3. The dyes are tested to determine if they bleed to water. If found to be fugitive, the dyes are set during the wet-cleaning process.

4. The garments are given special treatment in accordance with their fabric construction. For example, taffetas, sharkskins, and satins of acetate are seldom extracted because they would become so wrinkled that finishing would be difficult. Woolens are dried at room temperature to prevent shrinkage. Sizing and dressing oils are replaced where necessary. Different brushes are used for different types of fabrics.

5. The temperature of the water is controlled carefully to avoid bleeding of color and shrinkage of wool.

6. Strong alkalies and strongly alkaline soaps are never used. Instead, neutral soaps and synthetic detergents are used as cleansing agents.

7. Special treatment is given to spots and stains before wet cleaning. For example, milk, blood, and albumin stains are treated with an enzyme. Ink, dye, and Mercurochrome stains are removed with suitable agents.

8. White garments that have become yellow or badly stained are bleached.

9. Garments are given the least possible mechanical action, whether hand brushed while lying on a flat surface, or processed in a machine.

What Determines If An Item Should Be Wet Cleaned?

If a garment contains much general perspiration, the odor as well as the stain can be removed more satisfactorily by wet cleaning than by spotting it locally.

Many stains that require prolonged soaking can be handled more efficiently in the wet-cleaning department. For instance, if ink has been spilled in large areas on a colored dress, the stain could be removed by spotting, but there would be more danger of damaging the color and fabric in the area than if the entire garment were placed in a soaking bath and then wet cleaned.

Garments that require bleaching should be wet cleaned. If a garment has become yellowed, it must be immersed in a bleach bath for a period of time. Most white garments eventually fall into this class.

The construction, dyestuff, or sizing of a garment may make spotting difficult. For example, some types of spun rayon, especially those containing permanent sizing, are very difficult to spot. Or a dye may be so fugitive that a color ring may remain in the garment after spotting, whereas, after wet cleaning, the color would be even, though there might be a slight general loss of dyestuff.

Some garments contain an excessive amount of sizing. When spotted, sizing rings form. If spotting or prespotting and rerunning in the dry-cleaning department do not remove the rings, it is necessary to wet clean the garment.

Wet cleaning is the most practical method for removing the type of embedded soil that cannot be removed in dry cleaning. Soil of this nature usually contacts a garment when the fibers are moist and hence swollen, and becomes embedded as the fibers contract when the garment dries. It is well known that the dry solvents do not alter the size or shape of the textile fibers, which therefore hold the embedded soil within them. On the other hand, wet cleaning swells the fibers so that the soil may be worked out. In dresses, embedded soil is usually located at the waistline, at the placket where the slide fastener is located, and at the seat of the skirt, in jackets and coats, and the cuffs, elbows and creases in the sleeve.

Some fabrics or household items must be wet cleaned rather than dry cleaned. For example, wet cleaning is the preferred-care method for glass curtains and draperies, for electric blankets because of the wired coils or heating elements, and for the majority of vinyl fabrics on the market.

The cleaning industry has long considered wet cleaning a necessary part of plant procedure, a process that often restores a garment to wearability when other methods have failed.

The dry cleaner in certain cases should call the consumer before he wet cleans some items because of the risk involved:

1. Fabrics in which the finish will be lost, for example, nonpermanent moiré, ciré, chintz or any other fabric that will lose sizing or finish that cannot be replaced.

2. Fabrics in which there will be general loss of color or bleeding, for example, prints that have bled in home washing and will become lighter in color during correction of the bleeding, garments that may show general loss of color or unevenness of color after long soaking periods necessary for stain removal, and fugitive colors that might give difficulty in wet cleaning.

3. Articles that may shrink or become distorted, for example, some types of rayon curtains, faille, bengaline, knit-back pile fabrics, garments cut off the bias, and any article that cannot be finished satisfactorily after wet cleaning.

Despite the impressive advances made in dry cleaning, wet cleaning retains a position of great importance in the industry. The wide variety of textile products now in use necessitates a corresponding variety of cleaning techniques in which wet cleaning plays a major role.

SELF-SERVICE OR COIN-OPERATED DRY CLEANING

Perhaps the greatest breakthrough in clothing maintenance from the consumer's standpoint came about at the beginning of the 1960s. The automatic self-service dry cleaner or coin-operated dry cleaning was an entirely new concept.

Coin-operated dry cleaning is based on the same concepts of professional dry cleaning. There are two solvents used: perchlorethylene and fluorocarbon solvents. The latter was introduced in 1973.

Most coin-store dry cleaning machines are designed to accommodate an eight-pound load, but bulk is equally important as weight. Large bulky pieces should be loosely loaded so the cylinder is about half full, even if such a load weighs only six pounds. Garments need room to tumble in the cleaning solvent—and room to fluff out during drying.

Every load is cleaned and rinsed in purified solvent. Solvent is never reused until purified and filtered. Table 8–2 contains some tips for better coin dry cleaning.

Recognizing Fabrics That Require Special Handling

Unfortunately, there is no simple way troublesome fabrics can be identified. To avoid fabric damage, there are several items that sould not be dry cleaned in coin-operated machines:

Leather and suede.
Simulated vinyl.
Fabrics containing olefin fibers (polypropylene and polyethylene).
Fabrics containing vinyon (vinyls and vinyl copolymer).
Genuine fur garments.
Fiberglas draperies and bedspreads.
Saran and Saranspun curtains and draperies.

Table 8–2 Tips for Better Coin Dry Cleaning

- Check and follow cleaning instructions on garment labels and hang tags.
- Separate and clean light-colored fabrics separately from dark, fragile and sheer from heavy clothing.
- Brush lint from cuffs and pockets.
- Remove fancy buttons, belts, or trim.
- Remove all articles from pockets.
- Repair any tears, rips, or broken seams.
- Remove spots or stains as recommended.
- Do not overload the machine if you want good cleaning results.
- Remove articles immediately from the machine at the completion of the drying cycle.
- Hang garments on hangers to prevent wrinkling.

Coated drapery linings (vinyl film or aluminum coatings).
Fabrics stitched with rubber core yarns.
Rubber coated fabrics.
Metallic coated dress fabrics.
Resin-bonded pigment prints.

Fabrics that should be placed in a net bag are:

Silk and wool combinations (or turn inside out).
Textured acetate knits.
Chiffon.
Sweaters made of mohair, cashmere, Angora.
Moiré.
All knits or turn inside out.
Urethane coated (simulated leather) trimmed garments.
Beaded or fur trimmed garments.

All velvets, plain or crushed, should be turned inside out.

9

Fabric Care–
Specialty Cleaning

The term "Special Services" is used to describe renovation processes other than those performed during a regular dry-cleaning service as described in Chapter 8. Additional equipment, techniques, and methods are necessary to clean certain items of wearing apparel and household items. In fact, some business firms may specialize in one or more special services, for example, leather cleaning and finishing, fur cleaning, remodeling, and storage. Some of the various special services offered are discussed in this chapter.

BRIDAL GOWNS

Although bridal gowns are worn for a very short time, they are subjected to many things that can cause problems later on if they are not taken care of immediately. Usually the train and hemline of the gown becomes soiled while walking to and from the church, after or while dancing at the reception. Flowers and confetti may result in tannin and dye stains. Punch, champagne, cocktails and coffee can cause caramelized sugar stains. Perspiration, if allowed to age in the fabric, can cause fabric discoloration and disintegration.

Many brides want to preserve their gowns for sentimental reasons. There are specialists who process and package wedding gowns for safekeeping. Some firms make claims and even give warranties.

FURS

The term "furrier's method" is used to describe cleaning furs by revolving them in an absorbent compound that is impregnated with a liquid having the capacity to remove all soil.

The furrier's method is a safe method of cleaning furs. Neither lining nor pelts can be damaged. Dyes do not bleed and separation or stretching of the pelts does not occur. A fur coat cleaned the furrier's method is very soft.

Preparation for Cleaning

Fur items are inspected for rips and damage from wear—minor repairs are made. The linings are repaired before cleaning. Matted areas in the fur are combed to achieve hair separation. Buttons are covered with button covers to protect them against breakage. Ornamental-type buttons are removed. Before cleaning the fur, the linings are either hand sponged or sprayed. If linings are sprayed, a continuous sprayer is used to insure uniform application. Heavily soiled areas are hand sponged with a terry cloth sponge prior to spraying.

Figure 9-1 A fur-cleaning machine with automatic air injector used during the drumming and caging cycle. The jet air principle removes the cleaning compound automatically while tumbling. (Courtesy: Walter Haertel Co.)

Furs are classified as to type—fragile or regular—and color. Examples of furs that can be classified as regular are mouton, muskrat, seal or other heavy straight hair garments. The fragile classification includes the very expensive furs, such as sable, chinchilla, mink, persian lamb, caracul, and other curled furs.

The color classification is necessary because some dyes used on furs are not fast to the cleaning solution. Dyed furs are classified according to special color, for example, red, blue, and so on. Dyed furs are tested to determine the degree of bleeding if they are cleaned by an alternate solvent method. This method of cleaning is discussed later.

Furs cleaned by the furrier method are placed in a fur drum for drumming. This term is used to describe the revolving of the fur in the cleaning compound (see Figure 9–1). Fur cleaning compounds are formulated with a solvent and finely ground corncobs, powdered wood, or cellulose products such as nutshells.

The next process is called caging. This is a process in which the compound is removed from the fur. In modern equipment, air is injected into the drum during the caging cycle. The average cycle is 20 to 30 minutes. The garments are removed from the tumbler and compressed air is used to remove any excess compound remaining in the garment such as in the pockets.

Glazing and Finishing

Whether or not a fur is glazed or given a special finish depends on the classification. Glazing of fur is the after process of cleaning and compares to the pressing of cloth garments after dry cleaning. The liquid compounds used contain special ingredients which polish the fur and impart the desired sheen. It is either sprayed or brushed onto the fur and allowed to dry. The fur is then ironed. See Figure 9–2.

The use of the rotary iron is the most widely used finishing technique employed today. Its use eliminates all hand finishing and renews the original finish of the fur by taking out all tufting and matting as well as further polishing the guard hairs. Some furs can be improved by some treatment such as combing or carding.

Heavier furs such as beaver, mouton, and sheared raccoon, are finished with a rotary iron. All furs, except the curly type furs, show a marked improvement with ironing. There are some furs that require special care. Persians, caraculs, persian paw, and American broadtail do not require glazing or ironing.

Alaskan seal is ironed on the rotary iron but sometimes dry steam is used for the final glazing. This gives the garment a softer and smoother appearance.

The cleaning compound has a tendancy to cling more to mouton, so an antistatic product is used to facilitate the removal of excess cleaning material. After the cleaning process, but before ironing, sheared beaver is sprayed with a glaze, allowed to dry, and then ironed.

After cleaning, no further finishing is required on the broadtails. The moles and white ermines are ironed using a low temperature and very little pressure on the iron.

White ermine, Russian broadtail, and mole have very tender pelts and require special handling. They are cleaned in a bag with the cleaning compound. They are not caged to remove the compound. Instead it is blown from the fur with an air gun.

FINISHING THE LINING

If the lining is not fastened at the bottom, the coat is placed on an ironing board with the board inserted between the lining and pelt of the fur. The lining is then hand ironed with a steam iron. Usually the seat areas require the most attention. If the lining is tacked at the bottom, the coat is placed inside out on a form or hanger. The lining is pulled away from the leather side of the fur, and then the steam iron is run quickly and lightly over the surface of the lining until the wrinkles disappear.

DURABILITY OF FURS

Properly cared for, a fur coat will last a long time. Length of wear depends on the care it receives and the kind of fur it is. Expensive chinchilla, for instance, will not last as long as inexpensive rabbit fur. The

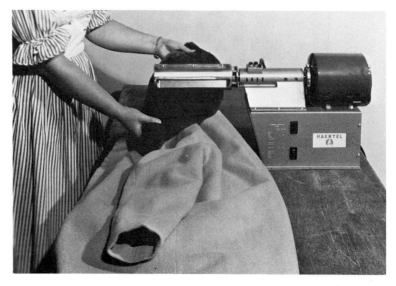

Figure 9-2 The rotary iron is a motor-driven, cylindrical iron. Heat is thermostatically controlled from 0° to 600°F depending on the type of fur to be finished. The fur is held against the revolving rotor to restore the original finish. (Courtesy: Walter Haertel Co.)

most perishable fur will outwear the strongest if the former is properly handled and cared for and the latter abused.

If a few seams part or a few small holes appear in the skin, take the garment to a reputable furrier and he can correct the trouble.

The Care of the Skins

Most fur troubles arise from improper care of the skin, which undergoes a highly technical process previous to manufacturing. The oil content of a skin determines both the life of a fur and its appearance. If the oil content is removed from the leather, the fur becomes brittle, dull, and lusterless.

The oil content gives the skin pliability, elasticity, and preserves and adds strength. The oils remain in the skin for many years unless it is abused. The removal of oil from the skin causes the leather to become hard and brittle. The fur becomes dull and valueless.

The following suggestions may increase the wear life of a fur garment:

1. Never place wet or damp furs near a stove, radiator, or heat register. Shake them gently and place on a hanger where they can dry slowly at room temperature. Use a padded hanger to conform to the shape of the neck and shoulders.

2. Hang furs in a closet where air can circulate. Avoid hanging furs near a steam pipe.

3. Sometimes the skin of a fur may stiffen. If this occurs, take the garment to a furrier to restore it to its former condition.

AVOID FRICTION

Avoid constant stroking of fur. Friction from the hand may singe the guard hairs. Never use a hairbrush or a comb on furs. Shaking the fur helps to open the fur fibers and helps to give protection against moths.

Jewelry, bags carried on the arm, or swinging against the sides may cause friction. The collar wears if constantly rubbed against a hat. Riding in automobiles causes wear on the lower back, the shoulder areas, and the sleeves from wrist to elbow.

AVOID STRAINS

Most fur garments are reinforced at places where strain is expected. When sitting down, see that it is not tightly buttoned. Try to avoid unnecessary strain across the hips and back.

SHEDDING AND CROCKING

Furs seldom shed, but in certain furs the hairs break off naturally. What may be thought to be either shedding or breaking hair is often just loose hair that the furrier has failed to remove.

Fur crocking is oxidation of the dye causing the dye to discolor or come off. Occasionally this occurs in new furs. What might be considered to be crocking is often merely an accumulation of dust or cosmetics. Having the fur cleaned will thoroughly remove this.

FADING OF COLORS If exposed to direct sunlight all furs will fade, whether natural or dyed. These changes are gradual. Keep furs out of strong sunlight and store them in summer.

Marten, mink, muskrat and other brown furs will turn lighter in color whether natural or dyed. White fox, ermine, and other white furs change to a slightly yellow tint. Others change color but not enough to be noticeable. A furrier can generally restore color by brushing dye on lightly.

STORAGE OF FURS Fur storage is a specialized business requiring a great deal of equipment and trained craftsmen who make fur care their sole business. Furs must be stored under exactly the right degree of humidity, for high humidity causes damage such as mold or mildew. Low humidity is equally dangerous. Dry air draws moisture and natural oils from pelts and fur hairs, thus shortening the life of the fur. Proper refrigeration, ventilation, fumigation, and other factors are equally important (see Storage, p. 363).

Retreatment– Fabric Sizing

Applying a sizing to garments restores their appearance, hand, and drape. The idea of sizing is not peculiar to dry cleaning. Probably the most familiar sizing is starch. When garments are washed, for example, all the water-soluble sizings are removed leaving the garment limp. A starch dip or spray is applied to restore body to the fabric. Starch is used widely in commercial laundering for the same purpose. People have come to expect cotton fabrics such as shirts to have a definite body and hand.

In dry cleaning, the problem of resizing is unique because of the requirements of the solvent system. Starch cannot be used because even though it is cheap and effective, it is not soluble in dry-cleaning solvent. The sizes available to the dry cleaner are either solutions or dispersions of various resins or gums, in either solvent or water.

There is one big difference in applying a finish in the textile mill and reapplying a finish to a fabric after laundering or dry cleaning. In the mill, the fabric is flat and a single thickness under controlled application conditions. In a garment or household item, one is working with double and triple thicknesses of fabric in a definite shaped form under uncontrolled application conditions (see Figure 9–3).

Figure 9-3 Retreatment of an embroidered Mouseline de Soie gown is achieved by spraying with a sizing. (Courtesy: International Fabricare Institute)

Retreatment– Flame Retardant

At the present time there is much interest in flame-retardant finishing. Some states or local fire marshals have passed legislation requiring it. Some customers are requesting that household articles such as bedspreads, furniture covers, and draperies be made flame retardant.

Reapplying a flame-retardant finish by a commercial laundry or dry cleaning plant is not a simple technology. The chemicals for achieving durable flame retardance are sold principally to textile finishing plants. The flame retardant finishes sold to dry cleaners and laundrymen so far are applicable to cotton fabrics only, and to some degree to rayon. They are nonpermanent if applied, which means they must be reapplied after each cleaning.

Retreatment–Moth Repellent

Most forms of moth life are destroyed by dry-cleaning solvent but once the solvent evaporates, moths can again attack a fabric.

Mothproofing agents give complete protection against moth damage when reliable agents are properly applied. Mothproofing agents can be applied by either spray or immersion methods.

Retreatment–Water Repellent

Textile mills apply water repellent finishes not only to rainwear fabrics but also to many other fabrics. For example, many men's suiting fabrics are made water repellent so the suits will be resistant to spots and stains.

347 *Fabric Care—Speciality Cleaning*

Some water repellent finishes are removed by dry cleaning or wet cleaning. Other finishes—called durable types—are not removed by dry cleaning or wet cleaning. Fabrics treated with the so-called durable finish lose their water repellency when dry cleaned. The reason is probably not because dry cleaning actually removes the finish, but because the fabric, when dry cleaned, retains a minute film of detergent that counteracts the water-repellent effect.

This has become important to dry cleaners. Many garments are sold with the claim that their water repellent or stain resistant characteristics will not be affected by dry cleaning. After they are dry cleaned and lose their water repellency, consumers feel the dry cleaner must have mishandled the garment.

The durable-type finishes are not removed by either dry cleaning or wet cleaning. This does not mean that all fabrics containing a durable water-repellent finish remain satisfactorily water repellent after dry cleaning. Although dry cleaning does not remove the finish itself, the detergents used in dry cleaning have some wetting out action and thus mask the effect of the original water-repellent finish. Moreover, even rinsing in distilled solvent does not remove the last traces of the detergent.

LEATHERS

The satisfaction one receives from wear and care of leather garments, leather-trimmed garments, and gloves is directly related to the selection and the care given the garment in wear. This explains why the upkeep of most leather garments exceeds the cost of upkeep of a fabric garment. The cost of upkeep of a leather garment should be taken into consideration when one is purchased.

Selecting Leather Garments

Good leather is the result of the skin quality, tanning quality, and finishing quality.

A top-quality skin is identifiable by being free from flaws, scars, barbed wire scratches, sores, seed marks, or thorns.

It is more difficult to make certain of good tanning and finishing. Weight and thickness may or may not relate to strength and durability. Poor quality leather soon loses its original appearance.

The consumer should do some comparative shopping to enable making a better selection. Learn to recognize the rich, soft surface that results from good tanning and finishing.

Quality grain leather has a rich, deep gloss through which the natural grain is visible. Its texture is soft and pliant. While no grain or suede leather is entirely free from crocking of color or leather dust, well-tanned and colored leather has a minimum amount.

Leather making is an exact science. Careful selection of raw skins minimizes the variation in quality that might result from the world-wide origin of the skins. Laboratory control insures manufacturing accuracy over each of the many complicated processes of preparation, tanning, and finishing.

Suede leather and grain leather are both the tanned skins of animals that are treated at the tannery with fine oils and dressings to make them soft and durable. These same oils make it possible to dye and finish suede and grain leather. The main difference between suede and grain leather is the way they are finished. Suede leather is a skin that is buffed by a special machine to raise a nap and give it that soft, velvety look and feel. This treatment is generally given to the underside or fleshy side of the skins, but it can also be given to the top or grain side. Grain or smooth leather is a skin treated with special dyes and finishes on the upper or top side of the skin to give it the soft, smooth feel and look.

Leather loses the oils as a result of wear, soil, and evaporation. The loss of oil is hastened by improper cleaning, improper storage, and excessive soiling.

Points to look for in a well-made leather garment are given in Table 9–1. Facts needed to make a selection in relation to care are

Table 9–1   Points to Look for in a Well-Tailored Garment

- Fullness of the cut to allow for freedom of movement—plenty of elbow room, adequate armholes, no skimping on material anywhere. Knife pleats, bellows, hinged sleeves are evidences of attention to the wearer's comfort.
- Adequate length, providing warmth around the waist. A leather jacket intended for cool-weather wear should have almost the same length as the coat of a business suit. This applies to both sleeve length and overall length.
- No skimping on quality—strong areas of leather at the seams to hold the threads.
- Well-shaped collar and cuffs. In children's garments, a generous turnup at the cuffs is a desirable feature, allowing for growing arms.
- Good quality lining. Grain leather garments are usually lined, covering up the inner "flesh" side. It makes the garment easier to put on and take off and provides greater comfort in wearing.
- Expert stitching with strong thread at the "break" in the collar and around the buttonholes. "Blind" stitching at cuffs and bottom is an attractive tailoring feature. There should be no loose threads.
- Finished seams, all belt loops firmly attached.
- High-quality fasteners, buttons, and buckles.
- Large, roomy pockets.
- No excess of flashy "hardware" in order to make up for skimping on leather.

Table 9-2 Points to Consider—Selection and Care

- Check on claims made for special finishes. Is water repellency of utmost importance? Fine leather fashions are usually not designed for hard-weather wear.
- Inspect the brightly colored garments for evenness of hue. Many of the bright shades possess poor colorfastness to light. After wear and before cleaning, examine an unexposed area, such as under the collar. Compare with an exposed area for color change.
- Check the garment carefully for thin places that may develop into holes. Leather cannot be mended too successfully.
- Do not let your garment get too soiled before cleaning. The deeper the soil is embedded, the more difficult it is to get good cleaning.
- Leather garments require special handling in cleaning. They cannot be cleaned as a regular cloth garment. Seek out a firm that specializes in leathers.

given in Table 9–2. Definition of leather terms are found in Appendix C.

Home Care of Suedes and Leathers

Wear a scarf to protect the neckline of a leather garment from makeup and hair oil. Protect leather from perspiration as it can cause discoloration.

Care should be used in decorating suede and leather garments with jewelry. Pin-type jewelry will punch or cut holes in the leather. Holes may also occur from sewing machine needles. Shortening or repairing suede or leather garments is best left to a skilled leather specialist.

Do not keep garments made of or trimmed with suede or grain leather in warm, airless places or in a plastic bag. Allow them to hang where air will circulate freely.

Avoid prolonged exposure to sun and light, since this may cause fading and oxidation.

Avoid heat when drying suede or grain leather that has become wet or damp from rain. Do not use abrasives to remove stains and spots. This results in ugly rings, discoloration, and other damage. Dye stains such as lipstick, ballpoint, and other inks are best removed by a leather cleaning specialist.

Never allow garments to become too soiled before having them cleaned. Age, heat, and other conditions set some stains, making it impossible to remove them safely.

Brush suede or suede trimmed garments frequently, using a dry, soft-bristled brush or a professional suede rubber sponge. Frequent brushing will remove surface oil and add luster to the suede. It also will help remove the fine suede dust (crocking) that is natural with new suede.

Scotch tape or masking tape is an ideal way to remove lint from knit or other fabric trim.

Extreme caution must be taken in pressing suedes. Set the iron for the lowest temperature—do not steam—and be sure to use a press cloth or heavy brown paper between the suede and iron. Press one panel at a time, keeping the iron moving constantly to avoid overheating. Upon completion, brush the entire garment thoroughly to raise the nap.

Accidental spillage of foodstuff, milk, blood, and the like, is best removed before it becomes dry. A soft cloth dampened in cool water will remove a great many water-soluble stains. A patting or blotting procedure is best. Let it dry at room temperature; flex the garment frequently while drying. When it is dry, brush it thoroughly.

Stains of an oily, greasy nature, such as vegetable oils or any hot salted greases, penetrates the skins quickly and leaves a permanent stain if not removed at once. Pat the affected area with a soft absorbent cloth to pick up all surplus grease.

Stains caused by fruit juices, coffee, tea, colas, and the like, that contain reducing sugars, perfume, and other liquids that contain alcohol will become set and turn brown from age and heat if not removed at once. These stains are very difficult, if not impossible, to remove. Treat these stains the same as accidental foodstuff spillage.

Garments made of or trimmed with smooth leather can be surface cleaned by using a sponge or soft cloth dampened in water containing a small amount of detergent. Wipe the surface clean, then dry with a clean towel. Allow to dry thoroughly. Then press the same as suede using the same precautions.

Professional Cleaning and Finishing of Leathers

All pieces of a matching ensemble should be brought to the leather cleaner at the same time, to assure that they will continue to match in color.

Leather company experts have worked with leading laundries, dry cleaners, and leather-cleaning specialists to develop a method of successfully dry cleaning leather.

After leather garments are marked in, they are prespotted. Leathers in general hold onto dirt and soil so stubbornly that it is always necessary to prespot them.

The basic spotting techniques used on fabrics are applicable to suede and grain leather with some limitations and exceptions.

If a leather coat has a fabric lining, this becomes a separate cleaning problem. In some cases, the lining must be completely removed and cleaned separately and then replaced after the leather portion of the garment is cleaned and finished. In some cases, the lining is hand burshed with a special detergent solution, cleaned, dried, and then masked with a special tape before the garment is sprayed and finished.

DRY CLEANING   Numerous methods of cleaning leather have been tried and abandoned over the years. Most of them required spraying with an oil-dye mixture to restore color. This is still required on some shades or colors in high fashion garments.

In recent years leather cleaners have turned to a system involving as its essential feature an oil-detergent mixture.

Grain leather garments are easier to handle than suedes. Suedes, including chamois, require more time in the cleaning process than grain leathers, although much the same procedures are followed.

PRESSING   A hot head press with no grid plate is used for pressing leathers. No steam is used. Steam pressure to the press is regulated not to exceed 50 pounds. Various shapes of pressing pads are used to get a good appearance of suede and leather. Pressure differs with the type of skin. For example, grain leathers made of horsehide or split cowhide require considerable pressure because of the thickness of the skin. Only very light pressure is applied to garments made of goat and kidskin, and the head of the press is covered with a moleskin or flannel cover cloth.

Suedes have to be brushed with a good bristle brush to raise the nap. Suedes may also have to be surface-treated with fine steel wool or fine emery cloth to remove any film or oxidized tissue from the surface.

DYEING AND FINISHING   Many of the dyes used to color leathers are partially removed in dry cleaning and must be replaced. This is what accounts for the price of cleaning service because each item is a special dye to match service. This requires expert mixing and color matching of dyes. When leather is combined with fabric in garment design, the fabric must be masked with special masking tape before the color is applied. Special equipment is necessary such as spray booths and guns, various mannequins or forms, expandable sleeve forms, and a complete stockroom of dyes for both grain and suede leathers. Once a grain leather garment has been sprayed and dried, it is ready for final inspection.

Although some cleaners may place leather garments in cellophane bags to protect them while they are transported to your home, they should be removed upon arrival to prevent color change and mildew. Most leather cleaners use paper bags.

Consumer Performance Problems

There are some peculiar situations in leather manufacture that may result in performance problems as listed below. Consumers should be aware of them.

CROCKING

It is generally known that leather is not entirely free from crocking or color offset. In recent years, the products of our best tanners have been markedly improved in this respect, but the consumer must expect that suede garments will shed a certain amount of dust caused by the abrasive work on the flesh side of the skin and that the color surface of grain finishes will wear off slightly. However, the continued popularity of suede year after year and the growing popularity of grain finishes proves that this is no handicap to repeat business for the retailer.

SKIN AND HIDE DEFECTS

Many skins contain defects caused by lice, ringworm, warble fly larvae, grub infestation, scars caused by wounds, and bruises from rough handling.

The manufacturer tries to eliminate these defects by using quality skins. He is able to mask many of them by treating the skin with an oil and dye or pigment. However, when the garment is cleaned, the defect may reappear as a light area on suede and dark area on grain leather.

There is no satisfactory way the cleaner can correct these conditions in the finished garment.

BELLY WRINKLES

Wrinkles that stop at the seams of specific panels in a garment are called "belly wrinkles." The defective panels come from the portion of the skin taken from the belly of the animal. The wrinkles are inherent. These skins are found mostly in inexpensive garments but can also be used in inconspicuous areas of expensive garments such as inside sleeve panels. The manufacturer is able to mask this condition when the skin is processed. However, when the garment is cleaned the wrinkles reappear. There is no satisfactory remedy.

THIN SKINS (SPLIT OR SHAVED SKINS)

Lightweight leather garments, especially women's suede garments, are often paper thin in some areas. These areas can usually be detected by their uneven nap. Holes can develop in these areas when cleaned. The defect is inherent in the skin.

ALUMINUM CHLORIDE DAMAGE (WHITE GLOVES AND WHITE SHEEPSKIN)

Aluminum chloride is used in the tanning process for producing white skins. When it is not correctly formulated and applied, an acid can develop, which weakens the skins. The leather cracks and peels. The damage usually becomes noticeable after the leather is exposed to the heat necessary in drying. This is a manufacturing defect. The damage cannot be corrected.

SUNFADE GARMENTS MADE ENTIRELY OF SUEDE

Garments show a loss of color in areas exposed to light during wear. Blue, green, and grey dyes are most sensitive to sun fading. The loss of color is due to the inherent sensitivity of the dye.

This color loss can be masked to some degree by redyeing, but it is usually impossible to restore the original color completely. The damaged leather either accepts the dye more readily or less readily than does the undamaged leather. In a combination of cloth and suede garments, this fading or color loss is difficult to detect because there are no unexposed areas to examine. The leather panels are completely exposed, so the loss of color occurs throughout. There is no satisfactory remedy.

COLOR LOSS IN DARK SUEDES

This is a uniform color loss over the entire garment. It occurs in both suedes and grain leathers, but it is easy to restore color to grain leather. Dark suedes lose more color than light suedes. Dark colored suedes are always suspect as bleeders. Special handling in cleaning can minimize this problem. Spray dyeing is required to make the garment wearable.

COLOR LOSS IN "BUSH COATS"

These coats are usually made of split cowhide. The surface of such a hide is rough—almost like suede. "Bush coats" lose color readily in cleaning, regardless of the method used. In some instances the oils are also removed, causing a harsh feel. Bush coats that can be dry cleaned are improved by spraying with a heavy coat of dye.

LOSS OF COLOR IN MULTIPLE-PIECE GARMENTS

A more notable loss or change of color occurs in one piece than in another of a multiple-piece garment when they are cleaned in separate loads. This condition can occur on all leather garments as well as on combination cloth and leather garments.

354 *Performance of Textiles*

All pieces of a multiple-piece garment should be cleaned in the same load. This applies to a two-piece suit or a jacket and belt or any other combination of more than one piece.

It is very difficult and often impossible to restore all such items to exactly the same color once one has faded more than the others.

COLOR LOSS DUE TO CLEANING OR CROCKING FROM BLACK SUEDES

This problem is found in expensive foreign tanned skins which have little or no nap. The deep black color is achieved by "loading" the skin with carbon black. This is not a dye. It is like a dust and will rub off or it will flow off in dry cleaning. A drastic loss of color occurs if you dry clean. No method has been developed by which the dry cleaner can replace the color once it is removed.

DYE TRANSFER (SUEDE DYE TRANSFERRING TO CLOTH)

Dye can transfer from suede leathers to the cloth portion of a garment during cleaning and drying. This transfer occurs most often in garments combining dark suede with light colored fabrics. This is an inherent characteristic of some dyes. Some of these garments can be restored by recleaning and rinsing in clear solvent. However, in most cases once the transferred dye has dried in the fabric, removal is impossible.

TRANSFER OF GRAIN LEATHER FINISH TO CLOTH

The grain leather finish on some trim softens in dry cleaning and drying and transfers to the fabric portion of the garment. Some types of finish used on leather in manufacturing lend themselves to this kind of transfer.

In most cases removal of the finish is not possible. However, sometimes it can be corrected by first recleaning the garment until the excess leather finish has been removed. Then a volatile dry solvent is applied followed by an oily type paint remover to the stained area.

RELAXATION SHRINKAGE

Shrinkage can be noted by fullness in the lining. Most leathers shrink when cleaned, but they can be handled with very little trouble and shaped back to the original size.

UNGLUED HEMS

If the hem of the garment has come unglued, the best procedure is to press the garment, recreasing the hem in its former position and reglue, using no more than necessary. Press the hem firmly with the heel of the hand as you go along. Hang the garment to dry.

355   *Fabric Care—Speciality Cleaning*

LINED GLOVES   The lining in some gloves is glued to the inside of the leather fingers. This construction is often found even in expensive gloves. The solvent affects the glue, and the lining comes loose. The success of replacing the lining depends on the construction of the glove.

RENTAL AND FABRIC CARE SERVICES   Career apparel is a new category of clothes in which fashion has been joined to function. The primary aim is to create a corporate fashion "look." Career apparel is specially designed for business clothing worn for reasons of aesthetics and identification, rather than for the protection of either the wearer or his personal clothing, as is the case with industrial uniforms.

The present size of the market for career apparel compared with wearing apparel is modest, but the surface has hardly been scratched. The potential is considered great. It is estimated that men and women wear an average of four garments per person twice a year—a summer and winter outfit, or eight garments per capita. The number of people who are industrial workers and unskilled service workers represent the image of a company. One can understand why dry cleaners and launderers were a logical group to enter this field as a supplier and as a caretaker of these garments.

Rental of formal wear is not new. It provides a needed service for individuals who require once in a lifetime or once a year formal attire to meet a social requirement.

REDYEING   This is a very specialized service that requires special equipment. Most dry cleaners do not have enough demand for this service to do it themselves. However, many dry cleaners accept work for redyeing and then send it to the wholesale dye houses (see Table 9–3).

The volume of garment dyeing has decreased in recent years. Perhaps the main reason is the increased use of polyester and other easy care materials in the makeup of today's garments. Fewer garments are made from wool or other natural fibers that redye rather easily.

Economics is a key factor in the dyeing business. In 1961, the recession played a big role in bringing more business to the redyeing trade. The redyeing business picks up when the nation's consumers are determined to save money. In most families, clothing and household furnishings are the first things economical consumers keep off the shopping list during difficult or hard times.

The psychology in regard to redyeing has changed considerably. Where once some families might be ashamed of redyeing because of

Table 9-3 Recommendations for the Best Redyeing Service

1. A garment or household item should be dry cleaned before it is sent to be dyed. The cleaner or dyer should dry clean and finish the item before it is returned to the consumer.
2. Measure knit garments before sending them to be dyed. Give the measurements to the cleaner or dyer so that the garment may be reblocked to shape after dyeing.
3. Be aware of conditions such as sun fading, holes or tears, thin, worn areas, and bad stains. Remember, redyeing does not cover up such damage. Stains should be removed before sending an article to the dyer.
4. Be selective in choosing colors for dyeing. A darker color should be selected to cover a lighter color or faded item. When selecting a pastel shade, the original color must be white or near white.
5. Remember: dyeing does not make a new garment out of an old one. It does extend its useful life beyond what is normally expected.
6. Some fabrics will shrink in dyeing unless they were originally preshrunk. However, many fabrics can be reshaped back to the original measurements. Check with a dyer if they give a guarantee for satisfactory redyeing.

social implications, the modern consumer has no such inhibitions about using a dollar-saving device for prolonging the useful life of clothes and furnishings.

REWEAVING

Reweaving is not often done in the dry-cleaning plant itself. When this service is offered the actual work is usually done by an outside reweaver. A good reweaver can repair relatively small damaged areas (such as cigarette burns) so that the damage is virtually invisible. Reweaving is a highly skilled service and it is usually very expensive. It is a good practice to get an estimate of the cost in order to determine if you feel the cost is justified in relation to the age or usefulness of the article to be rewoven.

TAILORING

Tailoring involves alterations of garments as well as actual making of garments. In most dry-cleaning plants tailoring is limited to garment alterations. Some large plants do have large alteration departments. In addition to servicing the consumer, they service retail stores who do not have an alteration or tailoring department.

Tailoring or major repairs is a convenient service for consumers. Many consumers want and need this kind of service. The availability of a paid repair service provides consumers with a more complete textile maintenance service.

HOUSEHOLD TEXTILES

Interior decorator fabrics, carpets, rugs, curtains, draperies, tapestries, slip covers, and upholstery fabrics require special care regularly. Usually these items have been carefully selected for color and style to complement a particular motif and, hopefully, they will maintain their original beauty for years to come.

Professional Service for Household Items

The size of the plant and the volume in household items processed usually determines the type of equipment to be used.

Draperies represent a large investment. They are subjected to many deteriorating factors during use. This is why a countergirl or routeman is required to inspect them carefully when they accept them for cleaning. Any fabric damage such as fading, yellow streaks, tendering, or questionable finishes should be called to the consumer's attention. This is why release is obtained before any work is undertaken.

Draperies are measured before dry cleaning and after finishing. If any shrinkage takes place in cleaning, steps are taken to stretch the drapery back to size if it is at all possible.

There are different makes and models of finishing equipment to restore a good appearance to draperies. Some are vertical, others horizontal in design. Some are operated manually; others automatically.

SATISFACTION BEGINS WITH SELECTION AND CARE

Today's shopper has available a huge variety of drapery fabrics and patterns from which to make a selection. Most of these are intended to give long, satisfactory service. However, some are created mainly for beauty rather than serviceability. It is wise to inquire about the durability of fabrics when making your selection (see Points of Selection and Care of Curtains and Draperies, Table 9–4).

In addition to the limitations of wearability in the fabrics themselves, there are various invisible causes which are constantly attacking the fabric and shortening its life.

Draperies or curtains may appear to be in perfect condition when sent for dry cleaning. Actually, however, they may be so deteriorated that even the moderate agitation necessary to remove soil causes them to fall into shreds. When this occurs, it is not carelessness or incompetence on the part of the cleaner but the result of one or more

Table 9–4 Points of Selection and Care of Curtains and Draperies

- Remember: household fabrics are excluded from the FTC Permanent Care Labeling Rule at this writing. See page 393
- Buy from a reputable store. Shop for quality merchandise.
- Buy material that is properly labeled. Buy dyed fabrics that are resistant to sun fading.
- Pick the right fabric for the job. For sunny locations, use fabrics that are resistant to sunlight deterioration. Do not use sheer fabrics as substitutes for shades or blinds. Synthetics are more resistant than cellulose fiber, silk least resistant.
- Line all draperies for protection against fading and fiber rotting or purchase draperies with coated finishes that give protection from sunlight.
- Window service conditions are severe. Colorfastness qualities should meet minimum requirements for satisfactory resistance to fading, laundering, and dry cleaning.
- Ask for sanforized or preshrunk fabrics.
- Atmospheric conditions cause "up and down" changes in measurements. This is an inherent characteristic of cotton and rayon fabrics. Permanent loss of floor or sill fit can only be prevented by use of completely stabilized fabrics or compensating dimensional allowances in the finished product such as double headings or double hems.
- When making curtains or draperies, use extreme care in sewing to avoid puckering. Select proper thread, use sharp needles, and check thread tension. Experiment for proper spacing of stitches and run at slow, constant speed. Remember: thread under tension shrinks in laundering and steam pressing.
- Good workmanship in the construction of draperies whether readymade or homemade is as important as the quality of the fabric itself.
- If possible, frequently rotate curtains and draperies from sunny windows to an unexposed side of the house to equalize the effect of the sun.
- Curtains and draperies last longer and look better when cleaned or laundered regularly at least once a year; synthetic fibers pick up dry soil (dust) due to static. Yellowing of cotton and rayon is caused by age.
- Follow cleaning and laundering requirements carefully.

use factors. When draperies do fail in use or care, we suggest you study item 67, International Fair Claims Guide For Consumer Textile Products, Appendix F(1) and the Balanced Drapery Depreciation Guide, Appendix F(2).

Nonimmersion Process

A relatively new process for cleaning draperies is called the nonimmersion process. First the draperies are put through a "dusting" cycle that incorporates air flow and a gentle tumbling action. This removes accumulated dust from the draperies. Then formulated, active, powdered granules are introduced into the cleaning cycle. The

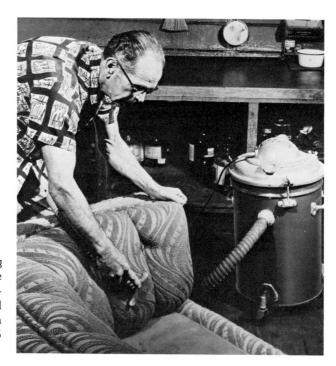

Figure 9-4 Furniture cleaning may be done either in the home or in a professional furniture cleaning plant. Special equipment and techniques are required to do a satisfactory job. (Courtesy: AIDS International)

granules absorb the soil, dirt and grease from the fabric. The third cycle of the process carries off the dirt-filled granules into a dust-collecting unit. The cleaning unit also permits the addition of bleaching agents, static eliminators, soil retardants, and agents that will remove smoke and other odors.

UPHOLSTERY CLEANING

Upholstery cleaning should be left to the professional cleaner. The consumer has a choice of sending out furniture to a business that specializes in upholstery cleaning or have the specialist come into the home.

The specialist must adapt his methods and techniques to the item to be cleaned, because of the variety of fabrics used and the variety of materials that are used for stuffings and paddings. The specialist must have equipment to (1) remove surface soil, (2) apply a cleaning solution to the fabric, (3) remove it quickly, and (4) dry it thoroughly (see Figure 9–4). When an upholstery fabric fails to give good performance in wear and cleaning, we suggest you study the Balanced Upholstery Depreciation Guide, Appendix F(3).

Care information of upholstery fabrics is omitted from the FTC's Permanent Care Labeling Rule, placing the responsibility on the consumer. For example, manufacturers of furniture make foam pillows and then slipcover them with upholstery fabrics using the zipper method of construction to obtain a better fit of the fabric to the foam. Some manufacturers never intended to have the consumer remove the covers for dry-cleaning. However, there are no permanently attached care instructions so that neither the consumer nor the cleaner is informed of proper care procedures. It is advisable to obtain in writing at the time of purchase the correct method of cleaning upholstered furniture. The expanded rule on Permanent Care Labeling includes upholstery fabrics, see page 393. This should eliminate consumer problems as described above.

Carpets and Rugs

Soils carried in by foot and deposited on carpets or rugs are particularly damaging to them. The abrasive materials wear down fibers dulling traffic areas.

Carpets and rugs should be vacuumed as frequently as possible. Daily vacuuming is helpful. Thorough vacuuming once a week is essential to rid the carpet of surface litter and gritty soils.

PLANT CLEANING

Loose rugs, such as Orientals or area rugs, can be cleaned better in professional plants that have specially designed equipment to remove embedded and greasy soils. Many plants have automatic equipment by which the rugs can be gently shampooed or jet cleaned, and scientifically dried under controlled conditions. Regular professional cleanings will keep rugs looking bright and their "wear-life" prolonged (see Figure 9–5).

ON-LOCATION CLEANING

This is also called "Wall-to-Wall Carpet Cleaning." Usually, it is not practical to remove wall-to-wall carpeting from the premises and send it to a professional plant for cleaning. Several systems have been devised to clean carpeting on location; each one has its own merits.

The professional cleaner determines what methods and procedures to use. His decisions are based on construction of the carpeting, depth and types of soils, and the length of time the carpet can be out of service.

Wet shampooing by a rotary scrubber, of which there are many types, is the most universal on-location method. Detergent solutions are put on the carpet by rotating brushes that massage the face fibers by controlled foamy solutions. A wet pick-up vacuum is used to remove excess moisture. The carpet is then dried overnight. Vacuuming is effective to raise the pile again.

Figure 9-5 Specialized equipment is used for cleaning rugs. Here an operator is feeding the rug into the machine where water and detergent and moving brushes clean it as it moves through the machine. (Courtesy: AIDS International)

Foam absorption is a process where foam is applied manually or by machine. The foam is used under controlled conditions by the technician who works the material into the carpet pile and removes it with sponges or by vacumming.

Dry cleaning is done by using special dry-cleaning compounds, usually solvents mixed with dry compounds, on the carpet, working them into the pile with specially designed machines and brushes. After a length of time, vacuuming removes the powder and soil from the carpeting.

There is another method of cleaning rugs, known as sonic cleaning. It utilizes a system of low sonic waves by which detergent solutions are injected into the carpet through vibrating, large flat plates. A separate vacuum removes the excess dirt-accumulated detergent solution.

There are "Do-It-Yourself" rental rug cleaning machines available in some drug stores and super markets that sell cleaning aids. It is important that the machines and products are used according to manufacturer's directions. The time, energy, and monetary expenditure in relation to the results obtained should be considered in order to determine if the "Do-It-Yourself" method is satisfactory. When the carpet fails to give satisfaction in use or care, we suggest you study the Balanced Carpet Depreciation Guide, Appendix F(4).

362   *Performance of Textiles*

ODOR AND SMOKE DAMAGE

The remedy of fire and smoke damage requires skills beyond ordinary cleaning and contracting. It pays to have a professional specialist.

There is more to odor than the smell. The location and types of material can present a problem. Odors can arise from smoke, ammonia fumes, stench bombs, tear gas, fuel oil spillage, burner puffbacks, skunks and other animals, decomposition and mustiness, floods and backed-up sewage, and other sources. Odors can cause problems with cotton, wool, silk, synthetic fabrics, and other materials such as furs, paper, building materials, rugs, upholstered furniture, feathers, jewelry, works of art, and many other kinds of tangible property located in such places as homes, storage vaults, banks, stores, factories, restaurants, offices, hospitals, schools, trucks, railroad cars, autos, ships, libraries, warehouses, food plants, and hotels.

The National Institute of Fire Restoration (NIFR) is an independent association of contractors and service firms that specialize in the treatment and repair of fire and smoke damage.

Wide-area spray deodorization is an effective quick-relief measure for fire and smoke damage. If properly performed it can permanently eliminate smoke odor in some cases, and enable stores, hotels, and homes to maintain operations after a fire. However, for most fire damage it provides only temporary relief unless followed by cleaning and other restoration processes.

In deodorization, as in other aspects of fire restoration, there are many variables for a simple formula to be applied with guaranteed success. Effective deodorization of smoke is always a combination of the right materials, the right method and the judgment that comes with experience. One of the most recent methods of deodorizing is the use of ozone (see Figure 9–6).

STORAGE

Storage service means storage of garments in adequate storage vaults. During the last few years, an increasing number of storage firms have installed burglar-proof and fireproof storage vaults constructed so that furs, coats, rugs, furniture, and other articles can be stored in them for protection.

Box Storage

A service offered by some professional cleaners is called "Box Storage." The cleaner provides a wardrobe storage hamper or a box or a low-cost storage bag. The packed container is then taken to the cleaner who cleans the garments, hangs them on hangers, and stores them in a storage vault with controlled humidity and temperature where they are safe and insect free. At the end of the season, the garments are returned to the consumer.

363   *Fabric Care—Speciality Cleaning*

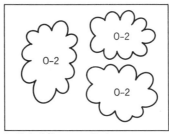

1. Air is 1/5 oxygen. Each oxygen molecule has two atoms (O–2).

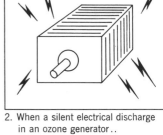

2. When a silent electrical discharge in an ozone generator..

3. ...strikes an oxygen molecule and splits it into two free atoms...

4. ...each free atom (O) then joins an unsplit oxygen molecule (O–2)...

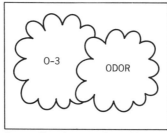

5. ...making the supercharged but short lived ozone molecule (O–3).

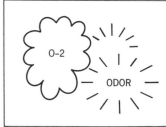

6. This intense oxidizing agent attacks bacteria that cause odor, mold, and the like, then returns to oxygen (O–2).

Figure 9-6 How ozone destroys odors.

Home Storage

Garments should be professionally cleaned and all spots removed before storing them at home. Remove belts from their loops and hang them from a coat hanger so the backing will not crack. Close all fastenings so garments will not hang out of shape. Then hang the clothes carefully or fold them into boxes.

Sweaters and knitted garments should be stored flat. Stuff them with tissue paper so fold marks will not be obvious. Pile can be distorted when pile garments are folded into boxes.

It has been noted in some instances that insect damage occurs on fabrics which contained no natural fibers. Wool and wool blends are usually involved, but insect damage has been noticed on fabrics that contained no wool or other natural fibers. Microscopic examination of the holes revealed the ''chew marks'' typical of insect damage. Unless the insect itself is available for examination, you cannot be sure just what type of insect—moths, carpet beetles, or other insect—caused the damage.

Insect damage may occur on synthetic fabrics if they are dirty, spotted, or stained. Holes may be caused by crickets, silverfish, or similar insects as well as moths or carpet beetles. Crickets and silverfish are known to damage cellulose, for example, particularly when starch, glue, or other attractive things are present. Carpet beetle and moth larvae have been known to chew through a nonwoolen material to get at wool underneath. Experiments show that the presence of synthetic fabrics in a garment is not in itself assurance that the garments will not be attacked by insects.

In home storage, sprinkle a reliable moth preventive into the clothes containers or closets or have the dry cleaner mothproof garments after cleaning. The most commonly used products for the protection of stored fabrics consist of naphthalene or paradichlorobenzene in balls, flakes, or powder, which are harmless to fabrics if used as directed.

There have been instances where garments have changed in color while hanging in a closet when the closet contained paradichlorobenzene for the prevention of insect damage. Is the color change caused by paradichlorobenzene? It has been found that certain dyes may be affected by moth preventive products.

Once garments are cleaned and mothproofed, they must be sealed from air and mositure to be completely safe. Storage areas should be kept cool and dry and should be out of the sunlight to discourage the hatching of insects.

Cedar chests and cedar-lined closets are satisfactory when moth eggs are already out of garments. While the cedar will not kill moths or silverfish, insects avoid garments surrounded by cedar. Allow spaces in storage compartments. Careless storage can be a hazard. NEVER PUT CLOTHING AWAY DIRTY. Dirt and food stains are an insect's invitation to destroy clothing.

SPECIAL ITEMS

Dry cleaners are often asked to clean special items, such as stuffed toys, lampshades, pillows, down-filled pillows, and sleeping bags.

Down-Filled Garments

Quilted down-filled garments can be dry cleaned in either petroleum, synthetic, or fluorocarbon solvent. The main problem in processing them is the formation of swales and streaks that occur when detergent or other nonvolatile material is left in the fabric. Check to see that the item is free of solvent odor.

Feathers

Feathers are very difficult to clean and finish. Excessive twisting may occur as the result of wear. Moisture from perspiration, rain or damp air can cause twisting in some of the feather trim, particularly marabou and ostrich. They curl and twist badly. Coq feathers should not be steamed. In some cases, the feathers must be removed for cleaning and then replaced after cleaning. Feathers that are glued to the fabric cannot be cleaned because the glue is solvent soluble. Feathers may discolor from adhesive.

Lampshades

Lampshades are difficult to clean because of the use of glue instead of sewing in making the shade, fabrics that get water or sizing rings very easily, and metal forms that rust.

Neckties

Neckties have become an expensive item in a man's wardrobe. Their appearance and wear life may be extended by periodic cleaning. Specialists in tie cleaning have forms to shape ties in the finishing process. There are also adjustable forms that can be either compressed or expended to fit into the tie.

Pillow Cleaning

Pillows can develop a bad odor from the accumulation of perspiration from the head. The stuffing becomes matted. Pillow cleaning by a professional involves removal of the stuffing from the ticking, cleaning the stuffing, replacing it in a brand-new ticking. Special equipment is needed to offer this service.

Sleeping Bags

Most sleeping bags can be dry cleaned satisfactorily if the proper precautions are used. The exception is a sleeping bag with a waterproof coating of plastic or rubber, which can usually be wet cleaned.

During dry cleaning or wet cleaning, some sleeping bags will lose their water repellency, making it necessary to re-treat them. Sleeping bags must be thoroughly deodorized before their use.

Stuffed Toys and Animals

Most stuffed toys can be cleaned with water and enough detergent to give a good suds. Stuffed toys and animals contain a number of different types of filling materials including sponge rubber.

The filling materials other than sponge rubber are the most troublesome. They often contain a water-soluble coloring, which will transfer to the outer fabric if it becomes wet. This discoloration is often difficult or impossible to remove, a factor that limits the amount of soil removal possible.

10
Labeling—Voluntary and Mandatory

Textile merchandise is labeled to (1) identify the product, (2) aid the businessman in selling his product, (3) aid the consumer in making an intelligent selection, and (4) aid the consumer, the professional dry clearner, and the laundryman in properly caring for the item.

The responsibility for effective labeling lies with fiber and fabric manufacturers, converters, and suppliers for providing specific and clear instructions for the use and care of their fibers and fabrics, the garment manufacturers for obtaining good labels and attaching them to the article produced, retailers for retaining the labels on the article so the consumer can read and use the information, and consumers. Consumers are responsible for reading labels and hangtags carefully, asking for and using informative labels and hangtags, patronizing retailers and mail-order firms that label their merchandise well, telling the salesperson, buyer, and store manager how helpful their labels are, and asking for more and better informative labels. The most popular way of informing the consumer is through the use of labels and hangtags.

Manufacturers may label fabrics and clothing by a printed label pasted onto the item, a hangtag attached to the item, a woven or printed label permanently attached, printed identification on the bolt or roller, spool, or wrapper, or woven or printed identification on the selvage.

Wearing apparel is usually labeled by (1) attaching a cardboard hangtag to the item by a string (the hangtag may give the consumer factual and promotional information and may be easily removed from the item) or (2) attaching a ribbon or cloth label in a seam or on a facing of the garment by machine stitching or heat fusion. Some labels are stamped on the item giving information such as size on the neckline and the brand size.

VOLUNTARY LABELING

Informative

An informative label supplies pertinent information to help the consumer make a wise choice and care for the item. It may state fiber content, fabric construction, special finishes that give specific appearance and serviceability, and performance properties. It may also give special instructions or precautions on care. The factual information may be based on laboratory tests and may include the size of the item as well as the manufacturer's name.

Informative labeling may also include information required by federal legislation, such as the Textile Fiber Products Identification

Act, or a statement that the article has met standards similar to those of Standard L-22, Performance Requirements for Textile Fabrics, issued by the American National Standards Institute.*

Brand A brand label is a distinctive mark, design, or symbol used to identify the goods of a particular seller or manufacturer. Trademark names fall in this type of labeling.

Certification The label indicates that the item has been tested by a laboratory, usually one independent of the manufacturer of the product. Each laboratory may establish its own fixed standards of quality. These certification labels are often referred to as "seals of approval" labels. Examples are The Good Housekeeping Seal of Approval, Parent's Magazine, and the International Fabricare Institute's Seal for Washability and Drycleanability. Usually no information is given on the label except that the article has been approved or guaranteed by a particular laboratory or agency.

Union In addition to an informative, brand, or certification label, there may also be a union label. This assures the consumer that the garment was made under fair working conditions. Unions operating in the clothing area are the Amalgamated Clothing Workers of America, International Ladies Garment Workers Union, and United Garment Workers of America.

Registered Number System (RN) A sewn-in label, RN 6821, or any other number found in a garment, means that the manufacturer obtained a registration number from the Bureau of Consumer Protection of the Federal Trade Commission. This number, rather than the manufacturer's name, is used to identify the source of the item.

The RN system poses interesting problems in administration and merchandising. The Bureau of Consumer Protection is burdened by the administration detail. It has received numerous inquiries from consumers trying to find out the identity of manufacturers so they can register their consumer complaints. However, some manufacturers and associates representing manufacturers have asked the

---

* Formerly the American Standards Association and the USA Standards Institute (see Chapter 1). L-22 has been transferred to Committee D13 of the American Society for Testing and Materials.

Federal Trade Commission to retain the registered number identification system for labeling clothing. They claim that no damage to consumers has been demonstrated under the system.

The manufacturers' concern is that if the Commission abolished the numbering system, it will require that the name of the manufacturer be on the label. The manufacturers claim that this would be a competitive hardship on retailers because it would destroy private label retailing. Also, competing retailers could readily determine the source of competitors' merchandise.

Retailers, in order to offer distinctive merchandise, carefully seek out manufacturers that will contribute to their stores' image. They wish to keep the identity of the manufacturer a secret to prevent their competitors from pirating "the creative genius of a competitor" rather than investing their own man-hours in the arduous task of finding just the right merchandise supplier.

MANDATORY LABELING

Various federal laws relating to textiles and furs include provisions for mandatory labeling of these items, with consequent requirements for supervision and enforcement. These functions have been assigned to various agencies, although most of the Acts are now assigned to the Federal Trade Commission.

Federal Trade Commission Regulatory Functions

Until 1973, the Bureau of Textiles and Furs of the Federal Trade Commission and the Office of Flammability of the Department of Commerce, were responsible for the administration of and compliance with the Wool Products Labeling Act, the Fur Products Labeling Act, the Flammable Fabrics Act, the Textile Fiber Products Identification Act, and the Trade Regulation Rule on Care Labeling of Textile Wearing Apparel.

In 1970, the Federal Trade Commission (FTC) created two new bureaus: the Bureau of Competition and the Bureau of Consumer Protection. The Bureau of Textiles and Furs was moved to the Bureau of Consumer Protection. The guidance and rules function of the Bureau of Industry Guidance was moved to the Bureau of Competition and Consumer Protection. (The Bureaus of Restraint of Trade and of Deceptive Practices were abolished.) The Care Labeling Rule is also administered under the Bureau of Consumer Protection.

In 1973, the Federal Commission for Product Safety (an independent agency) was established, and the responsibility for the Flammable Fabrics Act was moved to that agency.

Trade Practice Rules and Regulations

The Federal Trade Commission has, from time to time, set up certain trade practice rules with regard to textile fibers. Many of these rules were eliminated after the Textile Fibers Identification Act became effective, since the new Act covers the provisions of the trade practice rules, with the exception of the provision relating to silk weighting.

The Federal Trade Commission still requires that disclosure of any metallic weighting, loading, or adulterating materials in silk other than the dyeing and finishing materials necessary to produce the desired color or finish.

The Federal Trade Commission has also regulated the use of terms to describe shrinkage of cotton fabrics only. It specifies that fabrics must be labeled in such a way that consumers will not be led to believe that goods have been preshrunk to a greater degree than is actually true. For example, if a label states that shrinkage is less than 2.0 percent and a fabric shrinks to a greater degree, the fabric is mislabeled.

General notice of any proposed rule making is published in the *Federal Register.* If an oral hearing is held in connection with the proposed rule making, interested persons may appear and express their views and may suggest amendents, revisions, and additions. Written statements may also be accepted.

After consideration of all relevant matters of fact, law, policy, and discretion, including all relevant matters presented by interested persons in the proceeding, the Commission then adopts and publishes in the Federal Register a rule or order to become effective not less than 30 days after the date of publication.

The Federal Trade Commission issues administrative interpretations of the textile and fur laws for the guidance of industry in order that they may comply with the legal requirements. The industry guides provide the basis for voluntary and simultaneous abandonment of unlawful practices by industry.

The industry guides may be promulgated by the Commission either on its own initiative or by any interested person or group, when the industry guide would be in the public interest and would bring about more widespread and equitable observance of laws administered by the Commission.

As with the trade regulation rules, the Commission may conduct investigations, make studies, and hold conferences or hearings.

In cases arising under the textile and fur laws and rules where it appears to the Commission to be in the public interest to do so, the Commission will apply to the courts for injunctive relief against the unlawful sale of products under question.

WOOL PRODUCTS LABELING ACT

The Wool Products Labeling Act of 1939 became law in October 1940 and now operates under amendments of 1965. This federal law requires that all articles containing wool shall be so labeled. If the wool fiber is mixed with other fibers, the percentage of wool must be stated on the label. The kind of wool (reused, reprocessed) must also be stated if the wool is not new or "virgin," but there is no provision in the law requiring a statement as to the quality of the wool fiber used.

The Federal Trade Commission has issued 35 rules and regulations for industry guidance under the Wool Products Labeling Act.*

Definitions

The following definitions are included in the Wool Products Labeling Act:

Wool means the fiber from the fleece of the sheep or lamb or hair of the Angora or cashmere goat (and may include the so-called specialty fibers from the hair of the camel, alpaca, llama, and vicuna) that has never been reclaimed from any woven or felted wool product.

Reprocessed wool means the resulting fiber when wool has been woven or felted into a wool product that has subsequently been made into a fibrous state without ever having been utilized in any way by the ultimate consumer.

Reused wool means the resulting fiber when wool or reprocessed wool has been spun, woven, knitted, or felted into a wool product that has subsequently been made into a fibrous state after having been used in some way by the ultimate consumer.

Wool product means any product, or any portion of a product, which contains, purports to contain, or in any way is represented as containing wool, reprocessed wool, or reused wool.

The law does not require that specialty fibers (Angora, cashmere, camel, and the like) be indicated by name on labels, since they may be labeled as wool, but where they are named, the percentage must be given. If the specialty fibers have been reprocessed or reused, this information must be stated on the label.

In July 1973, the Senate passed a bill (S. 1816) to amend the Wool Products Labeling Act of 1936. It suggests substituting the term "recycled wool" for the terms "reprocessed wool" and "reused wool" where these terms appear in the Act. The term "recycled" is recommended for both terms since the fiber used in the production of "reprocessed wool" or "reused wool" goes through similar me-

---

* Rules and regulations under the Wool Products Labeling Act of 1939 (as amended November 20, 1965.) L-4453 Rev. FTC, Washington, D.C.

chanical processes in order to be used in the remanufacture of wool products. At this writing, the FTC Staff members have recommended that the Act not be amended. The bill is still pending in Congress.

FUR PRODUCTS LABELING ACT

The Fur Products Labeling Act (effective 1952) requires that purchasers be informed on labels, invoices, and in advertising of the true English name of the animal from which the fur came, its country of origin, and whether the fur product is composed of used, damaged, or scrap fur, or fur that has been dyed or bleached. The Act further requires that the terminology in the Fur Products Name Guide, amended in 1967 and issued by the Federal Trade Commission, be used in setting forth the animal name. A 1969 amendment to the Act added further provisions in the regulation of furs that are pointed, dyed, bleached, or otherwise artificially colored. The FTC rules prohibit the use of fictitious prices in labeling and advertising.

Definitions

The following definitions are included in the Fur Products Labeling Act:

Fur means any animal skin or part thereof with hair, fleece, or fur fibers attached thereto, either in its raw or processed state, but shall not include such skins as are to be converted into leather or which in processing shall have the hair, fleece, or fur fiber completely removed.

Used fur means fur in any form that has been worn or used by an ultimate consumer.

Fur product means any article of wearing apparel made in whole or in part of fur or used fur; except that such term shall not include such articles as the Commission shall exempt by reason of the relatively small quantity or value of the fur or used fur contained therein.

Waste fur means the ears, throats, or scrap pieces which have been severed from the animal pelt, and shall include mats and plates made therefrom.

FLAMMABLE FABRICS ACT

Each year there are 3000 to 5000 deaths and 150,000 to 250,000 injuries from burns associated with flammable fabrics.* The people who do survive undergo physical suffering and long and costly medical treatment. Some are disfigured for life; others suffer emotionally.

* Fourth Annual Report to the President and the Congress on the Studies of Deaths, Injuries and Economic Losses Resulting from Accidental Burning of Products, Fabrics, or Related Materials, Fiscal Year 1972, Bureau of Product Safety, Food and Drug Administration, Department of Health, Education and Welfare.

Flammability in textiles, plastics, foams, and coatings, which contributes to these injuries and deaths, has led to a growing public concern and regulation by government and industry. A Flammable Fabrics Act was passed in 1953 and amended in 1954 and 1967. The Federal Consumer Product Safety Commission, created in 1972, administers the Act. The Commission collects all burn data, develops standards and test methods, and enforces compliance with the Act.

Before 1972, the Act provided for the Secretary of Commerce to create an Office of Flammable Fabrics and to appoint an advisory committee of leaders in industry, business, and consumer affairs. The Office of Flammable Fabrics, located in the National Bureau of Standards, was responsible for research and development of test methods. Other agencies involved early with implementing the Flammable Fabrics Act were the Federal Trade Commission and the Department of Health, Education and Welfare.

The basic responsibility for establishing the need for standards and flammability tests for end products is the responsibility of the Federal Consumer Product Safety Commission.

To develop a standard, the agency must:

1. Issue a notice that there may be a need for a new standard. All interested parties then have a chance to present their views.

2. Issue a second notice establishing a proposed standard for flammability levels for the end product(s) under consideration. Interested parties may respond.

3. Publish a final notice setting forth the details of the standard and test method that becomes effective one year later or a suitable time following publication. After a one-year period, it becomes unlawful to produce and sell products which do not meet the established standards (see discussion on flammability, Chapter 5, Part IV).

There is still a need to develop flammability test methods that have a better correlation with actual occurrences of flaming, burning, charring and melting.

Fabric Hazards

The Public Health Service, Department of Health, Education and Welfare reports that in the case of 300 instances of clothing-burn accidents, it was found that 70 percent of all burn cases involving males resulted from ignition of shirts (45 percent) and trousers (26 percent). More than 80 percent of the cases involving females resulted from ignition of their nightwear (41 percent), sweaters (17 percent), blouses (15 percent), and bathrobes (11 percent).

In cases involving children under 10 years of age, the most

common types of clothing that burned were nightclothes (40 percent) and shirts or blouses (35 percent).

Types of fiber in the clothing that ignited, with burns resulting, were cotton, 87 percent; nylon, 7 percent; "synthetic" not otherwise classified, 3 percent; wool, 2 percent; and cotton-polyester blends, 2 percent.

Flame-Retardant Fabrics

Flame retardation has high priority in the textile industry as more and more items of wearing apparel and household furnishings are included in flammability regulations. Some manufacturers are modifying their fibers and putting flame-resistant chemicals into the solution before it is made into a fiber. Others are blending fibers to achieve a fire-resistant fabric. Still others are developing new finishes to apply to the surface of the fabric and still retain the aesthetic, comfort, and care characteristics consumers want.

Proposed legislation will require fabric manufacturers and importers to certify that their products meet U.S. flammability standards. The bill, as written, requires both manufacturers and importers to conduct tests on their products to ensure that they meet these standards.

In addition to the federal laws, other jurisdictions often have laws relating to flammability. These laws may differ from one city, county, and state to another. Some of the tests are contradictory. State laws change so you should check for the most recent information.

The burden of testing is on the manufacturer. Testing is costly, and uniformity is still lacking. Many groups are working on flammability standards. As each group decides to set a particular standard, it may develop a new test method with different requirements from existing methods. Sometimes the same type of product undergoes two different types of testing to meet two different standards of flammability. For example, 19 different domestic tests have been established by different groups for flammability.

Labeling for Flammability

Although the Flammable Fabrics Act does not establish guidelines for permanent care labeling, the Act implies that manufacturers must put a clear and conspicuous label on their apparel, warning consumers if the flame-retardant properties will be lessened or destroyed by home or commercial laundry. The flammability standard for children's sleepwear does require permanent care labeling as well as the flame-resistant labeling.

It is the responsibility of the manufacturers to test their products in order to ascertain how many washings the flame-retardant finish will actually take. The retailer is also obliged to test and warrant the products he sells, or he can be forced to remove goods from sale and from store catalogs.

In 1975,* The Consumer Product Safety Commission approved six labeling and recordkeeping changes to the children's sleepwear regulations. The amendments and policy statements for the most part were formal reaffirmations to exemptions granted earlier. Two of the policy statements implement the Commission's former decision on a petition submitted by the American Apparel Manufacturers Association.

According to the policy statements:

1. Regulations for the size 7 to 14 standard do not prohibit use of fabric manufactured before May 1, 1975, effective date of the standard. Also, when such fabric is used in manufacture of garments, the inability of the manufacturer to record the fabric production unit is not a violation of the regulation.

2. Regulations under the 0 to 6X and the 7 to 14 standard do not require the garment production unit (GPU) identification to be on a separate label. The policy states, however, that when the GPU is on a label containing other information, the other information must not interfere with the GPU identification.

3. Complying garments manufactured before the May 1, 1975 effective date that do not meet certain provisions of the standard can be displayed with fully complying garments.

Amendments to the standards were as follows:

1. The minimum letter size of the "GPU lettering must be 'legible and clear, although the lettering must be no smaller than other lettering appearing in the same label.'"

2. The garment manufacturer also would be allowed to maintain sales records by either GPU number or style number. If the records are maintained by style number, and there is a recall of one or more production units, the manufacturer must notify all purchasers of the style. The purchasers may elect to return either all items of the style or all the items of the production unit(s).

3. Noncomplying garments can be advertised with complying garments, but it must be clearly stated that they do not meet the Flammable Fabrics Standard. This provision expires May 1, 1978.

In November 1975, the Consumers Product Safety Commission announced that it had taken action to amend the enforcement regulations on children's sleepwear sizes 0 through 6X and size 7 through

* *Federal Register,* 40-12811.

14 to modify the requirements for the size of lettering to indicate the garment production unit identification and the requirements of sales records of items in interstate commerce. The Commission granted the petition of the American Apparel Manufacturers Association with the proviso (1) that the lettering for garment production unit be as large as that used for any other information appearing on the label and (2) that sales records that identify the items be sold by style as an alternative by garment production unit.

TEXTILE FIBER PRODUCTS IDENTIFICATION ACT

The Textile Fiber Products Identification Act became law and went into effect on March 3, 1960.

The purpose of the law is "to protect producers and consumers against misbranding and false advertising of the fiber content of textile fiber products. . . " This law was in addition to the already existing Wool Products Labeling Act.

How Are Items Identified?

To comply with the Textile Fiber Products Identification Act, manufacturers are required to stamp, tag, label, or use some other means of identification giving the following information:

1. The fiber or combination of fibers used in the item. Fibers must be designated with equal prominence whether natural or manufactured fibers. Fibers must be identified by their generic name (see definition below) in order of predominance by weight if the weight is 5 percent or more of the total fiber weight.

2. The percent of each fiber present, by weight, in the total fiber content must be given. This is exclusive of ornamentation not exceeding 5 percent by weight of the total fiber content. If the ornamentation is 5 percent or less, it may be designated as "other fiber" or "other fibers."

3. Manufacturers must state on upholstered products, such as mattresses, cushions, and the like, if the stuffing has been used as stuffing in another upholstered product, mattress, or cushion.

4. The tag, label, or stamp must carry the name or other identification of the manufacturer of the product or one or more persons subject to the Act.

5. If the item is imported, the name of the country where the product was made or processed must appear on the label.

Additional information that the manufacturer may wish to place on the tag or label is permissible as long as it does not violate the Act.

What Items Are Covered By the Act?

The Federal Trade Commission has ruled that the Act applies to the following textile products: wearing apparel; accessories such as scarfs, handkerchiefs, umbrellas, and parasols; household linens, including tablecloths, napkins, doilies, dresser and furniture scarfs, towels, washcloths, dishcloths, and ironing board covers; home furnishings, including curtains, draperies, slipcovers, and coverlets for furniture, afghans, and throws, floor coverings, stuffings in upholstered products, mattresses, and cushions; miscellaneous items including sleeping bags, hammocks and flags; and narrow fabrics except packaged ribbons.

What Items Are Excluded from the Act?

Articles excluded or exempted from the provisions of the Act include linings or interlinings incorporated primarily for structural purposes and not for warmth (except that exemption does not apply if any representation of fiber content is made in advertisements or labels); stiffenings, trimmings, facings, and interfacings; filling or padding incorporated primarily for structural purposes and not for warmth (except the exemption does not apply if any representation of fiber content is made in advertising or labels); upholstery stuffing; and outer coverings of furniture and mattresses.

Other items that are exempt include backings of and paddings or cushions to be used under floor coverings; bandages, surgical dressings, and other textile products the labeling of which is subject to the requirements of the Federal Food, Drug and Cosmetic Act of 1938; waste materials not intended for use in a textile fiber product; textile fiber products incorporated in shoes, overshoes, or similar outer footwear; and textile fiber products incorporated into headwear, handbags, luggage, brushes, lampshades, toys, adhesive tapes and adhesive sheets, and cleaning cloths impregnated with chemicals or diapers.

The list of exemptions also includes belts, suspenders, armbands, permanently knotted ties, garters, diaper liners, labels, looper clips for handicraft purposes, book cloth, artist canvases, tapestry cloth, and shoe laces; coated fabrics and portions of textile fiber products made from them; textile fiber products manufactured by operators of company stores and offered for sale and sold exclusively to own employees as ultimate consumers; secondhand household textile articles that are discernibly secondhand or are marked to indicate their secondhand character; and nonwoven products of a disposable nature intended for one-time use only.

The Federal Trade Commission may exclude other textile fiber products that have an insignificant textile fiber content where such disclosure of textile fiber content is not necessary for the protection of the consumer.

Remnants and products made from remnants of fabrics that are of unknown fiber content may be so labeled. The same is true for textile fiber products made from miscellaneous scraps, rags, and waste material.

Generic Names and Trade Names

A generic name is a "family" name. It designates one or more fibers in a group that basically has the same chemical composition. In the Rules and Regulations under the Textile Fiber Products Identification Act, the Federal Trade Commission defines 21 generic names—from acrylic to vinyon.*

Other generic names may be added to the list as new fibers appear.

Many manufacturers also call their fiber by a given term or registered name. These registered names cannot be used by any other manufacturer. However, if a manufacturer uses his trademark on a stamp, label, or tag, he must use it in conjunction with the specific generic name. Obviously, there are many more trademarks than generic names—more than 700 textile trademarks are registered. In addition to the trademarks registered for fibers, names are registered to identify different methods of textile processing of yarns and finishes.

Labeling Under the Act

The Textile Fiber Products Identification Act covers other rules and regulations. For example, the term "fur fiber" is defined and its use limited. Terms such as "virgin" and "new" are limited in their use.

In statement of percentage composition, the Federal Trade Commission established a tolerance of 3 percent on the basis of total fiber weight of the product exclusive of permissible ornamentation. Products varying more than 3 percent are considered misbranded unless the deviation results from unavoidable variation in manufacture and despite the exercise of due care.

SPECIFIC LABELING PROBLEMS

Because the labeling of certain products presents specific problems, the Federal Trade Commission has also established regulations applying to elastic yarn or materials; floor coverings containing backings, fillings, and paddings; trimmings of household textile articles; products containing linings and interlinings; fillings and paddings; textile fiber products containing superimposed or added fillers; pile fabrics and products composed of pile fabrics; and samples and swatches.

* Rules and Regulations Under The Textile Fiber Products Identification Act (as amended November 1, 1974) FTC L-5031, Washington, D.C.

Enforcement of the Act

The Textile Fiber Products Identification Act is enforced by the Federal Trade Commission, which can obtain an injunction to restrain a person from unlawful acts and can prohibit imports when the law is broken. To aid in enforcement, manufacturers must keep records of fiber content, and persons substituting a label must keep records for at least three years. Manufacturers, distributors, and retailers have had problems in complying with the provisions of the Act. Criminal penalties include a fine of not more than $5000, imprisonment for not over one year, or both.

CARE LABELING RULE

The Federal Trade Commission's Trade Regulation Rule on Care Labeling went into effect on July 3, 1972. It requires "a label or tag permanently affixed or attached . . . to the finished article, which clearly discloses instructions for the care and maintenance of such article." Hence, the Rule is often referred to as the Permanent Care Labeling Rule.

The FTC states that labels should use words and phrases, not symbols, to spell out care instructions. Because of continuing and rapid technological development in the apparel industry, it would be extremely difficult to devise a symbol system that would be flexible enough to accommodate future developments in care and maintenance without constantly adding new symbols.

It is important to know which articles should have permanent care labels; which items are exempt.

What Does the Rule Require?

The Commission has tried to produce a regulation that is workable for both the producer and consumer. The rule requires that most articles of wearing apparel bear permanent labels (see exceptions below), permanent care labels be supplied with over-the-counter fabrics to be used for clothing (see exceptions below), all fabrics or apparel manufactured after July 3, 1972 carry these labels, and imported garments and fabrics bear permanent-care labels.

What Does the Rule Exempt?

Manufacturers may petition the Federal Trade Commission for exemption from the rule for apparel whose "utility or appearance would be substantially impaired by a permanently attached label." Exemptions include hosiery, handgear, headgear, footgear, disposable items, items that need no care, completely washable items that cost $3 or less, plus the following, if exempted by petition to FTC—furs and leathers, household textiles considered decorative and ornamental, remnants cut and shipped by the manufacturer as "mill ends," white and solid-colored underpants and undershirts (except those containing wool), children's white slips up to size $16\frac{1}{2}$, socks (except those containing wool), men's work aprons, baby bibs, and handkerchiefs.

Items not included are see-through (sheer) or other items that would be substantially impaired (these may be exempted by petition to the FTC), remnant piece goods under 10 yards in length, not cut from larger bolts, pieces, or rolls at the retail store, and over-the-counter trims and bindings.

Specifications for Labels

Labels must disclose fully, clearly, and thoroughly the regular care of the garment or fabric; inform how to wash, iron, dry, bleach, dry clean and use any other procedures that are considered regular care; carry a warning if an usual care method appears to apply, but does not; stay attached and be readable for the reasonable life of a garment; be easy to locate; be in words, not symbols; and apply to all the findings (thread, buttons, zipper, trim) on the garment.

Articles in sealed packaging require that the permanent care label be visible through the wrap or a duplicate of the instructions must be made discernible on the surface of the package by means of a tag, or by printing directly on the package.

THE RULE SPECIFIES WHAT SHOULD NOT BE ON LABELS

Labels must not use promotional language, such as "never needs ironing." (The label must state at what temperature to iron in case the consumer wants to iron.)

Labels must not omit warning against dry cleaning if the garment cannot be dry cleaned. The FTC takes the position that the consumer assumes that if a garment is washable, it is also dry cleanable.

Labels must not be negative (such as "no bleach"). The label must be positive—tell the consumer what to do. For example,

Machine Wash, Warm
Line Dry
Do Not Use Chlorine Bleach

Interpretation— Clarification of the Rule

The Federal Trade Commission issued, along with the Rule, "A Statement of Basis and Purpose." Several points in it relate to textile care.

The FTC recognizes that there are two kinds of care and maintenance: regular care and maintenance, as required in the general use of the product, and spot care and maintenance, as required for the removal of anything accidentally spilled on the product. The Commission is aware of the difficulties of communicating information on stain-removal procedures to the consumer and has made no requirement for "Spot Care" in the rule.

MULTIPIECE GARMENTS

The Rule does not specify that each piece of a multipiece garment be labeled. For example, in an ensemble of two or more pieces (like the coat and trousers or skirt of a suit) only one label is required.

If only the unlabeled piece of an ensemble is sent to the dry cleaner, he should be informed of the care instructions contained on the label attached to the other piece of the ensemble.

WHITE GARMENTS

White fabrics are considered to be bleachable according to fiber content. If a manufacturer's product is not bleachable, this must be so indicated on the label. Since the FTC considers it a normal care practice not to bleach colored fabrics, the manufacturer is not required to warn against bleaching of colored garments.

Care Practices

The FTC takes the position that certain care practices are assumed to be common knowledge to consumers and, hence, need not be stated on the label: all fabrics are ironable under normal ironing conditions and all washable fabrics may also be dry cleaned, unless the label specifies otherwise. The Rule specifically provides washing instructions for permanent care labeling, but omits reference to dry cleaning.

A 1973 survey conducted by the Department of Clothing and Textiles, Purdue University, showed that 77.7 percent or three out of every four homemakers believe that if a garment can be washed or dry cleaned the label should specify both methods of maintenance. Out of the 962 Midwestern homemakers surveyed, 72.4 percent stated that they would not dry clean garments labeled "wash," while 89.3 percent indicated they would not wash garments labeled "dry clean."

Terms Used on Labels

As already mentioned, the FTC Rule avoids specific requirements for care instructions. A further weakness of the Rule is that it is not directly related to any standards of care and maintenance. To supplement the Rule, several textile industry standards of performance and testing are in common use. One of these, a Voluntary Industry

CONSUMER CARE GUIDE FOR APPAREL

	WHEN LABEL READS:	IT MEANS:
MACHINE WASHABLE	Machine wash	Wash, bleach, dry and press by any customary method including commercial laundering and dry cleaning
	Home launder only	Same as above but do not use commerical laundering
	No Chlorine Bleach	Do not use chlorine bleach. Oxygen bleach may be used
	No bleach	Do not use any type of bleach
	Cold wash / Cold rinse	Use cold water from tap or cold washing machine setting
	Warm wash / Warm rinse	Use warm water or warm washing machine setting
	Hot wash	Use hot water or hot washing machine setting
	No spin	Remove wash load before final machine spin cycle
	Delicate cycle / Gentle cycle	Use appropriate machine setting; otherwise wash by hand
	Durable press cycle / Permanent press cycle	Use appropriate machine setting; otherwise use warm wash, cold rinse and short spin cycle
	Wash separately	Wash alone or with like colors

	WHEN LABEL READS:	IT MEANS:
NON-MACHINE WASHING	Hand wash	Launder only by hand in luke warm (hand comfortable) water. May be bleached. May be drycleaned
	Hand wash only	Same as above, but do not dryclean
	Hand wash separately	Hand wash alone or with like colors
	No bleach	Do not use bleach
	Damp wipe	Surface clean with damp cloth or sponge
HOME DRYING	Tumble dry	Dry in tumble dryer at specified setting — high, medium, low or no heat
	Tumble dry Remove promptly	Same as above, but in absence of cool-down cycle remove at once when tumbling stops
	Drip dry	Hang wet and allow to dry with hand shaping only
	Line dry	Hang damp and allow to dry
	No wring No twist	Hang dry, drip dry or dry flat only. Handle to prevent wrinkles and distortion
	Dry flat	Lay garment on flat surface
	Block to dry	Maintain original size and shape while drying
IRONING OR PRESSING	Cool iron	Set iron at lowest setting
	Warm iron	Set iron at medium setting
	Hot iron	Set iron at hot setting
	Do not iron	Do not iron or press with heat
	Steam iron	Iron or press with steam
	Iron damp	Dampen garment before ironing
MISCELLANEOUS	Dryclean only	Garment should be drycleaned only, including self-service
	Professionally dry clean only	Do not use self-service drycleaning
	No dryclean	Use recommended care instructions. No drycleaning materials to be used.

This care Guide was produced by the Consumer Affairs Committee, American Apparel Manufacturers Association and is based on the Voluntary Guide of the Textile Industry Advisory Committee for Consumer Interests.
The American Apparel Manufacturers Association, Inc.

7/72

Figure 10-1

Guide for Improved and Permanent Care Labeling of Consumer Textile Products, was published in 1967 by the Industry Advisory Committee on Textile Information. It clarifies terms used in permanent care instructions. The Guide includes 56 care listings for washing, 11 for ironing, and 13 for dry cleaning.

Later the Consumer Affairs Committee of the American Apparel Manufacturers Association (AAMA) published an edited version of the Industry Guide (see Figure 10–1). The AAMA, the National Retail Merchants Association, and the American Retail Federation then used this glossary of terms to create 14 basic care labels that are appropriate for most merchandise subject to the rule. All three associations are encouraging apparel manufacturers to use these labels.

Guidelines for Permanent Care Labels

For the wording of the permanent care instructions on labels and on how and where to attach them in garments, manufacturers follow the guidelines published jointly by the American Apparel Manufacturers Association, the American Retail Federation, the National Retail Merchants Association, and the Textile Distributors Association. The guidelines cover the following points:

TYPES OF LABELS

Instructions may be woven into the labels or printed on them. The labels may be mitered in shape or rectangular. They may be loop labels, sewn at both ends so the middle of the label may loop away from the garment. They may be fused flat against the fabric without the use of sewing threads (see Figure 10–2).

Care instructions may be printed directly on the garment provided they remain legible for the life of the garment.

The label material must not ravel during laundering or dry cleaning and must remain readable for the life of the garment.

Care instructions may appear on the reverse side of the permanent label. If this is the case, the label face should state: "Care Instructions on Reverse Side."

The size of the label will depend on specific instructions. For example, those with detailed instructions will be larger. But in every case, the wording must be legible.

LABEL PLACEMENT

There are no mandatory rules for placement of labels. The following guide has been given as a suggestion only (see Figure 10–3).

Figure 10-2 Types of labels.

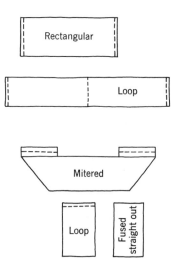

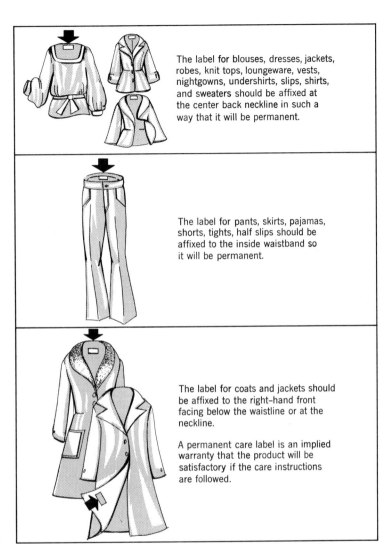

The label for blouses, dresses, jackets, robes, knit tops, loungeware, vests, nightgowns, undershirts, slips, shirts, and sweaters should be affixed at the center back neckline in such a way that it will be permanent.

The label for pants, skirts, pajamas, shorts, tights, half slips should be affixed to the inside waistband so it will be permanent.

The label for coats and jackets should be affixed to the right–hand front facing below the waistline or at the neckline.

A permanent care label is an implied warranty that the product will be satisfactory if the care instructions are followed.

Figure 10-3

Labeling of Piece Goods

In the area of over-the-counter fabrics for the home sewer, tailor, or custom designer, compliance with the FTC Rule on Care Labeling of Textile Wearing Apparel rests on both the textile manufacturer and the retailer.

The Rule states that over-the-counter piece goods must have appropriate care instructions which are printed on coded labels, permanently legible, and given to the consumer at time of purchase. The labels are supposed to match the code number on the end of the

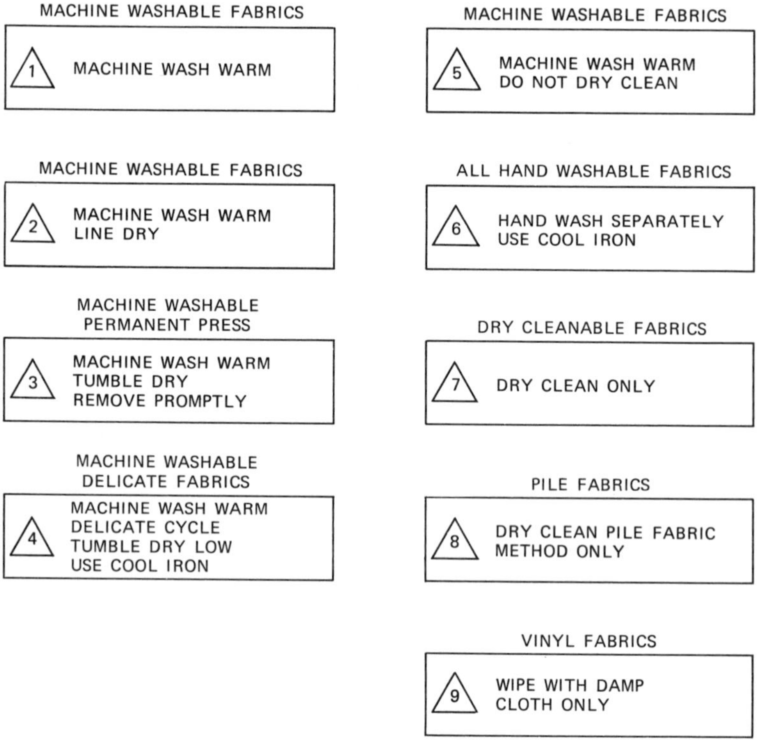

MACHINE WASHABLE FABRICS

1. MACHINE WASH WARM

MACHINE WASHABLE FABRICS

5. MACHINE WASH WARM
DO NOT DRY CLEAN

MACHINE WASHABLE FABRICS

2. MACHINE WASH WARM
LINE DRY

ALL HAND WASHABLE FABRICS

6. HAND WASH SEPARATELY
USE COOL IRON

MACHINE WASHABLE
PERMANENT PRESS

3. MACHINE WASH WARM
TUMBLE DRY
REMOVE PROMPTLY

DRY CLEANABLE FABRICS

7. DRY CLEAN ONLY

MACHINE WASHABLE
DELICATE FABRICS

4. MACHINE WASH WARM
DELICATE CYCLE
TUMBLE DRY LOW
USE COOL IRON

PILE FABRICS

8. DRY CLEAN PILE FABRIC
METHOD ONLY

VINYL FABRICS

9. WIPE WITH DAMP
CLOTH ONLY

Figure 10-4 Triangle system of labeling for over-the-counter fabrics. These coded labels were developed by the Textile Distributors Association for use with over-the-counter fabrics.

bolt. The labels are to be sewn onto the finished garment by the home sewer.

Care instructions are not printed on selvages because not all fabrics are printed. Moreover, selvages are usually trimmed from the fabric during cutting of the garment. Coded labels make for greater flexibility in terms of giving the consumer exact care instructions. This places a responsibility on the retailer to see that the consumer receives the proper coded label.

The Textile Distributors Association has developed a set of nine such labels that any fabric manufacturer may use (see Figure 10–4).

It is very important that home sewers buy thread, lining, zippers, trim, and other accessories that have care instructions compatible with those for the fabric used for a garment. If consumers neglect to do this, they may be disappointed when a garment fails to give good service in laundering or dry cleaning. For example, if a fabric is selected that is dry cleanable, but the lining and trim are not, the consumer will be disappointed in the appearance of the garment when it is dry cleaned. There is no way the manufacturer of component parts can control what the consumer puts together at the fabric counter.

Problems of Terminology for Terms and Definitions

At present, if an item fails to give good performance in care, the burden of proof falls on the consumer even though the Rule states that the person or organization that directed or controlled the manufacture of the finished article is responsible for care labeling of apparel.

The Consumer Care Guide for Apparel of the Consumer Affairs Committee, American Apparel Manufacturers Association, list 29 recommendations on home washing, drying, and pressing and 3 recommendations under the heading of "Miscellaneous" that define the terms "Dry Clean Only," "Professionally Dry Clean Only," and "No Dry Clean." The Triangle Label System (see Figure 10–4), the coded labeling system for over-the-counter wearing apparel fabrics, developed and distributed by the Textile Distributors Association provides 7 recommendations for home care and 2 recommendations for professional care. The Textile Distributors Association recommends code △ for dry cleaning that states "Dry Clean Only" and ⚠ for pile fabrics that states, "Dry Clean Pile Fabric Method Only." This last recommendation is for fur-pile fabrics or deep-pile fabrics that require special handling. Velvets, velveteens, and corduroy are classed as pile fabrics. These certainly do not need to be handled by the recommendations made for deep-pile fur fabrics.

Triangle ⚠ is for vinyl fabrics. The recommendation is "Wipe with Damp Cloth Only." Vinyls have been a problem in dry cleaning, but the professional dry cleaner has handled many vinyl and vinyl-trimmed garments satisfactorily in wet cleaning. Some manufacturers are now producing dry-cleanable vinyls.

The FTC acknowledges that a particular instruction need not be specifically detailed provided it can be shown to be really understandable to consumers. In the FTC's view, any term indicating washability implies dry cleanability unless the label specifically states "Do Not Dry Clean" or includes the limiting term "Only" after the washing instructions.

CONFUSING LABELS

Consumers and dry cleaners are going through a dilemma of confusing labels since the FTC Trade Regulation Rule on Care Labeling of Textile Wearing Apparel went into effect. For example, many inquiries have been made about the label that reads: "Dry Clean

DRY CLEAN
ONLY
Do not use petroleum
solvents or coin
Operated dry cleaning

(S)

100% WOOL

with leather

Figure 10-5 The above labels are contradictory. The label tells the consumer to dry clean the garment but not to use the dry-cleaning solvents used in professional or coin-operated cleaning.

Only. Do not use petroleum solvents, or the coin-operated methods of dry cleaning" (see Figure 10–5). "Dry Clean in Stoddard solvent only" would have been clearer. Manufacturers of wearing apparel have used the objectionable label not understanding the reference made to petroleum solvent. Thus it is evident that the labels were placed on merchandise to meet the requirement that the garment be labeled but not because the item was tested for dry cleaning and found to have limitations on cleanability in one solvent system. This label language eliminates the use of both the principal dry-cleaning solvents, yet it says "Dry Clean Only."

Some other labels that are causing concern are: "Do Not Wash," "Dry Clean," and "Use a Non-Solvent-Based Cleaning Fluid."

The latter label is confusing to dry cleaners. "What is a non-solvent-based cleaning fluid?" they ask. It must be a gas. The cleaning industry knows of no system of cleaning with a gas. Known dry-cleaning fluids dissolve oily soils. Therefore, they are "solvent-based" and would be barred from use by this strange label.

Another label states: "Professionally Dry Clean Without Using Petroleum Solvents. Do Not Tumble Dry. Do Not Wring or Press With Heat. Hang to Dry and Steam Lightly. Press Top, if Necessary."

This label also confuses cleaners. Accepted tests for dry cleanability are made with perchlorethylene, because what is cleanable in perc is also cleanable in petroleum solvent. Essentially they are alike but petroleum is less likely to damage lightly held colors or plasticized products. So why exclude this gentler solvent if dry cleaning is recommended?

This label appeared on a leather-trimmed, fleece-lined raincoat:

Dry Clean Only
It is advisable that the leather and/or suede trimming be covered by cloth while under hot steam while being dry cleaned in order to avoid color bleeding.

The hot steam would be used during pressing, if at all, not "while being dry cleaned."

Even do-it-yourself labels and hangtags can be quite involved, such as the following:

- Machine or hand wash separately in warm water using a mild soap or detergent.
- Do not use bleach or cold water detergent or any caustic soap.
- Do not soak, rub, or twist—rinse thoroughly.
- Hang to dry or dry in dryer immediately after normal washing cycle. Never put away damp.
- Avoid excessive sun exposure.

Surely there is a simpler explanation.

The following label relieves the manufacturer of any responsibility:

Sorry . . .
Because of the widespread use of detergents and cleaning methods, and since we cannot control those methods of washing and cleaning, we cannot guarantee the washability or cleanability of any garment.

Still another reads:

> *Dry Cleaning Instructions*
> - Cleaning—Dry Clean Only Using Mineral Turpentine Perchlene.
> - Ironing—Use a light cloth on the top of the material when ironing with 180° Fahrenheit to 270° Fahrenheit.

Cleaners reading this ask, "What is mineral turpentine perchlene?"

Dry cleaners like this label:

> *For Do It Yourselfers*
> Hand or machine wash with mild soap in lukewarm water. Rinse thoroughly. Drip dry on wooden hanger. Iron at rayon setting. Do not wring or spin dry.
> *For Leisure Lovers*
> Relax and let your dry cleaner do it.

Cost of Permanent Care Labeling

There are three specific cost factors to consider in permanent care labeling: the cost of the labels and the cost to apply them, the cost of testing the article to determine how it will perform, and the cost entailed in the implied warranty behind the label.

Who pays for permanent care labeling? It is no secret that the ultimate cost is borne by the consumer. One leading mail-order company puts the total cost of the simplest, smallest, permanently attached label, as outlined by the FTC's Trade Regulation Rule Relating to Care Labeling of Textile Wearing Apparel at $237 million. Another manufacturer said his company expects to spend between $400,000 and $500,000 a year on care labeling. The FTC has stated that cost estimates for permanently attached labels vary from "tremendous" to "incalculable." It has been estimated that the cost will be as high as 8 percent on lower-priced garments.

The federal agency also points out that consumers believe the elimination of loss resulting from improper care will more than offset the added initial cost and, ultimately, will result in a net saving.

Weakness of the Rule

It is estimated that 27 billion items must carry permanent care labels. Even so, the Rule omits the large area of household textiles, furs, and leathers. Another weakness of the Rule is that it requires only one piece of a multiunit garment to be labeled. The Rule lacks strength also because it is not tied to any care standards of performance.

The FTC staff recognizes that its Rule does not specify guidelines for manufacturers to follow in preparing care labels. In fact, consideration is being given to establishing guidelines.

Meanwhile, two national nongovernmental standards are available to serve as guidelines for care labeling: the Recommended Practice Standards for Permanent Care Labeling of the American Society for Testing and Materials, D-3136 (1972) and the American National Standards Institute, L-28.1 (1972).

The FTC staff concedes that the Rule is not working effectively in over-the-counter fabric sales. Consumers are not asking for care labels, but the FTC staff takes the position that the consumer should not need to ask for care labels. It is the responsibility of the retail store to give the label to the consumer. The FTC staff recognizes that this responsibility is not spelled out in the Rule, and consideration is being given to whether or not the Rule should place responsibility on the retailers.

The FTC staff has conducted private surveys concerning compliance with the Rule to determine its strengths and weaknesses.

Commission Issues Proposed New Care Labeling Rule

The FTC announced proposed revisions in its trade regulations rule requiring care labeling of wearing apparel (*Federal Register*, Vol. 41, No. 17, January 26, 1976). The proposed revisions would expand in certain respects the present Care Labeling Rule (which became effective on July 3, 1972) and retain, but clarify, other provisions.

Major proposed revisions would:

1. Expand the rule's coverage to include, among other things, household furnishings, and leather and suede wearing apparel.
2. Require that labels contain various disclosures designed to give the consumer clearer and more complete care instructions.
3. Provide a uniform glossary of terms used in care instructions.

The proposed revised rule is based primarily on the 9000 comments received in response to the Request for Comment. Most of the comments were from consumers. Many comments discussed the degree of compliance with the present rule; others suggested changes to improve its effectiveness.

Ninety percent of those commenting found that permanent care labels are attached to articles of wearing apparel as presently required; however, 75 percent indicated that labels are not being furnished to consumers with piece goods purchased at the retail level. The piece goods provision in the proposed rule has thus been modified to specify the responsibilities of manufacturers in this regard. Section 423.2 of the proposed rule would require manufacturers of piece goods to devise care instructions and supply care labels to the retailer. The issue of how further to ensure that consumers obtain these labels with piece goods at the point of retail purchase has been raised in a series of questions.

Many consumers favored extension of the coverage of the rule to include items other than textile wearing apparel. Eighty-five percent favored extension of the rule to cover textile household furnishings (draperies, curtains, upholstered furniture, linens, carpets, rugs, etc.), 94 percent favored the inclusion of leather and suede wearing apparel, 91 percent favored the inclusion of piece goods used to make any textile article, 76 percent favored the inclusion of yarn sold over-the-counter, and 70 percent favored the inclusion of intermediate components (fabric and other components used in the making of finished products for which care labels are required.)

Thus, the proposed rule would require that household furnishings, and leather and suede wearing apparel contain permanently attached care labels. Manufacturers of piece goods used to make any finished product covered by the proposed rule and yarn sold over-the-counter would have to supply care labels to retailers. The proposed rule would also require the manufacturers of carpets and rugs to provide care instructions to retailers of such products. In connection with the sale of any intermediate component, care instructions would have to be supplied by the component manufacturer to the finished product manufacturer for the component in question.

The proposed rule continues to exclude handwear, headwear, footwear, so-called "decorative items," piece goods "remnants" and thread from its coverage.

The Commission also received extensive comment on the nature of the care instructions themselves. Although 85 percent of those responding noted that typical care instructions are clear as far as they go, 56 percent indicated that such instructions are often inaccurate. Also, 79 percent found care information on labels to be incomplete or vague (e.g., washing instructions without drying instructions). The proposed rule would require, in general, that washing instructions be more specific and include drying instructions in every case, and bleaching and ironing instructions when appropriate. Solvent specifications are to be given with dry cleaning instructions when necessary. Additionally, since 54 percent of those commenting found "low labeling" to be a frequent problem and since 93 percent of those addressing the question favored alternative care instructions on certain items where needed (in this case, washing and dry cleaning instructions), the proposed rule would require the inclusion of washing and dry-cleaning instructions on care labels where applicable on finished household furnishings and certain items of outerwear. Finally, 64 percent of those commenting preferred the use of words, as opposed to symbols, on care labels. The proposed rule would permit symbols but only so long as words are included that fulfill the requirements of the rule.

With regard to care labeling terminology and appropriate definitions for such terminology, 79 percent felt that the rule should provide a uniform reference for terms used in care instructions. The proposed rule provides for such a reference in the glossary of terms developed by the American Society for Testing and Materials.

Abrasive or coarse labels on wearing apparel, potentially irritating to the skin were cited as a problem by 81 percent of those commenting on that question. Provision in the proposed rule has been made for a relaxation of the present requirement that permanent labels be readily accessible to the user in cases where the label is coarse or abrasive. In such cases the permanent label may be placed in an inaccessible location only so long as the same care instructions are printed or displayed on the outside of the garment when sold at retail.

Under the proposed rule, previously granted exemptions will stand as long as the products exempted still meet the criteria on which they were based; however, more explicit provisions for new exemptions are given. Standards of proof have been refined and made more specific. Provision is made for waiver of care labeling for certain items that are sold to rental service companies and hospitals, nursing homes, and other similar institutions.

According to FTC procedure, interested parties have been invited to propose disputed issues for consideration at a public hearing to be scheduled at a later date. A Public Policy Forum, National Conference on Care Labeling was held in Washington, D.C., July 1976.

Symbols on Care Labels

Many imported garments from Canada, Great Britain, and Europe now contain labels bearing care instructions in the form of symbols. These are intended to overcome language problems. Several different symbol labeling systems now used in different parts of the world are in the process of being consolidated through the International Organization for Standardization.

The leading symbol system of care labeling are Canadian, Dutch, and British. All systems use symbols of the same basic shape but they vary somewhat in content. There are five basic symbols in general use:

 Wash tub, which gives instructions about laundering or washing.

 Triangle, which signals instructions for bleaching.

 Square, which relates to drying.

 Hand iron, which introduces pressing or ironing instructions.

Circle or dry cleaning cylinder, which is the basis for dry-cleaning instructions.

In the Canadian and Dutch systems, red, amber and green colors are used.

Red means stop—don't carry out the action represented by the symbol. For added emphasis a red symbol is usually canceled out with an "X."

Amber means that some caution is necessary.

Green means that no special precautions are needed.

The British use a one-color system. All symbols are printed in black ink.

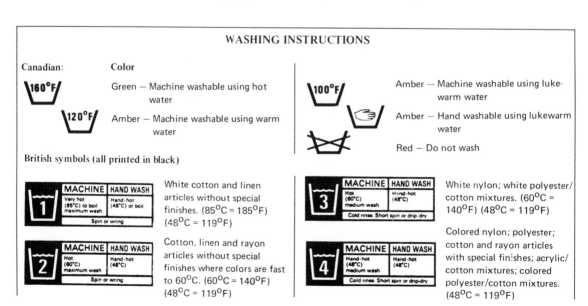

WASHING INSTRUCTIONS	
Canadian:	
Color	
160°F — Green — Machine washable using hot water	100°F — Amber -- Machine washable using lukewarm water
120°F — Amber — Machine washable using warm water	Amber — Hand washable using lukewarm water
	Red — Do not wash

British symbols (all printed in black)

MACHINE / HAND WASH	Description
1 — MACHINE: Very hot (85°C) to boil maximum wash / HAND WASH: Hand-hot (48°C) or boil — Spin or wring	White cotton and linen articles without special finishes. (85°C = 185°F) (48°C = 119°F)
2 — MACHINE: Hot (60°C) maximum wash / HAND WASH: Hand-hot (48°C) — Spin or wring	Cotton, linen and rayon articles without special finishes where colors are fast to 60°C. (60°C = 140°F) (48°C = 119°F)
3 — MACHINE: Hot (60°C) medium wash / HAND WASH: Hand-hot (48°C) — Cold rinse. Short spin or drip-dry	White nylon; white polyester/cotton mixtures. (60°C = 140°F) (48°C = 119°F)
4 — MACHINE: Hand-hot (48°C) medium wash / HAND WASH: Hand-hot (48°C) — Cold rinse. Short spin or drip-dry	Colored nylon; polyester; cotton and rayon articles with special finishes; acrylic/cotton mixtures; colored polyester/cotton mixtures. (48°C = 119°F)

396

 Cotton, linen and rayon articles where colors are fast to 40°C (104°F) but not at 60°C (140°F).

 Wool, including blankets and wool mixtures with cotton or rayon; silk (40°C = 104°F).

Acrylics; acetate and triacetate including mixtures with wool; polyester/wool blends. (40°C = 104°F).

Washable pleated garments containing acrylics, nylon, polyester or triacetate; glass fiber fabrics (40°C = 104°F).

Dutch:

 Green — Hot washing permitted. 95°C (203°F)

 Green — Moderately hot water permitted, 60°C (140°F).

 Amber — For lukewarm washing like wool. 40°C (104°F).

Red — Do not wash.

BLEACHING INSTRUCTIONS

Canadian:
Amber — Use chlorine bleach as directed on the container label.

 Red — Do not use chlorine bleach.

Dutch:
 Green — Bleaching with hypochlorite (chlorine bleach) if necessary is permitted.

 Red — No bleaching with hypochlorite (chlorine bleach).

DRYING INSTRUCTIONS

Canadian:
Green — It may be dried in a tumble dryer at medium to high setting.

 Amber — It may be dried in a tumble dryer at low setting.

 Green — It should be hung to dry.

Green — It should be hung soaking wet to drip dry.

Amber — It should be dried on a flat surface.

IRONING INSTRUCTIONS

Canadian:
 Green — A setting up to cotton and linen may be used.

 Amber — A setting of medium should be used.

 Amber — A setting of low should be used.

Red — Do not press or iron.

Dutch:
 Green — Hot ironing permitted.

Amber — No hot ironing.

 Red — No ironing.

British:
 Black — Hot 210°C (410°F) Rayon, modified rayon, cotton, linen.

 Black-Warm 160°C (320°F) Polyester mixtures, wool.

Black — Cool 120°C (248°F) Acrylic, nylon, acetate.

 Black — Do not iron.

DRYCLEANING INSTRUCTIONS

Canadian:

Green — It may be drycleaned.

Amber — It may be drycleaned, but tumble drying should be at a low temperature.

Red — Do not dryclean.

Dutch:

Green — Use of any solvent permitted.

Amber — Use of perchlorethylene or petroleum solvent permitted.

Amber — Only use of petroleum solvent permitted.

Red — Do not dryclean.

British:

Black — Any solvent may be used, including trichlorethylene.

Black — Any solvent may be used except trichlorethylene.

Black — Use petroleum or fluorocarbon solvents only.

Black — Do not dryclean.

INTERNATIONAL APPROACH TO CARE LABELING

The International Standardization Organization (ISO) with headquarters in Geneva, Switzerland, is concerned with the development of voluntary international agreement on standards of all kinds.

Participating countries in ISO standards projects are represented by their national standards organizations, called member bodies, which authorize qualified delegates to represent them in formal committee activities. In all, 14 countries are represented by more than 75 delegates. The member body in the United States is the American National Standards Institute.

The ISO Technical Committee, TC-38, handles all types of textile standards through many subcommittees. Subcommittee SC-11 is specifically charged with developing standards for care labeling. Its primary object is to develop an international symbol system of care labeling. A draft proposal on care labeling was tentatively approved at The Hague meeting in 1973, subject to final editing and corrections by committee members.

In 1975, 62 member bodies of ISO were asked to vote on the draft of International Standard for Care Labeling (ISO/DIS 3758). The United States cast a negative vote.

To understand why, it should be realized that the draft standard "evolved" mainly in Europe over a period of more than 25 years. In seeking to bring together the many points of view and general commitment of most of the European countries to a strictly symbol system of labeling, the process of true internationalization with countries outside of Europe, mostly the English-speaking countries, introduced questions of practicality and acceptability. It is not likely that sufficient negative votes will prevent adoption of the standard. However, this does not make the standard any more acceptable for international trade and communication for the following reasons:

1. No symbol for drying is required as in the Canadian system to convey information considered important to the consumer and fabric care specialist in U.S. labeling standards (i.e., "Do not tumble dry," etc.).

2. The four required symbols for washing, bleaching, pressing, and dry cleaning must always be shown, even when they must be indicated as not applicable by crossing out the inappropriate symbol. This is contrary to U.S. practice of labeling only restrictive processes (i.e., "Do not dry clean" on washable garments that otherwise are assumed to be dry cleanable, etc.).

3. The customary European symbols largely incorporated in the proposed draft standard are copyrighted by an organization not controlled by ISO. This appears to be contrary to an ISO directive that only ISO can license a country to use an ISO standard of any kind. The United States insists on free and unrestricted use of ISO-licensed privileges having no commercial benefit to others.

4. The symbol for "chlorine bleaching" is incorrectly referenced and appears to ignore use of other types of bleaches common in many countries. The reaction in chlorine bleaching processes is "anidation," not "chlorination" as stated.

5. The pressing temperature limit of 200°C (392°F) in the proposed standard is inadequate for pressing cotton and linen. The United States does not disagree with the lower limits of 110°C (230°F) and 150°C (302°F) required for pressing synthetics.

6. The United States opposes symbols that provide for a solvent specification on the grounds that the consumer has little opportunity to patronize dry cleaners according to the solvent they use. The U.S. position has always specified the more severe of the three solvents used to evaluate dry cleanability of textile products (i.e., perchlorethylene versus petroleum and fluorocarbon solvents).

The negative U.S. vote on this ballot should not be interpreted to mean that the United States is against the idea of an international standard for care labeling. The U.S. position simply suggests that the proposed standard in its present form is incomplete and premature and that it will fail of its purpose by being largely European oriented in content rather than aimed at serving the labeling needs of all countries.

International Language System Also Under Development

At the last meeting of ISO Subcommittee SC-11, TC 38, in The Netherlands, in 1973, which approved the draft standard presently undergoing international balloting, the U.S. delegation succeeded in obtaining approval to develop a symbols-related international language system of references to care practices for permanent care labeling of textiles. The proposed system is based on the Recommended Practice Standard D-3136 of the American Society for Testing and Materials (ASTM). A draft proposal by a U.S.-directed working committee of SC-11 has been completed and will be subject to the procedures for balloting the same as ISO/DIS 3758, which specifies use of symbols only.

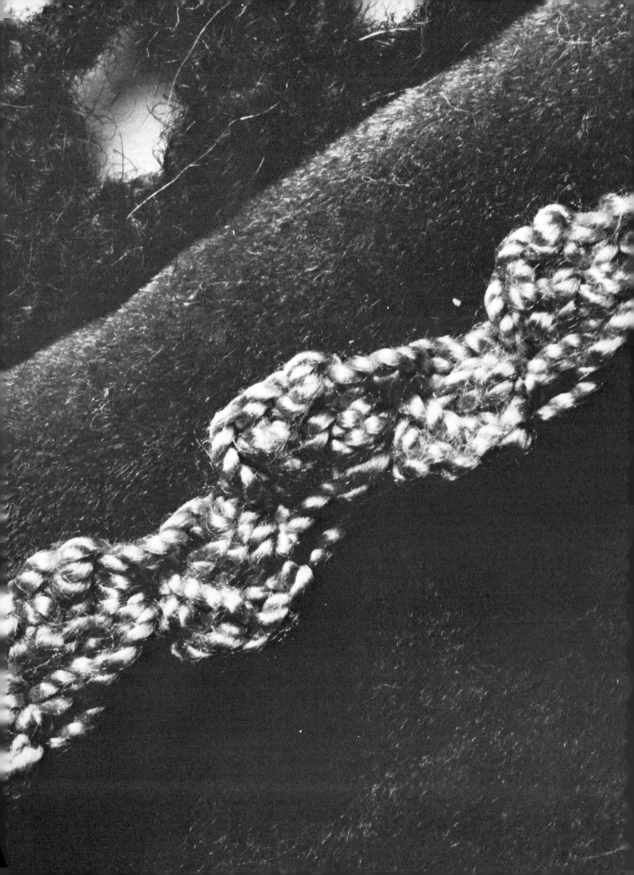

11

Government Programs Related to Textiles and the Consumer

The 1960s and 1970s saw an old economic cause take on new significance. More or less dormant since the 1930s, the consumer movement was stimulated by many of the same forces that were shaping the changing American environment in general: the population explosion, growing affluence, rising educational levels, economic expansion and technical and scientific advancement, mass marketing techniques, an increasingly complex marketplace, and changing social and personal values.

These forces are continuing, and accompanying them are a growing concern for the consumer's needs, desires, and responsibilities. Consumer-oriented activity by government, industry, and education will also intensify.

CONSUMER RIGHTS

In 1962, President John F. Kennedy stated four basic consumer rights: the right to be informed, the right to choose, the right to safety, and the right to be heard. It was soon recognized that a fifth right should be added: the right to be protected.

In his message to the Second Session of the 90th Congress (February 1968), President Lyndon B. Johnson took up the matter of consumer protection, saying:

> A hundred years ago, consumer protection was largely unnecessary. We were a rural nation then; a nation of farms and small towns. Even in the growing cities, neighborhoods were closely knit.
>
> Most products were locally produced and there was a personal relationship between the seller and the buyer. If the buyer had a complaint, he went straight to the miller, the blacksmith, the tailor, the corner grocer. Products were less complicated. It was easy to tell the excellent from the inferior.
>
> Today all this is changed. A manufacturer may be thousands of miles away from his customer—and even further removed by distributors, wholesalers and retailers. His products may be so complicated that only an expert can pass judgment of their quality. We are able to sustain this vast and impersonal system of commerce because of the ingenuity of our technology and the honesty of our businessmen.
>
> But this same vast network of commerce, this same complexity, also presents opportunities for the unscrupulous and the negligent.
>
> It is the government's role to protect the consumer—and the honest businessman alike—against fraud and indifference. Our goal must be to assure every American consumer a fair and honest exchange for his hard-earned dollar.

In short, President Johnson echoed what President Kennedy had said, "a consumer has four basic rights: the right to be fully informed about products he buys, the right to choose among several varieties, the right to safety and the right to be heard."

These rights started a new era of consumerism and new consumer-oriented legislation and government programs in the United States.

In April 1974, President Gerald R. Ford requested each of the departments and agencies in the executive branch to analyze their entire decision-making process to determine how additional consumer involvement could make federal agencies more responsive to the needs of the American consumer.

In April 1975, James T. Lynn, Director, Office of Management and Budget, and Virginia H. Knauer, Special Assistant to the President for Consumer Affairs, submitted such a plan. The plans developed by the departments and agencies are published in the *Federal Register*.* They were disseminated to consumers and all other interested groups.

A review of the plans indicates that there are common recommendations for improving consumer representation:

1. Creation or continuation of an organizational mechanism for consumer affairs.

2. Guidelines to the operating bureaus on how to improve consumer representation.

3. Greater involvement of line management in opening up the decision-making process to consumer input.

4. Early public announcement of issues under consideration to foster consumer input at an early stage in policy development.

5. Additional consumer representation on various advisory councils.

6. Specialized consumer information and educational materials to assist consumers.

7. Better coordination with national, state, and local consumer groups and other special interests groups.

8. Increased involvement of agency field offices.

9. Increased use of consumer complaints as an information tool for policy and program development.

Implementing the plans began immediately by holding regional conferences beginning January 1976.

* "Consumer Representation," *Federal Register,* (Agencies proposed plans) Vol. 40, No. 229, 11–26–75, pp. 55091 to 55273.

EXECUTIVE BRANCH OF GOVERNMENT AND CONSUMER CONCERNS

During the 1960s, the government became increasingly aware of the consumer's needs for more information and protection.

"I am today taking action to assure that the voice of the consumer will be 'loud, clear, uncompromising and effective' in the highest councils of the Federal Government." With this statement, President Johnson established the President's Committee on Consumer Interests and the position of Special Assistant to the President for Consumer Affairs.

The President's Committee on Consumer Interests issued a summary report (1967) which listed the consumer's concern as arising from:

> An inability to judge quality, chiefly because of rapid changes in the nature of the products and the increased variety of products and services offered for sale;
>
> A lack of information about where to seek recourse when a product or service is unsatisfactory or when he believes he has been misled or defrauded; and
>
> Confusion about how prices are determined in the American free-enterprise economy and why some of them rise. Concern about quality deterioration.
>
> A lack of knowledge of what consumer services and information are provided by the Federal Government and how to use these services.
>
> A lack of basic education and materials on how to buy, especially among persons with limited incomes.

Early in 1966, Esther Peterson, the first Special Assistant for Consumer Affairs, urged the creation of the Industry Advisory Committee for Textile Information, to work with the government in exploring areas of greatest consumer needs.

Following two years of intensive study, the Industry Advisory Committee submitted the Voluntary Guide for Improved and Permanent Care Labeling of Consumer Textile Products.* This document was formally adopted in 1967 and accepted by Betty Furness, who was the Special Assistant for Consumer Affairs at that time.

In the introduction, the Guide states that it is not concerned with textile products made of familiar material, the care of which is conventional and well known, but is, however, concerned with those textile products that possess unusual or exceptional qualities and that should be given special care. The glossary of care terms included in the Guide is an attempt to establish a uniform care terminology.

---

* A Voluntary Industry Guide for Improved and Permanent Care Labeling of Consumer Textile Products, National Retail Merchants Association, 100 West 31st Street, New York, New York 10001.

Based on the glossary, which is intended primarily for use by manufacturers and retailers, the American Apparel Manufacturers Association's Consumer Affairs Committee developed a "companion piece" for consumers.*

In 1971, President Nixon, by Executive Order 11583, outlined the mission and purpose of the Office of Consumer Affairs and the Consumer Advisory Council. At this time, the Office of Consumer Affairs was moved from the Executive Offices of the White House to the Department of Health, Education and Welfare. The duties and functions of the office were not changed or amended with the move. The Director of the Office of Consumer Affairs and the Special Assistant to the President for Consumer Affairs was held by the same individual, Mrs. Virginia Knauer.

After nearly 12 years of debate and controversy over the concept of federal-level consumer agencies, Congress passed legislation that would create an independent Consumer Protection agency. Three major bills were under consideration. Common to the bills are provisions for (1) vesting the agency with broad responsibilities for identifying consumer problems, (2) conducting its own studies, (3) developing programs, and (4) recommending legislation to Congress. There have been sharp differences over how strong the agency should be and what functions it should perform. At this writing, the measure faces presidential veto. Because of an amendment tied to organized labor's exemption from the powers of the proposed agency, the bill has been sent back to committee.

DEPARTMENTS, BUREAUS, COMMISSIONS, AND AGENCIES IN THE FEDERAL GOVERNMENT

The government is a large and complex system of departments, bureaus, commissions, and agencies. In the area of textiles, there is both interrelationship and autonomy. Consumers generally have little knowledge or understanding of the influences of governmental organizations and programs on the individual either directly or indirectly. In the following pages, the obvious relationships of government programs to textiles and clothing have been "sifted" out. Each discussion could be researched in depth by the interested student.

U.S. Department of Commerce

The mission and function of the Department of Commerce is to provide a wide range of services to business and consumers. Only those related to clothing and textiles are discussed here: The National Busi-

---

* Recommended Terms for Permanent Labels on Consumer Textiles, American Apparel Manufacturers Association, 1611 North Kent Street, Arlington, Virginia 22209.

ness Council for Consumer Affairs, the National Bureau of Standards, the National Fire Prevention and Control Administration, the Patent Office, the Bureau of the Census, and the Business and Defense Services Administration.

NATIONAL BUSINESS COUNCIL FOR CONSUMER AFFAIRS

On August 5, 1971, by Executive Order 11614, the National Business Council for Consumer Affairs was established to advise the President, the Office of Consumer Affairs, the Justice Department, the Federal Trade Commission, and other government agencies, through the Secretary of Commerce, on programs of business relating to consumer affairs.

As set forth in this order, the Council is authorized to identify and evaluate current and potential consumer problems, provide a forum for business and government on consumer issues, identify, recommend, and encourage action by business to meet legitimate consumer grievances, provide liaison among members of the business community on consumer affairs matters, and advise on actions of federal, state, and local agencies involving policies of consumer affairs. The organization of this council is shown in Figure 11–1.

THE NATIONAL BUREAU OF STANDARDS (NBS)

The National Bureau of Standards was established in 1901 in the Department of Commerce to provide technical assistance to industry, government and educational institutions. This assistance involved the development, maintenance, and dissemination of fundamental standards of physical measurement and the systematic and accurate determination of physical constants and important properties of matter and materials.

Today, in addition to providing a central base for a consistent and compatible system of physical measurement, NBS serves as a focal point within the federal government for assuring maximum application of the physical and engineering sciences to the advancement of technology in industry and commerce. To accomplish these objectives, the NBS conducts research and provides central national services in three broad program areas: basic measurement standards, materials research and engineering standards, and applied technology.

These programs are described as follows:

1. The Institute for Basic Standards provides the central basis within the United States for a complete, consistent system of physical measurement.

2. The Institute for Materials Research develops standard reference materials, new and advanced methods for measuring the prop-

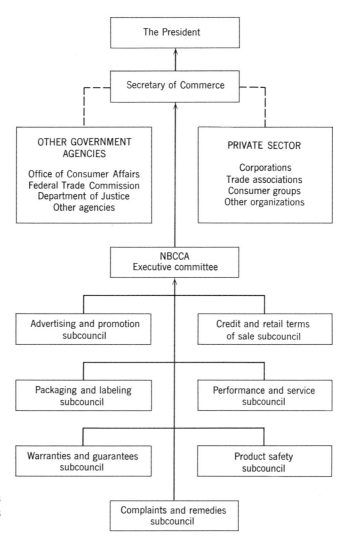

erties of materials, and generates critical data on well-characterized materials for industry and the scientific and technological communities of the nation.

3. The Institute for Applied Technology provides technical services to industry and government in the development of performance criteria and test methods for materials, devices, structures, and systems and promotes technological innovation in the public and private sectors.

4. The Center for Radiation Research conducts programs in basic

409 *Government Programs Related to Textiles and the Consumer*

standards, materials research, and applied technology utilizing radiation and nuclear scientific techniques.

5. The Center for Computer Sciences and Technology provides scientific and technical support to federal agencies in the fields of computers and information processing.

6. The Center for Consumer Product Technology was established for the development of test methodology for satisfying some of the product performance information needs of the consumer and government agencies at all levels. Current activities involve (1) energy conservation work with the home appliance industry to assist consumers in the selection and use of efficient appliances, (2) product safety work with the Consumer Product Safety Commission to assist in reducing the risk of injury from consumer products, and (3) product performance work with the Law Enforcement Assistance Administration to help local units in making cost-effective purchase decisions.

7. The Office for Information Programs promotes dissemination and accessibility of scientific information generated within NBS and other government agencies, and administers the National Standard Reference Data System.

One of the most recent NBS programs that affects every consumer is information and education on the metric system of weights and measures and changing over from the customary language of inches and pounds to the metric language of meters and kilograms. Bill 8674 was passed by the House on September 5, 1975. It still must pass the Senate. Even with passage by Congress, the compliance to the bill will be voluntary rather than mandatory.

NBS Serves the Textile Industry The government, through the participation of its NBS members in the work of the American Society for Testing and Materials (ASTM) and the American Association of Textile Chemists and Colorists (AATCC), assists other general interest groups and producer and consumer groups.

Government employees also participate in the development and revision of American Standards L-22 and L-24, sponsored by the American National Standards Institute (ANSI) and the American Society for Testing and Materials, which give the performance requirements of textile fabrics and institutional textiles. These standards are used by the textile and apparel industries as guides in establishing the appearance and performance properties of their products.

Federal Test Method Standards and Federal Specifications, promulgated by the General Services Administration, are developed with the cooperation of individual federal agencies. These specify the physical and chemical requirements and applicable test methods for controlling the quality of textile and apparel items used by federal agencies. In addition, they are often used by industry as guides for quality control.

A major contribution of the federal government to the textile industry resulted from the expenditure of funds for a U.S. Department of Commerce Civilian Industrial Technology Program (CIT) to benefit the textile and apparel industries. These industries were selected for government-sponsored research for many reasons: the fragmented nature of the textile industry and small size of the majority of apparel manufacturing companies, the small investment in research and development, the lack of technological advancement in techniques and equipment, the loss of foreign markets, declining employment and failures, and the great need for industry-oriented research.

The broad intention of the program was to increase the rate of technical innovation by increasing the level of technical competence and the use of new technology.

The Advisory Committee for Textile and Apparel Research (ACTAR), a committee of the National Academy of Sciences and National Research Council, advised and recommended courses of action for the program which was administered by the Textile and Apparel Technology Center (TATC) of the Institute for Applied Technology of the National Bureau of Standards. The industries also played active roles in the programs in recommending ways to encourage industry cooperation, by participating in task groups, and in recommending approval or disapproval of the research projects proposed.

Some 30 projects were funded and administered under the CIT program. Among them were:

Systems Analysis—three projects on textile problems, a textile company and an apparel company

New Markets for Textile Materials

State of the Arts—Limp Fabrics

Creation of Working Models—Limp Fabrics

Instrumental Color Control

Computer-Based Information Thesaurus

Information Workshops—one on textiles, another on apparel

Mechanics of Seaming

Survey of Needle Heat

Aiding in the Independence of the Apparel Research Foundation, Inc.

Journal of the Apparel Research Foundation

Tests for Apparel Fabrics

Sewing Threads for the Apparel Industry

NBS Serves the Consumer

The consumer directly depends on NBS work in many aspects of his daily routine. Goods and services are generally exchanged in measured quantities, for example, a yard of fabric, 360 milliliters of detergent.

All of these measures are based on standards maintained by the NBS. Basic measurements help us to make decisions. What iron should be purchased? What capacity water tank is needed for the new washer? Should an electric or gas dryer be purchased? Much of the NBS work, such as the standards and test methods developed for flammable fabrics, directly affects the health and safety of consumers.

NATIONAL FIRE PREVENTION AND CONTROL ADMINISTRATION

Congress passed the Federal Fire Prevention and Control Act that was signed into law in November 1974. The National Fire Prevention and Control Administration is located in the Department of Commerce. Its main objective is to reduce fire losses in the United States. It consists of a Research and Development Branch, a National Fire Data Center, the National Fire Academy, and the National Fire Education Center.

The Research and Development Branch is involved in pure research with the NBS. Its main objective is to develop better equipment for firefighters.

The National Fire Data Center collects and analyzes accurate fire incident data. In-depth analyses are done at the Center and in some studies in cooperation with the Office of Information and Hazard Analysis in the NBS.

The National Fire Academy has as its purpose the establishment of a national program for training fire fighters who will go back and do similar training at the regional or state level.

The National Fire Educational Center undertakes programs of public education.

OFFICE OF CONSUMER AFFAIRS

In 1976, an Office of Consumer Affairs was established in the Department of Commerce (Office of Ombudsman, Consumer Affairs Division). At this writing the Office is so new it is impossible to comment on its objectives and functions, which are to supply consumer input information of department policy and answer consumer inquiries. You can obtain information by writing to the Department of Commerce.

PATENT OFFICE The Patent Office, which administers the patent laws enacted by Congress, plays a key role in invention and innovation. It examines applications and grants patents, publishes and disseminates patent information, and maintains search files of U.S. and foreign patents and a Patent Search Center for public use. Additionally, it issues trademarks.

The Textile Group of the Patent Office is divided into three segments known as Art Units: (1) Textile—Weaving and Knitting, (2) Sewing and Apparel, and (3) Winding and Reeling.

The weaving and knitting and winding and reeling units direct attention to fabric construction, the sewing and apparel unit to garment manufacturers. For example, inventors apply for patents by writing a letter of application. Apparel items are divided into 10 categories: guards and protectors; body braces and supports; garment protectors; burial, fur, and bathing garments; body garments; hand and arm coverings; head coverings; skirts, stockings, bustles, and the like; supporters and retainers; and general structures.

Many processes used to produce fabrics, bindings and trim are patented. You might find a study on early patent rights very interesting.

BUREAU OF THE CENSUS The Bureau of the Census is responsible for timely information on manufacturers. It publishes reports for industry groups and individual industries and for geographic divisions, states, and large standard metropolitan areas. Such reports include information on employment, man-hours, payrolls, value added by manufacture, expenditure for new plants and equipment, cost of materials, end-year inventories, and value of products shipped. All of these affect the final cost of an item to the consumer.

BUSINESS AND DEFENSE SERVICES ADMINISTRATION The Business and Defense Services Administration, of which the Office of Textiles is a part, "is concerned with promoting and fostering the development of domestic business and industry. Its objectives are to provide information, services and assistance essential to business growth and technical development within the framework of the free enterprise system."

Most of the activities of the Office of Textiles are involved with international trade—the promotion of exports and the limitation of imports.

This office is also involved with the administration of the Flammable Fabrics Act, and works closely with the Consumer Product Safety Commission, and the National Bureau of Standards.

413 *Government Programs Related to Textiles and the Consumer*

U.S. Department of Labor

The Department of Labor has as its objectives "to foster, promote and develop the welfare of the wage earners of the United States, to improve their working conditions, and to advance their opportunities for profitable employment." It is responsible for promoting safe, healthy working conditions, administering compensation benefits for employees injured on the job, and for providing safeguards for working women and children.

WOMEN'S BUREAU

The Women's Bureau of the Department of Labor develops policies and programs to promote the welfare of the more than 29 million women in the labor force, to encourage better use of womanpower, and to provide information to state and community leaders.

BUREAU OF LABOR—MANAGEMENT RELATIONS

The Bureau of Labor—Management Relations enforces Federal legislation affecting conditions of employment and certain labor-management activities. It also provides a climate in which workers and employers can work out their differences.

BUREAU OF LABOR STATISTICS

The Bureau of Labor Statistics acts as the Department's chief economic fact finder by collecting, analyzing, and distributing information on employment, unemployment, wages, prices, jobs, and conditions of work. For example, it employs girls and women to shop for apparel but none of them buy anything. They look at enough clothing to outfit an entire family, visit hundreds of stores throughout the nation, and talk to buyers, merchandise managers, and store owners. They repeat the shopping trips for several months, with the price tag their primary interest. Their findings contribute to the monthly Consumer Price Index, which charts the rise and fall of the purchasing power of the consumer's dollar.

The Bureau states that clothing has probably changed more in terms of variety and types on the market in the past 10 years than in any previous 10 years.

When there is a lapse of time between publishing the Price Index, the list of items sometimes fails to reflect changes in fashion. Pantyhose, for example, was a popular item for some time before it was included in the Index.

The Bureau also looks for the changes in the types of stores where clothing is sold and for shifts in the amount of money spent on clothing in comparison with food and shelter.

The list of clothing checked for price is geared to middle-income wage earners. High fashion and exclusive clothing is not included.

The specifications for each apparel item are detailed. Item 32-644, for instance, is a girl's skirt, but not just any girl's skirt. Item 32-644 must be A-line or hiphugger, of a soft-finished fabric, such as flannel or tweed, and may be bonded with acetate tricot. The yarn must be either "all new woolen, except flannel may have 15 to 20 percent nylon or acrylic."

Its hem may be up to two inches and may have tape. The seams must be plain, with pinked or plain edges, the waistband must be double fabric and may be elasticized, and the skirt must have a zipper closure. In addition, it may have a self or plastic belt or other minor trim or detail.

Another factor taken into consideration is whether a particular item is nationally advertised, since big advertising budgets could contribute to the cost.

Each pricer must follow four basic rules:

1. The item must meet specifications.
2. It must be available in "salable" quantities, that is, it must cover a specified size range.
3. It must be in good condition. No "seconds" or irregulars are included.
4. It must be the volume "seller" among items meeting specifications.

If the pricer sees four coats in one store that meet the requirements, the buyer is asked which is the best seller. That is the one that is priced.

The Consumer Price Index is due for a change.* With Congressional funding, the Bureau of Labor Statistics wants to make radical changes in the way it samples apparel and other products, and the stores covered at the point of sale. Continuous updating is recommended.

A long-time criticism has been the "product mix" contained in the Consumer Price Index sampling. It doesn't necessarily represent what's being bought at a given moment. The new Consumer Price Index of 1977 will use a revised market basket 3 or 4 years old rather than 10 years old. Along with sampling changes there will also be changes in the types of stores sampled.

The textiles component of the Wholesale Price Index is also going under important revisions to bring it closer into line with present market conditions and to relate it to be more representative of current fiber use.† Government officials will work closely with such

* Richard Wightman, "Bureau of Labor Statistics Seeks to Overhaul the CPI," *Women's Wear Daily,* October 22, 1975.

† Richard Wightman, WPI Textiles Data to be Closer to Present Market, *Daily News Record,* October 22, 1975.

organizations of the American Textile Manufacturers Institute, American Yarn and Spinners Association, and the Thread Institute to update the index.

There are currently around 100 items priced in the textiles component of the current WPI but the product mix—and the weight given to the various products—is based on statistics gathered from manufacturers by the Census Bureau in 1973.

The current Index lacks emphasis on many textile products that have become more important over the past decade or which, in some instances, have been introduced since 1963. Revisions will include manufactured fiber goods and blends, knit goods, tufted carpet yarns, spun, carpet, and apparel yarns, and polyester and polyester blends.

U.S. Department of Agriculture (USDA)

The Department of Agriculture has been called a "people's department"—a department for producers and users of the essentials of living. Although the primary objective of this department is service to U.S. farmers and ranchers, the American consumer is the real beneficiary of the products and service of the USDA.

In a relatively short time, U.S. agriculture has undergone an amazing revolution. As the nation's biggest industry, it assures the consumer of an abundance of fiber and of good nutritious food. Several of the USDA programs are directly related to textiles and consumer education.

AGRICULTURAL RESEARCH SERVICE (ARS)

Agricultural research has been a function of the federal government since 1839, when Congress appropriated $1000 to the Patent Office for "the collection of agricultural statistics, and for other agricultural purposes."

Today, the chief research agency of USDA is the Agricultural Research Service. ARS employs about 3600 scientists and engineers in research positions, and has a total staff of about 8100.

This research agency is divided into four regions: (1) Southern, (2) Western, (3) North Central, and (4) North Eastern. All cotton research is carried out in the Southern region, with the Southern Regional Research Center (SRRC) located in New Orleans. Wool research is conducted in the Western region at the Western Regional Research Center in Albany, California. The Textiles and Clothing Laboratory in Knoxville, Tennessee, is located in the Mid-Atlantic area. Each region is divided into areas, with area directors. Research communication between Textiles and Clothing and SRRC does not go entirely through area directors. Research leaders in both locations communicate and cooperate horizontally in matters pertaining to textile research.

COOPERATIVE EXTENSION SERVICE

The Cooperative Extension Service is a three-way partnership. The state land-grant university, the U.S. Department of Agriculture and the county governments share in planning and financing Extension work. To make sure that local people have a voice in planning, many local citizens volunteer to serve as advisors.

The land-grant university is headquarters for the staff of specialists in agriculture, home economics, youth work, marketing, resource development, and related subjects. They work with county agents.

More than 3000 Extension offices throughout the nation make up a vast facility for extending knowledge to all Americans.

Some 4000 Extension Service home economists conduct thousands of classes and workshops each year, helping people become better consumers. They train more than one million adult volunteer leaders to assist them with the extension program. They disseminate information over radio, television and in newspapers. The 4-H Club program of the Extension Service is designed specifically to help young people.

SPECIAL ASSISTANT FOR CONSUMER AFFAIRS

Late in 1973, a position of Special Assistant for Consumer Affairs was created in the USDA. The Special Assistant was appointed to represent, at the highest levels of the Department, the concerns of consumers as they relate to all USDA programs and to advise administrators on "issues and actions which have a bearing upon consumers." The Department felt that there was a great deal to be done to communicate with consumers since there has been a great deal of confrontation and misunderstanding between the USDA and consumers.

U.S. Department of Health, Education and Welfare (HEW)

The Office of Consumer Affairs is now located in the Department of Health, Education and Welfare. The purpose and objectives of this office are discussed on page 405.

Until 1973, this Department was actively involved in carrying out the mandate of the Flammable Fabrics Act. These functions have now been transferred to the Consumer Product Safety Commission.

U.S. Department of Defense

Federal specifications and standards for Army and Navy military personnel are developed at the U.S. Department of the Army Research and Development Laboratories at Natick, Massachusetts. The Air Force maintains a Materials Laboratory at Wright-Patterson Air Force Base in Dayton, Ohio. These, along with qualified products lists, qualified laboratory lists, and military handbooks are available from the Defense Personnel Support Center or Naval Publications and Forms Center in Philadelphia.

INDEPENDENT AGENCIES

Federal Trade Commission (FTC)

In 1914, Congress enacted two laws. The Federal Trade Commission Act created a regulatory agency to proceed in the public interest against unfair methods of competition in commerce. The Clayton Act prohibited certain discriminatory and acquisitive practices where it could be shown that competition was suppressed. In 1938, the FTC Act was expanded to include. "unfair or deceptive acts or practices in commerce." As the Commission proceeded in its regulatory role, it was given other enforcement responsibilities, such as the proper labeling of wool, fur, and textile fiber products.

Although the Commission has specific responsibilities for law enforcement, this does not alter its fundamental purpose to guide business, rather than to prosecute violators.

The agency was organized and commenced functioning on March 16, 1915. It embodied a wholly new concept in law enforcement: enlightenment, persuasion, and prohibition without punishment.

Any action brought by the FTC must be invested with public interest. Although individuals and business concerns frequently invite the Commission's attention to acts of wrongdoing, the Commission never undertakes the investigation of a case without answering the question, "Does this matter involve sufficient public interest for the FTC to proceed?"

The FTC has no power of its own to imprison, fine, or assess or award damages. Its maximum authority is to issue an order to "cease and desist," and even this order can be appealed to the courts within 60 days after it is issued. After that time it becomes final. Only if the order is violated can the FTC, acting through the Department of Justice, seek penalties of up to $5000 a day for each violation.

The Commission's five members are appointed by the President and confirmed by the Senate. Not more than three may belong to the same political party. Their seven-year terms are staggered to assure continuity of experience, as well as to keep the Commission nonpartisan.

In 1950, administration of the FTC was made the responsibility of a chairman. The appointments of key personnel, such as bureau heads, require approval by a majority of the Commission.

DECEPTIVE PRACTICES

In 1938, Congress passed the Wheeler-Lea Act which, among other things, broadened the FTC's authority to halt in interstate commerce unfair or deceptive acts or practices, regardless of whether they injured competition.

The work of the Commission in this area would be overwhelming if it were not for the assistance of (1) the vast majority of businessmen who voluntarily comply with the law themselves and, through organized effort, encourage others to do likewise, (2) advertising media and advertising agencies that maintain high ethical standards, and (3) private and civic organizations that identify and expose deceptive practices. The FTC encourages all the assistance it can get from these three sources. In addition, it conducts its own active programs supporting voluntary compliance with the law. These include trade practice rules, advisory opinions, industry guides, trade regulation rules, and public announcements. All FTC complaints and orders, as well as initial decisions, are summarized in news releases issued after the actions are taken.

GUARANTEES AND BAIT   False advertising of guarantees without disclosure of the limitations they contain results in misrepresentation of an item to the consumer. The Commission has issued a general guide on the whole subject of guarantees and their advertising. The guide prohibits use of the word "Guaranteed" in an advertisement unless the limitations also are disclosed.

Disreputable merchandisers may also use "bait" advertising, another form of deception. Here the scheme is to advertise a popular article at a ridiculously low price simply for the purpose of luring consumers into a store. The scheme is deceptive when the bargain bait cannot be purchased, and salesmen attempt to switch the consumers to higher-priced substitutes. This technique has been under continuous observation by the FTC.

Probably the most publicized antideceptive cases brought by the FTC are those concerning false advertising on television. The Commission uses the same legal yardstick to determine whether the advertising is false or misleading regardless of how it is disseminated. If a TV picture succeeds in giving the consumer the impression that a product has virtues it lacks or falsely disparages a competing product, then the FTC might take action.

WARRANTIES   On July 4, 1975, the 1974 Magnuson-Moss Warranty Act became effective. Under the new law a written warranty must mean what it says. Purchasers must get the performance promised in a written warranty.

Congress instructed the Federal Trade Commission to work out the standards and details needed to implement the provisions of the

Act. For this purpose, the FTC proposed rules dealing with what information appears in the warranty, making warranty information available to shoppers before they make purchase decisions, and handling dispute settlement mechanisms.*

Neither the new law nor the rules proposed under the law require manufacturers to offer written warranties. Instead, they set standards for anyone who does. The proposed rules cover only written warranties for consumer products that cost more than $5.

Terms and conditions of the rule are as follows:

A written warranty must provide the following information, simply, in comprehensible language, in a single document:

- Name and address of warrantor.
- The time when the warrantor will perform his duties if other than Monday through Saturday, 9 A.M.–6 P.M.
- Identify of person(s) protected by the warranty, including limitations, if any: for example, protecting only the initial owner.
- Precisely what the warranty covers and what it excludes.
- When or under what circumstances the warranty commences, and the duration of the coverage on the product itself or any of its parts.
- What the warrantor will do in case of defect or failure (repair, replace or refund if a full warranty; which items and services will and will not be paid for or provided if a limited warranty).
- The time within which the warrantor will perform any obligations under the warranty after receiving notice of defect or failure.
- Anything the purchaser must do in order to secure warranty performance, including paying any expenses.
- Steps to take and who to contact to get warranty services performed, including names, address, telephone, etc.
- The fact that a dispute settlement mechanism is available, if one has been set up, and requirements for using it before pursuing legal remedies.
- If words like "life" or "lifetime" are used, the life referred to must be disclosed.
- If an owner registration or similar card is used, the warrantor must make it clear if the return of the card is a condition of warranty coverage. If it is, the warranty must say so. If it is not, the warranty must disclose that fact and must indicate its purpose, such as "marketing research" or "product safety registration."

All warranties must include one of the following statements about express and implied warranties:

---

* Call For Comment: Warranties, Federal Trade Commission.

This warranty gives you specific legal rights. You may also have implied warranty rights, including an implied warranty of merchantability which means that your product must be fit for the ordinary purposes for which such goods are used. In the event of a problem with warranty service or performance, you may be able to go to a small claims court, a State court, or a Federal district court.

This warranty gives you specific legal rights. You also have implied warranty rights. In the event of a problem with warranty service or performance, you may be able to go to a small claims court, a State court, or a Federal district court.

Large or outstanding type must be used:

- To warn consumers if limits are placed or implied warranty rights and all conditions on relief for damages.
- To name any state with laws that make such modifications unenforceable.

The warrantor must:

- Supply sellers with materials they need to see that consumers can compare warranty terms before making purchase decisions.
- Upon request, provide prospective consumers with copies of any warranties requested.
- For products costing over $5, disclose clearly and conspicuously this statement: "The retailer has a copy of the complete warranty on this product. Ask to see it."
- In addition, for products costing over $10, disclose clearly and conspicuously the designations "full-warranty" or "limited" warranty.

These designations must appear on the principal display panel of the product container and on the product itself, by means of a tag, sticker, or other attachment.

In the store, the seller must not obscure or remove any warranty information attached to a consumer product. The seller must make an indexed binder available to shoppers in each department. The binder must contain up-to-date copies of each warranty for the products sold there (even if this forces the retailer to request copies from the warrantor). Each binder cover must say: "You may obtain a copy of any of the warranties contained in this book from the warrantor."

In catalogs and in mail order materials where any warranted product is offered for sale, the seller must:

- Designate whether the warranty is full or limited.
- Offer the written warranty free, and state where to request it.
- Follow up by providing a copy of any written warranty requested.

Sales made from door to door on any product covered by a written warranty, the salesman must give the consumer a copy of the warranty before making a sale. Consumers may keep the warranties even if they don't buy the product.

The law also provides for dispute settlement mechanisms. In December 1975, the FTC issued rules designed to better equip consumers to make wise buying decisions.

The rules, effective January 1, 1977, require warrantors to make available to retailers materials such as tags, stickers, signs, and displays giving customers the information they need for comparative shopping.

Retailers have the option of selecting one of four means of making warranty information available to their customers. They may display warranties near products, maintain binders filled with warranty information, display products in packages with warranties on them, or display signs with general warranties on them.

The first two rules—those governing warrant items and presale availability of warranty information—went into effect December 31, 1976. The third rule—covering dispute settlement mechanisms—took effect July 4, 1976.

TEXTILES AND FURS The FTC's greatest concentration in halting false and misleading practices results from enforcement of special statutes requiring truthful labeling and advertising of woolens, furs, and textile fiber products. Here the FTC has a different role than under the FTC Act: it determines standards and actively polices them by inspection, whereas in its broader mission under the FTC Act to halt unfair and deceptive acts and practices in commerce, it performs a regulatory role and can be selective in choosing which matters have the greatest public interest.

The Bureau of Textiles and Furs was transferred to the Bureau of Consumer Protection in the realignment of the FTC in 1970.

The importance of the work in this area is understandable when you realize that more than 100 different industries make textile products. Sales run into billions of dollars, second only to food and shelter. Some 175,000 distributors in the fur business are subject to the Fur Products Labeling Act. The highly competitive conditions in the textile and fur industries make the inspector's job difficult. Both textiles and furs lend themselves to deception in quality or composition, which is hard for most buyers to detect. For example, the quality of a textile is hard to predict by the percentages of wool, reused wool, or man-made "miracle" fibers present in textile products. In the case of furs, deception may occur whether they have been tip dyed or otherwise treated to pass for more desirable fur from the same or even different animal. Foreign producers of textiles not familiar with U.S. requirements on labeling and invoicing have made the policing of competitive imports difficult.

RESTRAINT OF TRADE   The FTC has the power to enforce antitrust laws in areas of restraint of trade. Unfair or monopolistic practices of competition in commerce include the following:

1. Combinations or agreements of competitors to raise or otherwise control prices, tamper with the price structure or divide sales territories, or curtail competitors' sources of supply.

2. Restrictions by a seller on the freedom of independent consumers of his product to deal in competing products.

3. Payment of excessive prices for raw materials for the purpose and with the effect of eliminating weaker competitors dependent on the same source of supply.

4. Boycotts or combinations to force sellers into giving preferential treatment to some traders over their competitors.

5. Agreements among competitors to restrict exports or imports.

6. The knowing receipt of discriminatory allowances or unlawful payments by a consumer from his suppliers.

7. Inducing breach of contract between competitors and their consumers.

8. Secret bribery of buyers or other employees of consumers.

VOLUNTARY COMPLIANCE   The FTC's programs for the guidance of industries and individual businessmen are based on the assumptions that a great many violations result from ignorance. The Commission takes the position that a violation avoided is at least as much in the public interest as a violation halted.

The oldest of these programs is the Trade Practice Conference (TPC). This procedure was adopted to provide a particular industry with clear-cut rules on how the laws administered by the FTC apply to the special and to the general practices of that industry.

These rules do not have the force of law, but they do put the industry's members on notice that abiding by the rules is an excellent way to avoid punitive action by the Commission for a law violation. They also alert reputable members of the industry to the protection that the law affords them.

INDUSTRY GUIDES   A later procedure was developed to supplement the TPC method. This involves issuance of industry guides. They have a more limited scope but reach beyond a single industry. Guides are issued to clarify single-industry problems. Industry guides also contribute to public education.

ADVISORY OPINIONS   Until 1962, advice on the legality of proposed courses of action was made available to businessmen only by members of the FTC staff. Such advice was not binding on the Commission. Advice was sought only infrequently by business concerns that wanted something more definite than an educated guess before investing large sums of money. The commission decided to give formal advisory opinions that would, subject to reasonable conditions, be binding on the Commission. Whenever it is practicable to do so, the FTC will, in response to a request made in good faith, render its advisory opinion in advance of the propsed course of action, subject only to the right to reconsider its advice in the unlikely event that this would be necessary in the public interest.

TRADE REGULATION RULES   Another innovation designed to give businessmen clear-cut guidance on requirements of the law was the Commission's decision in 1962 to issue trade regulation rules. Such rules represent conclusions of the Commission after appropriate hearings as to the illegality of particular practices. Their formulation is accomplished in a more conspicuous way than are similar judgments in individual casework. When notice is published that the Commission intends to issue a trade regulation rule dealing with a particular practice, businessmen are not under the misapprehension that the rule will be binding only on somebody else. They will have an opportunity to present their views at hearings on the proposed rule, and they also know that, once it is issued, the Commission may rely on the rule to resolve any relevant issue.

Trade practice conference rules, industry guides, advisory opinions, and trade regulation rules are instruments provided to businessmen for keeping their own houses in order. In 1970, the guides and rules functions of the Bureau of Industry Guidance were moved to the Bureau of Consumer Protection.

ECONOMIC AND STATISTICAL STUDIES   The FTC also has the authority and the duty to explore economic problems in depth. It can demand and get information from corporations, compile, and analyze it, and make public the facts and the conclusions. The Commission undertakes studies at the direction of the President, Congress, or on its own initiative.

COMPLAINT HANDLING   How does a case start at the FTC? What happens to it along the way? Where does it end? It could begin with an individual or business that feels it has been treated unfairly.

Other sources are Congress, other federal, state, or local government agencies, trade associations, and the Commission acting on its own initiative. Applications or complaints are reviewed to determine whether they are in the public interest or are a probable violation of law and an investigation is begun. This may start with ordinary correspondence, by a demand on a corporation to file a special report, or by referring the case to one of FTC's field offices to be investigated firsthand by an attorney-investigator. Based on the additional information obtained, a decision is then made on whether (1) to close the case, (2) to handle the matter informally by obtaining from the person or company an assurance of discontinuance, or (3) to seek a formal cease-and-desist order.

If it is decided to issue a formal complaint, the case usually goes to the FTC's Division of Consent Orders where negotiations are conducted to settle the case by consent. If the individual or business contests the charges, the complaint is announced and public hearings are held. At the conclusion of these hearings, the FTC deliberates and soon thereafter publicly announces its decision, either to issue a cease-and-desist order or to dismiss some or all of the charges. After 60 days, the plaintiff must comply or appeal the decision to a U.S. Court of Appeals.

In making its judgments, the Commission takes no sides. The case stands or falls on the facts presented and the validity of the arguments presented.

Consumer Product Safety Commission

On October 27, 1972, President Nixon signed the Consumer Product Safety Act, creating an independent federal regulatory agency to protect consumers from unreasonable risk or injury from hazardous products. The agency is headed by five commissioners, each serving seven-year terms. They are appointed by the President and confirmed by the Senate and have the authority to set safety standards for consumer products and ban those products presenting undue risk of injury. The Act also established a 15-member Product Safety Advisory Council, which includes representatives of the business community, the consuming community, and federal, state, and local government agencies. The Commission administers all the work on flammable fabrics previously carried out by the Federal Trade Commission, the Department of Health, Education and Welfare, and the National Bureau of Standards (see Figure 11–2).

SCOPE OF THE CONSUMER PRODUCT SAFETY ACT

The Consumer Product Safety Act applies to all products produced or distributed for sale. It not only covers those products actually sold, but also includes products manufactured for lease or distributed to consumers without charge. Industrial products not normally used by

Figure 11-2 Organization of the Consumer Product Safety Commission.

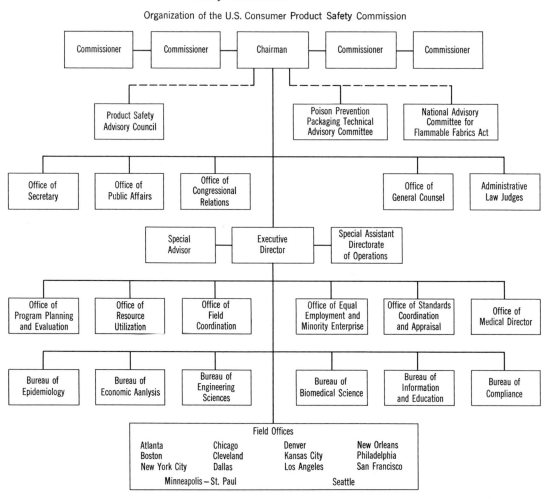

Organization of the U.S. Consumer Product Safety Commission

| Commissioner | Commissioner | Chairman | Commissioner | Commissioner |

Product Safety Advisory Council

Poison Prevention Packaging Technical Advisory Committee

National Advisory Committee for Flammable Fabrics Act

Office of Secretary — Office of Public Affairs — Office of Congressional Relations — Office of General Counsel — Administrative Law Judges

Special Advisor — Executive Director — Special Assistant Directorate of Operations

Office of Program Planning and Evaluation — Office of Resource Utilization — Office of Field Coordination — Office of Equal Employment and Minority Enterprise — Office of Standards Coordination and Appraisal — Office of Medical Director

Bureau of Epidemiology — Bureau of Economic Aanlysis — Bureau of Engineering Sciences — Bureau of Biomedical Science — Bureau of Information and Education — Bureau of Compliance

Field Offices

Atlanta	Chicago	Denver	New Orleans
Boston	Cleveland	Kansas City	Philadelphia
New York City	Dallas	Los Angeles	San Francisco
Minneapolis–St. Paul		Seattle	

426 *Performance of Textiles*

consumers are excluded from the scope of the new law. The Act also excludes a number of consumer products that are already regulated by other safety laws.

The Act's coverage extends to all aspects of the manufacture and marketing of a consumer product. In this regard, manufacturers, distributors, retailers, and private labelers are affected by the new law. The Act applies also to importers of consumer products.

DEVELOPING STANDARDS
Consumer product safety standards may be promulgated when the Commission finds that standards are necessary to prevent or reduce risk of injury through use of a product. It gives the commission broad information-gathering powers to help it determine whether or not to initiate the standard-setting process. The Commission must consider petitions to set safety standards from any interested person. This provision guarantees to consumers the right to participate in the Commission's processes, as well as bring suit should the Commission refuse to institute the requested rule-making proceedings. However, no suits may be brought under this provision until three years from the date the Act was enacted.

When the Commission determines that a safety standard for a consumer product is desirable it may either publish its intention to adopt an existing standard or invite offers to develop a new standard. It may develop standards on its own only if after inviting offers it does not receive acceptable offers within 30 days, if it finds that there already exists an adequate safety standard, or if the manufacturer of the product is the only one who offers a standard. Safety standards may include specifications for performance, composition, contents, design, construction, finish, packaging, and labeling. The Act makes clear that standards should be expressed in terms of performance where at at all possible.

Unless the Commission proposes the adoption of an already-existing standard, it must accept the offer of any technically competent group. The Act contains a provision for authorizing the Commission to contribute to the costs of developing the safety standard if it determines that its contribution will result in the development of a more satisfactory standard.

The Commission must publish a proposed safety rule within 210 days after publishing its development notice. If it finds that the product poses unreasonable risk of injury through use and that no feasible safety standard would adequately protect the public, it may order banning the product from sale or distribution in commerce

Within 60 days after publication of the proposed product safety rule, the Commission must act either to adopt or withdraw the proposal. The product safety rules are to be promulgated according to the rulemaking procedures set out in the Administrative Procedure Act. The legislation broadens these procedures somewhat by guaranteeing that all interested persons have an opportunity for oral as well as written presentation of their views.

The Act requires that the Commission declare—in any safety standard that it issues—findings concerning (1) the nature of the risk involved, (2) the number of products subject to the rule, (3) the public's need for the products involved, (4) the effect of the rule on the availability of the product, and (5) the effect of the rule on existing commercial practices. Furthermore, the Commission must prove that the rule is necessary to eliminate or reduce risk of injury, that the rule is in the public interest, and, in the case of a ban order, that no standard can be promulgated that will adequately protect the public.

The Commission also has the authority under the Act to prohibit manufacturers from stockpiling any product to which a rule applies in order to avoid the effect of the Product Safety Act.

Any person adversely affected by the actions of the Consumer Product Safety Commission may seek judicial review. The Commission's action in issuing a product safety rule will be affirmed only if the Commission has specifically made the findings specified above and these findings are incorporated into the body of the rule. The Commission's findings must be supported by substantial evidence on the record.

EMERGENCY POWERS

The Act gives the Commission emergency power to deal with products posing unreasonable risk of personal injury or death through use. Should the Commission find that the product is an imminently hazardous one, it may bring an action in the U.S. District Court having jurisdiction in which the product is located to seize and condemn the product and take whatever other action is appropriate to protect the public adequately.

This action may be taken even though there may be a safety rule applicable to the product or the time needed to develop such a rule. The Act does require that after the Commission takes emergency action, it must initiate proceedings to determine whether a safety standard will remove the hazard.

CERTIFICATION OF CONFORMANCE

Under the Act, manufacturers and private labelers must provide to their distributors or retailers certificates specifying applicable standards and affirming the product's conformance to those standards, stating the name of the manufacturer and place of manufacture. If the original shipment is broken up for delivery to more than one retailer, copies of the certificate must be provided to those parties within the distribution chain.

In the case of a product with more than one manufacturer or private labeler, the Commission may issue appropriate rules designating the person responsible for issuing the certificate.

The Commission may also promulgate rules dealing with the labeling of any consumer products, including products not subject to a safety rule. The Act gives the Commission authority to require that consumer products bear labels identifying the manufacturer or private labeler, and the date and place of manufacture. The label would also have to spell out the provisions of any applicable standard and certify that the product meets these standards. The Commission may permit this information to be in code as long as the code can be translated to interested persons.

The Commission may require that it be notified of a manufacturer's intent to market a new consumer product. This does not mean that in giving the Commission this authority, it was the intent of Congress to require premarket clearance by the Commission. Instead, this provision was included as a means of keeping the Commission informed of new products offered to consumers so that it can take the appropriate action in the case of hazardous products. This information is also necessary for the Commission to determine whether it is desirable to begin proceedings to develop a safety standard.

CORRECTING PRODUCT FAILURE

The Act clearly sets forth the seller's duty to inform the Commission should a product fail to comply with an applicable standard or pose a substantial hazard. If, after a formal hearing, the Commission determines that the product does present a hazard, it may order that notice of this fact be given to the public and that the manufacturer, distributor, or seller take remedial action. The maker or seller may then repair or change the product to bring it into conformity with the applicable standard, replace the product with a nondefective product, or refund the purchase price. However, before remedial action is taken, the plan of remedy must be submitted to the Commission for approval.

UNLAWFUL ACTS AND PENALTIES

It is unlawful for any person to manufacture for sale, offer for sale, distribute in commerce, or import any consumer product that is not in conformity with an applicable safety standard or that has been banned by the Commission. The broad language of this provision insures that the Act will reach each aspect of the manufacture and marketing of a product.

The Act makes it unlawful to refuse the Commission access to records or fail to furnish information and technical data as required by various sections of the law. The Act also provides for inspection of the premises by the Commission. It is unlawful to fail to provide a certificate of conformance or to falsify such a certificate. It is unlawful to fail to comply with a remedial order pertaining to notification of nonconforming products and repair, replacement, or refund. Finally, the Act makes the failure to comply with the antistockpiling provisions unlawful.

The Act subjects anyone committing any of the above prohibited acts to civil penalties of up to $2000 for each violation with a maximum penalty of $500,000 for any related series of violations. The Act also includes provisions for criminal sanctions including fines of not more than $50,000 and imprisonment for not more than one year. In addition to the civil and criminal sanctions, the Commission may enjoin the distribution in commerce of any product failing to meet the requirements of the applicable safety order. Also included are provisions that allow any interested party to sue for the enforcement of a safety standard. Finally, any person injured as a result of a violation of a safety standard may sue in the federal courts for damages.

STATE VERSUS FEDERAL STANDARDS

When a consumer product safety standard has been promulgated under this Act, no state may establish or allow to continue in effect any standard or regulation designed to deal with the same risk, unless the state standard is identical to the federal standard. The Commission may, however, after notice and full opportunity for the oral presentation of views by interested parties, grant an exemption to this provision if it finds that compelling local conditions require a higher level of performance than that imposed by the federal standards and that such an exemption will not unduly burden interstate commerce.

APPLICATION TO TEXTILES

The Consumer Product Safety Act gives broad powers to the Commission. This agency has also been given the responsibility for all aspects of the Flammable Fabrics Act. (See Appendix A for a partial list of Consumer Product Safety Commission offices.)

However, in October 1975, the House of Representatives passed legislation requiring the Consumer Product Safety Commission to submit its flammability safety standards to Congress for review. Congress then has 30 days to pass a resolution if it objects to the safety standard.

The amendment provides that "the commission shall transmit to Congress each consumer safety standard promulgated under this act and each rule, regulation and order promulgated by the committee."

Earlier the House approved another amendment to H.R. 6844, the Consumer Product Safety Improvements Act of 1975, that provides that representatives of the Natural Fiber Manufacturers Association and the Man-made Fiber Producer Association, as well as manufacturers of apparel and interior furnishings, must be members on the Flammable Fabrics Advisory Board.

General Services Administration

Federal specifications and standards are promulgated by the Standardization Division, Federal Supply Service, General Services Administration. These documents indicate physical and chemical requirements and applicable test methods for controlling the quality of textile and apparel items used by two or more federal agencies. This does not include items considered to be strictly military or special service items. These documents are mandatory for use by all federal agencies and are available to the public.

DEPARTMENTAL SPECIFICATIONS AND STANDARDS

Departmental specifications and standards for textile and apparel items are developed and issued by individual federal agencies primarily for their own use, but may also be used by other agencies. (A list of Federal Information Centers is given in Appendix H.)

THE COURTS
Small Claims Courts

When direct negotiation or arbitration fails, the only recourse a consumer has for claims of product failure is due process of law. However, in many cases the sum of settlement is relatively small and involves time and costly lawyer's fees necessary for a court procedure.

Most states have a small claims court to settle such disputes, but these courts are not necessarily existent in all towns and cities. The small claims procedure for settling a claim is simple and informal. A lawyer is unnecessary and, in some courts, is not allowed. Court fees are low, usually ranging from $3 to $15.

A trial date is usually set within 10 days or two weeks after a claim is filed, and seldom more than a month.

Court procedures vary from state to state, but the maximum claim limit across the country in a small claims court ranges from $100 to $1000. Some go as high as $3500. The average limit in 100 cities surveyed recently was found to be $350.

A small claims court can only be used to sue for money—not for the furnishing of goods or services, the return of property, or negligence unless a monetary value can be attached to these claims.

Although states have a legal age minimum of 18 or 21 years for filing suit in a small claims court, a consumer under the legal age requirement may file suit through an adult—a parent, a relative, or a friend who must also appear at the trial.

If the claimant cannot appear, regardless of age, power of attorney to sue or act can be delegated to an adult.

PROCEDURE FOR SMALL CLAIMS CASES

First, the court in the court district where the person or firm being sued resides can be located by checking the telephone directory under local, county, or state governments. Small claims courts are often a part of other courts or their functions may be filled by the local justice of the peace.

Second, it should be ascertained whether the court can handle this type of claim and whether it has jurisdiction over the party to be sued.

If the claim is considered appropriate, a modest court fee to cover the cost of the complaint and the summons will be charged to the claimant. A form requiring the claimant's name and address, the name and address of the defendant, and the amount claimed in the suit must be filled out accurately.

Once the complaint is filed, the claimant will be informed when to appear for trial. The court sends a summons to the defendant with information as to date, time, place of hearing, and details of the suit. In the event the defendant offers to settle out of court to the satisfaction of the claimant, the court should be notified of such action.

The claimant should collect and assemble bills of sale, invoices, receipts, and other evidence to substantiate the claim. Any available corroborating witnesses should be contacted for court appearance. Should a witness refuse to appear in court, a subpoena may be issued by the court clerk insuring that witness' testimony. A written testimony may be submitted by a witness unable to appear in court.

If an expert's testimony is desired, an inquiry as to the fee charged for said testimony should be obtained.

Observation of a small claims court procedure before appearance in court by a claimant can be helpful.

JUDGE OR ARBITRATOR

Two options are offered: the case may be heard before a judge or an arbitrator. An arbitrator is an experienced, private lawyer who volunteers his services.

The disadvantage in arbitration is that there is no recourse to appeal. This may not be too serious since appealing a judge's decision can be very expensive.

After each side has presented its evidence, a decision may be made immediately or several days later. A call to the clerk of the court will ascertain who won and the amount of the settlement.

The court may award less than the amount of the suit. Even if the claimant wins, how can collection be made?

In some instances, the winner in a court case cannot collect because the party sued may be unwilling to pay, has gone out of business, or is broke and has claimed bankruptcy. If the defendant is able to pay but refuses, collection is possible with the help of a local government official or the claimant can have the court place a lien on the bank account or property of the defendant. This latter measure is not easily accomplished.

There is a growing movement in many states for reforming the small claims court procedures by instituting committees in courts of justice of state houses of delegates and state senates.

OTHER GOVERNMENT INVOLVEMENT WITH TEXTILE AND APPAREL INDUSTRIES

Other government agencies that interrelate with the textile and apparel industries and affect the consumer indirectly are the Senate Sub-Committee on Trade Problems; the Office of Special Representation for Trade Negotiations, Executive Office of the President; the Department of State, Bureau of Economic Affairs, Fibers and Textile Division; the U.S. Tariff Commission, Textile Division; and the Bureau of Customs, Department of the Treasury. Any student majoring in textiles should become aware of the functions and workings of government in the above-mentioned areas because they do affect the textile industry.

State Consumer Protection Offices

Forty-six states, the Virgin Islands, and the Commonwealth of Puerto Rico now have consumer offices. The responsibilities and powers of each office varies from advisory only to actual enforcement of consumer protection laws. Within each state, responsibility for the consumer office may be in one or several branches of the government. A list of these offices are given in Appendix H. In addition to these state offices, many cities and counties have consumer offices with varying responsibilities and power.

12

Business-Industry, Professional-Technical Programs Related to Textiles and the Consumer

435

Consumerism is the word of the decade. For some businesses it means harassment and economic hardship. For others, it is a challenge. However you see it, it cannot be ignored. It is a fact of business life.

President Nixon's consumer advisor charged that our nation is riddled with "consumer illiteracy" of disastrous proportion and that little is being done to train the public in the art of buying.

"National Goals and Guidelines for Research in Home Economics," the report of a study sponsored by the Association of Administrators of Home Economics, outlines the situation in this way:

> Advances of the fiber, textile and textile-related industries in the past 20 years have provided today's consumer with an almost infinite variety of choices. Expansion and development in these fields have been accomplished by marked increases in industry-based research.
>
> Because of the competitiveness within the industry and the loose coordination among industries (producers and suppliers of fiber, fabrics, clothing and furnishings) the consumer often encounters problems he cannot solve.
>
> One aspect of the problem is communication between the consumer and the industry. Another is the need for objective evaluation of end use performance, a service which frequently receives minimal attention from industry. Research in both these areas can increase consumer satisfaction with textiles and textile products and can complement and supplement industrial research.

H. Bruce Palmer, president of the Council of Better Business Bureaus also stated the need for communication:

> Business is an economic institution made up of people who are consumers. In fact, each of us is both consumer and producer. Any attempt to deal with a person as a consumer or producer in isolation widens the fissure between business and people to a dangerous proportion.

This chapter explains how communication is carried on among civic and business groups, among scientific, trade, and manufacturers' associations, and among commercial, retail, and magazine laboratory programs that affect the consumer directly or indirectly. The aim is to obtain better performance of clothing and household textiles. Many professional groups spend time, money, and effort to bridge the gap of communication between business, industry, and the consumer. This chain of communication is long and complex as shown in Figure 12–1.

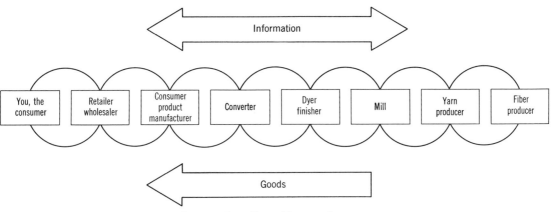

Figure 12-1 From fiber producer to you.

CIVIC OR BUSINESS GROUPS

Council of Better Business Bureaus, Inc. (CBBB)

In August 1970, the Council of Better Business Bureaus, Inc., a national organization, was formed by consolidating the National Better Business Bureau and the Association of Better Business Bureaus International. Its dual mission is to become an effective national, self-regulatory force for private enterprise and to demonstrate a sincere and visible concern for consumers.

Offices of the CBBB are maintained in New York City and in Washington, D.C. The Executive Office in New York maintains contact with major corporations, advertising agencies, and the media. National activities, including broad consumer education programs and voluntary self-regulation of national advertising, are administered in this office. The Operations Office in Washington coordinates the activities of the 150 Better Business Bureaus. It develops and administers programs and procedures aimed at improving and standardizing the operations of member bureaus and handles national casework, including consumer inquiries, complaints, and trade practice codes. The Washington office also works closely with government regulatory agencies and trade associations and keeps abreast of government activities of concern to consumers and business.

The Council established 14 major goals for the 1970s to fulfill its responsibility to consumers and business.

1. Help Better Business Bureaus improve and expand their services to consumers.

2. Standardize operating procedures for bureaus.

3. Increase the number of bureaus and expand geographical areas each bureau can serve effectively.

437   *Business-Industry Professional Programs*

4. Establish specific qualifications for bureau membership.

5. Assist bureaus to intensify monitoring, correction, or elimination of misleading local advertising.

6. Establishing a mechanism for voluntary self-regulation of national advertising.

7. Tie bureaus into the Consumer Information Data Bank.

8. Develop and expand consumer education programs.

9. Develop greater consumer participation in BBB activities.

10. Increase the number of consumer councils and panels.

11. Establish a National Consumer Information Resource Center.

12. Improve channels of communication between consumers and national business.

13. Expand and develop national trade practice programs and establish consumer arbitration panels.

14. Develop a creative and aggressive advertising and public relations program.

LOCAL BETTER BUSINESS BUREAUS (BBB)

The backbone of the Council is the 150 Better Business Bureau members located throughout the country and abroad. The BBB movement began in 1912 with "Vigilance Committees for Truth in Advertising" in local advertising clubs. The committees later became bureaus and expanded into the broader sphere of monitoring, investigating and correcting misleading and deceptive advertising and business practices.

Better Business Bureaus are self-regulatory agencies that seek the voluntary cooperation of business. When illegal practices are uncovered, and the business offender refuses to cooperate with the Bureau, the matter is referred to the appropriate law-enforcement agency. Frequently, the Bureau will appear in such cases to testify against the offender. Also, bureaus have close working relationships with governmental agencies, such as the Federal Trade Commission, consumer protection agencies, and state attorneys general.

BBBs are organized as nonprofit corporations financed entirely by membership dues or subscriptions paid by responsible business and professional firms in the community. Reputable firms are solicited for membership to maintain and expand services provided by the BBB.

The BBB helps consumers directly by providing information about a company before the consumer does business with it, helping to resolve a complaint there might be against a firm, providing good consumer information to help make intelligent buying decisions, and offering consumer arbitration to resolve disputes between buyer and seller.

In addition, the Bureau provides assistance by (1) fostering ethical advertising and selling practices, (2) monitoring advertising and selling practices, (3) alerting consumers to bad business and advertising practices when the business in question will not cooperate with the BBB to eliminate the abuse, (4) distributing consumer information through radio, television and printed literature, (5) providing speakers for schools, civic groups and business organizations, and (6) providing the media with public information materials on consumer subjects.

An illustration of how the BBB works for the consumer is best exemplified by an actual case.

The BBB of New York warned retailers and consumers that "aluminum" stockings were being panned off by an unidentified salesman as runproof and that they were a fraud.

The BBB was first notified about the matter by a store manager who put out $30 for more than a dozen packages of the stockings, which the salesman said had been made in Switzerland as "aluminized perflon thread," after the salesman convinced him they were runproof by running a knife blade over them.

The manager explained that he found out the very next day that the stockings were not runproof when the free pair his wife had gotten from the salesman developed a run as soon as she put them on. The packages that were later sold over the counter were promptly returned by consumers who complained that they were of incredibly bad quality.

The BBB received other complaints from small retailers saying they had been victimized in the same manner.

The BBB said that the labeling on the package appeared to be a violation of the Textile Fiber Products Identification Act. The package did not state where the stockings were made nor did it disclose the fiber content. It merely stated: "Befrelung . . . Aluminum, Perflon" and underneath, the words "Unzerbrechlich . . . elegant, feinmaschig, haltbar," meaning "unbreakable, elegant, fine mesh, durable."

All efforts to track down the salesman were unsuccessful, but the BBB did issue a warning to retailers and consumers.

Arbitration Programs

Many BBBs have established consumer arbitration programs as a means of voluntarily resolving business and consumer disputes. The bureaus have attempted to resolve such disputes by mediation. This method is usually successful, and the majority of disputes continue to be settled in this manner. In cases where resolution is not achieved through mediation, arbitration can be used. In the past, the consumer's only alternative to mediation was the courts, which takes time and money. Arbitration can quickly resolve a problem, and it is, of course, legally binding.

Arbitration is the process whereby two or more parties in disagreement submit their dispute to an impartial third party or panel for a decision. The participating parties must agree in advance, in writing, to abide by the decision of the arbitrator. Arbitration is legally binding and cannot be appealed through the courts, except in rare cases where bias, corruption, or prejudice on the part of the arbitrator can be proven (see Figure 12–2).

Figure 12-2

HOW ARBITRATION WORKS

1 THE COMPLAINT
Customer takes complaint to businessman—only if this fails does he go to the Better Business Bureau

Customer   Businessman

2 BETTER BUSINESS BUREAU
BBB tries to resolve cases informally—if not, arbitration is offered

Customer   BBB   Businessman

3 SUBMISSION AGREEMENT
Parties sign binding agreements to arbitrate agreed issues in dispute and submit to the BBB arbitration program.

Customer   BBB   Businessman

4 CHOOSING AN ARBITRATOR
The parties involved in the dispute will select a single arbitrator from a pool of volunteers. The volunteers will be attorneys from the Baton Rouge Bar Association who have agreed to assist the BBB with this important program.

5 INSPECTION
If appropriate, an inspection of the product, repair job or construction site is conducted with the BBB furnishing technical expertise as needed.

BBB   Arbitrator   Expert
Customer   Businessman

6 THE PROCEEDINGS
Informal proceedings are before an arbitrator. Both parties may be represented, have witnesses and give supporting evidence.

BBB   Arbitrator
Customer   Businessman
Witnesses

7 THE AWARD
The decision may resolve all issues in favor of one party or it may be "split" between the parties. In most states, a court of law will enforce an award without rehearing the case.

Arbitrator
Customer   Businessman

Arbitration, as a concept, dates back many centuries. It has, of course, been used in labor negotiations and business contracts for many years, but it is only recently that it has been recognized as a very effective method for resolving buyer-seller disputes. Many BBBs around the country have been setting up arbitration programs to deal with complaints that cannot be resolved through their traditional mediation efforts. In many cities large segments of the business community have agreed to "precommit" to arbitration. This means they have consented to arbitrate any consumer complaint ever filed against them at a local BBB.

The advantages of such a program are many. The most obvious is the speed and efficiency factor. A case can be presented for arbitration, the hearing held, and an award handed down all within a period of weeks. Formal litigation can require far longer periods than this. Another significant factor is the expense involved. In most instances the arbitration proceedings will be conducted at no cost to the disputants, and even in cases where expenses might be involved, these charges are minimal. Additionally, arbitration is legally binding. The arbitrator's award marks the conclusion of the case.

Persons active in the consumer field have long felt the need for a fresh alternative. Many of the complaints received by the BBB fall into a so-called "gray area." In such instances, the source of dissatisfaction cannot easily be attributed to either the buyer or the seller, and often the adjustment possibilities are not easily discernible. The businessman may reply to the consumer promptly, reasonably, and in detail; however, the explanation and a particular adjustment may not satisfy him, and he might wish to pursue the matter further. Typical complaints that fall into this nebulous category include dry-cleaning disputes, particularly cases in which a garment has suffered damage and the cleaner maintains he followed the dry-cleaning labels, service complaints in which the consumer feels that excess work was done but the company feels this work was necessary in order to properly diagnose the problem, and appliance complaints involving the replacement of new parts that the consumer may question.

JOINT PROGRAMS OF ARBITRATION

In some communities the state or county Office of Consumer Affairs and the BBB have established a joint consumer arbitration program.

The role of the BBB and the Office of Consumer Affairs in these proceedings is solely administrative. The two offices suggest the arbitration alternative in appropriate cases only after normal complaint-handling efforts have been unsuccessful and the parties still disagree and seek further action. If the disputing parties desire to arbitrate, they must sign agreements in advance. These agreements outline the basic cause of conflict, specific background information, and a proposed settlement that would be acceptable to each participant. The parties also agree to be bound by the decision of the arbitrator. Upon receipt of these signed agreement forms, the Office of Consumer Affairs and the BBB send to each party an identical list of five potential arbitrators. The parties must strike out those names that are unacceptable to them and rate the remaining names in order of preference. The arbitrator is then selected from among the candidates both parties find mutually acceptable. Upon the appointment of the arbitrator, a date for the hearing is scheduled, at the convenience of participants. The arbitrator conducts the hearing according to the rules set up by the two offices and within a specific time-period renders a written award.

Arbitrators serve without pay. Their sole compensation is derived from the satisfaction of playing a major role in cementing solid business-consumer relations.

Some bureaus have established Consumer Affairs Councils, which offer a forum through which consumer needs and problems can be heard and acted on. The forum also provides an opportunity for the consumer to become informed and better educated as to his buying rights and his buying responsibilities. Members of a Consumer Affairs Council are members of consumer groups, low-income groups, civic organizations, communication media, press, radio and television, labor, professional groups, business, industry, and government, as well as educators and clergymen.

The BBB uses many specialized public information tools, such as pamphlets, newsletters, films, speakers' bureaus, posters, newspapers, radio and television, and educational literature. Some bureaus have purchased and equipped buses with all these tools and take the program into the low-income areas of the community.

CHAMBER OF COMMERCE OF THE UNITED STATES

Many communities have a local Chamber of Commerce. Perhaps the most valuable division of local chambers is the Ethics Division. This is particularly true in communities that do not have a BBB.

The local Chambers of Commerce of all communities cooperate with each other through their affiliation with the national U.S. Chamber of Commerce. Program guidance begins at the national level.

The U.S. Chamber of Commerce, backed by years of study by its Council on Trends and Perspectives and its Consumer Issues Committee, has made several important recommendations to the business community urging greater concern with the legitimate needs of the consumer. For example, in its report, "Business and the Consumer—A Program for the Seventies," the Chamber makes the following points:

- Private industry will need to become more sensitive to the public's changing value systems, and will have to give greater attention to the problems of the consumer.
- Private industry will need to create new research institutions and "early warning" mechanisms to identify and analyze potential consumer issues before they arise, so that more effective advance action can be taken.
- Consistent with past trends, higher performance levels and greater public scrutiny of business can be expected in the future.

The Chamber's Consumer Issues Committee sums up the situation in its "Business-Consumer Relations Code" (shown in the box),

---

BUSINESS-CONSUMER RELATIONS CODE

We Reaffirm the Responsibility of American Business to:

1. Protect the health and safety of consumers in the design and manufacture of products and the provision of consumer services. This includes action against harmful side effects on the quality of life and the environment arising from technological progress.

2. Utilize advancing technology to produce goods that meet high standards of quality at the lowest reasonable price.

3. Seek out the informed views of consumers and other groups to help assure customer satisfaction from the earliest stages of product planning.

4. Simplify, clarify and honor product warranties and guarantees.

5. Maximize the quality of product servicing and repairs and encourage their fair pricing.

---

6. Eliminate frauds and deceptions from the marketplace, setting as our goal not strict legality but honesty in all transactions.

7. Ensure that sales personnel are familiar with product capabilities and limitations and that they fully respond to consumer needs for such information.

8. Provide consumers with objective information about products, services and the workings of the marketplace by utilizing appropriate channels of communication, including programs of consumer education.

9. Facilitate sound value comparisons across the widest possible range and choice of products.

10. Provide effective channels for receiving and acting on consumer complaints and suggestions, utilizing the resources of associations, chambers of commerce, better business bureaus, recognized consumer groups, individual companies and other appropriate bodies.

Adopted by the Chamber of Commerce of the United States, February 26, 1970.

which establishes a set of rules and standards on which a more positive relationship between business and consumers can be based.

In addition to its other activities, the national Chamber of Commerce is endeavoring to develop meaningful programs to increase the understanding and cooperation between the consumer and business on the local community level. To this end, it has issued a challenge to its 2700 local chapters in the form of a booklet entitled, "Let's Revitalize Business-Consumer Relations!"

In the booklet, the need for positive action is clearly recognized. It is pointed out that while consumers are reasonably well satisfied with the products and services of American business by and large, there has been an increasing tide of consumer complaints and questions in recent years.

Government, consumer organizations, labor unions, and others may exploit this discontent in ways that produce antibusiness reactions. This situation requires more effective communications with consumers, which the Chamber's Executive Advisory Panel believes can be done most successfully by local Chambers of Commerce.

The national Chamber of Commerce is also recommending a more active support for the BBBs in their efforts to create a complaint mechanism and to effect greater communication by bringing the disputing parties face to face. In connection with expanding business-consumer dialogues, the national Chamber of Commerce is urging its individual branches to support—and enlist the support of—other interested parties in the community.

As a part of the Business-Consumer Relations Program, the Chamber published a "Consumer Conference Guide on Clothing." It is designed as a guide for local Chambers of Commerce who are interested in maintaining good relationships between consumers and business. Sometimes the local Chambers sponsor forums on textiles and clothing for the benefit of consumers, educators and business.

SCIENTIFIC ASSOCIATIONS
Development of Standards

The development of standards and the dissemination of technical information relating to textiles are the major services of scientific associations for the consumer.

A standard may be thought of as a set of "rules of the game," for activities relating to social, religious, educational, technical, or any other feature of society. Some of the standards for social behavior may be legally enforced—for example, laws protecting life and property. Other social standards are generally adhered to by custom or common consent. These include requirements of table etiquette or rules for participants in sports and games, and many business practices that consumers have come to expect.

Technical or engineering standards set forth various practices or expectations in technical fields. They are designed to describe the characteristics of materials used in products, the performance that may be expected from products, and minimum levels of safety. Standard test methods tell how to measure the characteristics of materials and products and their performance and safety.

Just as with standards of social behavior, some technical standards are mandatory and can be legally enforced; others—the vast majority—are voluntary. For example, the standards governing flammability of certain fabric products, including rugs and children's sleepwear, are mandatory. On the other hand, although most manufacturers of appliances, such as irons, washers, and dryers, meet certain published standards, they are not legally required to do so.

Standards can benefit consumers by reducing costs, increasing product convenience and by specifying levels of safety and performance. Many products are designed to meet certain standards, but they are not always so labeled. For this reason the consumer is often unaware of the extent to which standardization affects him. For example, some manufacturers may follow the American National Standards Institute Standard L-22, Performance Requirements for Textile Fabrics, but this compliance may never be mentioned on a label or hangtag.

Federal law now requires that some products meet certain specified safety standards or they cannot be marketed within the United States. The measure of protection afforded by these mandatory safety standards (e.g., the Flammable Fabrics Act) accrues automatically to every purchaser.

Some safety standards are referenced in some laws, ordinances, or building codes and, therefore, are mandatory in some states and localities, but not in others. For example, some states ban the use of phosphate detergents.

Products that meet voluntary safety standards sometimes bear the mark of a certifying organization. For example, the symbol UL, that appears on most electrical appliances manufactured in the United States, indicates that the product complies with safety standards set by Underwriters' Laboratories, Inc.

Functional performance refers to a product's capacity to perform its intended purpose. Since safety aspects are normally defined in performance terms, the term "functional performance" is used to differentiate clearly between "safety performance" and design features.

Most standards for functional performance apply to matters of definition, test methods, and information disclosure; however, some have performance requirements based on standard test methods. Since suppliers sometimes make claims about the functional performance capabilities of the products they offer, these standards serve the purpose of giving such claims precise meaning, common verifiability, and recognized importance to assist the purchaser in choosing between competing products.

Functional performance for a variety of attributes that frequently bear on consumer satisfaction includes materials used in the product, design and construction, strength, energy supply and control, temperature, noise and vibrations, and convenience factors that do not directly affect the safety or proper operation of the product but do make it easier to use. How the American National Standards Institute establishes National Consensus Standards is shown in Figure 12–3.

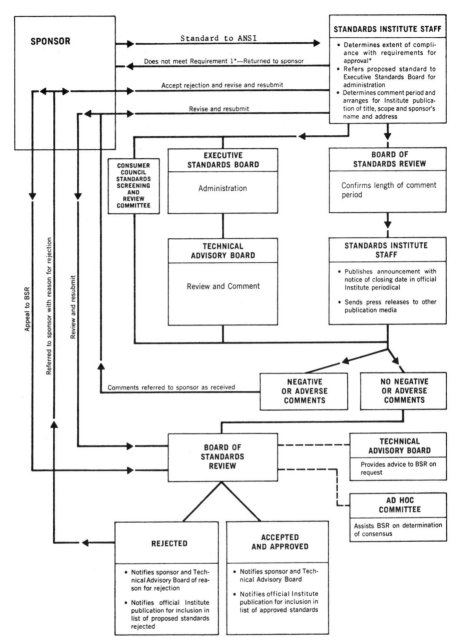

Figure 12-3 How the American National Standards Institute establishes national consensus standards. (Courtesy of American National Standards Institute)

American National Standards Institute (ANSI)

The American National Standards Institute (successor to the American Standards Association and the USA Standards Institute) is the coordinating organization for this nation's voluntary standards system. It is a federation of industrial, trade, technical, labor and professional organizations, government agencies, and consumer groups engaged in the development and promulgation of voluntary standards. ANSI is the clearinghouse and coordinator for more than 200 major organizations and government agencies that are involved in producing standards. It approves many of these as American National Standards. See Figure 12–4.

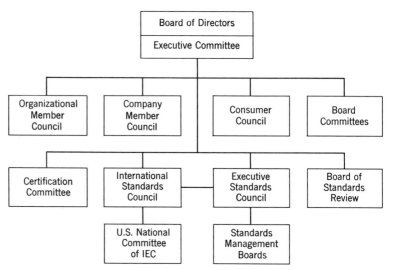

Figure 12-4 The Organization of the American Standards Institute. Courtesy of American National Standards Institute.

Board of Directors:	The governing and policy-making body of the Institute.
Executive Committee:	Acts for the Board of Directors between meetings of the Board.
Organizational Member Council and Company Member Council:	Ensure participation of their members in ANSI programs and provide a communication channel between their members and constituents and ANSI's Board on programs and policies of the Institute; help determine standards needs.
Consumer Council:	Responsible for consumer input to standards programs; ensures that standards meet the needs of consumers by reviewing and rating all applicable standards during approval

	process; also conducts consumer information programs.
Board Committees:	Help the Board of Directors fulfill its responsibilities; include committees on finance and goverment liaison and support.
Certification Committee:	Develops and operates programs leading to national accreditation of certification programs.
International Standards Council:	Responsible for technical and administrative policies and budget recommendations for ANSI's international activities.
Executive Standards Council:	Manages the standardization activities coordinated by ANSI—promulgates operating procedures; initiates standards projects; stimulates expeditious completion of standards work; also manages and coordinates U.S. participation in ISO technical work.
Board of Standards Review:	Approves standards as American National Standards and acts on withdrawal and reaffirmation when it finds that a consensus exists among those substantially concerned with the scope and provisions of the standards under consideration.
U.S. National Committee of IEC:	Responsible for effective participation in the work of IEC and for operation of the technical advisory groups that develop the U.S. position on international electrotechnical standards.
Standards Management Boards:	Assist the Executive Standards Council in carrying out its management and coordination functions for standards development in the discipline or homogeneous technical sphere in which the particular SMB operates.

The purpose of ANSI is to promote the use of national standards in the United States, to coordinate standards of development, and to avoid duplication of effort in standards writing. ANSI also serves as a clearinghouse for information on American and foreign standards and represents American interests in international standardization work. American national standards, approved by ANSI, are voluntary national standards, arrived at by common consent of manufacturers, distributors, retailers, consumers and other affected groups.

Technical standards come from a variety of sources. Many are written by more than 400 trade associations and professional societies that issue their own standards. Most manufacturers also have "in-house" standards that define the company's own processes and methods of operation. Typically, standards are drafted by subcommittees composed of technical experts who have particular knowledge of the product or item in question. They are then subject to review and approval at committee or higher level of the organization, where consumer opinion may be sought or welcome.

Standards under consideration for listing as American National Standards are announced in the biweekly *ANSI Standards Action,* and a period of eight weeks is allowed for comments, criticism, and suggestions. Consumers may make comments on the proposed standards.

By far, the largest number of standards that are submitted to ANSI for approval originate with the American Society for Testing and Materials.

Other major standards-writing bodies that contribute numerous standards for ANSI listing include the National Fire Protection Association, a voluntary nonprofit organization formed to promote the science and improve the methods of fire protection and prevention, and Underwriters' Laboratories, Inc.

CONSUMER REPRESENTATION IN STANDARDS MAKING

ANSI was the first national standards organization to recognize the importance of establishing a system to incorporate the consumer's point of view into its operation. In 1928 provisions were made for consumer participation in the development of standards for consumer products. In June 1967 new emphasis on consumer interaction was initiated when ANSI added a Consumer Council to its operating structure. This Council was assigned the overall responsibility of serving in "educational, advisory and coordinating capacities in order to maintain effective representation of consumers in activities of the Institute."

The Council ensures that the interests of consumers are adequately represented in national and international standardization activities. It is composed of individuals representing Institute membership, consumer organizations, and other qualified groups.

The primary responsibilities of the Consumer Council are to:

1. Provide the Board of Directors with guidance on behalf of consumers with regard to matters of policy, procedure, and planning.

2. Conduct studies and surveys to identify consumer needs for standardization of consumer goods and services.

3. Make recommendations for development of standards and certification programs important to the advancement of consumer interests.

4. Serve the Institute as a contact between the general public, government, and industry in the area of standards and certification programs for consumer goods and services.

5. Promote the education to consumers so that an awareness may be developed of the objectives, programs, and standards activities of the Institute that are directed toward the interests of consumers and require their support and encouragement for maximum effectiveness.

6. Assist in achieving effective and adequate consumer interest representation in standards development activities.

7. Submit to the nominating committee of the Board of Directors the names of candidates to represent the Consumer Council on the Board.

8. Provide a channel through which a member of the Institute may petition the Board of Directors or the Executive Standards Council for a review of any proposed or existing American National Standard.

To help realize the goals and objectives, the Consumer Council established several committees, composed of highly qualified individuals in the field of consumer affairs.

STANDARDS SCREENING AND REVIEW COMMITTEE

The Standards Screening and Review Committee screens and reviews all consumer product and service standards that are submitted to ANSI for approval. The task is accomplished with the aid of consumers from the private sector, testing laboratories, and representatives of government procurement agencies.

The Committee is composed of individual members of the Consumer Council representing consumer-oriented organizations, independent testing laboratories, and retail testing laboratories. The government contributes expertise from the General Services Administration, the Veterans Administration, and the National Bureau of Standards. Each group reviews and evaluates proposed American National Standards in accordance with well-established guidelines formulated by the Standards Screening and Review Committee.

CONSUMER EDUCATION COMMITTEE

A third very active ANSI group, the Consumer Education and Public Relations Committee, planned a series of regional standards briefing seminars for consumers. The seminars facilitated the participation of qualified, informed consumers in the writing of voluntary standards.

CERTIFIED ACCREDITATION PROGRAM

Another program that can benefit the consumer is ANSI's Accredited Certification Program. There is a growing importance for good certification programs as a mechanism of self-regulation by the private sector and government regulation for compliance purposes. A standard is not of much use unless it is used, and certification programs are a mechanism to assure the use of, and compliance with, the standard. A good certification program will promote good quality-assurance practices and identify the products, services or persons that meet the standards. The ANSI certification activity is designed to encourage and expedite good certification programs which meet the strict requirements of the ANSI Certification Procedures.

WHAT IS CERTIFICATION?

"Certification" is the procedure by which a product, service, or person becomes certified.

"Certified," as defined by ANSI, means "attested by the producer/certifier under procedures of a certification program as satisfying the requirements of the reference standard."

Certification has two main purposes. First, it identifies the product as meeting the specified standard, and second, it provides a mechanism for a "standards assurance" program to assure that the product conforms, and continues to conform, to the requirements of the standard.

The actual accreditation is done in three stages.

Stage 1 consists of a review of the standard by the ANSI Certification Committee to see whether it is appropriate for certification. Next, the basic legal and other documents that define the program are reviewed by the Certification Committee to see if they meet the criteria set forth in the procedures.

Stage 2 consists of the validation of the actual operation of the program by visiting and inspecting the work of the sponsor, the administrator, and the testing laboratories or inspection agencies to be sure that the actual program is the same as the written program. At this stage, if the program passes the initial qualification tests, ANSI, after approval by the Board of Directors, accredits the program.

Stage 3 consists of a monitoring operation where ANSI periodically checks to see that the program is operating satisfactorily during the term of the accreditation contract.

Following is a brief summary of the more important criteria the program must meet:

1. It must be based on a standard "Appropriate for certification"—either an American National Standard, an International Organization for Standardization (ISO) Standard or an International Electrotechnical Commission (IEC) recommendation.

2. The testing or inspection must be done by a competent, independent third party.

3. There must be a competent, experienced administrator (this can be a laboratory), a professional, certification administration organization, or a trade association or technical society.

4. The sponsor must own and completely control a certification mark that appears on the product or service agreement together with certain other required information.

5. There must be a comprehensive testing and inspection program to be sure all products or services with the mark do conform to the requirements of the standard.

6. There must be a fair and equitable disputes or appeals procedure available to the participants.

THE CANVASS METHOD GAINS CONSENSUS

ANSI procedures provide the means of development of standards. The most commonly used method is the "canvass method" in which a standard is prepared by an outside organization, a trade association, a technical society, or a government agency and submitted to ANSI for approval. On receipt of the standard, ANSI sends the sponsor a list of organizations to canvass to determine whether or not they think the standard is a good one. Included in these organizations are all the groups who might be interested, with special emphasis on consumer groups. These latter might include the American Home Economics Association, the National Safety Council, Consumers Union, various government agencies, independent laboratories, retail laboratories, and institutional consumer groups. After canvassing, the sponsor answers all objections and may change the standard to meet the objections. All the documentation is then sent to ANSI for approval.

ANSI then sends the standard to its Board of Standards Review (BSR) which serves as the final approval agency for ANSI standards. The BSR immediately sends the standard to the Consumer Council for review by the Standards Screening and Review Committee and lists it for public review in the ANSI semimonthly publication, *Standards Action*. After all the comments are in, and if everything is satisfactory, the standard is finally issued as an American National Standard.

This procedure develops what is called a "consensus" standard as it represents consensus of all concerned parties: consumers, government, public interest, and manufacturers.

ANSI STANDARD FOR TEXTILES

The standard for textiles, drawn up by the consensus method, is known as American National Standard Performance Requirements for Textile Fabrics, L-22–1968. The sponsoring organization was the National Retail Merchants Association. However, this organization relinquished the program and the Secretariat moved from the ANSI headquarters to the Fashion Institute of Technology in 1970.

In 1973 the original Committee L-22 of ANSI dissolved as an ANSI committee and became a subcommittee of the American Society for Testing and Materials (ASTM), which already had a committee, D-13, on textile materials.

The former ANSI committee is now designated ASTM Subcommittee D-13.56 on Fabric Performance Requirements. The reasoning was that as an ATSM subcommittee, Committee L-22 would have better information input and wider consensus of textile apparel industry members. Those closer to the development of standards would have a voice in their acceptance.

Standards passed by the ASTM subcommittee would be listed by L-22. The proposed scope of the ASTM Subcommittee D-13.56 is "To implement the scope of Committee D-13 with particular reference to performance required of consumer products in specific market areas. These apply to individual applications of fabrics for home sewing, wearing apparel, and home furnishings. The subcommittee will establish appropriate performance levels, based on existing methods or on methods to be developed, to assure reasonable consumer satisfaction and to supply bases for care labels or certification programs. Performance characteristics may include ecological considerations, safety, and care, in addition to other properties of concern to the consumer in each specific end use. The fabric performance requirement levels should be usable as guides for manufacturers, which include the producer of component parts as well as the end product, and for distributors who influence such manufacturers so that the final product as well as components can be appropriate in performance for their intended markets."

The American Society for Testing and Materials (ASTM)

The American Society for Testing and Materials is a federation of more than 100 standards-developing committees, each of which operates in its own area of interest, limited either by product category or by area of technology. ASTM in itself has no special technical expertise; this is provided by those who work within its system. ASTM provides the organizational experience and skills to make this work meaningful. The function of the central headquarters is to coordinate the work of the committees, to help them with administration and paper work, to stimulate and guide their work where possible, to see that their work is done in accordance with the rules, to publish their work under the ASTM logo, and to represent them in dealing with other components of the voluntary standardization system and other segments of society.

Some believe that the voluntary consensus system* is superior to unilateral standards development by government or by any other single interest, for the following reasons:

1. Standards are the primary means by which the benefits of technology are accommodated to our society. No single element of society alone, whether in industry or government, is competent to make this accommodation to keep pace with a rapidly changing technology to minimize the drag on innovation.

2. A standard for which all interests feel some responsibility is most likely to be kept up to date.

3. When all voices are heard in the standards forum, the resulting standard is most likely to be unbiased.

4. A balanced interest group is most likely to produce standards that are authoritative.

5. A standard written by representatives from all affected segments of society is more likely to be used.

The ASTM Charter and Bylaws are the basis of the Society's organization and operation. Management is centered in the Board of Directors, whose members are elected for three-year terms. The board is headed by the president, who serves for one year and who is assisted by two vice-presidents who serve two-year terms. Policy is executed and administered by a full-time managing director whose staff numbers about 150.

MEMBERSHIP AND COMMITTEES

There are two general types of membership. The member may be an individual or a nonprofit institution (educational, public library or a scientific, engineering, or technical society). The Sustaining Member may be an individual or a business, governmental, research or professional organization, trade association, or a separate facility of one of these.

* How USA Standards Are Created, The Management of Standards, June 1967, pp. 162–166.

The technical committees, of which there are nearly 120, are national, and in many cases international in their makeup. These semiautonomous groups generate the standards.

One of the most important phases of committee activity is voting and balloting on proposed standards and their revision. The very basis for the integrity of ASTM standards is that each standard has been considered and voted on by a balanced representation of all parties at interest, including producers and consumers.

Since 1918, the American Society for Testing and Materials has actively participated in and supported the work of the American National Standards Institute.

CERTIFICATION

The demand is increasing, especially in the area of ultimate consumer products, for certification and labeling programs that are designed to ensure the purchaser that the product he buys conforms to a cited standard. ASTM has no certification program. However, some manufacturers do label their products with an ASTM standard designation, thus implicitly certifying that the product conforms to that standard. But ASTM plays no part in that certification—it is the individual producer's responsibility.

INTERNATIONAL STANDARDIZATION

A major step taken by ASTM to foster international standardization was the decision, in 1963, to "take a leading position in the effort to establish a common system of measurement throughout the world." ASTM then embarked on a program to introduce modern metric [International System (SI)] units of measurement alongside U.S. customary units.

As more nations become industrialized, and the international level of material affluence rises, international trade multiplies. Just as national standards serve domestic commerce, so will international standards be indispensable in the growing trade across national boundaries.

The increasing importance of international standardization activity is signaled by the fact that a number of countries in Western Europe are adopting the standards of the International Organization for Standardization (ISO) as their national standards wherever possible. Many of the developing countries are also looking to ISO as their source for standards. There is every reason to believe that the trend toward international standardization will continue in the future and, therefore, there is every reason to hope that U.S. industrial and governmental support for this work will grow to meet the demand.

The interest in and support of international standardization work varies from one industry to another; therefore, U.S. representation in ISO work is strong in some areas and weak in others.

PUBLICATIONS The official publication of ASTM is the *Annual Book of ASTM Standards.* Today's knowledge of materials testing is reflected in this reference work containing nearly 5000 standards that have been developed by the ASTM technical committees.

Over the years, the society has made available a large number of fundamental scientific publications including technical reports and papers that have contributed significantly to the knowledge of the properties of materials and the means of evaluating these properties. Some of these publications have been sponsored by the technical committees, either as an outgrowth of organized committee work, or through the participation of individual authors invited to contribute research information required by the committees to serve as a basis for the development of standards.

The American Association of Textile Chemists and Colorists (AATCC)

The American Association of Textile Chemists and Colorists is a technical and scientific society of 10,000 members who live and work in the United States and 51 other countries. Some 300 organizations in the textile, chemical, and related industries help support the Association as corporate members.

The objectives of the AATCC have remained unchanged since its founding in 1921: "To promote increase of knowledge of the application of dyes and chemicals in the textile industry, to encourage in any practical way research work on chemical processes and materials of importance to the textile industry, and to establish for the members channels by which the interchange of professional knowledge among them may be increased."

TEST METHODS The Association is internationally recognized for its standard methods of testing dyed and chemically treated fibers and fabrics to measure and evaluate such performance characteristics as colorfastness to light and washing, durable press, soil release, shrinkage, water resistance, flammability, and the many other stresses to which textiles may be subjected.

Practically all the dyes, finishes, and many chemicals produced in the United States are controlled and checked by AATCC test methods. These test methods are a major factor in ensuring the marketability and satisfactory consumer performance of the billions of yards of textiles that find their way across the retail counters and into the hands of the consumer.

COOPERATIVE RELATIONSHIPS

AATCC maintains cooperative relationships with many other technical and scientific organizations and with departments and agencies of the federal government. At the international level, the Association participates in the International Organization for Standardization in an effort to bring about worldwide uniformity in testing procedures. The Society of Dyers and Colorists and AATCC collaborate in the publication of the Color Index.

Members receive AATCC's monthly journal, *Textile Chemist and Colorist,* a leading publication in the field of the chemistry of textiles and color and, in addition, *Products,* an annual index of textile chemical specialties and American-made dyes and pigments. The *Technical Manual,* containing AATCC test methods, a bibliography, committee rosters and reports, and the AATCC *Membership Directory* are also available to members.

American Association for Textile Technology (AATT)

The American Association for Textile Technology was founded in 1934 as a professional society for textile technologists. In recent years its role has been expanded to reflect the growing interaction between the worlds of textile technology and textile marketing.

In addition, AATT is expanding its activities to reflect the relationship between the textile industry and the consumer of its products. Through its various activities, members in the technical sector explore the role of marketing in textiles. Similarly, marketing people are given insight into the technical aspects of the products they sell.

AATT keeps closely in touch with all regulations and requirements of the U.S. government and other regulatory agencies and, when appropriate, holds meetings, seminars, and conferences dealing with such matters to keep the industry well informed.

The association's many members represent every segment of the textile industry from fiber producer to retailer.

AATT is composed of five regional chapters: Appalachian, Gulf States, New England, New York, and Piedmont, plus student chapters at eight major textile schools. Chapters have also been formed in colleges and schools of home economics at universities across the nation.

The objective of AATT is to encourage mutual understanding in the fields of textile technology and marketing, the advancement of textile technology in all its branches, cooperation with established facilities for textile education, and the interchange and dissemination of professional knowledge among its members and with other industry groups.

AATT conferences and publications cover such topics as soil release finishes, nonwovens, knitting equipment, water-repellent finishes, fusibles, home laundering, consumerism, fabric evaluation, living with government regulations, flammability, permanent-care labeling, fiber to fashion, the role of the fiber producer, industrial fabrics, and knit fabrics.

The AATT also published "A Guide For Garment Evaluation," to meet the increased need for garment evaluation, which followed the care-labeling rule.

The guide was edited by the AATT Council on Technology from original work done by the Consumer Services Laboratory of Celanese Fibers Marketing Company. It reflects the thinking of most of the commercial and retail laboratories in the country and can be used as a guide with a reasonable degree of confidence that the results produced by this system will be consistent with retail and consumer requirements.

The guide contains procedures for evaluating dimensional stability of fabric and sewing techniques to infrom the manufacturer of potential problems before going into acutal production. It contains the essential standards and procedures of a garment evaluation program, as well as supplementary tests which can only be conducted by a fully equipped textile-testing laboratory. Information on colorfastness to light and substantiation of claims for special finishes are an especially important part of the guide.

TEXTILE AND RETAIL TRADE ASSOCIATIONS

American Apparel Manufacturers Association (AAMA)

The American Apparel Manufacturers Association, composed of members from 43 states, the District of Columbia and Puerto Rico, and 12 foreign countries, represents six times more apparel production than any other trade organization in the world. Total AAMA membership consists of approximately 500 of the nation's leading apparel firms, who employ more than 500,000 people. More than 200 firms hold AAMA Associate Memberships. These companies are the leading suppliers of goods and services to the domestic apparel industry.

All activity of the American Apparel Manufacturers Association is directed at helping to keep its membership the most profitable and the most progressive apparel manufacturers in the world. This objective is attained by:

1. Promoting and safeguarding members' common business interests through close liaison with the executive and legislative departments of the government and with federal administrative and regulatory agencies.

2. Collecting, interpreting, and disseminating information judged to be of value to both the industry and individual businesses.

3. Conducting seminars for top management and production personnel throughout each year in strategic locations.

4. Conducting an annual "Panorama for Progress," the world's largest convention of products and services utilized in the apparel manufacturing industry.

AAMA publishes a wide variety of special studies, reports, booklets, technical aids, and newsletters covering the many facets of management, production, sales, and distribution in the apparel field.

Emphasis is placed on AAMA's "Service Through Leadership" program, which draws the outstanding professional knowledge and experience of more than 500 apparel executives into service on the Association's 17 standing committees.

The AAMA has been very active in consumer interests. It has a Consumer Affairs Committee that is guided by some of the industry's outstanding executives. The function of this committee is to cooperate with industry, consumer, or governmental representatives in the development and implementation of programs designed to meet demonstrated consumer needs involving the apparel industry.

The Association's Material Quality Committee has a number of consumer-related functions among its objectives, for example, to recommend acceptable standard test methods based on end use and to endorse or suggest changes in such standards, to develop means of assuring that standards and specifications, as agreed to by buyer and seller, are met, and to analyze and evaluate material innovations.

This committee's consumer-industry oriented activities at present include a review of the American National Standards Institute's new L-22 Committee report on "Performance Requirements for Textile Fabrics," a joint project with the Bureau of Standards and the Apparel Research Federation (ARF) to review the recent publication by the Bureau and ARF of their booklet, *Evaluation of Apparel Materials and Components,* the development of recommendations concerning current fabric defect grading systems, including an evaluation of the "Four Point Grading System," and the determination of minimum standards on innovations in fabrics now coming out of the mills, such as knitwear for men's slacks.

AAMA formerly provided leadership, legal advice, and funds to the Apparel Research Foundation. However, the Foundation acted totally independent of AAMA. In 1972, ARF was abandoned because of lack of funds. Some of its programs continue to function under the AAMA's Apparel Research Committee.

Among one of the ARF projects was a survey of consumer satisfaction with apparel products that utilized in-depth consumer interviews. It was called the APL's (Apparel Performance Level Standards) program. This project continues under a subcommittee of the Material Quality Committee of AAMA.

AAMA was involved also in the formation of the President's Industry Advisory Committee on Textile Information. This interagency committee was established by the President primarily as a result of a meeting instigated by AAMA with related supplier and retail organizations. This Committee subsequently developed a care labeling guide for the textile industry, which was accepted by the Special Assistant to the President for Consumer Affairs and was called a landmark of voluntary interindustry cooperation to help meet a consumer need.

This interindustry committee is now known as the "Textile Industry Advisory Committee on Consumer Interest." As part of its constant effort to keep an open line to consumer reactions, AAMA has acted as a liaison for its members and consumers who have complaints on everything from zippers and buttons to sizing and styles. They have passed these complaints along to their manufacturer members. The Association is represented on the Consumer Affairs Committee of the Chamber of Commerce of the United States.

PROJECT SAFE   Project SAFE (Safe Apparel For Everyone) was launched by the American Apparel Manufacturers Association in 1971 as the apparel industry began to feel the impact of Federal regulations for flammability of children's sleepwear. AAMA has been working with consumer groups, members of the textile industry, government agencies, and AAMA member companies to create an understanding of the implications of the Flammable Fabrics Act and how the apparel-textile industry is meeting its regulations.

Project SAFE functions in five areas: interindustry efforts, government relations, education and public relations, legal liaison, and technical and research through the efforts of the nine subcommittees of the AAMA's Apparel Products Flammability Committee. Each aspect of the flammability regulations has broad effects on many segments of the industry.

Project SAFE achievements include encouragement of the formation of an Inter-Association Committee on Consumerism, production of a comprehensive Fact Sheet on Flammability, creation of a monthly *SAFE Report* and *SAFE Abstract* to advise AAMA members and others about legal and technical aspects of the flammability issue, initiation of research studies on fabric and garment flammability, consultation with the National Bureau of Standards on testing methods, and development of cooperation and communication with the U.S. Consumer Product Safety Commission in regard to administration of the Flammable Fabrics Act. Project SAFE will also continue its work in creating fabric flammability test methods and standards that are more realistic than those existing now in relation to actual safety hazards. The American Society for Testing and Materials is reviewing a new test concept developed by a Project SAFE committee.

American Textile Manufacturers Institute, Inc. (ATMI)

The American Textile Manufacturers Institute is the national trade association for the man-made, cotton, wool, and silk segments of the American textile industry. It exists because the industry's top management realizes the need for an effective organization that enables individual textile companies to approach their problems on an industrywide, national basis. It represents virtually all segments of the industry, including spinning, throwing, weaving, knitting, finishing, and marketing. ATMI started (in 1949) with a series of mergers of the American Cotton Manufacturing Association (with members located primarily in the south) and the Cotton Textile Institue (with members located primarily in the north). In 1958, ATMI consolidated with the National Federation of Textiles, bringing in the man-made fibers and silk industries, followed by consolidations with the Association of Cotton Textile Merchants of New York in 1964, the National Association of Finishers of Textile Fabrics in 1965, and finally with the National Association of Wool Manufacturers in 1971. ATMI is the industry's primary spokesman with the legislative and administrative branches of the federal government. ATMI's activities also range into such fields as public relations, international relations, economic information, education, marketing, and many more. To carry out its program, ATMI maintains offices in New York City, Washington, D.C., and Charlotte, North Carolina.

CONSUMER AFFAIRS COMMITTEE

The Consumer Affairs Committee concerns itself with the broad ramifications of the consumer movement and its effect on textile marketing. This committee has become most active on subjects such as packaging and labeling, warranties and guarantees, and flammability.

PUBLIC RELATIONS

AMTI's Public Relations Division provides a communications link between the textile industry and the American public. The program:

1. Includes conferences between industry leaders and editorial managements of important publications.
2. Produces educational filmstrips and motion pictures.

3. Creates and distributes taped public service messages to radio stations.

4. Prepares and distributes news releases.

5. Provides information on the industry to thousands of teachers and students.

6. Builds recognition for textiles through advertising campaigns in several publications.

7. Conducts an industry tour for writers or broadcasters.

8. Arranges for interviews between journalists and industry people.

9. Counsels and assists individual companies on public relations problems and activities.

10. Writes and distributes several pamphlets or booklets about industry problems or achievements.

Public relations develops programs to obtain recognition for industry achievements in areas like research, product development, environmental preservation, corporate philanthropy, and socio-economic importance of the industry.

TECHNICAL SERVICES AND EDUCATION

ATMI's technical services activities are involved with matters that are of common interest to all segments of the industry. Projects and studies in this area form a broad range that covers waste-water treatment, industrial noise, data processing, research, and other technical matters.

Generally, all technical services fall within the objectives of three committees: Research and Technical Services, Education, and Data Processing.

National Retail Merchants Association (NRMA)

The National Retail Merchants Association has a diversified membership that is composed of department stores, specialty stores, mass merchandisers, chains, and independents. More than 1000 retail executives set NRMA policy, give direction to its professional staff, and serve as voluntary consultants to the membership.

NRMA provides its membership with (1) counsel and assistance on problems in every job function in retailing, whether those functions are handled by personnel in a vast merchandising complex or one person in a single store, (2) provides a forum for the interchange of new ideas, departures from traditional operating methods, advanced technical, control, marketing, and human relations information, and (3) conducts major studies charting and appraising retailing's ever-changing directions. Its publications provide key information on virtually every aspect of speciality and department store management and operation.

The range of NRMA's activities and services is indicated by its boards, groups, and committees, the Committee on Consumer Affairs being one of the most important.

Stores, NRMA's magazine, goes to every member every month and gives retailing counsel. During the course of each year, thousands of retail executives participate in NRMA programs scheduled in more than a dozen cities throughout the country.

NRMA's annual convention brings merchant leaders together to share success techniques. At a time when the volume and diversity of legislation and regulations affecting retailing are at an all-time high, NRMA is an effective and respected retailer voice in Washington.

National Knitted Outerwear Association

The National Knitted Outerwear Association is the only national organization of knitted outerwear firms in the country. It is a federation of regional groups of manufacturers, distributors and contractors of sweaters, swimwear, knitted shirts, infants' wear, and other articles of outer apparel. It was founded in 1918 as the medium through which the industry could offer its cooperation to the government's War Industries Board during World War I; and it has since then continued actively to offer its service to the members of the industry continuously and to the government when critical times required it.

The Assoication's principal purpose is to promote the welfare of the knitted outerwear and swimwear industry as a whole and the business interests of the individual manufacturers, distributors, contractors, suppliers, and selling agents who are identified with it.

It is concerned primarily with fostering trade and commerce among its active and associate members, correcting trade abuses, establishing sound trade customs and procedures and high ethical standards of business dealings, conducting technical studies and disseminating information of trade value, assisting in the settlement of disputes or the adjustments of differences between its members and others, and—among the most important—representing the industry's interests before various government agencies.

The Association publishes a weekly publication, *Knitted Outerwear Times;* an annual year book, *Knitted Outerwear Yearbook;* and a *Buyer's Guide Directory.* Additionally, it publishes findings of research studies, issues technical bulletins, and publishes textbooks on knitting.

TEXTILE TRADE ASSOCIATIONS

There are many textile trade associations that publish information about their products. This information helps the consumer understand the properties of particular fibers and what can be expected of them in wear and care. Some of these groups are the National Cotton Council of America, Cotton, Inc., Linen Trade Association, Man-Made Fiber Producers Association, Inc., International Silk Association of America, and the Wool Bureau.

International Fabricare Institute (IFI)

The International Fabricare Institute is the merger of two of the oldest trade associations in the United States: The American Institute of Laundering and the National Institute of Drycleaning. Its 13,500 members are institutional, linen supply, industrial, and family laundry and dry-cleaning firms throughout the United States and more than 50 foreign countries. In the United States alone, they handle over 85 percent of all laundry and dry-cleaning business. Affiliate membership is open to manufacturers, retailers, textile technical departments of colleges and universities, and government agencies.

The main offices of the Institute are located in Joliet, Illinois, the Research Center in Silver Spring, Maryland. IFI maintains a Textile Analysis Laboratory in Silver Spring with a branch office in Glendale, California. A trade school is maintained in Joliet, Illinois.

HOW THE INSTITUTE WORKS FOR CONSUMERS

The Research Department is responsible for issuing technical bulletins to industry on dry-cleaning detergents, spot and stain removal, finishing of garments, and household textiles. Good plant practices for maximum and best use of equipment helps its members do a better job for the consuming public.

The Consumer Relations Department publishes fabric and fashions bulletins for its members, Better Business Bureaus, consumer protective agencies, retail stores, and educators. In 1976, the department established a Professional Consumer Members program in the IFI. Members receive a monthly MEM-PACK of IFI bulletins. The use of the Textile Analysis Department has been opened to this class of members.

The Institute's Trade Relation Program and Seal Program work directly with the various segments of the textile and manufacturing industries to try to improve the performance of textile merchandise.

The Institute interacts with industry for the benefit of the consumer. If an item fails to give good performance in care, the burden of proof falls on the consumer even though the FTC Rule on Care Labeling of Textile Wearing Apparel states that the person or organization that directed or controlled the manufacture of the finished article is responsible for care labeling of apparel. The following true case illustrates the complexity of the problem.

Insulated sports garments made by a very reputable American firm and similar garments that were imported were labeled "Dry Clean Only." A few that were labeled "Do Not Dry Clean" dry cleaned satisfactorily. The reason for the warning is unknown. Those that were labeled "Dry Clean Only" did not always dry clean without damage. In the latter category, two problems—discoloration and blotches—were noted. The dry cleaner could overcome the problem of discoloration, but the blotches were permanent. The nylon or polyester shell fabric was coated with a finish that was affected by dry-cleaning solvents.

This type of labeling does not comply with the Rule on Care Labeling. The consumer who is told the garment did not dry clean satisfactorily held the dry cleaner responsible. The dry cleaner took the position that the merchandise should be returned to the store where it was purchased. The consumer took it to the store and was told that her dry cleaner must be a very poor cleaner because the label stated the merchandise could be dry cleaned. Where did this leave the consumer?

It is very difficult for one individual to take a complaint to the Federal Trade Commission to get redress. The time, effort, and frustration even at a loss of $80 to $100 does not always appear worth it.

The next recourse for the consumer is to work through the Better Business Bureau, the Ethics Division of the Chamber of Commerce, or a consumer protection agency. This also can be very time consuming. Many communities have neither a Better Business Bureau nor a consumer protection agency. Some communities may have Centers of Dispute Settlement sponsored by American Association of Arbitrators. The last alternative the consumer has is the small claims court (see p. 431).

A GUIDE FOR ARBITRATING COMPLAINTS

IFI's International Fair Claims Guide for Consumer Textile Products was first introduced in 1961 as an adjustments formula for the settlement of damage claims. Its success was immediate and far reaching. It is widely used today by dry cleaners, launderers, insurance adjusters, retailers, Better Business Bureaus, civil authorities, and others in many countries (see Appendix F).

In 1964, the Guide was expanded to include criteria for determining responsibility for damage to consumer textile products. This called for a special body of information on terminology, labeling, causes of damage, and new concepts of product classification unavailable from any other source. For this reason, the document has come into wide demand for educational uses, as well as for arbitration purposes.

A consensus process was followed in the development of the Guide similar to procedures used by formal standards-making bodies. Cooperating organizations included the Council of Better Business Bureaus, Association of Home Appliance Manufacturers, National Retail Merchants Association, American Home Economics Association, Menswear Retailers of America, a national U.S. insurance adjusting agency, a mail-order firm, a textile process licensing company, a fiber producer, and a committee of four noted consultants representing consumer, retail, and textile manufacturing interests.

The 1973 edition contains a special section on new developments in care labeling brought about by the Federal Trade Commission Rule on Care Labeling of Textile Wearing Apparel effective July 3, 1972, and by the growing use of symbol systems of labeling in many countries.

The document is now formally presented by the International Fabricare Institute for voluntary use in all countries because (1) all apparel products exported to the United States must comply with the FTC rule and (2) the Guide has achieved wide international acceptance for its criteria on textile performance questions in general.

How Does the Guide Work? The concept of serviceability of a garment is based on how long it lasts, how it should last, behavior during wear, and appearance after laundering or dry cleaning. There is a concept called "implied serviceability." The National Retail Merchants Association defines implied serviceability this way: "In the sale of merchandise there is an implied warranty that such goods will afford reasonable service in use and unless otherwise specified be cleaned and refreshed by customary methods."

If a garment can be cleaned by normal laundering or dry-cleaning methods, the guide states that it is not necessary for the manufacturer to put specific instructions on the label attached to the garment. However, if the garment must be handled in a special way, then a permanent care instruction should be attached to the garment.

The guide also introduces the concept of life expectancy for clothing and textile products. Estimates are given as to how long each garment may be expected to be worn. Normal wear, care, and change in fashion influence life expectancy of clothing. The value for an adjustment is based on a percentage of replacement cost and depends on how much the "life expectancy" of the item has been used up and the condition of the garment at the time the claim is made. These factors have been worked out and set up in tables. This method is used for figuring a reasonable estimate of the amount of loss.

CERTIFICATION OF FABRICS FOR CLEANABILITY

In this age of consumerism, class action, and politics in the marketplace, more and more emphasis is being put on companies to be more mindful of the consumer interest, such as the need for permanent care labels and compliance with safety requirements. More than ever before consumers need to know that garments are truly dry cleanable and washable.

The Certified Dry Cleanable Seal and the Certified Washable Seal are awarded to manufacturers whose fabrics or merchandise are tested in IFI's Certified Seal Laboratory. The seal is earned only if the goods meet specified standards.

With the ever-increasing number of fibers and fabrics there is a greater need for reliable guides for consumer protection and for enabling professional launderers and dry cleaners to protect their consumers' wearing apparel and household items.

The testing program, geared to test serviceability, assures washability or dry cleanability and satisfactory service throughout the normal wear life of the item if it is certified.

Tests include (1) dimensional change (shrinkage and stretching) tensile strength (the strength of a fabric in both dry and wet state), (2) colorfastness to water, solvent, perspiration, crocking or rubbing off of color, light, and oxides of nitrogen (gases in the atmosphere that cause color change), (3) durability of applied designs and finishes, (4) chlorine retention, (5) soil resistance, (6) yarn distortion, (7) abrasion resistance, and (8) pilling.

Component parts such as buttons, zippers, thread, lining, padding, emblems and the like, are also tested. Some items submitted for test are not tested for all the conditions listed above. Tests are selected on the basis of performance needs in the use or wear life expected of the item.

The International Fabricare Institute's test service under the Seal program also gives guidance to the manufacturer as to care label instructions.

National Automatic Laundry and Cleaning Council (NALCC)

The National Automatic Laundry and Cleaning Council was organized in 1960 when the urgent need was recognized for combined effort to oppose restrictive legislation to help increase volume and profits and to work generally for the promotion and growth of the self-service laundry and dry cleaning industry. NALCC has grown to become the service center and clearinghouse for the self-service industry on many problems. Included are all phases of legislation, consumer education, public relations, sales promotion, waste disposal, and statistics, with special emphasis on programs to serve store-owner members.

NALCC provides many types of promotional "tools" for members to use to reach the more than 40 million families that have not yet used coin-store services.

The Association of Interior Decor Specialists (AIDS)

The Association of Interior Decor Specialists, Inc., popularly known as AIDS International, was organized to bring together everyone who is engaged in the installation, cleaning, repairing, and restoration of all textile materials used in the interiors of every kind of structure. The goals of the Association and the reasons for its existence are to educate AIDS International members and their employees and to instruct the general public on the care of their interior decor fabrics—carpets, draperies, rugs, upholstery, wall coverings, and all other textile materials specified for interiors by designers or owners.

Education of consumers is carried out by articles written by members and staff employees, press releases, in-person interviews with trade and consumer magazine editors and newspaper editors, and by radio and television appearances by the staff or members. AIDS International also prepares consumer publications, such as explanatory leaflets and booklets.

Association of Home Appliance Manufacturers (AHAM)

The Association of Home Appliance Manufacturers is a nonprofit association of companies manufacturing more than 90 percent of the major and a majority of the portable appliances produced in this country each year (see Figure 12–5).

Through name changes and reorganizations, AHAM traces its history as a manufacturers' trade association, carrying on coordinated industry activity for more than 50 years. In 1966, AHAM was incorporated as a single-purpose appliance association, independent of other interests and representative of the entire industry, to serve home appliance manufacturers and the public.

A board of directors acts as the governing and policy-making body of the association, subject to control by the members. Program committees, staffed by more than 500 industry executives, parallel department specialists within the corporation. These committees develop industrywide programs in such areas as statistics, engineering standards, certification, consumer information, and government relations.

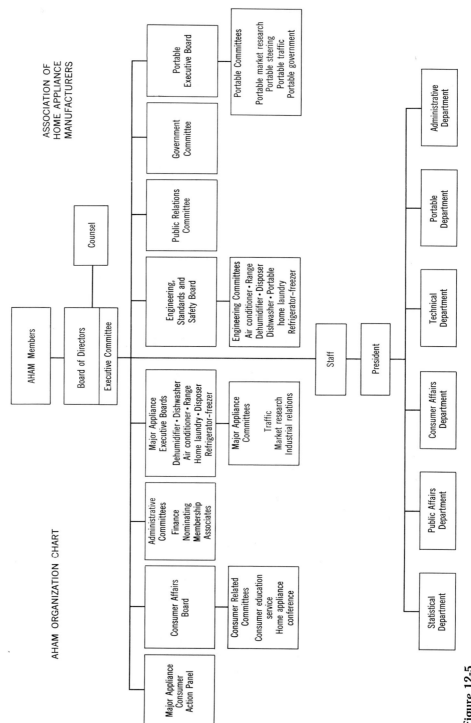

AHAM ORGANIZATION CHART

ASSOCIATION OF HOME APPLIANCE MANUFACTURERS

Figure 12-5

An association staff, headed by a president who sits on the board, is also organized by professional specialties. Engineers and legal, statistical, and communications personnel have the professional training and experience to carry out AHAM's activities.

The Association carries on activities and programs that its members feel can be done more efficiently collectively than individually. Through its consumer affairs activities, AHAM conducts a dialogue with consumers and consumer groups. It is assisted in these activities by the Major Appliance Consumer Action Panel, representing consumers at the highest level of industry.

This organization acts as the appliance industry spokesman, especially in the important area of government relations. Through the government committee, the industry can express its views on legislation, receive reports on government actions at all levels, and maintain liaison with government officials.

AHAM releases monthly factory sales figures, year-end totals and sales projections, and various special studies such as wage-and-benefit surveys, service studies, and specialized sales reports available only to participants in the studies.

AHAM has 18 standards covering home appliance performance and works closely with the Underwriters' Laboratories, American Gas Association, ANSI, and other groups in the promulgation of safety standards.

AHAM also sponsors certification programs on some appliances. Educational materials and teaching aids, consumer press releases, an Appliance Information Bureau to answer questions about appliances, and an annual National Home Appliance Conference are part of the information program.

Major Appliance Consumer Action Panel (MACAP)

In March 1970, eight nationally recognized consumer advocates agreed to join a privately sponsored effort "to voice consumers' views at the highest level of the major appliance industry." One month later the group was announced to the public as the Major Appliance Consumer Action Panel and its members began their work.

MACAP's sponsors are manufacturers of major appliances and retailers who sell appliances under their own brand names. The manufacturers and retailers support MACAP through three national trade associations: Association of Home Appliance Manufacturers, Gas Appliance Manufacturers Association, and the American Retail Federation.

MACAP panelists are invited to participate by the sponsors after being nominated by the existing panel. Each member is completely independent of the appliance industry, is an experienced practitioner in some aspects of the consumer arts, and is recognized for his or her leadership on behalf of consumers. In addition, the panel has made an effort to include in its membership individuals with expertise in a particular consumerrelated professional field. For example, members have a high level of competence in law, consumer finance, consumer education, consumer journalism, home equipment, or engineering.

MACAP had established goals for accomplishing greater consumer satisfaction with the appliance industry:

1. Complaint handling: reduce the time required to resolve consumer complaints reviewed by MACAP in the "study phase," identify and eliminate the problem areas in industry and MACAP procedures that prevent efficient and timely resolution of complaints, and improve MACAP's procedures for auditing "closed-resolved" consumer files in order to better evaluate the panel's effectiveness.

2. Appliance service: focus attention on the major industry problems preventing timely and quality servicing of appliances and encourage industry to develop and implement some positive programs designed to improve the service of appliances.

3. Warranties: review the progress made by the appliance industry in complying with the industry guidelines on warranty content and advertising and study the provisions and administration of warranties with the objective of making recommendations to industry for improvements.

4. Consumer education: encourage the distribution and utilization of consumer education materials developed by MACAP (see Figure 12–6).

The following is a typical case of complaints and the route of communication between the consumer, MACAP, and the manufacturer:

WASHER AND DRYER Consumer comment: "Washer delivered and installed with suspension part missing. Manufacturer claims not to be responsible, so replaced with another appliance. Dryer was reparied and it working satisfactorily."

Review of the file showed that the consumer did not previously indicate the washer was delivered with parts missing. The manufacturer offered to repair the appliance for $15 plus cost of parts, but the consumer advised the manufacturer that he did not have the money.

Consumer comment: "There has been much correspondence but no results. Too much time wasted to continue the action."

Review of the file indicates consumer's last letter in file alleged "buck passing" by manufacturer, but stated he did not want to waste further time. He hoped, however, that he could contribute to preventing same problem for others. File was closed, unresolved.

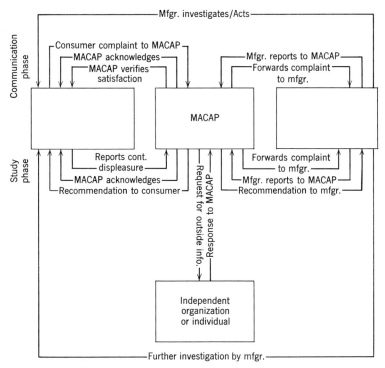

Figure 12-6 Flowchart of communications channels in MACAP. Complaint handling procedure illustrates the flow of communications in MACAP complaint-handling procedure. Ninety-six percent of complaints are resolved in communications phases.

WASHER

Consumer comment: "Lousy service on washer."

Staff phoned consumer to get specific complaint. Consumer indicated appliance was repaired and operating satisfactorily, but he was chagrined with delays and cost of service. However, he has built a new home and will soon be leaving appliance behind. He is impressed with MACAP's follow-up.

FIBER
PRODUCERS

The leading fiber producers, such as Celanese Corporation, AvTex Fibers, Inc.; formerly FMC Corporation, the DuPont Company, Eastman Chemical Corporation, and others, maintain large quality control laboratories that indirectly benefit the consumer. Many engage in licensed trademark programs from fiber to fabric. These programs set up standards that the fiber or fabric must meet before it can be labeled with the companies' trademarks. This kind of program assures the consumer of quality and gives technical guidance and control to the manufacturer. Many of these companies have extensive consumer educational programs that help consumers learn more about the products they buy.

Trademarks and Testing

Some fiber producers maintain elaborate programs for fabric testing and licensing trademarks. These producers recognize that fibers and fabrics do not automatically end up as fashionable products which will perform to the consumer's complete satisfaction. Achieving and maintaining high standards of quaility and performance require constant creative and technical attention.

Providing accurate information about textiles is a basic tenet of the marketing philosophy.

Certification

New textile industries appear on the manufacturing scene from time to time. An example is the bonded fabric segment of the textile industry.

When bonded fabrics were first introduced about 10 years ago, they seemed to offer so many good performance qualities that they gained instant popularity. To keep up with the demand, finishers—even those without the right equipment or know-how—entered this new business. Volume soared to 400 million yards a year. When improper bonding techniques were used, the troubles started: face fabrics and linings separated; blistering, puckering, and inordinate shrinkage appeared; and garments without proper care instructions were dry cleaned or washed when they should not have been.

Dissatisfied customers and the retail stores who had to cope with bonded fabrics just stopped buying. The bottom dropped out of the market, forcing many finishers to drop out of the industry. Twenty-five companies remained and continued to produce the 150 million yards of reliable goods that were still in demand. Many of them, along with converters, mills, and suppliers, felt there was a larger potential for good bonded-piece goods if only they could retain public confidence.

The Celanese Fiber Marketing Company, in conjunction with the Foam Fashion Forum, which includes chemical companies, mills, and fiber and foam producers, cosponsored a rigidly controlled fabric certification program through the medium of a newly formed group called the Bonded Fabrics Council of which the Certified Bonders Guild was also a member organization. The council was administered by the International Fabricare Institute, and the Better Fabrics Testing Bureau provided the council's official testing laboratories.

The prime purpose of the testing and certification program was to give absolute assurance to manufacturers, stores, and consumers as to quality of the bonded fabrics and garments purchased.

Hangtags were issued to Council members on a controlled, numbered basis for every two yards of fabric that met the standards. Garments or piece goods carrying the tag gave guarantee for the bonding.

The weakness of this program, as with some other certification programs of the past, is that if business is bad, the cost of the program to the manufacturer comes under scrutiny and is dropped. Also, hangtags may never survive the distribution route and may be lost before they ever reach the consumer.

Guarantees and Warranties

Guarantees and warranties are generally synonymous; they are promises in writing to the consumer, usually stating that the product is free from defects in materials or workmanship. Most guarantees protect the consumer against having to pay for repairs or replacement if the product proves to be defective within a specified length of time. Guarantees are made by the manufacturer or seller to inform the consumer of the guarantor's responsibilities for his product.

Almost all large appliances, such as washers and dryers, come with guarantees. A manufacturer or seller may guarantee any product. Guarantees on clothing and fabrics usually apply to certain characteristics such as fade-resistance, rather than to "defects in materials and workmanship."

The time span of a guarantee should be clearly stated, such as 30 days, six months or one year. Many guarantees are for one year. Large appliance guarantees may provide for replacement of parts over an extended period of time, such as five years. Many guarantees offer longer coverage for parts than for labor. The consumer should always read the guarantee to see how long the entire product, as well as individual parts, is guaranteed. Some guarantors can estimate the expiration date of the guarantee according to when that model was manufactured or sold. Some guarantees carry either the date of purchase or the expiration date. The dated sales slip or guarantee that bears a date can determine the expiration date. Retention of the sales slip gives proof of purchase if the guarantee is lost.

Comparing guarantees should be an important part of a shopping ritual. Comparing the reliability of the company behind the guarantee is just as important. A purchaser purchases a guarantee. It costs money to fulfill the terms of a guarantee, and that cost must be included in the price paid.

A consumer should be particularly wary of so-called unconditional warranties. There are virtually always conditions, and all promises should be in writing.

Consumer Advisory Committees

CONSUMER ADVISORY PANEL TO A TEXTILE MILL

Springs Mills, looking at the rising tide of consumerism, decided in late 1971 to do something to build bridges of understanding between consumers, business and industry, educational communities and government.

Company executives felt that there was value in learning more about how today's textile industry is perceived by a moderate, informed group of long-time consumer advocates.

At the same time, Springs had heard college professors repeatedly express their need for more direct communications with the textile business.

Viewing these educators as an underutilized link between the consumer and business, Springs brought together a Consumer Advisory Panel composed of six persons highly respected by the National Association of College Professors of Textiles and Clothing, two from each of the three national regions.

The panel was invited to meet with company executives for a free exchange of attitudes, ideas, and information.

The objective was to improve communications and understanding between Springs, the campus, and consumers.

Such a program provides two-way communications. The educator can become aware of the problems, decisions, and tradeoffs faced by textile companies in an era of consumerism and rapid fashion changes. Management has the opportunity to become acquainted with campus insight into trends in consumer attitudes, problems, and life-styles. Most important, the educator is uniquely situated to interpret business to the consumer and vice versa, and to provide information and direction to both groups. This type of program can result in greater understanding of each other's problems and goals.

RETAIL STORES, MAIL-ORDER FIRMS

Retailers are demanding product performance. This requires pretested merchandise, properly described and with correct care instructions. For these reasons, retail stores, such as J. C. Penney Company, Macy's, Marshall Field and Company, Kaufman's and others, and mail-order firms, such as Sears Roebuck and Company and Montgomery Ward, are expanding their testing laboratories. Retail store buyers look to these laboratories as a resource to back up manufacturer's claims.

COMMERCIAL LABORATORIES

Some manufacturing firms are not large enough to support their own research and development or quality control laboratories. They must rely on independent commercial testing laboratories such as the Better Fabrics Testing Bureau, Fabric Research Laboratories, Inc., the U.S. Testing Bureau, and others to do their testing for them.

Underwriters' Laboratories, Inc. (UL)

Underwriter's Laboratories, Inc. is a nationwide, independent, non-profit organization testing for public safety since 1894. Its engineers test products voluntarily submitted by manufacturers to see whether the products meet its requirements for safety. A product is tested and analyzed for all reasonably foreseeable hazards.

If the product passes the Laboratories' investigation, UL field inspectors then follow up at the factory to be sure the manufacturer is producing and checking the product to meet their safety requirements.

Safety requirements are established and kept current by the Laboratories' professional engineers working with industry and governmental inspection authorities. Many of the UL standards are recognized as American standards. Underwriters' Laboratories firmly controls the issuance of labels, which can only be obtained through them. Their label states the product on which it appears is reasonably free from fire, electric shock, and related accident hazards. The consumer should look for it on a washer, dryer, and iron.

The Underwriters' Laboratories are guided by their Consumer Advisory Council. The purpose of the Council is to establish more meaningful communication with informed consumer interests in the product safety field.

Council members are drawn from various groupings within the American National Standards Institute, from representatives of organized consumer groups throughout the United States, from representatives of large mail-order and department stores who have knowledge of and reflect a close concern for consumers, from representatives of government who have responsibilities involving consumers, and from persons who were formerly associated with public safety activities.

The broad responsibilities of the Council are to advise Underwriters' Laboratories in establishing levels of safety for consumer products, to provide the Laboratories with additional user field experience and failure information in the field of product safety, and to aid in educating the general public in the limitations and safe use of specific consumer products.

The Council is one of the media through which Underwriters' Laboratories disseminates information concerning the detection of new and unusual hazards associated with products and conveys the limitations and restrictions to be exercised in the use of a product to insure its safety.

MAGAZINES

Some magazines pride themselves in helping the consumer through their testing laboratories and educational programs. *Good Housekeeping* magazine, for example, backs up its advertising and articles with the work done by its Institute. *Changing Times* and *Parents Magazine* publish consumer educational articles as well as consumer educational materials.

Good Housekeeping Institute

The Good Housekeeping Institute was first organized in 1901 as a service division of *Good Housekeeping* magazine. It has been a leader in consumer education and product evaluation. It consists of a number of laboratories involved with chemistry, engineering, textiles, leathers, plastics, appliances, and home care. There are also a sewing center, a beauty clinic, and a dozen kitchens. The Institute staff is responsible for investigating representative samples of products advertised in *Good Housekeeping* and for preparing service editorials to help consumers run their homes intelligently. Its staff numbers about 100 and includes chemists, engineers, dieticians, home economists, beauticians, and specialists in various areas.

Every issue of *Good Housekeeping* includes reports from the service editors of the Institute who pass along advice on the many products they work with in the laboratories. For example, whenever an article appears on how to buy and care for a product such as household textiles, clothing and accessories, the information is checked by the technical staff of the Institute, and much of it is based on laboratory investigations that have been conducted in the Institute. Even the fashions that appear in *Good Housekeeping* are carefully selected; before they are shown, samples of each must be investigated and judged to be a good one in the opinion of the Textile Department of the Institute.

Advertising as well as editorial content is carefully reviewed. No product can be advertised until representative samples of it have been investigated and found acceptable for advertising by the technical staff of the Institute. Not only must the product be a good one but packaging, label information, and all claims made for it in the magazine must be found accurate by the Institute's technical staff. When evaluating products, the staff uses applicable government and industry standards plus the Institute's own requirements. If meaningful standards do not exist for a particular product, then the Institute staff develops them, often devising new equipment for the purpose. When a product does not meet its requirements, or claims cannot be substantiated, advertising is not accepted. Each year several hundred thousand dollars' worth of advertising is refused because products do not perform satisfactorily or live up to the claims made for them. Also, advertising is sometimes refused because certain types of products are considered potentially dangerous or non-beneficial.

THE GOOD HOUSEKEEPING SEAL

Products that meet the Institute's standards can carry its Seal of Approval. All products accepted for advertising by the magazine are covered by a replacement or refund guarantee. No manufacturer can use the Seal on his product until it has met the requirements established by the technical staff of the Institute. Once the Seal has been earned, the advertiser can use it on packages, brochures, and point-of-sale displays under a one-year Seal Licensing Agreement. If the manufacturer so desires, the Seal may also be used in connection with advertising in other magazines and broadcast media.

HANDLING COMPLAINTS

Any consumer who buys a product that has been advertised in *Good Housekeeping* and is not satisfied with it can submit a complaint by writing to the Good Housekeeping Institute. Upon receipt of such a letter, a simple complaint form is sent to the complainant asking for a description of the product, when and where it was bought, the price paid, and the difficulty with it. When the filled-in form is returned to *Good Housekeeping,* a thorough investigation of the complaint is made. If circumstances allow, the product is shipped to the Institute at its expense for verification of the complaint. When shipment is not possible, then a representative of the Institute may go to the complainant's home to inspect the product. If it is found defective, the complainant may choose either a replacement or a refund of the price paid for it. All complaints are settled as soon as possible—usually within two to three weeks.

Consumer's Research

Consumer's Research, Washington, New Jersey, is an educational, nonprofit organization serving consumers. It makes scientific and engineering tests of many of the products that consumers buy and use, and reports its findings in monthly issues of Consumers' Research Magazine and in the *Consumer Bulletin Annual.* Products are rated by brand names as A. Recommended, B. Intermediate, and C.

Not Recommended. Considerable work is also done in developing test methods and devices; many of the methods have been made available for the use of government agencies, research institutions, testing laboratories and manufacturers.

An important aspect of the work of Consumers' Research is its service to schools, colleges and universities. *Consumer Bulletin* is used as an educational aid.

Consumers Union

Another organization whose objective is to help the consumer is Consumers Union, Mount Vernon, New York. Its magazine, *Consumer Reports,* is distributed to millions of consumers. Testing reports include textiles, electronics, and chemicals. With government now setting standards in a variety of industries, Consumers Union states it is not only involved in new consumer legislation but plans to see that government and industry develop strong consumer performance standards.

Consumers Union, with its two million circulation monthly product-rating magazine, has moved onto the Washington scene. It is planning to expand by setting up a separate nonprofit foundation called Consumer Interests Foundation. The foundation will do no product testing but instead will concentrate on broader consumer problem areas where the remedy is not a matter of shunning one product and buying another. Examples are how advertising affects the listener or reader, the issue of imports and the consumer, and how business and industry handle consumer complaints.

PROFESSIONAL ASSOCIATIONS

American Arbitration Association (AAA)

The American Arbitration Association was organized in 1926 to design and administer modern arbitration systems. However, merely offering arbitration facilities is not enough. The business community must be persuaded that it will benefit by using them. Thus the AAA, although nonprofit in nature, must also market its services.

A long line of court decisions has recognized the utility of the arbitration process. The right to enter into private contracts is basic to our economic system. Parties are also encouraged to settle their disputes. Voluntary arbitration is one of the options in the settlement process.

Arbitration reduces the number of disputes that must be filed in court, and it also appeals to businessmen. Executives are easily persuaded that they should be permitted to settle disputes privately—at a time, method, and place of their own choosing.

Arbitration is not instant: on the average, it takes from three to six months for a case to be completed. It is not free: it must be financed by the parties who use it and can occasionally be as expensive as a court trial. It permits the parties to use an impartial expert to decide what they meant when they wrote their contract or what agreement they would have reached if they had anticipated the change in circumstances that they now face. Arbitration is a business tool, not an official part of the judicial process.

There are definite advantages in using this system. AAA arbitration operates across state and national borders. Another advantage is the privacy enjoyed by the parties who do not wish to publicize their dispute.

Because the businessman is willing to rely on the expertise of his arbitrator, he can accept arbitration's simplicity and finality.

The arbitrator should be given broad powers to decide how the case will be presented to him. The arbitrator's decision is expected to be final, ending all further litigation. Modern arbitration systems have been designed to accommodate the business and the consumer.

Under AAA rules, the parties can exercise control over the selection of their arbitrator. If parties are unable to dispose of their dispute through settlement, they can obtain a list of recommended arbitrators from the AAA. From such a list, they can make a mutual selection.

A primary responsibility of the AAA is to develop the best possible panel of arbitrators. The availability of highly qualified arbitrators is the major test of the system, and its major attraction. The regional directors of the AAA know that they are judged on the quality of the lists of arbitrators that they submit to parties. There are now 27,000 arbitrators on the AAA National Panel: lawyers, engineers, architects, textile experts, chemical engineers, bankers, and experts in many other fields. Accurate information is maintained as to the arbitrator's background and his standing in his field.

The AAA tries to keep arbitrators generally knowledgeable about arbitration. They receive copies of the monthly *Arbitration News,* which informs them of recent developments. When an arbitrator is selected for a case, an *Arbitrator's Manual* is sent, explaining the duties. When the arbitrator appears for the hearing, a tribunal administrator gives a briefing of the hearing procedures. The arbitrators are not professional: they arbitrate because of their standing in their own profession.

In screening the panel, each of the 21 regional offices of the AAA relies on a regional advisory council made up of leading attorneys, businesspeople, and community leaders. Advisory committees from various industries perform a similar function, for example, the General Arbitration Council of the Textile Industry, made up of representatives of textile trade associations whose members use arbitration, nominates industry leaders to serve on the panel of textile arbitrators. The community is not required to use the AAA services.

A common cause for failure in arbitration is the continuing use of the so-called "party-appointed arbitrator" system. Here, each party is supposed to select an arbitrator. The party-appointed arbitrators are supposed to select the single neutral arbitrator. This procedure has numerous defects. A resisting party can cause serious delay. The role of the party-appointed arbitrator is uncertain and subject to abuse. This procedure invites errors that can seriously prejudice any award that may be forthcoming.

National Center for Dispute Settlement

As a new division of the American Arbitration Association, the National Center for Dispute Settlement is nongovernmental, independent, and nonprofit.

The Center has established a National Consumer Arbitration Advisory Council to assist in the promotion of arbitration as a means of resolving disputes arising between businessmen and consumers. It also assists business and consumer groups in developing comprehensive dispute settlement machinery.

The Center provides a neutral ground to which the community leaders, consumers, tenants, public or private agencies, landlords, or local businesspeople can bring unresolved conflicts. In addition, they assist these parties in developing new procedures through which future conflicts can be resolved more quickly and less expensively.

COOPERATIVE PROGRAMS WITH BETTER BUSINESS BUREAUS

In some states the AAA, in cooperation with Better Business Bureaus, establishes consumer arbitration rules in order to provide appropriate procedures for resolving consumer disputes. Businesspeople who make use of these procedures contribute to the high standards of a business community by offering a fair remedy to their consumers.

American Home Economics Association (AHEA)

The American Home Economics Association works for and with consumers. The Textile and Clothing Section of AHEA is interested in publishing research findings and educational literature. Its membership participates in the work of scientific organizations in developing test methods and standards of performance of fabrics and clothing. Its members also testify before Congressional committees in the interest of the consumer.

Fashion Group

The Fashion Group, Inc. is a noncommercial association of individuals engaged in fashion work, formed to advance the principles of applied art in industry and to foster good taste in fashion, to encourage the cooperation among those engaged in conceiving, designing, manufacturing, promoting, and distributing fashions, and, through education and the dissemination of useful information, to inspire a keener interest in fashion industries so that those engaged in the field of fashion may better serve themselves and the public at large. The national headquarters is located in New York City. The affairs are directed by elected officers, a board of directors, and an executive director and staff. There are 23 active fashion group chapters within the United States and seven groups operating outside of the country.

Society of Consumer Affairs Professionals in Business

Founded in May 1973 at Anaheim, California, the Society of Consumer Affairs Professionals in Business membership reflects a wide cross section of American business and has as its main purpose "to foster the integrity of business in its dealings with consumers, promote harmonious relationships between business and government and consumers, and advance the consumer affairs profession."

One of the Society's main objectives is to provide for an exchange of ideas, expertise, and opinions relevant to consumer affairs and to aid business in responding to consumer needs.

Electrical Women's Round Table (EWRT)

The Electrical Women's Round Table was incorporated in 1927 in New York State. Its founders were a small group of women who shared a common interest: all were employed in the electrical industry. They agreed to meet each month to share ideas and inspirations for their work.

By the late 1940s many other women in the industry had heard of the Round Table and expressed interest in forming similar groups. As a result, in September 1948 the Bylaws of the original group were revised to permit the formation of individual chapters.

From the original small group of women, the Electrical Women's Round Table has today grown to 20 chapters with more than 800 members. EWRT to this day retains the distinction of being the only independent national organization of women associated with the electrical industry.

OBJECTIVES

EWRT has the following objectives:

To establish professional associations among women whose business occupations are connected with the electrical industry or allied fields.

483 *Business-Industry Professional Programs*

To promote the growth potential of women in the electrical industry or allied fields.

To promote research and education in the electrical field.

To promote greater emphasis on the work women are doing for the companies or affiliations in the electrical industry or allied fields.

To advance consumer education.

To promote the wise and efficient use of electricity.

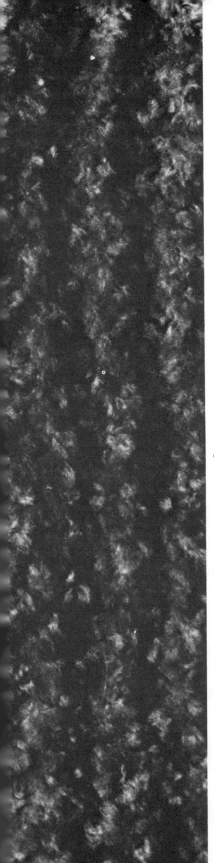

13

Consumer Involvement in the Performance of Textiles

THE CONSUMER'S RESPONSIBILITY

Everyone interested in improving relations between producers and users of consumer goods is increasingly aware that, important as they are, the efforts of government through new legislation and of industry through more pretesting and informative labeling are not in themselves sufficient to eliminate completely the failure of textile products in the hands of the consumer. The behavior of the consumer is just as important a factor as the actions of either government or industry.

How the consumer is behaving and how he will be behaving in the future is, of course, a matter of intense concern to industry, to government, and to educators as well as to consumers themselves. Individuals are not always aware of the effect of their actions when these are multiplied by millions of examples, nor are individuals always aware of the characteristics or the profile of the larger groups to which they belong.

In an analysis of the consumers of 1975 and beyond, *U.S. News and World Report** called these consumers the "new breed":

> "A generation of savvy and skeptical shoppers" interested in a "new functionalism" in the products they buy. Tomorrow's consumers, as the newsmagazine sees them, will be:
>
> *Younger.* The 24–35 age group is the fastest growing segment of the population. Changing values in this group will mean more "unmarrieds" and smaller families. More "middle class." By 1980, 26 million families—or 42 percent of all—will have incomes in excess of $15,000 a year. Life styles will become more sophisticated, more affluent.
>
> *Articulate.* Consumers will demand a more active role in deciding the nature and quality of goods and services.
>
> *Mobile.* People will be less reluctant to move to new localities, likely to make more vacation trips.
>
> *Simplicity.* Tastes favor a return to more basic, natural and functional products. Designs that are efficient and uncomplicated will sell best.
>
> *Changing female roles.* Fewer women will accept the traditional mother-housewife role.
>
> *Creative.* There will be more emphasis on "creative expression" in home life, work, and recreation. That will benefit do-it-yourself crafts, home improvements, sewing, baking, home canning.
>
> *Suspicious.* Consumers will exhibit distrust and skepticism toward government and industry, and will be more likely to complain about faulty products and misleading advertising.
>
> *Impatient.* People have been conditioned to expect "instant gratification," will continue to demand that products and services be readily available at all hours of every day.

* Anon., "A New Breed of Consumers Will Be Calling the Turn," *U.S. News and World Report,* Vol. 79 No. 2 (July-1975). Copyright 1975 U.S. News and World Report, Inc.

Educated. By 1980, an estimated 40 cents of every U.S. dollar will be spent by homes where the head of the family has had at least some college training.

Environmentally conscious. Energy efficiencies and ecological considerations will be increasingly important, with impact on more and more purchasing decisions.

Casual. Look for less emphasis on formality in dress and fashion, home care and entertaining.

Moreover, the prediction continues, as inflation and economic pressures reduce the amount of discretionary income—the amount left after paying for food, rent, transportation, and taxes—people are moved closer together in their interests, attitudes, and in what they consider important, as well as in what they will pay for certain items and in their determination to obtain the best buy for their money.

THE ROLE OF THE INDIVIDUAL CONSUMER

Consumer rights entail consumer responsibilities. Consumers must learn to recognize these obligations and be willing to accept them if they are to receive the greatest satisfaction from the products they buy.

The Consumer

Rights	Responsibilities
To information	To become informed
To choice	To compare alternatives and buy wisely
To performance	To follow care recommendations
To safety	To guard against carelessness
To recourse	To register legitimate complaints

The Individual's Responsibility for Selection and Care

Consumers who subscribe to the "new functionalism"—or to old-fashioned thrift for that matter—will succeed only if they invest time and thought in purchasing textiles and other products. These efforts include analysis of the consumer's needs and knowledge of the textiles products plus use of the safeguards and protections that are increasingly a part of the marketplace and, of course, intelligent use of the product once it has been purchased.

Proper care instructions on textile and apparel products are extremely valuable, but, to be effective, the consumer must read, understand, and follow these instructions.

Product flammability safety requires that the consumer remove matches and flammable liquids from within easy reach of children and that adults use them with caution.

489 *Consumer Involvement in the Performance of Textiles*

The Individual's Recourse in Cases of Product Failure

In the late 1960s and early 1970s, government, business, and industry made great efforts to devise methods and plans of arbitrating or settling consumer complaints. Regardless of the procedure or methods taken, all have been instigated in good faith to protect the consumer.

COMPLAINING EFFECTIVELY

Sometimes the manufacturer is at fault if a product fails in use. When a new fiber, fabric, finish, or decorative design is made, manufacturers go through a period of experimentation. They are stimulated to develop a new product because of consumer wants or needs. Ideas for new products often come from consumers. Once the idea is born, an experimental fabric or garment is made. It is tested by a limited number of people to get consumer reaction. If there are no major complaints, the product is manufactured and put into a limited number of stores and sold. These are called test areas. Consumer reactions and complaints are studied; then the manufacturer changes

Figure 13-1

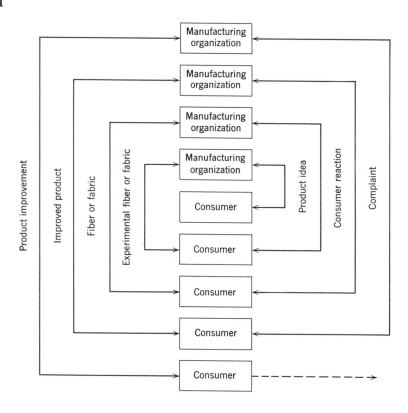

the product to improve it. Finally it is sold to consumers everywhere. Study the chart, Product Improvement (Figure 13–1).

Fabric and garments may fail to give good performance because of:

1. *Tough price competition.* Manufacturers try to reduce quality as much as possible in order to reduce price.

2. *Lack of quality control and use of standards in testing of fabrics.* Some firms do not maintain testing laboratories. Some do not employ methods of setting and meeting quality levels for satisfactory performance.

3. *Lack of understanding on the part of the manufacturer.* Some do not understand what is involved in consumer wear and care of clothing and household textiles.

When something does go wrong, how can a consumer complain effectively?

The simple, basic rules to follow in making a complaint are:

1. Put the complaint in writing and keep a carbon copy. A letter clarifies complaints and puts them on record.

2. Address the letter to the Customer-Relations Department of the firm. Faster service will be received.

3. Type the letter. Complaint department supervisors state that a typed letter gets faster action than does a handwritten letter.

4. State facts clearly. Curb emotions.

5. Return article in a clean condition.

6. Include duplicate or sales ticket and labels, if available.

7. Avoid sarcasm and profanity.

8. Be honest in reporting. False statements are easily recognized.

9. Be good natured. Consumers will get much farther if they seem to be acting fairly and objectively.

The Individual's Creative Input

Consumers play a positive role in the textile marketplace by their purchase—or nonpurchase—of specific items. Many consumers can also play a role in influencing what will appear on the market. They can express their wishes and suggestions directly to the manufacturers. Many consumers can participate in panels, workshops, studies, and in advisory councils to both industry and government.

THE ORGANIZATION PATH

Consumer Programs in Organizations

Consumer education and consumer problems and interests have traditionally been a part of the programs of many general-interest organizations, such as the General Federation of Women's Clubs or the American Association of University Women. For many professional associations, such as the American Home Economics Association, consumer interests are an integral part of their program and objectives. Committees, special programs, dissemination of information through the organizations' periodicals or journals have aimed chiefly at educating their members so that they will be more competent in their selection of goods and services.

Consumer Organizations

The National Consumers League,* the nation's oldest consumer group, was founded in 1899 to organize consumer pressure to fight for economic justice. Louis Brandeis and Felix Frankfurter served as the League's counsels. Eleanor Roosevelt was a vice-president. A nonprofit membership organization, the League today works to secure consumer rights through a program of advocacy, research, education, arbitration† and legislative action.

With a decline in confidence in all institutions, including the print and broadcast media, consumer groups started organizing in the late 1960s and early 1970s. Among such groups, devoted exclusively to consumer interests, are the Action For Children's Television, the Center for Auto Safety, the Center For Science in the Public Interest, the Conference of Consumer Organizations, the Consumer Action For Foods and Drugs, the Consumer Federation of America, the National Consumer Congress, the Consumer Union of US, Inc., and Council of Children, Media and Merchandising.

The Conference of Consumer Organizations (COCO)‡ was formed by leaders of community and state organizations who have felt the need for improved communications, closer cooperation, and coordinated effort in consumer action programs at the state and local levels throughout the country. They formed COCO to help themselves and to help others who seek to develop more effective community and state consumer organizations or to form new ones.

The COCO Steering Committee was formed in January 1974 when eight representatives of community and state consumer groups agreed to the principles of the Conference of Consumer Organiza-

* National Consumers League, 1785 Massachusetts Avenue N.W., Washington, D.C. 20036.

† *Arbitration of Consumer Complaints, A Casebook,* National Consumers Committee for Research and Education, 1411 Hopkins Street, N.W., Washington, D.C. 20036.

‡ COCO, Box 4277, Tucson, Arizona 85717.

tions. The Steering Committee met in May and December of 1974 to complete organizational arrangements. In November 1974, the Steering Committee invited other organizations and individuals similarly interested in consumer affairs to join COCO.

Such groups adopt activist tactics that go beyond the educational programs of the general interest and professional groups. They may attempt to influence the marketplace through boycotts, strikes, and the like and attempt to influence legislation or other regulatory action. Established groups, such as the Consumer Federation of America and Consumers Union, became active in consumerism in the past decade. Consumers Union, however, has some conflict between action in the new consumerism and emphasis on its long-time program of testing and reporting on products. Volunteer citizen-consumer action groups at the local level are organized to handle consumer grievances locally.

Consumer cooperatives also serve consumers through their traditional system of consumer control and sharing.

THE COOPERATIVE PATH

The cooperative path of consumers with government and with business and industry is one of the most promising approaches to mutual satisfaction and benefit. Such a group is the Consumer Sounding Board organized by the American National Standards Institute, Inc. The Sounding Board provides to technical committees (that develop consumer product performance or safety standards) a means of conferring with a cross section of ultimate consumers. The Consumer Sounding Board is intended to provide a dependable report of broad consumer experience, attitude, and opinion for the use of standards development committees regarding the product involved. Volunteers from a Consumer Sounding Board may be given special informational briefings on how a consumer may become a competent member of a technical committee which is working on a voluntary product performance or safety standard.

THE OMBUDSMAN OR ADVOCATE

Another phenomenon of the consumer movement of the past decades has been the emergence of the consumer advocates. Ralph Nader, the most famous, won instant fame as the author of *Unsafe At Any Speed,* an exposé of the auto industry, and quickly branched out to practically all areas of consumer interest in activities that have won him the description of "consumer advocate." He has formed his own organization to conduct investigative studies and carry on action programs in areas of consumer interest.

The President's Consumer Advisor and persons in similar positions in state and local governments are expected to represent the consumer at the appropriate level of government. In this respect they serve as consumer ombudsmen. However, they also present the views of the Administration to the consumer and explain government programs to consumers.

THE AUTHORITY

While a consumer advocate is by definition an activist, the authority or expert aims to inform rather than incite action. Perhaps the best known representative of this category of persons is Sylvia Porter in the field of economics and finance, including individual and family economics.

Research studies into the roles and effectiveness of both the consumer advocates and the consumer interests authorities at particular times would be of considerable interest to students.

LEGISLATIVE INFLUENCE

Representatives of the consumer groups mentioned in this chapter do influence textile legislation—or at least have opportunities to present their views to the legislative bodies when bills relating to labeling, safety, and the like are being considered. The effectiveness of their presentation would also make a good topic for a research study.

The educator has a great challenge in helping consumers deal wisely with textiles and other consumer products. Perhaps it is even more important for consumers to understand and evaluate the functions of consumer groups and consumer spokesmen as carefully as they consider the activities of business and of government.

CONSUMER PRODUCT INFORMATION SOURCES

The following list of Consumer Product Information Sources apply to all products, not necessarily textiles.

Government Sources

Consumer Information, an index of selected federal publications of consumer interest, quarterly publication of Consumer Product Information Center. Address: Consumer Information, Public Documents Distribution Center, Pueblo, Colorado 81009.

GCA Consumer News, Office of Consumer Affairs, Department of Health, Education and Welfare, published twice monthly. Address: Consumer News, Office of Consumer Affairs, Washington, D.C. 20201. Phone: (202) 962-1608. Subscriptions: $2 a year from Superintendent of Documents, Government Printing Office, Washington, D.C. 20402. Also publishes *Consumer Education Bibliography* and *Consumer Legislative Monthly Report.*

U.S. Consumer Product Safety Commission, 1750 K Street N.W., Washington, D.C. 20207. Phone: (202) 634-7700. Staff offices at 5401 Westbard Avenue, Bethesda, Maryland 20016. News releases and monthly *NEISS News,* information on product safety from the National Electronic Injury Surveillance System toll-free "hot line" for all information, complaints, and inquiries: in Maryland call (800) 492-2937, elsewhere (800) 638-2666.

Consumer Alert, Federal Trade Commission, Washington, D.C. 20580. General consumer protection. Also publishes *FTC News Summary.*

Consumers Guide series of pamphlets on consumer products, from the National Bureau of Standards Consumer Information Series, Department of Commerce. Available individually from U.S. Government Printing Office.

NBS-CIS-1	*Fibers and Fabrics*	65 cents
NBS-CIS-2	*Adhesives*	52 cents
NBS-CIS-3	*Tires*	50 cents

Guide to Federal Consumer Services, Department of Health, Education and Welfare, Office of Consumer Affairs, Washington, D.C.

Special Newsletters

Of Consuming Interest, newsletter on consumer goods and services, Federal-State Reports, P.O. Box 986, Court House Station, Arlington, Virginia 22216. Published weekly, $72 per year.

The Standards Institute Consumer Voice: Information on ANSI Voluntary National Standards, Consumer Affairs Department, American National Standards Institute, 1430 Broadway, New York, New York 10018.

Production Safety Letter, 1080 National Press Building, Washington, D.C. 20004. Phone: (202) EX 3-3830. $150 per year. Topical general interest.

Consumer Education Forum, ACCI Newsletter, and *Journal of Consumer Affairs,* American Council on Consumer Interests, 238 Stanley Hall, University of Missouri, Columbia, Missouri 65201. $10 per year.

Packaging and Labeling, update and reference on developments in packaging and labeling. Federal-State Reports, P.O. Box 986, Courthouse Station, Arlington, Virginia 22216. Published weekly, $175 per year.

Periodicals *Media and Consumer,* general interest periodical. Subscription: $12 per year from Media and Consumer Foundation, P.O. Box 850, Norwalk, Connecticut 06852.

Consumer Reports, information and comparative ratings on various consumer products. Subscription: $8 per year. P.O. Box 1000, Orangeburg, New York 10962. *CR* is publication outlet of Consumers Union, 256 Washington Street, Mount Vernon, New York 10550.

Consumer Research Magazine (formerly *Consumer Bulletin*), information and comparative ratings on various consumer products. Subscription: $8 per year, Consumer Research, Inc., Washington, New Jersey 07882.

ASTM Standardization News, published monthly by American Society for Testing and Materials, 1916 Race Street, Philadelphia, Pennsylvania 19103. Subscription: $9 per year.

Directory *Capital Contacts In Consummerism,* a "Who's Who" of key consumer contacts in congressional committees, federal departments, regulatory agents, national consumer activist groups, consumer affairs publications, state consumer affairs offices, 1975. Published by the Washington Communications Counselors, 1701 K Street N.W., Washington, D.C. 20006. 1975. $11.00.

Consumer Sourcebook by P. Wasserman and J. Morgan. A directory and guide to government organizations, associations, centers, and institutes, media services, company and trademark information, and bibliographic material relating to consumer topics, sources of recourse, and advisory information, 1975. Published by Gale Research Company, Book Tower, Detroit, Michigan 48226. $35.00.

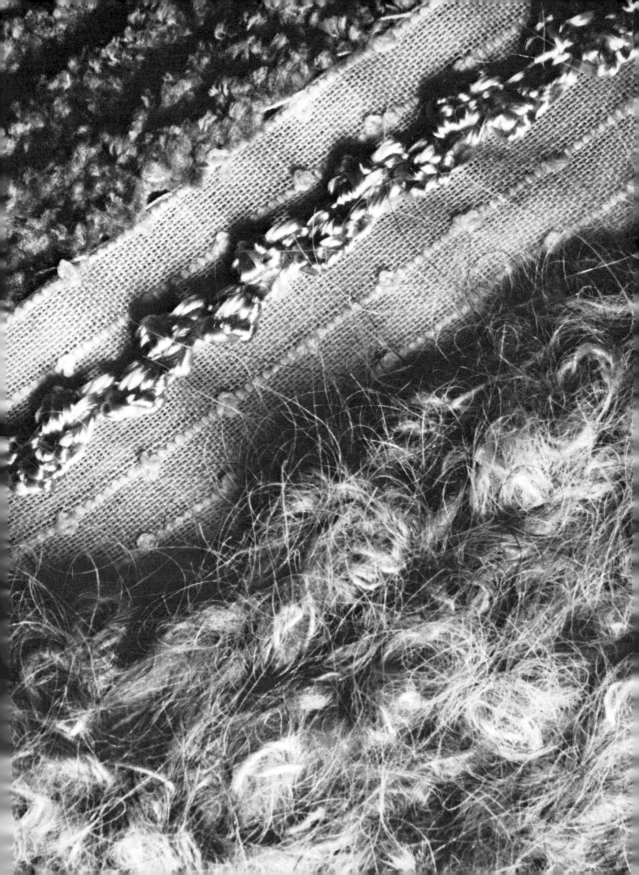

Appendix

CONTENTS

A
Commercial, Industrial, Government, and Private Testing Laboratories

COMMERCIAL, INDUSTRIAL, GOVERNMENTAL

Better Fabrics Testing Bureau, 101 West 31st Street, New York, New York 10001

Directory of Testing Laboratories, Commercial-Institutional, Special Technical Publication STP 330, American Society for Testing and Materials, 1916 Race Street, Philadelphia, Pennsylvania 19103— $3.75

Fabric Research Laboratories, Inc., 1000 Providence Highway, Dedham, Massachusetts 02026

Qualified Laboratory List, No. 21, January 1975; Defense Personnel Support Center, 2800 South 20th Street, Philadelphia, Pennsylvania 19101

Underwriters' Laboratories, Inc., 207 East Ohio Street, Chicago, Illinois 60611

U.S. Testing Company, Inc., Textile Research Department, 1415 Park Avenue, Hoboken, New Jersey 07030

RETAIL

Macy's Bureau of Standards, R.H. Macy Company, 151 East 34th Street, New York, New York 10001

Marshall Field and Company, Testing Laboratory, 111 North State Street, Chicago, Illinois 60690

J.C. Penney Company, Inc., 1301 Avenue of the Americas, New York, New York 10019

Sears Roebuck and Company, Merchandise, Development and Testing Laboratory, Department 817, 925 South Homan Avenue, Chicago, Illinois 60607

Sears Roebuck and Company, New York Textile Laboratory, Department 817, 360 West 31st Street, New York, New York 10001

B
Fiber Trademark Names; Fiber Producers and Associations

Acetate	Acele	Filament yarn	E. I. du Pont de Nemours and Co., Inc.
	Ariloft	Filament yarn	Eastman Kodak Co., Tennessee Eastman Co. Div.
	Avicolor	Solution-dyed filament	Avtex Fibers Inc.
	Celacloud	Crimped staple fiberfill	Celanese Fibers Marketing Co., Celanese Corp.
	Celanese	Staple filament, cigarette filter, and fiberfill	Celanese Fibers Marketing Co., Celanese Corp.
	Chromspun	Solution-dyed filament yarn	Eastman Kodak Co., Tennessee Eastman Co. Div.
	Estron	Filament yarn and cigarette filter tow	Eastman Kodak Co., Tennessee Eastman Co. Div.
	Estron SLR	Filament yarn	Eastman Kodak Co., Tennessee Eastman Co. Div.
	FMC	Filament yarn	Avtex Fibers Inc.
	Loftura	Slub voluminized Filament yarn	Eastman Kodak Co., Tennessee Eastman Co. Div.
	SayFR	Fire resistant Filament acetate	Avtex Fibers Inc.
Acrylic	A-Acrilan	Staple and tow	Monsanto Textiles Co.
	Acrilan	Staple and tow	Monsanto Textiles Co.

	Bi-Loft	Fibers, filaments	Monsanto Textiles Co.
	Creslan	Staple and tow	American Cyanamid Co.
	Orlon	Staple and tow	E. I. du Pont de Nemours and Co. Inc.
	Zefran	Acrylic, dyeable, and producer colored	Dow Badische Co.
Aramid	Kevlar	Filament	E. I. du Pont de Nemours and Co., Inc.
	Nomex	Filament and staple	E. I. du Pont de Nemours and Co., Inc.
Biconstituent Fiber	Source	Biconstituent nylon-polyester	Allied Chemical Corp., Fibers Division
	Monvelle	Biconstituent nylon-spandex	Monsanto Textiles Co.
Fluorocarbon	Teflon	Fluorocarbon	E. I. du Pont de Nemours and Co., Inc.
Metallic	Lurex	Yarn of slit film	Dow Badische Co.
Modacrylic	A-Acrilan	Staple and tow	Monsanto Textiles Co.
	Acrilan	Staple and tow	Monsanto Textiles Co.
	Elura	Modacrylic	Monsanto Textiles Co.
	Orlon	Staple and tow	E. I. du Pont de Nemours & Co., Inc.
	Sef	Modacrylic	Monsanto Textiles Co.
	Verel	Modacrylic	Eastman Kodak Co., Tennessee Eastman Co. Div.
Nylon	Actionwear	Nylon	Monsanto Textiles Co.
	Anso	Nylon filament and staple soil-resistant carpet yarn	Allied Chemical Corp., Fibers Division
	Antron	Nylon	E. I. du Pont de Nemours & Co., Inc.
	Astroturf	Nylon	Monsanto Textiles Co.
	Ayrlyn	Continuous filament	Rohm and Haas Co., Fibers Div.

Beaunit Nylon	Nylon filament, staple, and tow, plied and heat set 2500 denier and white and space dyed	Beaunit Corp.
Blue "C"	Nylon	Monsanto Textiles Co.
Bodyfree	Static-resistant filament apparel yarn	Allied Chemical Corp., Fibers Division
Cadon	Filament yarn and multilobal monofilament	Monsanto Textiles Co.
Cantrece	Nylon	E. I. du Pont de Nemours & Co., Inc.
Caprolan	Yarns, monofila- ments, and textured yarns	Allied Chemical Corp., Fibers Division
Captiva	Textured fila- ment hosiery yarn	Allied Chemical Corp., Fibers Division
Cedilla	Textured nylon filament yarn	Fiber Industries, Inc., Marketed by Celanese Fibers Marketing Co., Celanese Corp.
Celanese	Nylon	Fiber Industries, Inc., Marketed by Celanese Fibers Marketing Co., Celanese Corp.
Cordura	Nylon	E. I. du Pont de Nemours & Co., Inc.
Courtaulds Nylon	Nylon producer Crimped nylon yarn	Courtaulds North America, Inc.
Crepeset	Patented contin- uous monofila- ment that develops a regular crimp, also avail- able in anticling yarn	American Enka Co.
Cumuloft	Textured fila- ment carpet yarn	Monsanto Textiles Co.

Enka	Nylon fila- ment, staple	American Enka Co.
Enkaloft	Textured multi- lobal continuous filament carpet yarn and staple	American Enka Co.
Enkalure	Multilobal con- tinuous filament apparel yarn and textured delayed soiling carpet yarn	American Enka Co.
Enkalure II	Textured multi- lobal soil-hiding continuous fila- ment carpet yarn and staple.	American Enka Co.
Enkalure III	Anticling fine denier nylon	American Enka Co.
Enkasheer	Continuous monofilament torque yarn for ladies' stretch hosiery (patented process)	American Enka Co.
Guaranteeth	Apparel and home furnishings nylon and poly- ester yarn	Allied Chemical Corp. Fibers Division
Monvelle	Biconstituent nylon-spandex	Monsanto Textiles Co.
Multisheer	Multifilament producer-textured stretch yarn for panty hose	American Enka Co.
Phillips 66 Nylon	Multifilament nylon yarn	Phillips Fibers Corp.
Phillips 66 Nylon BCF	Bulk continuous filament yarn	Phillips Fibers Corp.
Qiana	Nylon	E. I. du Pont de Nemours & Co., Inc.
Random-Set	Heat set BCF nylon	Rohm and Haas Co.

Random-Tone	Fashion and styling yarns of BCF nylon fiber	Rohm and Haas Co.
Shareen	Nylon mono-filament textured yarn	Courtaulds North America Inc.
Source	Biconstituent nylon-polyester	Allied Chemical Corp., Fibers Division
Stria	Bulked nylon carpet yarn, modified twist	American Enka Co.
Stryton	Variable denier continuous filament nylon yarn	Phillips Fibers Corp.
Super Bulk	Heat-set, high-bulk continuous filament nylon carpet yarn; luxurious thick look of spun nylon	American Enka Co.
Tango	Fine denier nylon	Allied Chemical Corp., Fibers Division
Twix	Bulk nylon carpet yarn, modified twist	American Enka Co.
Ultron	Nylon	Monsanto Textiles Co.
Variline	Variable denier continuous filament yarn (patented process)	American Enka Co.
Zefran	Nylon	Dow Badische Co.
Olefin Herculon	Continuous multifilament, bulked continuous multifilament staple and tow	Hercules Inc., Fibers Div.
Marvess	Staple, tow, and filament yarn	Phillips Fibers Corp.
Marvess III BCF	Bulk continuous filament yarn	Phillips Fibers Corp.
Polyester Avlin	Filament yarn and staple	Avtex Fibers Inc.

Blue "C"	Polyester	Monsanto Textiles Co.
Dacron	Filament yarn, staple, tow, and fiberfill	E. I. du Pont de Nemours & Co., Inc.
Encron	Continuous filament yarn, staple, fiberfill	American Enka Co.
Encron MCS	Staple with modified cross section	American Enka Co.
Encron 8	Octalobal polyester that reduces glitter	American Enka Co.
Enka	Filament and staple	American Enka Co.
Esterweld	Polyester	American Cyanamid Co.
Fiber 200	Polyester	Avtex Fibers Inc.
Fortrel	Filament yarn, staple, tow, and fiberfill	Marketed by Celanese Fibers Marketing Co., Celanese Corp.
Fortrel 7	Continuous filament fiberfill	Fiber Industries, Inc., Marketed by Celanese Fibers Marketing Co., Celanese Corp.
Golden Touch	High-denier per filament Encron polyester for luxurious hand	American Enka Co.
Guaranteeth	Apparel and home furnishings nylon and polyester yarn	Allied Chemical Corp., Fibers Division
Kodel	Filament yarn, staple, tow, and fiberfill	Eastman Kodak Co., Tennessee Eastman Co. Div.
Quintess	Polyester multifilament yarns	Phillips Fibers Corp.
Source	Biconstituent nylon-polyester	Allied Chemical Corp.
Spectran	Polyester	Monsanto Textiles Co.
Strialine	Slub-effect, variable dyeing Encron polyester	American Enka Co.

	Textura	Producer textured polyester yarn	Rohm and Haas Co., Fibers Div.
	Trevira	Polyester	Hoechst Fibers Inc.
	Vycron	Filament, staple, tow, and fiberfill	Beaunit Corp.
	Zefran	Polyester	Dow Badische Co.
Rayon	Avicolor	Solution-dyed filament and staple	Avtex Fibers Inc.
	Aviloc	Adhesive-treated high-strength rayon yarn	Avtex Fibers Inc.
	Avril	High wet modulus staple	Avtex Fibers Inc.
	Avril FR	Fire-resistant, high wet modulus rayon	Avtex Fibers Inc.
	Beau-Grip	Specially treated viscose high-tenacity yarn	Beaunit Corp.
	Briglo	Bright luster continuous filament yarn	American Enka Co.
	Coloray	Solution-dyed staple	Courtaulds North America Inc.
	Encel	High wet modulus staple	American Enka Co.
	Englo	Dull luster continuous filament yarn	American Enka Co.
	Enka	Rayon	American Enka Co.
	Enkrome	Patented acid-dyeable staple and continuous filament yarn	American Enka Co.
	Fiber 40	High wet modulus staple	Avtex Fibers Inc.
	Fiber 700	High wet modulus staple	American Enka Co.
	Fibro	Staple	Courtaulds North America Inc.

	Fibro DD	Deep-dyed rayon staple fiber	Courtaulds North America Inc.
	Fibro FR	Flame-retardant rayon staple fiber	Courtaulds North America Inc.
	FMC	Rayon	Avtex Fibers Inc.
	I.T.	Improved tenacity staple	American Enka Co.
	Jetspun	Solution-dyed continuous filament yarn	American Enka Co.
	Kolorbon	Solution-dyed staple	American Enka Co.
	SayFR	Fire-resistant filament rayon	FMR Corp., Fiber Division
	Skyloft	Bulked continuous filament yarn	American Enka Co.
	Softglo	Semidull luster continuous filament yarn	American Enka Co.
	Super White	Optically brightened rayon	American Enka Co.
	Suprenka	Extra high-tenacity continuous filament industrial yarn	American Enka Co.
	Suprenka Hi Mod	Extra high-tenacity high-modulus continuous filament	American Enka Co.
	Xena	High wet modulus staple	Beaunit Corp.
	Zantrel	High wet modulus staple	American Enka Co.
	Zantrell 700	High wet modulus staple	American Enka Co.
Spandex	Lycra	Spandex	E. I. du Pont de Nemours & Co. Inc.
	Monvelle	Biconstituent nylon-spandex	Monsanto Textiles Co.
Triacetate	Arnel	Filament yarn and staple	Celanese Fibers Marketing Co., Celanese Corp.

This list of trademarks indicates trademarks used by members that do not come within the Federal Trade Commission definition of "fiber trademark" but that may be used, from time to time, to identify the source of certain manmade fibers or other products of the company.

Trademark	Member Company
ACT	Allied Chemical Corporation, Marketed by Specialty Chemicals Division
ADORATION	E. I. du Pont de Nemours & Co., Inc.
ANGELREST	Fiber Industries, Inc., Marketed by Celanese Fibers Marketing Company, A Division of Celanese Corporation
ANTELETTE	Fiber Industries, Inc., Marketed by Celanese Fibers Marketing Company, A Division of Celanese Corporation
ASTROTURF	Monsanto Textiles Company
AVISCO	Avtex Fibers Inc.
BEAUNIT	Beaunit Corporation
BYTRECE	E. I. du Pont de Nemours & Co., Inc.
CELABOND	Celanese Fibers Marketing Co., Celanese Corp.
CELAIRE	Celanese Fibers Marketing Co., Celanese Corp.
CELANESE	Celanese Fibers Marketing Co., Celanese Corp.
CELANNA	Celanese Fibers Marketing Co., Celanese Corp.
CELASPUN	Celanese Fibers Marketing Co., Celanese Corp.
CHEMSTRAND	Monsanto Textiles Company
COURTAULDS	Courtaulds North America Inc.
CUPROFINO	Beaunit Corporation
DU PONT	E. I. du Pont de Nemours & Co., Inc.
DYE I	Monsanto Textiles Company
EASTMAN	Eastman Kodak Company, Tennessee Eastman Company Division
EKTAFILL	Eastman Kodak Company, Tennessee Eastman Company Division
ELURA	Monsanto Textiles Company
ENKA	American Enka Company
FMC	Avtex Fibers Inc.
HERCULES	Hercules Incorporated
HYTEN	E. I. du Pont de Nemours & Co., Inc.
LEKTROSET	IRC Fibers Company, Subsidiary of American Cyanamid Company
LOKTUFT	Phillips Fibers Corporation, Subsidiary of Phillips Petroleum Company
LOWLAND	American Enka Company

LYRIC		Eastman Kodak Company, Tennessee Eastman Company Division
REEMAY		E. I. du Pont de Nemours & Co., Inc.
SERENE		Fiber Industries, Inc., Marketed by Celanese Fibers Marketing Co., A Division of Celanese Corporation
SPUNIZE		Allied Chemical Corp., Fibers Division
SUPERBA		Fiber Industries, Inc., Marketed by Celanese Fibers Marketing Company, A Division of Celanese Corporation
TASLAN		E. I. du Pont de Nemours & Co., Inc.
TYPAR		E. I. du Pont de Nemours & Co., Inc.
TYVEK		E. I. du Pont de Nemours & Co., Inc.
WEAR-DATED		Monsanto Textiles Company
ZEFSTAT		Dow Badische Company
ZEFWEAR		Dow Badische Company

FIBER PRODUCERS AND ASSOCIATIONS

Natural Fibers

Cotton	Cotton, Inc. 1370 Avenue of the Americas New York, New York 10019	
	National Cotton Council of America Box 12285, Memphis, Tennessee 38112	
	Supima Association of America 350 Fifth Avenue, New York, New York 10001	
Linen	Belgian Linen Association 280 Madison Avenue, New York, New York 10016	
	Irish Linen Guild 1271 Avenue of the Americas New York, New York 10020	
Wool	American Sheep Producers Council 200 Clayton St., Denver, Colorado 80206	
	American Wool Council 1460 Broadway, New York, New York 10038	
	Mohair Council of America 151 W. 40th St., New York, New York 10018	
	Wool Bureau 360 Lexington Ave., New York, New York 10017	
Silk	International Silk Association 299 Madison Ave., New York, New York 10017	

**Members, Man-made Fiber
Producers Association, Inc.**

Allied Chemical Corp., Fibers Div.,
One Times Square, New York, New York 10036

American Cyanamid Co., Fibers Div.,
Berdan Ave., Wayne, New Jersey 07470

American Enka Company, A Part of Akzona, Inc.
Enka, North Carolina 28728

Beaunit Corporation
261 Madison Ave., New York, New York 10016

Celanese Corp., Celanese Fibers Marketing Co.
1211 Ave. of the Americas, New York, New York 10018

.Dow Badische Company
Williamsburg, Virginia 23185

E. I. du Pont de Nemours & Co., Inc.
Textile Fibers Dept., Wilmington, Delaware 19898

Eastman Kodak Co., Tenn. Eastman Co. Div.,
Marketed by Eastman Chemical Products Inc.
Kingsport, Tennessee 37662

Hercules Inc., Fibers Div.,
910 Market St., Wilmington, Delaware 19899

Hoechst Fibers Incorporated
1515 Broadway at Astor Plaza, New York, New York 10036

Monsanto Textiles Company
800 N. Lindbergh Blvd., St. Louis, Missouri 63166

Phillips Fiber Corporation
Subsidiary of Phillips Petroleum Co.
P.O. Box 66, Greenville, South Carolina 29602

Rohm & Haas Co., Fibers Div.,
Independence Mall West, Philadelphia, Pennsylvania 19105

C
The Microscope

**USE OF THE
MICROSCOPE**

There is a right way and a wrong way to handle a microscope. Proper technique of operation makes it possible to operate a microscope with the greatest possible ease and efficiency. Study Figure C–1 and become familiar with the parts of a microscope.

The microscope is an optical instrument capable of producing a magnified image of a small object. The three important parts of the

Figure C-1 Optical and mechanical features of the microscope. (Courtesy: American Optical Corporation)

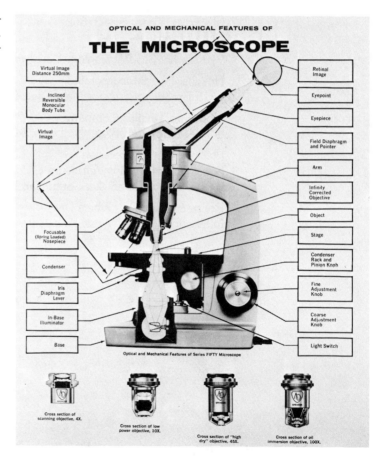

microscope consist of (1) a condenser, (2) an objective, and (3) an eyepiece. The condenser is a system of lenses or mirrors designed to collect, control, and concentrate light. The objective is the primary magnifying system of a microscope. The lense system forms a real, inverted, and magnified image of the object. The eyepiece is a lens or system of lenses for increasing magnification in a microscope by magnifying the image formed by the objective. The final image is virtual except when projected on a plane surface as in microprojection.

Place several fibers on a glass slide. Cover with a drop of water and a cover glass. To focus a microscope, place a low-power objective on the slide that is placed on the stage.

Swing the substage mirror so that the object is illuminated as evenly as possible. Use the coarse adjustment to focus down until the objective comes very close to the cover glass. DO NOT LET THE OBJECTIVE TOUCH THE COVER GLASS. This should be done while sighting across the slide from one side.

Look through the microscope and focus up very slowly with the coarse adjustment until the fibers come into view. This makes it easy to locate the specimen. When the tube nears the correct focus, the fibers appear as shadowy lines moving across the field of view. Move the slide very slowly because the microscope magnifies not only objects but motion as well.

The focusing should be deliberate enough so that the focal point will not be passed. Avoid the temptation to focus down with the coarse adjustment. This should never be done until considerable experience in manipulating the instrument has been obtained. A slip of the fingers may ruin the front lens of an objective or spoil the specimen on the slide. It is a good practice never to do this while looking through the instrument.

Make the final focus with the fine adjustment. These adjustments vary in construction in different models. Exercise care in focusing, because you must look through the eyepiece while the operation is being performed. Any actual contact of objective and slide should be avoided.

It should be noted that with any motion of the slide the microscope reverses the direction, so that if the specimen is pushed to the right, it appears to move to the left and vice versa.

When a revolving nose piece is used, the higher powered objectives are "parfocalized" so that an object may be found and focused with a low-powered objective, and when the higher-powered lens system is rotated into position, only a slight alteration of the fine adjustment is needed to get the correct focus.

The intensity of illumination may be made by adjusting the light, condenser, substage, or diaphragm.

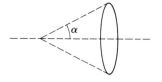

The ability of the microscope to pick out fine detail is of greater importance than either magnification or definition. You should not be interested in how big you can make the fiber appear but how much actual structure or detail you can make visible.

A quantity known as the "numerical aperture" is the measure of the resolving power of an objective. Theoretically the numerical aperture (N.A.) is the product of the lowest index of refraction (n) in the object space by the sine of half the angular aperture of the objective.

The cone of light proceeding from the specimen toward the objective is spread out by diffraction so that it is larger and of less uniform distribution than it would be otherwise. Each part of the cone carries the possibility of showing some portion of the specimen, and a complete image will not be formed unless all of the enlarged cone is admitted to the objective and transmitted by it. Obviously the numerical aperture of the objective is of importance here.

The magnifying power of the microscope depends on the size of the final image formed compared with the size of the object being examined. If a microscope is said to magnify 100 times, it means that the picture that is seen is 100 times as long and 100 times as wide as the object would appear if it were taken from the stage and placed 10 inches from the eye.

In order to express how much larger an object appears when seen through the microscope than when seen by the naked eye, a standard distance must be taken, because an object appears to the naked eye to be of different sizes at different distances.

Therefore, some standard must be taken for comparison purposes, and 10 inches has been universally adopted. The magnifying power of a microscope denotes the relative size of the picture compared with that of the original object when placed 10 inches from the eye.

If a microscope has a magnifying power of 100, such magnification may be produced by different methods. The object glass may magnify the object 20 times in the primary image, and the eyepiece increasing the primary image 5 times will give a total of 100. This magnification may also be produced by a lower-power object that magnifies the object 10 times and a higher-power eyepiece that magnifies it again by 10. The same result is obtained in magnifying power but a different result insofar as the quality of the image.

Another method of varying the magnifying power is to increase the distance between the object glass and the eyepiece. To accomplish this, the microscope is supplied with a drawtube that allows the tube length to be varied.

Magnification (M) is calculated as follows:

CALCULATION OF MAGNIFICATION, *M*

$$M = \frac{\text{length of image}}{\text{length of object}} = \frac{\text{optical tubelength}}{\text{focal length of objective}}$$

= (Magnification of eyepiece) (Magnification of objective)

= $(10\times)(43\times) = 430$

Magnification, low power : $10\times$ to $100\times$
medium power : $100\times$ to $500\times$
high power : $500\times$ to $1500\times$

The resolving power of a microscope is a measure of the fineness of detail that it will depict in the image that it forms, quite apart from the magnifying power. The microscope must have sufficient magnifying power to show such detail visible to the eye, but no amount of extra magnifying power is of use unless the resolving power is sufficient to produce an image containing the detail. Resolving power depends on the size of the cone of light that forms each point of the image.

Resolution is defined as the fineness of detail revealed by an optical device. Resolution is usually specified as the minimum distance by which two lines in the object must be separated before they can be revealed as separate lines in the image.

The theoretical limit of resolution is determined from the equation:

$$d = \frac{0.61\,\lambda}{n\,\sin\alpha}$$

where: d = minimum distance between object points observed as distinct points in the image
λ = wavelength of illumination
n = minimum refractive index of media between the object and the objective length
α = angular aperture/2

There is only one position in relation to the lenses where an object can be placed to give a perfectly clear picture. This position is generally called the focus, and the microscope is said to be "in focus" when it is so adjusted that the object is in this position.

The penetration or depth of an object or the number of different layers of an object that can be seen sharply at the same time with a microscope is very small. With lenses of a high aperture, and therefore a high magnifying power, the penetration decreases at a very rapid rate, and the power of seeing different planes sharply must depend on adjusting the instrument. It has been said that the depth of focus of a high-power microscope is really the fine focusing adjustment.

Depth of focus is defined as the depth of thickness of the image space that is simultaneously in acceptable focus.

Numerical Examples

Lens System	Numerical Aperture N.A.	Resolution μm	Depth of Focus μm
Human eye	0.01	50	00
Microscope (250×)	0.25	1.0	4
Electronmicroscope	0.002	0.003	1.5

A cross-sectional view of a fiber, in conjunction with a longitudinal view, gives a total picture that enables one to confirm fiber identification. Cross-sectional views show up the internal structure to an advantage. The preparation of cross sections of fibers can be achieved by several methods: (1) embedding the fiber in paraffin, (2) embedding the fiber in cork, (3) fabric cross section, (4) yarn sections, (5) metal plate sections, and (6) microtome sections.

A RAPID METHOD OF PREPARING FIBER CROSS SECTIONS*

Cross sections of fibers and yarns can be prepared rapidly by embedding the fibers in polyethylene. Polyethylene provides an ideal embedding medium for preparing cross sections: its light transmitting properties are good, it does not readily accept dyes and stains, it provides sufficient rigidity to resist the cutting blade, and it can be handled without crumbling. Polyethylene can be used with a variety of fixatives and mounting media since it is unaffected by the usual solvents used in microscopy. The temperature required to mold this plastic is much lower than the melting point of most textile fibers.

The polyethylene embedding technique requires a sharp microtome knife or single-edge razor blade with a holder to cut sections. A microtome designed for textile work is preferred and will provide thin, uniform sections. If a microtome is not available, a microtome knife should be used and cuts made with the aid of a low power binocular microscope or simple magnifier with an illuminator. A razor blade will cut better if washed free of antirust compounds and sharpened on a piece of leather. Knives should always be sharpened on a whetstone after use and edges wiped with a soft chamois before being put away.

* "A Rapid Method of Preparing Fiber Cross-Sections," 1974 Intersectional Technical Paper Competition, Hudson-Mohawk Section, *Textile Chemists and Colorists,* Vol. 7, No. 6 (June 1975).

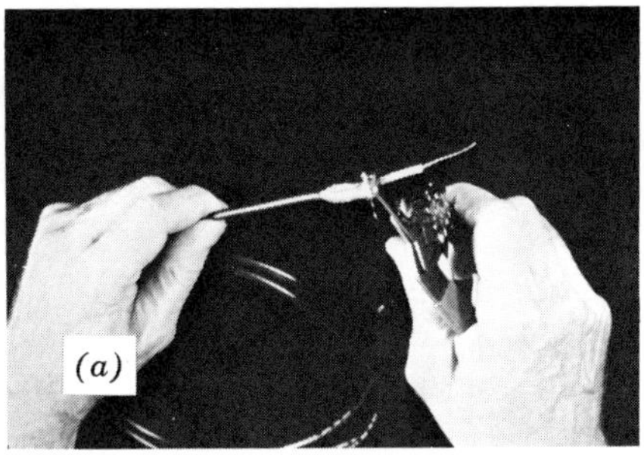

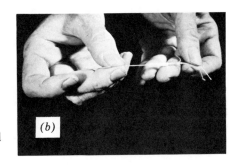

Figure C-2a Polyethylene embedding tube is obtained by stripping a commercially available RG 58-AU coaxial cable with a wire stripper. The 0.8-mm hole will accommodate most commonly used yarns.

Figure C-2b The yarn to be sectioned is pulled through a polyethylene tube with a sewing needle.

Figure C-2c The tube with the inserted yarn is placed in a square of aluminum foil; the foil is then folded.

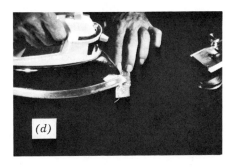

Figure C-2d Both sides are pressed with a hot hand iron. Alternatively, the foil may be placed in the center of a scorch tester, heated for 20 sec on each side and allowed to cool.

517

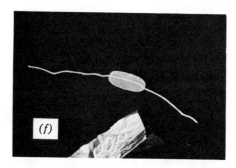

Figure C-2e To remove crimp from the yarn, the yarn can be taped and stretched before pressing with a hand iron.

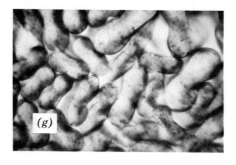

Figure C-2f Appearance of the specimen after flattening and heating.

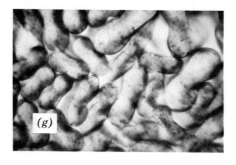

Figure C-2g Photomicrograph of typical yarn cross section prepared by this technique.

A tube of polyethylene approximately 12 millimeters long, 2 millimeters outside diameter and with a 0.8-millimeter hole is used in this method. Such a tube is obtained by stripping a commercially available RG 58/AU coaxial cable of its outer sheath and then removing the polyethylene insulation with a wire stripper. The 0.8-millimeter hole will accommodate most commonly used yarns. This coaxial cable may be obtained from any electronic or TV supply store (see Figure C–2a).

Procedure   The following steps are used to prepare cross sections.

The yarn to be sectioned is pulled through the polyethylene tube with a sewing needle threaded with ordinary sewing thread. This is accomplished by entwining the yarn in the thread and then drawing the thread and the yarn through the tube (Figure C–2b).

The tube with the inserted yarn is placed in a square of aluminum foil (Figure C–2c), then folded and flattened with a hot hand iron (Figure C–2d). Both sides should be pressed to center the yarn in the flattened tube.

Crimp can be removed from the yarn by stretching the yarn and taping portions of the yarn extending from the ends of the tube to an index card, sliding the aluminum foil under the tube, folding the card, and pressing (Figure C–2e).

A scorch tester set at 204°C can also be used; this method is preferred because both top and bottom surfaces are heated simultaneously. The foil is placed in the center of the scorch tester, and heated for 20 seconds on each side and then allowed to cool. The thickness should be slightly greater than the slot of the microtome to insure a tight fit. If the polyethylene is too thick, further pressing may be necessary.

The flattened tube (Figure C–2f) is trimmed with a razor blade and inserted in a microtome. Sections are sliced with a single-edged safety razor blade in a holder or a microtome knife. Very little pressure is exerted, and a bias motion prevents curling of the slice.

Freehand sections may be cut by stapling or tacking the flattened tube to a piece of plywood and slicing while observing the tube through a low-powered microscope.

A drop or two of glycerine or oil is placed over the sliced sections prior to covering with a cover glass. Permanent slides can be made with Canadian balsam or albumin fixative followed by cementing the edge of the cover glass.

An example of a fiber cross section produced by the polyethylene technique is shown in Figure C–2g.

Longitudinal View at 250×   Cross-Sectional View at 500×

PHOTOMICROGRAPHS OF MAN-MADE TEXTILE FIBERS

ACETATE FIBERS

Acele* (secondary acetate)
3.8 denier per filament
bright luster

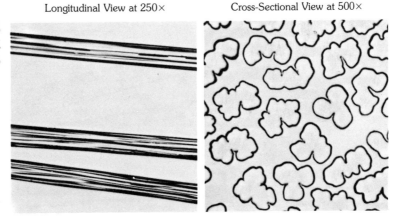

*Du Pont's registered trademark for its acetate fiber

"Arnel" (triacetate)
2.5 denier per filament
dull luster

 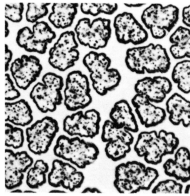

ACRYLIC FIBERS

"Acrilan" regular
3.0 denier per filament
bright luster

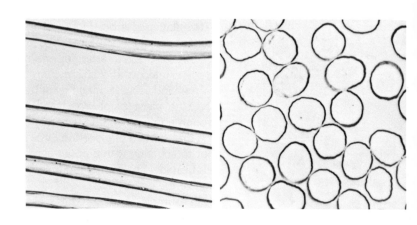

"Creslan"
3.0 denier per filament
semidull luster

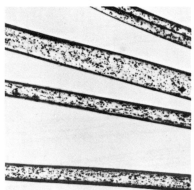 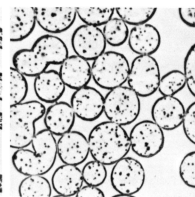

520

Longitudinal View at 250×   Cross-Sectional View at 500×

Orlon* regular
3.0 denier per filament
semidull luster

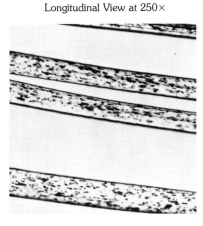
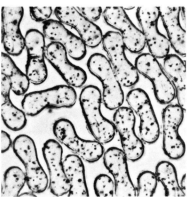

Orlon Sayelle†
3.0 denier per filament
semidull luster

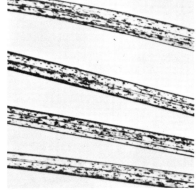
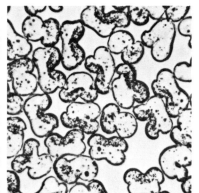

"Zefran"
3.0 denier per filament
semidull luster

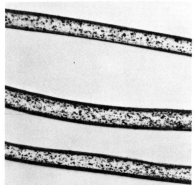
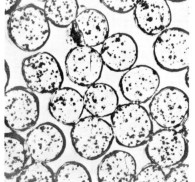

*Du Pont's registered
trademark for its acrylic
fiber
†Du Pont's registered
trademark for its
bicomponent acrylic fiber

521

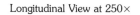

MODACRYLIC FIBERS

"Verel" regular
3.0 denier per filament
dull luster

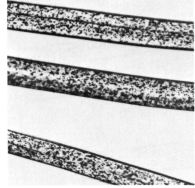
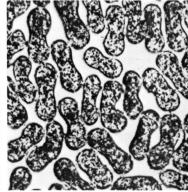

NYLON FIBERS

Antron*
15 denier per filament
bright luster

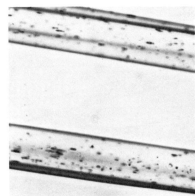
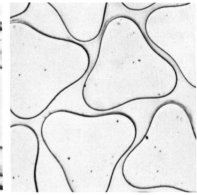

Nylon 6
3.1 denier per filament
semidull luster

*Du Pont's registered trademark
for its trilobal multifilament nylon
6-6 yarn

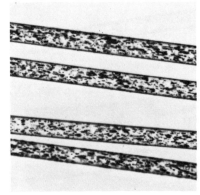
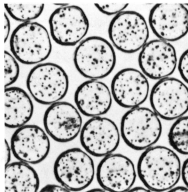

Nylon 6-6 regular
3.1 denier per filament
semidull luster

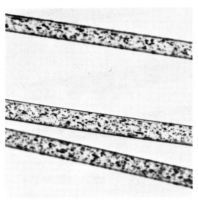
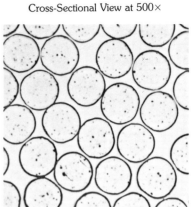

Nylon 6-6 Du Pont Type 501
18 denier per filament
semidull luster

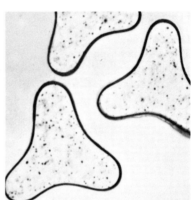

OLEFIN FIBERS

Polyethylene
90* denier per filament
natural luster

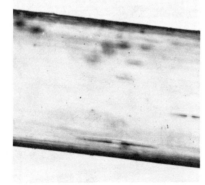
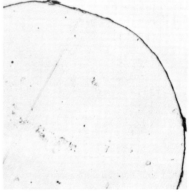

*4 to 5 mil (diameter monofila-
ment yarn)

Polypropylene
3.0 denier per filament
natural luster

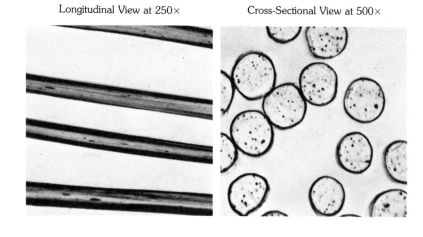

POLYESTER FIBERS

Dacron* regular
3.0 denier per filament
semidull luster

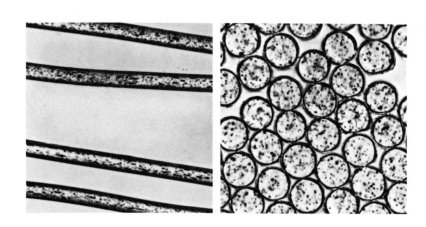

Dacron Type 62
1.4 denier per filament
semidull luster

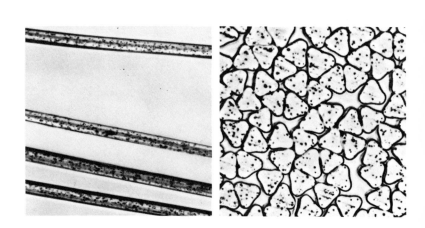

*Du Pont's registered trademark
or its polyester fiber

524

Dacron Type 64
3.0 denier per filament
semidull luster

"Kodel"
2.3 denier per filament
semidull luster

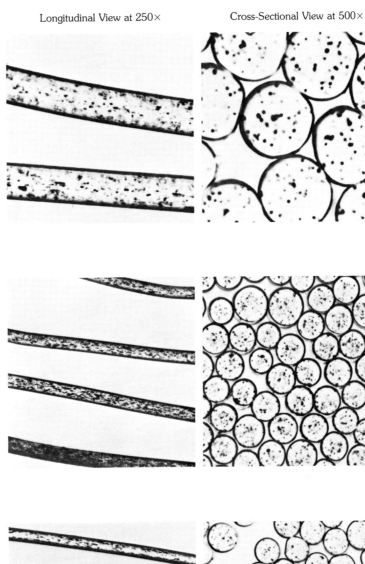

"Vycron"
1.5 denier per filament
semidull luster

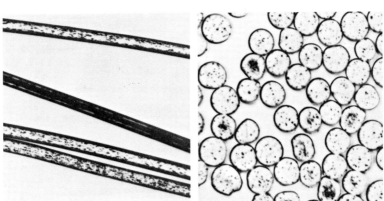

RAYON FIBERS

Cuprammonium
1.3 denier per filament
bright luster

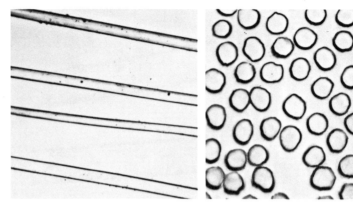

Viscose regular
3.8 denier per filament
bright luster

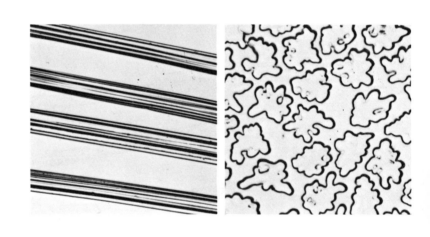

SARAN FIBER

Saran
16 denier per filament
natural luster

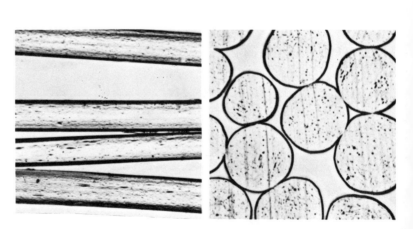

SPANDEX FIBERS

Lycra*
12 denier per filament
dull luster

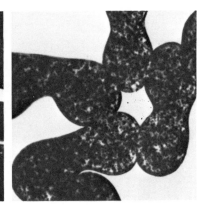

COTTON FIBERS

Cotton, mercerized
1.5* denier per filament
natural luster

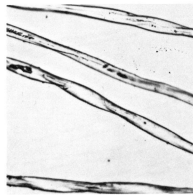
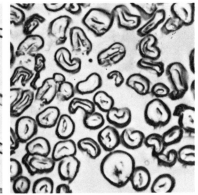

Cotton, not mercerized
1.5† denier per filament
natural luster

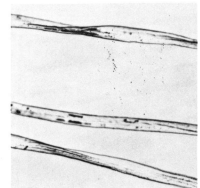

*Du Pont's registered trademark
for its spandex fiber

†Approximate average denier per
filament

FLAX FIBER

Flax, bleached
3.0* denier per filament
natural luster

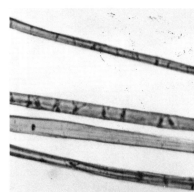 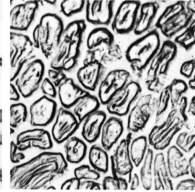

SILK FIBER

Silk, boiled-off
1.2* denier per filament
natural luster

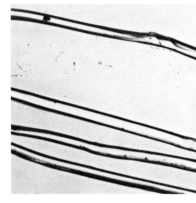 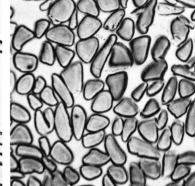

WOOL FIBERS

Cashmere
3.0* denier per filament
natural luster

*Approximate average denier per
filament

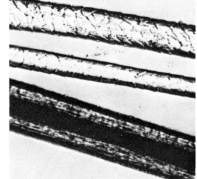 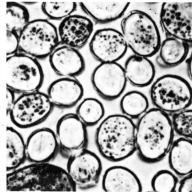

Mohair
6.5* denier per filament
natural luster

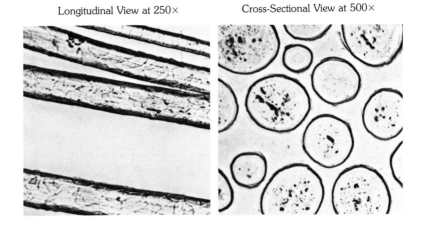

Regular (Merino)
4.0* denier per filament
natural luster

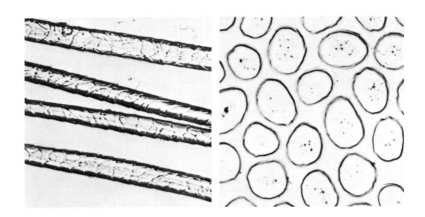

*Approximate average denier per filament.

D
Fiber Identification
Using Stain No. 4*

Test Procedure   Wet out material thoroughly in hot water before dyeing. Enter the fabric or yarn into a boiling 1.0 percent solution of DuPont Fiber Identification Stain No. 4, using a 20:1 bath to fiber ratio. Run bath at the boil for one minute, remove material, rinse lightly, and dry. Should there be any difficulty in distinguishing "Dacron" polyester fiber from "Orlon" acrylic fiber Type 42, return the material to the bath, add 5.0 percent of sulfuric acid and boil for five minutes. The "Dacron" will yield a gold shade and the "Orlon" will appear as a dull orange.

* Available from the Dyes and Chemicals Division, Organic Chemicals Department, E.I. du Pont de Nemours and Company, Inc.

Acetate	
"Acrilan" 1656	
"Arnel"	
Cotton	
Cyanamid Acrylic Fiber Type 61	
"Dacron" 54	
"Dacron" 64	
Nylon	
"Orlon" 42	
Silk	
"Verel"	
Viscose	
Wool	

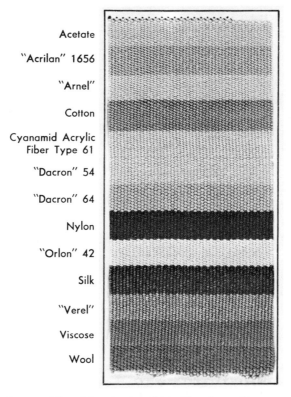

Dupont Fiber Identification Stain No. 4 provides a simple means for identifying individual fibers quickly, whether alone or used in a blended fabric. The stainings shown are representative of the results normally obtained on some of the fibers encountered in textile use. Variations in quality, preparation, or processing may cause differences from the stainings shown and further analysis is recommended.

531

E
Metric and Temperature Conversion Charts

Table E-1 Temperature Conversion Chart

°C	°F	°C	°F	°C	°F	°C	°F	°C	°F	°C	°F
0	32.0	37	98.6	74	165.2	111	231.8	148	298.4	185	365.0
1	33.8	38	100.4	75	167.0	112	233.6	149	300.2	186	366.8
2	35.6	39	102.2	76	168.8	113	235.4	150	302.0	187	368.6
3	37.4	40	104.0	77	170.6	114	237.2	151	303.8	188	370.4
4	39.2	41	105.8	78	172.4	115	239.0	152	305.6	189	372.2
5	41.0	42	107.6	79	174.2	116	240.8	153	307.4	190	374.0
6	42.8	43	109.4	80	176.0	117	242.6	154	309.2	191	375.8
7	44.6	44	111.2	81	177.8	118	244.4	155	311.0	192	377.6
8	46.4	45	113.0	82	179.6	119	246.2	156	312.8	193	379.4
9	48.2	46	114.8	83	181.4	120	248.0	157	314.6	194	381.2
10	50.0	47	116.6	84	183.2	121	249.8	158	316.4	195	383.0
11	51.8	48	118.4	85	185.0	122	251.6	159	318.2	196	384.8
12	53.6	49	120.2	86	186.8	123	253.4	160	320.0	197	386.6
13	55.4	50	122.0	87	188.6	124	255.2	161	321.8	198	388.4
14	57.2	51	123.8	88	190.4	125	257.0	162	323.6	199	390.2
15	59.0	52	125.6	89	192.2	126	258.8	163	325.4	200	392.0
16	60.8	53	127.4	90	194.0	127	260.6	164	327.2	202	395.6
17	62.6	54	129.2	91	195.8	128	262.4	165	329.0	204	399.2
18	64.4	55	131.0	92	197.6	129	264.2	166	330.8	206	402.8
19	66.2	56	132.8	93	199.4	130	266.0	167	332.6	208	406.4
20	68.0	57	134.6	94	201.2	131	267.8	168	334.4	210	410.0
21	69.8	58	136.4	95	203.0	132	269.6	169	336.2	212	413.6
22	71.6	59	138.2	96	204.8	133	271.4	170	338.0	214	417.2
23	73.4	60	140.0	97	206.6	134	273.2	171	339.8	216	420.8
24	75.2	61	141.8	98	208.4	135	275.0	172	341.6	218	424.4
25	77.0	62	143.6	99	210.2	136	276.8	173	343.4	220	428.0
26	78.8	63	145.4	100	212.0	137	278.6	174	345.2	222	431.6
27	80.6	64	147.2	101	213.8	138	280.4	175	347.0	224	435.2
28	82.4	65	149.0	102	215.6	139	282.2	176	348.8	226	438.8
29	84.2	66	150.8	103	217.4	140	284.0	177	350.6	228	442.4
30	86.0	67	152.6	104	219.2	141	285.8	178	352.4	230	446.0
31	87.8	68	154.4	105	221.0	142	287.6	179	354.2	232	449.6
32	89.6	69	156.2	106	222.8	143	289.4	180	356.0	234	453.2
33	91.4	70	158.0	107	224.6	144	291.2	181	357.8	236	456.8
34	93.2	71	159.8	108	226.4	145	293.0	182	359.6	238	460.4
35	95.0	72	161.6	109	228.2	146	294.8	183	361.4	240	464.0
36	96.8	73	163.4	110	230.0	147	296.6	184	363.2		

Table E-2 Metric Conversion Chart[a]

Approximate Conversions TO Metric Measures			Approximate Conversions FROM Metric Measures		
When You Know	Multiply by	To Find	When You Know	Multiply by	To Find
LENGTH			**LENGTH**		
inches	2.5	centimeters	millimeters	0.04	inches
feet	30	centimeters	centimeters	0.4	inches
yards	0.9	meters	meters	3.3	feet
miles	1.6	killometers	meters	1.1	yards
			kilometers	0.6	miles
AREA			**AREA**		
sq inches	6.5	sq centimeters	sq centimeters	0.16	sq inches
sq feet	0.09	sq meters	sq meters	1.2	sq yards
sq yards	0.08	sq meters	sq kilometers	0.4	sq miles
sq miles	2.6	sq kilometers	hectares (10,000		
acres	0.4	hectares	m²)	2.5	acres
MASS (weight)			**MASS** (weight)		
ounces	28	grams	grams	0.035	ounces
pounds	0.45	kilograms	kilograms	2.2	pounds
short tons (2000 lb)	0.9	tonnes	tonnes (1000 kg)	1.1	short tons
VOLUME			**VOLUME**		
teaspoons	5	milliliters	milliliters	0.03	fluid ounces
tablespoons	15	milliliters	liters	2.1	pints
fluid ounces	30	milliliters	liters	1.06	quarts
cups	0.24	liters	liters	0.26	gallons
pints	0.47	liters	cubic meters	35	cubic feet
quarts	0.95	liters	cubic meters	1.3c	cubic yards
gallons	3.8	liters			
cubic feet	0.03	cubic meters			
cubic yards	0.76	cubic meters			
TEMPERATURE (exact)			**TEMPERATURE** (exact)		
Fahrenheit temperature	5/9 (after subtracting 32)	Celsius temp	Celsius temperature	9/5 (then add 32)	Fahrenheit temperature

[a] The National Bureau of Standards has prepared a plastic wallet card that contains these data needed for converting from customary to metric units and vice versa. The price is 10 cents each, $6.25 per hundred. Order prepaid from the Superintendent of Documents, U.S. Government Printing Office, Washington, D.C. 20402 or from local U.S. Department of Commerce Field Offices as SD Catalog No. C13.10:365.

F
Claim Guides

INTERNATIONAL FAIR CLAIMS GUIDE FOR CONSUMER TEXTILE PRODUCTS:* AN ABBREVIATED VERSION

What Is This Guide For?

When you have a complaint about damaged clothing, it can be more complicated than you might think. If the damage shows up while the garment is at the drycleaner's, you might assume it is his fault and he should compensate you. He may disagree. And he may be right.

If he tells you to take it to the store where you bought it and ask for your money back, you may find this doesn't work either.

To help solve this all too common customer dilemma, the National Institute of Drycleaning (now the International Fabricare Institute) developed a Guide to help determine who is liable and for how much. It's called "The International Fair Claims Guide for Consumer Textile Products" and is 20 pages long. This is an excerpt.

In developing it the Institute consulted the Association of Better Business Bureaus, American Home Laundry Manufacturers Association, National Retail Merchants Association, American Home Economics Association, Menswear Retailers of America, insurance adjusters, Better Business Bureaus, claims court judges, laundrymen and drycleaners in settling these sticky matters.

The Guide has wide acceptance in other countries as well as the U.S.

Implied and Specified Serviceability

The National Retail Merchants Association defines "implied serviceability" this way: "In the sale of merchandise there is an implied warranty that such goods will afford reasonable service in use and unless otherwise specified be cleansed and refreshed by customary methods."

The Guide takes the position that if a garment contains no permanently affixed label giving care instructions—or if such a label has been removed, then we should assume that it can be "cleansed and refreshed" by "customary" or "normal" methods for a gar-

* International Fabricare Institute, Box 490, Joliet, Illinois 60434.

ment of its type. These "normal" renovation methods are listed in Table F-1.

However, when the garment maker turns out a product which must be handled in some special way, then a sewn-in care-instruction label should explain. Such instructions should appear not on a hang-tag which will become separated from the garment. They should be a permanent part of the garment or textile product. In the U.S. this is now required in wearing apparel under a Federal Trade Commission ruling.

The Guide says: "A man's suit is normally rated as drycleanable, not washable. If represented as washable, drycleaning is still properly an assumed capability. But if it is labeled Do not dryclean, no one should undertake to dryclean it without assuming full responsibility for results."

In other words, a permanent label should identify special capabilities (washable in the case above), and any limitations in care capabilities such as "Dryclean Only" or "Do Not Dryclean." Absence of a label implies a warranty that the "normal" renovation method may be employed. This "normal" method should be agreed on and be widely publicized. IFI suggests these "normal" procedures in Table F-1.

Table F–1   Implied Serviceability Designations and Life Expectancy Rates

Item		Renovation Method	Rate (yrs.)	Item		Renovation Method	Rate (yrs.)
	Men's & Boy's Wear			7.	Leather jackets and coats		5
1.	Bathing suits	Hand wash	2		Suede and grain leather		
2.	Coats and jackets		4		products require special		
	Cloth, dress	Dry clean			care in cleaning.		
	Cloth, sport	(See #20)			Colors normally subject		
	Pile (imitation fur)	Dry clean. Cold tumble only. No steam.			to fading and some loss in cleaning. Suedes and most grain leathers		
	Fur	Fur clean	10		restorable by application		
	Leather and suede	(See #7)			of color and finishing		
	Plastic	(See #10)			products.		
3.	Formal wear	Dry clean	5	8.	Neckties	Dry clean	1
4.	Gloves			9.	Sleepwear		2
	Fabric	Med. wash; dry-clean	1		White goods	Hot wash	
	Leather	Leather clean only	2		Colored goods	Med. wash	
5.	Hats			10.	Plastic apparel—(See #11)		3
	Felt and straw	Clean by hat renovation specialists only. Water resist.	2		Imitation leather and suede	Hand wash; no press	
				11.	Rainwear		
	Fur	Fur clean	5		Film and plastic coated fabrics	Hand wash; no press	2
6.	Jackets	(see #2 or #11)					

Item		Renovation Method	Rate (yrs.)	Item		Renovation Method	Rate (yrs.)
	Fabric				Wash suits	Med. wash; dry clean	2
	Unlined	Med. wash, dry clean	3	22.	Sweaters		3
	Lined and quilted	Dry clean			Wool and synthetics	Hand wash; dry flat only; dry clean; wet clean	
	Rubber	Wipe down with damp cloth; no press	3				
				23.	Underwear		2
12.	Robes				White	Hot wash	
	Silk or wool	Dry clean	3		Colored	Med. wash	
	Other:		2	24.	Uniforms		1
	Unlined	Med. wash; dry clean			Unlined and work types	Med. wash; dry clean	
	Lined	Dry clean			Lined and dressy	Dry clean	
13.	Shoes			25.	Vests		2
	Can be cleaned and polished, resoled, heeled. Thread in uppers holds sections securely for normal service life without undue breakage.				Fancy & regular	Dry clean	
				26.	Windbreakers	(See #11)	
				27.	Work clothing		2
	Men's		3		Customarily shows noticeable signs of wear to greater or lesser degree depending on amount of use. Color may be expected to appear rubbed off in areas. Fabric has strength to withstand strains of use and laundering at 160F with heavy duty soap.		
	Boy's		1				
14.	Shirts						
	Dress and plain sports		2				
	White and partly colored	Hot wash					
	Colored	Hot wash; no bleach					
					Women's & Girl's Wear		
	Sports (fancy)			28.	Aprons		
	Cotton and blends	Med. wash; dry clean	3		Regular	Med. wash; bleach white only.	1
	Wool or Silk	Dry clean; hand wash	2		Fancy	Hand wash; dry clean	4
15.	Shorts	(See #17)		29.	Blouses and		
16.	Ski jackets	(See #11)			Dress & Sports		
17.	Slacks and shorts	(including matching sets)			White cotton	Hot wash; dry clean	3
	Wool or wool blends	Dry clean	4		White synthetics and all colored	Med. wash; dry clean	2
	Cotton	Med. wash; dry clean	2				
	Synthetics	Dry clean	2	30.	Coats and jackets	(See #2)	
18.	Sneakers	Med. wash; bleach; Air or tumble dry	0	31.	Dresses		
					House and sports	Med. wash; dry clean	1
19.	Socks		1				
	Wool	Hand wash			Afternoon	Dry clean	3
	Other	Med. wash			Street	Dry clean	2
20.	Sport coats				Evening or cocktail:		
	Wool and wool blends	Dry clean	4		High fashion	Dry clean; special handling of delicate and decorated styles	3
	Cotton and synthetics	Dry clean	2				
21.	Suits						
	Summer weight				Basic	Dry clean	5
	Wool or wool blends	Dry clean	3	32.	Gloves		
	Cotton and synthetics	Dry clean	2		Fabric	Med. wash separate; dry clean	1
	Winter weight	Dry clean	4		Leather	Leather clean	2

Table F–1 (*Continued*)

Item	Renovation Method	Rate (yrs.)	Item	Renovation Method	Rate (yrs.)
33. Hats			52. Uniforms		1
Felt	Clean by special hat-renovation methods	1	Unlined and work types	Med. wash; dry clean	
			Lined and dressy	Dry clean	
Straw	Same unless trim detail precludes cleaning	2	53. Wedding gowns	Dry clean	[a]
			54. Windbreakers	(See #11)	
Fur	Fur clean	5	55. Work clothing	(See #27)	
34. Housecoats and robes			**Children's Wear**		
Lightweight cottons and synthetics	Mild wash; dry clean	1	56. Coats	Dry clean	2
			57. Coat sets	Dry clean	2
Quilted and heavy	Dry clean	3	58. Dresses	Med. wash; dry clean	2
35. Jackets	(See #2 or #11)		59. Hats, bonnets	Dry clean	1
36. Negligee			60. Playclothes	Med. wash	1
Cotton and nylon types	Med. wash	2	61. Snow suits		2
			Wool and wool blends	Dry clean	
37. Sleepwear		2	Cotton and synthetics	Med. wash; dry clean	
White goods	Hot wash		62. Suits	Dry clean	2
Colored goods	Med. wash		63. Undergarments		1
38. Rainwear	(See #11)		White goods	Hot wash	
39. Robes	(See #34)		Colored	Med. wash	
40. Scarves		2	**Household Furnishings**		
Wool	Dry clean		64. Bedspreads		3
Other	Mild wash; dry clean		Cotton, synthetics	Med. wash; dry clean	
Fur	Fur clean	5	65. Blankets		
41. Shoes			Heavy wool and synthetic fabrics	Mild wash; dry clean	10
Dress and walking	(See #13)	2	Lightweight	Mild wash; dry clean	5
Work		1	Electric	Mild wash	5
Evening, formal		5	66. Curtains		
42. Shorts	(See #44)		Sheer	Med. wash; dry clean	3
43. Skirts		2	Glass fiber	Hand wash; wet clean	
Winter and fall	Dry clean-wet clean		67. Draperies		
Resort and summer	Med. wash; dry clean		Lined	Dry clean	5
44. Slacks and shorts			Unlined	Med. wash; dry clean	4
Lounging and tailored	Dry clean	2	Sheer	Med. wash; dry clean	3
Active sport	Hand wash; dry clean	2	Glass fiber	Hand wash; wet clean	4
Dress	Dry clean	3	Linings (attached)	Same as drapery	4
45. Sneakers	(See #18)		Linings (separate)	Med. wash; dry clean	4
46. Socks	(See #19)		68. Sheets and pillow cases		2
47. Sport coats	(See #2)		White and colored	Hot wash	
48. Suits			69. Slipcovers	Med. wash; dryclean	3
Basic	Dry clean	4	70. Table linen		
High fashion	Dry clean. Special handling on delicate and decorated styles	3	Fancy	Mild wash	5
			Service		
			(white)	Hot wash	2
			(partly colored)	Hot wash	
49. Sweaters	(See #22)		(colored)	Med. wash	
50. Swim wear	Hand wash	2	71. Towels		
51. Underwear			All types	Hot wash	2
Slips	Mild wash; bleach white cottons	2	72. Upholstery fabrics		5
Foundation garments	Med. wash	1	Hand cleanable with drycleaning solvent or foam cleaners. Color and finish resistant to water.		
Panties	Med. wash; bleach white cottons	1			

[a] Indefinite life expectancy.

Life Expectancy and Evaluation

The Guide introduces the concept of "life expectancy" for clothing and textile products. Table F-1 estimates how many years each type of product might normally be expected to retain its full usefulness. Changes in fashion and normal wear-out time influence life expectancy. These factors were considered in arriving at the figures shown in the table.

According to Table F-2, adjustment values are based on a percentage of replacement cost rather than original purchase price. This percentage of replacement cost depends on the degree to which the "life expectancy" of the lost or damaged product has been used up and the condition of the product at the time of the loss. All this is worked out in Tables F-1 and F-2. This formula provides a reasonable estimate of the amount of the loss.

Using the Guide in Tax Deductions

When you donate a garment to recognized charities, in the U.S.A. you can claim an income tax deduction in the amount of its "fair market value." The Fair Claims Guide's tables provide a reasonable way to figure "fair market value." If you don't get a receipt from the

Table F-2   Calculation of Claims Adjustment Values

Life Expectancy rating of article (from Table F-1)						Adjustment Values		
1	2	3	4	5	10			
Age of article in months					Age of article in years	% of Replacement Cost		
						Excellent 100%	Average 100%	Poor 100%
0 to 4	0 to 4	0 to 4	0 to 4	0 to 4	Less than 1 year	100%	100%	100%
4 to 7	4 to 7	4 to 10	4 to 13	4 to 16	2 to 4 years	75%	75%	60%
7 to 9 [a]	7 to 13 [a]	10 to 19	13 to 25	16 to 31	4 to 6 years	70%	60%	45%
9 to 11 [a]	13 to 19	19 to 28	25 to 37	31 to 46	6 to 8 years	50%	40%	30%
11 to 13 [a]	19 to 25	28 to 37	37 to 49	46 to 61	8 to 11 years	30%	20%	15%
13 mos. & older	25 mos. & older	37 mos. & older	49 mos. & older	61 mos. & older	11 years and older	20%	15%	10%

[a] Use only with "Average" column in figuring Adjustment Value.
Note: Ages are given to, but not including the 1st day of the month or year shown.

charity, you should keep a memorandum describing the donated items and when and to whom they were given.

The Full Fair Claims Guide The 20-page International Fair Claims Guide for Consumer Textile Products contains definitions of all the terms appearing in these tables and it considers many different claim situations, providing a reasonable rule to follow in each.

If you would like to have the complete document, the International Fabricare Institute would be glad to send it to you. Just send us your name and address plus 50¢ to cover handling. Ask for "Fair Claims Guide."

Step by Step Use of Tables

1. Determine the cost of replacing the article. This is called Replacement Cost.

2. Determine the Actual Age of the article in months (in years for "ten year" items).

3. Determine the condition of the article as Excellent, Average, or Poor.

4. Select from Table F-1 the Life Expectancy rating of the article.

5. Refer to the column in Table F-2 at the top of which is shown the Life Expectancy rating selected in Step 4. Read down in this column to the box showing the Actual Age and across to the Adjustment Value.

6. In Table F-2 select the box under "Adjustment Values" which applies according to condition of the article.

7. Multiply the percent figure given in Table F-2 by the Replacement Cost figure determined in Step 1. This will be the Adjustment Value.

> *Example 1*—High fashion cocktail dress. Replacement cost—$200. Life Expectancy—3 years (Table F-1.) Actual age—30 months (Table F-2). Condition—Excellent. Adjustment Value—30% or $60. (Table II.)
>
> *Example 2*—Man's leather coat. Replacement cost—$80. Life Expectancy—5 years. Actual Age—5 months. Condition—Excellent. Adjustment Value—75% or $60.
>
> *Example 3*—Man's wool slacks. Replacement Cost—$18. Life Expectancy—3 years. Actual Age—60 months. Condition—Poor. Adjustment Values—10% or $1.80.
>
> *Example 4*—Custom-made, lined draperies. Replacement Cost—$250. Life Expectancy—5 years. Actual Age—48 months. Condition—Average. Adjustment Value—20% or $50.

BALANCED DRAPERY DEPRECIATION GUIDE*

The Balanced Drapery Depreciation Guide has been compiled by the National Institute of Fire Restoration of AIDS International to take the above factors into account and give a realistic life expectancy for a given set of draperies.

Sources of Deterioration in Drapery Fabrics

The main deteriorating factors are light, and the combustion residues from heating and cooking. They affect fabrics differently, depending on the fiber, weave, dyes used, and the presence or absence of a lining.

For example, cotton fabric that is exposed to strong sunlight for six months may lose over 75 percent of its strength. The same exposure to fiberglass would incur only a 20 percent loss of strength. A lining preserves drapery fabrics by placing a barrier between the fabric and sunlight. Fabrics of the same composition may deteriorate at different rates, because heavier weaves tend to outlast light, finely woven fabrics.

The other major cause of fiber degradation is the build up of airborne soil and residue from heating and cooking. These residues combine with moisture and heat to form dilute acids which damage fibers and fade colors. Regular cleaning, especially in the Springtime, can minimize this damage by removing the residues before the heat and moisture of Summer speed up the reaction.

This Balanced Drapery Depreciation Guide has been compiled by the National Institute of Fire Restoration to take the above factors into account and give a realistic life expectancy for a given set of draperies.

Step 1 **IN THE TABLE BELOW, FIND THE FABRIC COMPOSITION OF YOUR DRAPERY AND CIRCLE THE APPROPRIATE NUMBER.**

	UNLINED			LINED
	Light Weave	Medium Weave	Heavy Weave	
Cotton	17	15	12	7
Rayon	23	21	18	11
Fortisan	5	4	4	4
Acetate	27	25	21	13
Celaperm	20	18	15	9
Chromespun	19	17	14	8

* The guide is based on actual field appraisals.

	UNLINED			LINED
	Light Weave	Medium Wave	Heavy Weave	
Arnel	17	15	12	7
Nylon	8	6	6	6
Dacron	5	4	4	4
Orlon	5	4	4	4
Saran	5	4	4	4
Fiberglass	6	5	5	5
Silk	25	23	20	12
Unknown Fiber (average)	14	12	9	6

ENTER THE CIRCLED NUMBER IN THE FIRST BOX BELOW

Step 2 **IN EACH OF THE BOXES BELOW, WRITE FACTOR THAT CORRESPONDS TO YOUR DRAPERY.**

1. FABRIC STRENGTH

2. SUNLIGHT EXPOSURE Factor
   Heavy
      More than two hours per day of direct   5
      sunlight
   Moderate   Yours
      One to two hours per day of direct sunlight   3
   Slight
      Less than one hour per day of direct sun-   2
      light
   Shaded
      No direct sun or reflected light. Fully pro-   1
      tected by roof overhang, porch, etc.

3. FUEL   Yours
   Electric Heat & Range   0

   Gas Heat & Range   1

   Oil Heat   2

4. HEATING SYSTEM   Yours

    Radiant Floor or Ceiling   0

    Baseboard or Radiator   1

    Hot Air   2

5. FREQUENCY OF CLEANING   Yours

    Every two years   0

    Every three years or less   1

SUM OF FACTORS
TOTAL DEPRECIATION PER YEAR   %

BALANCED UPHOLSTERY DEPRECIATION GUIDE*

A. HOW DOES IT LOOK?
Examine the upholstery for soiling, stains, or fading. Then select the category that best describes this piece of furniture.

WHERE TO LOOK: (see illustration)
1. Arms—top and front edge
2. Cushions (both sides)
3. Headrest area
4. Skirt front
5. Back area hidden by cushion (for fading comparison with exposed areas)

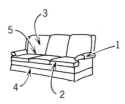

THIS UPHOLSTERY LOOKS:
BRAND NEW   RATING
No shading, soiling, blemish, or any other departure   0
from new

* This guide has been compiled under the direction of the National Institution of Fire Restoration Division of AIDS International and is based on actual field appraisals.

NEARLY NEW
Any slight departure from a new appearance, but no stains or noticeably soiled areas — 3

LIGHTLY USED
Any variation of brightness or cleanness when exposed areas are compared with an area protected by cushion or pleat — 6

MODERATELY USED
Soiling or shading in any of above inspection areas; light stains may be visible; furniture has a "used" look — 9

HEAVILY USED
Very noticeable soiled or stained areas, immediately visible to the casual observer — 20

CIRCLE THE APPROPRIATE RATING NUMBER & ENTER IT IN BOX A ON PAGE 545

B. HOW DOES IT WEAR?
Examine the following areas for wear, difference of texture, or previous damage:

WHERE TO LOOK: (see illustration)
1. Cording & edges of arms, back, cushions
2. Top of arms
3. Both sides of cushions

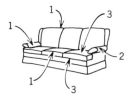

THIS UPHOLSTERY SHOWS:

NO WEAR — RATING
No visible wear, change in texture, or other departure from new — 0

LIGHT WEAR
Slight wear is discernible when exposed fabric is compared to unused or hidden areas; difference in texture is visible in some areas — 5

MODERATE WEAR
Loose threads, minor snags, abrasions, or roughness of — 15

fabric, missing buttons, loose cording; the item shows definite signs of wear

HEAVY WEAR
Padding shows through fabric, obvious snags or evidence of previous repair, fabric is threadbare in any area, generally worn or unattractive condition   50

CIRCLE THE APPROPRIATE RATING NUMBER & ENTER IT IN BOX B ON PAGE 545

C. HOW OLD IS IT?
In the table below find the age of your piece of furniture. Circle the fabric age factor. Write this factor in Box C on page 545.

Age of Furniture
(Fabric age, if reupholstered)

Age		Factor
1 year old	....	7
2 years old	....	14
3 years old	....	21
4 years old	....	28
5 years old	....	34
6 years old	....	40
7 years old	....	46
8 years old	....	51
9 years old	....	56
10 years old	....	60
11 years old	....	63
12 years old	....	66
13 years old	....	68
14 years old	....	70
15 years old	....	72
16 years old	....	74
17 years old	....	76
18 years old	....	78
19 years old	....	79
20 years & over	....	80

BOX A: FABRIC APPEARANCE ☐

+

BOX B: FABRIC WEAR ☐

+

BOX C: FABRIC AGE ☐

_____

TOTAL DEPRECIATION ☐
(Sum of Boxes A, B, & C)

BALANCED CARPET DEPRECIATION GUIDE*

1. Surface Appearance Factor

Read the descriptions below, then examine the carpet. Pay special attention to the entrance and "traffic" areas. Examine the steps, if carpeted in the same material.

This Carpet Looks:

BRAND NEW
No shading, soiling, blemish, or any other departure from new appearance — 0

NEARLY NEW
Barely noticeable shading or difference in color between traffic areas and protected areas; slight departure from new appearance — 2

LIGHTLY SOILED
Slight soiling or fading in traffic areas as compared with unused or protected areas — 4

MODERATELY SOILED
Soiling in traffic areas; presence of stains; any discoloration that gives the carpet a "used" look — 7

HEAVILY SOILED
Carpet is definitely in need of cleaning; stains or soiling are obvious — 10

EXTREMELY HEAVILY SOILED
Carpet has immediately noticeable stains, fading, or other discoloration that is unsightly — 25

* This guide has been compiled under the direction of the National Institute of Fire Restoration Division of AIDS International and is based on actual field appraisals.

WHICH CATEGORY BEST DESCRIBES THIS CARPET BEFORE DAMAGE?

WRITE THE NUMBER HERE

2. Visible Wear Factor

Read the descriptions below, examine the carpet as you did for surface appearance. In addition to those areas, also examine the carpet seams.

This Carpet's Condition Is:

BRAND NEW
No sign of wear, no shading; carpet still retains the sheen and and perfect uniformity of brand new goods   0

NEARLY NEW
Carpet is in perfect condition, but lacks the sheen and perfection of a brand new carpet; no wear is discernible   3

SLIGHTLY USED
Some shading or difference in the pile can be detected in traffic areas, near entrance doors or on stair treads, but not immediately noticeable to the casual observer   6

MODERATELY USED
Shading, flattened pile, or traffic pattern is not objectionable, but definitely noticeable   10

WELL-WORN
Flattening and wear of pile is getting to the stage where the carpet is beginning to look unattractive near doorways, over carpet seams or stair treads   25

HEAVILY WORN
Pile is completely worn away in some areas, to the degree that the backing is visible   50

WHICH CATEGORY BEST DESCRIBES THIS CARPET BEFORE DAMAGE?

WRITE THE NUMBER HERE

3. Age Factor Find the age of your carpet in years, and circle the factor listed beside it.

AGE	FACTOR
1 year old	9
2 years old	13
3 years old	17
4 years old	21
5 years old	25
6 years old	29
7 years old	33
8 years old	37
9 years old	41
10 years old	45
11 years old	49
12 years old	53
13 years old	57
14 years old	61
15 years old	65
16 years old	69
17 years old	71
18 years old	73
19 years old	74
20 years old	75

WRITE THE AGE FACTOR FOR THIS CARPET HERE [ ]

G
Fur and Leather Terms

FUR TERMS For a more complete definition of fur terms, please consult the Fur Dictionary, Zimmerman Products Company, 2519 Burnet Avenue, Cincinnati, Ohio 45219.

Alaskan Seal—Soft, short, fine and closely furred skin with an even pile and supple leather. Dyed black and brown. Good service. Requires special cleaning.

Beaver—Sheared—Short, dense, dark to pale brown. Good service.

Caracul—Curls looser than in Persian. Many shades. Good to fair service.

Chinchilla—Soft, dense, lustrous fur. Color is delicate blue-grey with darker under-fur. Fair service.

Coney (Dyed Rabbit)—Short, straight-haired fur—dressed and dyed to resemble many furs. Fair to low serviceability.

Hair Seal—Short hair—no under fur, flat and sleek. Natural color is greyish on back or spotted dyed brown or grey. Fair to low in service.

Hudson Seal (Sheared Dyed Muskrat)—Trade Name—Sheared and dyed. Short dense fur. Usually more serviceable than other dyed Muskrats since this fur is dyed before it is fatted and fatted again before last dyeing, therefore leather is stronger. Short dense fur. Black to resemble Alaskan Seal. Good service.

Mink—Short dense fur with lustrous guard hair. All colors. Flexible, light weight. Good service.

Mink Sides—Nearly any color. Made of smaller pieces. Very lustrous dense fur. Fair service.

Kolinsky Mink—Long guard hair. Lustrous texture as other mink, only usually longer hair. Fair service.

Mouton (Dyed Lamb)—Very heavy, dense, sheared fur. Heavy pelt. Luster is artificial. Usually dyed brown. Good service.

Muskrat, Natural—Same as dyed, only a lighter shade in under fur. Fair service to good.

Muskrat, Dyed—Short, dense, even fur with long guard hair, strong leather. Fair to good service.

Muskrat, Sheared—Usually a light color (beige). Looks similar to other sheared furs only shorter under fur. Fair service.

Nutria—Soft fur, resembling Beaver but shorter. Blue-brown in color, sometimes dyed. Must be glazed to luster as it is naturally dull. Fair service.

Ocelot—Short, straight, tawny colored hair. Black, brown and white oblong spots. Quality judged by flatness of fur and coloring. Fair to low service.

Plucked Otter—A lighter brown, similar in appearance to sheared raccoon. Good service.

Arianna Otter—Very short hair. Brown in color. Good service.

Persian Lamb—Usually dyed black, grey or some brown. Has knuckle curl and coarse hair with lustrous appearance. Should be soft and pliable. Good to fair service.

Persian Paw—Similar to Persian. Made of smaller pieces made into long plates, reinforced to stay cloth. Quite serviceable.

Raccoon, Sheared—Has dense lustrous under fur. Brownish, dark to light. Good service.

Grey Squirrel—Straight hair, dense under fur. Fine texture and lustrous guard hair. Many shades, dyed. Fair to low service.

LEATHER TERMS*

Hides and Skins

Antique—A mottled finish on textured kidskin with a soft hand.

Alligator—Alligator, crocodile and related types.

Buckskin—Deer and elk skins, with the outer grain removed.

Bullhide—Hide from a male bovine capable of reproduction.

Cabretta—A hair-type sheepskin; specifically from Brazil.

Calfskin—Skin from a young bovine, male or female.

Capeskin—From a sheep raised in South Africa.

Carpincho—A water rodent native to South America, like pigskin.

Cattlehide—General term for hides from a bovine of any breed or sex, but usually mature; includes bullhide, steerhide, cowhide, and sometimes kipskins.

* Leather Facts, New England Tanners Club, Peabody, Mass. 01960 (1965).

Cordovan—From a section of a horsehide called the shell.

Cowhide—Hide from a mature female bovine that has produced a calf.

Cuir Sauvage or Tache Cuir Sauvage—French phrase that means stained like a wild animal. The leather is cow or sheepskin with a smooth, glossy finish.

Deerskin—Deer and elk skins, with the grain intact.

Doeskin—From sheep or lambskins, usually with the grain removed.

Flesher—The underneath (flesh side) layer of a sheepskin that has been split off. Used to make chamois.

Goatskin—Skin from a mature goat.

Hair Sheep—Sheep from several species whose "wool" is hairlike.

Heifer—A female bovine, under three years of age, that has not produced a calf.

Hide—The whole pelt from large animals (cattle, horses, etc.)

Horsehide—Hide from a horse or colt.

Kangaroo—From the Australian kangaroo or wallaby.

Kidskin—Skin from a kid, or young goat.

Kipskin—Skin from a bovine, male or female; intermediate in size between a calf and mature animal.

Lambskin—Skin from a lamb or young sheep.

Lizard—Any of a great number of the lizard family.

Mocha—Middle East hair sheep, usually with the grain removed.

Ostrich—From the two-legged animal native to North Africa.

Peccary—From a wild boar native to Central and South America; like pigskin.

Pelt—An untanned hide or skin with the hair on.

Pigskin—Skin from pigs and hogs.

Rawstock—General term for hides or skins that a tanner has received in a preserved state preparatory to tanning; a tanner's inventory of raw material.

Sharkskin—From certain shark species.

Shearlings—Wooled sheep and lambskins, tanned with the wool intact.

Sheepskin—Skin from a mature sheep.

Shine Leathers—Glazed, varnished, or bronzed finishes to bring out the natural glow of the skin to give it sparkle and shine.

Skin—The pelt from small animals (calf, sheep, goat, etc.).

Skiver—The thin grain layer split from a sheepskin.

Snake—Any one of the snake species.

Steerhide—Hide from a mature male bovine, incapable of reproduction, that has been raised for beef.

Walrus—Skin from a walrus; also sometimes sealskin.

Water Buffalo—Flat-horned buffalo primarily from the tropics.

Tanning Processes

Aniline Finish—Full-grain leather that has been colored with dyestuffs rather than pigments. Usually topped with a protein, resin, or lacquer protective coating; can also be waxed.

Bark Tanned—See "Vegetable Tanned."

Boarded—A grain effect produced by folding a skin grain against grain and mechanically rolling the two surfaces back and forth against each other.

Chrome Tanned—Leathers that have been tanned with soluble chromium salts, primarily basic chromium sulfate. Currently the most widely used tannage in the United States.

Combination Tanned—Leathers tanned with more than one tanning agent. For example, initially chrome-tanned followed by a second tannage (called a "Retan") with vegetable materials.

Embossed—A mechanical process of permanently imprinting a great variety of unique grain effects into the leather surface. Done under considerable heat and pressure.

Full Grain—Grain leather in which only the hair has been removed. Usually carries either an aniline or glazed finish.

Glazed Finish—Similar to an aniline finish except that the leather surface is polished to a high luster by the action of glass or steel rollers under tremendous pressure.

Grain Leather—Hides and skins that have been processed with the grain or outer surface dressed for end use.

Imitation—A variety of materials that have been made to resemble genuine leather. The great bulk of these are rubber or plastic coated fabrics. It is unlawful to use terms connoting leather to describe imitations.

Leather—The pelt of an animal that has been transformed by tanning into a nonputrescible, useful material.

Mineral Tanned—Leathers that have been tanned by any of several mineral substances, notably the salts of chromium, aluminum, and zirconium.

Oil Tanned—Leathers tanned with certain fish oils. Produces a very soft, pliable leather such as chamois.

Pigment Finish—A process of coloring and coating the leather surface with colored pigments dispersed in film-forming chemicals called binders. The latter can be tailor made to produce surfaces that are highly resistant to wear, fading, and the like.

Retan—See "Combination Tanned."

Side Leather—Cattlehide grain leather that, prior to processing, has been cut in half forming two "sides." Purpose is to reduce the size to better accommodate tannery equipment. Represents the largest volume of commercial leather currently produced.

Snuffed—Grain leather that, in addition to hair removal, has had the outer surface lightly removed by buffing.

Split—The underneath layer of side leather that has been "split" off. Devoid of a natural grain, it may be either sueded or the pigment finished and embossed.

Suede—Leathers that are finished by buffing the flesh side (opposite the grain side) to produce a nap. Term refers to the napping process and is unrelated to the type of skin used.

Synthetic—See "Imitation."

Top Grain—See "Full Grain."

Vegetable Tanned—Leathers that have been tanned with vegetable materials that are derived from certain plants and woods, often called "Bark" tannins.

H
Government Agencies;
Trade Associations;
Scientific, Civic, and
Professional Associations

U.S. DEPARTMENT OF AGRICULTURE, WASHINGTON, D.C. 20250

Regional Offices

Southern Utilization Research and Development Division, Agricultural Research Service, U.S.D.A., P.O. Box 53326 New Orleans, Louisiana 70153
(Conducts extensive research on cotton textiles.)

Western Utilization Research and Development Division, Agricultural Research Service, U.S.D.A.
2850 Telegraph Avenue, Berkeley, California 94705
(Conducts extensive research on wool textiles.)

North Eastern Research and Development Division, Agricultural Research Servide, U.S.D.A.
Agricultural Research Center, Maryland 20301

North Central Research and Development Division, Agricultural Research Service, U.S.D.A.
200 West Peoria Parkway, Peoria, Illinois 61614

Agricultural experiment stations. Located at state land-grant colleges and universities.

Consumer Product Safety Commission, Washington, D.C. 20207

Federal Trade Commission, Washington, D.C. 20580

General Services Administration, Washington, D.C. 20405

Government Printing Office, Washington, D.C. 20402

Office of Consumer Affairs, Washington, D.C. 20201

U.S. Department of Commerce, Washington, D.C. 20230

U.S. Department of Defense, Washington, D.C. 20301

U.S. Naval Supply Depot, Philadelphia, Pennsylvania 19120

U.S. Department of Health, Education and Welfare
Office of Consumer Affairs, Washington, D.C. 20240

U.S. Department of Labor, Washington, D.C. 20210

U.S. Patent Office, Washington, D.C. 20231

The Center for Consumer Product Technology
U.S. Department of Commerce, National Bureau of Standards
Washington, D.C. 20234

STATE CONSUMER PROTECTIVE AGENCIES

Alaska (AG)	Nebraska (AGR)
Arizona (AG)	Nevada (CO)
Arkansas (AG)	New Hampshire (AG)
California (AG-IND)	New Jersey (AG)
Colorado (AG)	New Mexico (AG)
Connecticut (AG-IND)	New York (AG-GOV)
Delaware (AG-IND)	North Carolina (AG)
Florida (AG-AGR)	North Dakota (AG)
Georgia (IND)	Ohio (AG)
Hawaii (GOV)	Oklahoma (IND)
Idaho (AG)	Oregon (AG-CO)
Illinois (AG)	Pennsylvania (AG-AGR)
Indiana (AG-CO)	Rhode Island (AG-IND)
Iowa (AG)	South Dakota (AG)
Kansas (AG)	Texas (AG-IND)
Kentucky (AG-IND)	Utah (AG-IND)
Louisiana (AGR)	Vermont (AG)
Maine (AG)	Virginia (AG-GOV-AGRCO)
Maryland (AG)	Washington (AG)
Massachusetts (AG-GOV-IND)	West Virginia (AG-L)
Michigan (AG-GOV-IND)	Wisconsin (AG-AGR)
Minnesota (AG-CO)	Wyoming (IND)
Mississippi (AG-AGRCO)	Puerto Rico (AG)
Missouri (AG)	Virgin Islands (IND)

CODE

AG	Office of the Attorney General
AGR	Department of Agriculture
AGRCO	Department of Agriculture and Commerce (one department)
GOV	Office of the Governor
CO	Department of Commerce
L	Department of Labor
IND	Independent Office

In addition to these state offices, 53 cities and 18 counties have consumer offices with varying responsibilities and power.

PARTIAL LIST OF CONSUMER PRODUCT SAFETY COMMISSION OFFICES

This list could be much longer, but these agencies are the ones that appear to most interest the consumers who write to the U.S. Consumer Product Safety Commission. To report a product hazard or a product-related injury, write to the U.S. Consumer Product Safety Commission, Washington, D.C. 20207. In the continental United States, call the toll-free consumer safety hotline, 800-638-2666.

For more information, you also may contact the Commission's area offices:

Atlanta Area Office
Consumer Product Safety Commission
1330 West Peachtree St., N.W.
Atlanta, Georgia 30309
404-526-2231

Boston Area Office
Consumer Product Safety Commission
408 Atlantic Avenue
Boston, Massachusetts 02110
617-223-5576

Chicago Area Office
Consumer Product Safety Commission
230 S. Dearborn St.
Rm. 2945
Chicago, Illinois 60604
312-353-8260

Cleveland Area Office
Consumer Product Safety Commission
21046 Brookpark Road
Cleveland, Ohio 44135
216-522-3886

Dallas Area Office
Consumer Product Safety Commission
Rm. 410C, 500 South Ervay
Dallas, Texas 75201
214-749-3871

Denver Area Office
Consumer Product Safety Commission
Suite 938, Guaranty Bank Building
817 17th Street
Denver, Colorado 80202
303-837-2904

Kansas City Area Office
Consumer Product Safety Commission
Suite 1500, Traders National Bank Building
1125 Grand Avenue
Kansas City, Missouri 64106
816-374-2034

Los Angeles Area Office
Consumer Product Safety Commission
3660 Wilshire Boulevard, Suite 1100
Los Angeles, California 90010
213-688-7272

Minneapolis Area Office
Consumer Product Safety Commission
Rm. 650 Federal Building, Fort Snelling
Twin Cities, Minnesota 55111
612-725-3424

New Orleans Area Office
Consumer Product Safety Commission
Suite 414, International Trade Mart
2 Canal Street
New Orleans, Louisiana 70130
504-589-2102

New York Area Office
Consumer Product Safety Commission
6 World Trade Center
6th Floor
New York, New York 10048
212-264-9400 or 212-264-9401

Philadelphia Area Office
Consumer Product Safety Commission
10th Floor, 400 Market Street
Philadelphia, Pennsylvania 19106
215-597-9105

San Francisco Area Office
Consumer Product Safety Commission
Suite 500, 100 Pine Street
San Francisco, California 94111

Seattle Area Office
Consumer Product Safety Commission
392 Federal Building
912 Second Avenue
Seattle, Washington 98174
206-442-5276

FEDERAL INFORMATION CENTERS

ALABAMA

Birmingham
322-8591
Toll-free tieline
to Atlanta, Ga.

Mobile
438-1421
Toll-free tieline
to New Orleans, La.

ARIZONA

Tucson
622-1511
Toll-free tieline
to Phoenix, Ariz.

Phoenix
(602) 261-3313
Federal Building
230 N. First Ave.
85025

ARKANSAS

Little Rock
(501) 378-6177
Toll-free tieline
to Memphis, Tenn.

CALIFORNIA

Los Angeles
(213) 688-3800
Federal Building
300 N. Los Angeles St.
90012

Sacramento
(916) 449-3344
Federal Building—
U.S. Courthouse
650 Capitol Mall
95814

San Diego
(714) 293-6030
202 C. Street 92101

San Francisco
(415) 556-6600
Federal Building
U.S. Courthouse
450 Golden Gate Ave.
94102

San Jose
(408) 275-7422
Toll-free tieline
to San Francisco,
Calif.

COLORADO

Colorado Springs
(303) 471-9491
Toll-free tieline
to Denver, Colo.

Denver
(303) 837-3602
Federal Building
U.S. Courthouse
1961 Stout St.
80202

Pueblo
(303) 544-9523
Toll-free tieline
to Denver, Colo.

CONNECTICUT

Hartford
(203) 527-2617
Toll-free tieline
to New York, N.Y.

New Haven
(203) 624-4720
Toll-free tieline
to New York, N.Y.

FLORIDA

Fort Lauderdale
(305) 522-8531
Toll-free tieline
to Miami, Fla.

Miami
(305) 350-4155
Federal Building
51 Southwest First Ave.
33130

Jacksonville
(904) 354-4756
Toll free tieline
to St. Petersburg, Fla.

St. Petersburg
(813) 893-3495
William C. Cramer
Federal Building
144 First Ave. S.
33701

Tampa
(813) 229-7911
Toll-free tieline
to St. Petersburg, Fla.

West Palm Beach
(305) 833-7566
Toll-free tieline
to Miami, Fla.

GEORGIA

Atlanta
(404) 525-6891
Federal Building
275 Peachtree St. N.E.
30303

HAWAII

Honolulu
(808) 546-8620
U.S. Post Office
Courthouse & Customhouse
335 Merchant St. 96813

ILLINOIS

Chicago
(312) 353-4242
Everett McKinley Dirksen
Building
219 South Dearborn St.
60604

INDIANA

Indianapolis
(317) 633-8484
Federal Building
U.S. Courthouse
46 East Ohio St.
46204

IOWA

Des Moines
(515) 282-9091
Toll-free tieline
to Omaha, Neb.

KANSAS

Topeka
(913) 232-7229
Toll-free tieline
to Kansas City, Mo.

Wichita
(316) 263-6931
Toll-free tieline
to Kansas City, Mo.

KENTUCKY

Louisville
(502) 582-6261
Federal Building
600 Federal Place
40202

LOUISIANA

New Orleans
(504) 527-6696
Federal Building
Room 1210
701 Loyola Ave.
70113

MARYLAND

Baltimore
(301) 962-4980
Federal Building
31 Hopkins Plaza
21201

MASSACHUSETTS

Bsoton
(617) 223-7121
John F. Kennedy
Federal Building
Government Center
02203

MICHIGAN

Detroit
(313) 226-7016
Federal Building
U.S. Courthouse
231 West Lafayette St.
48226

MINNESOTA

Minneapolis
(612) 725-2073
Federal Building
U.S. Courthouse
110 South Fourth St.
55401

MISSOURI

Kansas City
(816) 374-2486
Federal Building
601 East Twelfth St.
64106

St. Joseph
(816) 233-8206
Toll-free tieline
to Kansas City, Mo.

St. Louis
(314) 622-4106
Federal Building
1520 Market St.
63103

NEBRASKA

Omaha
(402) 221-3353
Federal Building
U.S. Post Office &
Courthouse
215 N. 17th St. 68102

NEW JERSEY

Newark
(201) 645-3600
Federal Building
970 Broad St. 07102

Trenton
(609) 396-4400
Toll-free tieline
to Newark, N.J.

NEW MEXICO

Albuquerque
(505) 843-3091
Federal Building
U.S. Courthouse
500 Gold Ave., S.W.
87101

Santa Fe
(505) 983-7743
Toll-free tieline
to Albuquerque, N. Mex.

NEW YORK

Albany
(518) 463-4421
Toll free tieline
to New York, N.Y.

Buffalo
(716) 842-5770
Federal Building
111 West Huron St.
14202

New York
(212) 264-4464
Federal Office Building
U.S. Customs Court
26 Federal Plaza 10007

Rochester
(716) 546-5076
Toll-free tieline
to Buffalo, N.Y.

Syracuse
(315) 476-8545
Toll-free tieline
to Buffalo, N.Y.

NORTH CAROLINA

Charlotte
(704) 376-3600
Toll-free tieline
to Atlanta, Ga.

OHIO

Akron
(216) 375-5475
Toll-free tieline
to Cleveland, Ohio

Columbus
(614) 221-1014
Toll-free tieline
to Cincinnati, Ohio

Cincinnati
(513) 684-2801
Federal Building
550 Main Street 45202

**Cleveland
(216) 522-4040**
Federal Building
1240 East Ninth St.
44199

**Dayton
(513) 223-7377**
Toll-free tieline to
Cincinnati, Ohio

**Toledo
(419) 244-8625**
Toll-free tieline
to Cleveland, Ohio

OKLAHOMA

**Oklahoma City
(405) 231-4868**
U.S. Post Office &
Federal Office Building
201 N.W. 3rd St. 73102

**Tulsa
(918) 584-4193**
Toll-free tieline
to Oklahoma City, Okla.

OREGON

**Portland
(503) 221-2222**
208 U.S. Courthouse
620 Southwest Main St.
97205

PENNSYLVANIA

**Philadelphia
(215) 597-7042**
Federal Building
600 Arch Street
19106

**Pittsburgh
(412) 644-3456**
Federal Building
1000 Liberty Ave.
15222

**Scranton
(717) 346-7081**
Toll-free tieline
to Philadelphia, Pa.

RHODE ISLAND

**Providence
(401) 331-5565**
Toll-free tieline
to Boston, Mass.

TENNESSEE

**Chattanooga
(615) 265-8231**
Toll-free tieline
to Memphis, Tenn.

**Memphis
(901) 534-3285**
Clifford Davis Federal
Building
167 N. Main St. 38103

TEXAS

**Austin
(512) 472-5494**
Toll-free tieline
to Houston, Tex.

**Dallas
(214) 749-2131**
Toll-free tieline
to Fort Worth, Tex.

**Fort Worth
(817) 334-3624**
Fritz Garland Lanham
Federal Building
819 Taylor St. 76102

**Houston
(713) 226-5711**
Federal Building
U.S. Courthouse
515 Rusk Ave. 77002

**San Antonio
(512) 224-4471**
Toll-free tieline
to Houston, Tex.

UTAH

**Ogden
(801) 399-1347**
Toll-free tieline
to Salt Lake City, Utah

**Salt Lake City
(801) 524-5353**
Federal Building, U.S.
Post Office. Courthouse
125 So. State St. 84111

WASHINGTON

**Seattle
(206) 442-0570**
Arcade Plaza
1321 Second Ave. 98101

WISCONSIN

**Milwaukee
(414) 271-2273**
Toll-free tieline
to Chicago, Ill.

The Federal Information
Centers are a joint
venture of the U.S.

General Services
Administration and
the U.S. Civil
Service Commission.

In cities served by tielines,
the number listed will
connect you with the
nearest Federal
Information Center at
no charge.

TRADE ASSOCIATIONS American Apparel Manufacturers Association
1611 North Kent Street, Arlington, Virginia 22209

American Dye Manufacturers Institute, Inc.
74 Trinity Place, New York, New York 10006

American Printed Fabric Council
1440 Broadway, New York, New York 10018

American Textile Manufacturers' Institute, Inc.
1501 Johnston Building, Charlotte, North Carolina 28201

American Transfer Printing Institute
51 Madison Avenue, New York, New York 10010

Association of Home Appliance Manufacturers
20 North Wacker Drive, Chicago, Illinois 60606

Association of Interior Decor Specialists, Inc.
4420 Fairfax Drive, Arlington, Virginia 22209

Association of Knitted Fabrics Manufacturers
1450 Broadway, New York, New York 10018

Belgian Linen Association
280 Madison Avenue, New York, New York 10016

The Bonded Fabric Council
350 Fifth Avenue, Room 5623, New York, New York 10001

Carpet and Rug Institute, P.O. Box 2048, Dalton, Georgia 30720

Chemical Fabrics and Film Association
60 E 42nd Street, New York, New York 10017

Color Association of the United States, Inc.
200 Madison Avenue, New York, New York 10016

Cotton, Inc., 1370 Avenue of the Americas,
New York, New York 10019

Corduroy Council of America,
15 East 53rd Street, New York, New York 10022

Denim Council, 155 East 44th Street, New York, New York 10017

Durene Association of America,
350 Fifth Avenue, New York, New York 10001

Fabric Laminators Association
110 West 40th Street, New York, New York 10018

Gas Appliance Manufacturers Association
1901 North Ft. Meyer Drive, Arlington, Virginia 22209

International Fabricare Institute:

Headquarters: Dores and Chicago Avenue, Joliet, Illinois 60434

Research Center: 12251 Tech Road, Silver Spring, Maryland 20904

International Color Authority
24 East 38th Street, New York, New York 10016

International Silk Association (U.S.A.), Inc.
299 Madison Avenue, New York, New York 10017

International Nonwovens and Disposables Association
10 East 40th Street, New York, New York 10017

Irish Linen Guild
1271 Avenue of the Americas, New York, New York 10020

Knitted Fabrics Institute, Inc.
1450 Broadway, New York, New York 10018

Knitted Outerwear Manufacturers Association
350 Fifth Avenue, Room 492, New York, New York 10001

Lace Importers Association
420 Lexington Avenue, New York, New York 10017

Leavers Lace Manufacturers of America
1112 Union Trust Building, Providence, Rhode Island 02903

Man-Made Fiber Producers Association
1150 Seventeenth Street, NW, Washington, D.C. 20036

Men's Fashion Association of America
1290 Avenue of the Americas, New York, New York 10019

Narrow Fabrics Institute, Inc.
Room 618, 271 North Avenue, New Rochelle, New York 10801

National Automatic Laundry and Cleaning Council
7 South Dearborn Street, Chicago, Illinois 60603

National Association of Manufacturers
277 Park Avenue, New York, New York 10017

National Cotton Council of America
1918 North Parkway, Memphis, Tennessee 38112

National Fire Protection Association
60 Batterymarch Street, Boston, Massachusetts 02110

National Knitted Outerwear Association
51 Madison Avenue, New York, New York 10001

National Retail Manufacturers Association
100 West 31st Street, New York, New York 10001

National Safety Council
425 North Michigan Avenue, Chicago, Illinois 60611

Silk and Rayon Manufacturers Association
608 Fabian Building, Peterson, New Jersey 07505

Soap and Detergent Association
475 Park Avenue South at 32nd Street, New York, New York 10016

Society of the Plastics Industry, Inc.
250 Park Avenue, New York, New York 10017

Supina Association of America
603 First National Building, El Paso, Texas 79901

Textile Distributors Association
1040 Avenue of the Americas, New York, New York 10018

Vinyl Fabrics Institute
60 E. 42nd Street, New York, New York 10017

Wool Bureau,
360 Lexington Avenue, New York, New York 10017

Yarn Spinners Association, Inc.
Box 99, Gastonia, North Carolina 28052

SCIENTIFIC ASSOCIATIONS

American Association of Textile Chemists and Colorists
P.O. Box 12215, Research Triangle, Durham, North Carolina 27709

American Association for Textile Technology, Inc.
295 Fifth Avenue, New York, New York 10016

American National Standards Institute, Inc.
1403 Broadway, New York, New York 10018

American Society for Testing and Materials
1916 Race Street, Philadelphia, Pennsylvania 19103

Institute of Textile Technology, Charlottesville, Virginia 22902

Textile Research Institute
P.O. Box 625, Princeton, New Jersey 08540

CIVIC ASSOCIATIONS

Council of Better Business Bureaus, Inc.
1150 17th Street NW, Washington, D.C. 20036

U.S. Chamber of Commerce, 1615 H Street N.W., Washington, D.C. 20006

PROFESSIONAL ASSOCIATIONS

American Home Economics Association
2010 Massachusetts Avenue N.W., Washington, D.C. 20036

American Arbitration Association
140 West 51st Street, New York, New York 10020

Consumer Federation of America
P.O. Box 19354, 20th Street Station, Washington, D.C. 20036

Fashion Group of America, Inc. of New York
9 Rockefeller Plaza, New York, New York 10020

Major Appliance Consumer Action Panel
20 North Wacker Drive, Chicago, Illinois 60606

Society of Consumer Affairs Professionals in Business
1150 17th Street N.W., Washington, D.C. 20036

I
Textile Periodicals

American Dyestuff Reporter, SAF International, Inc.
44 East 23rd Street, New York, New York 10010

American Fabrics and Fashion Magazine
Doric Publishing Company, Inc.
24 East 38th Street, New York, New York 10016

American Textile Reporter Bulletin, Clark Publishing Co.
106 East Stone Avenue, P.O. Box 88, Greenville, South Carolina 29602

Daily News Record, Women's Wear Daily, and *Home Furnishings Daily*
7 East 12th Street, New York, New York 10003

Journal of Home Economics
Official Organ of the American Home Economics Association
2010 Massachusetts Avenue NW, Washington, D.C. 20036

Knitting Times, Official Publication of the National
Knitted Outerwear Association
51 Madison Avenue, New York, New York 10010

Modern Knitting Management, Rayon Publishing Corporation
303 Fifth Avenue, New York, New York 10016

Modern Textiles, Rayon Publishing Corporation
303 Fifth Avenue, New York, New York 10016

Textile Chemists and Colorist, Journal of the American
Association of Textile Chemists and Colorists
P.O. Box 12215, Research Triangle Park, North Carolina 27709

Textile Marketing Letter, Clemson University
Clemson, South Carolina 29631

Textile Organon, Textile Economics Bureau, Inc.
489 Fifth Avenue, New York, New York 10017

Textile Technology Digest, Institute of Textile Technology
Charlottesville, Virginia 22904

Textile World, McGraw-Hill Publications
1175 Peachtree Street NE, Atlanta, Georgia 30309

Textracts, J.B. Goldbert
225 East 46th Street, New York, New York 10017

Bibliography

Sources of references were footnoted in the text. Additional references are listed here.[*]

INTRODUCTION–AN OVERVIEW

Labarthe, Dr. Jules. Mellon Institute, Pittsburgh, Pa., "Madame, Do You Return Your Goods?" Paper prepared and delivered at Fourth Annual Home Economics Spring Weekend, Penn State College, April 17–18, 1953.

Labarthe, Dr. Jules. "Ten Thousand and One Complaints," *Textile Research Journal,* Vol. XXIV, No. 4 (April 1954), pp. 328–342.

Scheir, Sig. "Gauzy Fashion Fabric: Fashion Preempts Quality in Latest Craze," *Daily News Record,* Vol. 5, No. 202 (October 15, 1975).

IFI's Technical Bulletin T-503 "Textile Damage Analysis Statistics for 1974," (1975).

1. THE ROLE OF TEXTILE TESTING

AATCC Technical Manual. Current volume, American Association of Textile Chemists and Colorists, Research Triangle Park, North Carolina.

Boothe, J. E. *Principles of Textile Testing.* Chemical Publishing Co. Inc., New York (1969).

[*] Copyright of bulletins published by the National Institute of Drycleaning is now the property of the International Fabricare Institute.

Hollis, Lorelei, "A Compilation and Evaluation of Laboratory Test For a College Textile Course Using Limited Equipment." University of Oklahoma, Master's Thesis (1970).

Odlum, Laura M. and Mary H. Cebik. Perspective For the Home Economics Profession, Southern Regional Education Board, Atlanta, Georgia (1975).

Skinkle, John H. *Textile Testing.* Chemical Publishing Co. Inc., New York (1949).

Textile Laboratory Equipment List, American Home Economics Association, Washington, D.C. 20009.

2. METHODS FOR FIBER IDENTIFICATION

Infrared Spectroscopy

AATCC Monograph No. 3, "Analytical Methods for a Textile Laboratory," AATCC, Research Triangle Park, North Carolina (1968), pp. 303–383.

Identification of Textile Materials, 5th Edition. The Textile Institute, Manchester England (1965) pp. 74–85.

Meridith, R. and J. W. S. Hearle. *Physical Methods of Investigating Textiles.* Textile Book Publishers, Inc., New York (1959) pp. 53–87.

Gas Chromatography

AATCC Monograph No. 3, "Analytical Methods for a Textile Laboratory," AATCC, Research Triangle Park, North Carolina (1968), pp. 259–263.

Ettre, Leslie S. and Albert Zlatkis. *The Practice of Gas Chromatography.* Wiley-Interscience, New York (1967).

Identification of Textile Materials, 5th Edition. The Textile Institute, Manchester, England (1965), pp. 86–90.

Senos, Hiroshi, Shim Touge, and Tsugio Takeuchi. "Pyrolysis Gas Chromatographic Analysis of 6–66 Nylon Copolymers," *Journal of Chromatographic Science* (May 1971).

Walker, John A., Minor T. Jackson, and James Maynard. *Chromatographic Systems.* Academic Press, New York (1972).

Fiber Analysis

"Identification of Fibers in Textile Materials," *Bulletin X156* (1961), E. I. duPont de Nemours and Company.

Technical Manual, American Association of Textile Chemists and Colorists, current edition.

Thermal Analysis

AATCC Monograph No. 3, "Analytical Methods for a Textile Laboratory," AATCC, Research Triangle Park, North Carolina (1968), pp. 385–436.

Identification of Textile Materials, 5th Edition. The Textile Institute, Manchester, England (1965), pp. 91–94.

Fiber Microscopy

AATCC Yearbook and Technical Manual, current volume.

Beck, Conrad. *The Microscope.* E. Van Nostrand Company, New York (1923).

Chamot, Emile M. and Clyde W. Mason. *Handbook of Chemical Microscopy,* Wiley, New York (1958).

Cook, J. Gordon. *Handbook of Textile Fibers,* 4th Edition. Merrow Publishing Co. Ltd., Watford, Herts, England (1964).

Gage, Simon Henry. *The Microscope.* Comstock Publishing Company, Inc., Ithaca, New York (1974).

Swartz, E. R. *Textiles and the Microscope.* McGraw-Hill Book Company, Inc. New York (1934).

3. FIBER AND YARN ANALYSIS

Kaswell, Ernest R. *Textile Fibers, Yarns and Fabrics.* Reinhold Publishing Corporation, New York (1963).

Skinkle, John H. *Textile Testing.* Chemical Publishing Company, Inc., New York (1949).

4. ANALYSIS OF PHYSICAL FABRIC PROPERTIES

Physical Properties Bibliography. American Association of Textile Chemists and Colorists, AATCC Technical Center, P.O. Box 12215, Research Triangle Park, North Carolina 27709.

Pizzuto, J. J., Arthur Price, and Allen C. Cohen. *Fabric Science.* Fairchild Publications, Inc., New York (1974).

5. TESTING FOR PRODUCT PERFORMANCE

Part 1—Aesthetic Appearances

"All Purpose Weather Coats—Ski Jackets, Snowmobile Suits, Skating Outfits," *NID Fabrics–Fashions Bulletin FF-211.*

"Alkaline, Color Change," *NID Technical Bulletin T-104.*

"Anti-Perspirants and Deodorants," *Consumers' Research Bulletin* (September 1953), pp. 9–12.

"Atmospheric Gas Fading," *NID Fabrics–Fashions Bulletin FF-141.*

"Chameleon Fabric," *NID Fabrics–Fashions Bulletin FF-142.*

"Color Change to Abrasion," *NID Fabrics–Fashions Bulletin FF-128.*

"Color Changes," *NID Fabrics, Fashions Bulletin FF-125.*

"Color Changes," *NID Fabrics–Fashions Bulletin FF-98.*

"Color Change On Wool," *NID Technical Bulletin T-192.*

"Color Change—Perspiration," *NID Fabrics–Fashions Bulletins FF-118, FF-119.*

"Color Damage, Cold Wave Solution," *NID Technical Bulletin T-254.*

Egerton, G. S. "The Action of light on Cellulose Acetate, Rayon and Nylon Dyed with Duranol, Dispersal, S.R.A. and Solacet Dyes," *ibid.,* Vol. 64, No. 10 (October 1948), p. 336.

Egerton, G. S. "The Action of Light on Cellulose Acetate, Rayon and Nylon dyed and Dyed with Some Vat Dyes," *The Journal of Textile Institute,* Vol. 39, No. 8 (August 1948), pp. 293 and 298

"Fibrillation," *NID Fabrics–Fashions Bulletin FF-168.*

"Fishy Odors," *NID Technical Bulletin T-385.*

"Glazed Chintz," *IFI Fabrics–Fashions Bulletin FF-247.*

Laughlin, Joan. "Dimensions of Fabric Texture as Preceived Through the Visual and Tactile Senses, Exploratory Study Using Multidimensional

Sealing," Research Report, American Home Economics Association Annual Meeting (1975).

"Loss of Brightness in Fluorescent Dyes," *NID Fabrics–Fashions Bulletin FF-60.*

"Loss of Color in Blue Cottons," *NID Fabrics–Fashions Bulletin FF-11.*

"Loss of Color," *NID Technical Bulletin T-252.*

"Loss of Moire Designs," *NID Fabrics–Fashions Bulletin FF-175.*

"Loss of Prints on Sweaters," *NID Fabrics–Fashions Bulletin FF-90.*

"Loss of Screen-Printed Designs," *NID Fabrics–Fashions Bulletins FF-179, FF-184.*

"Loss of Ciré Finish," *IFI Fabrics–Fashions Bulletin FF-246.*

"Madras and Madras-Type Fabrics," *NID Fabrics–Fashions Bulletin FF-223.*

"Multi-Colored Dacron," *NID Fabrics–Fashions Bulletin FF-85.*

"Durable Press," *NID Fabrics–Fashions Bulletins FF-168, FF-189, FF-213.*

"Odor—Permanet Press," *NID Fabrics–Fashions Bulletins FF-125, FF-168.*

"Odor, Perspiration," *NID Fabrics–Fashions Bulletin FF-118.*

"Pilling of Soft Wools," *NID Technical Bulletin T-198.*

"Resin Bonded Pigment Colors," *NID Fabrics–Fashions Bulletins FF-46, FF-90, FF-85.*

Seholefield, F. and C. K. Patel. "The Action of the Light on Cotton Dyed With Vat Dyestuffs," *Journal of Society of Dyers and Colourists,* Vol. 44 (1928), pp. 268–274.

"Snagging In Sheer Tricot Knits," *NID Fabrics– -Fashions Bulletin FF-54.*

"Solvent-Soluble Dyes," *NID Fabrics–Fashions Bulletin FF-46.*

"Sublimation of Dye," *NID Practical Operation Tips Bulletin p–92.*

"Sunfade," *IFI Textile Analysis Bulletin TAB-14.*

"Wrinkling In Nylon," *NID Technical Bulletin T-179.*

Part 2—Durability   *Abrasion of Flocked Fabrics, IFI Technical Bulletin T-506.*

"Abrasion, Permanent Press Finish," *NID Fabrics–Fashions Bulletin FF-189.*

Abrasion, Polyester-blend Fabrics, NID Textile Analysis Bulletin TAB-16.

"Abrasion, Silk Organdy," *NID Fabrics–Fashions Bulletin FF-70.*

"Acid Damage to Blends," *IFI Textile Analysis Bulletin TAB-32.*

"Acid Damage, Flocked Suede," *NID Fabrics–Fashions Bulletin FF-79.*

"Alkaline Damage to Wool," *IFI Textile Analysis Bulletin TAB-40.*

Ashton, D., D. Clibbens, and N. E. Probert. "Some Experimental Observations on the Photochemical Degradation of Dyed Cotton," *Journal of the Society of Dyers and Colorists,* Vol. 65, No. 12 (December 1949), pp. 650–681.

"Bonded Wool," *NID Technical Bulletin T-258.*

"Chafing of Silk," *NID Technical Bulletin T-287.*

"Corduroy," *NID Fabrics–Fashions Bulletin FF-168.*

Egerton, G. S. "The Role of Hydrogen in the Photochemical Degradation of Cotton Sensitized by Vat Dyes and Some Metallic Oxides," *ibid.,* Vol. 39, No. 8 (August 1948), p. 305.

"Fabric-to-Fabric Bonded Fabrics," *NID Fabrics–Fashions Bulletins FF-139, FF-140, FF-157.*

"Fabric To Foam," *NID Fabrics–Fashions Bulletins FF-63, FF-80, FF-112, FF-126, FF-132, FF-135.*

"Flocked Velvet," *NID Fabrics–Fashions Bulletin FF-201.*

"Light Damage in Yellow Prints," *NID Fabrics–Fashions Bulletin FF-235.*

"Malimo Fabrics," *NID Fabrics–Fashions Bulletins FF-176, FF-192, FF-215.*

"Malipol Fabrics," *NID Fabrics–Fashions Bulletins FF-208, FF-210.*

"Seam Slippage," *NID Fabrics–Fashions Bulletins FF-136, FF-163.*

"Shoulder Pads," *NID Technical Bulletin T-253.*

"Simulated Leathers and Suede," *NID Fabrics–Fashions Bulletins FF-91, FF-101, FF-116, FF-98, FF-92.*

"Simulated Fur Fabrics," *NID Fabrics–Fashions Bulletins FF-19, FF-20, FF-29, FF-49, FF-128, FF-149, FF-212.*

"Splitting of Trousers," *NID Fabrics–Fashions Bulletin FF-189.*

"Splitting of Wool/Silk Combinations," "Cotton/Nylon Combinations," *NID Fabrics–Fashions Bulletins FF-4, FF-23.*

"Sunlight Damage," *IFI Fabrics, Fashions Bulletins FF-234; "Draperies," FF-235.*

"Velour," *NID Fabrics–Fashions Bulletin FF-194.*

"Velvets," *NID Fabrics–Fashions Bulletins FF-222, FF-223, FF-111, FF-212.*

"Wool/Silk Combinations," *NID Fabrics, Fashions Bulletins FF-4, FF-173.*

"Yarn Slippage," *NID Fabrics–Fashions Bulletins FF-70, FF-163, FF-188.*

Part 3—Comfort "Aero-Cellular Finish," *NID Fabrics–Fashions Bulletin FF-152.*

Dowlen, R., G. Pauley, and M. Hurley. "Complex Fabric Deformation: Drape of Apparel Fabrics," Research Report, American Home Economics Association Annual Meeting 1975.

"Elastic Waistbands," *NID Fabrics–Fashions Bulletin FF-5.*

"Elastic Yarns," *IFI Textile Analysis Bulletin TAB-44.*

"Insulated Drapery Fabrics," *NID Fabrics–Fashions Bulletin FF-213.*

"Insulating Finish," *NID Fabrics–Fashions Bulletin FF-380.*

"Metal Coating," *NID Fabrics–Fashions Bulletin FF-64.*

"Polyurethane Coating," *NID Fabrics–Fashions Bulletin FF-172.*

"Pouff Fabrics," *NID Fabrics–Fashions Bulletin FF-155.*

"Rubber Coating," *NID Fabrics–Fashions Bulletins FF-56, FF-83.*

Serba P. J. and R. F. Feldman. "Electrostatic Charging of Fabrics at Various Humidities," *J. of the Text. Inst.,* 55, T-288-298 (1964).

Static Electricity, NFPA Publication 77M (1961), National Fire Protection Association, 60 Batterymarch Street, Boston, Massachusetts.

"Vinyl Coating," *NID Fabrics–Fashions Bulletins FF-110, FF-146.*

Part 4—Safety (Textile Flammability) Gregory, J. M. and George H. Hatte. "Flammability and Fire Resistant Characteristics of Selected Drapery and Curtain Fabrics," *Journal of Home Economics,* Vol. 64, No. 3 (March 1972), p. 37.

Krasny, John F. and James H. Winger." Current Status of Flammability Test Development at the National Bureau of Standards," Products Center for Fire Research, National Bureau of Standards (1974).

Martin, Albert R. "Flame Retardant Finishing—Not a Simple Technology," *Technical Bulletin T-485* (1972).

"Spontaneous Ignition Hazard of Foam Rubber Products," *National Fire Protection Association Fire News* (August 22, 1957).

Summers, Teresa A. "Flammable Characteristics of Multilayer Fabrics Observed Through the Use of 16mm Movie Film," Research Report, American Home Economics Association Annual Meeting (1975).

Textile Flammability: A Handbook of Regulations, Standards and Test Methods, American Association of Textile Chemists and Colorists.

Part 5—Care   "Bleaching Chart," *NID Practical Operating Tips Bulletin P-16.*

"Bleaching Silk," *IFI Practical Operation Tips Bulletin P-57.*

"Bleaching, Hydrogen Peroxide," *NID Technical Bulletin T-501.*

"Chlorine Bleach to Cotton," *NID Technical Bulletin T-414.*

"Dye Bleeding—Corduroy," *IFI Fabrics, Fashions Bulletin FF-253.*

"Dye Bleeding—Denim," *IFI Fabrics, Fashions Bulletin FF-245.*

"Heat Shrinkage—Dacron," *NID Fabrics–Fashions Bulletin FF-85.*

"Heat Shrinkage—Knits," *NID Fabrics–Fashions Bulletins FF-207, FF-208.*

"Heat Shrinkage—Modacrylics," *NID Fabrics–Fashions Bulletin FF-242.*

"Heat Shrinkage—Olefin," *NID Fabrics–Fashions Bulletins FF-134, FF-147.*

"Heat Shrinkage—Polyethylene," *NID Fabrics–Fashions Bulletin FF-147.*

"Heat Shrinkage—Polypropylene," *NID Fabrics–Fashions Bulletins FF-134, FF-147.*

"Heat Shrinkage—Polyvinyl Chloride," *NID Fabrics–Fashions Bulletin FF-147.*

"Heat Shrinkage—Vinyon," *NID Fabrics–Fashions Bulletin FF-147.*

"Holes From Bleaching," *IFI Textile Analysis Bulletin TAB-22.*

"Heat Shrinkage—Acrylic Knits," *NID Fabrics–Fashions Bulletin FF-153.*

"Heat Shrinkage—Cushion Covers," *NID Fabrics–Fashions Bulletin FF-216.*

"Linen Damage From Bleach," *IFI Technical Analysis Bulletin TAB-22.*

"Oxidizing Bleach," *IFI Technical Analysis Bulletin TAB-22.*

"Rayon Damage," *IFI Technical Analysis Bulletin TAB-22.*

"Reducing Bleaches," *NID Practical Operation Tips Bulletin P-43*

"Shrinkage-Angora," *NID Technical Bulletin T-293.*

"Shrinkage-Bonded Fabrics," *NID Fabrics–Fashions Bulletin FF-140.*

"Shrinkage-Cashmere," *NID Fabrics–Fashions Bulletin FF-28.*

"Shrinkage-Crepe," *NID Fabrics–Fashions Bulletin FF-188.*

"Shrinkage-Curtains," *NID Fabrics–Fashions Bulletin FF-234.*

"Shrinkage-Drapery Fabrics," *NID Fabrics–Fashions Bulletin FF-192.*

"Shrinkage-Face Fabrics with Press-on Linings," *NID Fabrics–Fashions Bulletin FF-136.*

"Shrinkage in Knits," *NID Fabrics–Fashions Bulletins FF-95, FF-99, FF-207, FF-221, FF-226, T-470.*

"Shrinkage in Lace," *NID Fabrics–Fashions Bulletin FF-146.*

"Shrinkage in Linen," *NID Fabrics–Fashions Bulletin FF-24.*

"Shrinkage in Linings," *NID Fabrics–Fashions Bulletin FF-17.*
"Shrinkage in Mali," *NID Fabrics–Fashions Bulletin FF-192.*
"Shrinkage in Mohair," *NID Fabrics–Fashions Bulletin FF-99.*
"Shrinkage in Metallic Yarns," *NID Fabrics–Fashions Bulletin FF-36.*
"Shrinkage in Polyester," *IFI Fabrics–Fashions Bulletin FF-221.*
"Shrinkage in Soft Wools," *NID Fabrics–Fashions Bulletins FF-148, FF-248.*
"Stretching in Crepe," *NID Fabrics–Fashions Bulletin FF-188.*
"Stretching in Knits," *NID Fabrics–Fashions Bulletins FF-84, FF-121, FF-153, FF-190.*
"Stretching in Matte Jersey," *NID Fabrics–Fashions Bulletin FF-230.*
"Stretching in Orlon Sweaters," *NID Fabrics–Fashions Bulletin FF-3.*
"Stretching in Rachel-Crocheted Knits," *NID Fabrics–Fashions Bulletin FF-190.*
"Water-Sensitive Dye" *IFI Textile Analysis Bulletin TAB-46.*
"Water-Soluble Dye," *IFI Textile Analysis Bulletin TAB-48.*

Part 6—Biological Resistance

Banville, Robert and Ethel McNeil. "Bactericides" *Applied Microbiology,* Vol. 14, No. 1 (January 1966), pp. 1–7.
"Chloride Damage to Silk," *NID Fabrics, Fashions Bulletin FF-119.*
Dickinson, J. C. and R. E. Wagg. "Bactericides," *J. Applied Bact.,* 30 (1967). p. 340.
Hess, R. "Bactericides," *Krankenhaus,* 52, (1960), 90–98.
"Insect Damage on Synthetic Fibers," *NID Technical Bulletin T-375.*
Jackson, Lloyd E. "Bactericides," *American Journal of Public Health,* Vol. 12, No. 6 (June 1922), pp. 507–509.
Martin, Albert R. *Should Drycleaners Use Bactericides,* Technical Bulletin T-463, National Institute of Drycleaning (1970).
McNeil, Ethel et al. "Bactericides," *American Dyestuff Reporter* Vol. 53 (Dec. 9, 1963), pp. 87–90.
"Moth Crystals and Color Change," *NID Technical Bulletin T-219.*
Rhodes, W. K. "Bactericides," *Der Fachverband,* 8, 55 (1968).
Sidwell, R. W., G. J. Dixon, and Ethel McNeil. "Bactericides," *Applied Microbiology,* 15 (1967), pp. 921–927.
"Skin Irritation," *NID Technical Bulletin T-421.*
Stuart, L. S. "Bactericides," *Soap and Chemical Specialties,* 33, (1957), p. 95.
U.S.D.A. Circular No. 466, March 1938 and Patents (Public) 1,961,108; 1,990,292; 2,012,686 and 2,017,805.
Wagg, R. E. "Bactericides," *Chemistry and Industry* (October 20, 1965), pp. 1830–34.

Part 7—Environmental Resistance

"Atmospheric Gas Fading: O-Fading," *NID Fabrics, Fashion Bulletin FF-141.*
"Color Change of Red Dyes," *NID Fabrics–Fashions Bulletins FF-66, FF-183.*
Italian Tweed Causes Problems," *NID Fabrics–Fashions Bulletin FF-59.*
Rogers, R. E. and M. Hays. "The Effect of Various Storage Conditions on a

Cotton, a Linen and a Woolen Fabric," *Textile Research,* Vol. 13 (1943), pp. 20–35.

Salvin, V. S. and R. Walker. "Service Fading of Disperse Dyestuffs by Chemical Agents Other Than Oxides of Nitrogen," *Textile Research Journal,* Vol. 25 (1955), pp. 571–585.

"Silk Prints Causing Problems," *NID Fabrics–Fashions Bulletin FF-72.*

"Sunfade," *IFI Textile Analysis Bulletin TAB-14.*

"Water Repellent Finish," *NID Fabrics–Fashions Bulletins FF-130, FF-131.*

"Water Repellent Finish," *NID Technical Bulletin T-420.*

"Water-Sensitive Dye," *IFI Textile Analysis Bulletin TAB-46.*

"Water-Soluble Dye," *IFI textile Analysis Bulletin TAB-48.*

6. FABRIC CARE—SPOT AND STAIN REMOVAL

A Guide For Home Spot Removal, International Fabricare Institute (1970).

Aids to Interior Decor Fabric Care–Carpets, Rugs, Draperies, Upholstery, AIDS International (1972).

"Carmelized Sugar Stains," *NID Technical Bulletins T-276, T-282, T-284* (1952).

Coleman, Bob. "A Guide to Modern Carpet Cleaning," *Carpet Industry Review,* Merchandising Division, Carpet and Rug Institute (1970).

Lyle, Dorothy Siegert. *Focus On Fabrics,* National Institute of Drycleaning (1964).

Randlett, Judson C. and William J. Nicklaw, "Spotting," *NID* (1956).

"Removing Stains From Fabrics, Home Methods," *Home and Garden Bulletin No. 62,* U.S. Department of Agriculture, U.S. Government Printing Office (1973).

Smith, Stanley L. "Don't Be Stumped by Stains, A Primer for Spot Removers," *NID* (1974).

Wentz, M., A. C. Lloyd, and A. Watt. "Experimental Removal of Stains," *Textile Chemists and Colorists,* Vol. 7, No. 10 (October 1975), p. 179.

7. FABRIC CARE–LAUNDERING

Abbott, Richard L. "Taking the Mystery Out of Fabrics," *Coin Launderers and Cleaners* (November/December 1971), pp. 20–32.

"Coin-Operated Laundry," *Small Business Reporter,* Bank of America NT and SA. (1973).

"Detergents In Depth," a symposium report, The Soap and Detergent Association (March 28–29, 1974).

Gill, Ward A. "The Coinamatic Industry—Optimism and Growth," National Automatic and Cleaning Council (unpublished paper), (1973).

Harris, Jay C. "Detergents and Emulsifiers," *ASTM Yearbook,* American Society for Testing Materials (1972).

How To Save Time–Work–Money, Self-Service Laundering and Dry-cleaning–The Coin-Op Way, National Automatic Laundry and Cleaning Council (1973).

"Laundry Detergents; Suddenly Chemical Problems Including Arsenic," *Consumer Bulletin* (June 1970), pp. 27–28.

Lyle, Dorothey Siegert. "Better Laundering—Help Your Customers Get It," *Coin Launders and Cleaners* (April 1972), pp. 36–34.

Lyng, Ann. "Issues and Trends In Textile Use and Care—The Detergent Veiwpoint," unpublished paper, 21st National Conference of the Electrical Women's Roundtable, Inc. (1973).

Mork, Lucille F. "Figuring Home Laundering Costs," *Family Economic Review,* U.S. Department of Agriculture, Agricultural Research Services (October 1964).

Mork, Lucille F. "The Cost of Doing Laundry at Home," *Family Economic Review,* U.S. Department of Agriculture, Agriculture Research Services (Fall 1975).

"New Developments in Home Laundering," *Textile Topics,* Celanese Educational Services, Celanese Corporation, Inc. (Fall 1968).

"New Laundry Products," *Textile Topics,* Celanese Educational Services, Celanese Corporation, Inc., (Spring 1973).

Phillips, Roland Jr. "Drycleaning," *NID* (1968).

Purchase, Mary E. "Phosphates and Detergents in Water Pollution," *Information Bulletin No. 12,* Physical Sciences, Department of Design and Environment Analysis, Cooperative Extension, New York State College of Human Ecology, Cornell University (March 1971).

"The Two Dimensions of Soil Redeposition, Greying and Yellowing," *NID Technical Bulletin T-412, 1958.*

"Redeposition," *NID Technical Bulletin T-368.*

"The Detergent Dilemma (reprint)" *Good Housekeeping* (January 1971).

"The New Generation Looks At You; Purdue University Study," *Coin Laundries and Cleaners* (October 1972), pp. 18–24.

"The Technology of Home Laundering," Monograph No. 108, American Association for Textile Technology (1973).

Textile Handbook, American Home Economics Association, Washington, D.C. (1974).

8. FABRIC CARE—DRY CLEANING

A Guide to the Properties and Use of Valclene Drycleaning Fluid, DuPont, A-67536 Rev. (August 1971).

Berg, Norbert J. "Wetcleaning," *NID* (1945).

Deranian, Helen. *Finishing Techniques for the Textile Maintenance Industry.* Barclay Publishing, Inc. (1968).

Fulton, George P. "Applied Science for Drycleaners," *NID.* (1951)

Johnson, Albert E. "Drycleaning," a Merrow Monograph (1971).

Lyle, Dorothy Siegert. "Coin-Operated Drycleaning," *Coin Launderer and Cleaner.* Vol. 27, No. 2 (1972).

Lyle, Dorothy Siegert. "Fabric Conditioning," *Coin Launderer and Cleaner,* Vol. 27 No. 3 (1972).

Martin, Albert E. "Valclene," *NID Technical Bulletin T-458.*

Martin, Albert E. "Drycleaning Machines for Fluorocarbon 113." *NID Technical Bulletin T-477.*

Phillips, Roland E. "Drycleaning," *NID.* (1966)

9. FABRIC CARE—SPECIALTY CLEANING

Aids to Interior Decor Fabric Care–Carpets, Rugs, Draperies, Upholstery, AIDS International (1972).

"Cleaning Wedding Gowns," *NID Practical Operating Tips Bulletin P-69.*

"Cleaning Leather Gloves," *NID Practical Operating Tips Bulletin P-38.*

"Cleaning Leather Garments Using Fat Liquor," *NID Practical Operating Tips Bulletin P-85.*

Coleman, Bob. "A Guide to Modern Carpet Cleaning," *Carpet Industry Review,* Merchandising Division, Carpet and Rug Institute (1970).

Cohen, Harry and George E. Linton. *Chemistry and Textiles for the Laundry Industry.* Textile Book Publisher, a Division of Interscience Publishers, Inc. New York, p. 165.

"Drycleaning Leathers Using a Detergent-Oil Charged System," *NID Practical Operating Tips Bulletin P-110.*

Eaton Leather Kit, Eaton Chemical Corporation, 1490 Franklin Street, Detroit, Michigan.

"Effect of Drycleaning On Durable Water Repellents," *NID Technical Bulletin T-313.*

"Finishing Leather Garments," *NID Practical Operating Tips Bulletin P-86.*

"Flame-Retardant Finishing—Not a Simple Technology," *NID Technical Bulletin T-485.*

"Flameproofing," *NID Technical Bulletin T-168.*

Fur Cleaning and Finishing, Walter Haertel Company, Minneapolis, Minnesota.

Fur Care and the Fur Dictionary, Zimmerman Products Company, Cincinnati, Ohio.

"Fur Cleaning," *Practical Tips Operating Bulletin P-47; Fabrics–Fashions Bulletin FF-20; Technical Bulletin T-196;* The National Institute of Drycleaning.

"Handling Leather Garments, Parts, I and II," *NID Technical Bulletins T-203, T-204.*

Hubbard, C. C. *How to Clean Rugs and Upholstery Fabrics.* J. J. Little and Ives Company, New York. (1930)

"Insect Damage on Man-Made Fibers," *NID Technical Bulletin T-375.*

Johnson, Albert and R. Hasenclever. "Curtain Window Fabric Damages—Some Causes and Cures," *Curtain and Drapery Department Magazine* (June 1960).

Leather Facts, New England Tanners Club, Peabody, Massachusetts.

Leather In Our Lives, Leather Industries of America, 411 Fifth Avenue, New York.

"Moth Crystals and Color Change," *NID Technical Bulletin T-219.*

"Refurbishing With Color," *Rohm and Haas Reporter* (May-June 1961), pp. 3–5.

"Should Drycleaners Use Bactericides?" *NID Technical Bulletin T-463.*

"Sizing," *NID Technical Bulletin T-373.*

"Test On Mothproofing Products," *NID Technical Bulletin T-226.*

"The Use of Valclene Drycleaning Fuids for Drycleaning Leathers and Suedes," *Bulletin V-4;* E. I. Dupont de Nemours and Co. Inc., Organical Chemicals Department.

The True Story of Genuine Leather, A. C. Lawrence Leather Company, Gloversville, New York, 10 M 53.

"Tips on Handling Leathers, Parts I and II," *NIP Practical Operating Tips Bulletins P-51,P-85.*

10. TEXTILE LABELING—VOLUNTARY AND MANDATORY

"A Voluntary Industry Guide for Improved and Permanent Care Labeling of Consumer Textile Products," National Retail Merchants Association (1967).

Abbott, Richard L. "Taking the Mystery Out of Fabrics," *The New Coin Launderer and Cleaner* (November/December 1971), p. 28.

"British Textile Care Labeling Scheme—Conditions of Use," The Home Laundering Consultative Council (1972).

"Care Labels Can Save You Money and Trouble," *Federal Trade Commission Buyers Guide No. 10* (1972).

Conner, Gail. "Care Label Mini-Survey," University of North Carolina (June 1973) (unpublished).

Care Labeling Guide, National Retail Merchants Association (1972).

Care Labeling for Textiles, Bureau of Consumer Affairs (1971).

"Confusing Labels," *IFI Fabrics, Fashions/Fact, Fiction Bulletins FFFF-5, FFFF-6.*

Consumer Care Guide for Apparel, American Apparel Manufacturers Association (1972).

Fact Sheets: No. 17, Flammable Fabrics; No. 23, Flammable Liquids; No. 24, Laundry Procedures for Flame-Resistant Fabrics; No. 25, Federal and State Standards for Fabric Flammability; No. 34, Space Heaters and Wood and Coal Burning Heating Stoves; No. 53, Upholstered Furniture. U.S. Consumer Product Safety Commission, Washington, D.C.

"Fire Retardants," Skeet Laboratories, Inc., Vol. I, *Textiles* (March 1972).

"FTC Calls for Ending R.N. Coding System," *IFI Fabrics, Fashion/Fact, Fiction Bulletins FFFF-5 FFFF-7* (1972, 1973).

"FTC Realignment—Correspondence on File, Look for That Label," *Consumer Bulletin No. 6* Federal Trade Commission (1972).

"FTC Says: Garments Labeled "Wash" Can Also be Drycleaned," *Coin Launderer and Cleaner* (September 1972), p. 32.

Guide to Fabric Flammability, U.S. Consumer Product Safety Commission, Washington, D.C. (April 1975).

"It's What the Customer Thinks That Counts," *IFI Special Reporter* (May 1973).

Klapper, Marvine. "The Label Business—Easy Street It's Not," *Women's Wear Daily* (July 3, 1973).

"New Standards to Insure Sleepwear," *Consumer Alert,* FTC, Vol. II, No. 7 (July/August 1972).

"Permanent Care Labeling, Parts I and II," *NID Fabrics, Fashion Bulletins FF-219, FF-220* (1973).

"Purdue Consumer Survey Shows FTC Labeling Inadequate," *Coin Launderer and Cleaner* (June 1973), p. 21.

Powderly, Daniel W. "Permanent Care Labeling—Potential Effects on Manufacturer and Converter Costs and Impact Upon Voluntary Standards," *AATT Technical Review and Register,* p. 63.

Rules and Regulations Under the Flammable Fabrics Act, Federal Trade Commission (1953), amended.

Rules and Regulations Under the Fur Products Labeling Act, Federal Trade Commission (1951), amended.

Rules and Regulations Under the Textile Fiber Product Identification Act, Federal Trade Commission (1960), amended.

Rules and Regulations Under the Wool Products Labeling Rule, Federal Trade Commission (1939).

Standard Definitions of Terms Relating To Care of Consumer Textile Products and Recommended Practices for Use of These Terms on Permanently Attached Labels, D 3136-72, American Society for Testing Materials (1972).

"Symbols On Care Labels," *NID Practical Operating Tips Bulletin P-109* (1972).

"Textile and Apparel Identification Number—FTC Terminates Confidential Status—Effective 10-17-74," *Federal Register,* Vol. 39, No. 140 (Friday, July 17, 1974), p. 26398.

Trade Practice Rules and Federal Register, Federal Trade Commission.

Triangle System of Labeling for Over-the-Counter Fabrics, Textile Distributors Association (1972).

Trade Regulation Rule Including a Statement of Its Basis and Purpose Care Labeling of Textile Wearing Apparel, Federal Trade Commission (1972).

"Who's Responsible for Consumer Safety," Educational Relations Department, J. C. Penny Co. (Spring/Summer 1975).

11. GOVERNMENT PROGRAMS RELATED TO TEXTILES AND THE CONSUMER

[Copies of military and federal specifications and standards, qualified products lists, military handbooks, *etc.* listed in the Department of Defense Index of Specifications and Standards (DODISS) can be obtained from Commanding Officer, Naval Publications and Forms Center, 580l Tabor Avenue, Philadelphia, Pennsylvania 19120.]

Consumer Alert, Federal Trade Commission, Vol. II, No. 4 (April 1972).

Consumer Product Safety Act, Public Law 92–573.

"Consumer Product Agency Makes Plans to Bow Out," United Press International, *The Washington Star* (December 14, 1975).

"Costly Metric System Conversion Not on Apparel Makers' Table," *Women's Wear Daily* (October 20, 1973).

Directory of State, County, City Consumer Affairs Office, Government Printing Office, Publication 1700–00119.

Executive Order No. 11583, Office of Consumer Affairs, The White House, February 24, 1971.

Fact Sheet No. 52, "Some Federal Consumer-Oriented Agencies," U.S. Consumer Products Safety Commission.

Here Is Your Federal Trade Commission, U.S. Government Printing Office.

Johnson, Stephen M. "FTC Proposed Warranty Reg. Attacked by ARF President," *Daily News Record* (September 19, 1975).

State Consumer Action Summary '72, Government Printing Office; Publication 413–00002.

The President's Committee on Consumer Interest, U.S. Printing Office 1967–0258–971 (March 1967).

The President's Consumer Message, Office of The White House, February 24, 1971.

Warranties, FTC Call for Comment, Federal Trade Commission.

Wightman, Richard. "Bureau of Labor Statistics Seek to Over-haul the CPI," *Women's Wear Daily* (October 22, 1975).

Wightman, Richard. "WPI Textile Data to be Chosen to Present Market," *Daily News Record* (October 22, 1975).

12. BUSINESS-INDUSTRY, PROFESSIONAL–TECHNICAL PROGRAMS RELATED TO TEXTILES AND THE CONSUMER

"A Guide for Garment Evaluation," *American Association for Textile Technology, Monograph No. 107.*

ANSI Progress Report 1975, American National Standards Institute (1975).

"Business Industry—Professional Association Involvement," *Textiles and the Consumer* (1972).

Cairns, John A. "IFI—A Great New Marketing Force," *The Clemson University Marketing Letter* (February 1973).

Coulson, Robert. "Marketing A Modern Commercial Arbitration System," Vol. 54, No. 2 (August/September 1970).

"Does Consumer Arbitration Really Work?" *Changing Times* (July 1973).

Guide for Permanent Care Labeling, National Retail Manufacturers Association, 1972.

"International Fair Claims Guide for Consumer Textile Products," *IFI* (1973).

"Let's Revitalize Business-Consumer Relations," *A Program Guide for Local Chambers of Commerce,* U.S. Chamber of Commerce (1972).

Questions and Answers for Consumers, National Association of Manufacturers, (1972).

Serving the Appliance Industry and Homemaking Public, American Home Appliance Manufacturers (1972).

Testing For Public Safety, Underwriters' Laboratories (1972).

Twenty Questions (and Answers) About Consumer Arbitration, The Council of Better Business Bureaus, Inc. (1972).

Uniform Rules for a National Program of Arbitration for Business and Customers, The Council of Better Business Bureaus, Inc.

U.S.A. Standards; Performance Requirements for Textile Fabrics, L-22, American National Standards Institute.

"What's Behind Good Housekeeping," *Good Housekeeping.* (Pamphlet)

13. CONSUMER INVOLVMENT IN THE PERFORMANCE OF TEXTILES

"Learn to Complain Effectively," *Fabrics–Fashions/Fact, Fiction, National Institute of Drycleaning Bulletin FFFF-2.*

The Consumer Tribune, Published by the Consumer Affairs Foundation, 150 Tremont Street, Boston, Massachusetts.

Index